The Presidency and the Political System

SEVENTH EDITION

Michael Nelson, *Editor*

Rhodes College

CQ PRESS

A Division of Congressional Quarterly Inc.
Washington, D.C.

CQ Press
1255 22nd Street, N.W., Suite 400
Washington, D.C. 20037

(202) 729-1900; toll-free, 1-866-4CQ-PRESS (1-866-427-7737)

www.cqpress.com

The Presidency and the Political System, Seventh Edition was typeset
by TechBooks
Cover design by Naylor Design Inc.

Printed and bound in the United States of America

06 05 04 03 02   5 4 3 2 1

The publisher wishes to thank Stanford University Press for the use of
Figures 17.4 and 17.5 on page 471. Copyright 2000 by the Board of
Trustees of the Leland Stanford Junior University.

Library of Congress Cataloging-in-Publication Data
The presidency and the political system / Michael Nelson, editor.—7th ed.
     p. cm.
Includes bibliographical references and index.
   ISBN 1-56802-673-0 (alk. paper)
   1. Presidents—United States. I. Nelson, Michael–

JK516 .P639 2003
352.23'0973—dc21

                                           2002009277

To my beloved wife, Linda.

She opens her mouth with wisdom,
and the teaching of kindness is on her tongue. . . .
Her children rise up and call her blessed;
her husband also, and he praises her.

PROVERBS 31:26, 28

Contents

Preface

Every syllabus for a college course notes the term and year the course is offered, usually in the upper right-hand corner of the first page. In many departments, this is simply a clerical entry: it really doesn't matter all that much whether you take Shakespeare in fall 2003 or spring 2006. Timing matters immensely, however, in a course on the American presidency. Indeed, what makes political science so interesting is that its subject (succinctly described by political scientist Harold D. Lasswell as "who gets what, when, and how") refuses to stand still. This point applies especially to the presidency, in which the nature of the institution is so closely intertwined with that of the person who, at any given moment, occupies it.

Consider just a few of the developments in the three years since this book's sixth edition was published: the historically unprecedented Bush-Gore election—and postelection—of 2000, the mixed record of success of President George W. Bush during his first eight months in office, and the tumultuous aftermath of the September 11, 2001, terrorist attacks on the World Trade Center and the Pentagon.

All of these political developments and more, along with the new contributions to the flourishing scholarly literature on the presidency and the political system they have inspired, are treated fully in this seventh edition. The book's nineteen chapters are organized into five parts: The Presidency in Comparative Perspective (a new section), Elements of Presidential Power, Presidential Selection, Presidents and Politics, and Presidents and Government.

To note that the authors have taken recent developments into account is not to say that this is a "current events" book—far from it. The presidency is an office with deep roots in history, shaped by decisions that were made at the Constitutional Convention of 1787 and by more than two centuries of change in the system since its founding. It also is shaped by the history and current functioning of the myriad parts of the American political system, such as Congress, the courts, the bureaucracy, interest groups, the media, public opinion, the electoral process, and the party system. This broader understanding of the presidency underlies all of the analyses of more recent events that the writers present.

The most noteworthy addition to the seventh edition is the roster of new contributors: Nigel Bowles, Matthew Dickinson, Suzanne Globetti, John D. Griffin, Marc J. Hetherington, Lawrence R. Jacobs, Richard M. Pious, Daniel J. Tichenor, and David A. Yalof. Topically, this edition devotes greater attention to the presidency in comparative perspective and considers how the examination of alternative systems of government can enhance understanding of the American presidency.

I do not agree with everything that every author has to say in this book; nor will any reader. But together the contributors constitute an all-star team of presidential scholars, and the intellectual substance of the chapters is fully matched by their readability. Through six previous editions, this book has been widely assigned in courses and extensively cited and reviewed in scholarly books and articles. Students may be assured of receiving the most comprehensive possible understanding of the presidency, and scholars will continue to find the essays valuable in conducting their research.

I am deeply grateful to those who helped in the preparation of the seventh edition, the authors first and foremost. Susan Sullivan and Jean Woy, formerly of Congressional Quarterly, and Erwin C. Hargrove of Vanderbilt University helped me to think through the themes and organization of the first edition, and Barbara de Boinville served as a helpful editor. Joanne Daniels, Nola Healy Lynch, and Tracy White contributed mightily to the second edition, as did Nancy Lammers, Kristen Carpenter Stoever, and Ann O'Malley to the third. Every edition since then has enjoyed the gently guiding hand of Brenda Carter. The fourth and fifth editions also benefited from the work of Joanne Ainsworth and Talia Greenberg, as did the sixth edition from the contributions of Gwenda Larsen, Belinda Josey, and Debbie K. Hardin. For their excellent work on the seventh edition, I offer heartfelt thanks to Charisse Kiino, Carolyn Goldinger, Elizabeth Jones, and Belinda Josey. Jay Sulzmann, my student, did a fine job preparing the index.

This seventh edition marks the twentieth anniversary of the first edition of *The Presidency and the Political System,* an occasion I wish to mark by acknowledging and thanking all who have written chapters for previous editions of the book: Roger G. Brown, Bruce Buchanan, Timothy E. Cook, W. Bowman Cutter, Roger H. Davidson, George C. Edwards III, James Fallows, Morris P. Fiorina, Benjamin Ginsberg, Michael B. Grossman, Willis D. Hawley, Samuel Kernell, Martha Joynt Kumar, Paul Light, John Anthony Maltese, Walter R. Mebane Jr., Mark A. Peterson, Joseph A. Pika, Beryl A. Radin, Lyn Ragsdale, Francis E. Rourke, Elizabeth Sanders, Robert Scigliano, Martin Shefter, Bartholomew H. Sparrow, Thomas Tillman, Jack L. Walker, and Thomas Weko.

Michael Nelson

Contributors

JOHN H. ALDRICH is Pfizer-Pratt University Professor of Political Science at Duke University. He has written or cowritten *Why Parties? Before the Convention, Linear Probability, Logit and Probit Models,* and an election series that includes *Change and Continuity in the 2000 Elections.* Aldrich has been president of the Southern Political Science Association and a fellow at the Center for Advanced Study in the Behavioral Sciences, and he is a fellow of the American Academy of Arts and Sciences. Current projects include studies of various aspects of campaigns and elections, political parties, Congress, and an assessment of the impact of globalization on democratic politics.

NIGEL BOWLES is a fellow of St Anne's College, Oxford, and a lecturer in the Department of Politics and International Relations at Oxford University. His publications include *The White House and Capitol Hill* and *The Government and Politics of the United States.* He is currently writing a book on Richard Nixon's presidency.

JOHN P. BURKE is professor of political science at the University of Vermont. He is the author of *Bureaucratic Responsibility* and *The Institutional Presidency* and coauthor of *How Presidents Test Reality: Decisions on Vietnam, 1954 and 1965* and *Advising Ike: The Memoirs of Attorney General Herbert Brownell.* His most recent works include *The Institutional Presidency: Organizing and Managing the White House from FDR to Clinton* and *Presidential Transitions: From Politics to Practice.*

MATTHEW J. DICKINSON is professor of political science at Middlebury College. He is the author of *Bitter Harvest: FDR, Presidential Power, and the Growth of the Presidential Branch* and has published numerous articles on the presidency, presidential decision making, and presidential advisers. His current research examines the growth of presidential staff in the post–World War II era.

SUZANNE GLOBETTI is a visiting assistant professor of government and legal studies at Bowdoin College. Her research interests include ideological campaign rhetoric and public ideology. Her work has appeared in the *American Journal of Political Science.*

JOHN D. GRIFFIN is an assistant professor of political science at the University of Notre Dame. He specializes in American political institutions, particularly the U.S. Congress. With John Aldrich, he is currently writing a book on the emergence of a competitive party system in the American South.

MARC J. HETHERINGTON is an assistant professor at Bowdoin College. He recently finished a year as a visiting research fellow at the Center for the Study of Democratic Politics, Princeton University, where this chapter was completed. He has published several articles and book chapters on political trust and is presently working on a book manuscript titled *Why Trust Matters: Declining Political Trust and the Demise of American Liberalism.*

LAWRENCE R. JACOBS is professor of political science at the University of Minnesota. His most recent book, *Politicians Don't Pander: Political Manipulation and the Loss of Democratic Responsiveness*, with Robert Shapiro, won awards from Harvard University's Joan Shorenstein Center on the Press, Politics, and Public Policy, the American Political Science Association, and the American Sociological Association. His research on health care policy was awarded a Robert Wood Johnson Investigator Award in Health Policy Research.

SIDNEY M. MILKIS is the James Hart Professor of Politics and senior scholar at the Miller Center of Public Affairs at the University of Virginia. His books include *The President and the Parties: The Transformation of the American Party System Since the New Deal, Political Parties and Constitutional Government: Remaining American Democracy, The American Presidency: Origins and Development, 1776–1998*, third edition (with Michael Nelson), *Presidential Greatness* (with Marc Landy), and *The New Deal and the Triumph of Liberalism* (with Jerome Mileur).

BRUCE MIROFF is professor and chair of political science at the State University of New York at Albany. His books include *Pragmatic Illusions: The Presidential Politics of John F. Kennedy, Icons of Democracy: American Leaders as Heroes, Aristocrats, Dissenters, and Democrats*, and *The Democratic Debate*, third edition (cowritten). He is currently engaged in research for a book on George McGovern's presidential campaign and the transformation of American liberalism.

TERRY M. MOE is professor of political science at Stanford University and senior fellow at the Hoover Institution. He is the author of *The Organization of Interests* and *Schools, Vouchers, and the American Public* and the coauthor of *Politics, Markets, and America's Schools*. He has written extensively on American political institutions and organization theory, with special attention to public bureaucracy, the presidency, interest groups, and the American education system. His articles on the presidency include "The Politicized Presidency," "Presidents, Institutions, and Theory," and "The Presidential Power of Unilateral Action."

MICHAEL NELSON is professor of political science at Rhodes College. His articles have appeared in, among other publications, the *Journal of Politics, Political Science Quarterly, Public Interest, Congress and the Presidency*, and *Washington Monthly*, where he formerly served as editor. More than forty of his articles have been anthologized in works of political science, history, and English composition, and he has won national writing awards for his articles on music and baseball. His most recent books are *Governing Gambling: Politics and Policy in State, Tribe, and Nation* (with John Lyman Mason) and *The Elections of 2000*. Other recent books include *Alive at the Core: Exemplary Approaches to General Education in the Humanities, The American Presidency: Origins and Development, 1776–1998* (with Sidney M. Milkis), and *Guide to the Presidency*, third edition.

BRUCE NESMITH is associate professor and chair of political science at Coe College. He teaches courses on American political institutions, political philosophy, and religion and U.S. politics. He is the author of *The New Republican Coalition: The Reagan Campaigns and White Evangelicals*. He is currently researching policy-making by the president and Congress.

RICHARD M. PIOUS is Adolph and Effie Ochs Professor at Barnard College and a professor in the Graduate School of Arts and Sciences, Columbia University. He is the author of *The American Presidency* and *The President, Congress, and the Constitution* and the coauthor of *The Oxford Guide to the United States Government*. He has recently written articles on crisis decision making and presidential failure and a law review article on Bill Clinton's impeachment.

PAUL J. QUIRK is professor of political science at the University of Illinois at Urbana–Champaign. He is the author of *Industry Influence in Federal Regulatory Agencies* and *The Politics of Deregulation*, along with numerous articles and essays on the presidency, presidential elections, public opinion, and public policymaking. He has served on the editorial boards of several leading journals, including the *American Political Science Review*, and was recently president of the Public Policy Section of the American Political Science Association. His current research concerns the processes and quality of policy deliberation in American politics.

BERT A. ROCKMAN is director of and professor in the School of Public Policy and Management at Ohio State University, where he is also professor of political science. He is coeditor of the journal *Governance*, author of *The Leadership Question: The Presidency and the American System*, coeditor of *The Bush Presidency: First Appraisals*, *The Clinton Presidency: First Appraisals*, and *The Clinton Legacy*. He is coauthor of *In the Web of Politics: Three Decades of the U.S. Federal Executive*. He is a past president of the Organized Section on Presidency Research of the American Political Science Association and president-elect of the Midwest Public Administration Association. He also has received the Richard E. Neustadt and Pi Sigma Alpha Awards.

STEPHEN SKOWRONEK is the Pelatiah Perit Professor of Political Science at Yale University. He is the author of *Building a New American State: The Expansion of National Administrative Capacities, 1877–1920* and *The Politics Presidents Make: Leadership from John Adams to Bill Clinton*. He is also managing editor of *Studies in American Political Development*.

DANIEL J. TICHENOR is assistant professor of political science at Rutgers University at New Brunswick. He is the author of *Dividing Lines: The Politics of Immigration Control in America*. His articles on interest groups, social movements, American national institutions, and policy politics have appeared in *Political Science Quarterly*, *Polity*, *Presidential Studies Quarterly*, *Studies in American Political Development*, and several edited volumes. He is currently completing a book on social movements and the presidency.

JEFFREY K. TULIS teaches political science at the University of Texas at Austin. He is the author of *The Rhetorical Presidency*, coauthor of *The Presidency in the Constitutional Order*, and coeditor of the Johns Hopkins Series on Constitutional

Thought. He is currently completing a book on institutional irresponsibility, provisionally titled *The Politics of Deference*.

DAVID A. YALOF is associate professor of political science at the University of Connecticut. His first book, *Pursuit of Justices: Presidential Politics and the Selection of Supreme Court Nominees*, won the 1999 Richard E. Neustadt Award as the best book on the presidency from the American Political Science Association's presidency research group. He is coauthor of *The First Amendment and The Media in the Court of Public Opinion*. His articles on connections between the branches of government have appeared in, among other publications, *Political Research Quarterly*, *Judicature*, and *Constitutional Commentary*. He is currently completing a book on the politics of investigating executive branch officials in the absence of an independent counsel.

1 Evaluating the Presidency

Michael Nelson

First impressions are important, in politics as in everything else. Numerous studies of political socialization have found that long before children have any real knowledge of what the federal government actually does, they already think of the president in terms of almost limitless power and goodness. In this chapter, Michael Nelson uncovers powerful traces of these first impressions in the later impressions of politically aware adults. Presidential scholars, White House correspondents, average citizens, members of Congress, and civil servants working in the federal bureaucracy—each of these important constituencies may seem at first blush to hold attitudes that are detrimental to presidential power. Closer inspection, however, reveals that each group's surface judgments overlie more fundamental orientations toward politics that exalt presidential power.

The November 1, 1948, issue of *Life* magazine is a collector's item because of a picture on page 37 that is captioned, "The next president travels by ferry over the broad waters of San Francisco bay." The picture is of Thomas E. Dewey. Of greater significance, however, is an article that begins on page 65 and is titled "Historians Rate U.S. Presidents." The article was written by Arthur M. Schlesinger Sr., who had called on fifty-five of his fellow historians to grade each president as either "great," "near great," "average," "below average," or a "failure." When Schlesinger tallied up the results, Abraham Lincoln, George Washington, Franklin D. Roosevelt, Woodrow Wilson, and Andrew Jackson scored as great presidents. Ulysses S. Grant and Warren G. Harding were rated as failures. The rest fell in between.

As interesting as the Schlesinger evaluations and their many imitators are, the important lessons to be learned from them may be more about the judges than their judgments, more about the presidency than about the presidents. What standards do scholars use to evaluate presidents? Against what image of the presidency do they measure the Lincolns and Hardings, the Reagans and

Clintons? What standards for evaluation are used by other important judges of the presidency: journalists, citizens, members of Congress, bureaucrats?

Answering these questions can tell us a lot, not only about the presidency's evaluators, but also about the presidency itself.[1] Presidents, after all, want the "verdict of history" that scholars eventually render to be favorable. In the short run, they need to win the support of journalists, the mass public, and congressional and bureaucratic officeholders if they are to succeed. To do so, presidents must understand the standards of evaluation that these groups apply to them.

Scholars: Strength amid Confusion

Schlesinger followed his 1948 survey of historians with another in 1962. The results were strikingly similar: the same pair of "failures" and, with the exception of Jackson, the same set of "greats." More important, so were the twin standards that historians in the late 1940s and early 1960s appeared to be measuring presidents against: strength and the desire to be strong. "Washington apart," Schlesinger wrote, "none of [the great presidents] waited for the office to seek the man; they pursued it with all their might and main." Once in office, their greatness was established because "every one of [them] left the Executive branch stronger and more influential than he found it." When dealing with Congress, they knew "when to reason and to browbeat, to bargain and stand firm, . . . and when all else failed, they appealed over the heads of the lawmakers to the people." Nor did the great presidents shy away from confrontations with the Supreme Court. They were, to be sure, inattentive to administration of the bureaucracy, but this freed them, according to Schlesinger, for the more important tasks of "moral leadership."[2] A 1968 survey by Gary Maranell not only confirmed Schlesinger's conclusion that "strength" and "activeness" were important criteria in the historians' model of the presidency but also found that "idealism" and "flexibility" were not.[3]

The historians' model was very much like that of the other group of scholars who write and talk about the presidency, political scientists.[4] Their view in the 1950s and 1960s was summed up nicely in the title of an article by Thomas Cronin: "Superman: Our Textbook President."[5] After reviewing dozens of American government textbooks written in those two decades, Cronin found that political scientists typically characterized the presidency as both omnipotent and benevolent. The idea that strength and goodness go hand in hand shone through, for example, in James MacGregor Burns's textbook assessment that "the stronger we make the Presidency, the more we strengthen democratic procedures."[6] It also animated the most influential book on the presidency of this period, *Presidential Power*. "A president's success" in maximizing power, wrote its author, Richard Neustadt, "serves objectives far beyond his own and his party's. . . . Presidential influence contributes to the energy of the government and to the viability of public policy. . . . What is good for the country is good for the president, and vice versa."[7]

Underlying the political scientists' model was a seemingly quasi-religious awe of the presidency. Clinton Rossiter began his book *The American Presidency* by confessing his "feeling of veneration, if not exactly reverence, for the authority and dignity of the presidency." He described Lincoln as "the martyred Christ of democracy's passion play" and quoted favorably the "splendid judgment" of the English radical political leader John Bright in 1861 that

there is nothing more worthy of reverence and obedience, and nothing more sacred, than the authority of the freely chosen magistrate of a great and free people; and if there be on earth and amongst men any right divine to govern, surely it rests with a ruler so chosen and so appointed.[8]

Herman Finer was equally reverent, although in a polytheistic way. Finer characterized the presidency not only as "the incarnation of the American people in a sacrament resembling that in which the wafer and the wine are seen to be the body and blood of Christ" but also as "belong[ing] rightfully to the offspring of a titan and Minerva husbanded by Mars."[9]

Thus strength and the desire to be strong, power and virtue, omnipotence and benevolence—all were tied together in what may be called (only half facetiously) the "Savior" model of the presidency. According to the model's underlying rationale, the president is the chief guardian of the national interest, not only in foreign policy (because no one else can speak and act for the nation), but also in domestic affairs because of the pluralistic structure of government and society. Members of Congress cater to influential interests within their constituencies, scholars argued, but the president can mobilize the unorganized and inarticulate and speak for national majorities against special interest groups.

Clearly, scholars' normative preference for presidential strength in the 1950s and 1960s had more to it than their value judgments about the proper distribution of power among the branches of government. It was rooted in their liberal policy preferences as well. Democratic historians outnumbered Republicans by two to one in the Schlesinger samples, for example. One of the reasons they found the strength of the presidents they labeled "great" so appealing was that, as Schlesinger put it, each of these presidents "took the side of liberalism and the general welfare against the status quo."[10] William Andrews observed a similar partisan and ideological bias among his fellow political scientists, many of whom had worked in liberal Democratic administrations. When it comes to the presidency, he concluded, "the constitutional theory follows the party flag."[11]

In sum, argued scholars of the Savior school through the mid-1960s, presidential strength and ambition would serve the national interest. How, then, to explain the nation's subsequent experience with Lyndon B. Johnson and Richard M. Nixon in the late 1960s and early 1970s? In foreign affairs the power of these presidents sustained a large-scale war in Vietnam long after public opinion had turned against it. The power of the president as "chief legislator," in Rossiter's phrase, prompted such hasty passage of Great Society social welfare programs that the programs' flaws, which might have been discovered in bargaining between the president and Congress, were not found until later. Many of these flaws were in administrative design and implementation, the very areas of activity that the Savior model had encouraged presidents to avoid. Finally, in 1972 and 1973 the host of abuses of presidential power known as Watergate occurred, forcing Nixon's resignation in August 1974.

The flawed presidencies of Johnson and Nixon convinced many scholars that presidential strength and the general welfare, far from being synonymous, were now more likely to appear as opposites: Satan to the earlier model's Savior. Arthur M. Schlesinger Jr. had helped to create the Savior model with his glowing biographies of Jackson, Roosevelt, and John F. Kennedy, especially in eulogistic passages such as this one from A Thousand Days: "Thinking of the young Roosevelts, lost suddenly in middle age, and of the young Kennedys, so sure and purposeful, one perceived an historic contrast, a dynastic change, like the Plantagenets giving way to the Yorks." In 1973 Schlesinger came back with a book berating the "imperial presidency."[12] Marcus Cunliffe called the office a "Frankenstein monster."[13] Nelson Polsby noted that the careers of most of the "great" presidents were tied up with total war.[14]

The new task for presidential scholars was to explain why strength in the presidency was likely to be harmful to the nation rather than helpful, as they previously had thought. Their search carried them into two primary areas: the person and the office.

The expedition into personality as a source of presidential pathology was led by James David Barber. Barber identified a presidential character type, the "active-negative," whose efforts to maximize power are born of a deep-seated and psychologically unhealthy need to dominate others.[15] When active-negatives encounter serious challenges to their power, as all presidents eventually do, they react rigidly and aggressively. Such was the case with Johnson and Nixon. The nation survived their presidencies, but considering the nature of modern nuclear weaponry, Barber argued, even one more active-negative could be one too many.

Other scholars looked to the office to explain why presidential strength was likely to be destructive. Cronin claimed that the "swelling of the presidency"—the sheer growth of the White House staff—had turned it into "a powerful inner sanctum of government isolated from the traditional constitutional checks and balances."[16] George Reedy suggested that "the life of the White House is the life of a court," in which the president "is treated with all the reverence due a monarch." He explained,

There is built into the presidency a series of devices that tend to remove the occupant of the Oval Office from all of the forces which require most men to rub up against the hard facts of life on a daily basis. . . . No one interrupts presidential contemplation for anything less than a major catastrophe somewhere on the globe. No one speaks to him unless spoken to first. No one ever invites him to "go soak your head" when his demands become petulant and unreasonable.[17]

Ironically, no sooner had the Satan model of a powerful but dangerous presidency taken hold among political scientists and historians than events again intruded: the unusually weak administrations of Gerald R. Ford (1974–1977) and Jimmy Carter (1977–1981). The immediate response of presidential scholars was not unlike that of the ancient Israelites when Samson transgressed and had his strength cut away: They beheld the new weakness and were distressed by it. The Samson model of the presidency—others called it the "imperiled" or "tethered" presidency—came in startling contrast to those that had preceded it.[18] The model ruefully portrayed a large and growing gap between what presidents can do and what they are expected to do.

The Samson model traced to two sources the presidency's apparent incapacity to deliver: the office's constitutional dependence on other political institutions for support and the recent decline in the ability or willingness of those institutions to provide it. According to Samson theorists, parties had grown too weak to help, Congress too decentralized to bargain with, the bureaucracy too fragmented and powerful to lead, and the media too adversarial for its spotlight to be an asset for the president. Among the public, single-issue groups harshly critical of government were proliferating, even as those parts of the population supposedly most inclined to support the president—the less educated, religiously fundamentalist, and strongly partisan—were dwindling in number. Thus presidents "had to work harder to keep the same popularity."[19]

Yet, even as the president's ability to meet demands for action was supposedly declining, the volume, intensity, and complexity of those demands were said to be increasing. Godfrey Hodgson argued that the American people expect too much of their president:

He must simultaneously conduct the diplomacy of a superpower, put together separate coalitions to enact every piece of legislation required by a vast and complex society, manage the economy, command the armed forces, serve as a spiritual example and inspiration, respond to every emergency.[20]

With demands on the presidency so high, Samson theorists argued in the late 1970s, no individual president could be expected to meet them. They cited the recent high turnover in the presidency as a sign of the weakness of the institution. Ronald Reagan's inauguration in 1981 made him the sixth president to be sworn into office in only twenty years.

But once in office, Reagan quickly refuted the Samson model of the presidency, just as the Johnson and Nixon administrations had the Savior model, and Ford and Carter had the Satan model. A political cartoon from the summer of 1981 depicts an angry professor storming out of a door marked "Political Science Department." Papers fly around the office in his wake, one the title page of a book manuscript marked, "The Limits of Power," another a newspaper with the headline "Stunning Tax, Budget Wins for Reagan." In the foreground a secretary explains to a startled student: "He just completed the definitive, 600-page work on why special-interest groups, weak parties, and a fragmented Congress make presidential leadership impossible." Reagan's landslide reelection in 1984 demonstrated that his dramatic legislative victories in 1981 were no fluke.

Savior, Satan, Samson—the sheer velocity of the turnover in these models since the 1960s would seem to indicate that the best one-word description of how scholars evaluate the presidency is *confusion*. The sources of this confusion are not hard to trace. Although the models purported to describe the enduring institution of the presidency, they were created in overheated response to specific presidents. In addition, each of the three models combined, albeit unwittingly, an empirical question (Is the presidency strong or weak?) with a normative one (Is this condition of presidential strength or weakness good or bad for the American political system?). Both types of questions are worth asking, but not in the same breath. Thus in the Savior model, which prevailed from the Roosevelt through the Kennedy administrations, the answers were: the presidency is a strong office, and this is good for the system. The Satan model displaced it when scholars, overreacting to the lessons of Johnson and Nixon, decided that the strength of the presidency, although great, was dangerous. Then, startled once again by the weak administrations of Ford and Carter, they went back to the drawing board and constructed the Samson model (the office is weak, which is bad).[21]

Yet underlying this confusion has been a recurring, if sometimes implicit, celebration of presidential strength. The Savior model exulted in the presence of strong presidential leadership; the Samson model mourned its apparent demise. Even the Satan school may be understood as the scholarly equivalent of a lovers' quarrel with the presidency. Although he warned of active-negative character types, for example, Barber placed his hopes for the country in the election of "active-positives," presidents who would seek to dominate the system out of zest rather than zeal. And in attacking the excessive power of the "imperial presidency," Schlesinger Jr. stopped short of endorsing any serious effort to limit the office constitutionally. Eisenhower's remarkable rise in stature among historians, from the bottom third of all presidents in 1962 to the top ten in several recent rounds of scholarly rankings, owes less to any new appreciation of what was long thought to be his passive style of leadership than it does to research that shows him to have been a deceptively strong "hidden-hand" leader.[22]

In the 1990s and 2000s strength as the standard for evaluations of presidents seems to be as firmly grounded in the minds of presidential scholars as it was in the heyday of the Savior model in the 1950s and 1960s. A 1996 survey of eminent historians and political scientists by Schlesinger Jr. revealed that "[t]he choice of best and worst presidents has remained relatively stable through the years." Explaining the high regard that the great presidents continue to enjoy among his academic colleagues, Schlesinger noted that little had changed since his father's 1948 and 1962 surveys. In the eyes of presidential scholars, he wrote, a great president was one who "took risks . . . provoked controversy . . . st[ood] in Theodore Roosevelt's 'bully pulpit.' "[23]

Journalists: Strength amid Cynicism

If *confusion* is the catchword for understanding changing scholarly views of the presidency, the comparable shorthand description of recent journalistic standards of evaluation is *cynicism*. Underlying this surface attitude, however, is an implicit exaltation of presidential strength. Like presidential scholars, the White House press corps tends to encourage a powerful executive.

Historically, journalistic cynicism toward the presidency can be traced to Vietnam and Watergate.[24] White House reporters felt that a breach of trust occurred in the late 1960s and early 1970s: They had been lied to repeatedly by presidents and their aides and, because they had reported those lies in their newspapers and news broadcasts in good faith, felt they had been used. Stephen Hess described "the residue of that era" among the Washington journalists he interviewed as "distrust of public institutions and politicians in general."[25] That distrust carried over into routine events such as the presidential press secretary's daily briefing, where, according to the former *Newsweek* editor Mel Elfin, "reporters vie with each other to see who can ask the toughest questions and never let Watergate happen to us again."[26]

A more deeply rooted and important source of cynicism among journalists, however, may be the "status frustration" of the White House press corps. This frustration has developed out of the growing imbalance between reporters' social and professional status, which is exalted, and the job itself, which is degrading.

Of the high status of the White House press corps, little needs to be said. The White House correspondent, notes one journalist, is "part of the whole social circle" of Supreme Court justices, cabinet secretaries, and prominent members of Congress.[27] Professionally, the presidency is among a handful of what Hess called "high-prestige beats" in Washington.[28] White House reporters are usually guaranteed prominent placement for their daily dispatches and tend to be high on the list of journalists who are invited to give lucrative lectures and write magazine articles or books. The presidential beat is also a gateway to better things in the profession. David Halberstam described the beat as "an institutional ticket. The guy who gets to the White House goes on to some bigger job," such as editor, columnist, or television anchor.[29]

In stark contrast to these external indicators of success and prestige is the job itself, which has been well described as "the body watch." The reporters they are watching is the president's, and the purpose of the watch is to find out everything that the president does, both officially and privately. To do so means staying near. As Elfin put it, "The worst thing in the world that could happen to you is for the president of the United States to choke on a piece of meat, and for you not to be there."[30]

Staying near, however, is a goal that usually can be achieved only in the most technical sense. The White House press room is just yards away from the Oval

Office, but the distance is seldom spanned. Reporters are forbidden to roam the halls of the White House and Executive Office Building in the time-honored modus operandi of their profession, and their access even to the office of the press secretary is limited to the assistants' outer sanctums. (During his brief tenure as Clinton's communications director, George Stephanopoulos tried to fence in reporters still more tightly, but ultimately relented under intense media pressure.) Charged by their editors to "body-watch" the president, reporters typically must rely on the secondhand reports of the press secretary, who comes out once a day to brief them, or on other presidential aides or visitors to the Oval Office, who may choose to speak to them or not. When reporters are allowed to see the president, it is almost always in a setting defined both physically and procedurally by the administration. Members of the White House press corps enjoy high status in part because they are so visible, but the irony is that "they are visible because of the large amount of time they spend waiting for something to happen—for the briefing to start, for the president to appear for a White House ceremony in the Rose Garden, for a visitor to arrive, for a statement or a transcript to be released."[31]

The frustration that journalists feel in a job whose main activities are stenographic is great. A briefing room full of White House reporters when the press secretary appears is not unlike a classroom full of middle school students who have just been informed that a substitute teacher is on the way. In their daily reports to the public, in which professional and editorial standards forbid overtly hostile displays, status frustration, joined to the hangover from Vietnam and Watergate, shows up in more subtle form. As one study of the subject records,

reporters now present news about the White House along with an item that casts doubt on the credibility of what has been said or on the reliability of the person who has said it. They indicate to their viewers that a cynical approach is a realistic approach when analyzing the motives of the president and his advisers.[32]

Cynicism boils over into blatantly negative coverage when a president's rectitude comes to be doubted. Nixon and Watergate, Ford and his early pardon of Nixon, Carter's reluctance to fire the scandal-tainted budget director Bert Lance, the Reagan administration's selling of arms to Iran and diversion of some of the proceeds to the contra rebels in Nicaragua—in all cases, suspicion of presidential wrongdoing provided a seeming license for journalists to place a black hat on the president's head and white ones on their own. Not surprisingly, they took out after Clinton in 1994, when questions were raised about the propriety of his and Hillary Rodham Clinton's investment in the Whitewater real estate development during his tenure as governor of Arkansas, and in 1998, when evidence emerged about his adulterous affair with one-time White House intern Monica Lewinsky. Journalists also tried their hardest to tie President George W. Bush and Vice President Richard B. Cheney to the Enron scandal in 2002.

Yet, on balance, most presidents still receive mostly favorable press coverage. As journalist and former White House staffer James Fallows noted in his 1996 book *Breaking the News*, "The 'toughness' of today's media is mainly a toughness of demeanor rather than a real toughness of reporting."[33] In their study of how CBS, *Time*, and the *New York Times* covered the presidency from 1953 to 1978, Michael Grossman and Martha Kumar found that about twice as many stories were favorable to the president as were unfavorable. The pattern they detected continued into the Reagan years, then fell off for the first president Bush and Clinton. Yet, if anything, the two-to-one ratio in favor of the presidency may understate the true situation. Flattering pictures of presidents in *Time*, the *Times*, and CBS outnumbered unflattering ones in Grossman and Kumar's research by margins of 33 to 1, 34 to 1, and 6 to 1, respectively.[34] Local and regional media, which the authors did not study, tend to be more supportive of the president than the national media. George W. Bush benefited from strong positive coverage in the aftermath of the September 11, 2001, terrorist attacks.

Even more pertinent to the issue of journalists' standards for evaluating the presidency are the kinds of actions by presidents that generate the most favorable coverage. According to Grossman and Kumar, reporters respond enthusiastically to presidential actions that convey strength. They list five categories of such stories:

1. appearing decisive—military leadership
2. appearing decisive—firing contrary subordinates
3. being in command—the president as expert
4. being in command—the president as effective intellectual
5. being recognized as a leader—foreign travel

In sum, when strong action—or the appearance of strong action—comes from the White House, journalists tend to applaud it. The extent to which this tendency has continued is evidenced by the title of the most influential book on Reagan and the press, *On Bended Knee* and the corresponding book about Clinton's media relations, *Spin Cycle*.[35] The tendency to celebrate presidential strength also was apparent in press coverage of George W. Bush before and after he launched the war on terrorism. Instead of "Bush," he became "the president" in news stories, and the gleeful reporting of "Bushisms"—that is, Bush's occasional grammatical errors and malapropisms—gave way to journalistic praise of the president's "plainspokenness."

Why do reporters who are cynical about the presidency continue to cover it favorably? One reason is occupational necessity. Most White House correspondents must file several stories every day. Because of the severe limitations that are placed on reporters' ability to gather information independently, the president or the press secretary is in a good position to define the agenda they cover. "They have this huge built-in element of control over you," explains one *Washington Post* reporter. "You're locked into this little press room with only a telephone connecting you to the rest of the White House, and they have the option of taking your calls or not. All you get is staged events—press conferences, briefings, photo opportunities."[36] Dom Bonafede of the *National Journal* observed during the Ford years that "every day when [press secretary Ron] Nessen gets out there he determines, with his opening statement, what the news is going to be for that day."[37]

Within a few months of taking office in 1981, the Reagan administration refined the task of information management to an art, alternating techniques of secrecy and publicity to shape the flow and even the "spin" (the public relations term for "meaning") of news. Reagan's team was so adroit that when Clinton got off to a bumpy start with the press in early 1993, his solution was to add one of the Reagan administration's leading spinmeisters, David Gergen, to his senior staff. George H. W. Bush invented yet another new twist. A stickler for secrecy, he nonetheless appeared before reporters more than any president since Franklin Roosevelt. Bush managed the news by putting out lots of information, virtually all of his own choosing. Thus, even when reporters tagged on a cynical twist, it was usually to a story that the White House had packaged.

Editors demand more than routine stories from their White House correspondents; they also expect an occasional exclusive to give them a leg up on the competition. These almost always come through leaks of information from members of the White House staff. Such leaks are usually intended to make the president look good. The personal success of presidential assistants, after all, is tied very closely to the political success of the president. But according to the late Peter Lisagor of the *Chicago Daily News*, reporters really have little choice but to use whatever they get:

The competition and competitive pressure is such that guys have to get a story. If they get something that someone else might not have—no matter how self-serving [for the White House] it may seem and no matter how hardnosed they may feel themselves to be—they may often go with the story.[38]

Considerations other than occupational necessity also contribute to reporters' favorable portrayal of a powerful presidency. Their worldview, or implicit conception of how the political system works, greatly affects how they perform their job. "Journalists define the center of government action as the executive," noted David Paletz and Robert Entman, and "personalize the institution as one man."[39] A study by Elmer Cornwell of front-page newspaper headlines from 1885 to 1957 found "a long-term upward trend [in presidency-centered coverage] in absolute terms and relative to news about Congress"; Alan Balutis's extension of Cornwell's data through 1974 found both trends growing stronger.[40] As for television, Doris Graber's study of network evening news programs in 1994 and 1995 found that they broadcast nearly five times as many stories about the president as about Congress and that the stories about Congress usually were shorter and appeared later in the program.[41] The favorable or unfavorable quality of presidential coverage may be less important than the coverage itself. Simply by dwelling on the presidency, the media reinforce images of its strength and importance.[42] Finally, reporters tend to look at government through the lens of electoral politics. They often describe relations between the presidency and other policy-making institutions, especially Congress, in terms of victories and defeats for the president. This, too, reinforces the notion that strong presidents who dominate the system are good presidents.

Citizens: Strength amid Contradiction

The American presidency combines the roles of chief of government and chief of state. As chief of government, the president is called on to act as a partisan political leader, in the manner of the British prime minister. As chief of state, the president is the equivalent of the British monarch: the ceremonial leader of the nation and the living symbol of national unity.

Because the presidency embodies both roles, the general public tends to evaluate presidents by standards that seem contradictory. According to Cronin, Americans want the president to be "gentle and decent but forceful and decisive," "inspirational but 'don't promise more than you can deliver,' " "open and caring but courageous and independent," a "common man who gives an uncommon performance," and a "national unifier-national divider."[43] George Edwards suggested several similar sets of contradictory public expectations about presidential style, including "leadership vs. responsiveness" and "statesman vs. politician."[44] Most of these apparent paradoxes are really one:

Americans want the president to be a chief of state who will unite them as well as a chief of government who will lead and thus divide them.

Expectations of presidential policy making also seem to be contradictory. On the one hand, the public expects the president to reduce unemployment, cut the cost of government, increase government efficiency, deal effectively with foreign policy, and strengthen national defense. In a survey taken shortly after Carter's election in 1976, 59 percent to 81 percent of the respondents, depending on the policy in question, said they expected Carter to accomplish these goals. The comparable figures following Reagan's 1980 election ranged from 69 percent to 89 percent. Similarly high expectations arose after Clinton was first elected in 1992.[45]

Yet the conventional wisdom among scholars is that the public also would prefer that Congress—the other, constitutionally equal branch that the voters elect—dominate the presidency in the policy-making process. For example, after reviewing a wide variety of poll data from as far back as 1936, Hazel Erskine concluded, "Whenever given a choice between congressional vs. presidential decision-making, the people tend to trust Congress over the chief executive. Whether the issue pertains to specific domestic or military matters, or to authority in general, seems immaterial."[46]

In apparent contradiction of their high expectations of presidential performance, then, Americans are *philosophical congressionalists*. But in truth, all this means is that when pollsters ask abstract questions about institutional relations, the public tends to side with Congress against the president. (It is hard to imagine that questions about the proper balance of power between the branches come up very often in ordinary conversation.)[47] When one looks at evidence about attitudes and feelings that bear more directly on political behavior, the balance shifts. The American people, like American scholars and journalists, want and admire strength in the presidency.

One finds first that Americans are *operational presidentialists*. Whatever they may say about proper institutional roles in theory, the presidents they like are the ones who take the lead and the Congresses they like are the ones that follow. Stephen Wayne provided evidence for the first half of this proposition in his report on a survey that asked people what qualities they admired most in their favorite president. "Strong" led the list by far; "forceful," "ability to get things done," and "decisive" ranked third, fifth, and seventh, respectively. "Concern for the average citizen," "honest," and "had confidence of the people" were the only often-mentioned qualities that were not clear synonyms for strength.[48] As for Congress, the only times that a majority of the respondents have approved of its performance in several decades of Harris and Gallup surveys have been when Congress was most responsive to strong presidential leadership.[49]

Americans can also be described as *emotional presidentialists*. Almost all of their political heroes from the past are presidents.[50] When candidates run for president, they promise to be like the best of their predecessors. In contrast, members of Congress—the "only distinctly native American criminal class," in Mark Twain's jest—serve in political folklore as the butt of jokes. Congressional aspirants tend to "run *for* Congress by running *against* Congress."[51]

Heroic feelings about the presidency show up most dramatically when a president dies. Surveys taken shortly after President Kennedy's assassination found Americans to be displaying symptoms of grief that otherwise appear only at the death of a relative or close friend. They "didn't feel like eating" (43 percent), were "nervous and tense" (68 percent), and felt "dazed and numb" (57 percent).[52] They also feared, for a short time at least, that the Republic was in danger.[53] Similar emotional outpourings seem to have accompanied the deaths in office of all presidents, whether by assassination or natural causes and whether they were popular or not. In Great Britain, it is a royal death, such as King George V's in 1936 or Princess Diana's in 1997, that occasions such deep emotions, not the death of the prime minister, the chief of government.[54]

The public's emotional attachment to the presidency has implications of its own for strong leadership. The honeymoon that a president enjoys with the people at the start of the term is, in a sense, an affirmation of faith in the office. New presidents almost always receive the early approval of millions of citizens who had voted against them, and some presidents are able to keep their public approval ratings at near-honeymoon levels for a year or more. As we will see, popularity with the voters is quite conducive to presidential leadership of Congress.

Presidents can also trade on the public's emotional support for the office in foreign affairs. Citizens will "rally 'round the flag" in the form of their chief of state in all sorts of international circumstances.[55] According to a study by Jong Lee, wars and military crises head the list of support-inspiring events, followed by new foreign policy initiatives, peace efforts, and summit conferences.[56] Nixon's public approval rating went up 12 percentage points after his October 1969 "Vietnamization" speech; Ford's jumped 11 points after he "rescued" the merchant ship *Mayaguez;* and Carter added 12 points to his rating as a result of the Camp David summit that brought Israel and Egypt together. Reagan enjoyed a number of such boosts: from 45 percent to 53 percent after the Grenada invasion in 1983 and from 62 percent to 68 percent after the 1986 bombing of

Libya, for example. In early 1991 Bush's approval rating soared higher (89 percent) than any previous president's after the U.S. victory against Iraq in the Gulf War. His record was broken by his son, George W. Bush, after he launched the war on terrorism in September 2001. The younger Bush's popularity rose from 51 percent to 90 percent and remained near that peak for months, the strongest and most sustained rally effect in the history of polling.

Rossiter summed up the symbolic and political importance of the presidency:

No president can fail to realize that all his powers are invigorated, indeed are given a new dimension of authority, because he is the symbol of our sovereignty, continuity, and grandeur. When he asks a senator to lunch in order to enlist support for a pet project, . . . when he orders a general to cease caviling or else be removed from his command, the senator and . . . the general are well aware—especially if the scene is laid in the White House—that they are dealing with no ordinary head of government.[57]

The evaluators of the presidency to whom Rossiter referred are not outside of government but are fellow officeholders. Like scholars, journalists, and the general public, members of Congress and bureaucrats evaluate the presidency in ways that are superficially detrimental to presidential leadership. Yet their underlying attitudes offer support for strong presidents.

Members of Congress: Strength amid Constituency Centeredness

Whether animated by a selfish urge to do well or a selfless desire to do good, the modern member of Congress wants to be reelected.[58] As Richard Fenno explained, "For most members of Congress most of the time, [the] electoral goal is primary. It is the prerequisite for a congressional career and, hence, for the pursuit of other member goals."[59] From 1946 to 2002 an average of more than 90 percent of all representatives sought another term in each election, as did approximately 85 percent of all senators.[60]

To be reelected, members must please their constituents, a task best accomplished by working in Congress to advance local interests as defined by local people. A Harris survey conducted for the House Commission on Administrative Review asked respondents whether they thought their representative should be primarily concerned with looking after the needs and interests of "his own district" or "the nation as a whole." They chose "own district" by a margin of 57 percent to 34 percent. About twice as many voters in another survey said that when a legislator sees a conflict between "what the voters think best" and "what he thinks best," the legislator should obey the voters. Additional studies confirm these findings.[61]

Personal ambition and constituents' demands powerfully influence how members of Congress behave in office. Most channel their energy and resources into activities that translate readily into votes. This creates an anomaly. Although Congress's main constitutional task is to legislate in the national interest, most of the activities that produce votes for members are nonlegislative, primarily "pork-barreling" and casework.[62] (Pork-barreling involves getting federal grant and project money for their home states and districts; casework is handling constituents' complaints about their personal experiences with the federal bureaucracy.) David Mayhew added "advertising" to the list of leading congressional activities: newsletters or questionnaires mailed home, personal visits, Web sites, and similar efforts "to create a favorable image but in messages having little or no issue content."[63]

What time is left for legislative activity generally is spent in two reelection-oriented ways. First, members propose laws that sound pleasing to the voters. This takes little effort but enables them to gain publicity in local media and to answer nearly any constituent's inquiry about policy or legislation with, "I introduced a bill on that very subject." Almost every member of Congress, for example, introduced or cosponsored a health care reform bill in 1994. (None passed.) At the same time, simply proposing laws commits them to none of the difficult, time-consuming, and largely invisible activities needed to get legislation over the hurdles of subcommittee, committee, and floor passage in each house.

Second, legislators work hard on those few areas of lawmaking that are of particular interest to the local constituency and to large campaign contributors. For example, the senators from a farm state can be certain that their effectiveness, not just their rhetoric, on agricultural issues will be monitored closely by opinion leaders back home. This explains why, for example, farm-state members dominate the Agriculture Committees in both houses and westerners dominate the Natural Resources Committee in the House and the Environment and Public Works Committee in the Senate.[64] Once on these committees, members often enter into mutually beneficial relationships with the interest groups and executive agencies in their policy "subgovernment." By supporting programs that interest groups favor, legislators obtain campaign funding and other electoral benefits. From agencies they receive special consideration for their constituents and influence over the distribution of patronage and contracts in return for generous appropriations and loose statutory reins.

Not surprisingly, representatives and senators also evaluate the presidency according to constituency-based criteria. To presidents who have an extensive legislative agenda, this can seem discouraging. Their difficulty in moving bills through a constitutionally bicameral legislature is compounded by Congress's culture of constituency service, which distracts members from serious legislative activity into the more electorally rewarding business of pork-barreling, casework, and advertising. Successful presidential leadership also requires that members direct their attention to national concerns. But congressional ambition is such that local issues, or the local effects of national issues, usually come first. Finally, most presidential initiatives call for legislative alteration of the status quo. Such proposals often conflict with the general satisfaction that each component of the various subgovernments, including the congressional committees and subcommittees, has with existing arrangements.

Nevertheless, in other, perhaps more important, ways Congress's constituency-centered culture enhances rather than inhibits presidential strength. These are the power to initiate, the power of popularity, and power in foreign policy.

Power to Initiate

During the past century, the public has placed ever-greater demands for action on the federal government, most of which have required the passage of new legislation. To satisfy each of these demands, Congress as an institution has had to move through the long, tortuous, and largely subterranean process of developing programs and steering them past its own internal obstacles to action. Representatives and senators naturally have wanted the legislative process to work, but as noted earlier, the pursuit of reelection takes them mainly into nonlegislative areas of activity.

Again and again since 1932, members of Congress have found their way out of this dilemma by turning to the presidency. Not only did Congress give Franklin Roosevelt a virtual blank check to deal with the Great Depression as he saw fit—in the fabled first hundred days, it passed more than a dozen pieces of Roosevelt-spawned legislation—Congress also authorized actions that allowed the president to institutionalize the role of policy initiator. The Bureau of the Budget was transferred from the Treasury Department to the newly created Executive Office of the President and was empowered to screen all departmental proposals for legislation before Congress could see them. In addition, the president was authorized to hire a personal political staff, largely for the purpose of developing and selling legislation to Congress.

In succeeding administrations, these trends continued. The Employment Act of 1946 called on the president (with the aid of the White House's new Council of Economic Advisers) to monitor the economy and recommend corrective legislation in times of economic distress. Similar congressional requests for presidential initiative were included in many other acts. When President Eisenhower, deferring to what he assumed would be Congress's preference, did not submit a legislative program in 1953, senators and representatives of both parties complained. Since then, every president has used the annual State of the Union address to shape Congress's policy agenda for the year. Remarkably, when Congress wanted to express its deep dissatisfaction with President Nixon's economic policies in 1971, it passed a law that forced on him the power to impose wage and price controls on the entire economy. When Congress wanted to place the burden on President Clinton to cut federal spending in 1997, it gave him the line-item veto. (The Supreme Court quickly found the line-item veto to be an unconstitutional delegation of power to the president.) In 2002, many legislators demanded that the president's Office of Homeland Security be converted into a cabinet department and granted new powers. Congress sometimes demands strength from the president even when the president does not want to act strongly.

Power of Popularity

The power to initiate legislation that members of Congress have ceded to the presidency in the interests of their own reelection is formidable in itself, but what of the power to get laws passed? Again, the constituency-centered culture of Congress can work to the advantage of presidential strength. The same congressional preoccupation with reelection that has led members to try to insulate their relationship with the voters from national political forces has also made them extremely sensitive to any national forces that might cost them votes. In particular, when legislators think that the president's support among the voters is high, they are more likely to follow presidential leadership.[65]

Perceptions of presidential popularity may grow out of a landslide election victory that is accompanied by unusually large gains for the president's party in Congress. Such gains invariably are attributed, accurately or not, to the president's coattails or to a mandate shared with Congress. Either way, the election creates a heightened disposition among legislators of both congressional parties to support the president's legislative agenda: copartisans because they want to ride the bandwagon, and at least a few electorally vulnerable members of the opposition party because they want to avoid being flattened by it. Such was the case following the landslide elections of Johnson in 1964, whose party gained thirty-seven seats in the House, and Reagan in 1980, when Republicans won thirty-three new seats in the House and took control of the Senate with a gain of twelve seats.

The obsession with reelection that governs legislators' reactions to election results sometimes causes them to respond in a similar manner to indexes of presidential popularity during a president's term. Because reelection-oriented members of Congress "are hypersensitive to anticipated constituent reaction" to their actions, it is not surprising that the amount of support Congress gives to a president's legislative agenda is related to some extent to his public approval rating.[66] Most presidents enjoy a honeymoon period of high voter approval at the start of the term. Broadly speaking, among recent presidents, Eisenhower, Kennedy, and Reagan maintained their initial popularity throughout their terms, Johnson and Nixon kept theirs for the first two years, and Carter and the elder Bush held their ground in the polls for at least the first year. Even after their approval ratings declined, all but Johnson were able to revive their initial popularity, at least for short periods.[67] Johnson and Reagan held on long enough to get their particularly dramatic legislative programs through Congress virtually intact, Johnson in 1964 and 1965 and Reagan in 1981.

Power in Foreign Policy

Congress's constituency-centered culture also encourages presidential strength in foreign policy. Historically, Congress has been assertive only on the foreign policy issues that concern voters the most, especially unpopular wars and policies that have a clear domestic politics coloration, such as foreign trade and support for nations, especially Israel, with vocal and well-organized ethnic lobbies in this country.

Until the cold war ended in the early 1990s, these issues were overshadowed by the worldwide conflict between the United States and the Soviet Union. The war on terrorism that Bush launched in 2001 has overshadowed them once again. For members of Congress to pursue an interest in foreign policy much further than their constituents' interests is to tempt electoral fate. In one recent period, three consecutive Senate Foreign Relations Committee chairs were defeated in reelection bids by opponents who charged that they cared more about world politics than about local concerns.

Bureaucrats: Strength amid Careerism

Career civil servants may seem to be the group whose favorable evaluations presidents need the least. In civics book theory, they are part of the president's executive chain of command and perform purely administrative, not policy-making, functions. In practice, however, Congress and the courts, not just the chief executive, have a rightful say over what bureaucrats do. And in modern society, bureaucracy increasingly has involved those who implement policy in the making of it.

Like members of Congress, career civil servants, who represent virtually 99 percent of the federal workforce, often are motivated by self-interest. "The prime commitments of civil servants," wrote Erwin Hargrove, "are to their career, agency, and program. The markers of success are autonomy for their bureaus and expansion of budgets."[68] Such self-interested commitments make life difficult for the department secretaries and other political executives whom the president appoints to manage the bureaucracy in pursuit of the administration's policies.

The stance of presidents and their executive appointees toward the career bureaucrats, observed James Fesler, includes "an assumption that the bureaucracy is swollen, a doubt of careerists' competence, and an expectation of their unresponsiveness to the administration."[69] This view of the unresponsive bureaucrat seemed to be validated by Joel Aberbach and Bert Rockman in their 1970 study of the political beliefs of high-ranking civil servants in several social service agencies.[70] Large majorities of the bureaucrats whom they interviewed disapproved of President Nixon's policies to reduce the social agencies' programs and budgets. This was especially true of the 47 percent who were Democrats, but the bulk of the 36 percent who were independents also opposed the president. These data seemed so supportive of the stereotype of the self-interested bureaucrat resisting the policies of the elected president that Nixon actually quoted the authors' *American Political Science Review* article in his memoirs: "Our findings . . . pointedly portray a social service bureaucracy dominated by administrators hostile to many of the directions pursued by the Nixon administration in the realm of social policy."[71]

But far from proving Nixon's point, Aberbach and Rockman actually laid the groundwork for a later study that appears to have refuted it. In 1976 Richard Cole and David Caputo conducted a similar survey and discovered that most high-level bureaucrats, including Democrats and especially independents, by then supported Nixon's policies. "We find the 'pull' of the presidency to be very strong," Cole and Caputo concluded.[72]

What accounts for the apparent willingness of career bureaucrats to respond to strong presidential leadership? In part the stereotype of bureaucratic self-interest has been overdrawn. As Fesler noted, most careerists feel obliged "to serve loyally the people's choice as president. Because senior careerists have been through several changes in administration, this is a well-internalized commitment."[73] Presumably, the stronger a president's leadership, the easier it is for loyal bureaucrats to follow.

A more important explanation may be the president's capacity to redefine the self-interest of career bureaucrats. Cole and Caputo reported that the Nixon administration played an unusually purposeful and active role in the job-promotion process within the upper reaches of the civil service. Civil servants sympathetic to the administration's policies were favored. This group included not only Republicans but also many independents and some Democrats who recognized that the administration meant business and therefore adapted their views in order to further their own careers.

Nixon's successors enjoy even greater resources for influencing the bureaucracy than he did. The Civil Service Reform Act of 1978, which was passed at the request of President Carter, created a seven thousand-member corps of senior civil servants—the Senior Executive Service—whom the president may transfer or demote more easily than in the past. Reagan, according to Terry Moe, made "explicitly political use of the Senior Executive Service, usually by removing career officials from important slots and filling them with partisans. He also used reductions in force as a legal means of eliminating whole bureaucratic units staffed by careerists."[74] Subsequent presidents have followed suit.

In sum, the civics books are not entirely wrong. Some bureaucrats follow the ethic of loyal service to the president because they believe in it. Others follow when promotions are based on faithful obedience to the president. In either event the result is the same: "Senior bureaucrats, like Supreme Court justices, 'follow the election returns.' "[75]

Summary and Conclusion

Presidential scholarship in recent decades has been marked by a bewildering succession of new models of the presidency, each the product of an admixture of empirical and normative assessments, each constructed in hasty overreaction to the most recent president. Journalists' coverage of the presidency has been tinged by a Vietnam- and Watergate-induced cynicism whose real source may be the status frustration of the modern White House press corps. Citizens pin their hopes for chief-of-state-like symbolic leadership and chief-of-government-like political leadership on one office, the presidency. Members of Congress view the White House through constituency-colored lenses, judging the presidency mostly by the narrow standard of personal reelection ambitions. Tenured civil servants, whose working life is committed to the bureaucracy, also tend to evaluate the presidency in terms of their own careers.

Each of these assessments, although true in part, is superficial. Underlying the scholars' confusion is an implicit appreciation that significant policy change, whatever its ideological direction, requires a strong president. The career needs and worldviews of journalists lead them, too, to exalt presidential strength. Citizens apparently want to have the contradictions in their expectations resolved through presidential actions that are strong and appear to be unifying. Legislators and bureaucrats realize, albeit reluctantly at times, that their career interests can be served by strong presidential initiatives.

On the whole, the underlying admiration for and celebration of presidential strength by scholars, journalists, citizens, members of Congress, and career bureaucrats should be a source of comfort to presidents and to all who have fretted in recent years about a decline in the authority of the presidency. But two cautionary notes need to be sounded.

First, strength means different things to different people. Scholarly celebrants of a strong presidency have traditionally dismissed the president's administrative duties as distractions from the real tasks of moral and political leadership. Yet many bureaucrats respond to strong presidential initiatives only when they seem likely to influence their own careers. Similarly, although the public tends to respond enthusiastically to strong presidential action of a unifying kind, journalists write most approvingly when a president defeats the political opposition.

Second, the urge that presidents such as Johnson, Nixon, and Clinton have felt to impress audiences both present and future as strong—and hence "great"—leaders may lead them to behave in ways that disserve themselves, the government, and the nation. "For fear of being found out and downgraded," wrote Nelson Polsby, "there is the temptation to hoard credit rather than share it . . . [and] to export responsibility away from the White House for the honest shortfalls of programs, thus transmitting to the government at large an expectation that loyalty upward will be rewarded with disloyalty down." The final and most dangerous temptation is "to offer false hopes and to proclaim spurious accomplishments to the public at large."[76]

The complete lesson for presidents who wish to exert strong leadership, then, is that they need not worry about threats from the rest of the political system. Their problems really begin only when the concern for appearing strong distracts them from the business of being president.

Notes

1. Some of the themes in this chapter are discussed in more detail by Erwin C. Hargrove and Michael Nelson in *Presidents, Politics, and Policy* (New York: Knopf, 1984).

2. Arthur Schlesinger, "Our Presidents: A Rating by 75 Historians," *New York Times Magazine*, July 29, 1962, 12ff.

3. Gary Maranell, "The Evaluation of Presidents: An Extension of the Schlesinger Polls," *Journal of American History* 57 (June 1970): 104–113.

4. A study of how social scientists rated presidents from Franklin D. Roosevelt through Richard M. Nixon found economists' rankings to be similar to those of political scientists and historians. Malcolm B. Parsons, "The Presidential Rating Game," in *The Future of the American Presidency*, ed. Charles Dunn (Morristown, N.J.: General Learning Press, 1975), 66–91.

5. Thomas Cronin, "Superman: Our Textbook President," *Washington Monthly* (October 1970): 47–54.

6. James MacGregor Burns, *Presidential Government: The Crucible of Leadership* (Boston: Houghton Mifflin, 1965), 330.

7. Richard Neustadt, *Presidential Power: The Politics of Leadership* (New York: Wiley, 1960). The theme of Neustadt's book is that, although presidents can do little by direct command, they can and should wield great power through skillful bargaining and persuasion.

8. Clinton Rossiter, *The American Presidency* (New York: Harcourt, Brace and World, 1960), 15–16, 108.

9. Herman Finer, *The Presidency* (Chicago: University of Chicago Press, 1960), 111, 119.

10. Schlesinger, "Our Presidents," 40.

11. William Andrews, "The Presidency, Congress, and Constitutional Theory," in *Perspectives on the Presidency*, ed. Aaron Wildavsky (Boston: Little, Brown, 1975), 38. For further evidence of partisan and ideological bias in scholarly assessments of the presidency, see Parsons, "Presidential Rating Game," and Christopher J. Bosso, "Congressional and Presidential Scholars: Some Basic Traits," *PS: Political Science and Politics* 22 (December 1989): 839–848.

12. Arthur M. Schlesinger Jr., *A Thousand Days* (Boston: Houghton Mifflin, 1965), 677; and Schlesinger Jr., *The Imperial Presidency* (Boston: Houghton Mifflin, 1973).

13. Marcus Cunliffe, "A Defective Institution?" *Commentary*, February 1968, 28.

14. Nelson Polsby, "Against Presidential Greatness," *Commentary*, January 1977, 63.

15. James David Barber, *The Presidential Character* (Englewood Cliffs: Prentice-Hall, 1972).

16. Thomas Cronin, *The State of the Presidency* (Boston: Little, Brown, 1975), 138.

17. George Reedy, *The Twilight of the Presidency* (New York: New American Library, 1970), chap. 1. See also Bruce Buchanan, *The Presidential Experience* (Englewood Cliffs: Prentice-Hall, 1978); and Irving Janis, *Victims of Group Think* (Boston: Houghton Mifflin, 1972).

18. Gerald Ford, "Imperiled, Not Imperial," *Time*, November 10, 1980, 30–31; and Thomas Franck, ed., *The Tethered Presidency* (New York: New York University Press, 1981).

19. Aaron Wildavsky, "The Past and Future Presidency," *Public Interest* 41 (fall 1975): 56–76.

20. Godfrey Hodgson, *All Things to All Men* (New York: Simon and Schuster, 1980), 239.

21. Seraph, a fourth model of the presidency as an institution that is and should be weak, has never dominated presidential scholarship. But it has its adherents. See, for example, Fred Greenstein, "Change and Continuity in the Modern Presidency," in *The New American Political System,* ed. Anthony King (Washington, D.C.: American Enterprise Institute for Public Policy Research, 1978); and Peter Woll and Rochelle Jones, "The Bureaucracy as a Check upon the President," *Bureaucrat* 3 (April 1974): 8–20.

22. Barber, *Presidential Character,* chap. 13; Schlesinger Jr., *Imperial Presidency,* chap. 11; Robert K. Murray and Tim H. Blessing, *Greatness in the White House* (University Park: Pennsylvania State University Press, 1988), 16; and Fred I. Greenstein, *The Hidden-Hand Presidency: Eisenhower as Leader* (New York: Basic Books, 1982).

23. Arthur Schlesinger Jr., "The Ultimate Approval Rating," *New York Times Magazine,* December 15, 1996, 47–51.

24. Pre-Vietnam and Watergate press attitudes are described by Tom Wicker in "News Management from the Small Town to the White House," *Washington Monthly,* January 1978, 19–26.

25. Stephen Hess, *The Washington Reporters* (Washington, D.C.: Brookings Institution, 1981), 78.

26. Quoted by Michael Baruch Grossman and Martha Joynt Kumar in *Portraying the President: The White House and the News Media* (Baltimore: Johns Hopkins University Press, 1981), 131.

27. Ibid., 206–207.

28. Hess, *Washington Reporters,* 49.

29. Quoted in Grossman and Kumar, *Portraying the President,* 183.

30. Ibid., 43.

31. Ibid., 36.

32. Ibid., 301.

33. James Fallows, *Breaking the News: How the Media Undermines American Democracy* (New York: Pantheon, 1996), 196.

34. Grossman and Kumar, *Portraying the President* chap. 10, and see fig. 12-1 for data on Reagan, Bush, and Clinton.

35. Ibid., 232–238; Mark Hertsgaard, *On Bended Knee: The Press and the Reagan Presidency* (New York: Farrar, Straus, and Giroux, 1988); and Howard Kurtz, *Spin Cycle: Inside the Clinton Propaganda Machine* (New York: Free Press, 1998).

36. Quoted by David Paletz and Robert Entman in *Media Power Politics* (New York: Free Press, 1981), 57.

37. Quoted in Grossman and Kumar, *Portraying the President,* 33.

38. Ibid., 182.

39. Paletz and Entman, *Media Power Politics,* 55.

40. Elmer Cornwell, "Presidential News: The Expanding Public Image," *Journalism Quarterly* 36 (summer 1959): 282; and Alan Balutis, "The Presidency and the Press: The Expanding Public Image," *Presidential Studies Quarterly* 7 (fall 1977).

41. Doris Graber, *Mass Media and American Politics,* 6th ed. (Washington, D.C.: CQ Press, 2002), 295–296.

42. Bruce Miroff, "Monopolizing the Public Space: The President as a Problem for Democratic Politics," in *Rethinking the Presidency,* ed. Thomas Cronin (Boston: Little, Brown, 1982), 218–232.

43. Thomas Cronin, "The Presidency and Its Paradoxes," in *The Presidency Reappraised,* 2d ed., ed. Thomas Cronin and Rexford Tugwell (New York: Praeger, 1977), 69–85.

44. George C. Edwards III, *The Public Presidency* (New York: St. Martin's, 1983), 196–198.

45. "Early Expectations: Comparing Chief Executives," *Public Opinion* (February/March 1981): 39; George C. Edwards III and Stephen J. Wayne, *Presidential Leadership*, 5th ed. (New York: St. Martin's Press, 1999), 103.

46. Hazel Erskine, "The Polls: Presidential Power," *Public Opinion Quarterly* 37 (fall 1973): 488.

47. Richard Fenno Jr., *Home Style: House Members in Their Districts* (Boston: Little, Brown, 1978), 245. According to Fenno: "Most citizens find it hard or impossible to think about Congress as an institution. They answer questions about it; but they cannot conceptualize it as a collectivity."

48. Stephen Wayne, "Great Expectations: What People Want from Presidents," in *Rethinking the Presidency*, ed. Cronin, 192–195.

49. Roger Davidson and Walter Oleszek, *Congress and Its Members*, 7th ed. (Washington, D.C.: CQ Press, 2000), 413–414.

50. Donald Devine, *The Political Culture of the United States* (Boston: Little, Brown, 1972), 128.

51. Fenno, *Home Style*, 168.

52. Paul Sheatsley and Jacob Feldman, "The Assassination of President Kennedy: Public Reactions," *Public Opinion Quarterly* 28 (summer 1964): 197–202.

53. Ibid., 197.

54. See, for example, Sebastian de Grazia, *The Political Community* (Chicago: University of Chicago Press, 1948), 112–115.

55. John Mueller, *War, Presidents, and Public Opinion* (New York: Wiley, 1973), 69–74, 122–140.

56. Jong R. Lee, "Rally Round the Flag: Foreign Policy Events and Presidential Popularity," *Presidential Studies Quarterly* 7 (fall 1977): 255.

57. Rossiter, *American Presidency*, 16–17.

58. See Morris Fiorina, *Congress: Keystone of the Washington Establishment*, 2d ed. (New Haven: Yale University Press, 1989), 37–47; and David Mayhew, *Congress: The Electoral Connection* (New Haven: Yale University Press, 1974).

59. Fenno, *Home Style*, 31.

60. Calculated from data presented in *Vital Statistics on American Politics*, 2001–2002, ed. Harold W. Stanley and Richard G. Niemi (Washington, D.C.: CQ Press, 2001), 53–55. In that same period, more than 90 percent of the representatives and nearly 80 percent of the senators who ran were reelected.

61. Morris Fiorina, "Congressmen and Their Constituents: 1958 and 1978," in *The United States Congress*, ed. Dennis Hale (Chestnut Hill: Boston College, 1982), 39; Davidson and Oleszek, *Congress and Its Members*, chaps. 4 and 5.

62. Fiorina, *Congress*, 41–49.

63. Mayhew, *Congress*, 49.

64. Kenneth A. Shepsle, *The Giant Jigsaw Puzzle: Democratic Committee Assignments in the Modern House* (Chicago: University of Chicago Press, 1978); Roger Davidson, *The Role of the Congressman* (New York: Pegasus, 1968), 121.

65. For a study of the complex relationship between presidential popularity and legislative success, see Mark A. Peterson, *Legislating Together: The White House and Capitol from Eisenhower to Reagan* (Cambridge: Harvard University Press, 1990), chaps. 4 and 5.

66. George C. Edwards III, *At the Margins: Presidential Leadership of Congress* (New Haven: Yale University Press, 1989).

67. Edwards, *Public Presidency,* 219–220.

68. Erwin C. Hargrove, *The Missing Link* (Washington, D.C.: Urban Institute, 1975), 114.

69. James Fesler, "Politics, Policy, and Bureaucracy at the Top," *Annals* 466 (March 1983): 32.

70. Joel Aberbach and Bert Rockman, "Clashing Beliefs within the Executive Branch: The Nixon Administration Bureaucracy," *American Political Science Review* 70 (June 1976): 456–468.

71. Richard Nixon, *RN* (New York: Grossett and Dunlap, 1978), 768.

72. Richard Cole and David Caputo, "Presidential Control of the Senior Civil Service," *American Political Science Review* 73 (June 1979): 399–412.

73. Fesler, "Politics, Policy, and Bureaucracy," 34.

74. Terry M. Moe, "The Politicized Presidency," in *The New Direction in American Politics,* ed. John E. Chubb and Paul E. Peterson (Washington, D.C.: Brookings Institution, 1985), 260–261.

75. Francis Rourke, "Grappling with the Bureaucracy," in *Politics and the Oval Office,* ed. Arnold Meltsner (San Francisco: Institute for Contemporary Studies, 1981), 137.

76. Polsby, "Against Presidential Greatness."

Part I The Presidency in Comparative Perspective

2 Comparing the Core Executive in Britain, France, and the United States

Nigel Bowles

"The oldest lesson in political science," notes Nigel Bowles, is that "we learn and understand more about one political system by comparing it systematically with others." Much can be learned about executive government in the United States by comparing it with executive government in, for example, Britain and France. At various times and in various combinations, Bowles argues, all three national executives may be understood through the lenses of one or more of four models of executive government he presents: "monocratic" (government by one person), "segmented" (government in which the chief executive leads in certain policy areas, while other members of the executive lead in others), "shared" (government in which leadership responsibility in each policy area is shared), and "bureaucratic coordination" (government in which permanent agencies dominate in their own policy areas). As was the case in all three countries in the aftermath of the September 11, 2001, terrorist attacks on the United States, the prominence of each of these four models of executive government "is heavily contingent upon exogenous developments."

Ever since Aristotle classified political systems in his great work *The Politics*, most political scientists have accepted that knowledge and understanding of any one political system are enriched by comparing it with other political systems. For example, the study of the development of social welfare policy in one country may become more meaningful by comparison of its origins, circumstances, and development in that country with analysis of those characteristics in another. The comparative method also helps shed light on major political developments: we can discover more about democratization in Brazil if we compare the processes of democratization there with such processes in other South American countries. A similar claim for the utility of the comparative method can be made for the study of privatization or of public sector reform in the 1980s and 1990s: comparison aids knowledge and understanding of why public sector reforms came to be adopted in so many countries at much the same time, how and why they differed in their forms and purposes, and the implications that such reforms have had for the nature and quality of democratic politics. Comparison can also enrich our knowledge and understanding of political institutions such as courts, legislatures, bureaucracies, and executives.

The comparative method in political science is most useful when it is *systematic*—when the origins, structures, powers, rules, or membership of an institution or set of institutions in one political system are systematically compared with those of one or more different systems. It is important that we know exactly what is being compared and why, and what useful inferences may and may not be drawn. This chapter examines the executive in three major western democracies. I pose the question—"How is the distribution of power within the core executives of Britain, France, and America to be understood at the beginning of the twenty-first century?"—and seek to answer it by comparative analysis.[1]

In 1990 political scientists Patrick Dunleavy and Rod Rhodes offered a framework for analyzing the core executive in Britain. Their framework consists of six models: Prime Ministerial, Prime Ministerial Cliques, Cabinet, Ministerial, Segmented, and Bureaucratic Coordination.[2] They defined the "core executive" to include ". . . all those organizations and structures which primarily serve to pull together and integrate central government policies, or act as final arbiters within the executive of conflicts between different elements of the government machine."[3]

Dunleavy and Rhodes's framework offers clear advantages. In particular, it is more nuanced than the traditional dichotomy between prime ministerial government and cabinet government. Robert Elgie used a modified form of their approach both in his work on France and in his comparative analysis.[4] In this chapter I use another modified version to assess the utility of four categories of executive government and apply them to Britain, America, and France. The four types are:

Monocratic Government: "presidential" government in the United States and in Fifth Republic France and "prime ministerial" government in Britain.

Segmented Government: leadership by the chief executive in certain policy areas and by members of the executive in other areas.

Shared Government: leadership by politicians interacting with each other, whether competitively or cooperatively.

Monocratic Government

France, Britain, and America have all been identified at one time or another
as monocratic. During the Third Republic (1870–1940) and Fourth Republic
(1946–1958), however, France exhibited not a trace of monocracy: the executive
was perpetually weak, sometimes to the point of paralysis. In Britain, neither
the prime minister nor cabinet ministers enjoyed any significant autonomy
from Parliament, whose greatest power was negative—denying the executive
the autonomy to govern.

Charles de Gaulle provided a solution to the Fourth Republic's manifest inadequacies by returning in 1958 from self-imposed political exile to preside over
the drafting of a new constitution for a Fifth Republic. Yet even during that
drafting, which was undertaken with the threat of civil war hanging over
France, it seemed unlikely that a monocratic regime would result. The new
constitution's authors sought a balance between a system of responsible
government based loosely on the British model and a president chosen by an
electoral college. Once elected president, however, de Gaulle set about undermining not only that intention, but also those French colonists in Algeria who
had misinterpreted his election to mean that Algeria would remain forever
French. By 1962 de Gaulle not only had maneuvered to bring about Algerian independence but also unconstitutionally forced and won the holding of a referendum to provide for direct election of the president of the Republic, with a
runoff election between the top two candidates if no candidate received a majority in the first round.

De Gaulle's referendum did not result in universal acceptance of the
regime's legitimacy. The left, especially the Communist Party, which regularly
won a fifth or more of the presidential vote between 1958 and 1974, regarded the
two-stage ballot for the presidency as a means to exclude it from power. That
was why the communists favored a parliamentary regime—at least until such
time as they could seize unfettered power permanently. Like others on the left,
the politician who later emerged as a leader of the French Socialist Party and as
president of the Republic from 1981 to 1995, François Mitterrand, also expressed
(or feigned) alarm at the institution of the presidency. In 1964 Mitterrand
disingenuously characterized it as representing a Gaullist *coup d'état permanent*. Valéry Giscard d'Estaing, Mitterrand's predecessor as president from 1974

to 1981, had similarly dissembled on the subject. Although they were not Gaullists, Giscard and Mitterrand nevertheless showed themselves in office to be zealous defenders of presidential prerogatives and pomp. As Vincent Wright observed, "François Mitterrand's virulent denunciations of presidentialism ceased when he became President. Already as First Secretary of the Socialist Party he had displayed his schizophrenic attachment to both republican ideals and monarchical methods."[6] The broader significance of Mitterrand's behavior was that the presidency had by 1981 achieved a legitimacy that had seemed improbable at the beginning of the Fifth Republic and would have seemed barely conceivable to most informed opinion leaders during the Third and Fourth Republics.

If monocracy *is* to be found in France, the strongest case for it is in the Fifth Republic during those periods when the president enjoyed favorable party majorities in the Assembly—under de Gaulle from 1958 to 1969, Georges Pompidou from 1969 to 1974, Giscard from 1974 to 1981, and Mitterrand from 1981 to 1986 and from 1988 until 1993, and Jacques Chirac from 1995 to 1997. The broader argument that France is monocratic finds support from François Goguel, who characterized the regime as "presidential," a synonym for monocratic.[7] Writing just two years after de Gaulle's death, Maurice Duverger went so far as to describe the regime as "monarchical." [8] As memories of de Gaulle, his politics, and the party he founded have faded, it has been harder to describe the French executive in such strong terms. De Gaulle governed with solidly favorable Assembly majorities. But conditions of cohabitation, in which a president governs with a prime minister chosen from among opponents, have since become common. During the cohabitations of 1986 to 1988, 1993 to 1995, and 1997 to 2002, monocracy has been conspicuous by its absence. Even when the president has an Assembly majority, the case for monocracy is clearer with respect to the president's political prestige rather than his direct responsibility for domestic decision making. In the gritty politics of policy implementation, the president of France has alongside him a prime minister with authority, power, and resources of his own.

The president may dismiss the prime minister, but it is a risky option. Among the reasons for which presidents have exercised the option have been unpopularity and incompetence (as when Mitterrand dismissed the hapless Edith Cresson in 1995) and popularity and competence (as when de Gaulle dismissed the supremely able Pompidou in 1969). To a president, either combination of qualities might appear to be a political threat. Nevertheless, the prime minister has enormous authority not only over policymaking and implementation, but also over the central organs of the state. That authority—the entitlement to act—grants him power, which is the capacity to influence others and to shape the direction of policymaking and implementation. Cohabitation has made even plainer that the distribution of authority and power in the French executive is contingent upon broader political circumstances. Those circumstances are, first, whether the president has a free hand in selecting a prime minister from his own party rather than having to choose one from a hostile Assembly majority; second, the political capacities and fortunes of the president and prime minister; and third, the calculations of each about his political prospects.

A significant element in such calculations is that leading French politicians regard the presidency as France's supreme electoral prize. In the Fifth Republic, many prime ministers have sought the presidency, but no president has sought to be prime minister. That difference is exemplified in the current executive: in the 2002 elections President Chirac sought to retain his post, while Prime Minister Lionel Jospin sought to displace him—hence their ferocious political competition between 1997 and 2002. If, under conditions of cohabitation, the differences of authority and power between the two executive posts are slight, the difference between their popular prestige remains great. As Olivier Duhamel wrote in 1986, "After having tried out over a century and a half all possible systems, we have adopted a Constitution pregnant with almost every system."[9] His point was that struggles over the nature of the executive power, which had in part provoked the French Revolution of 1789, were not settled by that revolution but instead were redirected and reframed by it. Duhamel is correct, but the possibilities emerging from the pregnant Fifth Republic's constitution have been fewer than he implies: the regime has never been parliamentary, and is becoming less monocratic.

Many have argued that the U.S. government is monocratic.[10] The presidency's prestige is immense. No other office matches the presidency on that count or for its consequential attraction to serious and ambitious politicians. Yet monocracy is not apparent, with the possible exception of Lincoln between 1861 and 1865, until the twentieth century. Until then, Congress was always central to politics and even to administration. Had the Framers of the Constitution sought to establish a monocratic system, the states would have rejected the attempt. In fact, pressure among the Framers at Philadelphia in 1787 for such a system was never strong. They had experienced both the perils of an unaccountable colonial executive before the Revolutionary War and the inadequacies of confederal government with no executive after the war, and they fully appreciated the risks attaching to executives with either too much or too little power. Their final draft of the Constitution provided for a mixed government: a popularly elected House, a Senate selected by the states, and a president chosen by an electoral college. Over the course of more than two centuries, democratic means of election have enveloped all three institutions, but their structural separation from each other has remained complete. That separation, and the logic of negotiation and bargaining to which it has given rise, continue. Although Congress may temporarily yield to presidential influence in time of national emergency, the legislature cannot as a matter of constitutional practice be marginalized.

A president's commands are rarely self-executing.[11] The president's unilateral authority has grown, however, as shown, for example, by the burgeoning of executive orders since 1933. The scope of these agreements has become so large, their exercise so frequent, and their domain so important that not only the president's legal authority but also his usable power have increased with them. For the most part, Congress has acquiesced in this major extension of presidential authority and usable power.[12] This development does not make the president a commander (except in war), nor does it invalidate the understanding of the United States as a separated system. Congress's capacity and incentive to participate authoritatively in public policy as a coordinate institution remain immense.

Although constrained by his cabinet colleagues' ambitions, a British prime minister's authority is extensive. He decides upon the cabinet's composition, recruiting and dismissing as he judges best, formally subject to no one and certainly not to Parliament. He may establish or abolish government departments. He can dominate the processes of government decision making and thereby of policy formation and execution by selecting the chairs of the major cabinet committees. He interprets the discussion at those committees more or less as he wishes. He has extraordinary and special responsibility for the security and intelligence services' operations and budgets. Unlike his cabinet colleagues, the prime minister has no ministerial responsibility for a department, but he does have political responsibility for the government's conduct, successes, and failures.[13] Churchill discovered, in the Conservatives' heavy election defeat of July 1945, that even his popular prestige protected him neither from political responsibility for the failings of prewar Conservative governments nor from the resistance of British soldiers who opposed the continuation in peacetime of government by the officer class that had led them during war. Nevertheless, the character and extent of the British prime minister's power are set by his relationship with five groups:

- the cabinet upon whose continuing support he ultimately depends;
- backbench MPs in his own party;
- interest groups whose relations with the party in Parliament and in the country are politically or financially important;
- the official opposition in the House of Commons; and
- the voting public.

Adverse opinion within the cabinet can cruelly expose a prime minister—that was, in part, Anthony Eden's fate in 1956 and 1957 after the ignominious failure of the Suez expedition, as it was Margaret Thatcher's after public resistance intensified over her imposition of a poll tax. In each case, cabinet members concluded that the prime minister had become an electoral liability. Strong opposition among backbench MPs more numerous than the government's majority in the House of Commons may threaten a government's survival. That was John Major's experience when a small group of Conservative MPs (among them, Ian Duncan-Smith, the current leader of the Conservative Party), who were bitterly opposed to European integration, deliberately risked the continuation of Major's government rather than accommodate their views on Europe to those of the prime minister and his cabinet.

The once considerable ability of interest groups, especially trade unions, to intimidate an incumbent government has been slight since the mid-1980s. Powerful unions, benefiting from substantial immunities under the law as it then stood, effectively destroyed the anti-inflation strategies of Harold Wilson's and James Callaghan's Labour governments of 1966–1970, 1974–1976, and 1976–1979, and of Edward Heath's Conservative government of 1970–1974, thereby undermining those governments' political credibility. Thatcher crushed union demands with enhanced police and security forces and then used her large parliamentary majorities to reduce radically the legal immunities of unions.

Weak parliamentary opposition in Britain strengthens an incumbent executive by default; a divided opposition emboldens it. Thatcher had the good fortune between 1980 and 1988 to face a divided and sometimes incompetent Labour opposition, as Tony Blair has faced a divided and largely incompetent Conservative one since 1997. Thatcher and Blair behaved as they did and promoted the public policies they did partly to maximize and exploit the opposition's divisions. Similarly, with public support, a prime minister and his senior colleagues can vanquish most opponents, as Thatcher and Blair did; without it, even a highly competent prime minister can do little, as Harold Macmillan discovered in the twelve months before he stood down as prime minister in October 1963. Ambitious cabinet members may exploit weakness in the cabinet, among backbench MPs, interest groups, the opposition, or the voting public to advance their own cause and to damage that of the prime minister. Tony Benn, the ambitious left-wing secretary of state for energy, sought to do just that to Prime Minister James Callaghan between 1976 and 1979. Benn failed to damage Callaghan, but both then and thereafter he succeeded in damaging the Labour Party's credibility with the voters and so contributed to the Labour government's defeat in 1979.

Segmented Government

Dunleavy and Rhodes stipulate that segmented government exists in Britain when ". . . the premier and the Cabinet operate in different policy areas, with ministers operating below the interdepartmental level at which cabinet machinery becomes involved."[14] Clearly, this category does not easily apply to France or the United States where cabinet government does not exist. Nevertheless, segmented government is a useful category because neither prime ministers nor presidents can possibly exercise authority or power across the entire swath of a government's responsibility. In France, "segmentation" refers to a division of responsibilities between the president and the prime minister; in America, to a similar configuration between the president and his political appointees in the federal agencies; and in Britain, to a division of responsibilities between the prime minister and members of the cabinet.

Before a British prime minister intervenes in matters beyond the government's overall strategy—the economy, foreign and security policy—he must persuade himself of three things: first, that he has a compelling political interest in intervening beyond these traditional areas of prime ministerial responsibility; second, that he has the political and bureaucratic resources to sustain his intervention; and third, that he has the tenacity to change policy not only to the government's political advantage but also to his own. That is what Blair has attempted in education and health policy, but it is far from certain that he will succeed, not least because he lacks the deep bureaucratic support that is always available to department ministers. Civil servants in, for example, the Department of Health report to that department's ministers, not to the prime minister. Accordingly, the ministers enjoy advantages over the prime minister in their own policy areas. They specialize; he does not. They rarely think about other departments' business, except that of their paymaster, the Treasury; he has to think about all the departments' business because he has political responsibility for problems wherever they occur. In politics it is usually the unexpected event that shapes prime ministers' and presidents' lives, and they need to be sensitive to potential disruptions whatever their source. But that leaves little time to initiate and sustain chief executives' interventions beyond their usual policy domain.

In fact, most public policies lie beyond an American, British, or French chief executive's combat radius: the costs of involvement are usually too high and the benefits too uncertain. To this extent, the segmented government idea is a statement of fact about modern government: most areas of public policy remain within the jurisdiction of ministers (in Britain and France) and cabinet secretaries and their subordinates (in America) as a matter of practical politics and administration. Complex systems of bureaucratized government programs demand ministerial specialization, sustained involvement, and, as a result, segmentation. Prime ministers and presidents cannot escape the fact and implications of the principle of division of labor within government.

The American federal executive provides an example of segmentation. George W. Bush's conduct of his office changed suddenly and irrevocably on September 11, 2001. When that day began, he was engaged in a photo opportunity with schoolchildren in Sarasota, Florida, pressing his agenda for education reform; by the end of that day, he had returned to Washington to preside over an administration whose purpose was radically redefined by the terrorist attacks upon New York and Washington. After September 11, the U.S. secretary of education would have to plow the furrow of education reform mostly without President Bush's active engagement.

The significance of war for segmented government in the United States is that it tends to focus the president's attention ever more closely upon his responsibilities as commander in chief. It makes it harder for him to venture into other areas of public policy and to sustain such ventures over time. In practice, every president has to choose where and when to make policy commitments. War reduces his scope for doing so. As a result, a president will not be able to commit his time and energy or that of his staff to making durable efforts to change federal policy in more than a few policy areas—not least because authority over most programs' character and funding lies with Congress. Effective control of day-to-day executive decisions about policy initiation rests with senior political appointees in federal agencies, not in the White House. Presidents typically make and sustain few interventions in policy areas that fall within the formal jurisdiction of their cabinet colleagues, except in the presidential trinity of the economy, foreign affairs, and security policy. There are exceptions to the rule. President Lyndon Johnson, for example, initiated new policies concerning civil and political rights, welfare, the environment, urban affairs, education, and immigration reform while conducting the war in Vietnam. Such exceptions are few in number.

In France, too, the segmented government model finds empirical support in the Fifth Republic, partly because of the conspicuous failures of the Third and Fourth Republics to accord sufficient authority to the president or prime minister to act. After the wartime horrors of German occupation and of the collaborationist Vichy regime, France's weak Fourth Republic was a replay of the failed Third, providing for a weak executive, a dominant legislature, and bitterly divided parties. Although France made extraordinary economic advances from 1946 to 1958, the twelve years of the Fourth Republic's life, it did so despite executive weakness, not because of it. Decolonization in general, and Algerian decolonization in particular, did in the 1950s what the German invasion had done in 1940: both crises revealed not only the executive's incapacity in the face of extreme threat but also the fragility of France's republican order.

To be sure, Algerian decolonization was so serious a problem that it might well have threatened a regime with a more resilient architecture and more focused executive authority. Indeed, it did just that to the Fifth Republic between 1958 and 1962. As president, de Gaulle took extraordinary risks both to protect his emergent policy of disengagement from Algeria and to preserve the regime from those in the army and elsewhere who opposed his policy. Not the least of the risks de Gaulle took were those to his personal safety: one of several assassination attempts occurred in 1962 at Petit-Clamart, where fourteen bullets passed through his car but left him untouched and, remarkably, unruffled. De Gaulle's conduct of policy toward Algeria laid the foundation for the universal recognition that foreign affairs in the Fifth Republic is, indeed, the president's *domaine réservée.* Samy Cohen provocatively argues in his book *La Monarchie Nucléaire* that the president's domination of foreign and defense policy in France has become so great that he has taken on the attributes of Zeus.[15] De Gaulle arrogated to himself the authority to develop French nuclear weapons policy, to shape Europe to French designs (an effort in which he largely failed), and to create for France a negotiating space between the West and the East (in which he partly succeeded).

Even under cohabitation, the prime minister is wholly marginal in these matters, playing only such role as the president deigns to permit him. In economic, social, and education policy, by contrast, the prime minister normally dominates: even de Gaulle permitted his three prime ministers very broad latitude to govern in all matters beyond his *domaine réservée*. Under both Mitterrand's presidency and Chirac's, the phases of cohabitation reinforced this Gaullist rule of segmentation. As prime minister from 1997 to 2002, Jospin was not merely an influential figure but an enormously important one in, for example, accelerating the processes of French privatization. But his influence upon foreign and defense policy was slight.

Shared Government

A British prime minister must at least give the impression that he shares in government with the cabinet, where senior members limit his power and silently remind him of his political mortality. A prime minister who forgets that rule risks downfall, as Margaret Thatcher discovered in 1990 when the Conservative cabinet forced her to resign. To avoid such a personal catastrophe, a prime minister must take steps to deter and deflect it, protecting his position tomorrow by behaving appropriately today.[16] Most cabinet ministers publicly disavow ambition, but all privately seek opportunities for advancement. In this respect, the British prime minister's circumstances differ from those of the U.S. or French president because each is protected from *coups* by fixed terms and of the French prime minister, who serves at the pleasure of the president rather than of ministerial colleagues. The British prime minister cannot safely behave as if he were a president.

The British prime minister therefore depends (at best) on his colleagues' ongoing confidence in him or (at worst) on their inability to act collectively to displace him. All prime ministers reflect upon the paradox of being surrounded by people who are at once colleagues, bound together by the doctrine of collective responsibility that requires each of them to support *every* decision of the cabinet, and potential political rivals. That reality is usually enough to give any prime minister pause. Even war does not inoculate a prime minister from removal, as Neville Chamberlain discovered when he was replaced by Churchill in May 1940.[17] Nor does a huge election victory guarantee immunity from striving colleagues' ambitions, as Clement Attlee found in 1947/1948. Only unflinching support from Ernest Bevin, the politically powerful foreign secretary, deterred would-be cabinet rebels from ousting Attlee as prime minister.[18]

Accordingly, a prime minister must constantly attend to his political relations with senior and politically resourceful cabinet colleagues, especially the chancellor of the Exchequer (the political head of the Treasury) and the foreign and home secretaries. During his first period as prime minister between 1964 and 1970, Harold Wilson perfected the nefarious art of keeping such potential conspirators off balance to reduce the risk that one or more of them might depose him. The stratagem worked, but at the price of distracting Wilson from important questions of public policy.[19] During his own premiership from 1976 to 1979, James Callaghan behaved differently—partly because of his different temperament, partly because there was no credible threat to him from cabinet colleagues, but mostly because, as he lacked a Commons majority for most of his three years in office, his first concern was to enable the government to survive. That helps to explain why Callaghan stood by Denis Healey, his intellectually formidable but politically embattled chancellor of the Exchequer, during a particularly fraught period in Britain's postwar financial history. Had Callaghan done otherwise, the government might well have fallen earlier than it did.

Everything of political importance is at stake in the relationship between the prime minister and the chancellor: the government's credibility with voters, financial and economic markets, and with political supporters and opponents in the House of Commons. Two examples, one from Thatcher's administration in the late 1980s and one from Blair's after 1997, illustrate the point. Thatcher deliberately undermined the political credibility of Nigel Lawson, her most successful chancellor, by appointing Alan Walters, a Europhobic economist, to her retinue of advisers at No. 10, even though she knew (or perhaps because she knew) that Walters's appointment was repugnant to Lawson. The chancellor's resignation damaged Thatcher and contributed substantially to the government's destabilization and her political demise in September 1990. The relationship between Blair and Gordon Brown, his chancellor of the Exchequer since 1997, is different. Each understands the risks, as Thatcher failed to do, of a prime minister and chancellor appearing to advance different agenda. Blair and Brown each needs the other to advance his own purposes. Each also threatens the purposes of the other. But the government collectively needs both to stay in post. A relationship that once was close is characterized by continuing mutual need and by clashing ambitions that have caused their dealings to become episodically rancorous, with the potential to damage them and the government.[20]

Shared government abounds in the United States—not within the executive, but between the executive and the legislature. Article II of the Constitution creates a single executive. The president shares "the executive power" with no one else. That is an enormous asset for him. But unlike a British prime minister, the president has no party colleagues in the legislature whose primary political purpose is to sustain his government or to enable him to prosper against the opposition. That massive buttress of executive government in Britain is absent in the U.S. government, which is monocratic but because of the separation of powers lacks the reliable support of party. The system is alternatively understood, in Richard Neustadt's famous formulation, as "separated institutions sharing powers."[21] Separation obliges the American president to do what a French president need not—concern himself constantly with Congress's capacity to weaken his program and undermine him politically. Even when what is misleadingly referred to as the "same" party is (equally misleadingly) in "control" of the presidency and both houses of Congress, no president can subject Congress to his sustained power. Congress's authority under Article I is simply too great. The corollary to the separation of powers is the doctrine of "checks and balances." The former refers to the allocation of authority, and the latter to the processes of law and policymaking that force the separate branches to share power, to interact, to negotiate and bargain, and to struggle for advantage. The U.S. Constitution affords the president opportunities to set the national agenda, but it also implies an obligation to negotiate with an autonomous Congress for that agenda's adoption: the president has no plausible political option other than to work incessantly with Congress to achieve his objectives. What the Constitution separates, the processes of policymaking force together into shared authority and power over government.

Sharing persists even in war: the president still depends upon Congress to declare war or to support his waging of it, including the appropriation of sufficient funds to finance the effort. Nevertheless, war or the threat of it plays to a president's constitutional strengths and, at least in the short term or while there is a prospect of victory, causes effective power to shift to the White House. The point is not simply about authority: when the United States is in peril, voters look to the chief executive to lead and reassure; they do not look to the 535-member bicameral legislature. Presidents exploit that political fact, and Congress finds the exploitation difficult to resist.[22] In cases of uncertainty about war aims or war means or of significant military failure, such as in the latter phases of the Korean War and in Vietnam after 1966, however, voters express their doubts by voting against the president's party in congressional midterm elections. That is what happened to Wilson in 1918, Roosevelt in 1942, Truman in 1950, and Johnson in 1966. Although only Wilson suffered the replacement of a Democratic congressional majority with a Republican one, all four presidents experienced heavy losses on Capitol Hill.

In France, by contrast, crises usually leave the executive's domination of the legislature undisturbed—whether under cohabitation or not. By invoking pertinent clauses of the Constitution, the government may circumvent the Assembly altogether, either by declaring legislation to be "urgent," opting to pass legislation in package form, or invoking the government's right to rule by ordinance.[23] Not only may the government bypass the Assembly in this way but also frequently does so. Academic writing on French politics, understandably preoccupied with questions of party and parliament during the Fourth Republic, is now directed overwhelmingly toward the state and the executive: the authors of one recent book concerned with academic "debates and controversies" in French politics give little space to the legislature.[24] The shared government model no more applies to executive-legislative relations in Paris than it does in London.

Many striving ministerial participants shared in power in the short-lived governments of the Third and Fourth Republics. Under the Fifth Republic, however, only two candidates merit inclusion: the president as head of state and the prime minister as head of government. As for the nature of the sharing, ambiguity saturates the French Constitution. Article 20 declares, "The Government shall decide on and conduct national policy" and "It shall have at its disposal the public service and the armed forces." Article 21 declares that the prime minister ". . . shall direct the activities of the government," be "responsible for national defense," "have power to make regulations," and make "appointments to civil and military posts." The same article grants the prime minister extensive powers of patronage.[25] This abundance of authority leads Vincent Wright to conclude, "Even on a minimalist reading, the Prime Minister [is] a key policy actor."[26] So he is. And the prime minister shares executive authority with the president, but the distribution of power between the two offices is more complicated than the constitutional text suggests.

We have already seen that the presence or absence of cohabitation shapes the distribution of executive power in France. However, the president always enjoys the advantage that derives from the special legitimacy of his direct election, unlike the prime minister who owes his position to being the president's choice. This asymmetry of legitimacy works, as de Gaulle intended it should, to underline the presidency's supremacy. The Constitution is a poor guide on this question as on much else: nowhere does it grant to the president the right to dismiss the prime minister. Article 8 merely declares, "The President of the Republic appoints the Prime Minister. He terminates his functions when the latter tenders the resignation of the Government."[27] In practice, however, because de Gaulle took it upon himself to dismiss Michel Debré in 1962, presidents have dismissed prime ministers at will. Mitterrand availed himself of the services of no fewer than seven prime ministers, of whom he dismissed five.

Bureaucratic Coordination

In all three countries, presidents and prime ministers come to appreciate the frustrations of their position and accept that although they have responsibility for all the policy areas, their ability to affect significantly the content of any policy area is limited. One of the many postulated explanations of what Dunleavy and Rhodes term the ". . . very limited control over the rest of the state apparatus" that the core executive in Britain enjoys is the authority and power of the bureaucracy.[28] In truth, in America, Britain, and France, the evidence suggests that bureaucracies exercise such authority and power over a policy only when core executives choose not to commit their own political resources to effecting change. In many policy areas, the constraints of international and national markets are more significant.

Bureaucrats' typical advantages over core executives are their *permanence* in office, the *experience* they gain through long exposure to a cluster of related policy areas, and the *expertise* that even the most junior bureaucrat is in principle capable of acquiring or for which he or she has been trained. These qualities potentially are assets for governments capable of drawing upon them as resources; they also are potentially liabilities because of the asymmetries to which they give rise with regard to ministers who are always *temporary* occupants of office and usually are both *inexperienced* in a particular agency's subject matter, and *inexpert*.

France's experience suggests that the combination of a change of regime and of the identity of the chief executive may result in major changes of policy. De Gaulle's ability to use the resources of the presidency between 1958 and 1962 to change policy toward Algeria is a striking example. Less dramatically, de Gaulle attempted to change policy toward Europe in order to project France as the leader of a Franco-German alliance at the heart of the European Economic Community (now the European Union) from which he excluded Britain. Although that policy was only partly successful, he did manage to withdraw France from NATO's integrated military command in 1965. In all three cases, the bureaucratic interests within the French government were powerful but divided and hence vulnerable to de Gaulle's maneuvering. In none of the three cases does the power of coordinated bureaucracies explain the course of French policy and politics.

Markets are often more powerful constraints on executive power. Mitterrand's attempt to shift economic policy in a socialist direction through the sweeping nationalization of companies and a host of policies aimed at reducing unemployment was short-lived. But it is not clear that what ended this attempt in 1983/1984 was bureaucratic resistance to democratic socialism. Resistance there was, notably in the Finance Ministry, but the power of international markets explains more of the outcome.

In Britain, too, the power of markets to constrain governments has often been apparent. Markets do not eliminate governments' ability to decide, but they do limit it. Whether under fixed exchange rates and capital controls (the policies that prevailed in Britain after World War II until the 1970s) or under floating exchange rates and free capital movement (as have prevailed since 1979), British governments have constantly found their freedom to make economic policy limited by markets. Market pressure precipitated the devaluations of the pound in 1947 and 1967, the large cuts in public expenditure in 1966 and the even larger cuts in 1976, and the exit from the European Exchange Rate Mechanism in 1992.

The power of bureaucracies is scarcely absent in London: the Treasury throughout the postwar period has interpreted its role as one of reducing public expenditure wherever possible in an effort to protect the pound from speculative attacks and to dampen inflationary pressure. Treasury orthodoxy has remained firmly in place, however subject it may be to doctrinal alteration. In other areas of government policy, bureaucratic interest and ability to resist change has also been apparent—nowhere more so than in the Ministry of Agriculture, Fisheries, and Food, which for decades assiduously protected the interests of large farmers against the interests of consumers.

But neither with respect to the power of markets nor to the power of bureaucratic interests is the case for the bureaucratic coordination model in Britain clear-cut. Markets constrain all governments, but the underlying cause of financial crisis in Britain in 1966 and 1976 was excessive government expenditure. The overspending was a matter of politicians' choosing rather than of bureaucrats' obstructing. Similarly, Britain's ejection from the European Exchange Rate Mechanism in 1992 resulted from a Sterling/Deutschmark exchange rate that politicians (the prime minister, the chancellor of the Exchequer, and the foreign secretary, in particular) had chosen. Governments operating in markets are necessarily subject to market pressures, but markets do not eliminate the freedom of a prime minister or department ministers to act or choose. The Ministry of Agriculture, Fisheries, and Food was indeed for long the voice of its larger grain farmer clients, but it was entirely within the authority and power of ministers to alter that state of affairs, as Blair showed in 2001 when he abolished the department. British core executives have not typically been the prisoner of their bureaucracies: otherwise, radical policy departures in, for example, privatization and the contracting-out of public services in the 1990s would have been impossible. When British prime ministers and their administrations have firmly and decisively led, departments generally have followed.

The United States resembles France and Britain with respect to bureaucrats' inherent advantages of permanence, experience, and expertise. But it differs fundamentally with respect to the bureaucracy's design and in the consequential location and exercise of democratic authority over it. In France and Britain, the political executive creates, abolishes, and modifies the bureaucracy as it determines. These decisions have nothing to do with the legislature. In America, Congress creates, designs, empowers, and finances federal agencies and codifies their jurisdictions in law. The customary arguments on behalf of the proposition that power lies with bureaucracies are therefore complicated by agencies' prudent attention not just to the preferences of the president and his appointees within agencies but also to those of Congress—and especially to congressional committees.

Accordingly, the ability of the U.S. president and of his appointees to implement policy is usually constrained: federal agencies are not his to direct, program, and reorder because Congress has the power to resist him through committee oversight hearings and by the committees' regular processes of authorization and appropriation. In the case of regulatory commissions such as the Federal Reserve Board, Congress deliberately grants greater decision-making autonomy to bureaucrats than it typically does in the case of conventional administrative agencies. The Federal Reserve Board has shown that it is prepared to use its enhanced autonomy in making decisions about short-term interest rates. However, even in the case of regulatory commissions, senior officials are bound to take full account of congressional and presidential preferences.

Conclusion

The categories that Dunleavy and Rhodes use in their theory of the British core executive are not readily transferable to different countries, nor does categorization itself explain patterns of difference and similarity between countries or across time. Nevertheless, categorization clarifies those patterns and, as this chapter has shown, indicates something of the complexity in thinking about executives comparatively and some of the utility of doing so through a clear framework.

Three inferences may be drawn. First, the oldest lesson in political science is reaffirmed: we learn and understand more about one political system by comparing it systematically with others. Second, although the categories are analytically distinct, they are not mutually exclusive. For example, a comparative account explaining executive decision making in America, Britain, and France about establishing a coalition to oppose al-Qaeda in 2001 would draw on all four categories of executive government presented in this chapter: monocratic, segmented, shared, and bureaucratic coordination. Third, executive government in the three countries is heavily contingent upon exogenous developments. That is as true of the outbreak of foot and mouth disease in Britain in 2000, as it is of the Japanese attack upon Pearl Harbor in 1941, and of de Gaulle's sudden resignation from the French presidency in 1969. The nature of executive government within any single country may appear settled only to be suddenly disrupted by unanticipated phenomena and forces. Asked which were the most important influences upon him as prime minister of Britain, Harold Macmillan spoke for all chief executives by answering, simply, "Events, dear boy, events."

Notes

1. I use "Britain" as a more familiar term than "the United Kingdom" but not with the intention of excluding Northern Ireland from the chapter's scope.

2. Patrick Dunleavy and Rod Rhodes, "Core Executive Studies in Britain," *Public Administration* 68 (1990).

3. Ibid., 4.

4. Robert Elgie, "Models of Executive Politics," *Political Studies* 45 (1997); and Robert Elgie and Steven Griggs, *French Politics* (New York: Routledge, 2000).

5. Dunleavy and Rhodes, "Core Executive Studies in Britain," 19.

6. Vincent Wright, "The President and the Prime Minister," in *De Gaulle to Mitterrand*, ed. Jack Hayward (London: Hurst and Co., 1993), 105.

7. François Goguel, "The Evolution of the Institution of the French Presidency, 1959–1981," in *Constitutional Democracy: Essays in Comparative Politics*, ed. Fred H. Eidlin (Boulder: Westview Press, 1983).

8. Maurice Duverger, *La Monarchie républicaine* (Paris: Robert Laffont, 1974).

9. Olivier Duhamel, "L'hypothèse de la contradiction des majorités en France," in *Les Régimes Semi-Présidentiels*, ed. Maurice Duverger (Paris: Presses Universitaires de France, 1986), 271.

10. Arthur Schlesinger Jr., *The Imperial Presidency* (Boston: Houghton Mifflin, 1973).

11. Richard E. Neustadt, *Presidential Power and the Modern Presidents* (New York: Free Press, 1990), 11.

12. Kenneth R. Mayer, *With the Stroke of a Pen* (Princeton: Princeton University Press, 2001).

13. Anthony King, "The British Prime Ministership in the Age of the Career Politician," *West European Politics* 14 (1991): 36.

14. Dunleavy and Rhodes, "Core Executive Studies in Britain," 1.

15. Samy Cohen, *La Monarchie Nucléaire* (Paris: Hachette, 1986), 15.

16. King, "British Prime Ministership."

17. John Lukacs, *Five Days in London* (New Haven: Yale University Press, 1999).

18. Alan Bullock, *Ernest Bevin: Foreign Secretary 1945–1951*, vol. 3 (London, Heinemann, 1983), 455–456; and Kenneth Harris, *Attlee* (London: Weidenfeld, 1982), 347–350.

19. See, for example, Ben Pimlott, *Harold Wilson* (London: HarperCollins, 1992), 422–431.

20. See, for example, Peter Oborne, *Alastair Campbell* (London: Aurum Press, 1999), 168–172.

21. Neustadt, *Presidential Power and the Modern Presidents*, 29.

22. As was true of Senator Fulbright during the Vietnam War and of Senator Byrd during preparations for operations against al-Qaeda.

23. John Keeler, "Executive Power and Policy-making Patterns in France," *West European Politics* 16 (1993).

24. Elgie and Griggs, *French Politics*.

25. Sammy Finer, Vernon Bogdanor, and Bernard Rudden, *Comparing Constitutions* (Oxford: Clarendon Press, 1995), 219.

26. Wright, "The President and the Prime Minister," 104.

27. Finer, Bogdanor, and Rudden, *Comparing Constitutions*, 216.

28. Dunleavy and Rhodes, "Core Executive Studies in Britain," 15.

3 The American Presidency in Comparative Perspective: Systems, Situations, and Leaders

Bert A. Rockman

In the previous chapter, Nigel Bowles argued that to understand the American presidency, we must understand the national executives of other countries. In this chapter, Bert A. Rockman offers a three-part approach to conducting these comparative analyses. Because every national executive is part of a larger political system, first we must compare the U.S. system with the political systems of other countries; second, compare the situations that arise in different countries and that challenge the president and other national executives to respond; and, third, compare the leadership roles of the American president with the roles that other national executives are expected to play. One of Rockman's most provocative conclusions is that the obvious differences between the presidency and other national executive roles often mask more important underlying similarities.

What does the American presidency look like when viewed from the vantage point of other political systems? How does it differ from other leadership posts? What differences derive from the characteristics of political systems, such as their governmental arrangements and political cultures? Such questions demand a comparative systems perspective on political leadership. This chapter assesses the office of the presidency by looking at some of the conditions that act to enlarge or diminish its leadership capacities. In so doing we shall also be able to compare conditions relevant to the exercise of leadership across political systems. What kinds of situations make presidents more powerful? Which make them less so?

Another way to compare leadership roles is to analyze the styles of the leaders themselves as they differ across systems. Definitions of the job and leadership styles vary from president to president and from prime minister to prime minister. Their styles of leadership shape the contours of their roles. Style cannot be divorced, however, from situations and political systems; rather, it is shaped by and interacts with them. In short, our three elements for comparison—systems, situations, and leaders—are intertwined.

Although intertwined, these three elements are analyzed separately in this chapter to provide distinct bases for a comparative perspective. This perspective leads us to ask how systems structure leadership roles, what situations influence leadership possibilities, the extent to which situations are structured by systems, and how leaders themselves vary. How are leaders selected and their roles defined? By undertaking such an exercise, inexact as it may be, we can develop a more sophisticated perspective on the leadership role of the American presidency.

Systems

American political rhetoric lionizes the U.S. system of government. Scholars, however, are more inclined to be critical, believing that the American political system oscillates between periods of stark presidential aggrandizement and periods of sustained policy stalemate. When either of these tendencies peaks, a rash of reform proposals develops to emulate what are perceived to be more effective forms of governance in other democracies. For a long time the British system of party government provided the model. Its ability to concentrate power and accountability seemed wonderfully straightforward in contrast to the complicated American system. Yet when the United Kingdom was engulfed in political turmoil, labor troubles, and relative economic decline in the 1970s, the party government model lost some of its luster. The Scandinavian model of social corporatism and rationalized politics seemed attractive for a time because of its consensual and inclusive characteristics, but to emulate it would require a vast and probably impossible restructuring of American society and its social and political norms. In the 1980s Japan's evident economic success also attracted attention. Its appeal, however, was based more on the country's business and industrial management techniques than on its politics and government, which feature a heavy reliance on money, pork barrel spending, and subsidies to inefficient but politically important sectors of production.

In fact, emulation usually turns out to be a function of how well things are going in the country whose institutional arrangements are the object of reformers' affections. By these fickle standards, the United States and Britain each performed very well in the last half of the 1990s. Yet their institutional arrangements could hardly be more different.

A comparative approach requires an exploration of nuances, not a proclamation of the virtues of one institutional form over the other. We therefore begin with several broadly organized features of systems to guide our analysis, starting with the attributes of national power and concluding with the role of political culture and its influence on public expectation.

Power Attributes

The great military and economic power of the United States translates into immense political power. How these political resources are actually used is another matter, but there is no doubt that on the world scene and at international gatherings the United States is the principal actor among nation-states, more powerful than any other because its power reaches across international military, economic, and political spheres.

Under these circumstances it is nearly impossible for an American president to be anything less than important. The stature of U.S. presidents, however, reflects America's stature in the world far more than any president's relatively anemic capability to influence matters at home.[1] Even though no president is a free agent in world politics, a president is often able to define what a foreign policy crisis is and tends to have a freer hand in foreign rather than in domestic policy. Because presidents have the power to initiate action in foreign affairs, others must react to them. From the perspective of the United States as a leader in world affairs and the president's ability to initiate actions that become national commitments, the American president is an important and potentially powerful figure.

We need to distinguish between *importance* and *power*. The president of the United States is important because the country has great power and corresponding influence on world politics. Such prominence helps make U.S. presidents influential in international settings because collective action frequently requires Washington's consent. However, American presidents cannot always deliver in accordance with others' expectations, especially when domestic opposition is strong (the fast-track trade defeat suffered by the Clinton administration, for example) or when political costs are thought to be high (ground forces in Kosovo, for example).

Government Size

The size of the enterprise over which leaders preside says something about their power, or at least about the tools at their disposal. Presumably, the greater the government's share of societal resources, the more leverage it has in negotiations between public policy makers and private interests. Two points need to be stressed. First, the public sphere in the United States is historically small in relation to those in West European democracies. Second, the premises underlying the notion that big government makes for easier direction are not necessarily correct.

One of the elements of government size is the resource extraction, or taxing, arm of government, a function that can indicate only the relative size of the public sphere, not the distribution of activities within it. (A far higher proportion of government expenditures goes to the defense sector in the United States, even in the post–cold war era, than in comparable European countries.) In 1996, compared with twenty-eight other wealthy democracies located mostly in Europe, the United States tied with Japan in ranking just two places from the bottom in extracting public resources. Only Mexico and Turkey taxed less.[2] In fact, the fifteen European Union countries on average extract more than 50 percent more resources for the public sphere than is the case in the United States.[3] The federal government in absolute terms is large, but it is comparatively small in relation to the private sector and to the governments of other affluent democracies.

A large state, however, can be less than responsive to political direction from the top, especially if many of its expenditures are in the form of past program commitments. Ideally, leaders wish to set agendas free of past commitments. The accumulation of such commitments over time obviously limits the ability to change direction. Indeed, the meteoric growth in entitlements spending (health care, pensions, and various forms of income assistance) sets profound limits on funding new programs. A large state, consequently, may be merely a vastly overcommitted state and likely to be viewed by top political leaders more as an impediment in the path of leadership than a resource.

Government at the federal level in the United States is actually shrinking in most ways but not in total expenditures. This situation stems mainly from aggregate expenditure growth in entitlements as a result of demographic change— in other words, an older population draws more pension benefits and requires more health care. The discretionary spending share of the federal budget is in decline, and with it the prospect that presidents can come to Congress for new programs requiring significant federal expenditures. Previous commitments place a lien on the resources available to leadership and diminish the space for maneuver. This is the predicament with which the heads of other affluent democracies, as well as the president of the United States, are faced. On the whole, however, this constraint affects adversely the agendas of Democratic presidents more than Republicans because the former are more inclined toward government activism than the latter.

Centralization

Centralization of resources and authority can provide assets to top national political leaders. Yet there are different forms of centralization. One is the level of financial and political resources available to the central government in relation to other units of government. A reasonable presumption is that the higher the ratio of central government resources to those of regional and local governments, the greater the leverage of central political leaders. A second form of centralization involves the party apparatus that provides the political power the leadership needs to govern. A third form of centralization has to do with the relationship between leaders at the top and their cabinets.

Looking at the relative centralization of government, we find that the resources commanded by the central government in the United States are considerably less than those found in European states. The U.S. system, being a federal one, grants considerable autonomy to the state governments, an arrangement that also stems from the constitutional bargain required to cede some power to the new American federal government. In general, the United States tends to look like other Organization for Economic Cooperation and Development (OECD) federal states, with the central government taking close to 68 percent of total government revenues compared to the 73 percent average share of OECD federal governments. The far more numerous OECD states with unitary systems of government, however, allocate an average 87 percent of total revenues to the central government.[4]

These data have consequences for national political leaders. In 1981, when Ronald Reagan launched his successful campaign to cut federal taxes, supply-siders believed the dollars returned to the private sector would be used to stimulate investment and growth in the national economy. State governments frequently reacted to federal spending cuts, however, by increasing their own taxes.[5] Although the net effect of these countervailing activities is unclear, certainly the intended macroeconomic effects of presidential fiscal and tax policies were blunted.

Such outcomes are typical under a federal system. The U.S. system, however, is more decentralized than most. Unlike Germany's federal government, for instance, Washington has little ability to coordinate and homogenize public policies and budgets among the states. Most American presidents have found their administrations embroiled in conflicts between federal policy and one or more states or regions. The most notable of these conflicts in the post–World War II era was with southern states and communities over civil rights issues, especially school desegregation. More recently, conflicts have centered on land use in the West; energy production in several states, especially in the oil-producing Southwest; and, during the Reagan era, the tax policies and rates of the higher tax states of the Northeast and Upper Midwest. The states often prevail in such conflicts because of their ability to marshal political resources in Congress, an example of which was the relentless lobbying at the grassroots level to compel Democratic senators from oil- and gas-producing states to oppose President Clinton's proposed energy tax in 1993. Recently, the federal government has been ceding more policymaking back to the states, furthering tendencies toward heterogeneity in the American federal system.

Unitary governments, to be sure, are no panacea for central policies that meet with deep regional unpopularity. The United Kingdom under Prime Minister Tony Blair has devolved authority to Scotland and, to a lesser extent, to Wales. But being able to bring about this substantial constitutional change so swiftly and decisively was itself a reflection of the power of the central authority in the United Kingdom. In contrast, U.S. presidents intent on pursuing national policies find that goal more elusive than do their counterparts in Western Europe. This difference is at least as much a function of the great size and territorial diversity of the United States as it is a consequence of its political institutions. The institutions, however, express this diversity and facilitate it rather than tame or moderate it.

Another, more finely grained, form of centralizing resources for political leadership is the ability to enforce political discipline from the top. The model for such discipline, according to Richard Rose, is "party government," which he has defined as the "unique . . . claim to have the right to choose what solutions shall be binding upon the whole of society."[6]

One role of political parties, however, may be to prevent the leader either from straying from the party fold or creating a personal political machine.[7] To the extent that a party is highly institutionalized, it may compel the leader to adhere to party interests and values in return for its disciplined support. Party constituencies and leaders need to be mollified. That is the normal course of events everywhere. Occasionally, willful leaders, such as Margaret Thatcher, who succeeded in her leadership of the British Conservative Party by remaking the party in her image, and Helmut Schmidt, who had less success in remaking the German Social Democratic Party in his, seek to override or break some of the prevailing party constituencies. Centralized party support, which American reformers often see as a panacea for beleaguered presidents, comes at a high price and limits a leader's pursuit of innovations that may depart from accepted party policies and constituencies. The more institutionalized the parties are, the more they are likely to exert this gravitational pull on their leaders' aspirations. Leaders have to build and sustain coalitions both within and outside of their parties. In this regard, American presidents are not alone. In fact, because of the limited institutionalization of the parties in the United States, presidents are often able to penetrate their official party organizations rather thoroughly, thus ensuring the responsiveness of the national party machinery to them. It should be noted, too, that American parties for a variety of reasons have become more centralized in recent years, that each has become more internally cohesive, and that all of this has come to fruition at a time when divided government is the norm—a result more likely to limit than empower presidents.[8]

Yet a different form of centralization has to do with the relative concentration of resources available in the office of the leader. It is no straightforward matter to describe precisely what a resource is. That British prime ministers inhabit an office staffed with very few people who are personally subordinate to them does not mean that they are inherently less powerful than American presidents. Although many people work for U.S. presidents and are thus accountable to them, staff size is not the equivalent of leadership capacity. Indeed, staff size may even be inversely related to leadership capacity.[9] The growth of the modern White House staff reflects the need, as seen by most presidents, for presidential integration and direction of an otherwise fragmented government. The staff and other coordinating, budgetary, and monitoring organs of the Executive Office of the President (EOP) enhance the president's ability to counter the centrifugal tendencies of the departments and their political constituencies as expressed through Congress. It may be that this form of centralization arises for the sole reason that, without it, presidents would be completely at the mercy of these centrifugal forces and subgovernmental arrangements. Thus, the munificently staffed White House speaks less to the power of the presidency than to its weakness in the face of potentially competing actors within a highly fragmented system.

Presidential and Parliamentary Systems

What difference does governing structure make? What are the differences between presidential and parliamentary systems with respect to the supposedly contrasting roles of a president and a prime minister in a cabinet government as initiators of legislative proposals? Presumably, in a parliamentary system, once the cabinet decides, the deal is mostly done, but in the American system presidential proposals are just the beginning of a long and uncertain process in Congress. It is reasonable, therefore, to suppose that presidents are more constrained than prime ministers because of the legislature's independence from the executive.

This supposition, however, is in need of review. Advocates of parliamentary government, such as Lloyd N. Cutler, assume that either the parliamentary system or some well-disguised form of it will produce the cohesion and authority for presidents to govern in accordance with their agendas.[10] They assume that in parliamentary systems, unified party government, rather than government by coalition (the far more frequent case), would prevail. And they further assume that even where majority party government prevails, divisions within the ruling party would be minimal. Finally, the advocates of parliamentary government neglect the relevance of other actors—interest groups, for example, which in a party government system would ply their influence within the parties and through the bureaucracy rather than in the legislature.

Probably the most significant difference between the presidential and parliamentary systems is the manner in which the various interests and political factions struggle to shape the national agenda. Presidents tend to maximize and expand the agenda in public to accord both with their goals and with those of relevant party constituencies. Because of the separation between the executive and the legislature, the president's efforts to construct legislative majorities are necessarily open and visible. Such efforts generate confrontation, which makes presidents look more vulnerable when they lose and more potent when they win. In contrast, a prime minister is more typically engaged in striking inter- or intraparty bargains that the government can carry forward.[11] Once an agenda is formed, it is almost certain (assuming bargains are kept) that its most important elements will gain parliamentary approval. But such victories can be misleading because most of the cutting, shaping, and limitation of the agenda has occurred before the legislative stage. What is preshaped and thus basically certain of passage in a parliamentary system is shaped later in the presidential system and with more uncertainty about its ultimate disposition. This is, in the end, the real difference between the two kinds of systems.

Accountability

What forms of accountability undergird the systems that presidents and prime ministers lead? A broad summary of these accountability relationships is portrayed in Table 3.1. The pattern suggests that more of an insider's political

Table 3.1 Sources of Prime Ministerial and Presidential Accountability

Source of accountability	Extent of accountability	
	Prime ministers	Presidents
Party	Strong	Moderate to weak
Cabinet	Strong	Nonexistent
Legislature	Weak	Strong
Mass public	Strong	Very strong

game exists under a parliamentary/cabinet arrangement than under the American presidential arrangement.

Mass political accountability is strong for both kinds of leaders. In the parliamentary system the electoral verdict is, to a greater extent than in the presidential, about the parties. Prime ministers need to cultivate their parties but expect to have their support when they need it. Because U.S. presidents cannot assume cohesive support from their own party in Congress on any given issue, the uncertainty attached to building support makes them more susceptible than prime ministers to the effects of fluctuations in public opinion.

Presidents depend very little on cabinet or party approval, but they are greatly dependent on Congress, assuming that their activities require legislative approval. For prime ministers, however, party and cabinet are intimately connected—a connection that is much fainter in the United States, where the structures are less clearly demarcated. A presidential cabinet is not a collegial body of peers or fellow party leaders; rather, its members are decidedly a president's underlings. Presidents more often rely for counsel on friends (Bebe Rebozo for Richard M. Nixon, Charles Kirbo for Jimmy Carter); White House staff (Henry Kissinger for Nixon, Zbigniew Brzezinski and Hamilton Jordan for Carter); Washington icons (Averell Harriman and Clark Clifford for various Democratic presidents); or spouses (especially, but not exclusively, Hillary Rodham Clinton).

Party structures also differ. A president can control the formal party machinery at the national level, but even though the national party organizations have become more prominent, most of the action in American political parties remains at the state and local level. Prime ministers, in contrast, are much more dependent on, and therefore more accountable to, their cabinets and their parties.

In many ways, presidents are usually less, not more, inhibited than prime ministers. But presidents also tend to be more politically vulnerable because the process under which they operate is more visible and open and not easily controlled through prearranged agreements. Again, the two systems tend to create different behavioral incentives, although leaders will differ as to how they interpret these incentives.

A Unitary or Collective Executive

The idea that presidents should not be inhibited in carrying out their executive powers is firmly asserted in *The Federalist*, no. 70. Hamilton argued,

Those politicians and statesmen who have been the most celebrated for the soundness of their principles and for the justness of their views have declared in favor of a single Executive and a numerous legislature. . . .

Decision, activity, secrecy, and despatch will generally characterize the proceedings of one man in a much more eminent degree than the proceedings of any greater number.[12]

The concept of a cabinet with collective decision-making responsibilities was not to be fully comprehended until many years later in the evolution of parliamentary government. Collective cabinet responsibility required the development of mass-based political parties to fuel modern parliamentary democracy.

The executive power produced by the modern mass-based political parties and collective cabinet responsibilities, ironically, seems to have been greater than that realized through the Hamiltonian conception of a unitary executive. The cabinets of modern parliamentary governments, which comprise the leading members of a political party or coalition, stand or fall together. The cabinet must be brought along by the prime minister, and the different positions of its members reconciled. Once this is accomplished, parliamentary support can then typically be assumed.

Almost the exact opposite holds true in the presidential system. The cabinet members, being the president's subordinates, almost never make collective decisions. Decisions are the president's responsibility, even if the president feels compelled to use interdepartmental committees to make them. In this sense, the presidency is indeed the focus of governing energy that Hamilton wished to generate. Although presidents need not put together agreements in the cabinet (a process, given the protections accorded the press in the United States, likely to produce massive leaks from the disgruntled), their difficulties begin when they must persuade Congress to act on their behalf. Unity built around the dominance of an individual rather than collective executive merely displaces the locus of coalition building, making it more open and thus more likely to dissipate presidential energies in embarrassing political defeats.

The collective executive, in short, works through the modern political party. The unitary executive, however, cannot so easily channel energies in such a fashion. Even deeply partisan presidents cannot always count on support from the leaders of their party in Congress; the congressional leaders, in turn, may or may not be in a position to help presidents work out agreements. In a Constitution written before the advent of mass political parties, it was natural to assume, as Hamilton did, that one person could produce sufficient executive energy. This assumption may no longer be tenable.

Selection Processes and "Selectorates"

The process of selecting a presidential candidate in the United States is a virtual three-ring circus, but the rings are concentric. They move from smaller to larger audiences in a protracted process.

In modern politics, ambitious politicians have to draw attention to themselves or to their roles as political advocates. For the most part, European and Japanese politics are organized around party organization as the stream in which political ambition is spawned—a condition that once held in the United States, especially in the nineteenth and early twentieth centuries. Party is now, however, just one of the channels in the widened band through which politicians can beam their messages and direct their ambitions. As the candidacies of Jimmy Carter in 1976, Ross Perot in 1992 and 1996, and the more distant ones of Dwight D. Eisenhower and Wendell Willkie make clear, party is not always the dominant channel.

Two pertinent questions arise from this difference in the organization of leadership selection. Who are the selectors? And what difference does the nature of the "selectorate" make for candidates and their behavior?

The answer to the first question is relatively simple, but the simplicity is mostly superficial. The simple response is that selection is far more party controlled in other democratic polities than in the United States. The direct primary, a distinctly American phenomenon, tends to remove an especially important lever from party organization—the ability to select candidates. If the selectorate is broader for American presidential aspirants than for those who vie for equivalent posts in Europe, it is not always clear what the consequences of this difference are. Organization and money are important in American primary elections, and candidates who appeal to party activists are often able to generate more of both. In this sense, the primary election process actually can strengthen ideological consonance between candidates and party activists, particularly because it accords disproportionate influence to party activists.

It is therefore much easier to assert that American processes of candidate selection differ from those in other political democracies than it is to say what those differences mean. In the United States the process of candidate selection is both visible and lengthy. It requires a lot of money and sustained public interest. The process produces a larger number and possibly greater variety of candidates, and it is inevitably less controlled and predictable. When an incumbent seeks reelection, the attention of the president (and therefore of the administration) is riveted on creating effective political defenses (or attacks) for the numerous political judgment days (primaries and the general election) that lie ahead. When a sitting president is ineligible to run again or chooses not to, attention drifts from the administration to the succession.

Yet functional similarities between American and other democratic polities also exist, however differently they are manifested. All ambitious politicians must build bases of support so that when the opportunity strikes they are in a position to take advantage. Politicking, in this sense, does not occur all of a sudden. Rather, it is a continuous process. But the inside game does not always produce inside leaders, as the case of Thatcher indicates. In the view of Anthony King, Thatcher's chief point of recommendation for the Conservative Party leadership was that she was not Ted Heath, her predecessor.[13] Had she been an inside politician, it is unlikely that she would have been so injudicious as to have taken Heath on.

When reformers look for a fix, selection processes seem to be the natural target. One assumption that reformers make is that altering the selectorates will make the selected more moderate, more responsive, more likely to be victorious, more experienced, and more predictable. Such results are less than obvious, even if one could define these virtues more sharply. The greater likelihood is that those who are selected will vary widely within any selection process.

Political Culture and Expectations

Before emphasizing, and possibly overemphasizing, the peculiarities of the American environment and system, we need to mention some important cross-national similarities in modern mass politics. One is that the role of public expectations appears to be a generalized phenomenon of modern political life in all industrially advanced democratic systems. Mass expectations and governing realities are rarely compatible, particularly when times are bad. Maintaining political support thus appears to be a difficult undertaking in any system when bad news outraces the good. Dennis Kavanagh, for example, noted (at least until the advent of Tony Blair) that only two postwar British prime ministers maintained the support of more than half of the British public for two years or longer.[14] Michael Lewis-Beck has shown that in several European countries the fortunes of political leaders rest greatly on public perceptions of the state of the economy.[15] Both George H. W. Bush's precipitous fall in popular approval in the recession-shadowed latter stages of his presidency and Bill Clinton's reelection in the robust political economy of 1996 testify to the potency of public perceptions of economic well-being.

To be certain, the styles, structures, and norms of politics are not the same everywhere. Shared norms tend to moderate expectations and provide avenues for molding agreements, as in Norway and Sweden. But the flow of events still tends to dictate the margin of political safety for the incumbent leadership. Despite a much ballyhooed ameliorist style of politics, the rise of social turmoil and inflation in Sweden did affect the stability of political coalitions in the 1970s and 1980s. More recently, a Social Democratic government in Sweden that reduced social welfare benefits also suffered at the polls.

The great problem of modern democratic accountability is that the public is usually results-oriented and unrealistic about what governments can achieve at what cost. The public typically prefers, more or less everywhere, to retain entitlements, avoid tax increases, and balance budgets. That said, the public largely responds to what leaders put on the table. Hence, what gets put on the table by contending political elites is vital. What is uncertain is whether elites are made more or less responsible by political insulation, of which they have little in the United States, or whether the alternatives they offer are a function of their ideology. To be sure, the tax cuts that were the centerpiece of George W. Bush's first six months were never regarded as having the same priority by the public, which was more interested in protecting its entitlements. However, if tax cuts were offered, the public by healthy margins also approved of receiving them.

Political leaders are under pressure to satisfy high but contradictory expectations at the least cost to themselves. Politicians tend to be amenable to these appealing but contradictory expectations, which they often promote through their own flamboyant rhetoric. This malady is not peculiar to the United States, but the proximity of American political institutions and political leaders to popular pressures heightens the risk of irresponsible policymaking.

The great-power status of the United States, along with its relative physical isolation, also generates some unique expectations. Great-power status in an era of mass political consciousness leads to an episodic, albeit fleeting, jingoism. The combination makes for the worst of all possible worlds—paroxysms of fervor without sustained commitment. The American public is not of a single mind by any means, but its dominant tendency appears to be isolationist when engagement is likely to entail serious costs. Like other modern mass publics, Americans seem reluctant to be disturbed. Nowhere, including the United States, was public opinion deeply roused toward action to halt the civil war in the Balkans in the 1990s. Yet, although interventionism is more typically an elite-induced phenomenon, when it is perceived that America has been provoked, mass opinion will often support strong words and decisive (and, above all, immediately successful) actions, such as the invasions of Grenada in 1983 and Panama in 1989 and the antiterrorist strikes in Afghanistan that began in 2001. Keep the peace, talk tough when necessary, but get it over with fast. Notably, the brief and successful war against Iraq in 1991 was more popular once it was over than it was in the protracted period leading up to it. After an initial burst of support for the NATO bombing campaign in Yugoslavia, enthusiasm eroded as the campaign continued without producing immediate results. Only after the long bombing campaign produced a favorable outcome for NATO at virtually no cost to the NATO forces did the erosion of support come to a halt.

Beyond the unusual considerations that accompany great-power status, two additional and related aspects of the American system generally enhance unrealistic expectations about presidents. One is, as Hugh Heclo has suggested, the illusion of national unity that is created by presidential candidates who are trying to build electoral coalitions independent of their party base. The other is the false but widespread belief that the president is the whole of government. According to Heclo:

By fleetingly raising expectations concerning the leader's unifying and governing powers, the selection process in the United States may actually make credible government all the more difficult. In popular conception the president is selected to reign in supreme command; in reality he will often be pulling strings and hoping that something somewhere will jump.[16]

Heclo's discussion of the consequences of the American presidential selection process—its lack of political apprenticeship and consequently its emphasis on individualistic political entrepreneurship—resonates with some critiques of the American presidency.[17] These critiques portray a presidential office not only divorced from collective responsibility but also bereft of the sustaining power of collective institutions. Thus public aspirations, centered in a single individual, can only rarely be fulfilled. Because of the mismatch of aspirations and leadership resources, presidents (or those who speak for them and act on their behalf) seek to expand their resources and gain control over other institutions, notably the bureaucracy.[18]

In sum, expectations about leadership are founded essentially in the modern democratic ethos. Nevertheless, a view has developed that the American presidency is beset by unusually high expectations. This is partly because of the American projection of power in the world and the accompanying expectation that the president will keep intact both peace and national pride. But much of this diagnosis is grounded in the institutional nature of the American political system in general and the presidency in particular. The presidency is remarkably individualized and plebiscitary. Reformers' concerns about the president's abilities to exercise power often have neglected the issue of how such power would and should be exercised. Cut off from the sources of both counsel and constraint of which most prime ministers must avail themselves as part of a collective governing apparatus, presidents more likely would be granted power unrestrained by prudence. The direction of reform to empower presidents may unbalance the governing equation further by offering more powers for political mobilization and fewer incentives for prudent behavior.

Situations

Our analysis of systemic variations helps to illuminate the differences in the situations in which leaders find themselves. A quick tour of some of these varying situations includes short-run political coalitions, long-run political coalitions, and the role of crisis and foreign policy initiation.

Short-Run Coalitions

As noted earlier, the aficionados of party government in the United States typically have in mind the clear majority-rule situation—the Westminster model. But majority-party government is relatively rare in parliamentary systems. At a minimum, it rests on a winner-take-all, single-seat-district system that gives a seat to the candidate with either a plurality or a majority. Most parliamentary systems, however, have some mixed form of proportional representation and district voting. These properties tend to produce various kinds of coalition arrangements.

Under normal circumstances, U.S. presidents are themselves in a complex coalition arrangement in spite of their presumptive control of the executive and the existence of only two parties in Congress.[19] But a president's coalitions (unlike those of a prime minister) are fluid rather than wholly structured by party. What remains unclear is whether a president is any more disadvantaged than the head of a coalition government, who is certainly constrained by arrangements made by the parties forming the government. A president can ask for more, but with greater risk of failure. Continued failure, or, more important, the perception of failure, corrodes a president's political standing.

In any event, rarely in American politics do elections create even a moment of party government. But such moments can occur, and when they do they usually have huge legislative and policy consequences. One of the most critical conditions for producing party government has to do with the generation, dissipation, and regeneration of long-run political coalitions.

Long-Run Coalitions

The United States is the oldest competitive party system in the world and among the most volatile. Democrats and Republicans and their party ancestors have held different positions and taken on different constituencies during different eras of American history.[20] The process by which the partisan plates beneath the political surface shift over a period of time is referred to in the vocabulary of American politics as the cycle of realignment. The traditional pattern of realignment requires the slow exhaustion of prior party alignments, the emergence of new political appeals and constituencies and, ultimately, new patterns of voting. Typically, realigning moments are associated with unusual clarity in mass political cleavages and in partisan divisions among elites.[21] Considerable policy innovation usually occurs because of the relative ease of mobilizing political support in contrast to more normal times. These rare moments of realignment, in classic form, produce a kind of party government for a time in which substantial majorities in both houses of Congress are assembled in support of a party program. In modern times, this has meant support of the president's program.[22]

In the shorter term as well, exhaustion of political initiative can result from the decay of a prevailing coalition or party. The ability to cope with larger problems often declines when a party has been in power for a long time. Such symptoms arose in the final years of the various Conservative governments in Britain from 1951 to 1964 and, again, during the sunset of the tattered Labor government in the late 1970s—a government sustained only by the forbearance of smaller parties in not bringing the Callaghan government to an end. Similarly, the victory of the Likud coalition in Israel in 1977 reflected the development of new political forces at a time when the Israeli Labor coalition had also lost its energy and direction. The nature of the cycle is that parties long in government become stale in ideas and internally contentious. These forces brought the Conservatives to power in Britain in 1979 and brought them down in 1997. Similar processes brought down the Social Democrats in Germany in 1982 and the rival Christian Democrats in 1998.

Thus the processes of energizing, enervating, and revitalizing go on everywhere. As the political forces that generate a government wind down, initiative declines, caution replaces risk taking, and survivability displaces direction. Intraparty and intragovernmental rifts become more noticeable. In short, the prospects for governing on behalf of clear goals diminish.

In an absolute pinch, an exhausted government can usually be saved in parliament, if not with the electorate. That is an advantage that U.S. presidents rarely have. Regime exhaustion in the American system is more directly and overtly connected with political troubles in generating legislative support. But even though party discipline can buffet some of the most severe challenges to a parliamentary government, the effects of regime exhaustion on the political vitality of leadership are substantial. John Major's government from the mid-1990s until its end was not in the same situation enjoyed by his predecessor, Margaret Thatcher, 1979–1990, for the vast portion of her time in office; nor was Helmut Schmidt in 1981 and 1982 able to embark on the initiatives in Germany that Willy Brandt had done from 1969 to 1971. Similarly, George Bush (1989–1993) was in no position to energize policy change as Ronald Reagan had in 1981. "Political time"—the life cycle of regime creation and dissolution—is measured differently across political systems, but the basic concept has universal properties (see Chapter 5).

What for now remains puzzling in the American case is not whether realignment has taken place,[23] but whether one party stands to benefit from it—and if so, which one? After the 1994 midterm elections, it appeared that the Republicans had made a momentous breakthrough, having won both chambers of Congress for the first time in four decades. But in 1996, despite the Republicans retaining their congressional majorities, the incumbent Democratic president also won. And in subsequent elections the Republican majorities in each chamber dwindled to the point of a near standstill, eventually leading to a takeover of the Senate in 2001 by the Democrats because of the defection from the Republican ranks of one senator, James Jeffords of Vermont. In sum, although there have been realignments within the electorate in a continuous fashion (the migration of white southerners to the Republican Party and of working women to the Democratic Party), neither party has gained a distinct advantage. This means that neither the president nor the congressional leadership will prevail completely.

Crises

Can the American president act quickly and decisively in a crisis? Is there any inherent difference between the president's ability to do so and that of a cabinet in a parliamentary government? The word *inherent* in this question is important; but first we need to determine what a crisis is. A crisis generally is what someone in a leadership position declares it to be, but only if widespread agreement follows.

That was the case in the immediate aftermath of the terrorist hijackings and attacks on the World Trade Center and the Pentagon on September 11, 2001. Indeed, there was no need to convince anyone that a crisis of shocking proportions existed. In this radically altered environment, few questions were asked—at least publicly—about ceding to the president and the federal government prerogative powers of wartime authority. Even within the president's cabinet and White House staff, not to mention among members of relevant congressional committees, the information net was narrowed to a small "need-to-know" set of actors defined by the president. The police powers of the state also rapidly expanded to rein in potential terrorists. The answer to the question posed above then is obvious—yes, American presidents can act quickly and decisively in a crisis. But the downside for presidents is that over time what was once a crisis may become a morass. Attenuation of support may then follow unless positive results come quickly.

Crisis entails the existence of a new and unanticipated situation that carries with it strong decisional costs and risks. The Argentine invasion of the Falklands/Malvinas in 1982 produced a crisis in London because the costs of any reaction would be strong and risk-bearing. Either the fleet would go to war and risk defeat thousands of miles away or it would stay home and the Thatcher government, along with the British nation, would risk political humiliation. The elder Bush faced similar choices in the Persian Gulf in 1990 and 1991, and his son confronted those choices more recently. Yet a problem that all executive leaders face is that although making the right choices in a foreign policy crisis is unlikely to rescue them from broader political failures, making the wrong choices can help bring them down even if they have been otherwise successful.

In the short run, foreign policy crises are apt to generate greater support for leadership responses because they engage the entire nation. Yet the U.S. reaction to the Soviet invasion of Afghanistan at the end of 1979 demonstrates how closely foreign and domestic interests are linked and, therefore, exactly how fragile support for a president's crisis decisions may be. Grain farmers and their representatives in Washington protested when the Carter administration imposed an embargo of American wheat to the Soviet Union. Domestic crises are even less likely to elicit agreement on leadership response because they engage the attention of diverse interests, which see their concerns linked positively or, more often, adversely to proposed solutions.

Two aspects of crisis management are especially illustrative of the differences between presidential and parliamentary systems. In the American system, the ability to initiate action decisively is a presidential advantage, and, if the crisis is exceptionally brief, decision and action can usually be implemented to achieve some resolution. For example, movement from the defensive Desert Shield operation in the Persian Gulf in November 1990 to a war footing that served as a prelude to the offensive Desert Storm operation two months later decisively altered the burden of proof from the president to Congress. Inertia now favored the president. Still, when the president's action requires congressional approval or if there is litigation that challenges the constitutionality of the president's actions, the system of separation of powers can be limiting. The Supreme Court's rejection of Truman's seizure of the steel mills in the face of a threatened steelworkers' strike during the Korean War was an obvious case of the blunting of leadership initiative. Prime ministers, on the other hand, tend to feel the limits of response early because they have to carry their cabinets with them, especially if the government is a multiparty coalition. Presidents have an advantage when decisive and brief action is possible before others have an opportunity to act. The more protracted the action, the more the complexity of the American system tends to take effect, and the greater the inclination of normal politics to prevail. In parliamentary systems, the advantages and disadvantages appear to be the mirror image of the presidential system: initial action involves a fair amount of consultation, but fewer impediments arise thereafter.

Although American presidents can act quickly and decisively in crises, this does not mean that they will. Kennedy took his time during the Cuban missile crisis, both to size up alternatives and to reach a consensus among his advisers. Nor does it mean that after they act, presidents' initiatives will be accepted by the other branches of government. In May 1999, for example, a congressional resolution to end the U.S.-led NATO air war in Yugoslavia narrowly failed to pass the House in a tie vote (213–213). Moreover, decisiveness does not necessarily mean success. In 1956 British prime minister Anthony Eden acted decisively in Suez and failed. In 1982 during the Falklands/Malvinas crisis, Prime Minister

Thatcher acted decisively and succeeded. Similarly, in the *Mayaguez* incident of 1975, when a U.S. ship was seized by revolutionary Cambodian forces, Gerald Ford attempted to rescue American hostages and succeeded (despite substantial loss of life among the rescue team). But the luckless Jimmy Carter failed in an effort to rescue American hostages being held in the American Embassy in Tehran in 1980. Luck may be at least as good a guide as design.

Leaders

Like actors on a stage, political leaders vary in their temperaments and aptitudes. Some scripts are better suited for certain actors than others. The roles leaders are given to play have much to do with how they fare, and the roles they play are a function of both their system's institutions and historical accident. A consequence of the U.S. political system is that the American president has to play a variety of roles, and the qualities needed for some may contradict those needed for others. As it is with actors, leaders have some space to interpret and define their roles and at least a modest amount of latitude to decide what to stress. Unlike actors, however, leaders face uncertainties and choices for which they have not been scripted.

Leadership Roles

The American president, Clinton Rossiter pointed out in his classic book on the subject, wears many hats, and plays more roles than top leaders in other systems.[24] This is so because in the separation-of-powers system, American institutions do not have sharply differentiated functions. They share power and so have little division of labor. By contrast, modern parliamentary institutions, to differing degrees, tend to differentiate functions and concentrate power.[25]

Among the many hats worn by the American president, according to Rossiter, are those of chief of state, chief executive, chief diplomat, commander in chief, and chief legislator. Yet these are only the constitutional roles. Rossiter adds several others that have been grafted onto the modern presidency through practice: party chief, opinion leader and representative, manager of prosperity, leader of the Western alliance, and chief administrator. Of the five formal roles, the one that is most emphasized in contrasting the American system with others is that of chief legislator, an area of comparative disadvantage for presidents.

Presidents normally are the embodiment of their party and penetrate its national apparatus. Even the exceptions to this rule—Truman and Ford, who as vice-presidential successors had difficulties controlling their parties, and

Carter—ultimately were able to secure the apparatus and to win over the minds if not the hearts of their parties' elites. For political leaders in parliamentary systems, gaining personal control over their far better organized and institutionalized parties is more difficult. Within their parties European prime ministers are as much representatives or internal mediators as leaders.

Some of the American president's many roles—notably, commander in chief, chief diplomat, alliance leader, and prosperity manager (in an increasingly internationalized economy)—result from, or have become more important because of, the central role of the United States in world affairs. The president's functions as chief executive and administrator also have been altered. Since 1956, when Rossiter published *The American Presidency,* the role of the White House staff and the EOP has grown markedly in importance. Their growth gives the president an organizational presence, which permits greater presidential influence in the affairs of the executive branch. It also creates new problems of presidential management, such as who, among those who invoke the president's name, actually speaks for the president. In the halcyon days before the Iran-contra scandal, the Reagan White House seemed to suggest that it was far more important that the president be a chief (an expressive leader) than a chief executive (a manager).[26] That scandal, however, served as a strong reminder that a president cannot avoid being a chief executive. The management difficulties that so beset the first years of the Clinton presidency, in fact, suggest the importance of both functions. If the role of chief is ineffectively performed, no president can expect to be an effective chief executive. But without a head for details and some measure of organizational and staff discipline, a president's hopes for effective leadership may be derailed.

Presidents come wrapped in the cloak of the state and are not, as are prime ministers, merely the heads of governments. That could be one reason why presidential elections are so often greeted as a process of national legitimation and unity instead of just the outcome of a partisan struggle. Sporadic presidential efforts to appeal to populist instincts tend to diminish the pomp of the chief-of-state role and thus strip away the notion that the occupant of the office is someone special. Clinton waxed inelegantly about his preference in underwear on MTV—a minor blip, as matters turned out, compared to the X-rated accounts of the Monica Lewinsky affair. Playing on populist sentiments and, perhaps, his own instincts, Carter managed, to his detriment, to strip away all illusions of state majesty from the presidency. Ford and Truman also thought better of humility than majesty (having followed particularly "royal" presidencies). But as Rossiter put it, the American presidency is both the most and the least political of offices.[27] In its guise as chief of state, it is the least directly political—although astute presidents (none better than Reagan) know how to extract maximum political mileage from this aspect of the presidential role.

All political leaders are tasked with "managing prosperity." Their fortunes are tied to their success or sheer luck with the economy. Yet economic interdependence and the emergence of a global economy have made the economic forces to be managed less obviously manipulable. Global currency and securities markets place a significant constraint on governments' fiscal policies.

It is in the roles of chief legislator and opinion leader and representative that—aside from the party leadership role—institutional differences between prime ministers and presidents are at their purest. As we have seen, one of the main differences between a president and a prime minister is that a president builds political coalitions after legislation is introduced and a prime minister builds coalitions beforehand because party unity is paramount in a parliamentary/cabinet government. A president, in a highly unpredictable environment, is constantly engaged in calculating and recalculating legislative prospects and strategies and is therefore continuously involved in political mobilization to build and sustain coalitions.

Blending the roles of opinion leader (spokesperson for the people), chief of state, and keeper of the peace and the economy with more overt political roles such as chief legislator and party leader means that the president must bring highly diverse skills to the office. A good compass and the ability to articulate direction clearly are crucial requirements of the job. The test, however, as Rossiter observed, is how well all of these diverse elements are integrated—if indeed they are. Surely, in this regard, the president's job is the most complex of all leadership positions. It contains elements that provide it with both unusual power and unusual vulnerability.

Leadership Definitions

In view of the complexity of any leadership position, especially the American presidency, how can one define the job, and to what extent can definitions make a difference?

A leader in any organization of both reasonable complexity and competing goals and strategies is hostage to the priorities of others. However self-starting a leader may be, a president or prime minister is running a kind of variety show with different acts commanding attention. Some acts are staples; others vary according to the momentary rise of certain issues or perceived needs. Every variety show host needs a stand-up comedian and a singer, just as every government leader needs a finance minister and a foreign minister. But the priorities of a health or education minister, like the juggler or dancing bear, are not a constant booking for the leader.[28] Although a top leader must attend to the necessities of state, social policy is discretionary.

Two leaders—Thatcher and Reagan—stand out for their strong sense of what they wanted done and their ability to articulate their purposes clearly. It was difficult to misperceive their signals. For various reasons, leaders such as Major, Carter, Bush, and Clinton were not clearly directive. In all of these cases the governing parties were divided. In some cases (Bush, Clinton, and even Reagan), the governments were also divided. Temperament, however, may be at least as important as political division. Major sought to smooth over deep intraparty differences, whereas Thatcher dumped dissidents overboard. Unlike Reagan, who made decisions out of deep inner, perhaps even dogmatic, conviction, Carter was open to facts or arguments that could move a decision this way or that, thus creating uncertainty as well as providing an invitation for more acts to gain a spot on his "show." Much like Carter, Clinton was attracted to reasoning through different points of view, but he suffered initially, as did Carter, from putting forth an agenda more extensive than his level of political support allowed. The combination of policy ambition and weakness resulting from the 1994 decimation of his political resources moved Clinton toward compromise, frequently based on the agendas of his opponents, thus making him vulnerable to the charge of inconstancy.

The first President Bush also suffered from a weak political hand but had few policy ambitions.[29] At least in the first half of his term, Bush's desire for accommodation rather than confrontation (a desire that diminished after his fellow Republicans virtually impaled him for violating his "no new taxes" pledge in late 1990) reflected both the limits of his political circumstances—a Democratic Congress and no mandate—and a political personality that had a large "comfort zone" for accommodating seemingly dissonant policy choices. Except for Clinton's initial level of policy ambition, what has been said of Bush and his circumstances applied equally well to Clinton. The crucial difference is that Clinton became the master of policy triangulation and, despite resentment toward him from within his party's ranks, seemed to have more latitude with his party than Bush was able to achieve.

How presidents lead, then, is partly a function of who they are—that is, what their instincts and temperament lead them to do. But it is also a function of the conditions under which they govern—for example, how fragile or sturdy their political and governing coalition is or seems to be. Every leader inherits the activities set in motion by other political actors, including their predecessors. The extent to which leaders push against this parallelogram of forces is a function of governing institutions (which help determine the forces of resistance), the conditions under which they come to power, and their own tendencies, especially how they look at the world (black and white or shades of gray and risk-bearing or risk-averse). When a desire for change seems clear and when it is facilitated by institutions and electoral outcomes, a leader obviously has greater latitude. But a tendency to see things in large-scale visions rather than in operational details and to see things in black and white rather than gray also makes for a stronger push off the blocks. Reagan and Thatcher had that capacity. Neither suffered from doubt or from paralysis by analysis.

In George W. Bush's case, the conditions of his election might reasonably have produced caution, especially with narrow margins in Congress and Bush's own rhetoric of reconciliation. In his favor, at least until Senator Jeffords left the Republican ranks, was that he was the first Republican president to operate under a unified government since Eisenhower after the 1952 election. Bush chose centrist rhetoric but followed his party's drumbeat to the right on policy. Partisan forces were much stronger in 2001 than they were in 1953, and they tethered Bush more closely to his party. Eisenhower's personal stature also allowed him to operate "above" party in a way that was not possible almost fifty years later.

Just as the onset of World War II subordinated Roosevelt's New Deal agenda to the war effort, after the September 11 attacks, Bush's agenda was no longer his own. Ironically, Saddam Hussein had made the first Bush presidency seem more purposeful, and Osama bin Laden did the same for the younger Bush's presidency. But both Bush I and Bush II were mainly reacting to unforeseen events. Their agendas were taken hostage, but for a time the crises made each president look less political and more presidential.

In the end what difference does leadership make? The question tantalizes because we have no clear way of connecting leadership behavior to outcomes. Much depends on which aspects of leadership we deem situationally appropriate. To energize government, simplicity is of the essence. One need not be a philosopher-king, but one does need to be a king (or queen). That, at least, appears to be the lesson we derive from those who have succeeded in giving direction to government, regardless of its ultimate wisdom. The extent to which constraints fail to paralyze choice is partly a consequence of the willingness to take risks. The more risk-averse leaders are, the greater the constraints will seem to be.

We can infer the effects of leadership if we look carefully. Robert Putnam and his colleagues, for instance, illustrated both the limitations and the possibilities of leadership.[30] By studying various Italian regional governments, they conclude that performance is predicted almost perfectly by variation in broad indicators of regional, social, economic, and historical characteristics. When they look only at regions with similar characteristics, however, they also observe differences in performance among them. The first-cut variations in performance across the regions are clearly a function of the differential in resources available to govern effectively. The second-cut differences suggest that when these resources do not vary, skillful leadership (or, alternatively, its absence) makes a difference in the region's performance. In other words, the conditions for leadership should be looked at first. But outcomes are not the pure residual of those conditions. The outcomes also are affected by leaders. Thus, the manager of a last place baseball team may be every bit as skilled as the manager of the championship team, but the former typically has fewer resources to manage effectively than the latter. The relevant test of managerial skills therefore is whether one does better or worse than expected. Notably, the managers who win accolades (such as manager of the year) are rarely those who steer championship teams but are instead those who exceed their baseline expectations by a significant margin.

The possibilities for leadership are imbedded in factors over which leaders themselves have little direct control.[31] Leaders nowhere are free to do as they wish. Institutions and situations help to determine the range of possibilities, but leaders themselves have varying propensities to explore just how far ranging are the "arts of the possible."[32]

A Final Word

Comparison is the basis of judgment. False comparisons idealize at least one of the alternatives or generalize from momentary discomforts. The perspective provided by sound comparative analysis makes complex what seemed so simple. Stark contrasts recede on closer inspection. Sometimes institutions give us differences in form rather than in result.

The American political system generates a good deal of overt but often uncrystallized conflict. Because so much agenda-generating and coalition-building is done openly in the United States, conflict is more visible and presidents often appear to be stymied. But governing is nowhere an easy matter. Political leaders in all democracies are subject to public disapproval and diminished political resources. In the absence of a Stalinist concentration of power, politics makes governing hard, and democratic politics makes it harder still. Comparison helps us to avoid drifting off into idealizing alternatives when we think about political leadership in the United States. Above all, the capacity for leadership is not a constant quantity. Situational forces both stretch and constrain that capacity, and leaders vary a good bit in the extent to which they wish to test the boundaries of what is possible. The American president is neither wholly unique nor entirely similar to other democratic political leaders. Above all, like political leaders elsewhere, the American president is not immune from the global forces that, to some degree, have shifted power from the nation-state to regional supranational organizations, to international markets, and to central financial institutions.

Notes

1. Anthony King, "Foundations of Power," in *Researching the Presidency*, ed. George C. Edwards III, John H. Kessel, and Bert A. Rockman (Pittsburgh: University of Pittsburgh Press, 1993), 415–451.

2. *Revenue Statistics of OECD Member Countries, 1965–1997* (Paris: OECD Publications, 1996), 14.

3. Ibid., 79.

4. Ibid., 202. The cited figures include Social Security taxes extracted by the central governments.

5. Richard P. Nathan and Fred C. Doolittle, "The Untold Story of Reagan's 'New Federalism,'" *Public Interest* 77 (fall 1984): 96–105.

6. Richard Rose, "The Variability of Party Government: A Theoretical and Empirical Critique," *Political Studies* 17 (December 1969): 414.

7. James W. Ceaser, "Political Parties and Presidential Ambition," *Journal of Politics* 40 (August 1978): 708–741.

8. For the prevalence of divided government at the state as well as the federal level, see Morris Fiorina, *Divided Government*, 2d ed. (Boston: Allyn and Bacon, 1996). For strong party differences, see David C. King, "The Polarization of American Parties and Mistrust of Government," in *Why People Don't Trust Government*, ed. Joseph S. Nye Jr., Philip D. Zelikow, and David C. King (Cambridge: Harvard University Press, 1997), 155–178.

9. See King, "Foundations of Power."

10. Lloyd N. Cutler, "To Form a Government," *Foreign Affairs* 59 (fall 1980): 126–143.

11. Rose, "Variability of Party Government"; see also Anthony King, "Political Parties in Western Democracies: Some Skeptical Reflections," *Polity* 2 (fall 1969): 111–141.

12. Alexander Hamilton, in *The Federalist Papers*, no. 70, ed. Clinton Rossiter (New York: New American Library, 1961), 424.

13. Anthony King, "Margaret Thatcher: The Style of a Prime Minister," in *The British Prime Minister*, 2d ed., ed. Anthony King (Durham: Duke University Press, 1985), 96–140.

14. Dennis Kavanagh, "From Gentlemen to Players: Changes in Political Leadership," in *Britain: Progress and Decline,* ed. William L. Gwyn and Richard Rose, *Tulane Studies in Political Science* 17 (New Orleans: Tulane University Press, 1980), 90–91; see also Richard Rose, *The Capacity of the President: A Comparative Analysis* (Strathclyde, Scotland: Centre for the Study of Public Policy, 1984), 72–73.

15. Michael Lewis-Beck, "Comparative Economic Voting: Britain, France, Germany, Italy," *American Journal of Political Science* 30 (May 1986): 315–346.

16. Hugh Heclo, "Presidential and Prime Ministerial Selection," in *Perspectives on Presidential Selection,* ed. Donald R. Matthews (Washington, D.C.: Brookings Institution, 1973), 48.

17. Rose, *Capacity of the President;* Theodore J. Lowi, *The Personal President: Power Invested, Promise Unfulfilled* (Ithaca: Cornell University Press, 1985); and Bert A. Rockman, *The Leadership Question: The Presidency and the American System* (New York: Praeger, 1984).

18. See, for example, Richard P. Nathan, *The Administrative Presidency* (New York: John Wiley, 1983); and Joel D. Aberbach and Bert A. Rockman, "Clashing Beliefs within the Executive Branch: The Nixon Administration Bureaucracy," *American Political Science Review* 70 (June 1976): 456–468. A lengthy discussion of Reagan administration efforts to gain control of the bureaucracy is in Bert A. Rockman, "USA: Government under President Reagan," in *Jahrbuch zur Staats- und Verwaltungswissenschaft,* ed. Thomas Ellwein, Joachim-Jens Hesse, Renate Mayntz, and Fritz W. Scharpf (Baden-Baden: Nomos, 1987), 183–223. For a straightforward articulation of the president's need to gain control over the bureaucracy, see Terry M. Moe, "The Politicized Presidency," in *The New Direction in American Politics,* ed. John E. Chubb and Paul E. Peterson (Washington, D.C.: Brookings Institution, 1985), 235–272. And for evidence thereof, see Charles Tiefer, *The Semi-Sovereign Presidency: The Bush Administration's Strategy for Governing without Congress* (Boulder: Westview Press, 1994).

19. In assessing a number of studies that compare governmental policy-making capabilities across a variety of advanced democracies, Weaver and Rockman concluded, "The U.S. separation of powers system tends to cluster closely with the coalitional parliamentary regime types in terms of its associated risks and opportunities." R. Kent Weaver and Bert A. Rockman, eds., *Do Institutions Matter? Government Capabilities in the United States and Abroad* (Washington, D.C.: Brookings Institution, 1993), 450.

20. See, for instance, Benjamin Ginsberg, *The Consequences of Consent: Elections, Citizen Control and Popular Acquiescence* (Reading: Addison-Wesley, 1982).

21. For example, see Paul Allen Beck, "The Electoral Cycle and Patterns of American Politics," *British Journal of Political Science* 9 (April 1979): 129–156; and David W. Brady, "Critical Elections, Congressional Parties and Clusters of Policy Changes," *British Journal of Political Science* 8 (January 1978): 79–99.

22. See Stephen Skowronek, *The Politics Presidents Make: Leadership from John Adams to George Bush* (Cambridge: Belknap Press, 1993).

23. See Walter Dean Burnham, "Realignment Lives: The 1994 Earthquake and Its Implications," in *The Clinton Presidency: First Appraisals,* ed. Colin Campbell and Bert A. Rockman (Chatham, N.J.: Chatham House, 1996), 363–395.

24. Clinton Rossiter, *The American Presidency* (New York: Mentor Books, 1956).

25. Samuel P. Huntington, "Political Modernization: America vs. Europe," in *Political Order in Changing Societies,* ed. Samuel P. Huntington (New Haven: Yale University Press, 1968), 93–139.

26. Richard Rose, "The President: A Chief But Not an Executive," *Presidential Studies Quarterly* 7 (winter 1977): 5–20.

27. Rossiter, *American Presidency.*

28. See, in this regard, Richard Rose, "British Government: The Job at the Top," in *Presidents and Prime Ministers,* ed. Richard Rose and Ezra N. Suleiman (Washington, D.C.: American Enterprise Institute, 1980), 1–49.

29. See David Mervin, *George Bush and the Guardianship Presidency* (Houndmills: MacMillan, 1996).

30. Robert D. Putnam, Robert Leonardi, Raffaella Y. Nanetti, and Franco Pavoncello, "Explaining Institutional Success: The Case of Italian Regional Government," *American Political Science Review* 77 (March 1983): 55–74.

31. For a well-formulated statement of the power of legacies in constraining leadership and the possibilities of leadership, see Robert D. Putnam, *Making Democracy Work: Civic Traditions in Modern Italy* (Princeton: Princeton University Press, 1993).

32. See Erwin C. Hargrove, *The President as Leader: Appealing to the Better Angels of Our Nature* (Lawrence: University Press of Kansas, 1998); and Paul Brace and Barbara Hinckley, *Follow the Leader: Opinion Polls and the Modern Presidency* (New York: Basic Books, 1992).

Part II Elements of Presidential Power

4 The Two Constitutional Presidencies

Jeffrey K. Tulis

A political design of the presidency can be found in Article II of the Constitution. Yet, according to Jeffrey K. Tulis, two constitutional presidencies exist—not only the enduring, capital-C version that the Framers invented at the Constitutional Convention of 1787, the formal provisions of which remain substantially unaltered, but also the adapted lowercase-c constitution that Woodrow Wilson devised and that most presidents during the past century have followed. Sometimes, the fit between the formal and informal constitutional presidencies is close—for example, in the months following the September 11, 2001, terrorist attacks on the United States. But, Tulis argues, the two constitutional presidencies usually are in tension with each other. Both constitutions value "energy" in the presidency, but the exercise of popular rhetorical leadership that is proscribed by the Framers' Constitution is prescribed by Wilson's. As a result, Tulis concludes, "Many of the dilemmas and frustrations of the modern presidency may be traced to the president's ambiguous constitutional station, a vantage place composed of conflicting elements."

The modern presidency is buffeted by two "constitutions." Presidential action continues to be constrained, and presidential behavior shaped, by the institutions created by the original Constitution. The core structures established in 1789 and debated during the founding era remain essentially unchanged. For the most part, later amendments to the Constitution have left intact the basic features of the executive, legislative, and judicial branches of government. Great questions, such as the merits of unity or plurality in the executive, have not been seriously reopened. Because most of the structure persists, it seems plausible that the theory on which the presidency was constructed remains relevant to its current functioning.[1]

Presidential and public understanding of the constitutional system and of the president's place in it have changed, however. This new understanding is the "second constitution" under which presidents attempt to govern. Central to this second constitution is a view of statecraft that is in tension with the original Constitution—indeed it is opposed to the Founders' understanding of the presidency's place in the political system. The second constitution, which puts a premium on active and continuous presidential leadership of popular opinion, is buttressed by several institutional, albeit extraconstitutional, developments. These include the proliferation of presidential primaries as a mode of selection and the emergence of the mass media as a pervasive force.[2]

Many of the dilemmas and frustrations of the modern presidency may be traced to the president's ambiguous constitutional station, a vantage place composed of conflicting elements. The purpose of this chapter is to lay bare the theoretical core of each of the two constitutions to highlight those elements that are in tension between them.

To uncover the principles that underlie the original Constitution, this chapter relies heavily on *The Federalist*. A set of papers justifying the Constitution, the text was written by three of the Constitution's most articulate proponents, Alexander Hamilton, James Madison, and John Jay. The purpose of this journey back to the Founders is not to point to their authority or to lament change; nor is it meant to imply that all the supporters of the Constitution agreed with each of their arguments. *The Federalist* does represent, however, the most coherent articulation of the implications of, and interconnections among, the principles and practices that were generally accepted when the Constitution was ratified.[3]

The political thought of Woodrow Wilson is explored to outline the principles of the second constitution. Wilson self-consciously attacked *The Federalist* in his writings; as president he tried to act according to the dictates of his reinterpretation of the American political system. Presidents have continued to follow his example, and presidential scholars tend to repeat his arguments. Most presidents have not thought through the issues Wilson discussed—they are too busy for that. But if pushed and questioned, modern presidents would probably (and occasionally do) justify their behavior with arguments that echo Wilson's. Just as *The Federalist* represents the deepest and most coherent articulation of generally held nineteenth-century understandings of the presidency, Wilson offers the most comprehensive theory in support of contemporary impulses and practices.

The Founding Perspective

Perhaps the most striking feature of the founding perspective, particularly in comparison with contemporary political analyses, is its synoptic character.

The Founders' task was to create a whole government, one in which the executive would play an important part, but only a part. By contrast, contemporary scholars of American politics often study institutions individually and therefore tend to be partisans of "their institution" in its contests with other actors in American politics.[4] Presidency scholars often restrict their inquiries to the strategic concerns of presidents as they quest for power. Recovering the founding perspective provides a way to think about the systemic legitimacy and utility of presidential power as well. To uncover such a synoptic vision, one must range widely in search of the principles that guided or justified the Founders' view of the executive. Some of these principles are discussed most thoroughly in *The Federalist* in the context of other institutions, such as Congress or the judiciary.

The Founders' general and far-reaching institutional analysis was preceded by a more fundamental decision of enormous import. Federalists and anti-Federalists alike sought a government devoted to limited ends. In contrast to polities that attempt to shape the souls of their citizenry and foster certain excellences or moral qualities by penetrating deeply into the "private" sphere, the Founders wanted their government to be limited to establishing and securing such a sphere. Politics would extend only to the tasks of protecting individual rights and fostering liberty for the exercise of those rights. Civic virtue would still be necessary, but it would be elicited from the people rather than imposed on them.

Proponents and critics of the Constitution agreed about the proper ends of government, but they disagreed over the best institutional means to secure them.[5] Some critics of the Constitution worried that its institutions would actually undermine its limited liberal ends. Although these kinds of arguments were settled politically by the Federalist victory, *The Federalist* concedes that they were not resolved fundamentally because they continued as problems built into the structure of American politics.

Is a vigorous executive consistent with the genius of republican government? Hasty readers of *The Federalist* think yes, unequivocally. Closer reading of *The Federalist* reveals a deeper ambivalence regarding the compatibility of executive power and republican freedom.[6]

Demagoguery

The Founders worried especially about the danger that a powerful executive might pose to the system if power were derived from the role of popular leader.[7] For most Federalists, demagogue and popular leader were synonyms, and nearly all references to popular leaders in their writings are pejorative. Demagoguery, combined with majority tyranny, was regarded as the peculiar vice to which democracies were susceptible. Although much historical evidence supported this insight, the Founders were made more acutely aware of the problem by the presence in their own midst of popular leaders such as Daniel Shays, who led an insurrection in Massachusetts. The Founders' preoccupation with demagoguery may appear today as quaint, yet it may be that we do not fear it today because the Founders were so successful in institutionally proscribing some forms of it.

The original Greek meaning of *demagogue* was simply "leader of the people," and the term was applied in premodern times to champions of the people's claim to rule as against that of aristocrats and monarchs. As James Ceaser pointed out, the term has been more characteristically applied to a certain quality of leadership—that which attempts to sway popular passions. Because most speech contains a mix of rational and passionate appeals, it is difficult to specify demagoguery with precision. But as Ceaser argued, one cannot ignore the phenomenon because it is difficult to define, suggesting that it possesses at least enough intuitive clarity that few would label Dwight Eisenhower, for example, a demagogue, whereas most would not hesitate to so label Joseph McCarthy. The main characteristic of demagoguery seems to be an excess of passionate appeals. Ceaser categorized demagogues according to the kinds of passions that are summoned, dividing these into "soft" and "hard" types.

Soft demagogues tend to flatter their constituents, "by claiming that they know what is best, and makes a point of claiming his closeness (to them) by manner or gesture."[8] Hard demagogues attempt to create or encourage divisions among the people to build and maintain their constituency. Typically, this sort of appeal uses extremist rhetoric that panders to fear. James Madison worried about the possibility of class appeals that would pit the poor against the wealthy. But the hard demagogue might appeal to a very different passion. "Excessive encouragement of morality and hope" might be employed to create a division between those alleged to be compassionate, moral, or progressive, and those thought insensitive, selfish, or backward. Hard demagogues are not restricted to the right or to the left.[9]

Demagogues can also be classified by their object. In this instance the issue becomes more complicated. Demagoguery might be good if it were a means to a good end, such as preservation of a decent nation or successful prosecution of a just war. The difficulty is to ensure by institutional means that demagoguery would be used only for good ends and not simply to satisfy the overweening ambition of an immoral leader or potential tyrant. How are political structures created that permit demagoguery when appeals to passion are needed but proscribe it for normal politics?

The Founders did not have a straightforward answer to this problem, perhaps because there is no unproblematic institutional solution. Instead, they addressed it indirectly in two ways: they attempted both to narrow the range of acceptable demagogic appeals through the architectonic act of founding itself and to mitigate the effects of such appeals in the day-to-day conduct of governance through the particular institutions they created. The Founders did not choose to make provision for the institutional encouragement of demagoguery in time of crisis, refusing to adopt, for example, the Roman model of constitutional dictatorship for emergencies.[10] Behind their indirect approach may have been the thought that excessive ambition needs no institutional support and the faith that in extraordinary circumstances popular rhetoric, even forceful demagoguery, would gain legitimacy through the pressure of necessity.

Many references in *The Federalist* and in the ratification debates over the Constitution warn of demagogues of the hard variety who through divisive appeals would aim at tyranny. *The Federalist* literally begins and ends with this issue. In the final paper Hamilton offered "a lesson of moderation to all sincere lovers of the Union [that] ought to put them on their guard against hazarding anarchy, civil war, a perpetual alienation of the states from each other, and perhaps the military despotism of a victorious demagogue."[11] The Founders' concern with hard demagoguery was not merely a rhetorical device designed to facilitate passage of the Constitution. It also reveals a concern to address the kinds of divisions and issues exploited by hard demagoguery. From this perspective, the founding can be understood as an attempt to settle the large issue of whether the one, few, or many ruled (in favor of the many "through" a constitution), to reconfirm the limited purposes of government (security, prosperity, and the protection of rights), and thereby to give effect to the distinction between public and private life. At the founding, these large questions were still matters of political dispute. Hamilton argued that adopting the Constitution would settle these perennially divisive questions for Americans, replacing those questions with smaller, less contentious issues. Hamilton called this new American politics a politics of "administration," distinguishing it from the traditional politics of disputed ends. If politics were transformed and narrowed in this way, thought Hamilton, demagogues would be deprived of part of their once-powerful arsenal of rhetorical weapons because certain topics would be rendered illegitimate for public discussion. By constituting an American understanding of politics, the founding would also reconstitute the problem of demagoguery.[12]

If the overriding concern about demagoguery in the extraordinary period before the ratification of the Constitution was to prevent social disruption, division, and possibly tyranny, the concerns expressed through the Constitution for normal times were broader: to create institutions that would be most likely to generate and execute good policy or to resist bad policy. Underlying the institutional structures and powers created by the Constitution are three principles designed to address this broad concern: representation, independence of the executive, and separation of powers.

Representation

As the Founders realized, the problem with any simple distinction between good and bad law is that it is difficult to provide clear criteria to distinguish the two in any particular instance. It will not do to suggest that in a democracy good legislation reflects the majority will. A majority may tyrannize a minority, violating its rights; and even a nontyrannical majority may be a foolish one, preferring policies that do not further its interests. These considerations lay behind the Founders' distrust of "direct" or "pure" democracy.[13]

Yet an alternative understanding—that legislation is good if it objectively furthers the limited ends of the polity—is also problematic. It is perhaps impossible to assess the "interests" of a nation without giving considerable attention to what the citizenry considers its interests to be. This consideration lies behind the Founders' animus toward monarchy and aristocracy.[14] Identifying and embodying the proper weight to be given popular opinion and its appropriate institutional reflections is one of the characteristic problems of democratic constitutionalism. The Founders' understanding of republicanism as representative government reveals this problem and the Constitution's attempted solution.

Practically, the Founders attempted to accommodate these two requisites of good government by four devices. First, they established popular election as the fundamental basis of the Constitution and of the government's legitimacy. They modified that requirement by allowing "indirect" selection for some institutions (for example, the Senate, Supreme Court, and presidency)—that is, selection by others who were themselves chosen by the people. With respect to the president, the Founders wanted to elicit the "sense of the people," but they feared an inability to do so if the people acted in a "collective capacity." They worried that the dynamics of mass politics would at best produce poorly qualified presidents and at worst open the door to demagoguery and regime instability. At the same time, the Founders wanted to give popular opinion a greater role in presidential selection than it would have if Congress chose the executive. The institutional solution to these concerns was the electoral college, originally designed as a semiautonomous locus of decision for presidential selection and chosen by state legislatures at each election.[15]

Second, the Founders established differing lengths of tenure for officeholders in the major national institutions, which corresponded to the institutions' varying "proximity" to the people. House members were to face reelection every two years, making them more responsive to constituent pressure than members of the other national institutions. The president was given a four-year term, sufficient time, it was thought, to "contribute to the firmness of the executive" without justifying "any alarm for the public liberty."[16]

Third, the Founders derived the authority and formal power of the institutions and their officers ultimately from the people but immediately from the Constitution. The effect would be to insulate officials from day-to-day currents of public opinion, while allowing assertion of deeply felt and widely shared public opinion through constitutional amendment.

Fourth, the Founders envisioned that the extent of the nation itself would insulate governing officials from sudden shifts of public opinion. In his well-known arguments for an extended republic, Madison reasoned that large size would improve democracy by making the formation of majority factions difficult. But again, argued Madison, extent of the territory and diversity of factions would not prevent the formation of a majority if the issue were an important one.[17]

The brakes on public opinion, not the provision for its influence, are what cause skepticism today.[18] Because popular leadership is so central to modern theories of the presidency, the rationale behind the Founders' distrust of "direct democracy" should be noted specifically. This issue is raised dramatically in *The Federalist* no. 49, in which Madison addresses Jefferson's suggestion that "whenever two of the three branches of government shall concur in [the] opinion . . . that a convention is necessary for altering the Constitution, *or correcting breaches of it,* a convention shall be called for the purpose." Madison recounts Jefferson's reasoning: because the Constitution was formed by the people, it rightfully ought to be modified by them. Madison admitted "that a constitutional road to the decision of the people ought to be marked out and kept open for great and extraordinary occasions." But he objected to bringing directly to the people disputes among the branches about the extent of their authority. In the normal course of governance, such disputes could be expected to arise fairly often. In our day they would include, for example, the war powers controversy, the impoundment controversy, and the issue of executive privilege.

Madison objected to recourse to "the people" on three basic grounds. First, popular appeals would imply "some defect" in the government: "Frequent appeals would, in great measure, deprive the government of that veneration which time bestows on everything, and without which perhaps the wisest and freest governments would not possess the requisite stability." *The Federalist* pointed to the institutional benefits of popular veneration—stability of government and the enhanced authority of its constitutional officers. Second, the tranquility of the society as a whole might be disturbed. Madison expressed the fear that an enterprising demagogue might reopen disputes over "great national questions" in a political context less favorable to their resolution than the Constitutional Convention.

Third, Madison voiced "the greatest objection of all" to frequent appeals to the people: "The decisions which would probably result from such appeals would not answer the purpose of maintaining the constitutional equilibrium of government." Chief executives might face political difficulties if frequent appeals to the people were permitted because other features of the office (their singularity, independence, and executive powers) would leave presidents at a rhetorical disadvantage in contests with the legislature. Presidents will be "generally the objects of jealousy and their administrations . . . liable to be discolored and rendered unpopular," Madison argued. "The Members of the legislatures on the other hand are numerous. . . . Their connections of blood, of friendship, and of acquaintance embrace a great proportion of the most influential part of society. The nature of their public trust implies a personal influence among the people."[19]

Madison realized that there may be circumstances "less adverse to the executive and judiciary departments." If the executive power were "in the hands of a peculiar favorite of the people . . . the public decision might be less swayed in favor of the [legislature]. But still it could never be expected to turn on the true merits of the question." The ultimate reason for the rejection of "frequent popular appeals" is that they would undermine *deliberation* and result in bad public policy:

The *passions*, therefore, not the *reason*, of the public would sit in judgment. But it is the reason, alone, of the public, that ought to control and regulate the government. The passions ought to be controlled and regulated by the government.[20]

There are two frequent misunderstandings of the Founders' opinion on the deliberative function of representation. The first is that they naively believed that deliberation constituted the whole of legislative politics—that there would be no bargaining, logrolling, or nondeliberative rhetorical appeals. The discussions of Congress in *The Federalist* numbers 52 to 68 and in the Constitutional Convention debates reveal quite clearly that the Founders understood that the legislative process would involve a mixture of these elements. The founding task was to create an institutional context that made deliberation most likely, not to assume that it would occur "naturally" or, even in the best of legislatures, predominantly.[21]

The second common error, prevalent in leading historical accounts of the period, is to interpret the deliberative elements of the Founders' design as an attempt to rid the legislative councils of "common men" and replace them with "better sorts"—more educated and, above all, more propertied individuals.[22] Deliberation, in this view, is the by-product of the kind of person elected to office. The public's opinions are "refined and enlarged" because refined individuals do the governing. Although this view finds some support in *The Federalist* and was a worry of several anti-Federalists, the Founders' Constitution places much greater emphasis on the formal structures of the national institutions than on the background of officeholders.[23] Indeed, good character and high intelligence, they reasoned, would be of little help to the government if it resembled a direct democracy: "In all very numerous assemblies, of whatever characters composed, passion never fails to wrest the sceptre from reason. Had every Athenian citizen been a Socrates, every Athenian assembly would still have been a mob."[24]

The presidency was thus intended to be representative of the people, but not merely responsive to popular will. Drawn from the people through an election (albeit an indirect one), presidents were to be free enough from the daily shifts in public opinion so that they could refine it and, paradoxically, better serve popular interests. Hamilton expressed well this element of the theory in a passage in which he linked the problem of representation to that of demagoguery:

There are those who would be inclined to regard the servile pliancy of the executive to a prevailing current, either in the community or in the legislature, as its best recommendation. But such men entertain very crude notions, as well of the purposes for which government was instituted, as of the true means by which public happiness may be promoted. The republican principle demands that the deliberative sense of the community should govern the conduct of those to whom they intrust the management of their affairs; but it does not require an unqualified complaisance . . . to every transient impulse which the people may receive from the arts of men, who flatter their prejudices to betray their interests. . . . When occasions present themselves in which the interests of the people are at variance with their inclinations, it is the duty of the persons whom they have appointed to be the guardians of those interests to withstand the temporary delusion, in order to give them time and opportunity for more cool and sedate reflection.[25]

Independence of the Executive

To "withstand the temporary delusion" of popular opinion, the executive was made independent. The office would draw its authority from the Constitution rather than from another government branch. The Framers were led to this decision from their knowledge of the states, where, according to John Marshall, the governments (with the exception of New York) lacked any structure "which could resist the wild projects of the moment, give the people an opportunity to reflect and allow the good sense of the nation time for exertion." As Madison stated at the convention, "Experience had proved a tendency in our governments to throw all power into the legislative vortex. The executives of the states are in general little more than Cyphers; the legislatures omnipotent."[26]

Independence from Congress was the immediate practical need, yet the need was based on the close connection between legislatures and popular opinion. Because independence from public opinion was the source of the concern about the legislatures, the Founders rejected James Wilson's arguments on behalf of popular election as a means of making the president independent of Congress.

Executive independence created the conditions under which presidents would be most likely to adopt a different perspective from Congress on matters of public policy. Congress would be dominated by local factions that, according to plan, would give great weight to constituent opinion. The president, as Thomas Jefferson was to argue, was the only national officer "who commanded a view of the whole ground." Metaphorically, independence gave presidents their own space within, and their own angle of vision on, the polity. According to the founding theory, these constituent features of discretion are entailed by the twin activities of executing the will of the legislature and leading a legislature to construct good laws to be executed, laws that would be responsive to the long-term needs of the nation.[27]

Separation of Powers

The constitutional role of the president in lawmaking raises the question of the meaning and purpose of separation of powers. What is the sense of separation of power if power is shared among the branches of government? Clearly, legalists are wrong who have assumed that the Founders wished to distinguish so carefully among executive, legislative, and judicial power as to make each the exclusive preserve of a particular branch. However, their error has given rise to another.

Political scientists, following Richard Neustadt, have assumed that because powers were not divided according to the principle of "one branch, one function," the Founders made no principled distinction among kinds of power. Instead, according to Neustadt, they created "separate institutions sharing power."[28] The premise of that claim is that power is an entity that can be divided up to prevent any one branch from having enough to rule another. In this view, the sole purpose of separation of powers is to preserve liberty by preventing the arbitrary rule of any one center of power.

The Neustadt perspective finds some support both in the Founders' deliberations and in the Constitution. Much attention was given to making each branch "weighty" enough to resist encroachment by the others. Yet this "checks and balances" view of separation of powers can be understood better in tandem with an alternative understanding of the concept: powers were separated and structures of each branch differentiated to equip each branch to perform different tasks. Each branch would be superior (although not the sole power) in its own sphere and in its own way. The purpose of separation of powers was to make effective governance more likely.[29]

Ensuring the protection of liberty and individual rights was one element of effective governance as conceived by the Founders, but not the only one. Government also needed to ensure the security of the nation and to craft policies that reflected popular will.[30] These three governmental objectives may conflict; for example, popular opinion may favor policies that violate rights. Separation of powers was thought to be an institutional way of accommodating the tensions between governmental objectives.

Table 4.1 presents a simplified view of the purposes behind the separation of powers. Note that the three objectives of government—popular will, popular rights, and self-preservation—are mixed twice in the Constitution; they are mixed among the branches and within each branch so that each objective is given priority in one branch. Congress and the president were to concern themselves with all three, but the priority of their concern differs, with "self-preservation" or national security of utmost concern to the president.

The term *separation of powers* has perhaps obstructed understanding of the extent to which different structures were designed to give each branch the special quality needed to secure its governmental objectives. Thus, although the

Table 4.1 Separation of Powers

Objectives (in order of priority)	Special qualities and functions (to be aimed at)	Structures and means
CONGRESS 1. Popular will 2. Popular rights 3. Self-preservation	Deliberation	a. Plurality b. Proximity (frequent House elections) c. Bicameralism d. Competent powers
PRESIDENT 1. Self-preservation 2. Popular rights 3. Popular will	Energy and "steady administration of law"	a. Unity b. Four-year term and reeligibility c. Competent powers
COURTS 1. Popular rights	"Judgment, not will"	a. Small collegial body b. Life tenure c. Power linked to argument

Founders were not so naive as to expect that Congress would be simply "deliberative," they hoped its plural membership and bicameral structure would provide necessary, if not sufficient, conditions for deliberation to emerge. Similarly, the president's "energy," it was hoped, would be enhanced by unity, the prospect of reelection, and substantial discretion. As we all know, the Supreme Court does not simply "judge" dispassionately; it also makes policies and exercises will. But the Founders believed it made no sense to have a Court if it were intended to be just like a Congress. The judiciary was structured to make the dispassionate protection of rights more likely, if by no means certain.

The Founders differentiated powers as well as structures in the original design. These powers ("the executive power" vested in the president in Article II and "all legislative power herein granted" given to Congress in Article I) overlap and sometimes conflict. Yet both the legalists' view of power as "parchment distinction" and the political scientists' view of "separate institutions sharing power" provide inadequate guides to what happens and what was thought *ought* to happen when powers collided. The Founders urged that "line drawing" among spheres of authority be the product of political conflict among the branches, not the result of dispassionate legal analysis. Contrary to more contemporary views, they did not believe that such conflict would lead to deadlock or stalemate.[31]

Consider the disputes that sometimes arise from claims of "executive privilege."[32] Presidents occasionally refuse to provide information to Congress that its members deem necessary to carry out their special functions. They usually justify assertions of executive privilege on the grounds of either national security or the need to maintain the conditions necessary to sound execution, including the unfettered canvassing of opinions.

Both Congress and the president have legitimate constitutional prerogatives at stake: Congress has a right to know and the president a need for secrecy. How does one discover whether in any particular instance the president's claim is more or less weighty than Congress's? The answer will depend on the circumstances—for example, the importance of the particular piece of legislation in the congressional agenda versus the importance of the particular secret to the executive. There is no formula independent of political circumstance with which to weigh such competing institutional claims. The most knowledgeable observers of those political conflicts are the parties themselves: Congress and the president.

Each branch has weapons at its disposal to use against the other. Congress can threaten to hold up legislation or appointments important to presidents. Ultimately, it could impeach and convict them. For their part, presidents may continue to "stonewall"; they may veto bills or fail to support legislation of interest to their legislative opponents; they may delay political appointments; and they may put the issue to public test, even submitting to an impeachment inquiry for their own advantage. The lengths to which presidents and Congresses are willing to go was thought to be a rough measure of the importance of their respective constitutional claims. Nearly always, executive-legislative disputes are resolved at a relatively low stage of potential conflict. In 1981, for example, President Ronald Reagan ordered Interior Secretary James Watt to release information to a Senate committee after the committee had agreed to maintain confidentiality. The compromise was reached after public debate and "contempt of Congress" hearings were held.

It is important to note that this political process is dynamic. Viewed at particular moments, the system may appear deadlocked; looked at over time, considerable movement becomes apparent. Similar scenarios could be constructed for the other issues over which congressional and presidential claims to authority conflict, such as the use of executive agreements in place of treaties, the deployment of military force, or the executive impoundment of appropriated monies.[33]

Although conflict may continue to be institutionally fostered or constrained in ways that were intended by the Founders, one still may wonder whether their broad objectives have been secured and whether their priorities should be ours.

At the beginning of the twentieth century, Woodrow Wilson mounted an attack on the Founders' design, convinced that it had not achieved its objectives. More important, his attack resulted in a reordering of these objectives in the understandings that presidents have of their roles. His theory underlies the second constitution that buffets the presidency.

The Modern Perspective

Woodrow Wilson's influential critique of *The Federalist* contains another synoptic vision. Yet his comprehensive reinterpretation of the constitutional order appears, at first glance, to be internally inconsistent. Between writing his classic dissertation, *Congressional Government*, in 1884 and publishing his well-known series of lectures, *Constitutional Government in the United States*, in 1908, Wilson shifted his position on important structural features of the constitutional system.

Early in his career Wilson depicted the House of Representatives as the potential motive force in American politics and urged reforms to make it more unified and energetic. He paid little attention to the presidency or judiciary. In later years he focused his attention on the presidency. In his early writings Wilson urged a plethora of constitutional amendments that were designed to emulate the British parliamentary system, including proposals to synchronize the terms of representatives and senators with that of the president and to require presidents to choose leaders of the majority party as cabinet secretaries. Wilson later abandoned formal amendment as a strategy, urging instead that the existing Constitution be reinterpreted to encompass his parliamentary views.

Wilson also altered his views at a deeper theoretical level. Christopher Wolfe has shown that although the "early" Wilson held a traditional view of the Constitution as a document whose meaning persists over time, the "later" Wilson adopted a historicist understanding, claiming that the meaning of the Constitution changed as a reflection of the prevailing thought of successive generations.[34]

As interesting as these shifts in Wilson's thought are, they all rest on an underlying critique of the American polity that Wilson maintained consistently throughout his career. Wilson's altered constitutional proposals—indeed, his altered understanding of constitutionalism itself—ought to be viewed as a series of strategic moves designed to remedy the same alleged systemic defects. Our task is to review Wilson's understanding of those defects and to outline the doctrine he developed to contend with them—a doctrine whose centerpiece would ultimately be the rhetorical presidency.

Wilson's doctrine counterpoises the Founders' understanding of demagoguery, representation, independence of the executive, and separation of powers. For clarity, these principles will be examined in a slightly different order
from before: separation of powers, representation, independence of the executive, and demagoguery.

Separation of Powers

For Wilson, separation of powers was the central defect of American politics. He was the first and most sophisticated proponent of the now conventional argument that separation of powers is a synonym for "checks and
balances"—that is, the negation of power by one branch over another. Yet
Wilson's view was more sophisticated than its progeny because his ultimate indictment of the Founders' conception was a functionalist one. Wilson claimed
that under the auspices of the Founders' view, formal and informal political
institutions failed to promote true deliberation in the legislature and impeded
energy in the executive.

Wilson characterized the Founders' understanding as "Newtonian," a yearning for equipoise and balance in a machinelike system:

The admirable positions of the *Federalist* read like thoughtful applications of
Montesquieu to the political needs and circumstances of America. They are full of
the theory of checks and balances. The President is balanced off against Congress,
Congress against the President, and each against the Court. . . . Politics is turned
into mechanics under [Montesquieu's] touch. The theory of gravitation is
supreme.[35]

The accuracy of Wilson's portrayal of the Founders may be questioned. He
reasoned backward from the malfunctioning system as he found it to how they
must have intended it. Wilson's depiction of the system rather than his interpretation of the Founders' intentions is of present concern.

Rather than equipoise and balance, Wilson found a system dominated by
Congress, with several attendant functional infirmities: major legislation frustrated by narrow-minded committees, lack of coordination and direction of
policies, a general breakdown of deliberation, and an absence of leadership. Extraconstitutional institutions—boss-led political parties chief among them—
had sprung up to assume the functions not performed by Congress or the
president, but they had not performed them well. Wilson also acknowledged
that the formal institutions had not always performed badly, that some prior
Congresses (those of Webster and Clay) and some presidencies (those of

Washington, Adams, Jefferson, Jackson, Lincoln, Roosevelt, and, surprisingly, Madison) had been examples of forceful leadership.[36]

These two strands of thought—the growth of extraconstitutional institutions and the periodic excellence of the constitutional structures—led Wilson to conclude that the Founders had mischaracterized their own system. The Founders' rhetoric was "Newtonian," but their constitutional structure, like all government, was actually "Darwinian." Wilson explained:

The trouble with the Newtonian theory is that government is not a machine but a living thing. It falls, not under the theory of the universe, but under the theory of organic life. It is accountable to Darwin, not to Newton. It is modified by its environment, necessitated by its tasks, shaped to its functions by the sheer pressure of life.[37]

The Founders' doctrine had affected the working of the structure to the extent that the power of the political branches was interpreted mechanically and that many of the structural features reflected the Newtonian yearning. A tension arose between the "organic" core of the system and the "mechanical" understanding of it by politicians and citizens. Thus "the constitutional structure of the government has hampered and limited [the president's] actions but it has not prevented [them.]" Wilson tried to resolve the tension between the understanding of American politics as Newtonian and its actual Darwinian character to make the evolution self-conscious and thereby more rational and effective.[38]

Wilson attacked the Founders for relying on mere "parchment barriers" to effectuate a separation of powers. This claim is an obvious distortion of founding views. In *Federalist* no. 47 and no. 48, the argument is precisely that the federal Constitution, unlike earlier state constitutions, would not rely primarily on parchment distinctions of power but on differentiation of institutional structures.[39] Through Wilson's discussion of parchment barriers, however, an important difference between his and the Founders' view of the same problem becomes visible. Both worried over the tendency of legislatures to dominate in republican systems.

To mitigate the danger posed by legislatures, the Founders had relied primarily on an independent president with an office structured to give its occupant the personal incentive and means to stand up to Congress when it exceeded its authority. These structural features included a nonlegislative mode of election, constitutionally fixed salary, qualified veto, four-year term, and indefinite reeligibility. Although the parchment powers of Congress and the president overlapped (contrary to Wilson's depiction of them), the demarcation of powers proper to each branch would result primarily from political interplay and conflict between the political branches rather than from a theoretical drawing of lines by the judiciary.[40]

Wilson offered a quite different view. First, he claimed that because of the inadequacy of mere parchment barriers, Congress, in the latter half of the nineteenth century, had encroached uncontested on the executive sphere. Second, he contended that when the president's institutional check was used, it took the form of a "negative"—prevention of a bad outcome rather than provision for a good one. In this view, separation of powers hindered efficient, coordinated, well-led policy.[41]

Wilson did not wish to bolster structures to thwart the legislature. He preferred that the president and Congress be fully integrated into, and implicated in, each other's activities. Rather than merely assail Congress, Wilson would tame or, as it were, domesticate it. Separation would be replaced by institutionally structured cooperation. Cooperation was especially necessary because presidents lacked the energy they needed, energy that could be provided only by policy backed by Congress and its majority. Although Congress had failed as a deliberative body, it could now be restored to its true function by presidential leadership that raised and defended crucial policies.

These latter two claims actually represent the major purposes of the Wilsonian theory: leadership and deliberation. Unlike the Founders, who saw these two functions in conflict, Wilson regarded them as dependent on each other. In "Leaderless Government" he stated,

I take it for granted that when one is speaking of a representative legislature he means by an "efficient organization" an organization which provides for deliberate, and deliberative, action and which enables the nation to affix responsibility for what is done and what is not done. The Senate is deliberate enough; but it is hardly deliberative after its ancient and better manner. . . . The House of Representatives is neither deliberate nor deliberative. We have not forgotten that one of the most energetic of its recent Speakers thanked God, in his frankness, that the House was not a deliberative body. It has not the time for the leadership of argument. . . . For debate and leadership of that sort the House must have a party organization and discipline such as it has never had.[42]

It appears that the Founders and Wilson differed on the means to common ends. Both wanted "deliberation" and an "energetic" executive, but each proposed different constitutional arrangements to achieve those objectives. In fact, their differences went much deeper, for each theory defined deliberation and energy differently. These differences, hinted at in the previous quotation, will become clearer as we examine Wilson's reinterpretation of representation and independence of the executive.

Representation

In the discussion of the founding perspective, the competing requirements of popular consent and insulation from public opinion as a requisite of impartial judgment were canvassed. Woodrow Wilson gave much greater weight to the role of public opinion in the ordinary conduct of representative government than did the Founders. Some scholars have suggested that Wilson's rhetoric and the institutional practices he established (especially regarding the nomination of presidential candidates) are the major sources of contemporary efforts to create a more "participatory" democracy. However, Wilson's understanding of representation, like his views on separation of powers, was more sophisticated than that of his followers.[43]

Wilson categorically rejected the Burkean view that legislators are elected for their quality of judgment and position on a few issues and then left free to exercise that judgment:

It used to be thought that legislation was an affair to be conducted by the few who were instructed for the benefit of the many who were uninstructed: that statesmanship was a function of origination for which only trained and instructed men were fit. Those who actually conducted legislation and conducted affairs were rather whimsically chosen by Fortune to illustrate this theory, but such was the ruling thought in politics. The Sovereignty of the People, however . . . has created a very different practice. . . . It is a dignified proposition with us—is it not?—that as is the majority, so ought the government to be.[44]

Wilson did not think his view was equivalent to "direct democracy" or to subservience to public opinion (understood, as it often is today, as response to public opinion polls). He favored an interplay between representative and constituent that would, in fact, educate the constituent. This process differed, at least in theory, from the older attempts to "form" public opinion: it did not begin in the minds of the elite but in the hearts of the masses. Wilson called the process of fathoming the people's desires (often only vaguely known to the people until instructed) "interpretation." Interpretation was the core of leadership for him.[45] Before we explore its meaning further, it will be useful to dwell on Wilson's notion of the desired interplay between the "leader-interpreter" and the people so that we may see how his understanding of deliberation differed from the Founders'.

For the Founders, deliberation meant reasoning on the merits of policy. The character and content of deliberation would thus vary with the character of the policy at issue. In "normal" times, there would be squabbles by competing interests. Deliberation would occur to the extent that such interests were compelled to offer and respond to arguments made by the others. The arguments might be relatively crude, specialized, and technical or they might involve matters of legal or constitutional propriety. But in none of these instances would they resemble the great debates over fundamental principles—for example, over the question of whether to promote interests in the first place. Great questions were the stuff of crisis politics, and the Founders placed much hope in securing the distinction between crisis and normal political life.

Wilson effaced the distinction between "crisis" and "normal" political argument.

Crises give birth and a new growth to statesmanship because they are peculiarly periods of action . . . [and] also of unusual opportunity for gaining leadership and a controlling and guiding influence. . . . And we thus come upon the principle . . . that governmental forms will call to the work of the administration able minds and strong hearts constantly or infrequently, according as they do or do not afford at all times an opportunity of gaining and retaining a commanding authority and an undisputed leadership in the nation's councils.[46]

Wilson's lament that little deliberation took place in Congress was not that the merits of policies were left unexplored but rather that, because the discussions were not elevated to the level of major contests of principle, the public generally did not interest itself. True deliberation, he urged, would rivet the attention of press and public, whereas what substituted for it in his day were virtually secret contests of interest-based factions. Wilson rested this view on three observations. First, the congressional workload was parceled out to specialized standing committees, whose decisions usually were ratified by the respective houses without any general debate. Second, the arguments that did take place in committee were technical and structured by the "special pleadings" of interest groups, whose advocates adopted the model of legal litigation as their mode of discussion. As Wilson characterized committee debates,

They have about them none of the searching, critical, illuminating character of the higher order of parliamentary debate, in which men are pitted against each other as equals, and urged to sharp contest and masterful strife by the inspiration of political principle and personal ambition, through the rivalry of parties and the competition of policies. They represent a joust between antagonistic interests, not a contest of principles.[47]

Finally, because debates were hidden away in committee, technical, and interest based, the public cared little about them. "The ordinary citizen cannot be induced to pay much heed to the details, or even the main principles of lawmaking," Wilson wrote, "unless something more interesting than the law itself be involved in the pending decision of the lawmaker." For the Founders this would not have been disturbing, but for Wilson the very heart of representative government was the principle of publicity: "The informing function of Congress should be preferred even to its legislative function." The informing function was to be preferred both as an end in itself and because the accountability of public officials required policies that were connected with one another and explained to the people. Argument from "principle" would connect policy and present constellations of policies as coherent wholes to be approved or disapproved by the people. "Principles, as statesmen conceive them, are threads to the labyrinth of circumstances."[48]

Wilson attacked separation of powers in an effort to improve leadership for the purpose of fostering deliberation. "Congress cannot, under our present system . . . be effective for the instruction of public opinion, or the cleansing of political action." As mentioned at the outset of this section, Wilson first looked to Congress itself, specifically to its Speaker, for such leadership. Several years after the publication of *Congressional Government*, Wilson turned his attention to the president. "There is no trouble now about getting the president's speeches printed and read, every word," he wrote at the turn of the century.[49]

Independence of the Executive

The attempt to bring the president into more intimate contact with Congress and the people raises the question of the president's "independence." Wilson altered the meaning of this notion, which originally had been that the president's special authority came independently from the Constitution, not from Congress or the people. For the Founders, presidents' constitutional station afforded them the possibility and responsibility of taking a perspective on policy different from either Congress or the people. Wilson urged us to consider presidents as receiving their authority independently through a mandate from the people. For Wilson, presidents remained "special," but now because they were the only government officers with a national mandate.[50]

Political scientists today have difficulty in finding mandates in election years, let alone between them, because of the great number of issues and the lack of public consensus on them. Wilson understood this problem and urged the leader to sift through the multifarious currents of opinion to find a core of issues that he believed reflected majority will even if the majority was not yet fully aware of it.

The leader's rhetoric could translate the people's felt desires into public policy. Wilson cited Daniel Webster as an example of such an interpreter of the public will:

The nation lay as it were unconscious of its unity and purpose, and he called it into full consciousness. It could never again be anything less than what he said it was. It is at such moments and in the mouths of such interpreters that nations spring from age to age in their development.[51]

"Interpretation" involves two skills. First, the leader must understand the true majority sentiment underneath the contradictory positions of factions and the discordant views of the masses. Second, the leader must explain the people's true desires to them in a way that is easily comprehended and convincing.

Wilson's desire to raise politics to the level of rational disputation and his professed aim to have leaders educate the masses are contradictory. Candidly, he acknowledged that the power to command would require simplification of the arguments to accommodate the masses: "The arguments which induce popular action must always be broad and obvious arguments; only a very gross substance of concrete conception can make any impression on the minds of the masses."[52] Not only is argument simplified, but disseminating "information"— a common concern of contemporary democratic theory—is not the function of a deliberative leader in Wilson's view:

Men are not led by being told what they don't know. Persuasion is a force, but not information; and persuasion is accomplished by creeping into the confidence of those you would lead. . . . Mark the simplicity and directness of the arguments and ideas of true leaders. The motives which they urge are elemental; the morality which they seek to enforce is large and obvious; the policy they emphasize, purged of all subtlety.[53]

Demagoguery

Wilson's understanding of leadership raises again the problem of demagoguery. What distinguishes a leader-interpreter from a demagogue? Who is to make this distinction? The Founders feared there was no institutionally effective way to exclude the demagogue if popular oratory during "normal" times was encouraged. Indeed, the term *leader,* which appears a dozen times in *The Federalist,* is used disparagingly in all but one instance, and that one is a reference to leaders of the Revolution.[54]

Wilson was sensitive to this problem. "The most despotic of governments under the control of wise statesmen is preferable to the freest ruled by demagogues," he wrote. Wilson relied on two criteria to distinguish the demagogue from the leader, one based on the nature of the appeal, the other on the character of the leader. The demagogue appeals to "the momentary and whimsical popular mood, the transitory or popular passion," whereas the leader appeals to "true" and durable majority sentiment. The demagogue is motivated by the desire to augment personal power, and the leader is more interested in fostering the permanent interests of the community. "The one [trims] to the inclinations of the moment, the other [is] obedient to the permanent purposes of the public mind."[55]

Theoretically, these distinctions present a number of difficulties. If popular opinion is the source of the leader's rhetoric, what basis apart from popular opinion itself is there to distinguish the "permanent" from the "transient"? If popular opinion is constantly evolving, what sense is there to the notion of "the permanent purposes of the public mind"? Yet the most serious difficulties are practical ones. Assuming it is theoretically possible to distinguish the leader from the demagogue, how is that distinction to be incorporated into the daily operation of political institutions? Wilson offered a threefold response to this query.

First, he claimed his doctrine contained an ethic that could be passed on to future leaders. Wilson hoped that politicians' altered understanding of what constituted success and fame could provide some security. He constantly pointed to British parliamentary practice, urging that long training in debate had produced generations of leaders and few demagogues. Indeed, Wilson had taught at Johns Hopkins, Bryn Mawr, Wesleyan, and Princeton, and at each of those institutions he established debating societies modeled on the Oxford Union.[56]

Second, Wilson placed some reliance on the public's ability to judge character:

Men can scarcely be orators without that force of character, that readiness of resource, that cleverness of vision, that grasp of intellect, that courage of conviction, that correctness of purpose, and that instinct and capacity for leadership which are the eight horses that draw the triumphal chariot of every leader and ruler of freemen. We could not object to being ruled by such men.[57]

According to Wilson, the public need not appeal to a complex standard or theory to distinguish demagoguery from leadership, but could easily recognize "courage," "intelligence," and "correctness of purpose"—signs that the leader was not a demagogue. Wilson does not tell us why prior publics have fallen prey to enterprising demagogues, but the major difficulty with this second source of restraint is that public understanding of leaders' characters would come from their oratory rather than from a history of their political activity or from direct contact with them. The public's understanding of character might be based solely on words.

Third, Wilson suggested that the natural conservatism of public opinion, its resistance to innovation that is not consonant with the speed and direction of its own movement, will afford still more safety:

Practical leadership may not beckon to the slow masses of men from beyond some dim, unexplored space or some intervening chasm: it must daily feel the road to the goal proposed, knowing that it is a slow, very slow, evolution to the wings, and that for the present, and for a very long future also, Society must walk, dependent upon practicable paths, incapable of scaling sudden heights.[58]

Wilson's assurances of security against demagogues may seem unsatisfactory because they do not adequately distinguish the polity in which he worked from others in which demagogues have prevailed, including some southern states in this country. However, his arguments should be considered as much for the theoretical direction and emphases that they imply as for the particular weaknesses they reveal. Wilson's doctrine stands on the premise that the need for more energy in the political system is greater than the risk incurred through the possibility of demagoguery.[59] This represents a major shift, indeed a reversal, of the founding perspective. If Wilson's argument regarding demagoguery is strained or inadequate, it was a price he was willing to pay to remedy what he regarded as the Founders' inadequate provision for an energetic executive.

Conclusion

Both constitutions were designed to encourage and support an energetic president, but they differ over the legitimate sources and alleged virtues of popular leadership. For the Founders, presidents draw their energy from their authority. Their authority rests on their independent constitutional position. For Woodrow Wilson and for presidents ever since, power and authority are conferred directly by the people. *The Federalist* and the Constitution proscribe popular leadership. Wilson prescribed it. Indeed, he urged the president to minister continually to the moods of the people as a preparation for action. The Founders' president was to look to the people, but less frequently, and to be judged by them, but usually after acting.

The second constitution gained legitimacy because presidents were thought to lack the resources necessary for the energy promised but not delivered by the first. The second constitution did not replace the first, however. Because many of the founding structures persist while our understanding of the president's legitimate role has changed, the new view should be thought of as superimposed on the old, altering without obliterating the original structure.

Many commentators have noted the tendency of recent presidents to raise public expectations about what they can achieve. Indeed, public disenchantment with government altogether may stem largely from disappointment in presidential performance, inasmuch as the presidency is the most visible and important American political institution. Yet, rather than being the result of the personality traits of particular presidents, raised expectations are grounded in an institutional dilemma common to all modern presidents. Under the auspices of the second constitution, presidents must continually craft rhetoric that pleases their popular audience. Even though presidents are always in a position to promise more, the only additional resource they have to make good on their promises is public opinion itself. Because Congress retains the independent status conferred on it by the first Constitution, it can resist the president.

Naturally, presidents who are exceptionally popular or gifted as orators can overcome the resistance of the legislature. For the political system as a whole, this possibility is both good and bad. To the extent that the system requires periodic renewal through synoptic policies that reconstitute the political agenda, it is good. But the very qualities that are necessary to achieve such large-scale change tend to subvert the deliberative process, which makes unwise legislation or incoherent policy more likely.

Ronald Reagan's major political victories as president illustrate both sides of this systemic dilemma.[60] On the one hand, without the second constitution, it would be difficult to imagine Reagan's success at winning tax reform legislation. His skillful coordination of a rhetorical and a legislative strategy overcame the resistance of thousands of lobbies that sought to preserve advantageous provisions of the existing tax code. Similarly, Social Security and other large policies that were initiated by Franklin D. Roosevelt during the New Deal may not have been possible without the second constitution.

On the other hand, Reagan's first budget victory in 1981 and the Strategic Defense Initiative (SDI, also known as Star Wars) illustrate how popular leadership can subvert the deliberative process or produce incoherent policy. The budget cuts of 1981 were secured with virtually no congressional debate. Among their effects was the gutting of virtually all of the Great Society programs passed by Lyndon B. Johnson, which themselves were the product of a popular campaign that circumvented the deliberative process.

When Congress does deliberate, as it has on SDI, the debate is often structured by contradictory forms of rhetoric, the product of the two constitutions. The arguments presidents make to the people are different from those they make to Congress. To the people, President Reagan promised to strive for a new defense technology that would make nuclear deterrence obsolete. But to Congress, his administration argued that SDI was needed to supplement, not supplant, deterrence.[61] Each kind of argument can be used to impeach the other. Jimmy Carter found himself in the same bind on energy policy. When he urged the American people to support his energy plan, Carter contended that it was necessary to remedy an existing crisis. But to Congress he argued that the same policy was necessary to forestall a crisis.[62]

The second constitution promises energy, which is said to be inadequately provided by the first. This suggests that the two constitutions fit together to form a more complete whole. Unfortunately, over the long run, the tendency of the second constitution to make extraordinary power routine undermines, rather than completes, the logic of the original Constitution. Garry Wills has described how presidents since John F. Kennedy have attempted to pit public opinion against their own executive establishment. Successors to a charismatic leader then inherit "a delegitimated set of procedures" and are themselves compelled "to go outside of procedures—further delegitimating the very office they [hold]."[63] In Reagan's case, this cycle was reinforced by an ideology opposed to big government. "In the present crisis," Reagan said at his first inaugural, "government is not the solution to our problem; government is the problem." Although fiascoes like the Iran-contra affair are not inevitable, they are made more likely by the logic and legitimacy of the second constitution.

It was hard to imagine that any leader would embrace the second constitution more than Reagan did, but Bill Clinton surpassed him. According to George Edwards,

The Clinton presidency is the ultimate example of the rhetorical presidency—a presidency based on a perpetual campaign to obtain the public's support and fed by public opinion polls, focus groups, and public relations memos. No president ever invested more in measuring, and attempting to mold, public opinion. [This administration] even polled voters on where it was best for the First Family to vacation. This is an administration that spent $18 million on ads in 1995, a nonelection year! And this is an administration that repeatedly interpreted its setbacks, whether in elections or health care reform, in terms of its failure to communicate rather than in terms of the quality of its initiatives or the strategy for governing. Reflecting his orientation in the White House, Bill Clinton declared that "role of the President of the United States is message."[64]

The Clinton presidency was a roller coaster of political successes and failures. No doubt it will take scholars decades to make sense of Clinton's political choices and the public's reaction to them. No simple explanation is suitable to explain how this president, who was the head of his political party when the Democrats were badly defeated in 1994, rebounded so decisively in 1996, how he came to be impeached by the House in 1998 yet be acquitted by the Senate in 1999. A full analysis of these political undulations and their consequences for the polity would include, at a minimum, accounts of the president's character, his political acumen, the state of the economy and the world, and the actions of the Republican opposition. Without venturing to offer even the beginning of such an analysis, it may be helpful to suggest how the two constitutional presidencies may be a useful backdrop for a fuller narrative. The political dilemmas faced by Clinton and the choices he made to contend with them are, at least in part, a product of the uneasy conjunction of the two constitutions.

For example, the president's fidelity to the second constitution contributed to the most serious mistake that prompted the impeachment proceeding. Faced with an inquiry into his relationship with Monica Lewinsky, Clinton sought a rhetorical solution to his political difficulty. Oriented to the immediate demands of persuasion in a national plebiscite, Clinton relied on his bully pulpit. On the advice of his former pollster Dick Morris and friend and media adviser Harry Thomason, the president went on national television and forcefully denied that he had "sexual relations" with Lewinsky. That denial, more than the conduct it concealed, fueled congressional opposition and delegitimized his presidency in the eyes of many of his critics and even some of his allies.

Yet presidents are schooled by both constitutions even when they only consciously understand the second. President Carter discovered the Rose Garden strategy of retreating from public view when the demands of foreign policy placed him in a position to see the benefits of a political posture inherent to the first constitution.[65] Similarly, President Clinton rediscovered the first Constitution as the nation taught itself the constitutional meaning of impeachment.

As the impeachment drama unfolded, Clinton was uncharacteristically mute. He let his lawyers and other surrogates do the talking about impeachment-related matters while he attended to the nation's other business. The nation's resurrection of a nineteenth-century constitutional anachronism, impeachment, placed the president in a position from which he could see the political benefit of acting like a nineteenth-century president. Because the animating charge of the political opposition was that Clinton had disgraced his office—whether through his sexual behavior or his subsequent deceptions and alleged perjury—the president's conduct during the formal proceedings became a rhetorical or dramaturgical refutation of the main charge against him. The one exception to this presidential style, so characteristic of the first Constitution, seemed to prove its significance. When the president emerged from the White House to lead congressional allies in a show of support immediately following the House vote, he was severely criticized for politicizing a constitutional process. Clinton's conscious and seemingly instinctive understanding of leadership conflicted with the model of statesmanship inherent to the constitutional order. After that misstep, the president attempted to recapture the advantages that the dignity of the office provided him.

Yet it would be wrong to suggest that the first Constitution "saved" Bill Clinton in the long term. Because his understanding of political success was so tethered to the second constitution, for Clinton successful governance seemed to mean popular approbation in the present. Presidents of the first Constitution were schooled in a broader, forward-looking, understanding of success. Nineteenth-century presidents sought fame more than they craved popularity. They understood that their fame depended more on a retrospective assessment of the health of the entire constitutional order than on a calculus of immediate political objectives obtained. Clinton seemed to believe that his legacy would be measured principally by the products of his skillful use of the rhetorical arts in partisan contest. It is more likely that Clinton's legacy will be fashioned by his failure to fully understand the Constitution, even as he used it to his political advantage.

While political circumstance encouraged President Clinton to rediscover the first Constitution, political crisis has led President George W. Bush to a more rhetorical presidency than would be his natural inclination. President Bush is not a gifted orator. Like his father, the younger Bush has difficulty expressing himself elegantly, is prone to misstatement, and seems unable to deliver the proper cadences in formal speech. In the wake of the terrorist attack on America on September 11, 2001, however, Bush found it necessary to deliver a number of speeches to a grieving nation. Because it was altogether proper, even from the perspective of the first Constitution, that he do this, his words gained in politically constructed authority what they lacked in natural grace. The Constitution, its norms, institutions, and traditions, elevated an ordinary speaker, and ordinary man, to a station from which he was able to deliver extraordinarily effective leadership in the months following September 11. Although the modern rhetorical presidency sometimes undermines the Constitution by encouraging pseudocrises, it is also true that genuine crises reveal a polity whose first Constitution is improved by the demands and customs of the second.

Notes

1. Notable structural changes in the Constitution are the Twelfth, Seventeenth, Twentieth, and Twenty-second Amendments, which deal, respectively, with change in the electoral college system, the election of senators, presidential succession, and presidential reeligibility. Although all are interesting, only the last seems manifestly inconsistent with the Founders' plan. For a defense of the relevance of the constitutional theory of the presidency to contemporary practice, see Joseph M. Bessette and Jeffrey Tulis, eds., *The Presidency in the Constitutional Order* (Baton Rouge: Louisiana State University Press, 1981). See also David K. Nichols, *The Myth of the Modern Presidency* (University Park: Pennsylvania State University Press, 1994).

2. James W. Ceaser, *Presidential Selection: Theory and Development* (Princeton: Princeton University Press, 1979); Nelson Polsby, *Consequences of Party Reform* (New York: Oxford University Press, 1983); Doris A. Graber, *Mass Media and American Politics,* 6th ed. (Washington, D.C.: CQ Press, 2001); David L. Paletz and Robert M. Entman, *Media, Power, Politics* (New York: Free Press, 1981); and Harvey C. Mansfield Jr., *America's Constitutional Soul* (Baltimore: Johns Hopkins University Press, 1991), chap. 12.

3. This essay does not reveal the Founders' personal and political motives except as they were self-consciously incorporated into the reasons offered for their Constitution. The Founders' views are treated on their own terms, as a constitutional theory; Hamilton's statement in the first number of *The Federalist* is taken seriously: "My motives must remain in the depository of my own breast. My arguments will be open to all and may be judged by all." James Madison, Alexander Hamilton, and John Jay, *The Federalist Papers,* ed. Clinton Rossiter (New York: New American Library, 1961), no. 1, 36. For a good discussion of the literature on the political motives of the founding fathers, see Erwin C. Hargrove and Michael Nelson, *Presidents, Politics, and Policy* (New York: Knopf, 1984), chap. 2.

4. The most influential study of the presidency is by Richard Neustadt. See *Presidential Power: The Politics of Leadership from FDR to Carter* (New York: Wiley, 1979), vi: "One must try to view the Presidency from over the President's shoulder, looking out and down with the perspective of his place."

5. Herbert J. Storing, *What the Anti-Federalists Were For* (Chicago: University of Chicago Press, 1981), 83n.

6. *The Federalist,* no. 70, 423.

7. In the first number, "Publius" warns "that of those men who have overturned the liberties of republics, the greatest number have begun their career by paying obsequious

court to the people, commencing demagogues and ending tyrants." And in the last essay, "These judicious reflections contain a lesson of moderation to all the sincere lovers of the Union, and ought to put them upon their guard against hazarding anarchy, civil war, and perhaps the military despotism of a victorious demagogue, in the pursuit of what they are not likely to obtain, but from TIME and EXPERIENCE."

8. Ceaser, *Presidential Selection*, 12, 54–60, 166–167, 318–327. See also V. O. Key, *The Responsible Electorate* (New York: Random House, 1966), chap. 2; Stanley Kelley Jr., *Political Campaigning: Problems in Creating an Informed Electorate* (Washington, D.C.: Brookings Institution, 1960), 93; Pendleton E. Herring, *Presidential Leadership* (New York: Holt, Rinehart and Winston, 1940), 70; and *The Federalist*, no. 71, 432.

9. *The Federalist*, no. 10, 82; and Ceaser, *Presidential Selection*, 324.

10. Clinton Rossiter, *Constitutional Dictatorship: Crisis Government in the Modern Democracies* (Princeton: Princeton University Press, 1948), chap. 3.

11. *The Federalist*, no. 85, 527.

12. Harvey Flaumenhaft, "Hamilton's Administrative Republic and the American Presidency," in *The Presidency in the Constitutional Order*, ed. Bessette and Tulis, 65–114. The Civil War and turn-of-the-century progressive politics show that Hamilton's "administrative republic" has been punctuated with the sorts of crises and politics Hamilton sought to avoid.

13. *The Federalist*, no. 10, 77; no. 43, 276; no. 51, 323–325; no. 63, 384; and no. 73, 443. Moreover, the factual quest to find a "majority" may be no less contestable than dispute over the merits of proposals. Contemporary political scientists who provide ample support for the latter worry when they suggest that it is often both theoretically and practically impossible to discover a majority will—that is, to count it up—owing to the manifold differences of intensity of preferences and the plethora of possible hierarchies of preferences. Kenneth Arrow, *Social Choice and Individual Values* (New York: Wiley, 1963); and Benjamin I. Page, *Choices and Echoes in Presidential Elections* (Chicago: University of Chicago Press, 1978), chap. 2.

14. *The Federalist*, no. 39, 241; see also Martin Diamond, "Democracy and the Federalist: A Reconsideration of the Framers' Intent," *American Political Science Review* 53 (March 1959): 52–68.

15. *The Federalist*, no. 39, 241; no. 68, 412–423. See also James Ceaser, "Presidential Selection," in *The Presidency in the Constitutional Order*, ed. Bessette and Tulis, 234–282. Ironically, the Founders were proudest of this institutional creation; the electoral college was their most original contrivance. Moreover, it escaped the censure of and even won a good deal of praise from antifederal opponents of the Constitution. Because electors were chosen by state legislatures for the sole purpose of selecting a president, the process was thought more democratic than potential alternatives, such as selection by Congress. Compare Nichols, *Myth of the Modern Presidency*, 39–45.

16. *The Federalist*, no. 72, 435. The empirical judgment that four years would serve the purpose of insulating the president is not as important for this discussion as the principle reflected in that choice, a principle that has fueled recent calls for a six-year term.

17. *The Federalist*, nos. 9 and 10.

18. Gordon Wood, *The Creation of the American Republic: 1776–1787* (New York: Norton, 1969); Michael Parenti, "The Constitution as an Elitist Document," in *How Democratic Is the Constitution?* ed. Robert Goldwin (Washington, D.C.: American Enterprise Institute, 1980), 39–58; and Charles Lindblom, *Politics and Markets* (New York: Basic Books, 1979), conclusion.

19. *The Federalist,* no. 49, 313–317.

20. Ibid., 317.

21. See *The Federalist,* no. 57; Joseph M. Bessette, "Deliberative Democracy," in *How Democratic Is the Constitution?* ed. Goldwin, 102–116; and Michael Malbin, "What Did the Founders Want Congress to Be—and Who Cares?" (paper presented at the annual meeting of the American Political Science Association, Denver, September 2, 1982). On the status of legislative deliberation today, see Joseph M. Bessette, *The Mild Voice of Reason: Deliberative Democracy and American National Government* (Chicago: University of Chicago Press, 1994); William Muir, *Legislature* (Chicago: University of Chicago Press, 1982); and Arthur Maas, *Congress and the Common Good* (New York: Basic Books, 1983).

22. Wood, *Creation of the American Republic,* chap. 5; and Ceaser, *Presidential Selection,* 48.

23. *The Federalist,* no. 62; no. 63, 376–390; and Storing, *What the Anti-Federalists Were For,* chap. 7.

24. *The Federalist,* no. 55, 342.

25. *The Federalist,* no. 71, 432; Madison expresses almost the identical position in no. 63, where he stated,

> As the cool and deliberate sense of the community, ought in all governments, and actually will in all free governments, ultimately prevail over the views of its rulers; so there are particular moments in public affairs when the people, stimulated by some irregular passion, or some illicit advantage, or misled by the artful misrepresentations of interested men, may call for measures which they themselves will afterwards be most ready to lament and condemn. In these critical moments how salutary will be [a Senate].

26. John Marshall, *Life of George Washington,* quoted in Charles Thatch, *The Creation of the Presidency* (1923; reprint, Baltimore: Johns Hopkins University Press, 1969), 51; and Max Farrand, ed., *The Records of the Federal Convention of 1787,* 4 vols. (New Haven: Yale University Press, 1966), 2:35, 22, 32.

27. *The Federalist,* no. 68, 413; no. 71, 433; and no. 73, 442; see also Storing, "Introduction," in Thatch, *Creation of the Presidency,* vi–viii. Thomas Jefferson, "Inaugural Address," March 4, 1801, in *The Life and Writings of Thomas Jefferson,* ed. Adrienne Koch and William Peden (New York: Modern Library, 1944), 325.

28. Neustadt, *Presidential Power,* 26, 28–30, 170, 176, 204. See also James Sterling Young, *The Washington Community* (New York: Columbia University Press, 1964), 53. This insight has been the basis of numerous critiques of the American "pluralist" system, which, it is alleged, frustrates leadership as it forces politicians through a complicated political obstacle course. See also Jeffrey K. Tulis, "The President in the Political System: In Neustadt's Shadow," in *Presidential Power: Forging the Presidency for the Twenty-First Century,* ed. Robert Y. Shapiro, Martha Joynt Kumar, and Lawrence R. Jacobs (New York: Columbia University Press, 2000), 265–273.

29. Farrand, *Records,* vol. 1, 66–67; *The Federalist,* no. 47, 360–380; see also U.S. Congress, *Annals of Congress,* vol. 1, 384–412, 476–608. See generally Louis Fisher, *Constitutional Conflict between Congress and the President* (Princeton: Princeton University Press, 1985).

30. In many discussions of separation of powers today, the meaning of effectiveness is restricted to only one of these objectives—the implementation of policy that reflects popular will. See, for example, Donald Robinson, ed., *Reforming American Government* (Boulder: Westview Press, 1985).

31. See, for example, Lloyd N. Cutler, "To Form a Government," *Foreign Affairs* 59 (fall 1980): 126–143.

32. Gary J. Schmitt, "Executive Privilege: Presidential Power to Withhold Information from Congress," in *Presidency in the Constitutional Order*, ed. Bessette and Tulis, 154–194.

33. Richard Pious, *The American Presidency* (New York: Basic Books, 1979), 372–415; Gary J. Schmitt, "Separation of Powers: Introduction to the Study of Executive Agreements," *American Journal of Jurisprudence* 27 (1982): 114–138; and Louis Fisher, *Presidential Spending Power* (Princeton: Princeton University Press, 1975), 147–201.

34. Woodrow Wilson, *Congressional Government: A Study in American Politics* (1884; reprint, Gloucester, Mass.: Peter Smith, 1973), preface to 15th printing, introduction; Wilson, *Constitutional Government in the United States* (New York: Columbia University Press, 1908); and Christopher Wolfe, "Woodrow Wilson: Interpreting the Constitution," *Review of Politics* 41 (January 1979): 131. See also Woodrow Wilson, "Cabinet Government in the United States," in *College and State*, ed. Ray Stannard Baker and William E. Dodd, 2 vols. (New York: Harper and Brothers, 1925), 1:19–42; Paul Eidelberg, *A Discourse on Statesmanship* (Urbana: University of Illinois Press, 1974), chaps. 8 and 9; Harry Clor, "Woodrow Wilson," in *American Political Thought*, ed. Morton J. Frisch and Richard G. Stevens (New York: Scribner, 1971); and Robert Eden, *Political Leadership and Nihilism* (Gainesville: University of Florida Press, 1984), chap. 1.

35. Wilson, *Constitutional Government*, 22, 56; and Wilson, "Leaderless Government," in *College and State*, ed. Baker and Dodd, 337.

36. Wilson, *Congressional Government*, 141, 149, 164, 195.

37. Wilson, *Constitutional Government*, 56.

38. Ibid., 60; see also Wilson, *Congressional Government*, 28, 30, 31, 187.

39. *The Federalist*, nos. 47 and 48, 300–313. Consider Madison's statement in *Federalist* no. 48, 308–309:

Will it be sufficient to mark with precision, the boundaries of these departments in the Constitution of the government, and to trust to these parchment barriers against the encroaching spirit of power? This is the security which appears to have been principally relied upon by the compilers of most of the American Constitutions. But experience assures us that the efficacy of the provision has been greatly overrated; and that some more adequate defense is indispensably necessary for the more feeble against the more powerful members of the government. The legislative department is everywhere extending the sphere of its activity and drawing all power into its impetuous vortex.

40. Schmitt, "Executive Privilege."

41. Wilson, "Leaderless Government," 340, 357; Wilson, *Congressional Government*, 158, 201; and Wilson, "Cabinet Government," 24–25.

42. Wilson, "Leaderless Government," 346; at the time he wrote this, Wilson was thinking of leadership internal to the House, but he later came to see the president performing this same role. Wilson, *Constitutional Government*, 69–77; see also Wilson, *Congressional Government*, 76, 97–98.

43. Eidelberg, *Discourse on Statesmanship*, chaps. 8 and 9; and Ceaser, *Presidential Selection*, chap. 4, conclusion.

44. Woodrow Wilson, *Leaders of Men*, ed. T. H. Vail Motter (Princeton: Princeton University Press, 1952), 39. This is the manuscript of an oft-repeated lecture that Wilson delivered in the 1890s. See also Wilson, *Congressional Government*, 195, 214.

45. Wilson, *Leaders of Men,* 39; and Wilson, *Constitutional Government,* 49. See also Wilson, *Congressional Government,* 78, 136–137.

46. Wilson, "Cabinet Government," 34–35. See also Wilson, "Leaderless Government," 354; and Wilson, *Congressional Government,* 72, 136–137.

47. Wilson, *Congressional Government,* 69, 72.

48. Ibid., 72, 82, 197–198; Wilson, "Cabinet Government," 20, 28–32; and Wilson, *Leaders of Men,* 46.

49. Wilson, *Congressional Government,* 76; ibid., preface to 15th printing, 22–23.

50. Ibid., 187.

51. Wilson, *Constitutional Government,* 49. Today, the idea of a mandate as objective assessment of the will of the people has been fused with the idea of leader as interpreter. Presidents regularly appeal to the results of elections as legitimizing the policies they believe ought to reflect majority opinion. On the "false" claims to represent popular will, see Stanley Kelley Jr., *Interpreting Elections* (Princeton: Princeton University Press, 1984).

52. Wilson, *Leaders of Men,* 20, 26.

53. Ibid., 29.

54. I am indebted to Robert Eden for the point about *The Federalist.* See also Ceaser, *Presidential Selection,* 192–197.

55. Wilson, "Cabinet Government," 37; and Wilson, *Leaders of Men,* 45–46.

56. See, for example, Wilson, *Congressional Government,* 143–147.

57. Ibid., 144.

58. Wilson, *Leaders of Men,* 45.

59. Wilson, *Congressional Government,* 144.

60. I discuss this and other dilemmas more fully in *The Rhetorical Presidency* (Princeton: Princeton University Press, 1987). See also Jeffrey K. Tulis, "Revising the Rhetorical Presidency," in *Beyond the Rhetorical Presidency,* ed. Martin Medhurst (College Station: Texas A&M Press, 1996); and Jeffrey K. Tulis, "The Constitutional Presidency in American Political Development," in *The Constitution and the American Presidency,* ed. Martin Fausold and Alan Shank (Albany: State University of New York Press, 1991). For recent criticisms of these ideas along with my rejoinder, see Richard Ellis, ed., *Speaking to the People: The Rhetorical Presidency in Historical Perspective* (Amherst: University of Massachusetts Press, 1998).

61. Steven E. Miller and Stephen Van Evera, ed., *The Star Wars Controversy* (Princeton: Princeton University Press, 1986), preface.

62. Sanford Weiner and Aaron Wildavsky, "The Prophylactic Presidency," *Public Interest* 52 (summer 1978): 1–18.

63. Garry Wills, "The Kennedy Imprisonment: The Prisoner of Charisma,"*Atlantic,* January 1982, 34; and H. H. Gerth and C. Wright Mills, eds., *From Max Weber* (New York: Oxford University Press, 1958), 247–248.

64. George C. Edwards, "Campaigning is Not Governing: Bill Clinton's Rhetorical Presidency," in *The Clinton Legacy,* ed. Colin Campbell and Bert A. Rockman (New York: Chatham House Publishers, 1999), 37. Clinton quoted in Elizabeth Drew, *Showdown: The Struggle between the Gingrich Congress and the Clinton White House* (New York: Simon and Schuster, 1996), 19.

65. Tulis, *Rhetorical Presidency,* 174–175.

5 Presidential Leadership in Political Time

Stephen Skowronek

Some recent scholarship on the presidency has emphasized the cyclical aspects of the office. Stephen Skowronek explains one recurring sequence in presidential history—namely, the rise and fall of regimes, or governing coalitions—in terms of the passage of "political time." Each sequence begins when an established regime is defeated soundly in a presidential election, bringing to power a new coalition led by a new president, such as Andrew Jackson in 1828 and Franklin D. Roosevelt in 1932. The challenges to the president who would create a regime are to undermine the "institutional support for opposition interests," to restructure "institutional relations between state and society," and to secure "the dominant position of the new political coalition." As Skowronek argues, not all presidents succeed in this endeavor, and the efforts of even those presidents who do succeed eventually crumble as the new regime becomes old and vulnerable. Skowronek concludes by offering some thoughts about the place of the four most recent presidents—Ronald Reagan, George H. W. Bush, Bill Clinton, and George W. Bush—in the cyclical history of national regimes.

Three general dynamics are evident in presidential history. The locus of the first is the constitutional separation of powers. It links presidents past and present in a timeless and constant struggle over the definition of their institutional prerogatives, and suggests that, although much has changed in two hundred years, the basic structure of presidential action has remained essentially the same. A second dynamic can be traced through the modernization of the nation. It links presidents past and present in an evolutionary sequence culminating in the expanded powers and governing responsibilities of the "modern presidency," and it suggests that the post–World War II incumbents stand apart—their shared leadership situation distinguished from that of earlier presidents by the scope of government concerns, the complexity of national and international issues, and the sheer size of the institutional apparatus. The third dynamic is less well-attended by students of the American presidency. Its locus is the changing shape of the political regimes that have organized state-society relations for broad periods of American history, and it links presidents past and present at parallel junctures in "political time." [1] This third dynamic is the point of departure for our investigation.

To read American history with an eye toward the dynamics of political change is to see that within the sequence of national development there have been many beginnings and many endings. Periods are marked by the rise to power of new political coalitions, one of which comes to exert a dominant influence over the federal government. The dominant coalition operates the federal government and perpetuates its position through the development of a distinctive set of institutional arrangements and approaches to public policy questions. Once established, however, coalition interests have an enervating effect on the governing capacities of these political-institutional regimes. From the outset, conflicts among interests within the dominant coalition threaten to cause political disaffection and may weaken regime support. Then—beyond the problems posed by conflicts among these established interests—more basic questions arise concerning the interests themselves. As the nation changes, the regime's traditional approach to problems appears increasingly outmoded, and the government it dominates appears increasingly hostage to sectarian interests with myopic concerns, insufferable demands, and momentary loyalties. In all, the longer a regime survives, the more its approach to national affairs becomes encumbered and distorted. Its political energies dissipate, and it becomes less competent in addressing the manifest governing demands of the day.

Thinking in terms of regime sequences rather than linear national development, one can distinguish many different political contexts for presidential leadership *within* a given historical period. Leadership situations might be characterized by the president's posture vis-à-vis the dominant political coalition. In the modern Democratic period, for example, regime outsiders like Republicans Dwight D. Eisenhower and Richard M. Nixon faced different political problems from those confronted by regime insiders like John F. Kennedy and Lyndon B. Johnson.

Leadership situations might also be differentiated according to political time; that is, when in a regime sequence the president engages the political-institutional order. Presidents Franklin Roosevelt, John Kennedy, and Jimmy Carter—all Democrats who enjoyed Democratic majorities in Congress—may be said to have faced different problems in leading the nation as they were arrayed along a sequence of political change that encompassed the generation and degeneration of the New Deal order.

This view of the changing relationship between the presidency and the political system can easily be related to certain outstanding patterns in presidential leadership across American history. First, the presidents who traditionally make the historians' roster of America's greatest—George Washington, Thomas Jefferson, Andrew Jackson, Abraham Lincoln, Woodrow Wilson, and Franklin Roosevelt—all came to power in an abrupt break from a long-established political-institutional regime; and each led a movement of new political forces into control of the federal government.[2] Second, after the initial break with the past and the consolidation of a new system of government control, a general decline in the political effectiveness of regime insiders is notable. Take, for example, the sequence of Jeffersonians. After the galvanizing performance of Jefferson's first term, we observe increasing political divisions and a managerial-style presidency under James Madison. Asserting the sanctity of an indivisible Republican majority, James Monroe opened his administration to unbridled sectarianism and oversaw a debilitating fragmentation of the federal establishment. A complete political and institutional breakdown marked the abbreviated tenure of John Quincy Adams.

But is it possible to go beyond these general observations and elaborate a historical-structural analysis of political leadership in the presidency? What characteristic political challenges face a leader at any given stage in a regime sequence? How is the quality of presidential performance related to the changing shape of the political-institutional order? These questions call for an investigation that breaks presidential history into regime segments and then compares leadership problems and presidential performances at similar stages in regime development across historical periods. Taking different regimes into account simultaneously, this essay will group presidents together on the basis of the parallel positions they hold in political time.

The analysis focuses on three pairs of presidents drawn from the New Deal and Jacksonian regimes: Franklin Roosevelt and Andrew Jackson, John Kennedy and James K. Polk, and Jimmy Carter and Franklin Pierce. All were Democrats and thus affiliated with the dominant coalition of their respective periods. None took a passive, caretaker view of his office. Indeed, each aspired to great national leadership. Paired comparisons have been formed by slicing into these two regime sequences at corresponding junctures and exposing a shared relationship between the presidency and the political system.

We begin with two beginnings—the presidency of Franklin Roosevelt and its counterpart in political time, the presidency of Andrew Jackson. Coming to power on the displacement of an old ruling coalition, these presidents became mired in remarkably similar political struggles. Although separated by more than a century of history, they both faced the distinctive challenge of constructing a new regime. Leadership became a matter of securing the political and institutional infrastructure of a new governmental order.

Beyond the challenges of regime construction lie the ever more perplexing problems of managing an established regime in changing times. The regime manager is constrained on one side by the political imperatives of coalition maintenance and on the other by deepening divisions within the ranks. Leadership does not penetrate to the basics of political and institutional reconstruction. It is caught up in the difficulties of satisfying regime commitments while stemming the tide of internal disaffection. As a consequence, the president is challenged at the level of interest control and conflict manipulation. Our examination of the manager's dilemma focuses on John Kennedy and his counterpart in political time, James Polk.

Finally, we come to the paradoxes of establishing a credible leadership posture in an enervated regime. Jimmy Carter and Franklin Pierce both came to power at a time when the dominant coalition had degenerated into myopic sects that appeared impervious to the most basic problems facing the nation. Neither of these presidents penetrated to the level of managing coalition interests. Each found himself caught in the widening disjunction between established power and political legitimacy. Their affiliation with the old order in a new age turned their respective bids for leadership into awkward and superficial struggles to avoid the stigma of their own irrelevance.

All six of these presidents had to grapple with the erosion of political support that inevitably comes with executive action. But if this problem plagued them all, the initial relationship between the leader and his supporters was not the same, and the terms of presidential interaction with the political system changed sequentially from stage to stage. Looking within these pairs, we can identify performance challenges that are shared by leaders who addressed the political system at a similar juncture. Looking across the pairs, we observe an ever more tenuous leadership situation, an ever more constricted universe of political action, and an ever more superficial penetration of the political system.

Jackson and Roosevelt: Upheaval and the Challenge of Regime Construction

The presidencies of Andrew Jackson and Franklin Roosevelt were launched on the heels of major political upheavals. Preceding the election of each, a party long established as the dominant and controlling power within the federal government had begun to flounder and fragment in an atmosphere of national crisis. Finally, the old ruling party suffered a stunning defeat at the polls, losing its dominant position in Congress as well as its control of the presidency. Jackson and Roosevelt assumed the office of chief executive with the old ruling coalition thoroughly discredited by the electorate and, at least temporarily, displaced from political power. They each led into control of the federal establishment a movement based on general discontent with the previously established order of things.

Of the two, Jackson's election in 1828 presents this crisis of the old order in a more purely political form. New economic and social conflicts had been festering in the United States since the financial panic of 1819, but Jackson's campaign gained its special meaning from the confusion and outrage unleashed by the election of 1824. In that election, the Congressional Caucus collapsed as the engine of national political unity, and the once monolithic Republican Party disintegrated into warring factions. After an extended period of political maneuvering, an alliance between John Quincy Adams and Henry Clay secured Adams a presidential victory in the House of Representatives, despite Jackson's pluralities in both popular and electoral votes. The Adams administration was immediately and permanently engulfed in charges of conspiracy, intrigue, and profligacy in high places. Jackson, the hero of 1815, became a hero wronged in 1824. The Jackson campaign of 1828 launched a broadside assault on the degrading "corruption of manners" that had consumed Washington and on the conspiracy of interests that had captured the federal government from the people.[3]

In the election of 1932 the collapse of the old ruling party dovetailed with and was overshadowed by the Great Depression. The Democratic Party of 1932 offered nothing if not hope for economic recovery, and in this Roosevelt's candidacy found special meaning almost in spite of the candidate's rather conservative campaign rhetoric. The depression had made a mockery of President Herbert Hoover's early identification of his party with prosperity, and the challenge of formulating a response to the crisis broke the Republican ranks and threw the party into disarray. Roosevelt's appeal was grounded, not in substantive proposals or even partisan ideology, but in a widespread perception of Republican incompetence, if not intransigence, in the face of national economic calamity. As future secretary of state Cordell Hull outlined Roosevelt's leadership situation in January 1933: "No political party at Washington [is] in control of Congress or even itself ... there [is] no cohesive nationwide sentiment behind any fundamental policy or idea today. The election was an overwhelmingly negative affair."[4]

Thus Jackson and Roosevelt each engaged a political system cut from its moorings by a wave of popular discontent. Old commitments of ideology and interest were suddenly called into question. New commitments were as yet only vague appeals to some essential American value (republican virtue, economic opportunity) that had been lost in the indulgences of the old order. With old political alliances in disarray and new political energies infused into Congress, these presidents had an extraordinary opportunity to set a new course in public policy and to redefine the terms of national political debate. They recaptured the experience of being first.

But this situation is not without its characteristic leadership challenge. The leader who is propelled into office by a political upheaval in government control ultimately confronts the imperatives of establishing a new order in government and politics. This challenge is presented directly by the favored interests and residual institutional supports of the old order; once the challenge has been posed, the unencumbered leadership environment that was created by the initial break with the past quickly fades. Presidents are faced with the choice of either abandoning their new departure or consolidating it with structural reforms. Situated just beyond the old order, presidential leadership crystallizes as a problem of regime construction.

The president as regime builder grapples with the fundamentals of political regeneration—institutional reconstruction and party building. At these moments, when national political power has been shaken to its foundational elements, we see the president join at center stage a set of activities that other leaders, less favorably situated, engage only indirectly or piecemeal—destroying residual institutional support for opposition interests, restructuring institutional relations between state and society, and securing the dominant position of a new political coalition. Success in these tasks is hardly guaranteed. Wilson had to abandon this course when the Republicans reunited and preempted his efforts to broaden the Democratic base. Lincoln was assassinated just as the most critical questions of party building and institutional reconstruction were to be addressed, a disaster that ushered in a devastating confrontation between president and Congress and left the emergent Republican regime hanging precariously for the next three decades. Even Jackson and Roosevelt—America's quintessential regime builders—were not uniformly successful. Neither could keep the dual offensives of party building and institutional reconstruction moving in tandem long enough to complete both.

Andrew Jackson

Republican renewal was the keynote of Jackson's first term. The president was determined to ferret out the political and institutional corruption that he believed had befallen the Jeffersonian regime. This meant purging incompetence and profligacy from the civil service, initiating fiscal retrenchment in national projects, and reviving federalism as a system of vigorous state-based government.[5] Jackson's appeal for a return to Jefferson's original ideas about government certainly posed a potent indictment of the recent state of national affairs and a clear challenge to long-established interests. But there was a studied political restraint in his repudiation of the recent past that defied the attempts of his opponents to characterize it as revolutionary.[6] Indeed, while holding out an attractive standard with which to rally supporters, Jackson was careful to yield his opposition precious little ground on which to mount an effective counterattack. He used the initial upheaval in government control to cultivate an irreproachable political position as the nation's crusader in reform.

The transformation of Jackson's presidency from a moral crusade into a radical program of political reconstruction was instigated not by the president himself but by the premier institution of the old regime, the Bank of the United States.[7] At the time of Jackson's election, the bank was long established as both the most powerful institution in America and the most important link between state and society. It dominated the nation's credit system, maintained extensive ties of material interest with political elites, and actively involved itself in electoral campaigns to sustain its own political support. It embodied all the problems of institutional corruption and political degradation toward which Jackson addressed his administration. The bank was a concentration of political and economic power able to tyrannize over people's lives and to control the will of their elected representatives.

During his first years in office Jackson spoke vaguely of the need for some modification of the bank's charter. But because the charter did not expire until 1836, there appeared to be plenty of time to consider appropriate changes. Indeed, although Jackson was personally inclined toward radical hard-money views, he recognized the dangers of impromptu tinkering with an institution so firmly entrenched in the nation's economic life and hesitated to embrace untested alternatives. Moreover, he foresaw an overwhelming reelection endorsement for his early achievements and knew that to press the bank issue before the election of 1832 could only hurt him politically. After a rout of Henry Clay, the architect of the bank and the obvious challenger in the forthcoming campaign, Jackson anticipated a free hand to deal with the institution as he saw fit.

But Jackson's apparent commitment to some kind of bank reform and the obvious political calculations surrounding the issue led the bank president, Nicholas Biddle, to join forces with Clay. They orchestrated a preelection push to recharter the institution without any reforms a full four years before its charter expired. Biddle feared for the bank's future in a Jackson second term, and Clay needed to break Jackson's irreproachable image as a national leader and to expose his political weaknesses. An early recharter bill promised to splinter Jackson's support in Congress. If the president signed the bill, his integrity as a reformer would be destroyed; if he vetoed it, he would provide a sorely needed coherence to anti-Jackson sentiment.

As expected, the recharter bill threw Jackson enthusiasts into a quandary and passed through Congress. The bill pushed Jackson beyond the possibility of controlling the modification of extant institutions without significant opposition and forced him to choose between retreat and an irrevocable break with established government arrangements. He saw the bill not only as a blatant attempt by those attached to the old order to destroy him politically but also as proof certain that the bank's political power threatened the very survival of republican government. Accepting the challenge, he set out to destroy the bank. The 1828 crusade for republican renewal became in 1832 an all-fronts offensive to establish an entirely new political and institutional order.

The president's veto of the recharter bill clearly marked this transition. The political themes of 1828 were turned against the bank with a vengeance. Jackson said his stand would extricate the federal government from the interests of the privileged and protect the states from encroaching federal domination. He appealed directly to the interests of the nation's farmers, mechanics, and laborers, claiming that this great political majority stood to lose control over the government to the influential few. This call to the "common man" for a defense of the Republic had long been a Jacksonian theme, but now it carried the portent of sweeping government changes. Jackson not only was declaring open war on the premier institution of the old order but was also challenging long-settled questions of governance. The Supreme Court, for example, had upheld the constitutionality of the bank decades before. Jackson's veto challenged the assumption of executive deference to the Court and asserted presidential authority to make an independent and contrary judgment about judicial decisions. Jackson also challenged executive deference to Congress, perhaps the central operating principle of the Jeffersonian regime. His veto message went beyond constitutional objections to the recharter bill and asserted the president's authority to make an independent evaluation of the social, economic, and political implications of congressional action. In all, the message was a regime builder's manifesto for mobilizing a broad-based political coalition, shattering established institutional relationships between state and society, and transforming power arrangements within the government itself.

New political regimes, however, are not built by presidential proclamation. Jackson had his work cut out for him at the beginning of his second term. His victory over Clay in 1832 was certainly sweeping enough to reaffirm his leadership. In addition, having used the veto as a campaign document, Jackson could now claim a mandate to complete the work it outlined. But Clay had also used the veto as an issue, and the threat to the bank was fueling organized political opposition in all sectors of the country.[8] More important still, the Senate, which had been shaky enough in Jackson's first term, moved completely beyond his control in 1833, and his party's majority in the House returned in a highly volatile condition. Finally, the bank's charter had three more years, and bank president Biddle had every intention of exploiting Jackson's political vulnerabilities in the hope of securing his own future.

The election victory drew Jackson deeper into the politics of reconstruction. To maintain his leadership, he needed to neutralize the bank's significance for the remainder of its charter and to prevent any new recharter movement from emerging in Congress. His plan was to remove the federal government's deposits from the bank on his own authority and to transfer them to a select group of politically friendly state banks. The president would thus simultaneously circumvent his opponents and offer the nation an alternative banking system. The new banking structure had several potential advantages. It promised to work under the direct supervision of the executive branch, to forge direct institutional connections between the presidency and local centers of political power, and to secure broad political support against a revival of the national bank.

This plan faced formidable opposition from the Treasury Department, the Senate, and, most of all, from the Bank of the United States. Biddle responded to the removal of federal deposits with an abrupt and severe curtailment of loans. By squeezing the nation into a financial panic, Biddle hoped to turn public opinion against Jackson. The Senate followed suit with a formal censure of the president, denouncing his pretensions to independent action on the presumption of a direct mandate from the people.

The so-called Panic Session of Congress (1833–1834) posed the ultimate test of Jackson's resolve to forge a new regime. Success now hinged on consolidating the Democratic Party in Congress and reaffirming its control over the national government. The president moved quickly to assign blame for the panic to the bank. Having destroyed Biddle's credibility, he was able by the spring of 1834 to solidify Democratic support in the House and to gain an endorsement of his actions (and implicitly, his authority to act) from that chamber. Then, undertaking a major grassroots party-building effort in the midterm elections of 1834, Jackson and his political lieutenants were able to secure a loyal Democratic majority in the Senate. The struggle was over, and in a final acknowledgment of the legitimacy of the new order, the Democratic Senate expunged its censure of the president from the record.

But even as Congress was falling into line, the limitations of the president's achievement were manifesting themselves throughout the nation. Jackson had successfully repudiated the old government order, consolidated a new political party behind his policies, secured that party's control over the entire federal establishment, and redefined the position of the presidency in its relations with Congress, the courts, the states, and the electorate. The problem lay with his institutional alternative for reconstructing financial relations between state and society. From the outset, the state deposit system proved a dismal failure.

In truth, Jackson had latched on to the deposit banking scheme as much out of political necessity as principle. The president had been caught between his opponents' determination to save the bank and his supporters' need for a clear and attractive alternative to it. Opposition to Biddle and Clay merged with opposition to any national banking structure, and what might otherwise have been an interim experiment with state banking quickly became a political commitment. Unfortunately, the infusion of federal deposits into the pet state banks fueled a speculative boom and threatened a major financial collapse.

Hoping to stem this disaster, the Treasury Department began to choose banks of deposit less for their political soundness than for their financial health. Jackson threw his support behind a gradual conversion to hard money. In the end, however, the president was forced to accept the grim irony of his success as a regime builder. As Congress moved more solidly behind him, its members began to see for themselves the special political attractions of the state deposit system. With the passage of the Deposit Act of 1836, Congress expanded the number of state depositories and explicitly limited executive discretion in controlling them.[9]

Thus, although Jackson had reconstructed American government and politics, he merely substituted one irresponsible and uncontrollable financial system for another. Institutional ties between state and society emerged as the weak link in the new order. Jackson's chosen successor, Martin Van Buren, understood this all too well as he struggled to extricate the federal government from the state banks in the midst of the nation's first great depression.

Franklin D. Roosevelt

As a political personality, the moralistic, vindictive, and tortured Jackson stands in marked contrast to the pragmatic, engaging, and buoyant Franklin Roosevelt. Yet their initial triumphs over long-established ruling parties and the sustained popular enthusiasm that accompanied their victories propelled each into grappling with a similar set of leadership challenges. By late 1934 Roosevelt himself seemed to sense the parallels, writing to Vice President John Nance Garner, "The more I learn about Andy Jackson, the more I love him."[10]

The timing of this remark is noteworthy. In 1934 and 1935 Roosevelt's emergency program caused mounting discontent among the favored interests of the old order. Moreover, the president saw that the residual institutional bulwark of that order was capable of simply sweeping his programs aside. Like Jackson in 1832, Roosevelt was being challenged either to reconstruct the political and institutional foundations of the national government or to abandon the initiative he had sustained virtually without opposition in his early years of power.

The revival of the economy had been the keynote of Roosevelt's early program.[11] Although collectivist in approach and boldly assertive of a positive role for the federal government, the early policies of the New Deal did not present a broadside challenge to long-established political and economic interests. Roosevelt had adopted the role of a bipartisan national leader reaching out to all interests in a time of crisis. He carefully courted the southern Bourbons, who controlled the old Democratic Party, and directly incorporated big business into the government's recovery program. But if Roosevelt's program did not ignore the interests attached to and supported by the government arrangements of the past, it did implicate those interests in a broader coalition. The New Deal had also bestowed legitimacy on the interests of organized labor, the poor, and the unemployed, leaving southern Bourbons and northern industrialists feeling threatened and increasingly insecure.

This sense of unease manifested itself politically in the summer of 1934 with the organization of the American Liberty League. Although the league mounted an aggressive assault on Roosevelt and the New Deal, Roosevelt's party received a resounding endorsement in the midterm elections, actually broadening the base of enthusiastic New Dealers in Congress. The congressional elections vividly demonstrated the futility of political opposition, but in the spring of 1935 a more potent adversary arose within the government itself.

The Supreme Court, keeper of the rules of governance for the old regime, handed down a series of anti–New Deal decisions. The most important of these nullified the centerpiece of Roosevelt's recovery program, the National Industrial Recovery Act.

With the American Liberty League clarifying the stakes of the New Deal departure and the Court pulling the rug out from under the cooperative approach to economic recovery, Roosevelt turned his administration toward structural reform. If he could no longer lead all interests toward economic recovery, he could still secure the interests of a great political majority within the new government order.

Roosevelt began the transition from national leader to regime builder with a considerable advantage over Jackson. He could restructure institutional relations between state and society simply by reaching out to the radical and irrepressibly zealous Seventy-fourth Congress (1935–1937) and offering it sorely needed coherence and direction. The result was a second round of New Deal legislation. The federal government extended new services and permanent institutional supports to organized labor, small business, the aged, the unemployed, and later, the rural poor. At the same time, the president revealed a new approach to big business and the affluent by pressing for tighter regulation and graduated taxation.[12]

The scope and vision of these achievements far surpassed the makeshift and flawed arrangements that Jackson had improvised to restructure institutional relations between state and society in the bank war. But Roosevelt's comparatively early and more thoroughgoing success on this score proved a dubious advantage in subsequent efforts to consolidate the new order. After his overwhelming reelection victory in 1936, Roosevelt pressed a series of consolidation initiatives. Like Jackson in his second term, he began with an effort to neutralize the remaining threat within the government.

Roosevelt's target was the Supreme Court. He was wise not to follow Jackson's example in the bank war by launching a direct ideological attack on the Court. After all, Roosevelt was challenging a constitutional branch of government and could hardly succeed in labeling that branch a threat to the survival of the Republic. The president decided instead to kill his institutional opposition with kindness. He called for an increase in the size of the Court, ostensibly to ease the burden on the elder justices and to increase overall efficiency. Unfortunately, the real stakes of the contest never were made explicit, and the chief justice deflected the attack by simply denying the need for help. More important, the Court, unlike the bank, did not further exacerbate the situation. Instead, it reversed course in the middle of the battle and displayed a willingness to accept the policies of the second New Deal.

The Court's turnabout was a great victory for the new regime. It relegated to the irretrievable past the old strictures surrounding legitimate government activity that Roosevelt had been repudiating from the outset of his presidency. But in so doing, the justices eliminated even the implicit justification for Roosevelt's proposed judicial reforms. With the constituent services of the New Deal secure, Congress had little reason to challenge the integrity of the Court. Bound by his own inefficiency arguments, Roosevelt did not withdraw his proposal. Although stalwart liberals stood by the president to the end, traditional Democratic conservatives deserted him. A bipartisan opposition took open ground against Roosevelt, defeated the "Court-packing" scheme, and divided the ranks of the New Deal coalition. It was a rebuke every bit as portentous as the formal censure of Jackson by the Senate.

With Roosevelt, as with Jackson, the third congressional election of his tenure called forth a major party-building initiative. Stung by his defeat, the president sought to reaffirm his hold over the Democratic Party and to strengthen its liberal commitments. This effort was hindered, ironically, by Roosevelt's early and sweeping successes. Unlike Jackson in 1834, Roosevelt in 1938 could not point to any immediate threat to his governing coalition. The liberal program was already in place. The Court had capitulated, and despite deep fissures manifested during the Court battle, the overwhelming Democratic majorities in Congress gave no indication of abandoning the New Deal. Even the southern delegations in Congress maintained majority support for Roosevelt's domestic reform initiatives.[13] Under these conditions, party building took on an aura of presidential self-indulgence. Although enormously important from the standpoint of future regime coherence, at the time it looked like heavy-handed, selective punishment of personal enemies. In this guise, it evoked little popular support, let alone enthusiasm.

The party-building initiative failed. Virtually all of the conservative Democrats targeted for defeat were reelected, and the Republicans showed a resurgence of strength. As two-party politics returned to the national scene, the awkward division within the majority party between the old southern conservatism and the new liberal orthodoxy became a permanent feature of the new regime.

Despite these setbacks, Roosevelt pressed forward with the business of consolidating a new order, and a final effort met with considerable success. In 1939 the president received congressional approval of a package of administrative reforms that promised to bolster the president's position vis-à-vis the other branches of government. Following the precepts of his Committee on Administrative Management, the president had asked for new executive offices to provide planning and direction for government operations. Congress endorsed a modest version of the scheme, but although deflating Roosevelt's grand design, it clearly acknowledged the new governing demands presented by the large federal programs and permanent bureaucratic apparatus he had forged. The establishment of the Executive Office of the President (EOP) closed the New Deal with a fitting symbol of the new state of affairs.[14]

Polk and Kennedy: Reaffirmation and the Dilemmas of Interest Management

The administrations of Jackson and Roosevelt shared much in both the political conditions of leadership and the challenges undertaken. An initial upheaval, the ensuing political confusion, and the widespread support for a decisive break from the institutional strictures of the past framed America's quintessential regime-building presidencies. Opposition from the favored interests of the old order and their residual institutional supports eventually pushed these presidents from an original program to meet the immediate crisis at hand into structural reforms that promised to place institutional relations between state and society on an entirely new footing. After a second landslide election, Jackson and Roosevelt each moved to consolidate their new order by eliminating the institutional opposition and forging a more coherent base of party support. As the nation redivided politically, they secured a new ruling coalition, reset the political agenda, and institutionalized a new position of power for the presidency itself.

It is evident from a comparison of these performances that where Roosevelt's regime-building was triumphant, Jackson's faltered and vice versa: Roosevelt thoroughly reconstructed institutional relations between state and society, but his performance as a party builder was weak and his achievement flawed. Jackson left institutional relations between state and society in a dangerous disarray, but his performance and achievement as a party builder remain unparalleled. The more important point lies, however, beyond these comparisons. It is that few presidents can engage in a wholesale political repudiation of the past and address the political system at the level of institutional reconstruction and party building. Most presidents must use their skills and resources—however extensive these may be—to work within the already established government order.

Successful regime builders leave in their wake a more constricted universe for political leadership. To their partisan successors, in particular, they leave the difficult task of keeping faith with a ruling coalition. In an established regime, the majority-party president comes to power as a representative of the dominant political alliance and is expected to offer a representative's service in delegate style. Commitments of ideology and interest are clear, and the fusion of national political legitimacy with established power arrangements argues against any attempt to tinker with the basics of government and politics. Leaders are challenged, not to break down the old order and forge a new one, but to complete the unfinished business, adapt the agenda to changing times, and defuse the potentially explosive choices among competing obligations. They are partners in a highly structured regime politics, and, to keep the partnership working, they must orchestrate the fulfillment of promises and control impending disruptions. The political problem is to get innovation without repudiation and to present creativity as a vindication of orthodoxy.

The presidencies of James Polk and John Kennedy clearly illustrate the problems and prospects of leadership that is circumscribed by the challenge of managing an established coalition. Both men came to the presidency after an interval of opposition party control and divided government. The intervening years had seen some significant changes in the tenor of public policy, but there had been no systemic transformations of government and politics. Ushering in a second era of majority party government, Polk and Kennedy promised at once to reaffirm the commitments and revitalize the program of the dominant regime.

Neither Polk nor Kennedy could claim the leadership of any major party faction. Indeed, their credibility as regime managers rested largely on their second-rank status in regular party circles. Each schooled himself in the task of allaying mutual suspicions among the great centers of party strength. Their nominations to the presidency were the result of skillful dancing around the conflicts that divided the party. What they lacked in deep political loyalties they made up for with their freedom to cultivate widespread support.

Once the office was attained, the challenge of interest management was magnified. Each of these presidents had accepted one especially virulent bit of orthodoxy that claimed majority support within the party as a necessary part of the new regime agenda. Their ability to endorse their party's most divisive enthusiasm (Texas annexation and civil rights, respectively) without losing a broad base of credibility within the party was fitting testimony to their early education in the art of aggressive maintenance of the regime party. But their mediating skills did not alter the fact that each came into office with a clear commitment to act on an issue that had long threatened to split the party apart. In addition, Polk and Kennedy each won astonishingly close elections. There was no clear mandate for action, no discernible tide of national discontent, no mass rejection of what had gone before. The hair-breadth Democratic victories of 1844 and 1960 suggested that the opposition could continue to make a serious claim to the presidency and reinforced an already highly developed sense of executive dependence on all parts of the party coalition. With maintenance at a premium and an ideological rupture within the ranks at hand, Polk and Kennedy carried the full weight of the leadership dilemma that confronts the majority-party president of an established regime.

James K. Polk

For the Democratic Party of 1844, the long-festering issue was the annexation of Texas, with its attendant implication of a war of aggression for the expansion of slave territory.[15] Andrew Jackson, an ardent nationalist with a passion for annexation, had steered clear of any definitive action on Texas during the last years of his presidency. He had just consolidated the Democratic Party, and the threat of dividing it anew along sectional lines argued for a passive posture of merely anticipating the inevitable.[16]

Democratic loyalists followed Jackson's lead until 1843, when the partyless "mongrel president," John Tyler, desperate to build an independent political base of support for himself, latched onto the annexation issue and presented a formal proposal on the subject to Congress. With Texas finally pushed to the forefront, expansionist fever heated up in the South and the West and antislavery agitation accelerated in the North.

Jackson's political nightmare became a reality on the eve of his party's nominating convention in 1844. Martin Van Buren, Jackson's successor to the presidency in 1837 and still the nominal head of the Democrats, risked losing an all but certain nomination by coming out against the *immediate* annexation of Texas. Despite its carefully orthodox wording, the New Yorker's pronouncement roused a formidable opposition in the southern and western wings of the party and left the convention deadlocked through eight ballots. With Van Buren holding a large bloc of delegates but unable to get the leaders of the South and West to relinquish the necessary two-thirds majority, it became clear that only a "new man" could save the party from disaster. That man had to be firm on immediate annexation without being openly opposed to Van Buren. On the ninth ballot, James Knox Polk became the Democratic nominee.

Polk was well aware of the circumstances of his nomination. As leader of the Democratic Party in Tennessee and stalwart friend of Andrew Jackson, he had unimpeachable credentials as an orthodox party regular. He had served loyally as floor leader of the House during the critical days of the bank war and had gone on to win his state's governorship. But after Polk tried and failed to gain his party's vice-presidential nomination in 1840, his political career fell on hard times.

Calculating his strategy for a political comeback in 1844, Polk made full use of his second-rank standing in high party circles. Again he posed as the perfect vice-presidential candidate and cultivated his ties to Van Buren. Knowing that this time Van Buren's nomination would be difficult, Polk also understood the special advantages of being a Texas enthusiast with Van Buren connections. As soon as that calculation paid off, Polk ventured another. In accepting the presidential nomination, he pledged that, if elected, he would not seek a second term. Although he thus declared himself a lame duck even before he was elected, Polk reckoned he would not serve any time in office at all unless the frustrated party giants in all sections of the nation expended every last ounce of energy for the campaign—an effort they might not make if it meant foreclosing their own prospects for eight years.[17]

The one-term declaration was a bid for party unity and a pledge of party maintenance. But the divisions that were exposed at the convention of 1844 and their uncertain resolution in a Texas platform and a dark-horse nomination suggested that the party was likely to chew itself up under a passive caretaker presidency. If Polk were to avoid a disastrous schism in the party of Jackson, he would have to order, balance, and service the major contending interests in turn. He would have to enlist each contingent within the party in support of the policy interests of all the others. Polk submerged himself in a high-risk strategy of aggressive maintenance in which the goal was to satisfy each faction of his party enough to keep the whole from falling apart. The scheme was at once pragmatic and holistic, hardheaded and fantastic. The most startling thing of all is how well it worked.

The president opened his administration (appropriately enough) with a declaration that he would "know no divisions of the Democratic Party." He promised "equal and exact justice to every portion."[18] His first action indicated, however, that the going would be rough. Scrutinizing the cabinet selection process, Van Buren (whose electoral efforts had put Polk over the top) judged that his interests in New York had not been sufficiently recognized. The frustrated ex-president presumed a determination on the new president's part to turn the party toward the slave South. Polk tried to appease Van Buren with other patronage offers, but relations between them did not improve. From the outset Van Buren's loyalty was laden with suspicion.

The outcry over patronage suggests that any action the president took would cloud Polk's orthodoxy in charges of betrayal. Van Buren's accusations were but the first in an incessant barrage of such charges.[19] But Polk was not powerless in the face of disaffection. He had an irresistible agenda for party government to bolster his precarious political position.

Polk's program elaborated the theme of equal justice for all coalition interests. On the domestic side, he reached out to the South with support for a lower tariff, to the Northwest with support for land price reform, to the Northeast by endorsing a warehouse storage system advantageous to import merchants, and to the old Jackson radicals with a commitment to a return to hard money and a reinstatement of the independent treasury. (Van Buren had dedicated his entire administration to establishing the independent treasury as a solution to Jackson's banking dilemma, but his work had been undermined in the intervening four years.) It was in foreign affairs, however, that the president placed the highest hopes for his administration. Superimposed on his carefully balanced program of party service in the domestic arena was a missionary embrace of America's "Manifest Destiny." Reaching out to the South, Polk promised to annex Texas; to the Northwest, he promised Oregon; and to bind the whole nation together, he made a secret promise to himself to acquire California. In all, the president would complete the orthodox Jacksonian program of party services and fuse popular passions in an irresistible jingoistic campaign to extend the Jacksonian Republic across the continent.

Driven by the dual imperatives of maintenance and leadership, Polk sought to transform the nation without changing its politics. Party loyalty was the key to success, but it would take more than just a series of favorable party votes to make Polk's strategy of aggressive maintenance work. The sequence, pace, and symbolism of Polk's initiatives had to be assiduously controlled and coordinated with difficult foreign negotiations so that the explosive moral issues inherent in the program would not enter the debate. Sectional paranoia and ideological heresies had to be held in constant check. Mutual self-interest had to remain at the forefront so that reciprocal party obligations could be reinforced. Polk's program was much more than a laundry list of party commitments. If he did not get everything he promised in the order he promised it, he risked a major political rupture that would threaten whatever he did achieve. Here, at the level of executive management and interest control, the president faltered.

After the patronage tiff with Van Buren demonstrated Polk's problems with the eastern radicals, disaffection over the Oregon boundary settlement exposed his difficulties in striking an agreeable balance between western and southern expansionists. The president moved forward immediately and simultaneously on his promises to acquire Oregon and Texas. In each case he pressed an aggressive, indeed belligerent, border claim. He demanded "all of Oregon" (extending north to the 54° 40' parallel) from Great Britain and "Greater Texas" (extending south of the Nueces River to the Rio Grande) from Mexico.

The pledge to get "all of Oregon" unleashed a tidal wave of popular enthusiasm in the Northwest. But Great Britain refused to play according to the presidential plan, and a potent peace movement spread across the South and the East out of fear of impending war over the Oregon boundary. Polk used the belligerence of the "54° 40' or fight" faction to counter the peace movement and to prod the British into coming to terms, but he knew the risks of war on that front. An impending war with Mexico over the Texas boundary promised to yield California in short order, but a war with both Mexico and Great Britain spelled disaster.

When the British finally agreed to settle the Oregon boundary at the forty-ninth parallel, Polk accepted the compromise. Then, after an appropriate display of Mexican aggression on the Texas border, he asked Congress for a declaration of war on Mexico. Abandoned, the 54° 40' men turned on the president, mercilessly accusing him of selling out to the South and picking on defenseless Mexico instead of standing honorably against the British. A huge part of the Oregon territory had been added to the Union, but a vociferous bloc of westerners now joined the Van Burenites in judging the president deceptive and dangerously prosouthern. Polk had miscalculated both British determination and western pride. His accomplishment deviated from the pace and scope of his grand design and in so doing undermined the delicate party balance.

Polk's designs were further complicated by the effects of wartime sensibilities on his carefully balanced legislative program. The independent treasury and warehouse storage bills were enacted easily, but old matters of principle and simple matters of interest were not enough to calm agitated eastern Democrats. They demanded the president's assurance that he was not involved in a war of conquest in the Southwest. Polk responded with an evasive definition of war aims. There was little else he could do to ease suspicions.

More portentous still was the influence of the tariff initiative on wartime politics. Polk had to court northwestern Democrats to make up for expected eastern defections on a vote for a major downward revision of rates. To do so, he not only used land price reform as an incentive to end debate but also withheld his objections to a legislative initiative brewing among representatives of the South and West to develop the Mississippi River system. The northwesterners swallowed their pride over Oregon in hopeful expectation and threw their support behind the tariff bill.

After the bill was enacted, Polk vetoed the internal improvement bill. It had never been a part of his program and was an affront to Jacksonian orthodoxy. But the president's maneuverings were an offense to the West and all but eclipsed the veto's stalwart affirmation of Jacksonian principles. To make matters worse, the land bill failed. The president made good his pledge to press the measure, but he could not secure enactment. Burned three times after offering loyal support to southern interests, the northwesterners were no longer willing to heed the counsels of mutual restraint. The president's effort to bring the war to a quick and triumphant conclusion provided them with their opportunity to strike back.

The war with Mexico was in fact only a few months old, but that was already too long for the president and his party. To speed the advent of peace, Polk decided to ask Congress for a $2 million appropriation to settle the Texas boundary dispute and to pay "for any concessions which may be made by Mexico." This open offer of money for land was the first clear indication that the United States was engaged in—perhaps had consciously provoked—a war of conquest in the Southwest. With it, the latent issue of 1844 manifested itself with a vengeance. Northern Democrats, faced with growing antislavery agitation at home, saw unequal treatment in the administration's handling of matters of interest, intolerable duplicity in presidential action, and an insufferable southern bias in national policy. They were ready to take their stand on matters of principle.

It is ironic that Polk's implicit acknowledgment of the drive for California, with its promise of fulfilling the nationalistic continental vision, would fan the fires of sectional conflict. Surely he had intended just the opposite. The president was, in fact, correct in calculating that no section of the party would oppose the great national passion for expansion to the Pacific. But he simply could not curb party disaffection in the East, and unfulfilled expectations fueled dissatisfaction in the West. He was left to watch in dismay as the malcontents joined forces to take their revenge on the South.

Northern Democrats loyally offered to support the president's effort to buy peace and land, but added a demand that slavery be prohibited from entering any of the territory that might be acquired. This condition was known as the "Wilmot Proviso" after Democrat David Wilmot, a Van Buren enthusiast from western Pennsylvania. Once introduced, it splintered the party along the dreaded sectional cleavage. An appropriations bill with the proviso was passed in the House, but it failed in the Senate when an effort to remove the proviso was successfully filibustered. Now it was Polk's turn to be bitter. In a grim confession of the failure of his grand design, he claimed he could not comprehend "what connection slavery had with making peace with Mexico."[20]

Ultimately, Polk got his peace, and with it he added California and the greater Southwest to the Union. He also delivered on tariff revision, the independent treasury, the warehouse storage system, Oregon, and Texas. Interest management by Polk had extorted a monumental program of party service from established sources of power in remarkably short order. Indeed, except for the conclusion of peace with Mexico, everything had been put in place between the spring of 1845 and the summer of 1846. But the Jacksonian party had ruptured under the pressures of enacting this most orthodox of party programs. Polk's monument to Jacksonian nationalism proved a breeding ground for sectional heresy, and his golden age of policy achievement was undermined at its political foundations.

The failure of interest management to serve the dual goals of political maintenance and policy achievement manifested itself in political disaster for the Democratic Party. By the fall of 1846 the New York party was divided into two irreconcilable camps, with Van Buren leading the radicals, who were in favor of the Wilmot Proviso and opposed to the administration. Although Polk maintained an official stance of neutrality toward the schism, party regulars rallied behind Lewis Cass, a westerner opposed to the proviso. Cass's alternative— "popular" or "squatter" sovereignty in the territories—promised to hold together the larger portion of the majority party by absolving the federal government of any role in settling the questions of slavery extension and regional balance that were raised by Polk's transformation of the nation. When the Democrats nominated Cass in 1848, the Van Buren delegation bolted the convention. Joining "Conscience Whigs" and "Liberty Party" men, they formed the Free Soil Party, dedicated it to the principles of the Wilmot Proviso, and nominated Van Buren as their presidential candidate.[21]

Polk abandoned his studied neutrality after the convention. In the waning months of his administration he withdrew administration favors from Free Soil sympathizers and threw his support behind the party regulars.[22] But it was Van Buren who had the last word. Four years after putting personal defeat aside, loyally supporting the party, and electing Polk, he emerged as the leader of the "heretics" and defeated Cass.

John F. Kennedy

John Kennedy had every intention of spending eight years in the White House, but this ambition only compounded the leadership dilemma inherent in his initial political situation. Kennedy's presidential campaign harkened back to Roosevelt-like images of direction and energy in government. It stigmatized Republican rule as a lethargic, aimless muddle, and roused the people with a promise to "get the country moving again."

At the same time, however, the party of Roosevelt maintained its awkward division between northern liberals and southern conservatives. The candidate assiduously courted both wings, and the narrowness of his victory reinforced his debts to each. The president's prospects for eight years in the White House seemed to hinge on his ability to vindicate, in his first four, the promise of vigorous national leadership without undermining the established foundations of national political power.

Kennedy's "New Frontier" was eminently suited to these demands for aggressive maintenance. It looked outward toward placing a human being on the moon and protecting the free world from communist aggression. It looked inward toward pragmatic adaptations and selected adjustments of the New Deal consensus. Leadership in the international arena would bring the nation together behind bold demonstrations of American power and determination. In the domestic arena it would contain party conflict through presidential management and executive-controlled initiatives.

Kennedy's leadership design had more in common with Polk's pursuits than frontier imagery. Both presidents gave primacy to foreign enthusiasms and hoped the nation would do the same. Facing a politically divided people and a fractionated party, they both set out to tap the unifying potential of America's missionary stance in the world and to rivet national attention on aggressive (even provocative) international adventures. By so doing, they claimed the high ground as individuals of truly national vision. At the same time, each countered deepening conflicts of principle in the ruling coalition with an attempt to balance interests. They were engaged in a constant struggle to mute the passions that divided their supporters and to stem coalition disaffection. Resisting the notion of irreconcilable differences within the ranks, Polk and Kennedy held out their support to all interests and demanded in return the acquiescence of each in executive determination of the range, substance, and timing of policy initiatives.

Some notable differences are evident in the way these presidents approached regime management. Kennedy, not unaware of Polk's failings, avoided Polk's tactics.[23] Polk had gone after as much as possible as quickly as possible for as many as possible in the hope that conflicts among interests could be submerged through the ordered satisfaction of each. Kennedy seemed to feel that conflicts could best be avoided by refraining from unnecessarily divisive action. He was more circumspect in his choice of initiatives and more cautious in their pursuit. Interest balance translated into legislative restraint, and aggressive maintenance became contained advocacy. Kennedy's "politics of expectation" kept fulfillment of the liberal agenda at the level of anticipation.[24]

At the heart of Kennedy's political dilemma was the long-festering issue of civil rights for black Americans. Roosevelt had seen the fight for civil rights coming, but he refused to make it his own, fearing the devastating effect it would have on the precarious sectional balance in his newly established party coalition.[25] Harry S. Truman had seen the fight break out and temporarily rupture the party in 1948.[26] His response was a balance of executive action and legislative caution. When the Republicans made gains in southern cities during the 1950s, the prudent course Truman had outlined appeared more persuasive than ever. But by 1961 black migration into northern cities, Supreme Court support for civil rights demands, and an ever more aggressive civil rights movement in the South had made it almost impossible for a Democratic president to resist a more definitive commitment.

In his early campaign for the presidential nomination, Kennedy developed a posture of "inoffensive" support on civil rights.[27] While keeping himself abreast of the liberal position, he held back from leadership and avoided pressing the cause on southern conservatives. Such maneuvering became considerably more difficult at the party convention of 1960. The liberal-controlled platform committee presented a civil rights plank that all but committed the nominee to take the offensive. It pledged presidential leadership on behalf of new legislation, vigorous enforcement of existing laws, and reforms in congressional procedures to remove impediments to such action. Adding insult to injury, the plank lent party sanction to the civil rights demonstrations that had been accelerating throughout the South.

Although the Democratic platform tied Kennedy to the cause that had ruptured the party in 1948, it did not dampen his determination to hold on to the South. Once nominated, he reached out to the offended region and identified himself with more traditional Democratic strategies. Indeed, by offering the vice-presidential nomination to Lyndon B. Johnson, he risked a serious offense to the left. Johnson was not only the South's first choice and Kennedy's chief rival for the presidential nomination, but his national reputation was punctuated by conspicuous efforts on behalf of ameliorative civil rights action in the Senate. Kennedy himself seems to have been a bit surprised by Johnson's acceptance of second place. The liberals were disheartened.[28] Together, however, Kennedy and Johnson made a formidable team of regime managers. Riding the horns of their party's dilemma, they balanced the boldest Democratic commitment ever on the side of civil rights with a determination not to lose the support of its most passionate opponents. Their narrow victory owed as much to those who were promised a new level of action as to those who were promised continued moderation.

The president's inaugural and State of the Union addresses directed national attention to imminent international dangers and America's world responsibilities. Civil rights received only passing mention. Stressing the need for containment in the international arena, these speeches also reflected the president's commitment to containment in the domestic sphere. In the months before the inauguration Kennedy had decided to keep civil rights off his legislative agenda. Instead, he would prod Congress along on other liberal issues, such as minimum wage, housing, area redevelopment, aid to education, mass transit, and health care. The plan was not difficult to rationalize. If on the one hand the president pressed for civil rights legislation and failed, his entire legislative program would be placed in jeopardy, and executive efforts on behalf of blacks would be subject to even closer scrutiny. If on the other he withheld the civil rights issue from Congress, southerners might show their appreciation for the president's circumspection. His other measures might have a better chance for enactment, and blacks would reap the benefits of this selected expansion of the liberal legislation as well as the benefits of Kennedy's executive-controlled civil rights initiatives.

Thus Kennedy avoided personal involvement in a pre-inaugural fight in the Senate over the liberalization of the rules of debate. The effort failed. He did lend his support to a liberal attempt to expand the House Rules Committee, but this was a prerequisite to House action on Kennedy's chosen legislative program. The rules effort succeeded, but the new committee members gave no indication of an impending civil rights offensive.[29]

Feelings of resentment and betrayal among civil rights leaders inevitably followed the decision to forgo the bold legislative actions suggested in the party platform. But by giving substance to the promise of aggressive executive action, the president sought to allay this resentment and to persuasively demonstrate a new level of federal commitment. The administration moved forward on several fronts.

The centerpiece of the administration's strategy was to use the Justice Department to promote and protect voter registration drives among southern blacks. This promised to give blacks the power to secure their rights and also to minimize the electoral costs of any further Democratic defections among southern whites. On other fronts, the president liberalized the old Civil Rights Commission and created the Committee on Equal Employment Opportunity to investigate job discrimination. When Congress moved to eliminate the poll tax, the president lent his support. When demonstrations threatened to disrupt southern transportation terminals, Attorney General Robert F. Kennedy enlisted the cooperation of the Interstate Commerce Commission in desegregating the facilities. When black applicant James Meredith asserted his right to enroll at the University of Mississippi, the administration responded with protection and crisis mediation. Even more visibly, the president appointed a record number of blacks to high civil service positions.

Kennedy pressed executive action on behalf of civil rights with more vigor and greater effect than any of his predecessors. Still, civil rights enthusiasts were left with unfulfilled hopes and mounting suspicions. Ever mindful of the political imperatives of containing advocacy, the president was trying not only to serve the interests of blacks but also to manage those interests and serve the interests of civil rights opponents. Indeed, there seemed to be a deceptive qualification in each display of principle. For example, the president's patronage policies brought blacks into positions of influence in government, but they also brought new segregationist federal judges to the South. The FBI that provided support for the voter registration drive also tapped the telephone of civil rights activist Martin Luther King Jr. The poll tax was eliminated with administration support, but the administration backed away from a contest over literacy tests. Kennedy liberalized the Civil Rights Commission, but he refused to endorse its controversial report, which recommended withholding federal funds from states that violated the Constitution. Although he encouraged the desegregation of interstate transportation terminals, the president put off action on a campaign pledge to promote the desegregation of housing by executive order. (When the housing order was finally issued, it adopted the narrowest possible application and was not made retroactive.) And although the administration ultimately saw to the integration of the University of Mississippi, the U.S. attorney general first tried to find some way to allow the racist governor of the state to save face.

Executive management allowed Kennedy to juggle mutually contradictory expectations for two years. But as an exercise in forestalling a schism within the ranks, the administration's efforts to control advocacy and to balance interests ultimately satisfied no one and offered no real hope of resolving the issue at hand. The weaknesses in the president's position became more and more apparent early in 1963 as civil rights leaders pressed ahead with their own timetable for action.

Although civil rights leaders clearly needed the president's support, they steadfastly refused to compromise their demands or to relinquish de facto control over their movement to presidential management. The president and his brother became agitated when movement leaders contended that the administration was not doing all that it could for blacks. Civil rights groups, in turn, were outraged by the administration's implication that the movement comprised an interest like any other and that its claims could be pragmatically "balanced" against those of racism and bigotry in a purely political calculus. Independent action had already blurred the line between contained advocacy and reactive accommodation in the administration's response to the movement. Continued independence and intensified action promised to limit the president's latitude still further and to force him to shift his course from interest balancing to moral choice.

The first sign of a shift came on February 28, 1963. After a season of rising criticism of presidential tokenism, embarrassing civil rights advocacy by liberal Republicans in Congress, and portentous planning for spring demonstrations in the most racially sensitive parts of the South, the president recommended some mild civil rights measures to Congress. His message acknowledged that civil rights was indeed a moral issue and indicated that it no longer could be treated simply as another interest. But this shift was one of words more than action. Kennedy did not follow up his legislative request in any significant way.

Although civil rights agitation clearly was spilling over the banks of presidential containment, the prospect for passing civil rights legislation in Congress had improved little since Kennedy had taken office. His circumspect attitude toward civil rights matters during the first two years of his administration had succeeded in winning only modest support from southern Democrats for his other social and economic measures. On the one hand, several of the administration's most important victories—minimum wage, housing, and area redevelopment legislation—clearly demonstrated the significance of southern support. On the other, the president had already seen southern Democrats defect in droves to defeat his proposed Department of Urban Affairs, presumably because the first department head was to be black.[30] If Kennedy could no longer hope to contain the civil rights issue, he still faced the problem of containing the political damage that would inevitably come from spearheading legislative action.

Kennedy's approach to this problem was to press legislation as an irresistible counsel of moderation. This meant holding back still longer, waiting for the extreme positions to manifest themselves fully, then offering real change as the only prudent course available. He did not have to wait long. In 1963 a wave of spring civil rights demonstrations that began in Birmingham, Alabama, and extended throughout the South brought mass arrests and ugly displays of police brutality to the center of public attention. Capitalizing on the specter of social disintegration, the administration argued that a new legislative initiative was essential to the restoration of order and sought bipartisan support for it on this basis. Congressional Republicans were enlisted with the argument that the only way to get the protesters off the streets was to provide them with new legal remedies in the courts. Kennedy then seized an opportunity to isolate the radical right. On the evening of the day Gov. George Wallace made his symbolic gesture in defiance of federal authority at the University of Alabama (physically barring the entrance of a prospective black student), the president gave a hastily prepared but impassioned television address on the need for new civil rights legislation.

In late June the administration sent its legislative proposal to Congress. The bill went far beyond the mild measures offered in February. It contained significantly expanded voting rights protections and for the first time called for federal protection to enforce school desegregation and to guarantee equal access to public facilities. But even with this full bow to liberal commitments, the struggle for containment continued. The administration tried to counter the zeal of urban Democrats by searching for compromises that would hold a bipartisan coalition of civil rights support. When civil rights leaders planned a march on Washington in the midst of the legislative battle, the president tried without success to dissuade them.

Containing the zeal of the left was the least of the president's problems. Kennedy had struggled continually to moderate his party's liberal commitments and thus avoid a rupture on the right. With a landmark piece of civil rights legislation inching its way through Congress, the president now turned to face the dreaded party schism. His popularity had plummeted in the South. George Wallace was contemplating a national campaign to challenge liberal control of the Democratic Party, and an ugly white backlash in the North made the prospects for such a campaign brighter than ever. Conservative reaction, party schism, and the need to hold a base in the South were foremost in the president's thinking as he embarked on his fateful trip to Texas in November 1963.

Pierce and Carter: Disjunction and the Struggle for Credibility

For Polk and Kennedy, leadership was circumscribed by a political test of aggressive maintenance and the corresponding dilemmas of interest management. With a preemptive assertion of executive control, each attempted to orchestrate a course and pace for regime development that would change the nation without changing its politics. Their governing strategies involved them in convoluted conflict manipulations that were calculated to reconcile divergent coalition interests, stave off a political rupture, and move forward on outstanding regime commitments. Grounded in established power, leadership cast a dark cloud of duplicity over its greatest achievements.

Indeed, it would be difficult to choose the greater of these two presidential performances. Polk was able to deliver on an impressive array of policy promises, but his success was premised on excluding from the political arena the basic moral issue raised by these policies. Kennedy delivered little in the way of outstanding policy, but he ultimately acknowledged the great moral choice he confronted and he made a moral decision of enormous national significance. These differences notwithstanding, Polk and Kennedy dealt with the unraveling of interest management in a similar way. Executive control and a promise of delivering significant policy support to all the interests of the majority party gave way within two years to an effort to limit the effects of an open rupture. When interest management could no longer stave off disaffection and hold the old coalition together, these presidents took their stand with the larger part and tried to isolate the heretics.

The irony in these performances is that, although upholding their respective regime commitments and affirming their party orthodoxies, Polk and Kennedy raised serious questions about the future terms of regime survival and thus left orthodoxy itself politically insecure. Because Polk's nationalism and Kennedy's liberalism ultimately came at the expense of the old majority coalition, a new appeal to the political interests of the nation seemed imperative. In vindicating orthodoxy, Polk and Kennedy set in motion a pivotal turn toward sectarianism in regime development.

For the Jacksonian Democrats, the turn toward sectarianism grew out of a political defeat. The election of 1848 exposed the weaknesses of stalwart Jacksonian nationalism and spurred party managers to overcome the political damage wrought by sectional divisiveness. In 1850 Democratic votes secured passage of a bipartisan legislative package designed to smooth the disruptions wrought by the Polk administration.[31] This incongruous series of measures, collectively labeled the "Compromise of 1850," repackaged moderation in a way that many hoped would isolate the extremists and lead to the creation of a new Union Party. But the dream of a Union Party failed to spark widespread interest, and Democratic managers grasped the sectarian alternative. Using the compromise as a point of departure, they set out to reassemble their broken coalition. While supporting government policies that were designed to silence ideological conflict, they renewed a partnership in power with interests at the ideological extremes.[32]

For the New Deal regime, the turn came on the heels of a great electoral victory. Running against a Republican extremist, Lyndon B. Johnson swept the nation. But the disaffection stemming from the Kennedy administration was clearly visible: Southern Democrat Johnson lost five states in his own region to the Republican outlier. In 1965 and 1966 Johnson tried to fuse a new consensus with policies that ranged across the extremes of ideology and interest. He dreamed of superseding the New Deal with a Great Society, but his vast expansion of services to interests added more to government fragmentation than to regime coherence. He also hoped to supplant the old Democratic Party with a "party for all Americans," but his extension of regime commitments did more to scatter political loyalties than to unify them.[33]

By the time of the next incarnation of majority-party government (1852 and 1976, respectively), the challenge of presidential leadership had shifted categorically once again. By 1852 the nationalism of Jackson had degenerated into a patchwork of suspect compromises sitting atop a seething sectional division. By 1976 the liberalism of Roosevelt had become a grab bag of special interest services all too vulnerable to political charges of burdening a troubled economy with bureaucratic overhead. Expedience eclipsed enthusiasm in the bond between the regime and the nation. Supporters of orthodoxy were placed on the defensive. The energies that once came from advancing great national purposes had dissipated. A rule of myopic sects defied the very notion of government authority.

Expedience also eclipsed enthusiasm in the bond between the majority party and its president. Franklin Pierce and Jimmy Carter each took the term *dark horse* to new depths of obscurity. Each was a minor, local figure, far removed from the centers of party strength and interest. Indeed, each hailed from the region of greatest erosion in majority party support. Pierce, a New Hampshire attorney, who had retired from the Senate almost a decade before, was called to head the Democratic ticket in 1852 after forty-eight convention ballots failed to yield a consensus on anyone who might have been expected to actually lead the party. His appeal (if it may be so called) within regular party circles lay first in his uniquely inoffensive availability and, second, in his potential to bring north-eastern Free Soil Democrats back to the standard they had so recently branded as proslavery. Carter, a former governor of Georgia, was chosen to head the Democratic ticket in 1976 after mounting a broadside assault on the national po-litical establishment. To say he appealed to regular party circles would be to mis-take the nature of his campaign and to exaggerate the coherence of the Democratic organization at that time. Still, Carter offered the Democrats a can-didate untainted by two decades of divisive national politics, and one capable of bringing the South back to the party of liberalism.

The successful reassembling of broken coalitions left Pierce and Carter to ponder the peculiar challenge of leading an enervated regime. These presidents engaged the political system at a step removed from a claim to managing coali-tion interests and orchestrating agenda fulfillment. Tenuously attached to a government establishment that itself appeared dangerously out of step with the most pressing problems of the day, their leadership turned on a question so narrow that it is really prerequisite to leadership—that of their own credibility. Despite determined efforts to establish trustworthiness, neither Pierce nor Carter could reconcile his own awkward position in the old order with the awkward position of the old order in the nation at large. Caught between the incessant demands of regime interests and the bankruptcy of the assumptions about the government and the nation that had supported those interests in the past, neither could find secure ground on which to make a stand and limit the political unraveling that comes with executive action. What began in expedi-ence simply dissolved into irrelevance.

Franklin Pierce

In 1852 Franklin Pierce carried twenty-seven of the thirty-one states for a hefty 250 out of 296 electoral votes.[34] In the process, the Democratic Party strengthened its hold over both houses of Congress. Still, the Pierce landslide was more apparent than real, and the election was anything but a mandate for action. As a presidential candidate, Pierce had merely endorsed the work of a bipartisan group of Senate moderates. His campaign was confined to a simple declaration of support for the Compromise of 1850 and a pledge to resist any further agitation on slavery, the issue that underlay all other national concerns.

The Pierce campaign was nothing if not a dutiful bow to senatorial authority and moderate political opinion.

It is possible that the new president might have enhanced his position at the start of his term by taking a second bow to the center and placing the largesse of his office at the disposal of the Senate moderates. But other aspects of the election argued against this strategy. Pierce actually had received less than 51 percent of the popular vote. He won the presidency, not because the moderate center of national opinion rallied to his standard but because the party managers working in the field had reassembled support at the extremes of Democratic Party opinion. To the extremists, the Compromise of 1850 was a cause for suspicion rather than satisfaction; it was a matter of reluctant acquiescence rather than loyal support.

Pierce was sensitive to the precariousness of his victory but thought the logic of his situation was fairly clear. He believed the election of 1848 had shown it was not enough for the Democratic Party to stand with the moderates and let the extremes go their own way and that the narrow victory of 1852 amply demonstrated the electoral imperative of consolidating party loyalties across the spectrum of party opinion. He was gratified by the election's renewed display of party loyalty—however reluctantly given—and he found far-fetched and unimpressive the possibility that the centrists of both parties might join him on independent ground in a kind of national coalition government. He therefore decided to reach out to the old party coalition in an effort to heal the wounds of 1848 once and for all.

In a bold bid for leadership, Pierce held himself aloof from the moderate senators and set out to rebuild the political machinery of Jacksonian government under presidential auspices. As the mastermind of a party restoration, he hoped to gain respectability in his dealings with Congress, to take charge of national affairs, and ultimately—in 1856—to lay claim to the mantle of Andrew Jackson. The basic problem with this plan for establishing a credible leadership posture was that no interest of any significance depended on the president's success. Pierce had exhausted his party's national strength and legitimacy simply by letting the various party leaders elect him. These leaders had no stake in following their own creation and no intention of suspending their mutual suspicions to enhance the president's position. Pierce quickly discovered that his claim to the office of Andrew Jackson had no political foundation and that by asserting his independence at the outset, he had robbed the alternative strategy—a bow to senatorial power—of any possible advantage.

As for political vision, Pierce's goal of resuscitating the old party machinery was ideologically and programmatically vacuous. It was conceived as a purely mechanical exercise in repairing and perfecting the regime's core institutional apparatus and thereby restoring its operational vitality. There was no reference to any of the substantive concerns that had caused the vitality of the party apparatus to dissipate in the first place. Those concerns were simply to be forgotten. Pierce recalled Polk's dictum of "equal and exact justice" for every portion of the party but neglected the wide-ranging appeal to unfinished party business that had driven Polk's administration. He held up to the nation the vision of a political machine restored and purged of all political content.[35]

The rapid unraveling of the Pierce administration began with the president's initial offer to forget the Free Soil heresy of 1848 and provide all party factions in the North their due measure of presidential favor for support given in 1852. Much to the president's dismay, many of the New York Democrats who had remained loyal in 1848 refused to forgive the heretics and share the bounty. The New York party disintegrated at a touch, and in 1853 the Whigs swept the state elections.

Within months of Pierce's inauguration, then, the president's strategy for establishing his credibility as a leader was in a shambles. The Senate had not yet confirmed his candidate for the collectorship of the Port of New York, an important post, and if the party leaders withheld their endorsement (a prospect that Pierce's early standoffishness and the New York electoral debacle made all too real), the rebuke to the fledgling administration would be devastating. Pierce was at the mercy of the Senate. Worse, he had placed the Senate at the mercy of the radical states' rights advocates of the South. This small but potent faction of southern senators felt shortchanged by the distribution of patronage in their own region and resolved to use the president's appeal for the restoration of Free Soilers as a basis for their revenge. The administration's distribution of rewards in the North, they said, represented a heightened level of commitment to the Free Soil element, and they challenged their more moderate southern cohorts to extract an equal commitment to their region as well.

The radical southerners found their opportunity in Illinois senator Stephen Douglas's bill to organize the Nebraska Territory. Douglas pushed the Nebraska bill because it would open a transcontinental railroad route through the center of his own political base. His bill followed the orthodox party posture, a stance confirmed in the Compromise of 1850, stipulating that the new territory would be organized without reference to slavery and that the people of the territory would decide the issue. Southerners who had ostensibly accepted this formula for settling new lands by electing Pierce in 1852 were offended by the president's northern political strategy in 1853 and felt compelled to raise the price of their support in 1854. They demanded that the Douglas bill include a repeal of the Missouri Compromise of 1820 and thus explicitly acknowledge that slavery could become permanently established anywhere in the national domain. Douglas evidently convinced himself that the expected benefits of his Nebraska bill were worth the price extracted by the South. After all, it could be argued that the repeal would only articulate something already implicit in the doctrine of squatter sovereignty. The change in the formal terms of sectional peace would be more symbolic than real. In any case, Douglas accepted the repeal, and by dividing the Nebraska Territory in two (Nebraska and Kansas) hinted that both sections might peacefully lay claim to part of the new land.

In January 1854, less than a year into Pierce's administration, Douglas led his southern collaborators to the White House to secure a presidential endorsement for the Kansas-Nebraska bill. With Douglas's railroad and the confirmation of Pierce's New York collector nominee hanging in the balance, the cornerstone of the Pierce presidency gave way. In his very first legislative decision, the president was being told to disregard his electoral pledge not to reopen the issue of slavery and to tie his leadership to the repudiation of the Missouri Compromise. To endorse the handiwork of the party leaders was to risk his credibility in the nation at large. But if he chose to stand by his pledge, he was certain to lose all credibility within the party. Pierce chose to stand with the party leaders. Like Douglas, he apparently had convinced himself that the Kansas-Nebraska bill was consistent enough with the spirit of the Compromise of 1850 to not raise any new issues concerning slavery. He then offered to help Douglas convince the northern wing of the party. The administration's candidate for collector of the Port of New York was confirmed.

Between March 1853 and January 1854 Pierce tried and failed to prove himself to his party on his own terms; between January and May of 1854 he struggled to prove himself to his party on the Senate's terms. The president threw all the resources of the administration behind passage of the Kansas-Nebraska bill in the House. Despite a Democratic majority of 159 to 76, he fought a no-win battle to discipline a party vote. Midway into the proceedings, sixty-six of the ninety northern Democrats stood in open revolt against this northern Democratic president. A no-holds-barred use of presidential patronage ultimately persuaded forty-four representatives to give a final assent. Instead of perfecting the political machine, Pierce found himself defying a political revolution. Passage of the bill was secured through the support of southern Whigs. Forty-two northern Democrats openly voted no. Not one northern Whig voted yes.[36]

Pierce lost his gamble with national credibility in the winter of 1854. Exhausted after the passage of Douglas's bill, the administration then suffered northern revenge for the broken pledge of 1852. The Democrats lost every northern state except New Hampshire and California in the elections of 1854. The once huge Democratic majority in the House disappeared, and a curious new amalgam of political forces prepared to take over. Adding to the rebuke was the threat of civil war in the territories. Free Soil and proslavery factions rushed into Kansas and squared off in a contest for control. The president called for order, but his plea was ignored.

Pierce never gave up hope that his party would turn to him. But once the North had rejected his administration, the South had no more use for him, and the party Pierce wanted so desperately to lead became more anxious to get rid of him. When faced with the unmitigated failure of his leadership and his political impotence at midterm, Pierce seemed to gain his first sense of a higher purpose. He threw his hat into the ring for a second term with a spirited defense of the Kansas-Nebraska Act and a biting indictment of the critics of the Missouri Compromise repeal. He appealed to the nation to reject treason in Kansas, wrapped his party in the Constitution, and cast its enemies in the role of uncompromising disunionists bent on civil war.[37]

This was the president's shining hour. Rejecting the specter of party illegitimacy and the stigma of his own irrelevance, standing firm with the establishment against the forces that would destroy it, Pierce pressed the case for his party in the nation and with it, his own case for party leadership. Still, no one rallied to his side. The party took up the "friends of the Constitution" sentiment, but it hastened to bury the memory of the man who had articulated it. Pierce's unceasing effort to prove his significance to those who had called him to power never bore fruit. The Democratic convention was an "anybody but Pierce" affair.

Jimmy Carter

There is no better rationale for Jimmy Carter's mugwumpish approach to political leadership than Franklin Pierce's unmitigated failure. No sooner had Pierce identified his prospects for gaining credibility with revitalizing the old party machinery under presidential auspices than he fell victim to party interests so factious that the desperate state of national affairs was all but ignored. The sect-ridden party of Jackson proved itself bankrupt as a governing instrument. Its operators could not even recognize that they were toying with explosive moral issues of national significance. Pierce's plan to claim party leadership first and then to take charge of the nation dissolved with its initial action, pushing the president down a path as demoralizing for the nation as it was degrading to the office. The quest for credibility degenerated into saving face with the Senate over patronage appointments, toeing the line on volatile territorial legislation for the sake of Douglas's railroad, and forswearing a solemn pledge to the nation.

It was Jimmy Carter's peculiar genius to treat his remoteness from his party and its institutional power centers as a distinctive asset rather than his chief liability in his quest for a credible leadership posture. He called attention to moral degeneration in government and politics, made it his issue, and then compelled the political coalition that had built that government to indulge his crusade against it. In a style reminiscent of Andrew Jackson, Carter identified himself with popular disillusionment with political insiders, entrenched special interests, and the corruption of manners in Washington. He let the liberals of the Democratic Party flounder in their own disarray until it became clear that liberalism could no longer take the political offensive on its own terms. Then, in the 1976 Florida primary, Carter pressed his southern advantage. The party either had to fall in line behind his campaign against the establishment or risk another confrontation with the still greater heresies of George Wallace.

The obvious problem in Carter's approach to the presidency was that although it claimed a high moral stance of detachment from the establishment, it also positioned itself within an established governing coalition. This curiosity afforded him neither the regime outsider's freedom to oppose established interests nor the insider's license to support them. The tension in Carter's campaign between the effort to reassemble the core constituencies of the traditional Democratic regime and the promise to reform the government order that served it suggested the difficulties he would face establishing a credible leadership posture in office. Carter's narrow victory magnified those difficulties by showing the regime's supporters in Congress to be a good deal more secure politically than their strange new affiliate in the executive mansion.

On what terms, then, did Carter propose to reconcile his outsider's appeal with his position within the old order? The answer of the campaign lay in Carter's preoccupation with problems of form, procedure, and discipline rather than in the substance of the old order. It was not bureaucratic *programs,* Carter argued, but bureaucratic *inefficiency* that left the people estranged from their government. It was not the system per se that was at fault but the way it was being run. In the eyes of this late-regime Democrat, the stifling weight and moral decay of the federal government presented problems of technique and personnel, not substance.

Like Jackson's early efforts, Carter's reform program called for government reorganization, civil service reform, and fiscal retrenchment. But coming from an outsider affiliated with the old order, the political force and ideological energy of this revitalization program were largely nullified. What Jackson presented as an ideological indictment of the old order and a buttress for supporters newly arrived in power, Carter presented as institutional engineering plain and simple. Carter's Jackson-like appeal to the nation translated into an ideologically passionless vision of reorganizing the old order without challenging any of its core concerns.[38]

It is in this respect that the shaky ground on which Carter staked his credibility as a leader begins to appear a good deal more like that claimed by Franklin Pierce than their different party postures would at first lead us to suppose. Both pinned their hopes on the perfectibility of machinery. Carter would do for the bureaucratic apparatus of the liberal regime what Pierce had intended to do for the party apparatus of the Jacksonian regime—repair the mechanical defects and realize a new level of operational efficiency. By perfecting the apparatus, they hoped to save the old regime from its own self-destructive impulses and, at the same time, eliminate the need to make any substantive choices among interests. Political vitality was to be restored simply by making the engines of power run more efficiently.

Sharing this vision, Pierce and Carter also shared a problem of action. Neither could point to any interest of political significance that depended on his success in reorganization. Carter's plan for instilling a new level of bureaucratic discipline was not the stuff to stir the enthusiasm of established Democrats, and once the plan became concrete action, there was plenty for party interests to vehemently oppose. Carter's vision of institutional efficiency dissolved in a matter of weeks into institutional confrontation.

The Carter administration immediately engaged the nation in an elaborate display of symbolism that was designed to build a reservoir of popular faith in the president's intentions and confidence in his ability to change the tenor of government.[39] The economic difficulties the old regime faced in simply maintaining its programmatic commitments at current levels dampened whatever enthusiasm there was for reaching out to the interests with expansive new programs in orthodox Democratic style. The impulse to lead thus focused on an early redemption of the pledge to be different. With his "strategy of symbols," the president bypassed Congress and claimed authority in government as an extension of his personal credibility in the nation at large.

The first material test of this strategy came in February 1977, when Carter decided to cut nineteen local water projects from the 1978 budget. As mundane as this bid for leadership was, it placed the disjunction between the president's appeal to the people and his political support in government in the starkest possible light. For the president, the water projects were a prime example of the wasteful expenditures inherent in the old ways government did business. The cuts offered Carter a well-founded and much-needed opportunity to demonstrate to the nation how an outsider with no attachments to established routines could bring a thrifty discipline to government without really threatening any of its programmatic concerns. Congress—and, in particular, the Democratic leadership in the Senate—saw the matter quite differently. The president's gesture was received as an irresponsible and politically pretentious assault on the bread and butter of congressional careers. Its only real purpose was to enhance the president's public standing, yet its victims were those on whom presidential success in government must ultimately depend. The Democratic leaders of the Senate pressed the confrontation. They reinstated the threatened water projects on a presidentially sponsored public works jobs bill. Carter threatened to stand his ground, and majority party government floundered at the impasse.

As relations with Congress grew tense, the president's bid for national leadership became even more dependent on public faith and confidence in his administration's integrity. By standing aloof from "politics as usual," the administration saddled itself with a moral standard that any would find difficult to sustain. A hint of shady dealing surfaced in the summer of 1977, and by the fall, the symbolic supports of Carter's leadership were a shambles.

Like the water projects debacle, the Bert Lance affair is remarkable for its substantive insignificance. The administration's "scandal" amounted to an investigation of financial indiscretions by one official before he took office. But the Carter administration was nothing if not the embodiment of a higher morality, and the budget director was the president's most important and trusted political appointee. The exposé of Lance, whose hand was on the tiller of the bureaucratic ship, not only indicted the administration's claim to ethical superiority but also made a mockery of the Democratic Senate's nomination review process. Shorn of its pretensions to a higher standard, the administration's outsider status became a dubious asset. Attention was now directed to the apparent inability of the outsiders to make the government work and address the nation's manifest problems.

Despite these first-year difficulties in establishing a credible leadership posture on his own terms, Carter still refused to abdicate to the party leaders.

Indeed, as time went on, the intransigence of the nation's economic difficulties seemed to stiffen the president's resistance to social policy enthusiasms he felt the nation could no longer afford to support. There was to be no recapitulation of the Pierce-Douglas disaster in an alliance between Carter and Sen. Edward M. Kennedy, D-Mass. But what of the prospects for continued presidential resistance? The core constituencies of the Democratic Party—blacks and organized labor in particular—found the president's program of government reorganization and fiscal retrenchment tangential at best to their concerns. They had little use for a Democratic president who seemed to govern like a Republican, and their disillusionment added to the dismay of the congressional leadership. Stalwart liberals admonished the president not to forsake the traditional interests but to rally them and, in Kennedy's words, "sail against the wind."[40] If the nation's shaky economy made this message perilous for the - president to embrace, his awkward political position made it equally perilous to ignore.

Following the Lance affair, Carter did attempt to dispel disillusionment with an appeal to the neoliberal theme of consumerism. He had identified himself with consumer issues during his campaign and opened the second year of his administration with a drive to establish a consumer protection agency. The proposal could hardly be said to address the demands of the old Democratic constituencies, but it had enthusiastic backing from consumer groups, a general popular appeal, support from the Democratic leadership in Congress, and the rare promise of serving all these at little direct cost to the government. In consumer protection, Carter found the makings of a great victory, one that would not only wash away the memory of the first year but also define his own brand of political leadership. But the legislation failed, and with the failure his prospects for leadership all but collapsed.

Indeed, this defeat underscored the paradox that plagued Carter's never-ending struggle for credibility. Opposition fueled by business interests turned the consumer protection issue against the administration with devastating effect. Identifying government regulation of industry with the grim state of the national economy, business made Carter's neoliberalism appear symptomatic of the problem and counterproductive to any real solution.[41] Carter's own critique of undisciplined government expansion actually became the property of his critics, and the distinctions he had drawn between himself and the old liberal establishment became hopelessly blurred. Although this most distant of Democratic presidents was alienating the liberal establishment by his neglect of its priorities, he was being inextricably linked to it in a conservative assault on the manifest failings of the New Deal liberal regime. Carter's liberalism-with-a-difference simply could not stand its ground in the sectarian controversies that racked the liberal order in the 1970s. It was as vulnerable to the conservatives for being more of the same as it was vulnerable to the liberals for being different.

As tensions between the old regime politics and new economic realities intensified, all sense of political definition was eclipsed. Notable administration victories—the Senate's ratification of a bitterly contested treaty with Panama, the endorsement of a version of the much heralded administrative reorganization, the negotiation of an accord between Israel and Egypt—offered precious little vindication of the promise of revitalization. Moreover, the president's mugwumpish resolve to find his own way through deepening crises came to be perceived as rootless floundering. His attempt to assert forceful leadership through a major cabinet shake-up in the summer of 1979 only added credence to the image of an administration out of control. His determination to support a policy of inducing recession to fight inflation shattered the political symbolism of decades past by saddling a Democratic administration with a counsel of austerity and sacrifice and passing to the Republicans the traditional Democratic promise of economic recovery and sustained prosperity.

The administration was aware of its failure to engage the political system in a meaningful way well before these momentous decisions. By early 1979 the president had turned introspective. It was readily apparent that his credibility had to be established anew and imperative that the administration be identified with some clear and compelling purpose. Carter's response to the eclipse of political definition was not a Pierce-like defense of the old order and its principles. It was, if anything, a sharpened attack on the old order and a renewed declaration of presidential political independence.

In what was to be his most dramatic public moment, Carter appeared in a nationally televised appeal to the people in July 1979 with a revised assessment of the crisis facing the nation.[42] Carter began his new bid for leadership credibility by acknowledging widespread disillusionment with the administration and its "mixed success" with Congress. But the president detached himself from the "paralysis, stagnation, and drift" that had marked his tenure. He issued a strong denunciation of the legislative process and reasserted his campaign image as an outsider continuing the people's fight against degenerate politics. Attempting to restore the people's faith in themselves and to rally them to his cause, Carter all but declared the bankruptcy of the federal government as he found it. Thirty months in office seemed to reveal to him only how deeply rooted the government's incapacities were. It was the system itself, not simply its inefficiencies, that the president now placed in question.

Trying once again to identify his leadership with the people's alienation from the government, Carter again exposed himself as the one with the most paralyzing case of estrangement. The awkward truth in this presidential homily lent credence to the regime's most vehement opponents by indicting the establishment controlled by the president's ostensible allies. On the face of it, Carter had come to embrace a leadership challenge of the greatest moment—the repudiation of an entire political-institutional order—but beneath the challenge lay the hopeless paradox of his political position. The Democratic Party tore itself apart in a revolt against him and the sentiments he articulated. It rejected his message, discredited his efforts, and then, in its most pathetic display of impotence, revealed to the nation that it had nothing more to offer. Carter finally may have seen the gravity of the problems he confronted, but as the people saw it, he was not part of the solution.

Rethinking the Politics of Leadership

The politics of leadership is often pictured as a contest between the individual and the system. Political fragmentation and institutional intransigence threaten to frustrate the would-be leader at every turn. Success, if it is possible at all, is reserved for the exceptional individual. It takes a person of rare political skill to manipulate the system in politically effective ways. It takes a person of rare character to give those manipulations national meaning and constructive purpose.

Although the significance of the particular person in office cannot be doubted, this individual-centered perspective on leadership presents a rather one-sided view of the interplay between the presidency and the larger political system. It is highly sensitive to differences among incumbents, but it tends to obscure differences in the political situations in which they act. If presidential leadership is indeed something of a struggle between the individual and the system, it must be recognized that the system changes as well as the incumbent. Indeed, the political conditions for presidential action can shift radically from one administration to the next, and with each change the challenge of exercising political leadership is correspondingly altered.

Within any one historical period the shifting political contexts encountered by leaders are likely to appear idiosyncratic, and the political changes effected by each incumbent, erratic. To catch the patterns and sequences in the politics of leadership, we need to adopt a much broader view of the relevant historical experience than is customary. On this larger canvas, similar kinds of situations elicit from leaders similar premises and projects for political action. Moreover, the situations, premises, and projects that tend to recur over long stretches of time have correspondingly similar political effects. Presidential history in this perspective is episodic rather than evolutionary, with leadership opportunities gradually dissipating after an initial upheaval in political control of the government. Presidents intervene in—and their leadership is mediated by—the generation and degeneration of political orders, or partisan regimes. The clock at work in presidential leadership keeps *political* rather than historical time.

The leaders who stand out at a glance—Washington, Jefferson, Jackson, Lincoln, and Franklin Roosevelt—are closer to each other in the political conditions of leadership than they are to any of their respective neighbors in historical time. In political time each is a first, a regime builder. The regime builders ride into power on an upheaval in government control and test their leadership in efforts to secure the political and institutional infrastructure for a new governing coalition. Their success creates a new establishment, thrusts their partisan successors into the position of regime managers, and poses the test of aggressive maintenance.

As the analysis of the Jacksonian and New Deal regimes has shown, successive incarnations of majority-party government produce progressively more tenuous challenges for regime managers. Politically affiliated with already established commitments of ideology and interest, these presidents approach the ever more perplexing problems of managing the regime's commitments with ever more superficial governing solutions. Regime supporters, in turn, approach ever more perplexing leadership choices with ever less forbearance. Ultimately, visions of regime management dissolve into politically vacuous mechanical contrivances, and leadership is foreclosed by the political dilemmas of simply establishing the president's credibility. In this way, the exercise of presidential power drives each regime further into a crisis of legitimacy, gradually preparing the ground for another reconstructive breakthrough.

It is worth noting that the critical issue in each of the six cases reviewed was not the success or failure in enacting some momentous new program for national action. Franklin Pierce, in pitched battle, succeeded in enacting the Kansas-Nebraska Act but failed miserably as a political leader; in contrast, Franklin Roosevelt, arguably the most formidable political leader of the twentieth century, was thwarted time and again on matters of program, from the voiding of the "first" New Deal by the Supreme Court to the failure of his party purge. Nor has the critical issue in these cases been the success of the policies enacted in solving national problems. After all, the New Deal failed to pull the nation out of the Great Depression, and Andrew Jackson's alternative banking scheme exacerbated an economic depression. The incumbents in these two historical sequences are distinguishable from one another—and paired individually with counterparts in very different historical periods—by their ability to set the terms and conditions of legitimate political action. In this view, the critical issue on which presidential leadership turns is their political authority, their control over the meaning of their initiatives and accomplishments in the face of the contending interpretations of friends and foes alike. A president's authority over political definitions changes with the passage of political time and hinges in large measure on the relationship between the incumbent and received governing commitments.[43]

Thus the paradigmatic expressions of political leadership in the presidency come from incumbents, such as Jackson and Roosevelt, who stand free of the commitments of the recent past and are able to define their leadership projects against the backdrop of the manifest failures of a recently displaced governing coalition. Able to hammer relentlessly against a failed and discredited course of national action, they are best situated to reset the terms and conditions of legitimate national government.

For Polk and Kennedy, whose ascension to power revived and reaffirmed commitments drawn from the recent past, leadership was quite different. It was their job to make good on long-heralded promises, to continue the work of the established regime, and to implement a robust policy agenda. Leadership was a matter of managing interests and implementing policies in the manner best calculated to stave off warfare within the ranks. In exercising power on these terms, however, Polk and Kennedy were constrained by the authority of faithful followers to challenge their particular rendition of the true meaning and implications of received commitments. Their leadership sent sectarian schisms deep into the ranks of regime supporters.

The difficulties of exercising political leadership mounted apace under Pierce and Carter. They came to power affiliated with an old orthodoxy that was on the defensive. Each offered to repair the political machinery of a faltering regime, one whose basic commitments of ideology and interest were increasingly seen as the very source of the nation's problems. Caught between the demands of their nominal supporters for further action along the old course and frontal assaults on the old course from a resurgent opposition, these leaders were unable to establish clear warrants for any course of action, and their exercises of power accelerated the crises of legitimacy they were intended to abate.

Comparisons that move across broad stretches of history help us make sense of the shifting parameters of the politics of leadership that are notable within a historical period. Still, they leave a major question outstanding: What has been the effect of the secular changes that, over time, have transformed the organization of government power itself? Roosevelt did not simply repeat Jackson's performance. He directed his leadership against interests and institutions that were more firmly entrenched in government and more fully integrated into the social and economic life of the nation. For this reason he was more constrained as a reconstructive leader than Jackson. Although Roosevelt was able to set the general terms for a reordering of political commitments, his initiatives repeatedly went down to defeat. The new order was not imposed from the top down as in Jackson's case but was fashioned more systemically by interests and institutions beyond Roosevelt's direct control.

In the Pierce-Carter comparison, secular changes in the organization of American government seem to have had the opposite effect. Jimmy Carter had at his disposal institutional resources for independent action that Franklin Pierce could scarcely have imagined. When Stephen Douglas marched to the White House demanding that Pierce take on the party's latest enthusiasm as his own, the senator had the balance of government power on his side. As president, Pierce had no resources of comparable institutional weight with which to counter his party's leadership in Congress. But when Edward Kennedy demanded that Carter buck the conservative tide and take on new liberal commitments, Carter was able to resist by employing the political resources of the modern presidency to distance his administration from the liberal agenda and defeat the Kennedy challenge. It would seem then that secular changes in the organization of American government have cut in two directions at once. They serve both to delimit the possibilities for a presidentially imposed reconstruction of American government and politics and to bolster the independence of those who are nominally affiliated with previously established commitments of ideology and interest.

Comparisons among presidents leading at similar moments in political time provide insight into the divergent experiences of more recent incumbents as well. Taking advantage of Carter's difficulties, Ronald Reagan reclaimed the leadership stance of the great repudiator. Like Jackson and Roosevelt, Reagan used his authority as an opposition leader standing against a discredited regime to reconstruct the terms and conditions of legitimate national government.

George H. W. Bush, Reagan's designated successor, offered to affirm and continue the "Reagan Revolution," but like orthodox innovators in other periods, his leadership authority was compromised by factional disputes that erupted within his own ranks over the true meaning of the faith. His son, George W. Bush, has also styled himself as an orthodox innovator, and he seems determined to avoid his father's missteps by following through on that leadership stance more conscientiously. His agenda of "compassionate conservatism" seeks not only to revive and extend the commitments of the Reagan Revolution—tax cuts, missile defense, regulatory relief, pro-life family values—but also to embellish them with attractive new initiatives in education, health care, and Social Security that will broaden the regime's appeal and demonstrate the enduring vitality of orthodoxy as a source of new solutions to the problems of the day. The outstanding question is whether W's keen sensitivity to his father's political fate will help him avoid a similar defeat in his own bid for reelection. Before September 11, 2001, W's handling of issues from tax cuts to stem-cell research suggested a rather typical episode in orthodox innovation, complete with all the characteristic problems. What is interesting is that after the terrorist attacks, the president did not abandon orthodox innovation but used his enhanced authority to advance the most orthodox aspect of his initial program, the combination of tax cuts and defense spending. What remains to be seen is whether the new authority that stems from the president's constitutional position as commander in chief will translate over the long haul into new authority for his original political project and overcome the difficulties that traditionally adhere to it.

Even Bill Clinton's leadership, the volatility of which is hard to square with any of the three leadership patterns reviewed in this chapter, becomes more understandable when placed in political time. Taking advantage both of Reagan's repudiation of liberalism and the factional divisions among conservatives that opened up under his predecessor, Clinton gained a measure of the political independence that Carter could only aspire to. He fashioned himself a "New Democrat," forthrightly renounced both Reaganism and liberalism, and proclaimed a "third-way" hybrid that threatened to displace orthodoxy in all its forms. His efforts recall the experiences of other wild cards in presidential history, most especially Andrew Johnson and Richard Nixon, whose vigorous assertions of political independence also became mired in impeachment proceedings.

It is easy to overstate historical parallels, and there can be no doubt that advent of the "modern presidency," with its vast expansion of institutional resources and its advances in political technology, has had an important effect of its own on the politics of leadership. But as we reflect the experiences of our most recent incumbents back through political time, we see that these changes have yet to displace patterns that have been evident from the start. These patterns seem to set the range of possibilities for each president. They indicate the potential reach and practical limits of the presidency as a position of national political leadership. They are, in the final analysis, a commentary on the Constitution itself.

Notes

1. Other works investigating distinctly political patterns in presidential history include Erwin C. Hargrove and Michael Nelson, *Presidents, Politics, and Policy* (New York: Knopf, 1984); and James David Barber, *The Pulse of Politics: Electing Presidents in the Media Age* (New York: W. W. Norton, 1980).

2. Thomas A. Bailey, *Presidential Greatness: The Image and the Man from George Washington to the Present* (New York: Appleton-Century-Croft, 1966), 23–24. Bailey critically discusses the ratings by professional historians. The important point, however, is that the presidents who rated highest in the Schlesinger surveys of 1948 and 1962 all shared this peculiarly structured leadership situation at the outset of their terms.

3. Robert Remini, *Andrew Jackson and the Course of American Freedom, 1822–1832*, vol. 2 (New York: Harper and Row, 1981), 12–38, 74–142.

4. Quoted in Frank Freidel, *FDR and the South* (Baton Rouge: Louisiana State University Press, 1965), 42.

5. Remini, *Andrew Jackson*, 152–202, 248–256.

6. The famous veto of the Maysfield Road, for example, was notable for its limited implications. It challenged federal support for *intrastate* projects and was specifically selected as an example for its location in Henry Clay's Kentucky. On Jackson's objectives in civil service reform, see Albert Somit, "Andrew Jackson as an Administrative Reformer," *Tennessee Historical Quarterly* 13 (September 1954): 204–223; and Eric McKinley Erickson, "The Federal Civil Service under President Jackson," *Mississippi Valley Historical Review* 13 (March 1927): 517–540. Also significant in this regard is Richard G. Miller, "The Tariff of 1832: The Issue that Failed," *The Filson Club History Quarterly* 49 (July 1975): 221–230.

7. The analysis in this and the following paragraphs draws on the following works: Remini, *Andrew Jackson*; Robert Remini, *Andrew Jackson and the Bank War: A Study in the Growth of Presidential Power* (New York: W. W. Norton, 1967); Marquis James, *Andrew Jackson: Portrait of a President* (New York: Grosset and Dunlap, 1937), 283–303, 350–385; and Arthur M. Schlesinger Jr., *The Age of Jackson* (Boston: Little, Brown, 1945), 74–131.

8. Charles Sellers Jr., "Who Were the Southern Whigs?" *American Historical Review* 49 (January 1954): 335–346.

9. Harry Scheiber, "The Pet Banks in Jacksonian Politics and Finance, 1833–1841," *Journal of Economic History* 23 (June 1963): 196–214; Frank Otto Gatell, "Spoils of the Bank War: Political Bias in the Selection of Pet Banks," *American Historical Review* 70

(October 1964): 35–58; and Frank Otto Gatell, "Secretary Taney and the Baltimore Pets: A Study in Banking and Politics," *Business History Review* 39 (summer 1965): 205–227.

10. Quoted in James MacGregor Burns, *Roosevelt: The Lion and the Fox* (New York: Harcourt, Brace and World, 1956), 208.

11. The analysis in this and the following paragraphs draws on Burns, *Roosevelt,* and Freidel, *FDR and the South.*

12. Burns, *Roosevelt,* 223–241.

13. Freidel, *FDR and the South.*

14. Richard Polenberg, *Reorganizing Roosevelt's Government: The Controversy over Executive Reorganization, 1936–1939* (Cambridge: Harvard University Press, 1966).

15. The analysis in this and the following paragraphs draws on the following works: Charles Sellers, *James K. Polk: Continentalist, 1843–1846* (Princeton: Princeton University Press, 1966); John Schroeder, *Mr. Polk's War: American Opposition and Dissent, 1846–1848* (Madison: University of Wisconsin Press, 1973); Norman A. Graebner, "James Polk," in *America's Ten Greatest Presidents,* ed. Morton Borden (Chicago: Rand McNally, 1961), 113–138; and Charles McCoy, *Polk and the Presidency* (Austin: University of Texas Press, 1960).

16. Sellers, *James K. Polk,* 50.

17. Ibid., 113–114, 123.

18. Ibid., 282–283.

19. Ibid., 162–164; Joseph G. Raybeck, "Martin Van Buren's Break with James K. Polk: The Record," *New York History* 36 (January 1955): 51–62; and Norman A. Graebner, "James K. Polk: A Study in Federal Patronage," *Mississippi Valley Historical Review* 38 (March 1952): 613–632.

20. Sellers, *James K. Polk,* 483.

21. Frederick J. Blue, *The Free Soilers: Third Party Politics, 1848–54* (Urbana: University of Illinois Press, 1973), 16–80; and John Mayfield, *Rehearsal for Republicanism: Free Soil and the Politics of Antislavery* (Port Washington, N.Y.: Kennikat Press, 1980), 80–125.

22. McCoy, *Polk and the Presidency,* 197–198, 203–204.

23. Arthur M. Schlesinger Jr., *A Thousand Days: John F. Kennedy in the White House* (Boston: Houghton Mifflin, 1965), 675–676.

24. Carroll Kilpatrick, "The Kennedy Style and Congress," *The Virginia Quarterly Review* 39 (Winter 1963): 1–11; and Henry Fairlie, *The Kennedy Promise: The Politics of Expectation* (New York: Doubleday, 1973), esp. 235–263.

25. Freidel, *FDR and the South,* 71–102.

26. Herbert S. Parmet, *The Democrats: The Years after FDR* (New York: Oxford University Press, 1976), 80–82.

27. The analysis in this and the following paragraphs draws on material presented in the following works: Carl M. Bauer, *John F. Kennedy and the Second Reconstruction* (New York: Columbia University Press, 1977); Schlesinger, *Thousand Days;* Parmet, *Democrats,* 193–247; Bruce Miroff, *Pragmatic Illusions: The Presidential Politics of John F. Kennedy* (New York: David McKay, 1976), 223–270; and Fairlie, *Kennedy Promise,* 235–263.

28. Bauer, *John F. Kennedy,* 30–38; and Schlesinger, *Thousand Days,* 47–52.

29. Bauer, *John F. Kennedy,* 61–88; and Schlesinger, *Thousand Days,* 30–31.

30. Parmet, *Democrats,* 211; and Bauer, *John F. Kennedy,* 128–130.

31. Holman Hamilton, *Prologue to Conflict: The Crisis and Compromise of 1850* (Lexington: University of Kentucky Press, 1964), esp. 156–164.

32. Roy F. Nichols, *The Democratic Machine,* 1850–54 (New York: AMS Press, 1967).

33. Parmet, *Democrats*, 220–228.

34. The analysis in this and the following paragraphs draws on Roy F. Nichols, *Franklin Pierce: Young Hickory of Granite Hills* (Philadelphia: University of Pennsylvania Press, 1969); and Nichols, *Democratic Machine*, 147–226.

35. Nichols, *Franklin Pierce*, 292–293, 308–310; and Nichols, *Democratic Machine*, 224.

36. Roy F. Nichols, "The Kansas-Nebraska Act: A Century of Historiography," *Mississippi Valley Historical Review* 43 (September 1956): 187–212; and Nichols, *Franklin Pierce*, 292–324, 333–338.

37. Nichols, *Franklin Pierce*, 360–365, 425–434.

38. Jack Knott and Aaron Wildavsky, "Skepticism and Dogma in the White House: Jimmy Carter's Theory of Governing," *Wilson Quarterly* 1 (winter 1977): 49–68; and James Fallows, "The Passionless Presidency: The Trouble with Jimmy Carter's Administration," *Atlantic Monthly*, May 1979, 33–58, and June 1979, 75–81.

39. The analysis in this and the following paragraphs draws on the following works: Robert Shogun, *Promises to Keep: Carter's First Hundred Days* (New York: Thomas Y. Crowell, 1977); Haynes Johnson, *In the Absence of Power: Governing America* (New York: Viking, 1980); Robert Shogun, *None of the Above: Why Presidents Fail and What Can Be Done about It* (New York: New American Library, 1982), 177–250; Thomas Ferguson and Joel Rogers, eds., *The Hidden Election: Politics and Economics in the 1980 Presidential Campaign* (New York: Pantheon, 1981), 200–230; and Alan Wolfe, *America's Impasse: The Rise and Fall of the Politics of Growth* (New York: Pantheon, 1981), 200–230.

40. Shogun, *None of the Above*, 220.

41. Johnson, *Absence of Power*, 233–245.

42. *New York Times*, July 16, 1979, 1, 10.

43. See Stephen Skowronek, *The Politics Presidents Make: Leadership from John Adams to Bill Clinton* (Cambridge: Harvard University Press, Belknap Press, 1997).

6 Presidential Competence

Paul J. Quirk

The skills of political leadership that a president requires are a recurring theme of modern presidential scholarship. Most students of political skill have dwelt on leadership technique: bargaining, persuasion, rhetoric, management, and the like. Paul J. Quirk approaches the subject differently, asking "What must presidents know?" Quirk rejects as impossibly demanding the widely advocated "self-reliant" model that is patterned after Franklin D. Roosevelt. Although he is even less approving of the "minimalist" or "chairman of the board" model that Ronald Reagan adopted, Quirk notes that unusual circumstances allowed George W. Bush to pursue it with reasonable success during his first year in office. Quirk's own model calls for "strategic competence" of the kind practiced, at least part of the time, by Presidents Kennedy, Ford, George H. W. Bush, and Clinton, among others: presidents need not know everything. Mainly, they must know how to make good choices about what to know.

The presidency of George W. Bush calls attention to a simple yet rarely examined question about American government: What must the president know? To have a good chance to succeed politically and serve the country well, must presidents be highly knowledgeable on the issues and processes of government? Must they have long experience in national government or spend hours daily immersed in briefing papers? Or can they rely on other officials—especially the cabinet and White House staff—to provide the necessary expertise and information?

Bush, like his predecessor Ronald Reagan twenty years earlier, entered office notoriously lacking in specific information about the affairs of government.

This chapter is an extensively revised and elaborated version of "What Must a President Know?" by Paul J. Quirk in *Transaction/SOCIETY*, no. 23 (January/February 1983) © 1983 by Transaction Publishers. The author would like to acknowledge the following for their very helpful advice: Stella Herriges Quirk, Irving Louis Horowitz, A. James Reichley, Robert A. Katzmann, Martha Derthick, and Michael Nelson.

Critics ridiculed both presidents for their frequent misinformed comments and inability to speak about issues without a script. Most of the public did not mind. Reagan served two terms and left office a popular president, although his reputation eroded in succeeding years.[1] At the end of his first year in office, Bush enjoyed record public-approval ratings, mostly the result of his conduct of the war on terrorism. What difference does a president's knowledge make? Considering the enormous complexity of modern government, is adequate presidential knowledge even feasible?

Although the requirements for a competent presidency cannot be reduced to a formula, they should be possible to define in general terms. Drawing primarily from the experiences of presidents from Franklin D. Roosevelt to Reagan, I present three distinct and competing conceptions of the president's personal tasks and expertise—that is, of presidential competence. I criticize two of them—one an orthodox approach of long standing, the other originally associated with Reagan. I then offer a third model, based on a notion of "strategic competence," and discuss the requirements of that model in three major areas of presidential activity. In the last section, I test the relevance of the analysis by assessing the performance of the three presidents who followed Reagan: George H. W. Bush, Bill Clinton, and George W. Bush.

The Self-Reliant Presidency

Most commentary on the presidency assumes a concept of the president's personal tasks that borders on the heroic. Stated simply, the president must strive to be self-reliant and personally bear a large share of the burden of governing. And he must therefore meet intellectual requirements that are correspondingly rigorous.

The classic argument for the self-reliant presidency is presented in Richard Neustadt's *Presidential Power*.[2] In arguing for an enlarged concept of the presidential role, Neustadt stressed that the president's political interests, and therefore his perspective on decisions, are unique. Only the president has political stakes that arguably correspond with the national interest. For no other government official is individual achievement so closely identified with the well-being of the entire nation. Thus a president's chances for success depend on what he can do for himself: his direct involvement in decisions, his personal reputation and skill, his control over subordinates.[3]

It is in this spirit that students of the presidency often hold up Franklin Roosevelt as the exemplary modern president—if not for his specific policies or administrative practices, at least for his personal orientation to the job. A perfect "active-positive" in James David Barber's typology of presidential personalities, Roosevelt made strenuous efforts to increase his control and to improve his grasp of issues and situations.[4] For example, he would set up duplicate channels within the government to provide him information and advice. When this did not seem enough, he looked outside the government for people who could offer additional perspectives.[5] The ideal president, in short, is one with a consuming passion for control, and thus for information.

This image of the president—as one who makes the major decisions himself, depends on others only in lesser matters, and firmly controls his subordinates—appeals to the general public, which seems to evaluate presidents partly by how well they live up to this image. But is the self-reliant presidency sensible, even as an ideal? Both experience and the elementary facts of contemporary government indicate strongly that it is not.

Even for Roosevelt, self-reliance carried certain costs. In an admiring description of Roosevelt's administrative practices, Arthur Schlesinger Jr. concedes that his methods hampered performance in some respects. Roosevelt's creation of unstructured, competitive relations among subordinates, a method he used for control, caused "confusion and exasperation on the operating level"; it was "nerve-wracking and often positively demoralizing." Because Roosevelt reserved so many decisions for himself, he could not make all of them promptly, and aides often had to contend with troublesome delays.[6] The overall effect of Roosevelt's self-reliant decision making on the design, operation, and success of New Deal programs is open to question. Indeed, the New Deal is revered mainly for its broad assertion of government responsibility for the nation's well-being, not for the effectiveness of its specific programs. Roosevelt took pride in an observer's estimate that for each decision made by Calvin Coolidge, he was making at least thirty-five. Perhaps some smaller ratio would have been better.

In later administrations the weaknesses of the self-reliant presidency have emerged more clearly. Presidents who aspired to self-reliance have ended up leaving serious responsibilities badly neglected. Lyndon B. Johnson, another president with prodigious energy and a need for control, gravitated naturally to the self-reliant approach.[7] Eventually, however, he directed his efforts narrowly and obsessively to the Vietnam War. Meeting daily with the officers in charge, Johnson directed the military strategy from the Oval Office, at times going into such detail as to select specific targets for bombing. Every other area of presidential concern he virtually set aside. Although such detailed involvement would have been unobjectionable had there been any cause to believe it would help to resolve the conflict, the reverse seems more likely. Guided by the president's civilian subordinates, the military officers themselves should have been able to decide matters of strategy at least as well as the president, probably better. Moreover, Johnson's direct operational control of military strategy may have impaired his ability to take a broader, "presidential" perspective. After all, doing a general's job, to some inevitable degree, means thinking like a general. Johnson illustrated a dangerous tendency for self-reliance to become an end in itself.

Jimmy Carter, although less driven than Johnson, preferred self-reliance as a matter of conviction. It led him toward a narrowness of a different kind. From the first month in office, Carter signaled his intention to be thoroughly involved, completely informed, and prompt. "Unless there's a holocaust," he told the staff, "I'll take care of everything the same day it comes in." He spent long hours daily poring over stacks of memoranda and took thick briefing books with him for weekends at Camp David. Initially, he even checked the arithmetic in budget documents. Later he complained mildly about the number of memoranda and their length, but he still made no genuine effort to curb the flow.[8] Carter's extreme attention to detail cannot have contributed more than very marginally to the quality of his administration's decisions. Yet it took his attention from other, more essential tasks. Carter was criticized as having failed to articulate the broad themes or ideals that would give his presidency a sense of purpose—a natural oversight for a president who was wallowing in detail. He certainly neglected the crucial task of nurturing constructive relationships with other leaders in Washington.[9]

The main defect of the self-reliant presidency, however, is none of these particular risks; rather, it is the blunt, physical impossibility of carrying it out. Perhaps Roosevelt, an extraordinary man who served when government was still relatively manageable, could achieve an approximation of the ideal. But the larger and more complex government has become, the more presidents have been forced to depend on the judgments of others. Today, any important policy question produces enough proposals, studies, and advocacy to keep a policymaker who sought to master it all fully occupied. In any remotely literal sense, therefore, presidential self-reliance is not so much inadvisable as inconceivable.

Even as an inspirational ideal (like perfect virtue), the self-reliant presidency is more misleading than helpful. It can lead to an obsessive narrowness, and it is too far removed from reality to offer any concrete guidance. Rather than such an ideal, presidents need a conception of what a competent, successful performance would really consist of—one that takes the nature of government and the limits of human ability as they exist.

The Minimalist Presidency

A second approach to presidential competence rejects the heroic demands of self-reliance altogether. In this approach, the president requires little or no understanding of specific issues and problems and instead can rely almost entirely on subordinates to resolve them. This "minimalist" approach has rarely if ever been advocated as an appropriate strategy for presidents in general. Nevertheless, it commands attention both because the Reagan administration explicitly relied on such an approach and because, in certain respects, George W. Bush has followed in Reagan's footsteps.

Minimalism does not imply a passive conception of the presidency as an institution, like that of some nineteenth-century presidents. Accepting the Whig theory of government, they believed that Congress, as the most representative branch, should lead the country, and they left it to Congress to shape and pass legislation without much presidential advice.[10] The Whig theory has been abandoned in the twentieth century, and minimalism, as here defined, is not an attempt to restore it. With the help of a large personal staff, the Office of Management and Budget (OMB), and other presidential agencies in the Executive Office of the President, a minimalist president can exercise his powers as expansively as any.

Nor does minimalism describe the "hidden-hand" leadership ascribed to Dwight D. Eisenhower in the notable reinterpretation of his presidency by Fred Greenstein.[11] Long viewed as a passive president, who reigned rather than ruled, Eisenhower has been thoroughly misinterpreted, according to Greenstein's provocative thesis. In truth, Eisenhower, seeing a political advantage, merely cultivated this image. He worked longer hours, gave closer attention to issues, and exercised more influence than the public was allowed to notice. The hidden-hand style, Greenstein argues, generally permitted Eisenhower to accomplish what he wanted, while insulating him from controversy. Eisenhower was not a minimalist, but a closet activist.

The first recent minimalist president was Ronald Reagan, whose administration often flatly rejected the self-reliant approach. President Reagan's role in decision making, his spokesmen said during the first year, would be that of a chairman of the board. He would personally establish the general policies and goals of his administration, select cabinet and other personnel who shared his commitments, then delegate broad authority to them so that they could work out the particulars.[12]

In part, the limited role for the president was clearly designed to accommodate Reagan's limitations—especially his disinclination to do much reading or sit through lengthy briefings—and to answer critics who questioned his capability to serve as president. By expounding a minimalist theory, the Reagan administration was able to defend the president's frequent lapses and inaccuracies in news conferences as harmless and irrelevant. It is a "fantasy of the press," said the communications director, David R. Gergen, that an occasional "blooper" in a news conference has any real importance.[13]

Nevertheless, the administration presented this minimalist model not merely as an ad hoc accommodation but as a sensible way in general for a president to operate. The model has at least one claim to be taken seriously: unlike self-reliance, it has the merit of being attainable. For several reasons, however, it has serious problems as general model. Nor was it necessarily satisfactory even in Reagan's case.

Chairman-of-the-board notions notwithstanding, a minimalist president and his administration are likely to have serious difficulties reaching decisions that serve the president's fundamental goals. Most obvious, the president's subordinates may have their own agendas. Senior administration officials have interests of their own. Unless the president is fairly attentive, he will have trouble knowing when an ostensibly loyal subordinate is mainly serving some other constituency. The strategy makes selection of genuinely responsive senior officials exceptionally critical.[14]

For one thing, a minimalist president—or rather, the sort of president who would adopt a minimalist approach—is likely to overestimate his or her capabilities. By neglecting the complexities of policy arguments over the course of a political career, one misses the opportunity to learn the importance of careful analysis. In politics, at least, few people place a high value on discourse that is more sophisticated than their own habitual mode of thought.

That President Reagan showed no particular humility about his ability to make policy judgments was most apparent in his decisions about budgets, taxes, and the federal deficit.[15] In late 1981 Reagan's principal economic policy makers—the OMB director, David A. Stockman; the Treasury secretary, Donald Regan; and the White House chief of staff, James Baker—recommended unanimously that the president propose a modest tax increase to keep the budget deficit to an acceptable level.

After the last holdout, Regan, came on board, the press began to treat the president's concurrence as a foregone conclusion. To the humiliation of his advisers, however, Reagan instead followed his own instinct not to retreat and rejected their recommendation. The resulting 1983 presidential budget was so far in deficit that it was dismissed out of hand even by the Republican Senate, and the president ended up accepting a package of "revenue enhancements" that Congress virtually forced on him. In 1983 and 1984 Reagan repeatedly rejected pleas for a deficit-reducing tax increase that were made by Stockman and Martin Feldstein, the administration's second chairman of the Council of Economic Advisers (CEA) and its most distinguished economist.

Moreover, even if a minimalist president is willing to delegate authority and accept advice, his aides and cabinet members may have difficulty making up for his limitations. As they compete for the president's favor, they tend to assume his likeness. That is, they take cues from his rhetoric and descend to his level of argument. Advocates then emerge for almost any policy he is inclined to support. Such imitation apparently produced the scandals in the Environmental Protection Agency (EPA) that embarrassed the Reagan administration during the first term and led to the removal of numerous high-level officials. These officials, including the administrator of the agency, Anne Gorsuch Burford, interpreted Reagan's sweeping antiregulatory rhetoric to mean that, requirements of the law notwithstanding, they should hardly regulate at all.

The effect of Reagan's relaxed approach to policy decisions on the quality of debate in his administration is illustrated by a White House meeting on the defense budget in September 1981, recounted in Stockman's revealing memoir.[16] The OMB was proposing a moderate reduction in the planned growth of defense spending—still giving the Pentagon an inflation-adjusted increase of 52 percent over five years and 92 percent of its original request. In a presentation that Stockman calls "a masterpiece of obfuscation," Secretary of Defense Caspar W. Weinberger compared American and Soviet capabilities as if the OMB were refusing to endorse any increase. Almost all of his comparisons, displayed in elaborate charts, concerned weapons categories that Stockman was not trying to cut. Weinberger stressed that the B-52 bomber was outdated, even though the OMB supported full funding for the B-1 and Stealth bombers that were planned to replace it; and he detailed the superiority of Warsaw Pact forces in numbers of divisions, even though the OMB had agreed to fund the full complement of sixteen active divisions the Pentagon wanted. (The secretary concluded all of this by showing a blown-up cartoon depicting the OMB budget as "a four-eyed wimp who looked like Woody Allen, carrying a tiny rifle.")

In the end, Weinberger got his way. Whatever the merits of the decision, a well-prepared, attentive president would have dismissed such a presentation as largely irrelevant to what was actually in dispute. A defense secretary who anticipated such a presidential response would have felt compelled to address the real issues.

Finally, if a president openly delegates significant decisions and pliantly accepts subordinates' advice, the press is likely to shame him into taking charge. Because the public likes presidents who seem in command, it makes good copy for a reporter to suggest that aides are assuming the president's job—even though relying heavily on them may be a sensible adaptation to the president's personal limitations. The press sometimes challenged Reagan to demonstrate his involvement in decisions, and this may have led him to make more decisions in certain areas than he would have otherwise. During summit meetings with the Soviet president Mikhail Gorbachev, Reagan took his chances negotiating with the Soviet leader one-to-one on arms control, a subject of daunting complexity for any president.[17]

Naturally, it is possible for a minimalist president to resist the temptations and pressures to overstep his capability and impose his own ill-informed judgments in decision making and leave such matters to experts. But it probably requires a president with an unusual self-effacing personality and a willingness to bear the questioning about who is "the real president." Such a strategy would also make the president exceptionally dependent on his senior aides and cabinet members, who would have extraordinary opportunity to shape the president's goals and agenda according to their own preferences.

Neither self-reliance nor minimalism therefore offers a plausible general route to presidential competence. The question is whether there is another possible model that corrects the defects of both—making feasible demands on the president yet allowing for competent performance.

Strategic Competence

The third conception of presidential competence, set forth in the rest of this chapter, lies between the two extremes of minimalism and self-reliance. But it does not represent just a vague compromise between them. It is based on a notion of *strategic competence,* and derives definition from that notion.

Nor is the idea merely that presidents need to be competent in the choice of strategies, a truthful observation but hardly a useful one. Strategic competence refers to the idea that, in order to achieve competence, presidents must have a workable strategy for competence. This strategy, it seems, must take into account three basic elements of the president's situation.

1. The president's time, energy, and talent, and thus his capacity for direct, personal competence, must be regarded as a scarce resource. Choices must be made concerning what things a president will attempt to know.

2. Depending on the task (for example, deciding issues, promoting policies), the president's ability to substitute the judgment and expertise of others for his own and still get satisfactory results varies considerably. Delegation works better for some tasks than for others.

3. The success of such substitutions will depend on a relatively small number of presidential actions and decisions concerning the selection of subordinates, the general instructions they are given, and the president's limited interactions with them. How well delegation works depends on how it is done.

Achieving competent performance, then, can be viewed as a problem of allocating resources. The president's personal abilities and time to use them are the scarce resources. For each task, the possibilities and requirements for effective delegation determine how much of these resources should be used and how they should be employed.

In the rest of this chapter, I will work out the implications of strategic competence in three major areas of presidential activity: policy decisions, policy processes, and policy promotion.[18] The test of the model is twofold. For each area of presidential activity, does it provide adequately for competent performance? Taken as a whole, does it call for a level of expertise and attentiveness that an average president can be expected to meet?

Policy Decisions

When it comes to substantive issues, vast presidential ignorance is simply inevitable. No one understands more than a few significant issues very well. Fortunately, presidents can get by—controlling subordinates reasonably well and minimizing the risk of policy disasters—on far less than a thorough mastery. Some prior preparation, however, is required.

As a matter of course, each president has a general outlook or philosophy of government. His principal aides must share that outlook or represent a variety of views roughly centered on it. The main requirement beyond this is for the president to be familiar enough with the substantive policy debates in each major area to recognize the signs of responsible argument. This familiarity includes having enough exposure to the work of policy analysts and experts in each area to know, if only in general terms, how they reach conclusions and the contribution they make. The point is not that the president will then be able to work through all the pertinent materials on an issue, evaluate them properly, and reach a sound, independent conclusion—that is ruled out if only for lack of time. As he evaluates policy advice, however, the president will at least be able to tell which of his subordinates are making sense. Whatever the subject at hand, the president will be able to judge whether an advocate is bringing to bear the right kinds of evidence, considerations, and arguments, and citing appropriate authorities.

One can observe the importance of this ability by comparing two, in some respects similar, episodes. Both John F. Kennedy in 1963 and Ronald Reagan in 1981 proposed large, controversial reductions of the individual income tax, each in some sense unorthodox. But in the role played by respectable economic opinion, the two cases could not be more different.

Kennedy brought to bear the prescriptions of Keynesian economics, which by then had been the dominant school of professional economic thought for nearly three decades. The Kennedy administration took office when the economy was in a deep recession. From the beginning, therefore, Walter Heller, a leading academic economist and Kennedy's CEA chairman, sought tax reductions to promote economic growth—the appropriate Keynesian response even though it might increase the federal deficit. Already aware of the rationale for stimulation, Kennedy did not require persuasion on the economic merits, but he did have political reservations. "I understand the case for a tax cut," he told Heller, "but it doesn't fit my call for sacrifice." Nor did it fit the economic views of Congress or the general public—both of which remained faithful on the whole to the traditional belief in an annually balanced budget. But the CEA continued lobbying, and Kennedy—first partially, later completely—went along. Finally, in 1963 Kennedy proposed to reduce income taxes substantially.

The novelty of this proposal, with the economy already recovering and the budget in deficit, alarmed traditionalists. "What can those people in Washington be thinking about?" asked former president Eisenhower in a magazine article. "Why would they deliberately do this to our country?" Congress, which also had doubts, moved slowly but eventually passed the tax cut in 1964. The Keynesian deficits proved right for the time: the tax cut stimulated enough economic activity that revenues, instead of declining, actually increased.[19]

Aside from being a tax cut and being radical, Reagan's proposal bore little resemblance to Kennedy's. Pushed through Congress in the summer of 1981, the

Kemp-Roth tax bill (named for its congressional sponsors Rep. Jack F. Kemp and Sen. William V. Roth Jr.) represented an explicit break with mainstream economic thinking, both liberal and conservative. The bill embodied the ideas of a small fringe group of economists whose views the conservative Republican economist Herbert Stein dismissed in the *Wall Street Journal* as "punk supply-side economics." In selling the bill to Congress, which was submissive in the aftermath of the Reagan election landslide, the administration made bold, unsupported claims. Despite tax-rate reductions of 25 percent in a three-year period, it promised that the bill would so stimulate investment that revenues would increase and deficits decline. This resembled the claims for the Kennedy bill except that, under the prevailing conditions, nothing in conventional economic models or empirical estimates remotely justified the optimistic predictions. The Senate Republican leader Howard Baker, a reluctant supporter, termed the bill "a riverboat gamble." The gamble did not pay off. Within a year, policymakers were contemplating deficits in the $200 billion range—twice what they had considered intolerable a short time earlier and enough, nearly all agreed, to damage the economy severely.[20]

A president with some measure of sophistication about economic policy would have dismissed as economic demagoguery the extraordinary claims made for the Kemp-Roth bill.[21] He would have become aware of several things: that mainstream economists have worked out methods for estimating the effects of tax policies; that these estimates are imprecise and subject to a certain range of disagreement; but that, nevertheless, they are the best estimates anybody has. President Reagan undoubtedly knew (it would have been impossible not to) that most economists did not endorse Kemp-Roth. But it seems he had never paid enough attention to economic debate to recognize an important distinction between ideological faith and empirical measurement.

None of this is to suggest that presidents should set aside their ideologies and simply defer to experts, conceived somehow as ideologically neutral. Gerald Ford, another conservative president, had an abiding commitment to the free market and assembled a cabinet and staff largely from individuals who shared his perspective. Yet the Ford administration also insisted that sound professional analysis underlie its decisions and took pains to consider a variety of views. Ford's CEA chairman, Alan Greenspan, although a devout conservative, encouraged the president to meet with diverse groups of outside economists (including former advisers in liberal Democratic administrations). He relied on conventional economic models and forecasting methods to fashion his own advice to the president. None of this prevented Ford's conservatism from shaping the policies of his administration, which held down government spending, stressed controlling inflation more than reducing unemployment, and started the process of deregulation.[22]

In much the same way, Reagan achieved conservative goals (cutting tax rates and reducing government distortion of economic decisions)—along with some liberal ones (tax relief for low-income people)—in the historic Tax Reform Act of 1986. The president's proposal was based on a massive study of the tax system by economists and tax specialists in the Treasury Department, which had advocated such reforms since the 1960s, and it embodied a consensual judgment among experts both inside and outside of government that the proliferation of credits, exemptions, and deductions in the federal tax code was harmful to the economy.[23]

Adequate policy expertise cannot be acquired in a hurry. A president needs to have been over the years the kind of politician who participates responsibly in decision making and debate and who does his homework. This means occasionally taking the time to read some of the advocacy documents (such as hearing testimony and committee reports) that are prepared especially for politicians and their staff. Such documents respect the limits of a politician's sophistication and tolerance for detail and yet provide a fairly rigorous education.

If properly prepared, a president need not spend long hours immersed in memoranda, the way Jimmy Carter did. If, after a thorough briefing on a decision of ordinary importance, the president still does not see which course he prefers, he is probably just as well off delegating the decision or taking a vote of his advisers. Other tasks will make more of a contribution to his success than further reading or discussion on a decision that is a close call anyway.

Policy Processes

In addition to policy issues, presidents must be competent in the processes of policymaking.[24] Most presidential policy decisions are based on advice from several agencies or advisory groups in the executive branch, each with different responsibilities and points of view. To be useful to the president, all the advice must be brought together in a timely, intelligible way, with proper attention to all the significant viewpoints and considerations. Unfortunately, complex organizational and group decision processes like these have a notorious capacity to produce self-defeating or morally unacceptable results. The specific ways in which they go awry are numerous, but in general terms there are three major threats: intelligence failures, in which critical information is filtered out at lower organizational levels (sometimes because subordinates think the president would be upset by or disagree with it);[25] groupthink, in which a decision-making group commits itself to a course of action prematurely and adheres to it because of social pressures to conform;[26] and noncoordination, which may occur in formulating advice, in handling interdependent issues, or in carrying out decisions.[27]

Many of the frustrations of the Carter administration resulted from its failure to organize decision processes with sufficient care and skill. Carter's original energy proposals, which affected numerous federal programs, were formulated by a single drafting group under the direction of Energy Secretary James Schlesinger. The group worked in secrecy and isolation, as well as under severe time pressure, which the president had imposed. The resulting proposals had serious flaws that, combined with resentment of the secrecy, led to a fiasco in Congress. Such problems were typical. The Carter administration's system of interagency task forces for domestic policymaking generally was chaotic and not well controlled by the White House.[28] Moreover, the White House itself was weakly coordinated. Not only did Carter's White House have fewer high-level coordinators than Reagan's, but, as John Kessel's comparative study has shown, those it did have were less active in communicating with the rest of the staff.[29]

In foreign policy, the major criticisms of the Carter administration concerned its propensity for vacillation and incoherence. Those tendencies resulted largely from its failure to manage the conflict between the national security adviser, Zbigniew Brzezinski, and Secretary of State Cyrus R. Vance. Despite their different approaches to foreign policy, neither their respective roles nor the administration's foreign policy doctrines were ever adequately clear. One crucial issue was whether the American stance toward negotiating with the Soviets on strategic arms would be linked with Soviet activities in the Horn of Africa (as Brzezinski wanted) or decided solely for its direct effects on American strategic interests (the preference of Vance). Instead of being reconciled, both policies were stated in public, each by the official who favored it, which cast doubt on America's ability to act consistently on either of them.[30] In part this problem resulted from Carter's personal unwillingness to discipline subordinates—to insist, for example, that Brzezinski abide by the more modest role that in theory had been assigned to him.

In short, serious presidential failures will often result not from individual ignorance—the president's or his advisers'—but from an administration's collective failure to maintain reliable processes for decision. But what must a president know to avoid this danger, and how can he learn it?

The effort to design the best possible organization for presidential coordination of the executive branch is exceedingly complex and uncertain—fundamentally a matter of hard trade-offs and guesses, not elegant solutions. Rather than adopt any one organization plan or carefully study the debates about them, a president needs to have a high degree of generalized process sensibility. He should be generally conversant with the risks and impediments to effective decision making and strongly committed to avoiding them. He should recognize the potentially decisive effects of structure, procedures, and leadership methods. And he should be prepared to assign these matters a high priority. In short, the president should see organization and procedure as matters both difficult and vital.

The main operational requirements are straightforward. One or more of the president's top-level staff should be a process specialist—someone with experience managing large organizations, ideally the White House, and whose role is defined primarily as a manager and guardian of the decision process, not as an adviser on politics and policy.[31] Certainly, one such person is needed in the position of White House chief of staff; others, perhaps much lower in rank, are needed to manage each major area of policy. A suitable person is one who is sophisticated about the problems of organization design and the subtleties of human relationships—in addition to just being orderly. The president should invest such a person with the support and authority needed to impose a decision-making structure and help him or her insist on adherence to it. Because any organizational arrangement will have weaknesses, some of them unexpected, the president and other senior officials must give the decision-making process continual attention—monitoring its performance and making adjustments.

Finally, if any of this is to work, the president also must be willing to discipline his own manner of participation. A well-managed, reliable decision-making process sometimes requires the president to perform, so to speak, unnatural acts. In the heat of debate about a major decision, taking the trouble to enforce general plans about structures and roles does not come naturally. Senior officials inevitably will try to bypass established procedures—asking for more control of a certain issue or ignoring channels to give the president direct advice. To enforce the procedures appears to distract from urgent decisions. In any case, the president's temptation is to react according to the substantive outcome he thinks he prefers: if an official who is supposed to be a neutral coordinator has a viewpoint the president likes, let her be heard; if an agency will make trouble over a decision that seems inevitable, let it stay out of it. Presidents are also tempted to attend primarily to those issues that most interest them, that they understand best, or that they see as promising satisfying results—all of which may fail to reflect their relative importance.

On important decisions that require intensive discussion—decisions in major foreign policy crises, for example—the requirements are even more unnatural. To avoid serious mistakes, it is crucial not to suppress disagreement or close off debate prematurely. Thus, it is important for the president to assume a neutral stance until the time comes to decide. According to psychologist Irving Janis's study of the Kennedy administration's disastrous decision to invade the Bay of Pigs, the president unwittingly inhibited debate just by his tone and manner of asking questions, which made it obvious that he believed, or wanted to believe, the invasion would work.[32] The president must restrain tendencies that are perfectly normal: to form opinions, perhaps optimistic ones, before all the evidence is in, and then want others to relieve his anxiety by agreeing. He must have a strong process sensibility if only because, without it, he will lack the motivation to do his own part.

The performance of Reagan and his aides in organization and policy management was mixed. In establishing effective advisory systems, especially at the beginning of the administration, they did well. The administration's principal device for making policy decisions, a system of "cabinet councils," was planned and run largely by Chief of Staff James Baker, who had a knack for organization and previous experience in the Ford administration.[33] Each cabinet council was a subcommittee of the full cabinet, staffed by the White House and chaired by a cabinet member or sometimes the president. The system generally worked well in blending departmental and White House perspectives and reaching decisions in a timely manner, and it kept cabinet members attuned to the president's goals. Inevitably, adjustments were made with the passage of time. The White House Legislative Strategy Group ended up making many of the decisions. Among the cabinet councils, the one assigned to coordinate economic policy, chaired by Treasury Secretary Regan, assumed a broad jurisdiction. To a degree, Reagan played his part in making these arrangements work. He enforced roles—removing a secretary of state, Alexander Haig, who was prone to exceed the limits of his charter—and invested the chief of staff with the authority to run an orderly process.

Nevertheless, the Reagan administration often failed to make decisions through a reasonably sound, deliberate process. One difficulty was that some of the officials Reagan selected to manage decision making lacked the appropriate skills or disposition for the task. In 1985 he allowed an exhausted Baker and an ambitious Regan to switch jobs. Although Regan by then had plenty of experience, he was less suited than Baker to the coordinating role of a chief of staff, and he soon came under attack for surrounding himself with weak subordinates and seeking to dominate the decision process. Until the appointment of Frank D. Carlucci in December 1986, the administration went through a series of four undistinguished national security advisers—one of them, William P. Clark, a long-time associate of Reagan's with minimal experience in foreign policy.

On many occasions, an even more important source of difficulty was the conduct of the president himself. Instead of exercising self-restraint and fostering discussion, Reagan gave his impulses free rein. He ignored bad news and reacted angrily to unwelcome advice.[34] His role in decisions was unpredictable. Reagan's announcement in March 1983 of the effort to develop a "Star Wars" missile defense system was made, as John Steinbrunner says, "without prior staff work or technical definition . . . [and] rather astonished professional security bureaucracies throughout the world."[35] During the 1986 summit meeting in Reykjavçik, Iceland, Reagan again acted without prior staff work as he tentatively accepted a surprise Soviet proposal to do away with long-range nuclear weapons—a Utopian notion that ignored the vast superiority of Soviet conventional forces and was soon disavowed by the administration.

Finally, a lack of concern for the integrity of the decision process figured prominently in the Iran-contra scandal that emerged in late 1986, a disaster for U.S. foreign policy and the worst political crisis of the Reagan presidency. The secret arms sales to Iran were vehemently opposed by Secretary of State George P. Shultz and Defense Secretary Weinberger, who wrote on his copy of the White House memorandum proposing the plan that it was "almost too absurd for comment." To get around their resistance, the White House largely excluded the two officials from further discussions and carried out the sales, in some degree, without their knowledge. Moreover, to escape the normal congressional oversight of covert activities, the transfers were handled directly by the staff of the National Security Council, theoretically an advisory unit, instead of the Defense Department (DOD) or the Central Intelligence Agency (CIA). In short, the White House deprived itself of the advice of the two principal cabinet members in foreign policy, the congressional leadership on intelligence matters, and the operational staff of DOD and the CIA—any of whom would have been likely to point out, aside from other serious objections, that the weapons transfers almost inevitably would become public.

Good policy decisions, carefully made, are not enough. Presidents also need competence in policy promotion—the ability to get things done in Washington and especially in Congress.[36] For no other major presidential task, it seems, is the necessary knowledge any more complicated or esoteric. Nevertheless, it is also a task in which delegation can largely substitute for the president's own judgment and thus one in which strategic competence places a modest burden on the president.

To promote his policies effectively, a president must make good decisions on complex, highly uncertain problems of strategy and tactics. Which presidential policy goals are politically feasible and which must be deferred? With which groups or congressional leaders should coalitions be formed? When resistance is met, should the president stand firm, perhaps taking the issue to the public, or should he compromise? In all these matters what is the proper timing? Such decisions call for a form of political expertise that has several related elements (all of them different from those involved in winning elections): a solid knowledge of the main coalitions, influence relationships, and rivalries among groups and individuals in Washington; personal acquaintance with a considerable number of important or well-informed individuals; and a fine-grained, practical understanding of how the political institutions work. Clearly, this expertise can be acquired only through substantial and recent experience in Washington. Its lack, however, need not pose much difficulty. Like any technical skill, which in a sense it is, the necessary expertise can easily be hired; the president must only see his need for it.

Because the government has many jobs that require political skill, people with the requisite experience abound. Many of them (to state the matter politely) would be willing to serve in the White House, and by just asking around a president can get readings on their effectiveness. Most important, having hired experienced Washington operatives, a president can delegate to them the critical judgments about feasibility, strategy, and political technique. It is not that such judgments are clear-cut, but, unlike questions of policy, in these matters the boundary between the realm of expertise and that of values and ideology is easy to discern. Political strategy, in the narrow sense of how to realize given policy objectives to the greatest possible extent, is ideologically neutral. It is even nonpartisan: Republican and Democratic presidents attempt to influence Congress in much the same way.[37] In any case, a political expert's performance in the White House can be measured primarily by short-term results, that is, by how much the administration's policy goals are actually being achieved.

The value and the necessity of delegating policy promotion can be seen in a comparison of Carter and Reagan—two presidents who had no prior Washington experience. If there was a single, root cause of the Carter administration's failure (underlying even its mismanagement of decision making), it was its refusal to recruit people with successful experience in Washington politics for top advisory and political jobs in the White House.

One of the more unfortunate choices was that of Frank Moore to direct legislative liaison. Although he had held the same job in Georgia when Carter was governor, Moore had no experience in Washington and came to be regarded in Congress as out of his depth. Among Moore's initial staff, which consisted mostly of Georgians, two of the five professionals had worked neither in Congress nor as lobbyists. In organizing them, Moore chose a plan that had been opposed by the former Democratic liaison officials who had been asked for advice. Instead of using the conventional division by chambers and major congressional groups, Moore assigned each lobbyist to specialize in an area of policy. This kept them from developing the stable relationships with individual members of Congress that would enhance trust, and it ignored the straightforward consideration that not all the issues in which the lobbyists specialized would be actively considered at the same time.[38] The Carter administration's reputed incompetence in dealing with Congress might have been predicted: the best of the many Georgians on the Carter staff were able and effective, but others were not, and collectively they lacked the local knowledge to operate well in Washington.[39]

After this widely condemned failure of his immediate predecessor, it is not surprising that President Reagan did not make the same mistake. But it is still impressive how thoroughly he applied the lesson, even setting aside sectarian considerations for some of the top White House positions. James Baker, who was mainly responsible for political operations during the first term, had not only been a Ford administration appointee and campaign manager for George Bush but was also considered too moderate for a high-level position by many of Reagan's conservative supporters. The congressional liaison director, Max Friedersdorf, was a mainstream Republican who had worked on congressional relations for Nixon and Ford.[40] In short, the political strategy by which the "Reagan revolution" was pushed through Congress in 1981 was devised and executed by hired hands who were latecomers, at most, to Reaganism. Although there was some change in personnel in subsequent years, including the job switch by Baker and Regan, the organization and management of this function was essentially stable.[41]

Although the task of formulating strategy for policy promotion can be delegated, much of the hard work cannot. Nothing can draw attention to a proposal and build public support like a well-presented speech by the president. Furthermore, there are always certain votes available in Congress if the president makes the necessary phone calls or meets with the right members. The latter task is often tedious, however, if not somewhat degrading—pleading for support, repeating the same pitch over and over, and promising favors to some while evading requests from others. Presidents therefore often neglect this duty, a source of frustration for their staffs. Carter "went all over the country for two years asking everybody he saw to vote for him," his press secretary complained, "but he doesn't like to call up a Congressman and ask for his support on a bill."[42] Reagan, in contrast, spared no personal effort to pass his program. During the debate on funding for the MX missile in 1985, he had face-to-face meetings with more than two hundred members of Congress and followed up with dozens of phone calls. When House Republicans felt they were being ignored in negotiations on tax reform, he went to Capitol Hill to make amends. In the end, a president's effectiveness in lobbying and making speeches depends very much on his basic skills in persuasive communication. A lack of such skills cannot be made up by presidential aides, nor can it be overcome to any great extent by additional learning.

The Possibility of Competence

The presidency is not an impossible job. The requirements for personal knowledge, attention, and expertise on the president's part seem wholly manageable—but only if the president has a strategy for competence that puts his own, inherently limited capabilities to use where and how they are most needed.

With regard to the substance of *policy decisions,* it is enough if the president over the years has given reasonably serious attention to the major national issues and thus is able to recognize the elements of responsible debate. Waking before sunrise to read stacks of policy memoranda is neither necessary nor especially productive.

To maintain an effective *policy process,* the president mainly needs to have a strong process sensibility, that is, a clear sense of the need for careful and self-conscious management of decision making and a willingness to discipline himself as he participates in it. He need not claim any facility in drawing the boxes and arrows of organization charts himself. Although this substantive and procedural competence will not ensure that the president always makes the right decision—the one he would make with perfect understanding of the issues—it will minimize the likelihood of decisions that are intolerably far off the mark.

Finally, and easiest of all, the president must know enough to avail himself of the assistance of persons experienced in *policy promotion* in the political environment of Washington, and especially in dealing with Congress—whether they have been longtime supporters or not. Then he must respect their advice and do the work they ask of him.

Three Cases: George H. W. Bush, Bill Clinton, and George W. Bush

The requirements for presidential competence help to account for some of the successes and failures of the three most recent presidents. Both the elder Bush and Bill Clinton exhibited strengths as well as significant deficiencies with respect to strategic competence. What is perhaps most interesting, however, is that the younger Bush has embarked on a new experiment with the strategy of minimalism.

George H. W. Bush

The presidency of the elder George Bush is typically counted a failure, mostly because he ended his term with low popularity ratings and was defeated in his bid for reelection.[43] The main source of his loss of popularity, however, did not reflect on his competence. In spring 1991, even as Bush was basking in the glory of American victories in the cold war and the Persian Gulf, the economy slipped into a recession. Bush refused to support a tax cut or spending increase to prime the economy, a stance later portrayed by Clinton and the Democrats as showing a lack of concern about the nation's economic distress. In fact, Bush was following the advice of most economists, who warned that increasing an already oversized budget deficit would do harm in the long run.[44] The weak economy hung on through most of 1992, eroded Bush's standing with the public, and, more than anything else, caused his defeat in the election.[45]

Yet Bush's political difficulties also reflected his own actions. To be sure, he was highly competent in many respects. He was generally well versed on public policy. He appointed an experienced cabinet and staff and used reasonably orderly and informative decision processes.[46] And he was an eager self-starter in using his extensive personal contacts to promote his policies in Congress.

Bush fell short of strategic competence, however, in one area. Instead of disciplining his participation in decision making, he allowed personal predilections to shape advisory processes and determine decisions. First, he had a hard time maintaining balanced attitudes toward risk and conflict. He vacillated between extremes of caution and risk taking, conciliation and self-assertion. In 1989 Bush surprised observers by caving in, almost meekly, to congressional pressure on aid to the Nicaraguan contras; but then he aggressively invaded Panama under dubious authority of international law. He attacked Iraq with massive force in 1991, but then pulled back without securing a complete victory. According to a scathing critique by former president Richard Nixon, Bush shrank from the challenge of leading the country to provide economic support for democratization in Russia.[47] One of Bush's riskiest moves was his unconditional "read-my-lips" promise during the 1988 campaign that he would not raise taxes. His eventual abandonment of the promise as part of a 1990 deficit reduction agreement was a political disaster for Bush that placed a major burden on his reelection effort.

Second, Bush had little patience for thinking broadly about plans and purposes. Critics dismissed him as shallow and complained that he had no vision of the country's future. Bush rejected the criticism as irrelevant, belittling what he called "the vision thing." But, in fact, his overly concrete style of thinking constrained deliberation in the White House. Even in the early stages of Bush's term, the staff focused on reacting to events, neglecting broad goals and long-range plans.[48]

Finally, Bush also had little patience for thinking, whether broadly or narrowly, about domestic policy. He had reasons for preferring to spend his time on foreign affairs: his extensive experience in that area (as former U.S. envoy to China and CIA director), the lack of popular support for conservative reforms in domestic policy, fiscal barriers to new or expanded social programs, and the likelihood of conflict over domestic issues with a Democratic Congress. But instead of exercising self-discipline, Bush freely indulged his preference for foreign policy. He allowed his lack of interest in domestic issues to be generally known.[49] Remarkably, the Bush administration offered no legislative agenda in its first year.[50] At later stages, some senior officials tried to advance some innovative conservative domestic policies, but they were consistently defeated within the administration.[51]

In the end, Bush learned that the public will not allow presidents to ignore domestic policy. His lack of a domestic agenda was an effective issue for the Democrats in the 1992 campaign. Indeed, Bush was reduced to promising that he would replace his White House staff and work mainly on domestic problems in his second term. We cannot say that if Bush had exerted more self-discipline and achieved greater strategic competence in policymaking, he would have had more substantial policy accomplishments or would have won reelection, but we can say he would have improved his chances.

Bill Clinton

Bill Clinton's presidency is more difficult to rate as a success or failure. Clinton achieved some major policy successes, such as deficit reduction and the North American Free Trade Agreement, but also experienced major defeats on gay rights and health care reform. He suffered a crushing partisan defeat in the 1994 congressional elections, but bounced back to win reelection in 1996 and regain some seats for his party in the 1998 congressional elections. He eliminated the federal budget deficit, but only after Republican prodding. In the most distinguishing episode of his presidency, Clinton was impeached by the House of Representatives on charges of perjury and obstruction of justice in the Monica Lewinsky scandal and then handily acquitted in the Senate trial.

Whatever the ultimate judgment of this mixed record, Clinton's case differed from his predecessor's on two counts. First, Clinton had better luck with the economy. He enjoyed sustained popularity largely on the strength of an extraordinarily prolonged stretch of economic growth. Second, although Clinton exhibited marked deficiencies of strategic competence early in his presidency, he learned from his mistakes and made corrections in time to restore his standing with the voters.

In many respects, Clinton was a conspicuously gifted political leader.[52] From the outset of his presidency, he showed an extraordinary grasp of policy issues. In a televised economic summit conference shortly before the inauguration, Clinton traded ideas, seemingly on equal terms, with leading economists, business leaders, and other experts. He performed with energy and skill in promoting his policies, and was (like Reagan) an exceptionally effective public speaker.

With respect to one major task, however—management of decision processes—he began abysmally and got his bearings only later. In the first year of his presidency, Clinton failed profoundly to exercise strategic competence in managing decision making. His first chief of staff, Thomas F. "Mack" McLarty, was a lifelong Arkansas friend and successful businessman who had no Washington or government experience. McLarty was out of his element in White House politics. The president's chief counsel, Bernard Nussbaum, was a Wall Street lawyer with minimal experience in Washington.[53] Many Clinton staff members were even less qualified—people in their twenties or early thirties who had limited professional experience of any kind.[54] Strangely, the early

Clinton White House also failed to reflect the president's supposed ideological commitments. Dominated by liberal Democrats, it included very few of the relatively conservative Democrats for whom Clinton had been a spokesman before the 1992 campaign.[55]

The decision-making process in the early Clinton White House was haphazard, without much explicit management or planned structure. Decisions were arrived at informally, if not mysteriously.[56] In some areas, Clinton seemed to aspire to the self-reliant model, making up for the lack of structured advisory processes by investing enormous amounts of time in long-winded discussions with the staff.[57] In other areas, especially foreign policy, he was hardly involved at all. The administration made and announced major policy changes on Bosnia and Cuba without the president's even being apprised of them.[58] In one remarkable episode, Clinton put his wife, Hillary Rodham Clinton, and an academic policy analyst, Ira Magaziner—neither of whom had prior experience in executive branch policy-making processes—in charge of developing his 1993 health care reform plan.[59] The disorganized, inexperienced, and ideologically unbalanced White House staff contributed to a legion of political difficulties that beset Clinton in his first two years as president and contributed to a disastrous Democratic defeat in the 1994 congressional elections.

By the beginning of his second year, however, Clinton had come to understand the costs of careless management and began to bring order and a more conservative direction to the decision process.[60] Clinton found an experienced Washington hand and skilled manager to run the White House: Leon Panetta, the OMB director and former chair of the House Budget Committee. In addition, he brought in David Gergen, an outright conservative political analyst and former Republican White House aide, to consult on strategy. Nussbaum, the chief counsel, resigned in the Whitewater scandal, and Clinton picked Lloyd N. Cutler, a renowned Washington lawyer and former counsel to President Carter, to replace him. When these officials eventually left the White House, their replacements also had strong credentials.

After the reformation of his decision-making methods, Clinton was generally quite skillful and effective. Paying more attention to foreign policy, he undertook successful military interventions in Bosnia, Haiti, and Serbia. In political terms, he rarely sounded a wrong note. In 1995 Clinton had a "showdown," as Elizabeth Drew called it, with congressional Republicans over their "Contract with America" and especially the budget.[61] Politically, at least, Clinton won, successfully portraying Speaker of the House Newt Gingrich and the Republicans as attacking Medicare and forcing shutdowns of the federal government. In 1996 Clinton moved so far to the right that he co-opted much of the Republican agenda, including deficit reduction and welfare reform. In his second term, Clinton worked with the Republicans to balance the budget while continuing to exploit their less-popular positions on Medicare and Social Security. In the end, the gravest questions about Clinton's leadership, raised by the Monica Lewinsky scandal, concerned his character, not his competence.

Minimalism Revisited: George W. Bush

Although George W. Bush is the son of one president, his approach to the presidency has more closely resembled that of another, Ronald Reagan. Bush is, for the most part, a minimalist president. Compared with Reagan, however, he is more attuned to the president's modest role in the minimalist scheme.

Bush's resort to a chairman-of-the-board, minimalist strategy was warranted, if not compelled, by his limited experience, knowledge, and intellectual interest in most matters of government.[62] Bush's prior government experience, six years as governor of Texas, was less extensive than most presidents', but not dramatically different from that of Carter, Reagan, or Clinton. More important, he was far from a diligent student of government even during that brief period. The media poked fun at Bush's malapropisms, grammatical errors, half-expressed thoughts, and misinformed statements—collected for enthusiasts on the *Slate* Web site as the "Complete Bushisms." The apparent implication—that Bush was unintelligent—was certainly unwarranted, but some of his misstatements raised questions about his familiarity with basic information about government and public policy.[63] What was more clear than his intellectual gifts or lack of them were the accounts of his conduct as governor, which suggested that he rarely dealt with issues in much detail. Rather, he insisted on brief meetings and short memoranda to inform his decisions and left most of the specifics to his staff.[64] The job of governor also had given Bush very little exposure to the international issues that often dominate the president's attention. If Bush had taken it upon himself to evaluate the quality of the arguments in White House policy debates, as the strategic-competence model requires, he might often have lacked the background to make adequate judgments.

As if conscious of his personal limitations, however, Bush selected a vice-presidential running mate, Dick Cheney, and later surrounded himself with a White House staff and cabinet, who were all widely praised as capable and experienced. Many had worked in the campaigns or administrations of recent Republican presidents, especially the elder Bush.[65] Senior political counselor

Karl Rove and communications director Karen Hughes were experienced Bush family political hands. The chief of staff, Andrew Card, had been deputy chief of staff in the first president Bush's administration. Card and Rove ran the White House as a tight ship, centralizing control of its various offices, focusing attention on priority issues through the new Office of Strategic Initiatives, and making sure that meetings began and ended on time. As appropriate for a chief of staff, Card avoided a high-profile public role and served as an "honest broker" in policy deliberations. In foreign affairs, Bush appointed an academic with modest experience on the National Security Council staff, Condoleezza Rice, as national security adviser, and she assembled a staff more experienced than herself.[66] Secretary of State Colin Powell and Secretary of Defense Donald Rumsfeld both had had distinguished Washington careers.

More important, Bush was evidently comfortable allowing his heavyweight senior aides and cabinet members to define the direction of his administration. The transition process was run primarily by Cheney, while Bush waited in the wings at his Texas ranch. After the inauguration, Bush delegated policy decisions with minimal oversight on his part. He met with his budget team for a total of five hours to make all his decisions on his first budget proposal.[67] The episode amounted to the raising and spending of almost $7 billion per minute of meeting; more significant, considering the centrality of the budget, the president disposed of a substantial fraction of his important decisions for an entire year in the equivalent of an afternoon. In general, policy leadership was divided between Cheney, who focused on economic issues, and Rove, the main pipeline to the Christian Right, who focused on social issues. In contrast with Reagan, there were no reports of President Bush overruling his unanimous advisers, peremptorily constraining their options, or surprising them with an unexpected decision. Although Bush had the final say on major issues, he allowed other senior officials to refine and present the options according to their own lights.

Reflecting some of the general hazards of the minimalist strategy, two kinds of difficulties developed from Bush's approach. First, it elicited the expected criticism of the president as not being in charge. In reference to Cheney's leadership of the transition, a joke circulated—sardonically reversing an old chestnut about vice presidents—that Bush was "a heartbeat away from the presidency."

The White House used various tactics, some of them potentially costly, to overcome that impression. Bush reportedly devoted many hours of study and reflection to making a single, though highly controversial decision on federal support for stem cell research—a dubious allocation of the president's time. According to one administration official, for several weeks Bush "brought up the issue almost daily, even in meetings not directly related to the topic."[68] After September 11, 2001, a concerted effort was made to magnify the president's role in the war on terrorism.

The issues of military strategy, coalition management, and Middle East politics involved in the war were as remote from Bush's prior experience as any he would likely encounter as president. Yet the administration sought to present him as the principal architect of its strategy. After Cheney gave a masterful hour-long television interview on September 16 explaining the strategy, the White House kept him out of sight to avoid highlighting his central role.[69] In addition, Condoleezza Rice gave a reporter for the *New York Times* a quite likely inflated account of Bush's contribution to the administration's decision making. Describing a two-day gathering of top officials at Camp David in mid-September, she claimed that on the first day Bush sat, mostly in silence, through seven hours of "intense debate" over strategy for the war. On the second day, Rice and Bush met privately. In her recounting, Bush said, " 'Here's what I want to do,' " and dictated an elaborate, phased plan as she took copious notes, which formed the basis for the administration's strategy and the president's speech on the war.[70] The media critic for the *Washington Post* expressed skepticism— pointing out several recent news stories that depicted Bush as being "in charge" on the basis of White House insiders' unverifiable accounts of private meetings with the president.[71] Whatever the reality of the Camp David meetings, the episode reflected the pressure on Bush to appear to make his own decisions without relying too heavily on subordinates. The danger is that such pressure could push a relatively uninformed president to prove his independence by overruling his advisers.

The second difficulty was not simply a consequence of minimalism, but Bush's modest role in decision making probably contributed to it. In a mirror image of the Clinton case, Bush's policies during his first year lurched to the right from the posture of his presidential campaign. Like Clinton in 1992, Bush had campaigned as a moderate—advantageous positioning, especially for the general election. He defined himself as a "compassionate conservative." But the transition, led by the conservative Cheney with minimal involvement by Bush, produced a massively conservative administration.[72] Bush's leading policy advisers, Cheney and Rove, along with Rice in foreign affairs, were conservatives, as were most of the cabinet and White House staff.

Attorney General John Ashcroft had been the most conservative member of the Senate.

With few exceptions, Bush's major policy decisions in the first year catered to upper-income and conservative constituencies.[73] Bush adopted or advocated a large tax cut, with benefits skewed toward high-income taxpayers; an antimissile defense system; expanded oil and gas drilling in the Alaskan wilderness; withdrawal from the Kyoto accord on global warming; and prohibition of federal support for family planning, among other conservative positions. In some cases, such positions prompted a backlash or led to stalemate with Congress. The administration's airport security bill was held up for several weeks over Republican and Bush administration opposition to requiring that airport security personnel be federal employees. The Justice Department's methods of dealing with suspected terrorists (including indefinite detentions of more than one thousand individuals, without charges) were criticized as wholesale abandonment of constitutionally protected civil liberties. And despite a recession, the administration and Congress were unable to agree on an economic stimulus package during the 2001 legislative session. At a minimum, the Bush administration's hard-line conservative posture, if not modified, was certain to produce difficult questions in the 2004 election campaign about what had happened to "compassionate conservatism."

By and large, however, the first year of the Bush presidency was counted a political and policy success. Record high public approval ratings reflected the apparent competence and significant successes of the Afghanistan phase of the war on terrorism. And unlike Clinton's first year, there were no scandals or policy fiascoes. In short, the early indications were that, in Bush's case, minimalism worked.

If that judgment holds for the duration of Bush's presidency, it is arguably the kind of exception that proves the rule. For a president, George W. Bush has a remarkably easy-going personality. As an adviser described him during the election campaign, he is "a man confident enough to show what he doesn't know, [and] an executive who expects his advisers to know more than he does about their areas of expertise."[74] It is unlikely that someone as unassuming and deferential would ever have become president if not for the unusual circumstances of Bush's career: that he was the son of a president, was recruited to politics in mid-life by his father's influential friends, and catapulted to prominence largely on the strength of his father's name.[75] Such a personality has the least temptation to overstep the limits of a minimalist presidency. But that type is not likely to become president very often.

Notes

1. As one Republican political analyst has observed in an article for a conservative magazine, "The years . . . [since 1989] have not so far been kind to Reagan's standing, either with the general public or with scholars of the presidency." See A. James Reichley, "Reagan in Retrospect," *The World and I*, May 1994. Most of the diminution of Reagan's standing is the result of the budget deficits and other economic troubles of the 1990s.

2. Richard E. Neustadt, *Presidential Power: The Politics of Leadership* (New York: Wiley, 1960). Later editions, most recently in 1980, have updated the analysis and in some ways modified the argument.

3. Ibid., chap. 7.

4. James David Barber, *The Presidential Character: Predicting Performance in the White House*, 2d ed. (Englewood Cliffs: Prentice-Hall, 1977).

5. Arthur M. Schlesinger Jr., "Roosevelt as Administrator," in *Bureaucratic Power in National Politics*, 2d ed., ed. Francis E. Rourke (Boston: Little, Brown, 1972), 126–138.

6. Ibid., 132–133, 137.

7. On Johnson's personality and his presidency, see Doris Kearns, *Lyndon Johnson and the American Dream* (New York: Harper and Row, 1976).

8. James Fallows, "The Passionless Presidency," *Atlantic*, May 1979, 33–48.

9. See Nelson W. Polsby, *The Consequences of Party Reform* (New York: Oxford University Press, 1983), 108–109.

10. On the Whig theory and the changing conceptions of the presidency as an institution, see James L. Sundquist, *The Decline and Resurgence of Congress* (Washington, D.C.: Brookings Institution, 1981), chap. 2.

11. Fred I. Greenstein, *The Hidden-Hand Presidency: Eisenhower as Leader* (New York: Basic Books, 1982).

12. Dick Kirschten, "White House Strategy," *National Journal*, February 21, 1981, 300–303.

13. Quoted in "The Presidency and the Press Corps," by John Herbers, *New York Times Magazine*, May 9, 1982, 45ff.

14. G. Calvin Mackenzie, *The In-and-Outers: Presidential Appointees and Transient Government in Washington* (Baltimore: Johns Hopkins University Press, 1987).

15. Erwin C. Hargrove, *The President as Leader: Appealing to the Better Angels of Our Nature* (Lawrence: University Press of Kansas, 1999), chap. 6.

16. David A. Stockman, *The Triumph of Politics: How the Reagan Revolution Failed* (New York: Harper and Row, 1986), 276–295.

17. Fred I. Greenstein, *The Presidential Difference: Leadership Style from FDR to Clinton* (Princeton: Princeton University Press, 2001), chap. 10.

18. For the sake of brevity, I omit the president's problems and potential strategies for managing policy implementation by the bureaucracy. See Richard P. Nathan, *The Administrative Presidency* (New York: Wiley, 1983). This function depends heavily on the appropriate selection of political executives. See G. Calvin Mackenzie, *The Politics of Presidential Appointments* (New York: Free Press, 1980).

19. Arthur M. Schlesinger Jr., *A Thousand Days: John F. Kennedy in the White House* (Boston: Houghton Mifflin, 1965), 628–630, 1002–8.

20. At least one Reagan administration leader has been candid about the role of faith in its 1981 economic proposals. See William Greider, "The Education of David Stockman," *Atlantic*, December 1981, 27ff.

21. The same cannot be said of members of Congress, whom one expects to be more prone to demagoguery, and who came under intense political pressure, stimulated in large part by the president.

22. See A. James Reichley, *Conservatives in an Age of Change: The Nixon and Ford Administrations* (Washington, D.C.: Brookings Institution, 1981), chap. 18; Roger Porter, *Presidential Decision Making: The Economic Policy Board* (New York: Cambridge University Press, 1980), chap. 3; and Martha Derthick and Paul J. Quirk, *The Politics of Deregulation* (Washington, D.C.: Brookings Institution, 1985), chap. 2.

23. Timothy B. Clark, "Strange Bedfellows," *National Journal*, February 2, 1985. For a penetrating study of the politics of taxation, see John F. Witte, *The Politics and Development of the Federal Income Tax* (Madison: University of Wisconsin Press, 1985).

24. The president's task in managing decision making is more difficult than that of chief executives in some of the parliamentary democracies because they have more elaborate and better institutionalized coordinating machinery. See Colin Campbell and George J. Szablowski, *The Super-Bureaucrats: Structure and Behavior in Central Agencies* (New York: New York University Press, 1979). For insightful analyses of the influences on presidential ability to use information effectively, see John P. Burke and Fred I. Greenstein, *How Presidents Test Reality: Decisions on Vietnam, 1954 and 1965* (New York: Russell Sage Foundation, 1989); and Bert A. Rockman, "Organizing the White House: On a West Wing and a Prayer," *Journal of Managerial Issues* 5 (winter 1993): 453–464.

25. Harold Wilensky, *Organizational Intelligence: Knowledge and Policy in Government and Industry* (New York: Basic Books, 1967).

26. Irving Janis, *Victims of GroupThink: A Psychological Study of Foreign-Policy Decisions and Fiascoes* (Boston: Houghton Mifflin, 1972).

27. Fundamentally, all organization theory concerns the problem of coordination. See Anthony Downs, *Inside Bureaucracy* (Boston: Little, Brown, 1967), chap. 11; and Jay R. Galbraith, *Organization Design* (Reading, Mass.: Addison-Wesley, 1977). Problems of coordination in the executive branch are emphasized in I. M. Destler, *Making Foreign Economic Policy* (Washington, D.C.: Brookings Institution, 1980). For a general treatment of presidential staffing and organization, see James P. Pfiffner, *The Strategic Presidency: Hitting the Ground Running*, 2d ed. (Lawrence: University Press of Kansas, 1996).

28. Lester M. Salamon, "The Presidency and Domestic Policy Formulation," in *The Illusion of Presidential Government*, ed. Hugh Heclo and Lester Salamon (Boulder: Westview Press, 1982), 177–212.

29. For this and other Reagan-Carter comparisons, see John H. Kessel, "The Structures of the Reagan White House" (paper presented at the annual meeting of the American Political Science Association, Chicago, September 1–4, 1983). More generally on Carter, however, see Kessel, "The Structures of the Carter White House," *American Journal of Political Science* 22 (August 1983).

30. The resulting mutual recriminations constitute leading themes in the memoirs of the two officials. See Cyrus Vance, *Hard Choices: Critical Years in America's Foreign Policy* (New York: Simon and Schuster, 1983); and Zbigniew Brzezinski, *Power and Principle: Memoirs of the National Security Advisor, 1977–1981* (New York: Farrar, Straus, and Giroux, 1983).

31. Alexander George makes an influential argument for separating the roles of process manager and policy adviser in "The Case for Multiple Advocacy in Making Foreign Policy," *American Political Science Review* 66 (September 1972): 751–785; see also

Alexander George, *Presidential Decision Making: The Effective Use of Information and Advice* (Boulder: Westview Press, 1980).

32. Janis, *Victims of GroupThink,* chap. 2.

33. For an account of the Reagan administration's organizational strategy, see James P. Pfiffner, "White House Staff versus the Cabinet: Centripetal and Centrifugal Roles," *Presidential Studies Quarterly* 16 (fall 1986): 666–690.

34. Reagan's capacity for ignoring bad news is documented in Stockman, *Triumph of Politics;* and Laurence I. Barrett, *Gambling with History: Reagan in the White House* (New York: Penguin Books, 1984), esp. 174.

35. John D. Steinbrunner, "Security Policy," in *The New Direction in American Politics,* ed. John E. Chubb and Paul E. Peterson (Washington, D.C.: Brookings Institution, 1985), 351.

36. On the president's relations with Congress, see Anthony King, ed., *Both Ends of the Avenue: The Presidency, the Executive Branch, and Congress in the 1980s* (Washington, D.C.: American Enterprise Institute, 1983); Barbara Kellerman, *The Political Presidency* (New York: Oxford University Press, 1984); and Mark A. Peterson, *Legislating Together: The White House and Capitol Hill from Eisenhower to Reagan* (Cambridge: Harvard University Press, 1990).

37. For a historical treatment and analysis of organization for White House liaison, see Stephen J. Wayne, *The Legislative Presidency* (New York: Harper and Row, 1978).

38. Eric L. Davis, "Legislative Liaison in the Carter Administration," *Political Science Quarterly* 95 (summer 1979): 287–302. Eventually, organization of the staff by issues was dropped.

39. In *Consequences of Party Reform,* 105–114, Polsby details the Carter administration's major mistakes in dealing with Congress and argues persuasively that its difficulties were not to any great extent the result of internal changes in Congress.

40. Dick Kirschten, "Second Term Legislative Strategy Shifts to Foreign Policy and Defense Issues," *National Journal,* March 30, 1985, 696–699.

41. Samuel Kernell, *Going Public: New Strategies of Presidential Leadership,* 3d ed. (Washington, D.C.: CQ Press, 1997); and Theodore J. Lowi, *The Personal President: Power Invested, Promise Unfulfilled* (Ithaca, N.Y.: Cornell University Press, 1985).

42. Quoted by Polsby in *Consequences of Party Reform,* 109.

43. For early assessments of the Bush presidency, see Colin Campbell and Bert A. Rockman, eds., *The Bush Presidency: First Appraisals* (Chatham, N.J.: Chatham House, 1991); and Ryan J. Barilleaux and Mary E. Stuckey, eds., *Leadership and the Bush Presidency: Prudence or Drift in an Era of Change?* (Westport, Conn.: Greenwood Press, 1992).

44. See Paul J. Quirk and Bruce Nesmith, "Explaining Deadlock: Domestic Policymaking in the Bush Presidency," in *New Perspectives on American Politics,* ed. Lawrence C. Dodd and Calvin Jillson (Washington, D.C.: CQ Press, 1994), 200–201.

45. See Paul J. Quirk and Jon K. Dalager, "The Election: A 'New Democrat' and a New Kind of Presidential Campaign," in *The Elections of 1992,* ed. Michael Nelson (Washington, D.C.: CQ Press, 1993), 57–88.

46. Richard Cohen, "The Gloves Are Off," *National Journal,* October 14, 1989, 2508–12; and "Mr. Consensus," *Time,* August 21, 1989, 17–22.

47. Richard M. Nixon, "The Challenge We Face in Russia," *Wall Street Journal,* March 11, 1992, 14.

48. Paul J. Quirk, "Domestic Policy: Divided Government and Cooperative Presidential Leadership," in *Bush Presidency,* ed. Campbell and Rockman, 69–92.

49. Robert Shogun, *The Riddle of Power: Presidential Leadership from Truman to Bush* (New York: Penguin, 1982), chap. 10.

50. Quirk, "Domestic Policy," 69–92.

51. Fred Barnes, "White House Watch: Logjam," *New Republic*, May 11, 1992, 10–11; James Pinkerton, "Life in Bush Hell," *New Republic*, December 14, 1992, 22–27; Mickey Kaus, "Paradigm's Loss," *New Republic*, July 27, 1992, 16–22; Fred Barnes, "White House Watch: War Dividend," *New Republic*, March 25, 1991, 12–13; and Burt Solomon, "White House Notebook: Bush Plays Down Domestic Policy in Coasting towards Reelection," *National Journal*, March 30, 1991, 752–753.

52. Fred I. Greenstein, *The Presidential Difference: Leadership Style from FDR to Clinton* (Princeton: Princeton University Press, 2001), chap. 12.

53. W. John Moore, "West Wing Novice," *National Journal*, June 5, 1993, 1339–43. Two decades earlier, Nussbaum had worked on the Watergate prosecution team.

54. Burt Solomon, "White House Notebook: A Modish Management Style Means Slip-Sliding around the West Wing," *National Journal*, October 30, 1993, 2606–7; Colin Campbell, "Management in a Sandbox: Why the Clinton Administration Failed to Cope with Gridlock," in *The Clinton Presidency: First Appraisals*, ed. Colin Campbell and Bert A. Rockman (Chatham, N.J.: Chatham House, 1995), 51–87.

55. Fred Barnes, "Neoconned," *New Republic*, January 25, 1993, 14–16.

56. Burt Solomon, "Crisscrossed with Connections . . . West Wing Is a Networker's Dream," *National Journal*, January 15, 1994, 256–257.

57. Elizabeth Drew, *On the Edge: The Clinton Presidency* (New York: Simon and Schuster, 1994).

58. On Clinton's lack of attention to foreign policy, see Larry Berman and Emily O. Goldman, "Clinton's Foreign Policy at Midterm," in *Clinton Presidency*, ed. Campbell and Rockman, 290–324.

59. Paul J. Quirk and Joseph Hinchliffe, "Domestic Policy: The Trials of a Centrist Democrat," in *Clinton Presidency*, ed. Campbell and Rockman, 262–289; Theda Skocpol, *Boomerang* (New York: Norton and Company, 1996), 10; Lawrence R. Jacobs and Robert Y. Shapiro, *Politicians Don't Pander: Political Leadership, Public Opinion, and American Politics* (Chicago: University of Chicago Press, 2000), chap. 2.

60. Julie Kosterlitz, "Changing of the Guard," *National Journal*, March 6, 1993, 575; Burt Solomon, "Boomers in Charge," *National Journal*, June 19, 1993, 1472.

61. Elizabeth Drew, *Showdown: The Struggle between the Gingrich Congress and the Clinton White House* (New York: Simon and Schuster, 1996).

62. For a fuller discussion of Bush's qualifications for the office of president, see Paul J. Quirk and Sean C. Matheson, "The Presidency: The Election and the Prospects for Leadership," in *The Elections of 2000*, ed. Michael Nelson (Washington, D.C.: CQ Press, 2001). My understanding of Bush's first year in office benefited from research papers by a number of undergraduate students in my course on the American presidency at the University of Illinois at Urbana-Champaign.

63. At a campaign appearance, for example, Bush attacked the Democratic ticket for wanting the federal government to control Social Security, "like it's some kind of federal program." It is the largest federal domestic program and is fully administered by the federal government. *Slate*, "Complete Bushisms," at Slate.com, accessed December 2000.

64. Dan Balz and Terry M. Neal, "Bush as President: Questions, Clues, and Contradiction," *Washington Post*, October 22, 2000, A1.

65. Richard L. Berke, "Bush Shapes His Presidency with Sharp Eye on Father's," *New York Times,* March 28, 2001, A1.

66. Karen DeYoung and Steven Mufson, "Leaner and Less Visible NSC; Reorganization Will Emphasize Defense, Global Economics," *Washington Post,* February 10, 2001, A1.

67. Richard L. Berke, "Bush is Providing Corporate Model for White House," *New York Times,* March 11, 2001, A1.

68. Frank Bruni, "Bush Weighs a Decision on Stem Cell Research Amid Reminders of Suffering, *New York Times,* July 8, 2001, A12.

69. Eric Schmitt, "For Cheney, a Low Profile and a Major Role," *New York Times,* October 6, 2001, A1.

70. Jane Perlez, David E. Sanger, and Thom Shanker, "A Nation Challenged: The Advisers; From Many Voices, One Battle Strategy," *New York Times,* September 23, 2001, A1.

71. Howard Kurtz, "What Bush Said and When He Said It," *Washington Post,* October 1, 2001, C1.

72. Dana Milbank and Ellen Nakashima, "Bush Team Has 'Right' Credentials; Conservative Picks Seen Eclipsing Even Reagan's," *Washington Post,* March 25, 2001, A1.

73. Richard Stevenson, "Political Memo; Bush's Moves to Assure Right Ignite Storm on Left," *New York Times,* April 8, 2001, A22; and Juliet Eilperin, "For GOP House Moderates a Season of Discontent," *Washington Post,* July 22, 2001, A6.

74. Balz and Neal, "Bush as President."

75. For a partisan yet informative account of Bush's rise to the presidency by an adviser to Clinton, see Paul Begala, *Is Our Children Learning? The Case against George W. Bush* (New York: Simon and Schuster, 2000).

7 The Psychological Presidency

Michael Nelson

Several delegates to the Constitutional Convention of 1787 noted during the first week of debate that to invest power in a unitary office was to invest power in one person. Not until James David Barber wrote The Presidential Character, *however, was a systematic effort made to explore the psychological consequences of that important truism. Michael Nelson examines this influential book, along with another that Barber wrote about the voters' supposed contributions to the "psychological presidency," called* The Pulse of Politics. *Although Nelson finds Barber's theories wanting (the healthiest of Barber's character types, for example, are not always successful presidents), he praises Barber for drawing scholars' attention to the psychological aspects of the presidency and for encouraging political journalists to do the same in their coverage of presidential campaigns.*

The United States elects its president every four years, which makes it unique among democratic nations. During several recent election campaigns, *Time* magazine has run a story about James David Barber, which makes him equally singular among political scientists. The two quadrennial oddities are not unrelated.

The first *Time* article, which appeared in 1972, was about Barber's just-published book, *The Presidential Character: Predicting Performance in the White House,* in which he argued that presidents could be divided into four psychological types: "active-positive," "active-negative," "passive-positive," and "passive-negative." What's more, according to Barber via *Time,* by taking "a hard look at men before they reach the White House," voters could tell in advance what candidates would be like if elected: healthily "ambitious out of exuberance," like the active-positives; or pathologically "ambitious out of anxiety," "compliant and other-directed," or "dutiful and self-denying," like the three other, lesser types, respectively. In the 1972 election, Barber told *Time,* the choice was between an active-positive, George McGovern, and a psychologically defective active-negative, Richard M. Nixon.[1]

Nixon won the election, but Barber's early insights into Nixon's personality won notoriety for both him and his theory, especially in the wake of Watergate. So prominent had Barber become by 1976 that White House correspondent Hugh Sidey used his entire "Presidency" column in the October 4 issue of *Time* to tell readers that Barber was refusing to type candidates Gerald R. Ford and Jimmy Carter this time around. "Barber is deep into an academic study of this election and its participants, and he is pledged to restraint until it is over," Sidey reported solemnly.[2] Actually, more than a year before, Barber had told *U.S. News & World Report* that he considered Ford an active-positive.[3] Carter, who read Barber's book twice when it came out, was left to tell the *Washington Post* that active-positive is "what I would like to be. That's what I hope I prove to be."[4] And so Carter would be, wrote Barber in a special postelection column for *Time*.[5]

The 1980 election campaign witnessed the appearance of another Barber book, *The Pulse of Politics: Electing Presidents in the Media Age,* and, in honor of the occasion, two *Time* articles. This was all to the good, because the first, a Sidey column in March, offered more gush than information: "The first words encountered in the new book by Duke's Professor James David Barber are stunning: 'A revolution in presidential politics is under way.' . . . Barber has made political history before."[6] A more substantive piece in the magazine's May 19 "Nation" section described the new book's cycle theory of presidential elections. According to Barber, ever since 1900 steady four-year beats in the public's psychological mood, or "pulse," have caused a recurring alternation among elections of "conflict," "conscience," and "conciliation." *Time* went on to stress, although not explain, Barber's view of the importance of the mass media, both as a reinforcer of this cycle and as a potential mechanism for helping the nation to break out of it.[7]

In subsequent years, Barber wrote for and was written about in numerous other national publications. But it was *Time*'s infatuation with Barber that brought him a level of fame that comes rarely to political scientists. For Barber, fame came at some cost. Although widely known, his ideas are little understood. The media's cursory treatment of them has made them appear superficial or even foolish—instantly appealing to the naive, instantly odious to the thoughtful. Partly as a result, Barber's reputation in the intellectual community as an *homme sérieux* has suffered. In the backrooms and corridors of scholarly gatherings, one hears "journalistic" and "popularizer," the ultimate academic epithets, muttered along with his name. Indeed, in a 1991 assessment of contemporary scholarly research on the presidency, Paul Quirk observed of the whole field of presidential psychology that "researchers seem to have kept their distance from the subject as if to avoid guilt by association" with Barber.[8]

This situation is in need of remedy. Barber's theories may be seriously flawed, but they are serious theories. For all their limitations—some of them self-confessed—they offer one of the most significant contributions a scholar can make: an unfamiliar but useful way of looking at a familiar subject that we no longer see very clearly. In Barber's case, the familiar thing is the American presidency, and the unfamiliar way of looking at it is through the lenses of psychology.

Psychological Perspectives on the Presidency

Constitutional Perspectives

To look at politics in general, or the American presidency in particular, from a psychological perspective is nothing new. Although deprived of the insights (and spared the nonsense) of modern psychology, the Framers of the Constitution constructed their plan of government on a foundation of Hobbesian assumptions about what motivates *homo politicus*. (They called what they were doing moral philosophy, not psychology.) James Madison and most of his colleagues at the Constitutional Convention assumed that "men are instruments of their desires"; that "one such desire is the desire for power"; and that "if unrestrained by external checks, any individual or group of individuals will tyrannize over others."[9] Because the Framers believed these things, a basic tenet of their political philosophy was that the government they were designing should be a "government of laws and not of men." Not just psychology but history had taught them to associate liberty with law and tyranny with rulers who depart from law, as had George III and his colonial governors.

In the end the convention yielded to those who urged, on grounds of "energy" in the executive, that the Constitution lodge the powers of the executive branch in a single person, the president.[10] There are several reasons why the delegates were willing to put aside their doubts and inject such a powerful dose of individual character into the new plan of government. One is the Framers' certain knowledge that George Washington would be the first president. They knew that Washington aroused powerful and, from the standpoint of winning the nation's support for the new government, vital psychological responses from the people. As Seymour Martin Lipset has shown, Washington was a classic example of what sociologist Max Weber called a charismatic leader, a man "treated [by the people] as endowed with supernatural, superhuman, or at least specifically exceptional powers or qualities."[11] Marcus Cunliffe noted,

[B]abies were being christened after him as early as 1775, and while he was still President, his countrymen paid to see him in waxwork effigy. To his admirers he was "godlike Washington," and his detractors complained to one another that he was looked upon as a "demigod" whom it was treasonous to criticize. "Oh Washington!" declared Ezra Stiles of Yale (in a sermon of 1783). "How I do love thy name! How have I often adored and blessed thy God, for creating and forming thee the great ornament of human kind!"[12]

Just as Washington's "gift of grace" would legitimize the new government, the Framers believed, so would his personal character ensure its republican nature. The powers of the president in the Constitution "are full great," wrote Pierce Butler, a convention delegate from South Carolina, to a British kinsman,

and greater than I was disposed to make them. Nor, entre nous, do I believe they would have been so great had not many of the delegates cast their eyes towards General Washington as President; and shaped their Ideas of the Powers to be given to a President, by their opinions of his Virtue.[13]

The Framers were not so naive or shortsighted as to invest everything in Washington. To protect the nation from power-mad tyrants after he left office, they provided that the election of the president, whether by electors or members of the House of Representatives, would involve selection by peers—personal acquaintances of the candidates who could screen out those of defective character. And even if someone of low character slipped through the net and became president, the Framers believed that they had structured the office to protect the nation from harm. "The founders' deliberation over the provision for indefinite reeligibility," Jeffrey Tulis has shown, "illustrates how they believed self-interest could sometimes be elevated."[14] Whether motivated by "avarice," "ambition," or "the love of fame," Alexander Hamilton argued in *The Federalist*, a president will behave responsibly to secure reelection to the office that allows that desire to be fulfilled.[15] Underlying this confidence was the assurance that in a relatively slow-paced world, mad or wicked presidents could do only so much damage before corrective action could remove them. As John Jay explained, "So far as the fear of punishment and disgrace can operate, that motive to good behavior is amply afforded by the article on the subject of impeachment."[16]

Scholarly Perspectives

The Framers' decision to inject personality into the presidency was a conscious one. But it was made for reasons that eventually ceased to pertain. The destructive powers at a modern president's disposal are ultimate and swift; the impeachment process now seems uncertain and slow. Peer review never took hold in the electoral college. The rise of the national broadcast media makes the president's personality all the more pervasive. In sum, most of the Framers' carefully conceived defenses against a president of defective character are gone.

Clearly, then, a sophisticated psychological perspective on the presidency was overdue in the late 1960s, when Barber began offering one in a series of articles and papers that culminated in *The Presidential Character*.[17] Presidential scholars had long taken it as axiomatic that the American presidency is an institution shaped in some measure by the personalities of individual presidents. But rarely had the literature of personality theory been brought to bear, in large part because scholars of the post–Franklin D. Roosevelt period no longer seemed to share the Framers' reservations about human nature, at least as far as the presidency was concerned. Instead, historians and political scientists exalted not only presidential power but also presidents who were ambitious for power. Richard Neustadt's influential book, *Presidential Power*, published in 1960, was typical in this regard:

The contributions that a president can make to government are indispensable. Assuming that he knows what power is and wants it, those contributions cannot help but be forthcoming in some measure as by-products of his search for personal influence.[18]

As Erwin Hargrove reflected in post-Vietnam, post-Watergate 1974, this line of reasoning was the source of startling deficiencies in scholarly understandings of the office: "We had assumed that ideological purpose was sufficient to purify the drive for power, but we forgot the importance of character."[19]

Scholars also had recognized for some time that Americans' attitudes about the presidency, like presidents' actions, are psychologically as well as politically rooted. Studies of schoolchildren indicated that they first come into political awareness by learning of, and feeling fondly toward, the president. As adults, they rally to the president's support, both when they inaugurate a new one and in times of crisis.[20] Popular nationalistic emotions, which in constitutional monarchies are directed toward the king or queen, are deflected in American society onto the president. Again, however, scholars' awareness of these psychological forces manifested itself more in casual observations (Dwight D. Eisenhower was a "father figure"; the "public mood" is fickle) than in systematic investigation.

The presidencies of John F. Kennedy, Lyndon B. Johnson, and Richard Nixon altered this scholarly quiescence. Surveys taken shortly after the Kennedy assassination recorded the startling depth of the feelings that Americans have about the presidency. A large share of the population experienced symptoms classically associated with grief over the death of a loved one. Historical evidence suggests that the public has responded similarly to the deaths of all sitting presidents, young or old, popular or not, whether by murder or natural causes.[21]

If Kennedy's death illustrated the deep psychological ties of the public to the presidency, the experiences of his successors showed even more clearly the importance of psychology in understanding the connection between president and presidency. Johnson, the peace candidate who rigidly pursued a self-defeating policy of war, and Nixon, who promised "lowered voices" only to angrily turn political disagreements into personal crises, seemed to project their personalities onto policy in ways that were both obvious and destructive. The events of the 1960s and 1970s brought students of the presidency up short. As they paused to consider the "psychological presidency," they found Barber standing at the ready with the foundation and first floor of a full-blown theory.

James David Barber and the Psychological Presidency

Barber's theory offers a model of the presidency as an institution shaped largely by the psychological mix between the personalities of individual presidents and the public's deep feelings about the office. It also proposes methods of predicting what those personalities and feelings are likely to be in particular circumstances. These considerations govern *The Presidential Character* and *The Pulse of Politics,* books that we shall examine in turn. The question of how we can become masters of our own and of the presidency's psychological fate is also treated in these books, but it receives fuller exposition in other works by Barber.

Presidential Psychology

The primary danger of the Nixon administration will be that the President will grasp some line of policy or method of operation and pursue it in spite of its failure. . . . How will Nixon respond to challenges to the morality of his regime, to charges of scandal and/or corruption? First such charges strike a raw nerve, not only from the Checkers business, but also from deep within the personality in which the demands of the superego are so harsh and hard. . . . The first impulse will be to hush it up, to conceal it, bring down the blinds. If it breaks open and Nixon cannot avoid commenting on it, there is a real setup here for another crisis.

James David Barber is more than a little proud of that prediction, mainly because he made it in a talk he gave at Stanford University on January 19, 1969, the eve of Nixon's first inauguration. It was among the earliest in a series of speeches, papers, and articles whose purpose was to explain his theory of presidential personality and how to predict it, always with his forecast for Nixon's future prominently, and thus riskily, displayed. The theory received its fullest statement in *The Presidential Character.*

Character, in Barber's usage, is not quite a synonym for personality but it comes close.[22] To be sure, a politician's psychological constitution also includes two other components: an adolescence-born *worldview,* which Barber defines as "primary, politically relevant beliefs, particularly his conceptions of social causality, human nature, and the central moral conflicts of the time"; and a *style,* or "habitual way of performing three political roles: rhetoric, personal relations, and homework," which develops in early adulthood. But clearly Barber considers character, which forms in childhood and shapes the later development of style and worldview, to be "the most important thing to know about a president or candidate." As he defines the term, "character is the way the President orients himself toward life—not for the moment, but enduringly." It "grows out of the child's experiments in relating to parents, brothers and sisters, and peers at play and in school, as well as to his own body and the objects around it." Through these experiences, the child—and thus the adult to be—arrives subconsciously at a deep and private understanding of his or her fundamental self-worth.

For some, this process results in high self-esteem, the vital ingredient for psychological health and political productiveness. Others must search outside themselves for evidence of worth that at best will be a partial substitute. Depending on the source and nature of their limited self-esteem, Barber suggests, they will concentrate their search in one of three areas: the affection from others that compliant and agreeable behavior brings, the sense of usefulness that comes from performing a widely respected duty, or the deference attendant with dominance and control over other people. Because politics is a vocation rich in opportunities to find all three of these things—affection from cheering crowds and devoted aides, usefulness from public service in a civic cause, dominance through official power—it is not surprising that some insecure people are attracted to a political career.

This makes for a problem, Barber argues. If public officials, especially presidents, use their office to compensate for private doubts and demons, it follows that they will not always use it to serve public purposes. Affection-seekers will be so concerned with preserving the goodwill of those around them that they seldom will challenge the status quo or otherwise rock the boat. The duty-doers will be similarly hidebound, although in their case inactivity will result from the feeling that to be useful they must be diligent guardians of time-honored practices and procedures. Passive presidents of both kinds may provide the nation with "breathing spells, times of recovery in our frantic political life," or even "a refreshing hopefulness and at least some sense of sharing and caring." Still, in Barber's view, their main effect is to "divert popular attention from the hard realities of politics," thus leaving the country to "drift." And "what passive presidents ignore, active presidents inherit."[23]

Power-driven presidents pose the greatest danger. They will seek their psychological compensation not in inaction but in intense efforts to maintain or extend their personal sense of domination and control through public channels. When things are going well for power-driven presidents and they feel they have the upper hand with their political opponents, problems may not arise. But when matters cease to go their way, as eventually will happen in a democratic system, the power-driven president's response almost certainly will take destructive forms, including rigid defensiveness and aggression against opponents. Only those with high self-esteem will be secure enough to lead as democratic political leaders should lead, with persuasion and flexibility as well as action and initiative.

Perhaps more important than the theoretical underpinnings of Barber's character analysis is the practical purpose that animates *The Presidential Character:* to help citizens choose their presidents wisely. The book's first words herald this purpose:

When a citizen votes for a presidential candidate he makes, in effect, a prediction. He chooses from among the contenders the one he thinks (or feels, or guesses) would be the best president. . . . This book is meant to help citizens and those who advise them cut through the confusion and get at some clear criteria for choosing presidents.

How, though, in the heat and haste of a presidential election, with candidates notably unwilling to bare their souls for psychological inspection, are we to find out what they are really like? Easy enough, argues Barber. To answer the complex question of what motivates a political leader, just answer two simpler questions in its stead: active or passive? ("How much energy does the man invest in his presidency?"); and positive or negative? ("Relatively speaking, does he seem to experience his political life as happy or sad, enjoyable or discouraging, positive or negative in its main effect?")

According to Barber, the four possible combinations of answers to these two questions turn out to be almost synonymous with the four psychological strategies that people use to enhance self-esteem. The *active-positives* are the healthy ones in the group. Their high sense of self-worth enables them to work hard at politics, enjoy what they do, and thus be fairly good at it. Of the four eighteenth- and nineteenth-century presidents and the sixteen twentieth-century presidents whom Barber typed, he placed Thomas Jefferson, Franklin D. Roosevelt, Harry S. Truman, Kennedy, Ford, Carter, George H. W. Bush, and Bill Clinton in this category. The *passive-positives* (James Madison, William H. Taft, Warren G. Harding, Ronald Reagan) are the affection seekers. Although not especially hard-working, they enjoy the office. The *passive-negatives* (Washington, Calvin Coolidge, Eisenhower) neither work nor play; it is duty, not pleasure or zest, that gets them into politics. Finally, there are the power-seeking *active-negatives*, who compulsively and with little satisfaction throw themselves into their presidential chores.

In Barber's view, active-negative presidents John Adams, Woodrow Wilson, Herbert Hoover, Lyndon Johnson, and Richard Nixon all shared one important personality-rooted quality: They persisted in disastrous courses of action (Adams's repressive Alien and Sedition acts, Wilson's League of Nations battle, Hoover's depression policy, Johnson's Vietnam, Nixon's Watergate) because to have conceded error would have been to lose their sense of control, something their psychological constitutions would not allow them to do. Table 7.1 summarizes Barber's four types and his categorizations of individual presidents.

Not surprisingly, *The Presidential Character* was extremely controversial when it came out in 1972. Many argued that Barber's theory was too simple, that his four types did not begin to cover the range of human complexity. At one level, this criticism is as trivial as it is true. In spelling out his theory, Barber stated clearly that "we are talking about tendencies, broad directions; no individual man exactly fits a category." He offered his character typology as a method for sizing up potential presidents, not for diagnosing and treating them. In the midst of image-laden election campaigns, a reasonably accurate shorthand device is about all we can hope for. The real question, then, is whether Barber's shorthand device is reasonably accurate.

Barber's intellectual defense of his typology's soundness, quoted in full, is not altogether comforting:

Why might we expect these two simple dimensions [active-passive, positive-negative] to outline the main character types? Because they stand for two central features of anyone's orientation toward life. In nearly every study of personality,

Table 7.1 Barber's Character Typology, with Presidents Categorized According to Type

Energy directed toward the presidency	Affect toward the presidency	
	Positive	Negative
Active	Thomas Jefferson Franklin Roosevelt Harry Truman John Kennedy Gerald Ford Jimmy Carter George Bush Bill Clinton	John Adams Woodrow Wilson Herbert Hoover Lyndon Johnson Richard Nixon
	"consistency between much activity and the enjoyment of it, indicating relatively high self-esteem and relative success in relating to the environment. . . . shows an orientation to productiveness as a value and an ability to use his styles flexibly, adaptively."	"activity has a compulsive quality, as if the man were trying to make up for something or escape from anxiety into hard work. . . . seems ambitious, striving upward, power-seeking. . . .stance toward the environment is aggressive and has a problem in managing his aggressive feelings."
Passive	James Madison William Taft Warren Harding Ronald Reagan	George Washington Calvin Coolidge Dwight Eisenhower
	"receptive, compliant, other-directed character whose life is a search for affection as a reward for being agreeable and cooperative. . . .low self-esteem (on grounds of being unlovable)."	"low self-esteem based on a sense of uselessness . . . in politics because they think they ought to be. . . .tendency is to withdraw, to escape from the conflict and uncertainty of politics by emphasizing vague principles (especially prohibitions) and procedural arrangements."

Sources: Barber's discussions of all presidents but Clinton are in *The Presidential Character: Predicting Performance in the White House*, 4th ed. (Englewood Cliffs: Prentice-Hall, 1992). Clinton is characterized by Barber in Doyle McManus, "Key Challenges Await Clinton," *Los Angeles Times*, January 20, 1993, A6.

some form of the active-passive contrast is critical; the general tendency to act or be acted upon is evident in such concepts as dominance-submission, extraversion-introversion, aggression-timidity, attack-defense, fight-flight, engagement-withdrawal, approach-avoidance. In every life we sense quickly the general energy output of the people we deal with. Similarly we catch on fairly quickly to the affect dimension—whether the person seems to be optimistic or pessimistic, hopeful or skeptical, happy or sad. The two baselines are clear and they are also independent of one another: all of us know people who are very active but seem discouraged, others who are quite passive but seem happy, and so forth. The activity baseline refers to what one does, the affect baseline to how one feels about what he does.

Both are crude clues to character. They are leads into four basic character patterns long familiar in psychological research.[24]

In the library copy of *The Presidential Character* from which I copied this passage, there is a handwritten note in the margin: "Footnote, man!" But there is no footnote to the psychological literature, here or anywhere else in the book. Casual readers might take this to mean that none was necessary, and they would be right if Barber's types really were "long familiar in psychological research" and "appeared in nearly every study of personality."[25] But they are not and they do not. As Alexander George has pointed out, personality theory itself is a "quagmire" in which "the term 'character' in practice is applied loosely and means many different things."[26] Barber's real defense of his typology—it works; look at Nixon—is not to be dismissed, but one wishes he had explained better why he thinks it works.[27]

Barber's typology also has been criticized for not being simple enough, at least not for purposes of accurate preelection application. Where, exactly, is one to look to decide if deep down candidate Jones is the energetic, buoyant person her image makers say she is? Barber is quite right to warn analysts away from their usual hunting ground—the candidate's recent performances in other high offices. These offices "are all much more restrictive than the Presidency is, much more set by institutional requirements,"[28] and thus much less fertile cultures for psychopathologies to grow in. This is Barber's only real mention of what might be considered a third, equally important component of the psychological presidency: the rarefied, courtlike atmosphere—well-described in George Reedy's *The Twilight of the Presidency*[29]—that surrounds presidents and allows those whose psychological constitutions so move them to seal themselves off from harsh political realities.

Barber's alternative to performance-based analysis—namely, a study of the candidate's "first independent political success," or FIPS, in which a personal formula for success in politics was discovered—is not very helpful either. How, for example, is one to tell which IPS was first? According to Barber's appropriately broad definition of *political,* Johnson's first success was not his election to Congress but his work as a student assistant to his college's president. Hoover's was his incumbency as student body treasurer at Stanford. Sorting through a candidate's life with the thoroughness necessary to determine his or her FIPS may or may not be an essential task. But it is clearly not a straightforward one.

Some scholars question not only the scientific basis or practical applicability of Barber's psychological theory of presidential behavior but also the importance of psychological explanation itself. Psychology appears to be almost everything to Barber, as this statement from his research design for *The Presidential Character* reveals.

What is de-emphasized in this scheme? Everything which does not lend itself to the production of potentially testable generalizations about presidential behavior. Thus we shall be less concerned with the substance or content of particular issues . . . less concern[ed] for distant phenomena, such as relationships among other political actors affecting events without much reference to the president, public opinion, broad economic or historical trends, etc.—except insofar as these enter into the president's own approach to decision-making.[30]

But is personality all that matters? Provocative though Barber's theory may be, it seems to unravel even as he applies it. A "healthy" political personality turns out to be no guarantor of presidential success. Barber classed Ford, Carter, and Bush early in their presidencies as active-positives, for example. Carter, in fact, seemed to take flexibility—a virtue characteristic of active-positives—to such an extreme that it approached vacillation and inconsistency, almost as if in reading *The Presidential Character* he had learned its lessons too well.

Nor, as Table 7.2 shows, does Barber's notion of psychological unsuitability seem to correspond to failure in office. The ranks of the most successful

Table 7.2 "Great" Presidents and Barber's Character Typology

	Positive	*Negative*
Active	Thomas Jefferson Franklin Roosevelt Harry Truman	John Adams Woodrow Wilson Lyndon Johnson [Abraham Lincoln]
Passive		George Washington Dwight Eisenhower

Note: For purposes of this table, a "great" president is defined as one who ranked among the first ten in at least one of these four polls of historians: Steve Neal, "Our Best and Worst Presidents," *Chicago Tribune Magazine*, January 10, 1982, 9–18; Robert K. Murray and Tim H. Blessing, *Greatness in the White House: Rating the Presidents, Washington through Carter* (University Park: Pennsylvania State University Press, 1988); David L. Porter, letter to author, January 15, 1982; and Arthur M. Schlesinger Jr., "The Ultimate Approval Rating," *New York Times Magazine*, December 15, 1996, 47–51. Four others who achieved this ranking (Jackson, Polk, T. Roosevelt, and McKinley) are not included because Barber did not classify them according to his typology. Lincoln's name is bracketed because Jeffrey Tulis classified him using Barber's typology.

presidents in four recent surveys by historians include some whom Barber classified as active-positives (Jefferson, Truman, and Franklin Roosevelt), but also an equal number of active-negatives (Wilson, Lyndon Johnson, and John Adams) and others whom Barber labeled passive-negatives (Washington and Eisenhower).[31] The most perverse result of classifying presidents by this standard involves Abraham Lincoln, whom Jeffrey Tulis, correctly applying Barber's theory, found to be an active-negative.[32]

Hargrove found the active-positive category equally unhelpful because of its broad expanse:

Active-positive presidents vary so as individuals that the category lacks the capacity to analyze and explain actions of presidential leadership. A schema that puts Franklin Roosevelt and Jimmy Carter in the same cell tells us that they shared high self-esteem and the capacity to learn and adapt to circumstances, but it says nothing about the great differences in political skill between them or the psychological bases for such differences.[33]

One could raise similar doubts about categories that lump together Harding and Reagan (passive-positive) or Coolidge and Eisenhower (passive-negative).

Clearly, personality is not all that matters in the presidency. As Tulis noted, Lincoln's behavior as president can be explained much better by his political philosophy and leadership skills than by his personality. Similarly, one need not resort to psychology to explain the failures of active-negatives Hoover and, in the latter years of his presidency, Lyndon Johnson. Hoover's unbending opposition to instituting massive federal relief in the face of the Great Depression may have stemmed more from ideological convictions than psychological rigidity. Johnson's refusal to change his administration's policy in Vietnam could be interpreted as the action of a self-styled consensus leader trying to steer a moderate course between hawks who wanted full-scale military involvement and doves who wanted unilateral withdrawal.[34] These presidents' actions were ineffective but not necessarily irrational.

Theoretical and practical criticisms such as these are important, and they do not exhaust the list. Observer bias is another. Because Barber's published writings provide no clear checklist of criteria by which to type candidates, subjectivity is absolutely inherent. But the criticisms should not blind us to his major contributions in *The Presidential Character:* a concentration (albeit excessive) on the importance of presidential personality in explaining presidential behavior, a sensitivity to personality's role as a variable (power does not always corrupt, nor does the office always "make the man"), and a boldness in approaching the problems voters face in predicting what kind of president a candidate will be if elected.

Public Psychology

The second side of the psychological presidency—the public's side—was Barber's concern in *The Pulse of Politics: Electing Presidents in the Media Age.* The book is about elections, those occasions when, because citizens are deciding who will fill the presidency, they presumably feel (presidential deaths aside) their emotional attachment to the office most deeply. Again Barber presents us with a typology. The public's election moods come in three varieties: *conflict* ("we itch for adventure, . . . [a] blood-and-guts political contest"), *conscience* ("the call goes out for a revival of social conscience, the restoration of the constitutional covenant"), and *conciliation* ("the public yearns for solace, for domestic tranquility").[35] In this book the types appear in recurring order as well, over a twelve-year cycle: conflict, conscience, then conciliation.

Barber's question in *The Pulse of Politics*—what is "the swirl of emotions" with which Americans surround the presidency?—is as important and original as the questions he posed in *The Presidential Character.* But again, his answer is as puzzling as it is provocative. Although Barber's theory applies only to American presidential elections since 1900, he seems convinced that the psychological "pulse" has been beating deeply, if softly, in all humankind for all time. Barber discovers conflict, conscience, and conciliation in the "old sagas" of ancient peoples and in "the psychological paradigm that dominates the modern age: the *ego,* instrument for coping with the struggles of the external world [conflict]; the *superego,* warning against harmful violations [conscience]; the *id,* longing after the thrill and ease of sexual satisfaction [conciliation]." He finds this primordial pulse firmly reinforced in American history. Conflict is reflected in our emphasis on the war story ("In isolated America, the war-makers repeatedly confronted the special problem of arousing the martial spirit against distant enemies. . . . Thus our history vibrates with *talk* about war"). Conscience is displayed in America's sense of itself as an instrument of divine providence ("our conscience has never been satisfied by government as a mere practical arrangement"). Conciliation shows up in our efforts to live with each other in a heterogeneous "nation of nationalities." In the early twentieth century, Barber argues, these three themes became the controlling force in the political psychology of the American electorate, so controlling that every presidential election since the conflict of 1900 has fit its place within the cycle: conscience in 1904, conciliation in 1908, conflict again in 1912, and so on. What caused the pulse to start beating so strongly, he feels, was the rise of national mass media.

The modern newspaper came first, just before the turn of the century. "In a remarkable historical conjunction, the sudden surge into mass popularity of the American daily newspaper coincided with the Spanish-American War." Because war stories sold papers, daily journalists also wrote about "politics as war"—that is, conflict. In the early 1900s national mass circulation magazines arrived on the scene, taking their cues from the Progressive reformers who dominated the politics of that period. "The 'muckrakers'—actually positive thinkers out to build America, not destroy reputations"—wrote of "politics as a moral enterprise," an enterprise of conscience. Then came the broadcast media, radio in the 1920s and television in the 1950s. What set them apart was their commercial need to reach not just a wide audience but the widest possible audience. "Broadcasting aimed to please, wrapping politics in fun and games . . . conveying with unmatched reach and power its core message of conciliation."

As for the cyclic pulse, the recurring appearance of the three public moods in the same order, Barber suggested that the dynamic is internal: Each type of public mood generates the next. After a conflict election ("a battle for power . . . a rousing call to arms"), a reaction sets in. Conscience calls for "the cleansing of the temple of democracy." But "the troubles do not go away," and four years later "the public yearns for solace," or conciliation. After another four years, Barber claims, "the time for a fight will come around again," and so on.

In *The Pulse of Politics,* difficulties arise not in applying the theory (a calendar will do: if it is 2004, this must be a conciliation election), but in the theory itself. Barber needed an even more secure intellectual foundation for the cyclic pulse than for the character typology, because this time he not only classified all presidential elections into three types but also asserted that they recur in a fixed order. Once again, however, one finds no footnotes. If Barber grounded his theory in scholarly sources, then it is impossible to tell—and hard to imagine— what they are. Nor does the theory stand up sturdily under its own weight. If, for example, radio and television are agents of conciliation, why have we not had more conciliating elections since they became our dominant political media? Perhaps that is why some of the "postdictions" to which Barber's theory leads are as questionable as they are easy to make. Did conciliation really typify the bitterly fought election among Clinton, Bush, and H. Ross Perot in 1992, conflict the placid election involving Clinton, Robert Dole, and Perot in 1996, or conscience the mean-spirited campaign between Vice President Al Gore and Texas governor George W. Bush in 2000?

The most interesting criticism pertinent to Barber's pulse theory, however, was made in 1972 by a political scientist concerned with the public's presidential psychology, which he described as a "climate of expectations" that "shifts and changes." This scholar wrote,

Wars, depressions, and other national events contribute to that change, but there is also a rough cycle, from an emphasis on action (which begins to look too "political") to an emphasis on legitimacy (the moral uplift of which creates its own strains) to an emphasis on reassurance and rest (which comes to seem like drift) and back to action again. One need not be astrological about it.

A year earlier this same scholar had written that although "the mystic could see the series . . . marching in fateful repetition beginning in 1900 . . . the pattern is too astrological to be convincing." Careful readers will recognize the identity between the cycles of action-legitimacy-reassurance and conflict-conscience-conciliation. Clever ones will realize that both passages were written by James David Barber.[36]

Person, Public Mood, and the Psychological Presidency

A good deal about the public's political psychology, in fact, is sprinkled through *The Presidential Character,* and the more of it one discovers, the more curious things get. Most significant is the brief concluding chapter, "Presidential Character and the Moods of the Eighth Decade" (reprinted in the three subsequent editions of the book, most recently in 1992), which contains Barber's bold suggestion of a close fit between the two sides of his model. For each type of public psychological climate, Barber posited a "resonant" type of presidential personality. This seems to be a central point in his theory of the presidency. "Much of what [a president] is remembered for," he wrote, "will depend on the fit between the dominant forces in his character and the dominant feelings in his constituency." Further, "the dangers of discord in that resonance are severe."[37]

What is the precise nature of this fit? When the public cry is for action (conflict), Barber argued, "it comes through loudest to the active-negative type, whose inner struggle between aggression and control resonates with the popular plea for toughness. . . . [The active-negative's] temptation to stand and fight receives wide support from the culture." In the public's reassurance (conciliation) mood, he wrote, "they want a friend," a passive-positive. As for the "appeal for a moral cleansing of the Presidency," or legitimacy (conscience), Barber suggests that it "resonates with the passive-negative character in its emphasis on *not* doing certain things." This leaves the active-positive, Barber's president for all seasons.[38] Blessed with a "character firmly rooted in self-recognition and self-love," Barber's "active-positive can not only *perform* lovingly or aggressively or with detachment, he can *feel* those ways."[39]

What Barber first offered in *The Presidential Character,* then, was the foundation for a model of the psychological presidency that was not only two-sided but integrated as well, one in which the "tuning, the resonance—or lack of it" between the public's "climate of expectations" and the president's personality "sets in motion the dynamic of his Presidency." Barber concentrated on the personality half of his model in *The Presidential Character,* then firmed it up and filled in the other half—the public's—in *The Pulse of Politics.* And this is where things become especially puzzling. Most authors, when they complete a multivolume opus, trumpet their accomplishment. Barber did not. In fact, one finds in *The Pulse of Politics* no mention at all of presidential character, of public climates of expectations, or of "the resonance—or lack of it"—between them.[40]

At first blush, this seems doubly strange, because there is a strong surface fit between the halves of Barber's model. As Table 7.3 indicates, in the twenty-three twentieth-century elections after Roosevelt's in 1904 (Barber did not type twentieth-century presidents before Taft), presidential character and public mood resonated sixteen times. The exceptions—active-negative Wilson's election in the conscience year of 1916, passive-negative Coolidge's in conflictual 1924, active-negative Hoover's in the conscience election of 1928, passive-negative Eisenhower's in the conciliating election of 1956, active-negative Johnson's in conscience-oriented 1964, active-negative Nixon's in conciliating 1968, and passive-positive Reagan's in conflict-dominated 1984—perhaps could be explained by successful campaign image management, an argument that would also support Barber's view of the media's power in presidential politics. In that case, a test of Barber's model would be: Did these "inappropriate" presidents lose the public's support when it found out what they were really like after the election? In every presidency but those of Coolidge, Eisenhower, and Reagan, the answer would have been yes.

On closer inspection, however, it also turns out that in every case but these the presidents whose administrations were unsuccessful were active-negatives. But, Barber tells us, active-negative presidents fail for reasons that have nothing to do with the public mood. As for the model's overall success rate of sixteen out of twenty-three, it includes ten elections that were won by active-positives who, he says, resonate with every public mood. A good hand in a wild-card

Table 7.3 Resonance of Character Type and Public Mood in Presidential Elections, 1908–1996

Election			Winning Presidential Candidate	
Year	Public mood	"Resonant" character types	Name	Character type
1908	Conciliation	Passive–positive (Active–positive)	Taft	Passive–positive
1912	Conflict	Active–negative (Active–positive)	Wilson	Active–negative
1916	Conscience	Passive–negative (Active–positive)	Wilson	Active–negative
1920	Conciliation	Passive–positive (Active–positive)	Harding	Passive–positive
1924	Conflict	Active–negative (Active–positive)	Coolidge	Passive–negative
1928	Conscience	Passive–negative (Active–positive)	Hoover	Active–negative
1932	Conciliation	Passive–positive (Active–positive)	Roosevelt	Active–positive
1936	Conflict	Active–negative (Active–positive)	Roosevelt	Active–positive
1940	Conscience	Passive–negative (Active–positive)	Roosevelt	Active–positive
1944	Conciliation	Passive–positive (Active–positive)	Roosevelt	Active–positive
1948	Conflict	Active–negative (Active–positive)	Truman	Active–positive
1952	Conscience	Passive–negative (Active–positive)	Eisenhower	Passive–negative
1956	Conciliation	Passive–positive (Active–positive)	Eisenhower	Passive–negative
1960	Conflict	Active–negative (Active–positive)	Kennedy	Active–positive
1964	Conscience	Passive–negative (Active–positive)	Johnson	Active–negative
1968	Conciliation	Passive–positive (Active–positive)	Nixon	Active–negative
1972	Conflict	Active–negative (Active–positive)	Nixon	Active–negative
1976	Conscience	Passive–negative (Active–positive)	Carter	Active–positive
1980	Conciliation	Passive–positive (Active–positive)	Reagan	Passive–positive
1984	Conflict	Active–negative (Active–positive)	Reagan	Passive–positive
1988	Conscience	Passive–negative (Active–positive)	Bush	Active–positive
1992	Conciliation	Passive–positive (Active–positive)	Clinton	Active–positive
1996	Conflict	Active–negative (Active–positive)	Clinton	Active–positive

game is seldom a good hand in straight poker; Barber's success rate in the elections not won by active-positives was only six of thirteen. In conscience elections, only once did a representative of the resonant type (passive-negative) win, while purportedly less suitable active-negatives won three times.

Barber's Prescriptions

In *The Presidential Character* and *The Pulse of Politics* Barber developed a suggestive and relatively complete model of the psychological presidency. Why he failed even to acknowledge the connection between the theories in each book, much less present them as a unified whole, remains unclear. Perhaps he feared that the lack of fit between his mood and personality types—the public and presidential components—would have distracted critics from his larger points.

In any event, the theoretical and predictive elements of Barber's approach to the presidency are sufficiently provocative to warrant him a hearing for his prescriptions for change. Barber's primary goal for the psychological presidency is that it be "de-psychopathologized." He wants to keep active-negatives out of the White House and put healthy active-positives in. He wants the public to become the master of its own political fate, breaking out of its electoral mood cycle, which is essentially a cycle of psychological dependency. Freed of their inner chains, the president and the public, Barber has claimed, will be able to forge a "creative politics" or "politics of persuasion," as he has variously dubbed it. Just what this kind of politics would be like is not clear, but apparently it would involve greater sensitivity on the part of both presidents and citizens to the ideas of the other.[41]

It will not surprise readers to learn that Barber, by and large, dismisses constitutional reform as a method for achieving his goals. After all, if the presidency is as shaped by psychological forces as he says it is, then institutional tinkering will be, almost by definition, beside the point.[42] Change, to be effective, will have to come in the hearts and minds of people: in the information they get about politics, the way they think about that information, and the way they feel about what they think. Because of this, Barber has argued, the central agent of change will have to be the most pervasive—namely, media journalism, especially its coverage of presidential elections.[43]

It is in his prescriptive writings that Barber is on most solid ground, and his answers as good as his questions. Unlike many media critics, he does not assume imperiously that the sole purpose of newspapers, magazines, and television is to elevate the masses. Barber recognizes that the media are made up of commercial enterprises that must sell papers and attract viewers. He recognizes, too, that the basic format of news coverage is the story, not the scholarly treatise. Barber's singular contribution is his argument that the media can improve the way they do all of these things at the same time, that better election stories will attract bigger audiences in more enlightening ways.

The first key to better stories, Barber has argued, is greater attention to the candidates. Election coverage that ignores the motivations, developmental histories, and basic beliefs of its protagonists is as lifeless as dramas or novels would be if they neglected these crucial human attributes. Such coverage is also uninformative. Elections, after all, present choices among people, and as Barber has shown, the kinds of people candidates are influences the kinds of presidents they would be. Good journalism, according to Barber, would "focus on the person as embodying his historical development, playing out a character born and bred in another place, connecting an old identity with a new persona—the stuff of intriguing drama from Joseph in Egypt on down. That can be done explicitly in biographical stories."[44]

Barber is commendably diffident; he does not expect reporters to master and apply his own character typology. But he does want them to search the candidates' lives for patterns of behavior, particularly the rigidity that is characteristic of active-negatives. (Of all behavior patterns, rigidity, he feels, "is probably the easiest one to spot and the most dangerous one to elect.")[45] With public interest ever high in "people" stories and psychology, Barber probably is right in thinking that this kind of reporting would not only inform readers but would engage their interest as well.

As *Washington Post* editors Leonard Downie and Robert Kaiser point out, press coverage of recent elections has sometimes tried to fulfill Barber's expectations.[46] During the nomination stage of the 1988 campaign, the "character" issue drove two Democratic candidates from the field, much to the relief of most political leaders and (eventually) most voters. Former senator Gary Hart's extramarital escapades, which were revealed by the *Miami Herald,* were politically harmful less because of his moral weakness than because of the recklessness the incidents illustrated in his character. Serious doubts also were raised about Sen. Joseph Biden's intellectual and personal depth when the press discovered that he had lied to voters about his success in school and then had tried to pass off stories from an autobiographical speech by a British politician as events drawn from his own life. As for the Republican nominee, George Bush, he triumphed in part because he was able to lay to rest the so-called wimp factor—that is, the suspicion that he was too weak to be a successful president.

Coverage of the character issue took a different and, from Barber's perspective, lamentable turn in the 1990s. Moral, not psychological, character became the media's obsession. In 1992 Clinton's truthfulness and fidelity were called into question when an Arkansas acquaintance, Gennifer Flowers, publicly charged that she and Clinton had engaged in a long-standing extramarital affair while he was governor. Clinton denied the charge but conceded that he and his wife had endured some marital problems in the past. Soon after, letters in Clinton's own hand were published suggesting that he had dodged the draft during the Vietnam War. In contrast to their strong response to the candidates whose psychological character was questioned in 1988, however, voters overcame their doubts about Clinton's moral character and elected him—an active-positive, in Barber's reckoning[47]—as president. Coverage of the 1996 election, which matched two well-established figures, the incumbent Clinton and the long-familiar Senate Republican leader Robert Dole, was less character centered than its recent predecessors. But in 1998, Clinton's affair with former White House intern Monica Lewinsky dominated the national agenda.

In campaigning for their parties' presidential nominations in 2000, Al Gore and George W. Bush each worked hard to persuade the voters that he was a leader of strong moral character. Gore emphasized that he was a family man who regarded Clinton's affair with Lewinsky as "inexcusable." Bush did his best to inoculate himself against character charges by admitting long before the first vote was cast that he had been morally lax as a younger man. He regularly ended campaign speeches by raising his hand skyward and declaring, "Should I be fortunate enough to win, when I put my hand upon the Bible, I will swear to uphold the dignity and honor of the office." The *Post* "printed book-length series of articles about the lives and careers of both men."[48]

Character concerns of the psychological sort went a long way toward determining the outcome of the general election. Gore carried a reputation into the campaign as an aggressive, experienced, and skillful debater, a reputation Bush lacked. Yet Bush ended up benefiting considerably more from their three nationally televised debates than Gore did. In the first debate, Gore treated his opponent with disdain, often speaking condescendingly when it was his turn and sighing and grimacing while Bush spoke. Chastened by the adverse public response, Gore was deferential, almost obsequious during the second debate. He hit his stride in the third debate, but the inconsistency of his behavior from one debate to the next fed voters' doubts about who Gore really was. Bush was not strongly impressive in any of the debates, but voters saw the same man in all three of them. Gore, who entered the debate season leading Bush by around five percentage points in the polls, left it trailing by five points.[49]

Engaging readers' interest is Barber's second key to better journalism. What voters need to make voting decisions is matched by what they want—namely, information about who the candidates are and what they believe. According to a study of network evening news coverage of the 1972 election campaign, which Barber cites, almost as much time was devoted to the polls, strategies, rallies, and other "horse-race" elements of the election as to the candidates' personal qualifications and issue stands combined. As Barber noted, "The viewer tuning in for facts to guide his choice would, therefore, have to pick his political nuggets from a great gravel pile of political irrelevancy."[50] Critics who doubt the public's interest in long, fleshed-out stories about what candidates think, what they are like, and what great problems they would face as president would do well to check the thirty-five years of ratings for CBS's *60 Minutes*.

An electorate whose latent but powerful interest in politics is engaged by the media will become an informed electorate because it wants to, not because it is supposed to. This is Barber's strong belief. So sensible a statement of the problem is this, and so attractive a vision of its solution, that one can forgive him for cluttering it with types and terminologies.

Notes

1. "Candidate on the Couch," *Time*, June 19, 1972, 15–17; James David Barber, *The Presidential Character: Predicting Performance in the White House* (Englewood Cliffs: Prentice-Hall, 1972); a second edition was published in 1977, a third edition in 1985, and a fourth edition in 1992. Unless otherwise indicated, the quotations cited in this essay appear in all four editions, with page numbers drawn from the first edition.

2. Hugh Sidey, "The Active-Positive Searching," *Time*, October 4, 1976, 23.

3. "After Eight Months in Office—How Ford Rates Now," *U.S. News & World Report*, April 28, 1975, 28.

4. David S. Broder, "Carter Would Like to Be an 'Active Positive,' " *Washington Post*, July 16, 1976, A12.

5. James David Barber, "An Active-Positive Character," *Time*, January 3, 1977, 17.

6. Hugh Sidey, " 'A Revolution Is Under Way,' " *Time*, March 31, 1980, 20.

7. "Cycle Races," *Time*, May 19, 1980, 29.

8. Paul J. Quirk, "What Do We Know and How Do We Know It? Research on the Presidency," in *Political Science: Looking to the Future*, ed. William J. Crotty and Alan D. Monroe, vol. 4 (Evanston: Northwestern University Press, 1991), 52. Psychologists, on the other hand, have been paying more attention to the presidency. See, for example, Dean Keith Simonton, *Why Presidents Succeed: A Political Psychology of Leadership* (New Haven: Yale University Press, 1987); and Harold M. Zullow, Gabriele Oettingen,

Christopher Peterson, and Martin E. P. Seligman, "Pessimistic Explanatory Style in the Historical Record," *American Psychologist* 43 (September 1988): 673–681.

9. Robert A. Dahl, *A Preface to Democratic Theory* (Chicago: University of Chicago Press, 1956), 6–8.

10. The phrase is Alexander Hamilton's. See Alexander Hamilton, James Madison, and John Jay, *The Federalist Papers,* with an introduction by Clinton Rossiter (New York: New American Library, 1961), no. 70, 423.

11. Seymour Martin Lipset, *The First New Nation* (New York: Basic Books, 1963), chap. 1; and Max Weber, *The Theory of Social and Economic Organization* (New York: Oxford University Press, 1947), 358.

12. Marcus Cunliffe, *George Washington: Man and Monument* (New York: New American Library, 1958), 15. See also Richard Brookhiser, *Founding Father: Rediscovering George Washington* (New York: Free Press, 1996).

13. Max Farrand, *The Records of the Federal Conventions of 1787,* 4 vols. (New Haven: Yale University Press, 1966), 1:65.

14. Jeffrey Tulis, "On Presidential Character," in *The Presidency in the Constitutional Order,* ed. Jeffrey Tulis and Joseph M. Bessette (Baton Rouge: Louisiana State University Press, 1981), 287.

15. *Federalist,* no. 71 and 72, 431–440.

16. Ibid., no. 64, 396.

17. See, for example, James David Barber, "Adult Identity and Presidential Style: The Rhetorical Emphasis," *Daedalus* 97 (summer 1968): 938–968; Barber, "Classifying and Predicting Presidential Styles: Two 'Weak' Presidents," *Journal of Social Issues* 24 (July 1968): 51–80; Barber, "The President and His Friends" (Paper presented at the annual meeting of the American Political Science Association, New York, September 1969); and Barber, "The Interplay of Presidential Character and Style: A Paradigm and Five Illustrations," in *A Source Book for the Study of Personality and Politics,* ed. Fred I. Greenstein and Michael Lerner (Chicago: Markham, 1971), 383–408.

18. Richard E. Neustadt, *Presidential Power: The Politics of Leadership* (New York: Wiley, 1960), 185.

19. Erwin C. Hargrove, *The Power of the Modern Presidency* (New York: Knopf, 1974), 33.

20. See, for example, Fred I. Greenstein, *Children and Politics* (New Haven: Yale University Press, 1965); and John E. Mueller, *War, Presidents, and Public Opinion* (New York: Wiley, 1973).

21. Paul B. Sheatsley and Jacob J. Feldman, "The Assassination of President Kennedy: Public Reactions," *Public Opinion Quarterly* 28 (summer 1964): 189–215.

22. Unless otherwise indicated, all quotes from Barber in this section are from *Presidential Character,* chap. 1.

23. Ibid., 145, 206. In more recent writings, Barber's assessment of presidential passivity has grown more harsh. A passive-positive, for example, "may . . . preside over the cruelest of regimes." *Presidential Character,* 3d ed., 529–530.

24. Barber, *Presidential Character,* 12.

25. Thirteen years after *The Presidential Character* was first published, in an appendix to the third edition Barber described a variety of works to show that his character types "are not a product of one author's fevered imagination," but rather keep "popping up in study after study." In truth, most of the cited works are not scholarly studies of psychological character at all, nor are they claimed to be by their authors.

26. Alexander George, "Assessing Presidential Character," *World Politics* 26 (January 1974): 234–282.

27. Ibid. George argued that Nixon's behavior was not of a kind that Barber's theory would lead one to predict.

28. Barber, *Presidential Character*, 99.

29. George Reedy, *The Twilight of the Presidency* (New York: New American Library, 1970). See also Bruce Buchanan, *The Presidential Experience: What the Office Does to the Man* (Englewood Cliffs: Prentice-Hall, 1978).

30. James David Barber, "Coding Scheme for Presidential Biographies," January 1968, mimeographed, 3.

31. The surveys are reported in Steve Neal, "Our Best and Worst Presidents," *Chicago Tribune Magazine*, January 10, 1982, 9–18; Robert K. Murray and Tim H. Blessing, *Greatness in the White House: Rating the Presidents, Washington through Carter* (University Park: Pennsylvania State University Press, 1988); David L. Porter, letter to author, January 15, 1982; and Arthur M. Schlesinger Jr., "The Ultimate Approval Rating," *New York Times Magazine*, December 15, 1996, 47–51.

32. Tulis, "On Presidential Character."

33. Erwin C. Hargrove, "Presidential Personality and Leadership Style," in *Researching the Presidency: Vital Questions, New Approaches*, ed. George C. Edwards III, John H. Kessel, and Bert Rockman (Pittsburgh: University of Pittsburgh Press, 1993), 96.

34. Erwin C. Hargrove, "Presidential Personality and Revisionist Views of the Presidency," *Midwest Journal of Political Science* 17 (November 1973): 819–836.

35. James David Barber, *The Pulse of Politics: Electing Presidents in the Media Age* (New York: Norton, 1980). Unless otherwise indicated, all quotes from Barber in this section are from chapters 1 and 2.

36. The first quote appears in *Presidential Character*, 9; the second in "Interplay of Presidential Character and Style," n.2.

37. Barber, *Presidential Character*, 446.

38. Ibid., 446, 448, 451.

39. Ibid., 243.

40. Barber did draw a connection between the public's desire for conciliation and its choice of a passive-positive in the 1980 election: "Sometimes people want a fighter in the White House and sometimes a saint. But the time comes when all we want is a friend, a pal, a guy to reassure us that the story is going to come out all right. In 1980, that need found just the right promise in Ronald Reagan, the smiling American." James David Barber, "Reagan's Sheer Personal Likability Faces Its Sternest Test," *Washington Post*, January 20, 1981, 8.

41. James David Barber, "Tone-Deaf in the Oval Office," *Saturday Review/World*, January 12, 1974, 10–14.

42. James David Barber, "The Presidency after Watergate," *World*, July 31, 1973, 16–19.

43. Barber, *Pulse of Politics*, chap. 15. For other statements of his views on how the press should cover politics and the presidency, see James David Barber, ed., *Race for the Presidency: The Media and the Nominating Process* (Englewood Cliffs: Prentice-Hall, 1978), chaps. 5–7; Barber, "Not Quite the *New York Times*: What Network News Should Be," *Washington Monthly*, September 1979, 14–21; and Barber, *Politics by Humans: Research on American Political Leadership* (Durham: Duke University Press, 1988), chaps. 17–18.

44. Barber, *Race for the Presidency*, 145.

45. Ibid., 171, 162–164.

46. Leonard Downie Jr. and Robert G. Kaiser, *The News About the News: American Journalism in Peril* (New York: Knopf, 2002), 36.

47. James David Barber, "Predicting Hope with Clinton at Helm," *Raleigh News and Observer*, January 17, 1993. For a different view of Clinton, one that offers examples of "the driven investments of energy" characteristic of active-negatives, see Stanley A. Renshon, "A Preliminary Assessment of the Clinton Presidency: Character, Leadership and Performance," *Political Psychology* 15 (1994): 331–394.

48. Downie and Kaiser, *News About the News,* 36.

49. Barber, *Race for the Presidency,* 174, 182–183.

50. Michael Nelson, "The Election: Ordinary Politics, Extraordinary Outcome," in *The Elections of 2000,* ed. Michael Nelson (Washington, D.C.: CQ Press, 2001), 78–79.

Part III Presidential Selection

8 The Presidency and the Nominating Process: Politics and Power

Richard Pious

The Constitution defines the pool of possible presidents in any election as consisting of every "natural born Citizen" who has "attained to the Age of thirty-five Years, and been fourteen Years a Resident within the United States"—more than one hundred million people. The Constitution also says that "[t]he executive Power shall be vested in a President of the United States of America"—one person. Historically, it has been the job of the major political parties to narrow the field of possible presidents to the two candidates from whom the voters make their final choice. During the early nineteenth century, congressional caucuses did this job on behalf of their parties. Caucuses were then replaced by national party conventions dominated by state party bosses. The conventions continue to meet every four years, but since the 1970s they have been dominated by delegates chosen by the voters in primaries. In this chapter, Richard Pious reviews the history of the presidential nominating process and analyzes the kinds of candidates whom different processes have tended to favor. He worries that in the current, primaries-dominated process, "those who emerge with the nomination lack national executive experience, a situation that rarely occurs in other nations." Pious suggests that "a nominating system that restores some peer review and a greater role for party professionals and members of Congress"—the same groups that dominated earlier nominating processes—might yield more qualified presidential nominees.

Americans have never been satisfied with the way parties nominate presidential candidates. By a nearly five-to-one margin, voters in 2000 thought that party politicians and big contributors had more say than ordinary citizens about the candidates the Democrats and Republicans would select, and they felt powerless to affect a process they thought was too long, too boring, and too uninformative.[1] How can the nominating contests attract the best politicians?

How can parties select their nominees in a way that engages the voters and fosters the legitimacy and increases the democratic mandate of those who win? Throughout American history, parties have experimented with different answers to these questions, but what remains a constant in American politics is that no approach to candidate selection has been able to simultaneously maximize participation of the voters and the responsibility of the contenders' peers to judge their qualifications.

Transformation of the Nominating Processes

The Framers of the Constitution knew that George Washington would be chosen unanimously as the first president. They assumed that from then on the electoral college would "nominate" five candidates for the presidency, each probably representing one of the larger states, and that the House of Representatives would choose from among this group. During Washington's presidency, however, politicians coalesced into "factions" and then into the beginnings of national parties. In 1796 the electoral college was organized by Federalists supporting John Adams, and by anti-Federalists backing Thomas Jefferson. If elections were to be decided by the electoral college, the parties would need a method to nominate candidates beforehand.

King Caucus: Nomination by Congressional Party

Between 1800 and 1824 the organization of electoral college votes was entrusted to party members in Congress. They would meet after the congressional session was over, with Federalists in one party caucus and Republicans (the name taken by the anti-Federalists) in another. Each caucus would endorse a contender by plurality vote of those present and send word of their endorsements to the state parties.

These congressional caucuses gave an advantage to Washington insiders, such as cabinet secretaries or congressional leaders, who were known to members of Congress and who could lobby directly at the Capitol for the nomination. Governors and other officials in the states were at a disadvantage, and none ran for president during this period. The Founders themselves were at the forefront of presidential politics: two-thirds of those receiving electoral votes in the first eight presidential elections had been members of the Congresses convening under the Articles of Confederation during the 1780s.

Between 1801 and 1829 each new president—Thomas Jefferson, James Madison, James Monroe, and John Quincy Adams—had served previously as secretary of state, with all but Jefferson serving in his immediate predecessor's administration. Each secretary of state was able to win the Republicans' congressional caucus endorsement by defeating cabinet or congressional rivals. Each promised cabinet positions to prominent congressional party leaders or their friends. Within each cabinet ambitious men jockeyed for position, and tried to consolidate their influence in Congress by tailoring their policies and positions to please legislators from their party.

The result was the development of cabinet government. The president was surrounded by cabinet secretaries with their own followings in Congress. To get anything done, the president had to win the support of these men. Important presidential decisions were made in council, with presidents reading formal state papers outlining their arguments to the cabinet, followed by spirited discussion and then a vote on the president's proposal. If a president received little or no support in the cabinet, he would often postpone the decision or abandon the policy.

Although the presidents who served in this period were all experienced and intelligent, cabinet government was a prescription for a weak and indecisive presidency. James Madison, who at the constitutional convention had wanted a "council of state" to diffuse executive power, governed between 1809 and 1817 through the system of cabinet consensus, and the resulting power vacuum was filled by congressional "hawks" eager for war with Great Britain. With a reluctant and indecisive president at the helm, the country suffered military defeats in Canada and a British raid that destroyed the Capitol and the White House. The situation improved only when a desperate president nominated his secretary of state, James Monroe, to simultaneously serve as secretary of war, putting an end to cabinet decision making and bringing some unity to government policy.

Nominating Conventions: Nomination
by State Party Organizations

The rise of Jacksonian democracy in the 1820s led to the abandonment of the congressional caucus and with it an end to cabinet government. In the presidential election of 1824 Andrew Jackson did not win the congressional caucus endorsement, but he nonetheless won pluralities of the popular and electoral college votes. In the contingency election that followed, the House chose John Quincy Adams, who had been "nominated" by resolutions of a number of state legislatures (but also had not won the congressional caucus endorsement). Adams picked House Speaker Henry Clay to be his secretary of state and thus his presumed successor. An enraged Jackson charged that a corrupt bargain between Adams and Clay had denied him the White House.

Jackson ran again in 1828, promising to sweep away the remnants of the corrupt Republican Party. He did not even try to win the endorsement of "King Caucus" but simply nominated himself for the presidency, winning endorsements from state conventions and some state legislatures. Jackson was elected, and the consequences for presidential governance were enormous. Because he had not been nominated by members of Congress, he felt no accountability to a congressional party. As president he exercised constitutional prerogatives to block the legislature's majority, making use of the veto to make policy of his own. Because he had not needed to put congressional leaders in his cabinet to win a nomination, he downgraded the cabinet, not even meeting with it for much of his first term. Jackson established the principle that a president could issue orders to cabinet secretaries and fire them if they did not follow his policies.

King Caucus was gone, but what would replace it? The answer was provided by the advances in water and rail transportation that by the 1830s made interstate travel along the eastern seaboard safe, comfortable, quick, and inexpensive. Anti-Masons convened the first national convention in 1830 to organize themselves as a political party and held a presidential nominating convention in 1831. The new national Republican Party held a convention in December 1831, and the Democratic Party met in the Baltimore Athenaeum in May 1832. The Democrats nominated Martin Van Buren as Jackson's second-term vice president and passed a resolution concurring in the "nominations" for reelection that Jackson had received "in various parts of the Union" by Democratic state parties.

Conventions were not democratic expressions of the will of the rank and file. "Less than one hundred men in any convention . . . really dictate what occurs," Bronx County's Democratic party boss Ed Flynn admitted years later.[2] State and local party bosses held the delegates' proxies. In many states a "unit rule" required each delegation to "caucus" (hold a meeting off the convention floor), and a majority of delegates under the guidance of the leaders then determined how the entire state's votes were to be cast. Some delegations would remain uncommitted, voting for a "favorite son" governor or senator, until the bosses completed their bargains with a leading candidate's manager and threw their support his way. "I authorize no bargains and will be bound by none," Abraham Lincoln telegraphed his managers in 1860 at Chicago's Wigwam Hall, site of the Republican convention. "Damn Lincoln," one of his zealous managers responded, and won Indiana by offering to make Caleb Smith secretary of the interior; Pennsylvania by giving Simon Cameron the War Department; and

New York by offering Salmon Chase the Treasury Department. In 1932 Franklin Roosevelt's campaign manager, Jim Farley, made a deal with Virginia to put Sen. Claude Swanson in the cabinet; won Missouri by offering patronage to the Pendergast machine in Kansas City; won Louisiana by seating a delegation headed by its governor, Huey Long, who was involved in a credentials fight with a rival Louisiana faction; and won Texas by offering Roosevelt's main rival, John Nance Garner, the vice presidency.

During the era of boss-dominated conventions, the front-runner would try to build a critical coalition over several ballots by convincing uncommitted delegations to join his bandwagon. Other candidates might gang up to encourage defections from the front-runner's coalition. (Democrats from 1832 to 1936 required a two-thirds vote for nomination in order to block any nominee who could not appeal to both North and South.) A rival coalition might challenge the credentials of some of the front-runner's delegates, start a platform fight to try to split his coalition, or raise a divisive procedural issue. In the end, a deadlocked convention might reject all the leading contenders and choose a "dark horse." Typically, these nominees did well in the elections, with all but Republican Wendell Willkie in 1940 winning—which may say something for the political acumen of the bosses behind them.

The convention system profoundly affected the presidency: "What the party wants," James Bryce, a noted British commentator on American politics observed late in the nineteenth century, "is not a good president but a good candidate."[3] Delegates favored nominees of mediocre ability who often lacked national government experience, but who were known by state party bosses. Between 1836 and 1900 serious contenders at the major party conventions included thirteen governors and ten Union generals, most of whom had initially been given their military commissions because they were state politicians. Only two cabinet secretaries received delegate votes, although twenty senators—themselves elected by party leaders in the state legislatures—contended. The convention system offered an open invitation to bosses to engage in influence peddling and outright corruption in the administration of a president they had handpicked.

In the early and mid-twentieth century, as the United States assumed the responsibilities of a great power, party bosses rose to the occasion and nominated distinguished public servants, including Theodore Roosevelt, William Howard Taft, Woodrow Wilson, Herbert Hoover, and Dwight Eisenhower. Even then they sometimes slipped back to old habits—witness their nomination of Warren Harding. The pattern of governors and senators dominating the field continued: between 1900 and 1968, nineteen senators and twenty-one governors, but only three cabinet secretaries, two members of the House, and two generals, received a significant number of convention votes.

The Primary and Caucus System: Nomination
by the Party in the Electorate

A second set of changes in nominating politics arose from the erosion of the legitimacy and authority of the post–New Deal Democratic Party in the 1960s, which was caused by the unpopularity of the Vietnam War with party activists; the mobilization of newly enfranchised African American voters in the South; and the student movement on university campuses. Between 1968 and 1972 the Democrats transferred the power to decide on the composition of a state's convention delegates from the state party organization to its party in the electorate—that is, from the bosses to the voters.

The mechanism that made this transfer possible was the primary contest, defined as a vote within a party to determine the preferences of its members. The first presidential primary had been held in Florida, which in 1904 used a "preference primary" that allowed voters to indicate their choice for the presidential nomination, although the convention delegates were still chosen by party leaders. By 1916, twenty states had established primaries, but many were still Florida-style "beauty contests." In the 1920s, due to high cost and low voter participation, eight states dropped primaries and returned to the caucus system.

Because so few states actually permitted the voters to select convention delegates, until the 1972 nominating season contenders could lose a majority of the sixteen or so primaries or not enter them at all and still be nominated: only two-fifths of the top vote-getters in the primary season were nominated by the conventions between 1912 and 1968. Things reached a crisis point in 1968, when Vice President Hubert Humphrey won the Democratic nomination without entering a single Democratic primary; his support came from party bosses who controlled more than 60 percent of the delegates. To many rank-and-file Democrats, especially the antiwar activists supporting Sen. Eugene McCarthy, the system seemed outrageously undemocratic. Journalists focusing on "smoke-filled rooms" and boss-dominated conventions joined them in delegitimizing the system.

The Democrats subsequently established the Commission on Party Structure and Delegate Selection (the McGovern-Fraser Commission) and adopted rules for 1972. The state parties were required either to hold primaries to select delegates to the national convention or to hold open caucuses (meetings at which any registered Democrat could participate) to select delegates to state conventions that would subsequently choose delegates to the national convention. Using either system, rank-and-file voters, not party bosses, would select the delegates to the convention. Delegations would no longer be bound by the unit rule, which Democrats repealed in 1968. The unified state delegation controlled by party bosses gave way to divided delegations in which several candidates might gain convention votes if they did well in the open state contests. The Republicans soon followed suit with similar rules changes, and most state legislatures opted for primaries rather than open caucuses: the number of primaries zoomed from 15 in 1968, to 27 by 1976, and to 40 by 1992. In 2000, 38 states held primaries that chose approximately three-quarters of the elected convention delegates, with caucuses choosing the remainder.

Modern presidential nominating campaigns are organized by the contenders, not by state and local party bosses. A contender can run for president even without the backing of state party leaders by appealing to voters directly in primaries and caucuses. Those chosen to run for convention delegates in primaries and caucuses have been selected by, and remain loyal to, a particular person's organization, not to a local party organization. Put another way, the delegate no longer belongs to the leader of the party in his or her state, but rather is a contender loyalist who takes direction from the contender's organization at the convention.

The primary system has transformed the field of contenders. A strong stomach, personal wealth or access to well-heeled contributors, name recognition, organizational abilities, and ease in dealing with the media are essential. No group of bosses meeting in a convention backroom now determines the ideal qualities of the party nominee for the next election cycle, much less chooses the party's candidate. It makes no sense to speak of "Republicans choosing an outsider" or "Democrats deciding on a centrist" in an era when the decisions about who will run are made by politicians who happen to see the ideal president in the bathroom mirror.

The way candidates are nominated today does nothing to enhance the authority of the presidency, and in some ways it detracts from the power of incumbent presidents. Nominees are beholden to special interests and large campaign contributors, rather than to state party organizations. Indeed, they cannot even think of mounting a run for the nomination without access to huge amounts of campaign cash. The length of the primary season means contenders must engage in an exhausting endurance contest. They are encouraged by their media advisers to deal with all issues tactically rather than substantively. In turn, if they change their positions they are characterized by the media and voters as mere "politicians" who have no principles. Each nominee's character and private life are subject to media scrutiny often based on rumor and innuendo.

Who Gets Nominated?

Does the nominating process attract the most qualified candidates? Contenders usually come from a small group of career politicians, most of whom have experience in public office, access to large amounts of money, and (especially) experience in running a media campaign or otherwise influencing public opinion. What they often do not have is experience in national government, particularly within the executive branch they aspire to lead.

Contenders with Prior Political Experience

Incumbent presidents, the only contenders with experience in the office, won twenty-three convention renominations between 1836 and 1996, and, even before that, Adams, Jefferson, Madison, Monroe, John Quincy Adams, and Jackson were their party's choices for a second term. But not all incumbents want a second term, nor do all get renominated. Several pre–Civil War presidents, such as James K. Polk, Millard Fillmore, Franklin Pierce, and James Buchanan, pledged to serve a single term or were discouraged from continuing. John Tyler and Andrew Johnson were sympathetic to the opposition party and therefore were ditched at the first opportunity. Later, in the post–Civil War period, incumbents' chances for renomination improved. Republican presidents dominated the largely African American party organizations in the southern states through their control of federal patronage, and this enabled them to amass a great lead in convention delegates and virtually assure themselves renomination. Because of the increase in federal patronage and contracts channeled through state parties, vice presidents who succeeded to the presidency after Theodore Roosevelt found it fairly easy to win the support of state party leaders and capture their party's nomination. But in the era of primary contests, presidents who are unpopular with the party rank and file are vulnerable to challenges within their own party: Gerald Ford in 1976 and Jimmy Carter in 1980 had to stave off intraparty challengers who nearly defeated them. As a result of the split in their parties, both candidates lost in the general elections.

A party that does not renominate its incumbent president usually has no chance to win the general election. When Polk was not renominated in 1848, opposition Whigs won with Zachary Taylor; when Fillmore was dropped in 1852, opposition Democrats won with Franklin Pierce; when Buchanan retired in 1860, opposition Republicans won with Abraham Lincoln. Similarly, when Harry Truman and Lyndon Johnson faced stiff opposition and withdrew from the contest, it presaged victory by the Republicans.

A president may try to pass the nomination to an heir apparent or to block another contender, but most such attempts do not work. Calvin Coolidge did not want his secretary of commerce, Herbert Hoover, to succeed him, but Coolidge had no influence at the Republican convention of 1928. Eisenhower wanted Treasury Secretary Robert Anderson, but in 1960 Anderson declined to run, allowing Vice President Nixon to assume the mantle of heir apparent. Some presidents have helped heirs win the nomination and election, as Ronald Reagan did with George H. W. Bush. But often the heir apparent loses the election, as did Hubert Humphrey in 1968 and Al Gore in 2000. The president can make it clear that he is sympathetic to their efforts during the primary season, help them raise funds, and shape public policy to give them credit for accomplishments in the administration. But it may be difficult for both president and heir to make the transition after the nomination—because each may view himself as the titular head of the party, entitled to speak for it and set its policy. Nixon in 1960 pleaded with Eisenhower to take measures against a crippling recession, and Humphrey in 1968 wanted Johnson to stop the bombing in Vietnam—neither president did so until it was too late. In 2000 Gore and President Clinton were unable to mesh their campaign efforts successfully, and considerable friction existed between their staffers.

Vice presidents have become viable contenders for presidential nominations because they have been transformed from marginal figures with little to do in Washington into important presidential advisers, policy implementers, and party campaigners. Until the twentieth century most vice presidents were not presidential contenders. Between 1789 and 1900 only seven vice presidents became president, three by winning party nominations and getting elected (John Adams, Thomas Jefferson, and Martin Van Buren) and four by succession (John Tyler, Millard Fillmore, Andrew Johnson, and Chester Arthur). Of those who became president by succession, none subsequently won renomination.

Between 1901 and 1989, seven vice presidents became president: Theodore Roosevelt, Calvin Coolidge, Harry Truman, and Lyndon Johnson succeeded to the office and subsequently won renomination and election. Richard Nixon was nominated for president and lost the election in 1960; eight years later he was nominated and elected president. Bush won his party nomination and the subsequent election in 1988—the first time this had happened since Van Buren did it in 1836. Gerald Ford became vice president through the appointment procedures of the Twenty-fifth Amendment, succeeded to the presidency when Nixon resigned in 1974, and won the presidential nomination of his party in 1976. Three other vice presidents won their party's presidential nominations but lost the general election: Hubert Humphrey in 1968, Walter Mondale in 1984 (after a four-year hiatus), and Al Gore in 2000.

One might expect that secretaries of state, defense, and Treasury, heads of the most important cabinet departments, with executive experience in national government, would be odds-on favorites to win presidential nominations. But department secretaries were favored only in the congressional caucus system. Since the 1830s only five cabinet secretaries have been viable contenders at a national convention: in the era of media politics many are "mentioned" as potential contenders but few make the race, and since 1824 only Taft in 1908 and Hoover in 1928 won major party nominations while serving in the cabinet. Most presidents have not served in the cabinet and come into office with little or no national executive experience.

Some presidents have been members of Congress, but the majority take office having few connections with the legislators with whom they will have to work.[4] One or more senators are almost always in the field of contenders (fifty-nine through 2000), but hardly any become president. Only one senator in the nineteenth century (Benjamin Harrison) and two in the twentieth (Warren Harding and John F. Kennedy) were elected directly from the Senate. Just after Kennedy became president, some political scientists—generalizing from a sample of one—argued that senators were likely to win presidential nominations because they served in Washington, got national media attention, had high name recognition, and dealt with important national issues. For a time this generalization held up: between 1960 and 1972 every major party nominee was a current or former senator. Yet in 1964 and 1972, the nominee who was a sitting senator (Barry Goldwater in 1964 and George McGovern in 1972) proceeded to lose the presidential election by huge margins. The anti-Washington mood of the voters made such candidates, who were steeped in "legislative language" and practices, less attractive to voters than the incumbent president seeking reelection.

Only eight serious contenders have competed for a presidential nomination while serving in the House. Of these, just one, James A. Garfield, has ever been elected president, and that was in 1880. Some presidential nominees have served in the House at some point in their careers, but they moved on to other public office or returned to private life before running for the White House.

Governors have executive experience but not in national politics. Nevertheless, they have done well in winning presidential nominations. With the end of King Caucus, governors became part of the field, with forty-two serious contenders between 1844 and 2000. In the nineteenth century four won the presidency, including James Polk, Rutherford Hayes, Grover Cleveland, and William McKinley. The list of the six elected in the twentieth century includes Wilson, Franklin Roosevelt, Carter, Reagan, Clinton, and George W. Bush. Four of the five most recent presidents were governors.

Governors usually win nominations because of an anti-Washington mood in the electorate: they portray themselves as Washington outsiders ready to shake up the capital and as vigorous executives who know how to solve problems. Governors also seem to be better able to organize efficient campaigns and fund them adequately, often relying on a core of in-state private and corporate contributors who have dealt with their state governments.

Military Officers

Military officers rarely win presidential nominations. Fifteen have been contenders for the nomination, but only those who were successful commanders in major wars became president: Washington, Jackson, William Henry Harrison, Taylor, Grant, and Eisenhower. In the nineteenth century a number won nominations and were defeated. It is not likely that anyone would attempt to run directly from military service today because the media skills and financial connections a contender needs are not acquired in a military career. Instead, military heroes such as John McCain seek elective public office at a lower level after their service is ended and then try for the presidential nomination.

Geographical Politics

Through 1820 all the nominees of the congressional caucus were Virginians. In the era of boss-dominated conventions between 1836 and 1968, eleven of the Whig and Republican nominees came from Ohio and six from New York, while fourteen of the Democratic nominees came from New York alone. Of the sixty-eight major party nominations in this period, Republicans gave only four to candidates from small states, all of whom subsequently lost the election. Democrats nominated only three such candidates: two of them were elected (Franklin Pierce of New Hampshire in 1852 and Harry Truman of Missouri in 1948), while William Jennings Bryan of Nebraska squandered three nominations (1896, 1900, and 1908). Before the Civil War, several nominees chosen or endorsed by conventions came from the South, including Jackson, William Harrison, Polk, and Taylor. After the Civil War, southerners were deemed to be excluded from consideration. Until 1976 and Carter's nomination, the only southerners chosen were Wilson (born in Virginia, but whose political career was spent in New Jersey) and Lyndon Johnson, a Texan who emphasized his western rather than southern roots.

Since the reforms of 1972, the geographic spread has increased: candidates can come from anywhere, and neither the South nor small states are excluded from the talent pool. For the Republicans, the old New York/Ohio combination has given way to the success of candidates from large Sun Belt states, especially California (Nixon and Reagan) and Texas (both Bushes). For Democrats, the picture is mixed, but since 1964 the party has won the White House only when it has nominated southern centrists (Johnson, Carter, and Clinton). One reason for the geographic switch is that since the early 1980s the Sun Belt states have gained population, and the Snow Belt states have lost population. As this trend continued, the Sun Belt also increased in electoral college strength because the House is required to reapportion its seats after each census, which consequently shifts the numbers in state electoral college delegations.

Do parties need to nominate experienced Washington insiders who have lengthy track records in national politics and who are considered knowledgeable and intelligent? There is no evidence that voters care about these traits. Since the mid-twentieth century, the outsider who ran against the insider politics of Washington was more likely to win. Such victors include Eisenhower, Carter, Reagan, Clinton, and the younger Bush. In the thirteen contests between 1952 and 2000, the candidates with less Washington experience won four times and lost twice, one race involved two Washington outsiders, and six involved two insiders.

The Nominating Season

The presidential nominating process is a two-year marathon. A large group of potential participants is winnowed down to a small field of contenders from which a winner eventually emerges. Is this lengthy process, with its emphasis on media relations, polls, and the ability to raise huge amounts of money, the best way to ensure good candidates?

David Broder, a columnist for the *Washington Post*, once argued that an "inner-club" of newspaper editorialists and columnists acted as screening committee of "talent scouts" that identified presidential possibilities that party professionals might otherwise overlook. Early attention from the "club" of pundits may help a campaign establish its credibility, especially with large campaign contributors, but it is also true that changes in public attitudes have made the establishment media endorsement as much a liability as an asset. Many voters consider columnists part of the Washington establishment. Contenders may therefore prefer to bypass tough scrutiny on national issues by informed journalists in favor of "soft" interviews on late-night television and all-day radio talk shows in which empathy rather than knowledge bonds them to their viewers and listeners. In 1992 Bill Clinton went on Arsenio Hall's late-night program and played jazz riffs on the saxophone in front of a national audience of millions. That scene alone was worth far more than a thousand words from newspaper columnists.

Where the media could be useful—in providing peer review—they tend to falter. An examination of mainstream media coverage of contenders just before the primary season starts indicates that only a tiny percentage of stories explore the candidates' records, only one-quarter deal with their positions, and a majority of stories are concerned with fund-raising and political strategy and tactics—the horserace.[5]

Until the most recent elections, prenomination polls had a mixed record of predicting the nominees. Only five or six politicians achieve contender status in the preconvention polls in any election cycle.[6] In some nominating seasons a contender can come out of nowhere and win a nomination, and high standing in the early polls does not guarantee anyone the nomination. Jimmy Carter, an obscure former governor from Georgia, won the Democratic nomination and the presidency in 1976, even though he had not been included in the polls the previous year. In 1986 Michael Dukakis's name did not appear on a list of eighteen likely Democratic candidates in the Gallup polls, yet in 1988 he won the Democratic nomination. Pre-primary polls sometimes overstate a front-runner's strength: in 1984 the New York Times published poll results before the first set of primaries indicating that Walter Mondale held a commanding lead. Shortly thereafter Mondale was in the fight of his life against Gary Hart. In 1996 and 2000, however, a combination of pre-primary polls, early fund-raising, cash reserves, and regional strength was the best predictor of who actually would win the nomination.[7] If this pattern holds true in the future, contenders must become political heavyweights before entering the nominating contests. They cannot rely on pulling themselves up by their bootstraps once the voting begins.[8] And one of the best ways to become a political heavyweight is to attract campaign contributions.

"You need three things to run for public office," House Speaker Tip O'Neill used to say, "money, money and money." Nowhere is this more true than in presidential nominating politics. The Federal Election Campaign Amendments of 1974 placed a spending limit on each contender's pre-nomination campaign. The law also limits campaign contributions. No individual may contribute more than $1,000 and no political action committee or political party committee may contribute more than $5,000 to a contender in the preconvention period.

Each contender is eligible for matching funds from the federal Treasury, if he or she raises $5,000 in each of twenty states in amounts of $250 or less. The Treasury then matches, dollar for dollar, all contributions of $250 or less. The Supreme Court later ruled that a contender who chooses not to accept matching funds is not limited to the expenditure ceiling.[9] Candidates who receive less than 10 percent of the vote in two consecutive state primary contests would lose their eligibility for federal funding. In effect, the law helps winnow out the weaker candidates by drying up their funding almost immediately, thus narrowing the field to three or four candidates within a few weeks after the first contests are held. The system favors contenders who can raise large amounts of money before the primary season begins, an advantage that is amplified because they are the only contenders who will retain credibility with the media. The money advantage is real and decisive: since 1980 every contender who eventually won a major party nomination led the field in funds raised on December 31 of the year prior to the convention. (It may be the case, however, that the ability to raise the most funds is the result, not the cause, of a front-running candidacy.)

Caucus-Convention and Primary Contests:
Are They Democratic?

The reforms of the 1970s were designed to put more power into the hands of the parties in the electorate, and it is fair to ask if these reforms have done so.

Caucuses have become open-participation events rather than closed gatherings of party leaders and their supporters. Some states attract 10 percent to 15 percent of registered party voters, but the overall participation rate averages around 3 percent. With such low turnout, caucuses cannot represent the parties in the electorate in the states that use them. They are less an exercise in mass voter mobilization than a forum for organized interests who can get their members to the meetings.[10] Because the Iowa caucuses are the first contest held by any state for convention delegates, they help winnow the field of contenders substantially. The winner and second-place finishers in

Iowa receive much more media coverage than other contenders and usually enjoy a surge in campaign contributions. In 1984, for example, Gary Hart took second place and George McGovern finished third, with fewer than fifteen hundred votes separating them. Hart received a boost in his campaign from the press, while McGovern was ignored and soon dropped out. Winning Iowa may mean little, but doing poorly usually means quitting the race within a month.

Proponents of state primaries argue that since 1972 these contests have become mass participation exercises in intraparty democracy, with tens of millions of voters taking part. One-quarter to one-third of the eligible voters turn out in most competitive state contests. But turnout has been declining since the 1970s, and in 2000 it was only 10.1 percent of eligible voters. Moreover, fewer Americans are paying attention to media coverage of the primary season, with the percentages dropping from 28 percent in February 1988 to 18 percent in February 2000.[11]

By tradition (and now by national party rules), the first primary is held in New Hampshire. Because of the enormous media exposure the New Hampshire results generate for the winner, it is one of the most important contests.[12] Turnout is always high: more than 80 percent of those eligible in the state turned out to vote in 1996 and 2000. Victory in New Hampshire is no guarantee of success, however; it must be followed by many other primary victories. Conversely, losing in New Hampshire need not be fatal, as Walter Mondale demonstrated in 1984. In 1992 Bill Clinton did not win the state, but, by coming in second to the favored New England candidate (Sen. Paul Tsongas of Massachusetts), he won the contest in the eyes of the media.

The primary electorate is unrepresentative. Primaries draw a disproportionate number of voters from higher socioeconomic groups. Nor is the primary electorate representative of the racial diversity of the population because Iowa and New Hampshire, the earliest states, are disproportionately white. These states, with their relatively small populations, serve to winnow the field, but they also disadvantage voters from states that hold contests later, and they give greater influence to white voters than to minority groups. The biggest distortions are ideological: Democratic primary voters are more likely to be liberal than the pool of all Democratic registered voters, while Republican primary voters are heavily skewed toward the conservative end of the party's spectrum.

Defenders of the primaries counter that in all cases since 1972 the winner of the primary season (and the eventual nominee) has *become* the first choice of the party's voters as expressed in public opinion polls. The primary winner is transformed into the leader of the party by virtue of subjecting himself (and someday *herself*) to the endurance contest and coming out victorious.[13]

In 1988, fourteen southern and border states decided to hold their primaries on March 8. Six other states joined in as well, and more than one-third of the convention delegates were chosen on "Super Tuesday," creating not only a large regional primary but also a make or break contest. In 1992 Super Tuesday gave Bill Clinton front-runner status after his losses in Iowa and New Hampshire.[14] Other states moved up their primary dates, and by 1996 and 2000, more than half the delegates were chosen in the first five weeks of voting. The nominating contest is now over almost before it begins.

The bunching of state contests means that contenders must do well immediately or face quick elimination, given the high cost of campaigning, and this in turn favors those who are well funded and well organized from the beginning. Front-runners employ a twofold strategy: first, in the early primaries they try to eliminate rivals who offer voters the same regional or ideological appeal, and, second, in the "shakeout" period when states in a specific region hold contests on the same day, they must defeat the remaining opponents. Long-shot candidates, after intensive campaigning in Iowa or New Hampshire, may make an immediate breakthrough by doing well in those states.[15] The compressed primary season, however, may not leave enough time for the long-shot candidates to capitalize on these victories.

National Conventions

Convention delegates no longer exercise independent judgment, but simply confirm the results of the primary and caucus contests. Nevertheless, conventions still have significant functions: delegates must agree on a platform and approve the candidate's choice of a running mate. For a second-term incumbent's party, the convention symbolizes a ritualistic transfer of party leadership from the president to the candidate.

The most important thing the delegates must do at the convention is win over a national television audience that has tuned in for a coronation and not a confrontation. Intense intraparty friction or a convention bloodbath makes it far more difficult for a candidate to win the White House than does a unified, well-managed convention that symbolizes party unity and delivers the party message. Even a candidate who can get to the White House after a fierce convention battle, such as Dwight Eisenhower in 1952, may find memories of the fight impeding his ability to work with his rivals, as Eisenhower found to be the case with Sen. Robert Taft.

Delegate Demographics

The nominee at the convention must win over a television audience that is quite different demographically and ideologically from the convention delegates the viewers see on their television screens. The delegates are better educated and more affluent than most voters. More than two-thirds have finished college, and more than half the Democrats and one-third of the Republicans hold advanced degrees. Most have family incomes well above the average. Democrats have more Catholic, Jewish, and African American representation at their conventions than do Republicans, reflecting differences in their party's electoral coalitions. If the Democratic convention may appear to be too weighted toward minorities, the Republican convention may appear to have too many whites and not enough minorities, and, therefore, each party has to find a way to make its convention "look like America."

In most conventions, a majority of Republican delegates call themselves conservatives (60 percent in 1988 and 70 percent in 1992) with the remainder being self-described moderates. Democratic delegates are now fairly evenly divided between liberals and conservatives (the split was 47 percent liberal and 44 percent moderate in 1992), because since 1972 the party has moved from a liberal position to centrist. Democrats have to deal with issues of "cultural politics," and the agendas of women, young delegates, and gays, as well as many minorities (20 percent of the 1988 convention was African American) may lead some voters to assume that the Democrats do not represent white "middle Americans" or their values. Republicans must manage at their convention to avoid charges that they are a lily-white party.

Until the 1970s many governors and members of Congress attended conventions as leaders of their state delegations and could play an important role in forging the nominee's winning coalition and moderating party platforms. But after the 1972 reforms, members of the party-in-government stopped attending because they felt uncomfortable and unwelcome in the midst of so many activists. In 1968, 39 percent of Democratic House members and 68 percent of Democratic senators were delegates, but in 1980 only 15 percent of House Democrats and 14 percent of Senate Democrats attended. To provide more representation of the party-in-government, Democrats since 1984 have provided seats in state delegations for superdelegates: most Democratic members of the House and Senate are added automatically to their state delegations, along with each state's members of the Democratic National Committee. Superdelegates accounted for 14 percent of convention delegates in 1984 and 18 percent in 1992.[16] Their presence is supposed to restore to the nominating process some element of peer review—that is, exposing candidates to the judgment of the politicians who know them and have worked with them. In theory the superdelegates might hold the balance of power if no contender came into the convention with a majority of the delegates. But so far these delegates have always voted heavily for the front-runner, with congressional peer review playing no role in the selection of the candidate.

The "Scripted" Convention

How the delegates conduct themselves at the convention may divide or unify the party, bring it new supporters from the television audience, or, alternatively, alienate voters and show a party in disarray on the evening network news. Guided by the campaign managers of the presumptive nominee, the national party committee organizes the convention business into staged segments, or "podium events," including addresses by party notables, showcasing of elected officials running for other offices, presentation of documentary films about the nominee and past presidents, and floor demonstrations. In response, television networks cut away from podium events: they go to commercial breaks, discussions by their own anchors and commentators, and interviews with delegates on the floor or invited guests.

The scripted convention helps the nominee obtain a "bounce" in the form of higher poll ratings. Since 1964 the upward surge in the polls has averaged 6 percent (with the record held by Nixon, who gained 14.1 percent in 1968). In 2000 Bush enjoyed a significant nine-point bounce by improving his standing relative to Gore on various leadership characteristics.[17] But a candidate can also self-destruct if the viewing audience hates the script: Barry Goldwater destroyed his chances in 1964 when he told his cheering supporters that "extremism in the defense of liberty is no vice," thus allowing Lyndon Johnson to paint him as an extremist who would start World War III. (After the convention, when Goldwater commercials appealed to voters with the slogan, "In your heart, you know he's right," Democrats retorted with the line, "In your guts, you know he's nuts.") The unscripted 1972 Democratic convention, in which delegates were able to write their own platform, seemed too extreme for most voters, and McGovern's support in the polls declined, from 41 percent to 39 percent.

With the politics drained out of conventions, they have lost much of their audience. Primetime convention coverage in 1976 by the three major networks ran 142 hours; by 1996 it was down to less than 20 hours, with each network averaging an hour of programming nightly. ABC's Ted Koppel left the Republican convention in disgust, saying there was no news to be covered there. Convention coverage loses in ratings to more popular fare: in 1996 a third-time *Seinfeld* rerun syndicated to a local station outdrew the three networks' convention coverage by 3 to 1.

Because convention managers have transformed an exciting spectacle of real politics into a dull, stage-managed exercise of party propaganda, they have no one to blame but themselves for alienating and losing their audience. In 1976 the average viewership for the conventions was 28 percent of all households. By 2000 it had slipped to an average of 15 percent, and only a small percentage of viewers watched continuously for the entire hour. The efforts of convention managers to reach a large audience by converting political combat into a coronation has failed, as a combination of less coverage by the networks and waning interest by viewers has made the format of the scripted convention obsolete.

Nominating Politics and Governance in the Twenty-First Century

Every few years a small cottage industry of political scientists, media commentators, and professional campaign experts arises to talk about reforming the nominating system. A majority (57 percent) of the public would prefer a national primary over the present system, to reinforce the power of the voters.[18] They believe that holding a primary on a single day would increase turnout and make the process more representative. Others hold that it is useful to have primaries held in stages, so that no well-funded candidate can deliver an immediate knockout punch on a single day. Instead, they believe that a long primary period enables other candidates to catch up and nullify the advantage of the front-runner, so that at the end of the day the candidate who has demonstrated the best organizational and media ability over a lengthy period of time will emerge victorious.

Some critics of the primary system would prefer less democracy and more peer review by politicians who know the field of contenders personally and can make an accurate assessment of their character and abilities.[19] They argue that the self-selected field emphasizes the wrong kind of experience and downgrades expertise based on a long apprenticeship in national government. They believe that peer review by professional politicians is needed to filter out the intellectually or ethically challenged. Critics also note the irony that efforts to democratize the nominating process through the primary system have created a need for huge amounts of money to fund television commercials, which in turn provides interest groups with opportunities to trade campaign cash for favored treatment. The need to develop a large, media-savvy campaign organization means that the staffers who surround candidates are schooled in arts of media manipulation and are too inclined to equate media savvy with effective governance. The newly elected president will appoint a *West Wing* sort of White House staff that is too young and too inexperienced. Critics further argue that nominations are now settled on the basis of media manipulation of an unrepresentative primary electorate and that the contest for its votes divides the party and makes it difficult to unify it for the general election. The personal costs of entering the ring are so great that the process itself winnows down the field and discourages some individuals with extensive experience and excellent character. Put another way, Broder's law (named for the columnist) states that any candidate willing to do what it now takes to win the nomination and election is not safe to be trusted with the office.

Primaries promote an individualistic, media-centered approach to presidential politics, rather than encouraging a president to work closely with the congressional and state parties. When candidates win the nomination by going over the heads of party leaders and communicating directly to voters, they may decide they owe nothing to party leaders or workers—and the feelings will be reciprocated. To the extent that incompetent, inexperienced, egocentric, and unscrupulous campaign staffers attempt to use the media to fool voters, the authority of the presidency is diminished—especially when the "hook" used by journalists to report on the nominating campaign emphasizes candidate manipulation and the role of special interests in funding campaigns.

One reform often called for by critics of the nominating process is a return of party politics at the conventions. Some argue that as many as half of each state's convention delegation should consist of uncommitted delegates chosen by the state party professionals. The primary and caucus contests could winnow down the roster of contenders, but the politicians would make the final choice, and that in turn would force contenders to forge close links with the party organizations.

Defenders of the current system claim that the media exposes phonies. They point out that peer review and the politicking that goes with it often led to mediocre nominees in the past. They say that the constraints that bosses placed on presidents hardly served the public interest and that we are better off without the horse trading and corruption that attended old-style convention politics.

Today, presidents are constrained, but in different ways. They can bypass the bosses, but they no longer can ignore the interests of the party rank and file, because they will have to run the primary gauntlet to gain renomination.

Perhaps the most serious problem with our nominating system is that those who emerge with the nomination lack national executive experience, a situation that rarely occurs in other nations. In European parliamentary systems most party and government leaders have served long apprenticeships in national government before heading it. European prime ministers start on the "back benches" and demonstrate their talents in minor assignments. They then become junior ministers, assisting senior colleagues in running a department and defending its policies in debates, or they hone their skills as "shadow ministers" assigned to debate with the government on particular issues. In Germany they often have experience in state government and then in a national ministry, a pattern similar to France. In the United States there is no orderly line of succession, no opposition party leader, unifying the party and preparing for the time the electorate returns his party to power. The prior careers of most presidents have not prepared them for the challenges of working within the Washington community.

It may not necessarily be true that such lengthy preparation produces better decisions and policies in the European countries to which comparisons are usually made. And it may on balance be better to have a nominating system that is open to new talent, albeit inexperienced, because it may produce leaders who are responsive to new trends rather than enmeshed in the ways of the old Washington establishment. But it also seems reasonable to assume that the complexities of managing the U.S. economy and providing for national security in an age of terrorist threats are both strong arguments for a nominating system that finds candidates who are both experienced *and* responsive.

The argument between proponents and opponents of the modern nominating system has raged for more than three decades. In that time, divisive intraparty battles, media campaigns, and critical media coverage have had their effects: the appeal of the nominees to the voters has declined sharply, as have the turnouts in primaries and caucuses, and the need to raise enormous amounts of money has increased. Have the tradeoffs between intraparty democracy and accountability, on the one hand, and effective presidential leadership of party and Congress, on the other, become unacceptable? A nominating system that restores some peer review and a greater role for party professionals and members of Congress might be the hybrid that could restore its vitality.

Notes

1. Shorenstein Center Poll, "Vanishing Voter Project," news releases, June 1 and June 16, 2000; and CBS News/*NYT* Poll, May 10–13, 2000, in which only 21 percent of respondents thought they, rather than party leaders (26 percent) or contributors (46 percent) had the most influence on nominations.

2. Ed Flynn, *You're the Boss* (New York: Collier Books, 1962), 111.

3. James Bryce, "Why Great Men Are Not Elected President," in *The American Commonwealth*, ed. Louis M. Hacker (New York: G. P. Putnam's Sons, 1959), 27–34.

4. The following data are based on the author's calculations; "contenders" are defined as those receiving delegate votes at national nominating conventions.

5. "Project for Excellence in Journalism," Pew Center for the People and the Press, January 2000.

6. William Keech and David Matthews, *The Party's Choice* (Washington, D.C.: Brookings Institution, 1976), 14–19; Arthur Hadley, *The Invisible Primary* (Englewood Cliffs: Prentice-Hall, 1976).

7. Randall E. Adkins and Andrew J. Dowdle, "Break Out the Mint Julips?" *American Political Quarterly* 28 (April 2000): 251–269; Randall E. Adkins and Andrew J. Dowdle, "How Important Are Iowa and New Hampshire to Winning Post-Reform Presidential Nominations?" *Political Research Quarterly* 54 (June 2001): 431–444.

8. Randall E. Adkins and Andrew J. Dowdle, "Is the Exhibition Season Becoming More Important to Forecasting Presidential Nominations," *American Politics Research* 29 (May 2001): 283–288.

9. *Buckley v. Valeo,* 424 U.S. 1 (1976).

10. See Austin Ranney, "Participation in Precinct Caucuses," in James I. Lengle and Byron E. Shafer, *Presidential Politics,* 2d ed. (New York: St. Martin's Press, 1983), 175.

11. "Public Attentiveness to News Stories in Primary Season," Pew Research Center for the People and the Press, 2000.

12. Gary Orren and Nelson Polsby, *Media and Momentum* (Chatham, N.J.: Chatham House Publishers, 1987).

13. William H. Lucy, "Polls, Primaries and Presidential Nominations," *Journal of Politics* 35 (November 1973): 837; later calculations by author.

14. Barbara Norrander, *Super Tuesday* (Lexington: University of Kentucky Press, 1992).

15. John H. Aldrich, *Before the Convention* (Chicago: University of Chicago Press, 1980), 161.

16. Michael Goldstein, *Guide to the 1992 Presidential Election* (Washington, D.C.: CQ Press, 1991), 26.

17. Gallup Poll News Service, August 14, 2000.

18. "Vanishing Voter Project," Shorenstein Center Poll, January 12–16, 2000.

19. See the incisive critique of James Ceasar, *Presidential Selection* (Princeton: Princeton University Press, 1979).

9 The Presidency and the Campaign: Creating Voter Priorities in the 2000 Election

John H. Aldrich and John D. Griffin

Many voters form a preference for one of the major party candidates before nominations are final and the general election campaign begins. Voters who do not identify strongly with either political party are much more likely to be undecided over the course of the campaign. The candidates therefore focus their efforts on swaying undecided voters. Candidates appeal to these voters by selecting campaign themes that reflect their policy priorities. In doing so, the candidates offer party identifiers new reasons to justify their prior commitment to a candidate. The priorities of identifiers should then converge to those of independent voters. Finally, if the winning candidate implements major campaign themes, policy will be responsive to the preferences of independent voters, who constitute a plurality of the electorate.

The 2000 presidential election campaign was one of the closest in history, filled with reversals of fortune between the two major party candidates and ending in an extended period of near chaos as the nation followed the twists and turns of the events in Florida and the U.S. Supreme Court's decisions about the vote there. The candidates' strategies, especially that of Vice President Al Gore, were debated among pundits throughout the campaign itself. Afterward, in a heated confrontation between Bill Clinton and Gore,[1] Clinton argued that a campaign based on the successes of their administration, especially its robust economic performance and federal budget surpluses, would have reversed the outcome. Gore retorted that such a campaign would have raised the specter of the president's moral lapses, which was why Gore preferred to focus on education, health care, and Social Security. Naturally, if George W. Bush had lost the election, his strategy of running primarily on traditional Democratic issues such as these, along with the Republican issue of tax cuts, would have been roundly criticized.[2]

The strategies the candidates chose in an election campaign—what they emphasize and what they ignore—have important effects on voter choices and therefore on the outcome. The candidates' strategies depend on what they perceive the voters care about and ultimately on the candidates' willingness to raise some concerns among voters, while avoiding others. Despite the long tradition of arguing that campaigns have only "minimal effects" (as the central claim about media influence on voters is called),[3] campaigns are consequential. We reject the view that most voters know too little about public policy to be affected by the candidates' appeals in all but the most unusual cases. We especially reject the argument of some scholars that predicting election results based on *a priori* conditions, such as the state of the economy, is more accurate than asking voters how they will vote, which means that it is the *a priori* conditions that determine the electoral outcomes.[4] Instead, our view is that electoral conditions affect how voters respond to the candidates, and because electoral conditions are more stable, their explanatory power tends to be greater.

The 2000 campaign provides a wonderful test case for examining whether candidate strategies in a campaign are consequential and whether candidates are, in turn, constrained by voters' existing concerns. This campaign works as test case because the United States faced no problem of such transcendent importance in 2000 as to preempt the candidates' strategic possibilities. The nation was not at war, as it had been in 1972; not suffering serious economic problems, as in 1976 and 1980; not confronting any looming international problems, as in 1980. In 2000 the candidates could realistically imagine that they could focus voter concern on one policy area or another. Unlike in 1984, no incumbent was running who was so popular as to make the campaign too asymmetric (that is, one-sided) for candidate strategy to matter.[5] In short, in 2000, as has not been true in some recent elections, candidates had room to maneuver strategically.[6]

To explain how the electorate arrived at its policy priorities on election day, we focus on the behavior of the major party presidential candidates. We argue that the priorities of voters are *endogenous* to the information they receive from the candidates. That is, they grow out of what the candidates say. We assume, therefore, that the two candidates' campaigns and the news media's coverage of them have substantial effects on what people care about when they decide which candidate to support. This is, at least potentially, a far larger campaign effect than other scholars have claimed.[7]

Second, we argue that the candidates choose the issues they plan to emphasize based on the preferences of undecided voters. By and large, undecided voters are independents—they do not identify strongly, if at all, with either of the major political parties. The candidates' appeals to these independent voters, however, are not made in isolation. Party identifiers also receive these appeals and may embrace them as new reasons to reinforce their existing voting decision. If party identifiers abandon their original policy priorities in favor of those articulated by the candidate they support, the priorities of these identifiers will converge to mirror those of independents. Moreover, if this takes place among the identifiers of both political parties, the policy priorities of Democratic and Republican voters will also converge.[8]

Candidates' Pursuit of Undecided Voters

Let us begin by looking more closely at our argument that presidential candidates select the issues they plan to emphasize by ascertaining which issues are of most concern to undecided voters. Candidates reason that undecided voters will base their vote on a comparison of the candidates' policy priorities with their own. The policy priorities of voters who already have decided which candidate to support are of lesser concern because their votes are not in play.

This view of the way candidates select campaign themes differs from the "issue ownership" approach advanced by some other scholars. According to that theory, "The goal [of a campaign] is to achieve a strategic advantage by making problems which reflect owned issues the programmatic meaning of the election and the criteria by which voters make their choice."[9] That is, the theory predicts that candidates trumpet issues on which their party holds a natural advantage among voters and downplay issues on which their party is disadvantaged. Candidates hope that by focusing the election on the issues their party owns, they will retain the support of a great majority of their own partisans, swing a significant number of independents to their side, and, if things go well, steal away at least a few supporters of the opposing party.

In the issue ownership approach, the candidates and their strategists, not the voters, select the topics to be emphasized. Although this approach to understanding campaigns acknowledges that candidates may "ride the wave" of salient issues,[10] it otherwise assumes that they are unresponsive to the public's priorities. In contrast, if the candidates' decisions to emphasize some issues over others are rooted in the priorities of voters, and if winning candidates act on their campaign priorities after the election, we would expect public policies to be responsive to voters' concerns.[11]

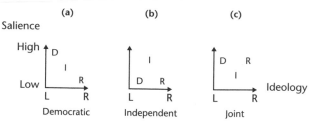

Figure 9.1 Types of Issue Ownership

Source: Compiled by the authors.

Figure 9.1 illustrates three types of issue ownership. The x axis represents the position of the parties on an issue along the left-right (liberal-conservative) ideological spectrum. The y axis represents the salience of the issue for identifiers with each of the parties. When an issue is more salient among one party's supporters than it is among supporters of the opposing party, as is the case among Democrats in Part a, under the traditional definition, that issue is "owned" by that party. An example among Democratic identifiers is poverty.

We supplement this definition of issue ownership with two additional cases. When an issue is more salient among independent voters than it is among identifiers of either party, shown in Part b, the issue is owned by independent voters. An example of such an issue is campaign finance reform. When an issue is of equal salience for supporters of both parties, but it is of lesser concern to independents, as shown in Part c, it is jointly owned by the two parties. Ownership matters because the candidate of the party that owns an issue can use it to the party's advantage in an election campaign.

The evidence we offer will demonstrate that the situation shown in Figure 9.1 (a) seldom arose in 2000—that is, most of the issues in the 2000 election were never, or were only temporarily, owned by one party.[12] Instead, two of the three most prominent issues in the campaign—education and health care—were owned at some point in the election by independent voters—the situation depicted in Figure 9.1 (b). The issue ownership approach therefore has nothing to say about many of the voters' major concerns in the 2000 election.

We extend the logic of issue ownership to matters on which neither party enjoys an advantage. In these instances, both of the major party candidates can embrace the issue in their efforts to sway independent voters. To show how this situation played out in the 2000 campaign, we first show that undecided voters are independent voters. Second, we identify independent voters' primary policy concerns in 2000. Third, turning to the candidates, we test whether they appealed to the most pressing concerns of independent voters. Fourth, we examine how all voters responded to the policy priorities the candidates articulated.

Undecided/Independent Voters

In the thirteen presidential elections between 1948 and 1996, 42 percent of the fifteen thousand voters interviewed for the National Election Studies (NES) survey said that they had decided which candidate they would vote for either when the candidates announced or by the time of the party primaries.[13] An additional 22 percent indicated that they made their decision by the time of the conventions. Less than 20 percent said they waited until the last two weeks of the campaign to make their choice. In truth, these numbers may underestimate the extent to which voters make up their minds early.[14]

Voters in the 2000 election departed from this pattern.[15] Only 25 percent of the voters had made up their minds by the time of the party primaries, perhaps due to the notable challenges by Sen. John McCain, R-Ariz., and former senator Bill Bradley, Democrat of New Jersey, to the front-runners. Nearly half of all voters had decided between Bush and Gore prior to the party conventions. Only one in eight waited until the final two weeks of the campaign. Yet these late-deciding voters determined the outcome of the election. They vastly exceeded in number the razor-thin margin that Bush held over Gore in Florida and in a number of other states.

The first step in our empirical analysis is to confirm that undecided voters tend to be voters who do not strongly identify with either of the major political parties. Other research has shown that voters who make early decisions in elections tend to be strong party identifiers.[16] The 2000 election was no exception. Figure 9.2 illustrates the effect of partisanship on the timing of voters' decisions. On the NES seven-point party identification scale, we grouped leaning Democrats, independents, and leaning Republicans as "independents," weak and strong Republican identifiers as "Republicans," and weak and strong Democratic identifiers as "Democrats."

The cumulative percentage of Democratic and Republican identifiers who "knew all along" for whom they would vote was more than twice the percentage of independent voters who did so, and this lead in decision time was never relinquished. In the period right after the nominating conventions, party identifiers remained 50 percent more likely than independents to have reached a voting decision. Comparing Democratic and Republican voters to each other reveals that both groups made up their minds at roughly the same rate. The Republicans were a bit faster, perhaps because their convention took place first.

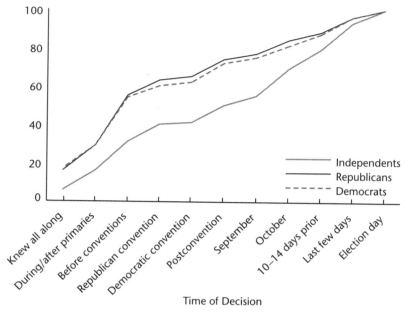

Figure 9.2 Timing of Vote Decision, by Party Identification

Cumulative Percent Decided

Time of Decision

Source: National Election Studies, Cumulative Data File, 1948–2000.

Priorities of Independents

What did independent voters consider important early in the election period? Table 9.1 reports the early priorities of the entire electorate using survey data from the Gallup Poll News Service. The polls were conducted March 10–12 and June 22–25, 2000. A respondent's policy priority is the issue he or she identified as the "most important problem facing the country today." Both surveys used an open-ended question format, and respondents were permitted to name only one issue as most important. Recall that, as Figure 9.2 shows, when the March poll was taken, approximately one in three party identifiers had decided how to vote, while less than one in five independents had done so. At the time the June poll was conducted, three in five party identifiers had reached a voting decision, but three in five independents remained uncommitted.

The twelve issues listed in Table 9.1 were chosen based on the frequency that independents named them over the course of the campaign. Taken together, these twelve issues account for approximately 70 percent of all responses in the March poll and 90 percent of all responses in the June poll. Ethics, education,

Table 9.1 Early Policy Priorities, 2000 Presidential Election (in percent)

			March 2000			
	Republican	*Rank*	*Independent*	*Rank*	*Democratic*	*Rank*
Education	11%	3	15%	1	17%	1
Taxes	13	2	12	2	8	4
Crime	8	4	10	3	14	2
Drugs	4	7	6	4	5	7
Ethics/morality	15	1	5	5	4	9
Economy	4	7	5	5	7	5
Medicare	3	9	5	5	5	7
Health care	6	5	4	8	11	3
Government	5	6	3	9	4	9
Poverty	2	10	2	10	6	6
Fuel prices	—		—		—	
FICA	—		—		—	
Total	71%		67%		81%	
N	304		358		345	
			June 2000			
	Republican	*Rank*	*Independent*	*Rank*	*Democratic*	*Rank*
Education	9%	5	13%	2	10%	3
Taxes	3	10	3	10	4	10
Crime	11	3	12	3	12	1
Drugs	7	6	5	8	8	4
Ethics/morality	19	1	16	1	7	7
Economy	6	7	6	7	6	8
Medicare	1	12	2	12	3	12
Health care	10	4	10	4	11	2
Government	13	2	7	5	6	8
Poverty	5	8	5	8	8	4
Fuel prices	5	8	7	5	8	4
FICA	3	10	3	11	4	10
Total	92%		89%		87%	
N	304		395		321	

Source: Gallup Organization.

Note: FICA aggregated with Medicare in March 2000 poll.

crime, and health care constituted the most salient issues in the minds of voters, with government, the economy, drugs, and poverty making up a (distant) second group. In March, independent voters owned the Medicare issue, and in June they owned education.[17]

A comparison of the two polls suggests that between March and June voters began to agree more about which issues were most important. A convenient way to measure just how closely the level of agreement was is through the correlation coefficient. These are measures that are exactly 0 if there is no correspondence at all between what voters said in March and in June, and they are at their highest value of 1 if the two lists agree exactly. In March, the correlation of Republican and independent mentions was .60, and it was .74 between Democratic and independent mentions. Republicans and Democrats, however, agreed little with each other about the nation's problems, with the correlation a much lower .27.[18]

By June, agreement was considerably higher. The priorities of Republicans and independents were correlated at an especially high .87. The priorities of Democrats and Independents also were rather highly correlated (.69). Although identifiers with the two parties had converged considerably with independents, Republicans and Democrats continued to exhibit different policy emphases compared with each other (at .48).[19]

When competing in the primaries, presidential candidates of the same party base their campaigns on different issue priorities, because their positions on issues typically differ little.[20] Presumably, the candidates do not stake out distinctive positions because primary electorates are relatively homogenous in their own positions. In contrast, we find that in the early period of the general election, voters in the full electorate differ in their positions *and* in their policy priorities.[21] In 2000 Republican voters placed a priority on the economy, problems with government, and ethical concerns more often than Democrats did. Democrats gave special priority to education, health care, poverty, drug use, fuel prices, and crime. Independent voters placed a priority on ethics, education, crime, and health care.

Speaking About the Issues

How did the candidates respond to independents' policy priorities, and how did voters react to the candidates' public messages? Candidates base their campaigns on the issues they choose to emphasize as well as on the positions they take on those issues.[22] If undecided voters identify certain issues as priorities, we would expect the candidates to speak more often and show more advertisements about these issues. As John Aldrich and R. Michael Alvarez have shown, "Voters are more likely to support the candidate who shares their concerns about the important problems facing the nation, and to shun candidates who are emphasizing other concerns in their campaigns."[23]

To examine these claims empirically, we coded Bush's and Gore's campaign speeches and their campaign advertisements between June 1 and October 7, 2000,[24] marking the frequency with which they raised each of the voters' twelve issue priorities. Figure 9.3 illustrates the relationship between the percentage of the candidates' speeches and television advertisements devoted to the twelve

Figure 9.3 Candidate Speeches/Advertisements and Mentions of Most Important Problem

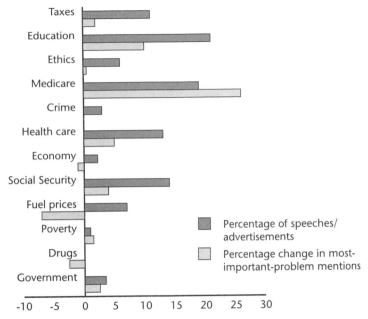

Sources: Shanto Iyengar, *In Their Own Words: Sourcebook for the 2000 Presidential Election* (Stanford: Stanford University, 2001); Gallup Poll News Service; Harris Polls; CBS News/*New York Times;* Fox News; and 2000 National Election Studies.

issues and the percentage change in the proportion of the electorate identifying each issue as the most important problem facing the country during the same period.[25] What do the data in the figure show?

First, a comparison of Figure 9.3 and Table 9.1 clearly shows that the issues that were of greatest importance to independent voters in June—namely education, ethics, and health care—were also the frequent subjects of the candidates' speeches and advertisements between June and October. Issues of lesser concern to independents, such as poverty, drugs, and the economy, were stressed less often. However, the candidates emphasized taxes, Medicare, and Social Security more than we anticipated, and crime less so. Undoubtedly, Bush and Gore focused on Medicare and Social Security because Florida has a large elderly population, and the state's twenty-five electoral votes figured heavily in the candidates' campaign strategies.

Second, the candidates did not always stress the same issues. Gore made most of the speeches reflected in Figure 9.3 concerning health care, and Bush gave most of the speeches concerning taxes. The candidates spoke nearly equally about education, Medicare, and Social Security. These data suggest that the effect of speeches on voters appears to be strongest when both candidates identify an issue as a priority. It may be that at least some voters discount a single candidate's emphasis on an issue as little more than a campaign ploy, but are more convinced that they should care about an issue if both candidates emphasize it.

Third, the more time Bush and Gore devoted to discussing an issue, the greater the percentage increase in the public's identification of that issue as important.[26] The candidates' investment of time discussing Medicare, health care, and problems in government produced especially large changes in the public's issue priorities. By devoting 18 percent of their speeches and advertisements to Medicare, for instance, the candidates increased public concern about the issue by more than 250 percent. Issues that the candidates largely ignored—crime, the economy, poverty, and drugs—experienced modest increases or declines in voters' identification of them as a most important problem.[27]

In sum, the presidential candidates in 2000 emphasized the issues that were of particular concern to independent voters. Further, the extent to which the candidates emphasized issues in their campaigns corresponded to the public's identification of these issues as the most important national problems. But were the public's concerns endogenous? In other words, were they shaped by the candidates? Or did rising public concern about these issues cause the candidates to focus on them? Because this question is of obvious importance to our understanding of the mechanisms of representation, we turn to it next.

Directionality

To determine whether voter priorities come in response to the campaigns or whether they are responses to other events, we analyze a longer data set. Scholars have observed that presidential campaigns are less active and receive less media coverage in the late spring and early summer of the election year than later in the election season.[28] If our causal argument is correct, the issues stressed by the candidates will be more salient to voters both earlier in the primary season and later in the fall, when the campaigns and the media are active, than in the late spring and early summer. That is, if voters do not receive ongoing appeals from the candidates, they likely will revert to their previous issue concerns, leading to a temporary decline in the effects of the campaign. The effects of campaigns on voter priorities should therefore be *convex over time*, as voters respond to campaign messages in February and March, revive their earlier concerns in May and June, and return to the issues the candidates emphasize in July and August. To examine whether this convexity exists in voter priorities, we examine three issues in twenty-eight Gallup polls between January 10 and October 31, 2000. These polls asked open-ended questions about voters' most important issue concerns and allowed respondents to name either one or two issues. The results are shown in Figure 9.4.

The first conclusion to be drawn from Figure 9.4 is that voters became more concerned about education, Medicare, and health care (in that order) as the campaign year progressed. Second, voters' concerns about these issues increased from January through the party primaries in February, March, and April, declined in late spring and early summer, and then rose again after the party conventions. The increase in voter concern about these issues in the first several months of the year reflected voters' responses to the candidates' primary campaigns. In late spring, when media coverage of the election lapsed and the Bush and Gore campaigns conserved their resources for the general election, voters' concerns about these issues subsided. After the conventions, when the candidates resumed their activity and the media returned to covering the race in earnest, voters' identification of these issues as their principal concerns rebounded. This evidence suggests that campaign activity, combined with media coverage, affects voters' identification of important national problems, a finding that is consistent with earlier work showing that voter identification of important national problems is responsive to the number of news stories on those issues, as well as with findings that politicians influence voter opinion.[29]

Another explanation for these results is that voters were less concerned about education, Medicare, and health care in late spring than at other times due to events that caused them to temporarily turn their attention elsewhere. But we can find nothing in the record that would have produced such changes.

Convergence on Priorities and the Vote

We have shown that Bush and Gore emphasized in their campaigns the issues that undecided voters were concerned about early in the 2000 election year. We also have demonstrated that voters became more concerned over time about the issues that these candidates emphasized in their campaigns. Now we examine whether party identifiers—voters who presumably decided between the candidates early in the year—adopted the issues advanced by the candidates as the issues about which they were most concerned. We think this is plausible,

Figure 9.4 Percentage of Population Identifying Issue as Most Important Problem, January 10–October 31, 2000

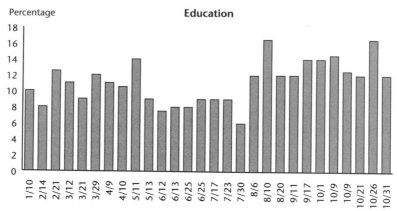

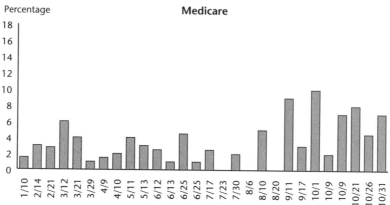

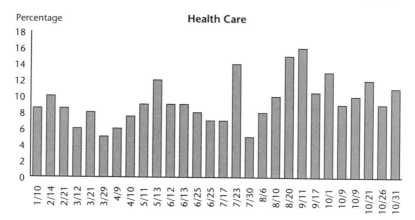

Sources: Gallup Poll News Service; Harris Polls; CBS News/*New York Times;* and Fox News; various dates.

Table 9.2 Similarity of Policy Priorities Among Party Identifiers and Independents, Fall 2000

	Republicans	Rank	Independents	Rank	Democrats	Rank
Education	13.51%	1	13.22%	1	15.46%	1
Health care	8.11	3	9.48	2	11.68	2
Medicare	10.81	2	7.76	3	11.34	3
Government	4.5	6	5.17	4	1.03	8
Poverty	1.8	9	4.60	5	3.78	6
Economy	4.5	6	4.31	6	5.16	4
Crime	5.41	5	4.31	6	4.81	5
Ethics/morality	7.66	4	4.02	8	3.09	7
Drugs	1.8	9	2.87	9	.34	12
Fuel prices	.45	12	1.44	10	.69	11
Social Security	3.6	8	1.44	10	1.03	8
Taxes	1.8	9	.86	12	1.03	8
Total	63.95%		59.48%		59.44%	
N	222		348		291	

Source: National Election Studies.

Note: Most important problem question asked in the preelection phase of the survey.

given prior research showing that individuals may be persuaded that a decision is incorrect, as well as research that individuals who are presented with contradictory information seek to resolve the conflict.[30]

The data in Table 9.2 allow us to examine this question. As in Table 9.1, we have tabulated the most important problems facing the country in the opinions of Republican, Democratic, and independent voters. In Table 9.2, however, these data come from polls conducted in September, October, and November 2000, as the campaign drew to a close.

A comparison of the fall data in Table 9.2 to the March and June data in Table 9.1 indicates that party identifiers and independents continued the convergence in their respective issue priorities that had begun earlier in the year. In the fall, the correlation of Republican priorities with the priorities of independent voters was .88, slightly higher in comparison to earlier in the year. The correlation between Democratic and independent voters was .94, or .20 higher than was observed in the spring. Perhaps most striking, the correlation of Republican and Democratic priorities was .89—up dramatically from .27 in March and .48 in June.[31]

In short, the policy priorities of identifiers with both parties as well as of independent voters converged to a single priority order. The echo produced by the candidates in the electorate was not a cacophony of voices, but a clear one.[32] Convergence was not perfect—Republicans still placed higher priority on morality problems than did Democrats, and Democrats placed higher priority on poverty than did Republicans. For the most part, however, supporters of

Table 9.3 Issue Priorities, by Vote Choice

	All Voters	Gore Voters	Bush Voters
Moral/ethical values	35%	17%	55%
Jobs/economy	26	36	16
Education	25	31	20
Social Security	21	25	26
Taxes	16	9	25
Abortion	14	12	17
Environment	10	14	2
Health care	8	11	5
Medicare	8	10	6
Budget surplus	6	6	6
Foreign affairs	5	5	5
Other	4	3	4

Source: Based on a national exit poll conducted by the *Los Angeles Times*, November 7, 2000.

Note: Question wording: "Which issues, if any, were most important to you in deciding how you would vote for president today?" (Up to two responses accepted). $N = 8,132$ (California oversample). http://www.pollingreport.com/election/htm.

both parties and independent voters agreed on what should be the main concern of national policymaking, even if the means to address these problems remained a matter of dispute. Moreover, in separate analyses we show that the priorities of Democratic, Republican, and independent voters not only converged, but also that they converged to the priorities of independents.[33]

These findings suggest a new interpretation of presidential mandates. The literature on presidential mandates is built on the theory that if a candidate for president emphasizes certain issues in the campaign and wins the election by a landslide, the likelihood increases that the new president and Congress will address those issues successfully.[34] Our results suggest that the vote percentage of the winning candidate is not the only indicator of whether the president has a mandate to enact his or her campaign themes. Rather, a presidential mandate may also exist when the electorate reaches agreement with each other as well as with the winning candidate about what the priorities of the new government should be.

Even if voters agree about the problems facing the country, if they do not base their vote on these priorities, we cannot be confident that elected officials will be responsive to their concerns. Table 9.3 displays the issues reported by voters on election day as most important to their voting decision in 2000.

As reflected in Table 9.3, many of the issues voters identified during the campaign as the country's most important problem—education, ethics, Social Security, health care, and Medicare—also formed the basis of their voting decisions. Noticeably, however, other issues that voters seldom mentioned in polls—abortion, the environment, and foreign affairs—were singled out as most important by a considerable number of voters. This finding serves as a reminder that the effects of campaigns on voter preferences, although considerable, may be limited.[35]

Conclusion

Independent voters hold a privileged position in two-party electoral competition. Under certain circumstances, the candidates' appeals to independent, often undecided, voters lead party identifiers to adopt the priorities of independents, producing a consensus in the electorate on what the national agenda should be. Voters in 2000 may have disagreed about how the government should address their policy priorities, but by the time of the election they appeared to agree on what those priorities should be.

Political campaigns are not divorced from postelection governance. For instance, the Bush administration's efforts to pass an education bill immediately after the election suggest that winning candidates do attempt to act on the issues they emphasized in the campaign. If the winning candidate takes action on voters' priorities once in office, the pre-campaign policy priorities of independents will take precedence in policymaking over the pre-campaign policy priorities of party identifiers. Because independent voters outnumber either Democrats or Republicans, the special attention that the candidates pay to independents does not necessarily raise concerns about whether elections are a successful mechanism of representation.

Notes

1. "Democrats See a Party Adrift as Presidential Loss Sinks In," *New York Times,* February 16, 2001, 1.

2. "The 2000 Campaign: The Strategy: Shifting Tactics, Bush Uses Issues to Confront Gore," *New York Times,* September 16, 2000, 1.

3. See, for example, Paul F. Lazarsfeld, Bernard Berelson, and Hazel Gaudet, *The People's Choice* (New York: Columbia University Press, 1944).

4. See, for example, Andrew Gelman and Gary King, "Why Are American Presidential Election Campaign Polls So Variable When Votes Are So Predictable?" *British Journal of Political Science* 23 (1993): 409–452.

5. See John H. Aldrich and Thomas Weko, "The Presidency and the Election Process: Campaign Strategy, Voting, and Governance," in *The Presidency and the Political System,* 2d ed., ed. Michael Nelson (Washington D.C.: CQ Press, 1988).

6. Specifically, although 64 percent of voters agreed on the top problem facing the United States in 1992 (the economy), and 53 percent did so in 1980 (inflation), just 16

percent of voters agreed on the top problem in 2000 (education). Gallup Organization, June 22, 2000.

7. See, for example, D. E. RePass, "Issue Salience and Party Choice," *American Political Science Review* 60 (1971): 389–400; Thomas M. Holbrook, "Campaigns, National Conditions, and U.S. Presidential Elections," *American Journal of Political Science* 38 (1994): 973–998; Thomas M. Holbrook, *Do Campaigns Matter?* (Thousand Oaks, Calif.: Sage Publications, 1996); and James E. Campbell, *The American Campaign: U.S. Presidential Elections and the National Vote* (College Station: Texas A&M University Press, 2000).

8. This account diverges from most studies by virtue of the role played by independents and undecided voters in shaping candidate behavior, rather than candidates responding to the concerns of the most active and engaged partisans. An early example is *The American Voter*, by Angus Campbell, Philip Converse, Warren Miller, and Donald Stokes (New York: Wiley, 1960).

9. John R. Petrocik, "Issue Ownership in Presidential Elections, with a 1980 Case Study," *American Journal of Political Science* 40 (1996): 825–850.

10. Stephen Ansolabehere and Shanto Iyengar, "Riding the Wave and Claiming Ownership Over Issues," *Public Opinion Quarterly* 58 (Autumn 1994): 335–357.

11. Prior work has shown that this aggregate-level representation takes place. See, for example, Benjamin I. Page and Robert Y. Shapiro, "Effects of Public Opinion on Policy," *American Political Science Review* 77 (1983): 175–190; and James A. Stimson, Michael B. Mackuen, and Robert S. Erikson, "Dynamic Representation," *American Political Science Review* 89 (1995): 543–565.

12. The theory of issue ownership allows for this eventuality, but its implications have not been pursued. Indeed, the major focus of this line of research has been on issues that have been owned by one party for extended periods of time.

13. The National Election Studies, Center for Political Studies, University of Michigan. Electronic resources from the NES website: www.umich.edu/~nes. (Ann Arbor: University of Michigan, Center for Political Studies, producer and distributor, 1995–2000; 1948–1998 Cumulative Data File).

14. The early experience of the Gallup poll shows that when respondents are permitted to secretly reveal the timing of their decision, the number of undecided voters is reduced by as much as one-third. Paul Perry, "Problems in Election Survey Methodology," *Public Opinion Quarterly* 43 (1979): 312–325.

15. National Election Studies, 2000 Pre/Post Election Study.

16. See, for example, Ithiel de Sola Pool, Bernard P. Abelson, and Samuel L. Popkin, *Candidates, Issues, and Strategies: A Computer Simulation of the 1960 Election* (Cambridge: Massachusetts Institute of Technology Press, 1965); Ithiel de Sola Pool, "The Effect of Communication on Voting Behavior," in *New Models for Communication Research*, ed. Wilbur Schramm (Beverly Hills, Calif.: Sage Publications, 1963).

17. In unreported results, in the June poll if independent leaners are grouped with party identifiers, the percentage of independent voters ($N = 146$) identifying health care as the most important problem (13 percent) also exceeds the percentage of Republicans (9 percent) and the percentage of Democrats (11 percent). Regrouping also does not disturb independents' ownership of education in the June poll.

18. These are Pearson correlations, with significance levels of $p = .01$, $p = .001$, and $p = .08$, respectively. The Spearman rank order correlation of Republicans and independents was .57 ($p = .01$); of Democrats and independents was .47 ($p = .01$); and of Republicans and Democrats was only .17 ($p = .06$).

19. Significance levels are $p = .000+$, .01, and .12, respectively. Spearman's correlations are .87 ($p = .000+$), .71 ($p = .01$), and .58 ($p = .05$), respectively.

20. John H. Aldrich and R. Michael Alvarez, "Issues and the Presidential Primary Voter," *Political Behavior* 16 (1994): 289–317.

21. RePass, "Issue Salience and Party Choice," also emphasized the impact of issue priorities in general elections.

22. Benjamin I. Page, *Choices and Echoes in Presidential Elections: Rational Man and Electoral Democracy* (Chicago: University of Chicago Press, 1978).

23. Aldrich and Alvarez, "Issues and the Presidential Primary Voter," 311.

24. Shanto Iyengar, *In Their Own Words: Sourcebook for the 2000 Presidential Election* (Stanford: Stanford University, 2001).

25. The "most important problem" percentage is based on fifteen surveys conducted by the Gallup Organization, Harris Polls, CBS News/*New York Times,* and Fox News between June 15 and October 9, 2000. All of the surveys used an open-ended format. Some of the surveys allowed only a single response; others allowed two responses. To estimate the percentage change, a linear time trend was fitted to the data for each issue, producing predicted values for June 1 and October 7. The difference between the predicted June and October values is the basis for the percentage change measure. These values were divided by ten for ease of presentation.

26. A vast literature on framing—see, for example, Thomas E. Nelson, Rosalee A. Clawson, and Zoe M. Oxley, "Media Framing of a Civil Liberties Conflict and Its Effect on Tolerance," *American Political Science Review* 91 (1997): 567–583—provides a causal mechanism for this result, as does a literature on persuasion. See, for example, Richard R. Lau, Richard A. Smith, and Susan T. Fiske, "Political Beliefs, Policy Interpretations, and Political Persuasion," *The Journal of Politics* 53 (August 1991): 644–675. For now, we are uncertain about why voters' policy priorities change. This finding is consistent with work showing that voters give most attention to issues that feature prominently in the media in the run-up to the election. See Shanto Iyengar, "Shortcuts to Political Knowledge," in *Information and Democratic Processes,* ed. John Ferejohn and James Kuklinski (Urbana: University of Illinois Press, 1990).

27. Declines with regard to some areas are inevitable if candidate activity is to have any effect.

28. Wayne Steger and Phoebe Connelly, "The Pie is Falling? Network News Coverage of Presidential Candidates, 1976 to 2000" (paper presented at the Midwest Political Science Association meeting, Chicago, April 2001).

29. Shanto Iyengar and Donald Kinder, *News that Matters: Television and American Opinion* (Chicago: University of Chicago Press, 1987); John R. Zaller, *The Nature and Origins of Mass Opinion* (New York: Cambridge University Press, 1992); and Lawrence R. Jacobs and Robert Y. Shapiro, *Politicians Don't Pander: Political Manipulation and the Loss of Democratic Responsiveness* (Chicago: University of Chicago Press, 2000).

30. See, for example, W. Edwards, H. Lindman, and L. J. Savage, "Bayesian Statistical Inference for Psychological Research," *Psychological Review* 70 (1963): 193–242; see also Leon Festinger, *A Theory of Cognitive Dissonance* (Evanston, Ill.: Row, Peterson, 1957).

31. In all cases, $p = .000+$. As for ordinal relationships, the Spearman rank order coefficient for Republicans and independents for September, October, and November was .77 ($p = .00+$), the only instance in which a correlation coefficient in Table 9.2 was smaller than one in Table 9.1. The Spearman correlation between independents and Democrats was .80 ($p = .00+$), compared with .74 in March and .69 in June. For

Republicans and Democrats it was .83 (p = .001), compared to .17 in March and .55 in June. Note that by election day, Democratic and Republican identifiers agreed more with each other in ordinal terms about which policy priorities were most important than either group of party identifiers agreed with independents.

32. V. O. Key, *The Responsible Electorate: Rationality in Presidential Voting, 1936–1960* (Cambridge: Belknap Press of Harvard University, 1968).

33. To determine which of the three groups had the most stable priorities, we compared the congruence of independent voter policy priorities in June and September/October with the congruence of policy preferences for each group of party identifiers across the two periods. Our analysis concludes that independent voters were less likely to change policy priorities than were party identifiers. The correlations between Republican and Democratic priorities in June and the fall were .24 (p = .45) and .31 (p = .32), respectively, while the correlation between independent voter priorities was .42 (p = .18). The Spearman rank order correlation between Republican and Democratic priorities in the two periods was .27 (p = .29) and .10 (p = .44), respectively, and .32 (p = .29) for independent voters.

34. See George C. Edwards, "Presidential Electoral Performance as a Source of Presidential Power," *American Journal of Political Science* 22 (1978): 152–168; Patricia Heidotting Conley, *Presidential Mandates: How Elections Shape the National Agenda* (Chicago: University of Chicago Press, 2001).

35. On the other hand, voters' reliance on abortion and the environment may be attributed to the efforts of interest groups targeting Nader supporters late in the campaign. See, for example, Jennifer Merolla, "Too Close for Comfort: Elite Cues and Strategic Voting in Multicandidate Elections" (Ph.D. diss., Duke University, forthcoming).

Part IV Presidents and Politics

10 The Presidency and Political Trust

Marc J. Hetherington and Suzanne Globetti

The relationship between the presidency and the public is interdependent. In the next chapter, Bruce Miroff looks at what presidents do to shape how the public perceives them. In this chapter, Marc J. Hetherington and Suzanne Globetti examine how public attitudes affect the presidency. In particular, they focus on why recent presidents have been, on average, markedly less popular than their predecessors—a consequential change because "unpopularity among the voters reduces a president's prestige within the Washington community, which, in turn, reduces the range of policies he can effectively pursue." Hetherington and Globetti trace the decline in public support for presidents to a larger trend: the declining trust Americans have in government as a whole. Crises such as the September 11, 2001, terrorist attacks on the United States can raise political trust temporarily, the authors argue, but the long-term decline in trust will continue as long as the political parties remain much more ideologically polarized than the voters.

Bill Clinton's sustained popularity in the face of ubiquitous scandals during his second term obscures the fact that contemporary presidents have been significantly less popular than presidents were in the 1950s and 1960s. The scandals aside, Clinton's relatively high popularity was easy to understand. He presided over the most robust economic expansion in the nation's history, with consumer confidence reaching an all-time high during his final year in office. In addition, Clinton had the good fortune of unlikable opponents. Only the most partisan Republicans would characterize Kenneth Starr, Newt Gingrich, and Tom Delay as more appealing than Clinton.

With Clinton's public approval soaring to 66 percent as he left office, many forget Clinton's unpopular beginning in 1993. By taking on divisive issues such as gays in the military and a major tax increase, he earned the worst public approval rating at the end of his first hundred days of any president in the modern era of polling, with an average rating of 54.6 percent. Clinton would have embraced such numbers from June 1994 to April 1995, a period in which his approval rating failed to reach 50 percent.[1] As for Clinton's successor, given the controversial nature of George W. Bush's election in 2000, his early low approval ratings were unsurprising, despite the quick passage of his tax cut. It seems that, absent extraordinary circumstances, such as the terrorist attacks of September 11, 2001, or the best economy in the nation's history, Richard Brody's observation still holds: contemporary presidents are 10 to 15 percentage points less popular than past presidents.[2]

The media may be one potential cause of this disparity. Brody suggests that when the media provide more negative coverage of the president, he becomes less popular. In addition, the media are more apt to provide negative coverage when there is dissensus among political elites. Since the 1970s, the press has become more negative about politics and politicians in general, especially members of Congress.[3] Because elites have become more ideologically polarized, presidents have become less popular—or so the reasoning goes. This explanation, however, fails to account for developments since the 1980s. During this time, the press continued to grow more negative, and battles between Republicans and Democrats became even more intense. Presidents, however, starting with Reagan, actually became a little more popular than their immediate predecessors, Richard Nixon, Gerald Ford, and Jimmy Carter. The explanation for chronically lower approval ratings, therefore, must be more complicated than media coverage alone.

One major reason that presidents are less popular today than they were in mid-twentieth century is that Americans trust their government significantly less than they did a generation or two ago. To the extent that most Americans thought about the government at all in the aftermath of World War II, they generally thought about it as a source of security, support, and benefits.[4] Starting in the mid- to late-1960s, however, Americans came to associate government with wasteful spending and gross bureaucratic ineptitude. Although the federal government certainly experienced its share of failures during this period, the public's continued scorn has long outlived the most infamous failures—the urban race riots of the 1960s, the Vietnam War, and Watergate.

As political trust continued to plummet through the 1970s, scholars desperately searched for signs of a legitimacy crisis, such as widespread support for revolutionary government change, but they found little convincing evidence.[5] Political scientists lost interest in studying political trust, ignoring the possibility that its decline had other important implications. In this chapter, we discuss one of declining trust's neglected implications, specifically how and why it undermines a president's popularity.

Popularity is critically important to a president's success in office. As Richard Neustadt noted, unpopularity among the voters reduces a president's prestige within the Washington community, which, in turn, reduces the range of policies that he can effectively pursue.[6] A lack of trust in the federal government may indirectly undermine a president's policy goals. As people become disenchanted with a "do-nothing" president, they continue to lose faith in the system as a whole. In short, a devastating cycle develops. Political distrust breeds the conditions for presidential disapproval, which leads to more political distrust. Indeed, declining political trust may provide the most plausible explanation of why the goals of political leaders are so much less ambitious today than they were thirty or forty years ago. Presidents of the 1960s aimed to master a "New Frontier" or create a "Great Society." Contemporary presidents—Democrats and Republicans alike—set their sights much lower.

What Is Political Trust and What Is the Shape of Its Decline?

What do terms such as *political trust* and *trust in government* mean? Scholars have generally used these terms synonymously and defined them as people's assessment of how well the federal government is doing compared with how well they *think* it should be doing. In other words, it is the ratio of people's perceptions of the government's performance to their expectations of how the government ought to perform.[7] People's expectations are generally high, and their perceptions of government performance usually fall short of expectations. Therefore, maintaining high levels of political trust is next to impossible, but the extent to which Americans today perceive the government as falling short of their expectations is remarkable, particularly in comparison to the 1960s.

The National Election Studies has asked four questions to assess individuals' political trust in every presidential election year since 1964. The text of the questions, followed by variables names we assigned to them, is as follows:

1. How much of the time do you think you can trust the government in Washington to do what is right—just about always, most of the time, or only some of the time? **Trust**

2. Do you think that people in government waste a lot of the money we pay in taxes, waste some of it, or don't waste very much of it? **Waste**

3. Would you say the government is pretty much run by a few big interests looking out for themselves or that it is run for the benefit of all the people? **Interest**

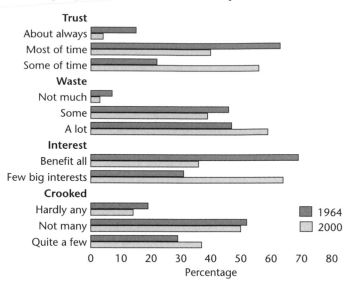

Source: American National Election Study, 1964, 2000.

4. Do you think that quite a few of the people running the government are crooked, not very many are, or do you think hardly any of them are crooked? **Crooked**

Figure 10.1 presents the frequency distributions for each item in 1964 and 2000. Although political trust in 2000 was higher than at any time since 1984, these data still suggest widespread skepticism about government. Only about 3 percent of the public believed that the government wastes "not very much" money, and only about 4 percent thought the government can be trusted "just about always." Indeed, a majority of respondents chose the most negative response option for each of the questions except "Crooked," and even in this case 37 percent think "quite a few" people running the government are crooked.

Comparing the frequencies from 2000 with those from 1964, we find several particularly striking results. In 1964 a majority of respondents did not choose the most negative response to any of the questions. Between 1964 and 2000 the percentage of people choosing the most negative response to each of the four questions increased by an average of 22 percentage points. The distribution of responses to "Interest" presents a near mirror image: approximately two-thirds were trustful in 1964, and nearly two-thirds were distrustful in 2000.

Rather than treating the four questions individually, scholars usually combine them to form a political trust index, and we can use this index to track how

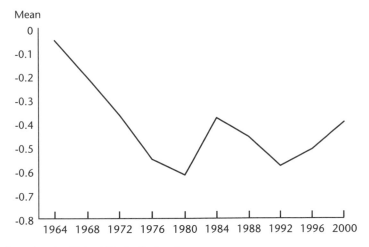

Figure 10.2 Changes in Political Trust, 1964–2000, Presidential Years

Source: American National Election Study, 1964, 2000.

trust has changed from year to year. Figure 10.2 shows consistent deterioration in the level of public trust between 1964 and 1980, followed by periodic upturns and downturns thereafter. Note that the beginning of the downturn in trust actually predates the domestic and foreign unrest usually offered as explanations: it took place between 1964 and 1966. Indeed, declining trust in government in the United States was part of a larger trend that also affected much of Western Europe during the mid- to late-1960s.[8] One plausible explanation for this widespread decline was public dissatisfaction with an expanding welfare state coupled with persistent social problems that government spending did not appear to be solving.[9] In the United States, for instance, political leaders since the 1960s have declared, but subsequently lost, "wars" against poverty, racism, inflation, stagflation, illegal drugs, and cancer. In short, as politicians routinely raised people's expectations about what government would do to levels well above what it might hope to deliver, people began to lose faith in the federal government.

To be sure, specific historical events also suggest potential explanations for the variation in political trust over time. Between 1968 and 1972 the public soured on the Vietnam War, and trust declined as U.S. involvement continued. One of the steeper drops in trust occurred between 1972 and 1976, at least in part because of the Watergate scandal. Beyond war and scandal, government performance also seems to affect political trust. When the economy bottomed out in the late 1970s, so did political trust. Conversely, during periods of economic expansion, such as the early 1980s and late 1990s, trust rebounded.

Figure 10.3 Average Presidential Approval, 1952–2000

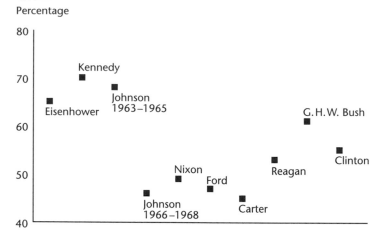

Source: Gallup Organization polls.

With the exception of the relatively short-lived rally resulting from the government's response to the terrorist attacks on New York and Washington, trust has never returned to where it was as recently as 1964. Jack Citrin and Donald Green suggested in 1986 that if the country got on a long winning streak—that is, if it witnessed prolonged peace and prosperity—high levels of trust might return.[10] Based on the small increases in trust relative to the larger decreases that have occurred since the 1960s, it appears that a winning streak would have to last generations to return the United States to the halcyon days of the early Johnson administration. In 2000, even with the most robust economy in the nation's history, Americans' political trust still failed to approach that of the 1960s.

It is no coincidence that support for the president has also dropped. Figure 10.3 shows this decline. Because the drop in trust began around 1966, we display the Johnson presidency in two parts, 1963–1965 and 1966–1968, so that we can assess whether the decline in presidential approval began then or later. Our measure of presidential approval is taken from the Gallup Survey, which asks people, "Do you approve or disapprove of the way [name of president] is handling his job as president." The president's approval rating is the percentage reporting that they approve.

The results shown in Figure 10.3 are striking. The Kennedy, Eisenhower, and early Johnson administration received the highest average approval ratings by far. Leaving aside George H. W. Bush, whose unusually high approval ratings during the Gulf War inflated his average, the gap in public approval of presidents before and after 1966 is around ten percentage points. Reagan and Clinton, two presidents under whom trust increased, are also the two most popular post-1966 presidents. As people become less trustful of the government in general, they apparently become less likely to support the incumbent president. And, as their feelings about the government in general recover, they become more positive about the president.

Why a Lack of Trust Ought to Undermine the President's Standing

Taken together, Figures 10.2 and 10.3 suggest a striking consonance between presidential approval and political trust. But does declining political trust explain lower presidential approval ratings, as we argue, or does reduced confidence in the president cause people to lose trust in government? The latter has long been the conventional wisdom among political scientists. Jack Citrin, for instance, shows that Republicans tend to trust the government more when there is a Republican president than when there is a Democratic president, and vice versa.[11] This finding caused political scientists to believe that changes in presidential approval caused changes in political trust. They reasoned that because the president is the head of the government, evaluations of him are likely to affect how people view the government as a whole. Indeed, many people likely view the president *as* the government. If a person approves of the president's performance, the argument went, then he or she might credit the government by trusting it more.

An even stronger argument suggests that causation flows in the reverse direction; in other words, less trust in government causes lower presidential approval, not the other way around. True, the president is the most visible part of the federal government, but he is only a part of it. In fact, some recent survey evidence shows that Americans increasingly discount the importance of individual presidents. In a July 13, 2000, press release titled "Fewer See Choice of President as Important," the Pew Research Center for the People and the Press reported that 30 percent of Americans agreed that it does not matter who is elected president, nearly double the percentage agreeing with that statement in the 1970s.[12] Apparently, much of the public holds a generalized notion of the government and its effectiveness quite apart from that of the president.

Such sentiment is important in distinguishing cause from effect. It makes more plausible the proposition that general feelings about the government inform feelings about specific actors in the government. Consider the thought process of someone responding to an opinion poll. When asked whether he or she approves of the job the president is doing, a politically distrustful respondent is likely to think that no one in the government is worth much, the president included. Hence the respondent is unlikely to approve of the president.

This reasoning is consistent with research in social psychology. Psychologists find that, when people make judgments, they tend to reason from feelings about things in general, such as stereotypes, to feelings about specific parts. General stereotypes about a particular racial group, for example, inform feelings about specific members of that group much more than experiences with specific group members affect the stereotypes. The same general-to-specific reasoning holds in politics as well. If a strong Democrat is introduced to a Republican politician and knows nothing else, the strong Democrat is more likely to evaluate the Republican poorly than if that politician were a Democrat. Along these lines, we expect that general feelings about the government (political trust) should affect feelings about specific parts of the government (the president).

Testing the Theory

Data are available that allow us to test whether declining political trust causes declining presidential approval, or whether declining approval causes declining trust. The most useful data come from panel studies in which the same people are asked the same questions on several different occasions. With a panel study, we can assess whether an attitude, such as political trust, that is measured at one time has an effect on other attitudes, such as feelings about the president, that are measured at a later time, or whether the reverse is the case. Panel studies are rare, but the National Election Study conducts them every so often, and we can use them to help determine cause and effect.

One way to test which attitude is the cause and which is the effect is to use what statisticians call a cross-lagged model. Figure 10.4 presents such a model. Arrows drawn from one variable to another represent a causal relationship. The numbers associated with the arrows represent the effect that a variable has on another. A star next to a number indicates a statistically significant effect.

In our model, we have two variables to explain—political trust and feelings about the incumbent president—both of them taken from respondents' answers to a survey administered by the National Election Study in 1992 for Part A and 1994 for Part B. As explanatory variables, we have the same respondents' answers to these same questions in 1991 for Part A of Figure 10.4 and 1992 for Part B. Obviously, people's responses to a question in 1991 are likely to be approximately the same if they are asked it again in 1992. For instance, people

Figure 10.4 Cross-Lagged Models: Political Trust and Feelings About the President, 1991–1992 and 1992–1994

A Cross-Lagged Model for 1991–1992

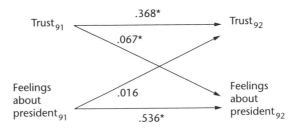

B Cross-Lagged Model for 1992–1994

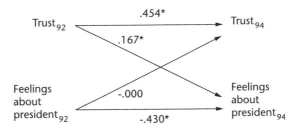

Sources: 1992 American National Election Study, enhanced with 1990 and 1991 data. 1994 American National Election Study, enhanced with 1992 and 1993 data.

* $p < .05$, two-tailed tests.

who liked George H. W. Bush or trusted the government in 1991 probably felt much the same way a year later. The statistical tests that reveal this relationship in Part A, therefore, are not surprising.

For our purposes, the more important arrows are those that cross in the middle. If an attitude measured in 1991 has a significant effect on another attitude measured in 1992, we can be fairly confident that the first attitude is a cause of the second, provided a good reason exists for thinking they are related. For example, if people's political trust measured in 1991 had a significant effect on their feelings about President Bush measured in 1992, we are fairly certain that trust was a cause of feelings about him.

The results presented in Part A suggest that political trust is a cause of feelings about the president. Even holding constant feelings about Bush in 1991, trust as measured in 1991 affected feelings about the president in 1992. Feelings about Bush in 1991, however, were not significantly predictive of political trust in 1992.

Because statistical results taken from surveys are sometimes an artifact of one particular study, it is best to replicate results using different data. We do this using panel data gathered in 1992 and 1994. The results appear in Part B of Figure 10.4. Once again, political trust measured in one year had a statistically significant effect on feelings about the incumbent president in a later year, but feelings about the president measured in a prior year had no effect on subsequent political trust.[13] Taken together, these results suggest that declining political trust since the 1960s has undermined presidential popularity.

Implications of Lower Presidential Approval

Political trust goes a long way in helping us understand the ten- to fifteen-point gap in public approval between recent presidents and presidents from the 1950s and early 1960s. Lower presidential approval, in turn, has implications for what the president can and cannot do. Neustadt noted the importance of a president maintaining public prestige or, in other terms, high job approval. Popularity is not an end in itself; rather, it buys the president influence in his dealings with others in the Washington community. When the public approves of the president, his bargaining power increases, and that allows him to pursue his program more aggressively. An unpopular president lacks the political capital necessary to convince other political actors and elites that his course is worth following.

Empirical support for Neustadt's theory is ample. For example, George Edwards finds a strong correlation between the president's popularity and his ability to win support for the legislation he champions in the House of Representatives.[14] Using a more fully developed theory and more advanced statistical techniques, Douglas Rivers and Nancy Rose demonstrate that the president increases his success rate in moving his agenda through Congress by one percentage point for each percentage point his approval rating goes up.[15] In short, public approval matters for presidents attempting to gain congressional support.

Rivers and Rose also demonstrate that approval is particularly important for a president who pursues an ambitious legislative agenda. Their study shows that the president spends some of his popularity with each item he supports. Because confronting a controversial issue is likely to alienate one constituency or another, the more issues the president addresses, the more groups he may alienate. These findings suggest that presidents need to emphasize all the non-legislative factors that might maximize their approval. Maintaining trust in government is one of those factors.

268 *Hetherington and Globetti*

This line of research clearly indicates the indirect effect the president's popularity has within the Washington community. The president's actions outside the capital can enhance that popularity. To secure public support for favored initiatives, presidents can "go public"—that is, appeal directly to the American public in televised speeches and press conferences. Although the president's ability to go public has been undermined in recent years by the proliferation of cable television, which draws viewers away from the major television networks that the president might hope to dominate, it remains a powerful device at the president's disposal.[16]

Examples of this leadership strategy abound. Ronald Reagan increased support for his proposed tax cuts in 1981 by taking his case directly to the people. The solidly Democratic House quickly fell into line. Bill Clinton also had some success going public early in his presidency to help secure congressional support for his deficit reduction package in 1993.

Samuel Kernell argues that the president's popularity is a key to how effective a president will be when he goes public. Because people will not rally behind the proposals of someone they think is doing a poor job, the policy goals of an unpopular president are probably best served by maintaining a low profile and not associating his name with favored legislation. The president's connection with a program might actually undermine support rather than encourage it. Indeed, during Clinton's unpopular phase, his public identification with the health care reform effort in 1994 was a blow to the future of the legislation. In contrast, presidents who are popular have the most success going public and winning public support.

In sum, whether presidents are appealing to Congress or to the American public, it is in their best interest to be popular. Popular presidents have significantly more success pursuing policy goals than those who are not.

What Does the Future Hold?

Low levels of political trust threaten the president's policy agenda, which has real implications for ordinary citizens. In view of the sorry state of political trust depicted in Figure 10.2, can future presidents hope to accomplish their legislative agendas? Or are presidents doomed to fail by a distrusting public? Answering these questions requires some discussion of what explains individuals' levels of political trust.

Events affect political trust, perhaps never more dramatically demonstrated than by the September 11 terrorist attacks, which had a tremendous effect on public attitudes. President Bush enjoyed a better than 80 percent public approval rating for a full six months until events in the Middle East apparently pushed his approval down ten or more points (at the time of this writing). In the days after the attack, trust in government increased to levels reminiscent of the mid-1960s. Such rally effects are not surprising—they often occur around political crises—but they are usually short-lived. Indeed, only three months after the attacks, the percentage of trusting responses to the traditional trust in government question had already dropped by 15 percentage points.[17] Although this poll was the last asking Americans about their trust in government before this book went to press, trust has likely continued to drop. People will be less likely to evaluate the government in terms of the military response to the attacks than they were in the weeks directly after them. Because the public's positive feelings about the military relative to other parts of the government likely explain the post–September 11 surge, more negative feelings about government are almost sure to return.

Other recent developments are not particularly encouraging for political trust either. Research suggests that trust increases when more people think that the government is doing well at solving what they consider the most important problems, with economic performance particularly important.[18] As we noted earlier, however, the runaway economic success of the late-1990s did not even come close to returning trust to its mid-1960s level, although it did increase it somewhat. Moreover, the cyclical nature of the economy keeps it from having consistently positive or consistently negative effects on political trust.

Political leaders can also increase trust when they provide policy alternatives that are consistent with the public's own preferences.[19] To the extent that people have measurable preferences on issues, forty years of research suggests that public opinion is neither liberal nor conservative. As E. J. Dionne has noted, Americans want commonsense centrist solutions to national problems.[20] As a result, when people see both political parties straying far from the ideological center, their trust in government drops.[21]

This observation is of some consequence because of recent trends among political elites. Driven by party activists who are motivated less by patronage than by ideology,[22] the Republican and Democratic Parties today are moving to the ideological poles, especially in Congress. Indeed, today's parties are more ideologically polarized than at any time during the last fifty years. Whether the issue is the environment, health care, taxes, campaign finance reform, or almost anything else, Republicans generally propose conservative solutions, and Democrats liberal ones.

Figure 10.5 Ideological Overlap Between Republican and Democratic Members of the House of Representatives, 81st–105th Congresses

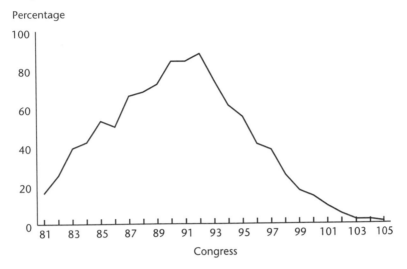

Percentage

Source: Compiled by the author.

We show the pattern of the two parties' ideological polarization in Figure 10.5. This figure uses data, called NOMINATE scores, that have been collected and calculated by Keith Poole and Howard Rosenthal.[23] These scores are designed to track the voting records of members of the House of Representatives over time. Each member gets a NOMINATE score for each two-year term based on how conservative or liberal his or her voting record was. The most liberal members receive the lowest scores; the most conservative members receive the highest scores; and more moderate members receive scores somewhere in between. If we sort the Republican and Democratic members into their party caucuses, we can use these scores to examine how ideologically distinct the congressional parties are, or, alternatively, how much they overlap.

When we use the term overlap, we mean the number of Democratic members who are more conservative than the most liberal Republican member. The measure of overlap that we present in Figure 10.5 is the number of House members who would have to convert to the other party to achieve complete ideological separation between the two parties. In the 1960s and 1970s, when the Democratic caucus included many southern conservatives and several northern Republicans were liberals, the amount of overlap was significant. Indeed, for eight consecutive Congresses during the 1960s and 1970s, more than sixty members would have needed to convert to achieve complete ideological separation.

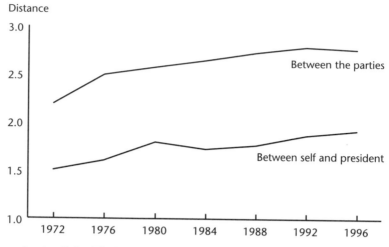

Figure 10.6 Perceived Ideological Distances Between Self and President and Between the Republican and Democratic Parties, 1972–1996

Distance

Between the parties

Between self and president

1972   1976   1980   1984   1988   1992   1996

Source: American National Election Study, Cumulative File.

Compare that with today. In the 105th Congress, only one Democratic member, Ralph Hall of Texas, would have had to switch for all the Republicans to be more conservative than all the Democrats.

Ideological polarization in Congress has affected public attitudes. First, people now view the president and the parties more ideologically. The National Election Study asks Americans to place themselves, the president, and both political parties on a seven-point scale ranging from extremely liberal at one end to extremely conservative at the other. When the ideological distance that people see between themselves and the president is small, the president fares better because more people share his ideology. Unfortunately for recent presidents, as Figure 10.6 shows, with the exception of Jimmy Carter in 1980, Americans have perceived an ever-increasing ideological distance between themselves and their presidents since 1972. If people do not share a president's ideology, they are surely less likely to support his program.

Figure 10.6 also demonstrates a steady increase in the ideological distance that people perceive between the major parties. The American public regarded both parties as centrist in the early 1970s, seeing little more than two points between them on the seven-point scale. More recently, this distance has widened to closer to three points, nearly a 50 percent increase. More easily distinguished parties and leaders, however, have some advantages. People who do not follow politics closely have less trouble choosing between them when the major parties provide "choices not echoes."[24] A good example is the 1964 presidential election. Lyndon Johnson won by a landslide because most Americans thought that Barry Goldwater was too far to the ideological right. People also find it easier to assign praise and blame to political leaders when an ideological divide separates the parties. George W. Bush's accomplishments before the terrorist attacks, especially his tax cut, came with almost no Democratic votes in Congress. People will have no trouble assigning credit or blame for his policies' perceived success.

More ideologically distinct parties have a downside in the public mind as well. As the parties have moved toward the ideological poles and Americans have correctly perceived these changes, their own ideological preferences have remained moderate. Indeed, to the extent that ordinary Americans have changed over time, they have grown even more centrist. Since the National Election Studies first started asking voters to place themselves on the seven-point liberal-conservative scale in 1972, the most popular response has always been the exact midpoint, labeled moderate or middle of the road. Moreover, the percentage of people choosing the most moderate option reached its all-time high in 1998, indicating that, when people think about themselves politically, they do not think in ideological terms.

The combination of ideological parties and a nonideological electorate is likely to have a negative effect on how people feel about government as a whole—that is, in political trust. As people come to see parties and politicians as ideologically out of touch, the government will surely pay a price through more negative public evaluations. Indeed, this is the crux of Dionne's explanation of why Americans hate politics. He persuasively argues that people believe the parties are providing extreme choices and unsound solutions. This state of affairs will have a negative impact on the presidency because the lower political trust generated by ideologically polarized parties will ultimately undermine presidential approval. In short, the combination of ideological parties and a nonideological voting public spells trouble for presidents in the future.

Conclusion

Our results suggest that reduced political trust today undermines a president's prospects for leadership. Moreover, recent developments in U.S. politics, such as the ideological polarization of the parties in Washington and the consistently moderate character of public opinion, create an environment in which trust is likely to decline again. Maintaining a robust economy, fighting a popular war, and avoiding major scandals will offset the decline, but these goals will be difficult to accomplish over the long term because of the cyclical nature of the economy and a news industry that has grown dependent on scandal. Presidents therefore will likely continue to feel the constraining effects of low political trust well into the future.

These constraining effects are likely to be viewed as more or less burdensome, depending on the president's party. Democrats typically attempt to implement more aggressive national public policies than Republicans, so high levels of trust in government will be more important to Democratic presidents than to Republicans. Recall that Neustadt, who prescribed that a president carefully marshal his resources to maintain public approval, was a formal or informal adviser to a string of Democratic presidents from Roosevelt to Kennedy. For Democrats to create new federal programs, the public will need to have faith in the president who proposes them and in the government responsible for administering them.

In contrast, a major component of the Republicans' philosophy has been to limit the size of the federal government. Their platforms support devolving power from the federal level to the state level, although success in this regard has been limited. Devolution does not require as much faith in the federal government for people to support it as, say, national health insurance does. In fact, low levels of trust in the federal government may even be useful in gaining public support for sending responsibilities from Washington to the states.[25] The Welfare Reform Act of 1996, easily the most significant new piece of social policy in the 1990s, owes much of its success to the public's loss of faith in the federal government.

At a minimum, the widespread distrust of the federal government provides Republicans a ready villain to campaign against. Recall that George W. Bush hit his stride in the 2000 campaign when he told Americans, "That's the difference in philosophy between my opponent and me. He trusts government. I trust you."[26] When political trust is low, Republicans, as the party of limited government, are more credible than Democrats in making this type of attack stick.

In this vein, it is interesting to note that the presidents who have sounded the trumpet for limited government as part of their governing strategy have often brought about increases in political trust and received relatively high approval ratings, no matter which party they represented. The two best examples are Ronald Reagan and Bill Clinton (at least after 1994). Reagan declared that "government is not the solution to our problem; government is the problem," and Clinton announced that "the era of Big Government is over." Although neither president did much to scale down the size of government, both benefited politically from these rhetorical flourishes and each was reelected. It is hard to disentangle whether people's renewed faith in government and support for these two presidents resulted from robust economic growth or their rhetoric of limited government. But, in view of America's liberal tradition, references to limited government should continue to receive a favorable response from most Americans. In fact, they may even make Americans trust the government more.

Republicans do, however, need to take care when deciding how to attack big government. Parts of the federal government are popular. People embrace programs that benefit most if not all Americans, such as Social Security, environmental protection, and spending on public education. Americans are mostly hostile to programs that redistribute money from the better off to the less well off.[27] Indeed, the GOP maintained strong support after its takeover of Congress in the 1994 election when it focused on cutting spending on social programs and reforming welfare. In their attempt to eliminate the Department of Education, however, Republicans enjoyed no success. When House Republicans shut the government down over general spending priorities in 1995, they felt a stinging rebuke from the public because they had gone beyond attacking the parts of government that people distrust.

The Republicans' misinterpretation of their 1994 mandate is understandable. The "Contract with America," on which congressional Republicans ran in 1994 was, in large part, about reducing the number and type of things that the federal government does. When political elites talk about the federal government in general, people tend to think about redistributive policies, of which most Americans disapprove.[28] Doing so attracted many votes in 1995. But rhetoric and governing are two different things. When the Republicans attempted to shrink federal responsibility across the board, they moved beyond what people distrust about government. It bears noting that they have not done particularly well in a federal election since.

Notes

1. See http://www.gallup.com/poll/trends/Ptjobapp_BC.asp for a summary of Bill Clinton's approval numbers.

2. Richard A. Brody, *Assessing the President: The Media, Elite Opinion, and Public Support* (Stanford: Stanford University Press, 1991).

3. Thomas Patterson, *Out of Order* (New York: Knopf, 1993).

4. Robert E. Lane, *Political Ideology: Why the American Common Man Believes What He Does* (New York: Free Press, 1962).

5. Arthur H. Miller, "Political Issues and Trust in Government, 1964–70," *American Political Science Review* 68 (September 1974): 951–972; and Arthur H. Miller, "Rejoinder to 'Comment' by Jack Citrin: Political Discontent or Ritualism?" *American Political Science Review* 68 (September 1974): 989–1001. See Jack Citrin, "Comment: The Political Relevance of Trust in Government," *American Political Science Review* 68 (September 1974): 973–988.

6. Richard E. Neustadt, *Presidential Power* (New York: Macmillan, 1990).

7. Gary Orren, "Fall From Grace: The Public's Loss of Faith in Government," in *Why People Don't Trust Government*, ed. Joseph S. Nye Jr., Philip D. Zelikow, and David C. King (Cambridge: Harvard University Press, 1997).

8. Seymour Martin Lipset and William Schneider, *The Confidence Gap: Business, Labor, and Government in the Public Mind* (New York: Free Press, 1983).

9. Jane Mansbridge, "Social and Cultural Causes of Dissatisfaction with U.S. Government," in *Why People Don't Trust Government*, ed. Nye et al.

10. Jack Citrin and Donald Philip Green, "Presidential Leadership and the Resurgence of Trust in Government," *British Journal of Political Science* 16 (October 1986): 431–453.

11. Citrin, "Comment: The Political Relevance of Trust in Government."

12. This report can be accessed at http://www.people-press.org/juneoorpt.htm.

13. With these results, we do not intend to suggest that changes in feelings about the president have no effect on changes in political trust over time. Theoretically, this makes little sense—people do use their feelings toward specific actors to inform their opinions about the government in general, at least to some degree. Indeed, using more sophisticated statistical techniques, Marc Hetherington has shown that feelings of trust and feelings about the president are arrived at simultaneously. See Marc J. Hetherington, "The Political Relevance of Political Trust," *American Political Science Review* 92 (December 1998): 791–808. But Hetherington also shows that trust's effect on feelings about the president is much stronger than the reverse effect. In fact, he shows that had political trust remained as high as it was in the late 1950s and early 1960s, Ronald Reagan would have had an approval rating at the end of his presidency almost identical to Dwight Eisenhower's, and Bill Clinton's late first-term numbers would have been almost the same as Lyndon Johnson's.

14. George C. Edwards III, "Presidential Influence in the House: Presidential Prestige as a Source of Presidential Power," *American Political Science Review* 70 (March 1976): 101–113.

15. Douglas Rivers and Nancy L. Rose, "Passing the President's Program: Public Opinion and Presidential Influence in Congress," *American Journal of Political Science* 29 (May 1985): 183–196.

16. Matthew A. Baum and Samuel Kernell, "Has Cable Ended the Golden Age of Presidential Television?" *American Political Science Review* 93 (March 1999): 99–114.

17. These data are taken from a *Time*/CNN/Harris Poll conducted December 19, 2001.

18. Hetherington, "Political Relevance of Political Trust"; and Citrin and Green, "Presidential Leadership and the Resurgence of Trust in Government."

19. Miller, "Political Issues and Trust in Government, 1964–70."

20. E. J. Dionne Jr., *Why Americans Hate Politics* (New York: Touchstone, 1991).

21. David C. King, "The Polarization of American Parties and Mistrust of Government," in *Why People Don't Trust Government*, ed. Nye et al.

22. John H. Aldrich, *Why Parties? The Origin and Transformation of Party Politics in America* (Chicago: University of Chicago Press, 1995).

23. Keith T. Poole and Howard Rosenthal, *Congress: A Political-Economic History of Roll Call Voting* (New York: Oxford University Press, 1997).

24. Benjamin I. Page, *Choices and Echoes in Presidential Elections: Rational Man and Electoral Democracy* (Chicago: University of Chicago Press, 1978).

25. Marc J. Hetherington and John D. Nugent, "Explaining Support for Devolution: The Role of Political Trust," in *What Is it About Government that Americans Dislike?* ed. John R. Hibbing and Elizabeth Theiss-Morse (New York: Cambridge University Press, 2001).

26. Bush used this rhetoric both on the stump and in television commercials. This particular quotation is taken from a campaign advertisement that the Bush campaign titled "Bush Trusts You."

27. This is a long-noted division in public opinion, owing its intellectual roots to early survey research by Lloyd A. Free and Hadley Cantril, *The Political Beliefs of Americans: A Study of Public Opinion* (New York: Clarion, 1968).

28. William G. Jacoby, "Public Attitudes toward Government Spending," *American Journal of Political Science* 38 (April 1994): 336–361.

11 The Presidential Spectacle

Bruce Miroff

To govern successfully, presidents have always needed political support from the public. What is new in the modern presidency is how hard they work to achieve it. As Bruce Miroff argues, the modern president "not only responds to popular demands and passions but also actively reaches out to shape them." The president does so in speeches and in symbol-laden events, which Miroff, borrowing from the language of cultural anthropology, calls "spectacles." Understood properly, for example, the highly popular war against Iraq that George H. W. Bush launched in February 1991 resembled nothing so much as a professional wrestling match, in which the audience (the American people) was gratified by the sight of the good guy (President Bush) overpowering the bad guy (Iraqi leader Saddam Hussein). For George W. Bush, the war against terrorism launched in response to the September 11, 2001, attacks on the World Trade Center and the Pentagon poses an even greater substantive and symbolic challenge.

One of the most distinctive features of the modern presidency is its constant cultivation of popular support. The Framers of the U.S. Constitution envisioned a president substantially insulated from the demands and passions of the people by the long duration of the term and the dignity of the office. The modern president, in contrast, not only responds to popular demands and passions but also actively reaches out to shape them. The possibilities opened up by modern technology and the problems presented by the increased fragility of parties and institutional coalitions lead presidents to turn to the public for support and strength. If popular backing is to be maintained, however, the public must believe in the president's leadership qualities.

Observers of presidential politics have come to recognize the centrality of the president's relationship with the American public. George Edwards has written of "the public presidency" and argued that the "greatest source of influence for the president is public approval."[1] Samuel Kernell has suggested that presidential appeals for popular favor now overshadow more traditional methods of seeking influence, especially bargaining. Presidents today, Kernell argued, are "going public," and he demonstrated their propensity to cultivate popular support by recording the mounting frequency of their public addresses, public appearances, and political travel. These constitute, he claimed, "the repertoire of modern leadership."[2]

This new understanding of presidential leadership can be carried further. A president's approach to, and impact on, public perceptions is not limited to overt appeals in speeches and appearances. Much of what the modern presidency does, in fact, involves the projection of images whose purpose is to shape public understanding and gain popular support. A significant—and growing—part of the presidency revolves around the enactment of leadership as a spectacle.

To examine the presidency as a spectacle is to ask not only how a president seeks to appear but also what the public sees. We are accustomed to gauging the public's responses to a president with polls that measure approval and disapproval of overall performance in office and effectiveness in managing the economy and foreign policy. Yet these evaluative categories may say more about the information desired by politicians or academic researchers than about the terms in which most members of a president's audience actually view the president. A public that responds mainly to presidential spectacles will not ignore the president's performance, but its understanding of that performance, as well as its sense of the more overarching and intangible strengths and weaknesses of the administration, will be colored by the terms of the spectacle.

The Presidency as Spectacle

A spectacle is a kind of symbolic event, one in which particular details stand for broader and deeper meanings. What differentiates a spectacle from other kinds of symbolic events is the centrality of character and action. A spectacle presents intriguing and often dominating characters not in static poses but through actions that establish their public identities.

Spectacle implies a clear division between actors and spectators. As Daniel Dayan and Elihu Katz have noted, a spectacle possesses "a narrowness of focus, a limited set of appropriate responses, and . . . a minimal level of interaction. What there is to see is very clearly exhibited; spectacle implies a distinction between the roles of performers and audience."[3] A spectacle does not permit the audience to interrupt the action and redirect its meaning. Spectators can become absorbed in a spectacle or can find it unconvincing, but they cannot become performers. A spectacle is not designed for mass participation; it is not a democratic event.

Perhaps the most distinctive characteristic of a spectacle is that the actions that constitute it are meaningful not for what they achieve but for what they signify. Actions in a spectacle are gestures rather than means to an end. What is important is that they be understandable and impressive to the spectators. This distinction between gestures and means is illustrated by Roland Barthes in his classic discussion of professional wrestling as a spectacle. Barthes shows that professional wrestling is completely unlike professional boxing. Boxing is a form of competition, a contest of skill in a situation of uncertainty. What matters is the outcome; because this is in doubt, we can wager on it. But in professional wrestling, the outcome is preordained; it would be senseless to bet on who is going to win. What matters in professional wrestling are the gestures made during the match, gestures by performers portraying distinctive characters, gestures that carry moral significance. In a typical match, an evil character threatens a good character, knocks him down on the canvas, abuses him with dirty tricks, but ultimately loses when the good character rises up to exact a just revenge.[4]

It may seem odd to approach the presidency through an analogy with boxing and wrestling—but let us pursue it for a moment. Much of what presidents do is analogous to what boxers do—they engage in contests of power and policy with other political actors, contests in which the outcomes are uncertain. But a growing amount of presidential activity is akin to wrestling. The contemporary presidency is presented by the White House (with the collaboration of the media) as a series of spectacles in which a larger-than-life main character and a supporting team engage in emblematic bouts with immoral or dangerous adversaries.

A number of contemporary developments have converged to foster the rise of spectacle in the modern presidency. The mass media have become the principal vehicle for presidential spectacle. Focusing more of their coverage on presidents than on any other person or institution in American life, the media keep them constantly before the public and give them unmatched opportunities to display their leadership qualities. Television provides the view most amenable to spectacle; by favoring the visual and the dramatic, it promotes stories with simple plot lines over complex analyses of causes and consequences. But other kinds of media are not fundamentally different. As David Paletz and Robert Entman have shown, American journalists "define events from a short-term, anti-historical perspective; see individual or group action, not structural or other impersonal long run forces, at the root of most occurrences; and simplify and reduce stories to conventional symbols for easy assimilation by audiences."[5]

The mass media are not, to be sure, always reliable vehicles for presidential spectacles. Reporters may frame their stories in terms that undermine the meanings the White House intends to convey. Their desire for controversy can feed off presidential spectacles, but it also can destroy them. The media can contribute to spectacular failures in the presidency as well as to successful spectacles.

Spectacle has also been fostered by the president's rise to primacy in the American political system. A political order originally centered on institutions has given way, especially in the public mind, to a political order that centers on the person of the president. Theodore Lowi wrote, "Since the president has become the embodiment of government, it seems perfectly normal for millions upon millions of Americans to concentrate their hopes and fears directly and personally upon him."[6] The "personal president" that Lowi described is the object of popular expectations; these expectations, Stephen Wayne and Thomas Cronin have shown, are both excessive and contradictory.[7] The president must attempt to satisfy the public by delivering tangible benefits, such as economic growth, but these will almost never be enough. Not surprisingly, then, presidents turn to the gestures of the spectacle to satisfy their audience.

To understand the modern presidency as a form of spectacle, we must consider the presentation of presidents as spectacular characters, their teams' role as supporting performers, and the arrangement of gestures that convey to the audience the meaning of their actions.

A contemporary president is, to borrow a phrase from Guy Debord, "the spectacular representation of a living human being."[8] An enormous amount of attention is paid to the president as a public character; every deed, quality, and even foible is regarded as fascinating and important. The American public may not learn the details of policy formulation, but they know that Gerald Ford bumps his head on helicopter door frames, that Ronald Reagan likes jellybeans, and that Bill Clinton enjoys hanging out with Hollywood celebrities. In a spectacle, a president's character possesses intrinsic as well as symbolic value; it is to be appreciated for its own sake. The spectators do not press presidents to specify what economic or social benefits they are providing; nor do they closely inquire into the truthfulness of the claims presidents make. (To the extent that they do evaluate the president in such terms, they step outside the terms of the spectacle.) The president's featured qualities are presented as benefits in themselves. Thus John F. Kennedy's glamour casts his whole era in a romanticized glow, Ronald Reagan's amiability relieves the grim national mood that had developed under his predecessor, and George W. Bush's traditional marriage rebukes the cultural decay associated with Bill Clinton's sex scandals.

The president's character must be not only appealing but also magnified by the spectacle. The spectacle makes the president appear exceptionally decisive, tough, courageous, prescient, or prudent. Whether the president is in fact all or any of these things is obscured. What matters is that he or she is presented as having these qualities, in magnitudes far beyond what ordinary citizens can imagine themselves to possess. The president must appear confident and masterful before spectators whose very position, as onlookers, denies the possibility of mastery.[9]

The most likely presidential qualities to be magnified will be those that contrast dramatically with the attributes that drew criticism to the previous president. Reagan, following a president perceived as weak, was featured in spectacles that highlighted his potency. The elder Bush, succeeding a president notorious for his disengagement from the workings of his own administration, was featured in spectacles of "hands-on" management. Clinton, supplanting a president who seemed disengaged from the economic problems of ordinary Americans, began his administration with spectacles of populist intimacy. The younger Bush, replacing a president notorious for personal indiscipline and staff disorder, presents a corporate-style White House where meetings run on time and proper business attire is required in the Oval Office.

Presidents are the principal figures in presidential spectacles, but they have the help of aides and advisers. The star performer is surrounded by a team. Members of the president's team can, through the supporting parts they play, enhance or detract from the spectacle's effect on the audience. For a president's team to enhance the spectacles, its members should project attractive qualities that either resemble the featured attributes of the president or make up for the president's perceived deficiencies. A team will diminish presidential spectacles if its members project qualities that underscore the president's weaknesses.

A performance team, Erving Goffman has shown, contains "a set of individuals whose intimate cooperation is required if a given projected definition of the situation is to be maintained."[10] There are a number of ways the team can disrupt presidential spectacles. A member of the team can call too much attention to himself or herself, partially upstaging the president. This was one of the disruptive practices that made the Reagan White House eager to be rid of Secretary of State Alexander Haig. A team member can give away important secrets to the audience; Budget Director David Stockman's famous confessions about supply-side economics to a reporter for the *Atlantic* jeopardized the mystique of economic innovation that the Reagan administration had created in 1981. Worst of all, a member of the team can, perhaps inadvertently, discredit the central meanings that a presidential spectacle has been designed to establish. The revelations of Budget Director Bert Lance's questionable banking practices deflated the lofty moral tone established at the beginning of the Carter presidency.

The audience watching a presidential spectacle is, the White House hopes, as impressed by gestures as by results. Indeed, the gestures are sometimes preferable to the results. Thus, a "show" of force by the president is preferable to the death and destruction that are the results of force. The ways in which the invasion of Grenada in 1983, the bombing of Libya in 1986, and the seizing of the Panamanian dictator Manuel Noriega in 1989 were portrayed to the American public suggest an eagerness in the White House to present the image of military toughness but not the casualties from military conflict—even when they are the enemy's casualties.

Gestures overshadow results. They also overshadow facts. But facts are not obliterated in a presidential spectacle. They remain present; they are needed, in a sense, to nurture the gestures. Without real events, presidential spectacles would not be impressive; they would seem contrived, mere pseudoevents. However, some of the facts that emerge in the course of an event might discredit its presentation as spectacle. Therefore, a successful spectacle, such as Reagan's "liberation" of Grenada, must be more powerful than any of the facts on which it draws. Rising above contradictory or disconfirming details, the spectacle must transfigure the more pliant facts and make them carriers of its most spectacular gestures.

Presidential spectacles are seldom pure spectacles in the sense that a wrestling match can be a pure spectacle. Although they may involve a good deal of advance planning and careful calculation of gestures, they cannot be completely scripted in advance. Unexpected and unpredictable events will occur during a presidential spectacle. If the White House is fortunate and skillful, it can capitalize on some of these events by using them to enhance the spectacle. If the White House is not so lucky or talented, such events can detract from, or even undermine, the spectacle.

Also unlike wrestling or other pure spectacles, the presidential variety often has more than one audience. Its primary purpose is to construct meanings for the American public. But it also can direct messages to those whom the White House has identified as its foes or the sources of its problems. In 1981, when

Reagan fired the air traffic controllers of the Professional Air Traffic Controllers' Organization (PATCO) because they engaged in an illegal strike, he presented to the public the spectacle of a tough, determined president who would uphold the law and, unlike his predecessor, would not be pushed around by grasping interest groups. The spectacle also conveyed to organized labor that the White House knew how to feed popular suspicions of unions and could make things difficult for a labor movement that became too assertive.

As the PATCO firing shows, some presidential spectacles retain important policy dimensions. One could construct a continuum in which one end represents pure policy and the other pure spectacle. Toward the policy end one would find behind-the-scenes presidential actions, including quiet bargaining over domestic policies (such as Lyndon Johnson's lining up of Republican support for civil rights legislation) and covert actions in foreign affairs (the Nixon administration's use of the CIA to "destabilize" a socialist regime in Chile). Toward the spectacle end would be presidential posturing at home (law and order and drugs have been handy topics) and dramatic foreign travel (from 1972 until the 1989 massacre in Tiananmen Square, China was a particular presidential favorite). Most of the president's actions are a mix of policy and spectacle.

The Triumph of Spectacle: Ronald Reagan

The Reagan presidency was a triumph of spectacle. In the realm of substantive policy, it was marked by striking failures as well as significant successes. But even the most egregious of these failures—public exposure of the disastrous covert policy of selling arms to Iran and diverting some of the profits from the sales to the Nicaraguan contras—proved to be only a temporary blow to the political fortunes of the most spectacular president in decades. With the help of two heartwarming summits with Soviet leader Mikhail Gorbachev, Reagan recovered from the Iran-contra debacle and left office near the peak of his popularity. His presidency had, for the most part, floated above its flawed processes and failed policies, secure in the brilliant glow of its successful spectacles.

The basis of this success was the character of Ronald Reagan. His previous career in movies and television made him comfortable with and adept at spectacles; he moved easily from one kind to another.[11] Reagan presented to his audience a multifaceted character, funny yet powerful, ordinary yet heroic, individual yet representative. He was a character richer even than Kennedy in mythic resonance.

Coming into office after a president who was widely perceived as weak, Reagan as a spectacle character projected potency. His administration featured a number of spectacles in which Reagan displayed his decisiveness, forcefulness, and will to prevail. The image of masculine toughness was played up repeatedly. The American people saw a president who, even though in his seventies, rode horses and exercised vigorously, a president who liked to quote (and thereby identify himself with) movie tough guys such as Clint Eastwood and Sylvester Stallone. Yet Reagan's strength was nicely balanced by his amiability; his aggressiveness was rendered benign by his characteristic one-line quips. The warm grin took the edge off, removed any intimations of callousness or violence.

Quickly dubbed the Great Communicator, Reagan presented his character not through eloquent rhetoric but through storytelling. As Paul Erickson has demonstrated, Reagan liked to tell tales of "stock symbolic characters," figures whose values and behavior were "heavily colored with Reagan's ideological and emotional principles."[12] Although the villains in these tales ranged from Washington bureaucrats to Marxist dictators, the heroes, whether ordinary people or inspirational figures like Knute Rockne, shared a belief in America. Examined more closely, these heroes turned out to resemble Reagan himself. Praising the heroism of Americans, Reagan, as representative American, praised himself.

The power of Reagan's character rested not only on its intrinsic attractiveness but also on its symbolic appeal. The spectacle specialists who worked for Reagan seized on the idea of making him an emblem for the American identity. In a June 1984 memo, White House aide Richard Darman sketched a campaign strategy that revolved around the president's mythic role: "Paint RR as the personification of all that is right with or heroized by America. Leave Mondale in a position where an attack on Reagan is tantamount to an attack on America's idealized image of itself."[13] Having come into office at a time of considerable anxiety, with many Americans uncertain (according to polls and interviews) about the economy, their future, and the country itself, Reagan was an immensely reassuring character. He had not been marked by the shocks of recent U.S. history—and he denied that those shocks had meaning. He told Americans that the Vietnam War was noble rather than appalling, that Watergate was forgotten, that racial conflict was a thing of the distant past, and that the U.S. economy still offered the American dream to any aspiring individual. Reagan (the character) and America (the country) were presented in the spectacles of the Reagan presidency as timeless, above the decay of aging and the difficulties of history.

The Reagan team assumed special importance because Reagan ran what Lou Cannon has called "the delegated presidency."[14] His team members carried on, as was well known to the public, most of the business of the executive branch; Reagan's own work habits were decidedly relaxed. Reagan's team did not contain many performers who reinforced the president's character, as did Kennedy's New Frontiersmen. But it featured several figures whose spectacle role was to compensate for Reagan's deficiencies or to carry on his mission with a greater air of vigor than the amiable president usually conveyed. The Reagan presidency was not free of disruptive characters—Alexander Haig's and James Watt's unattractive qualities and gestures called the president's spectacle into question. Unlike the Carter presidency, however, the Reagan administration removed these characters before too much damage had been done.

David Stockman was the most publicized supporting player in the first months of 1981. His image in the media was formidable. *Newsweek,* for example, marveled at how "his buzz-saw intellect has helped him stage a series of bravura performances before Congress," and acclaimed him "the Reagan Administration's boy wonder."[15] There was spectacle appeal in the sight of the nation's youngest ever budget director serving as the right arm of the nation's oldest ever chief executive. More important, Stockman's appearance as the master of budget numbers compensated for a president who was notoriously uninterested in data. Stockman faded in spectacle value after his disastrous confession in the fall of 1981 that budget numbers had been doctored to show the results the administration wanted.

As Reagan's longtime aide, Edwin Meese III was one of the most prominent members of the president's team. Meese's principal spectacle role was not as a White House manager but as a cop. Even before he moved from the White House to the Justice Department, Meese became the voice and the symbol of the administration's tough stance on law-and-order issues. Although the president sometimes spoke about law and order, Meese took on the issue with a vigor that his more benign boss could not convey.

In foreign affairs, the Reagan administration developed an effective balance of images in the persons of Caspar Weinberger and George Shultz. Weinberger quickly became the administration's most visible cold war hard-liner. As the tireless spokesperson and unbudging champion of a soaring defense budget, he was a handy symbol for the Reagan military buildup. Nicholas Lemann noted that although "Weinberger's predecessor, Harold Brown, devoted himself almost completely to management, Weinberger . . . operated more and more on the theatrical side."[16] His grim, hawklike visage was as much a reminder of the Soviet threat as the alarming paperback reports on the Russian behemoth that his Defense Department issued every year. Yet Weinberger could seem too alarming, feeding the fears of those who worried about Reagan's war-making proclivities.

Once Haig was pushed out as secretary of state, however, the Reagan administration found the ideal counterpoint to Weinberger in George Shultz. In contrast to both Haig and Weinberger, Shultz was a reassuring figure. He was portrayed in the media in soothing terms: low-key, quiet, conciliatory. In form and demeanor, he came across, in the words of *Time,* "as a good gray diplomat."[17] Shultz was taken to be a voice of foreign policy moderation in an administration otherwise dominated by hard-liners. Actually, Shultz had better cold war credentials than Weinberger, having been a founding member of the hard-line Committee on the Present Danger in 1976. And he was more inclined to support the use of military force than was the secretary of defense, who reflected the caution of a Pentagon burned by the Vietnam experience. But Shultz's real views were less evident than his spectacle role as the gentle diplomat.

The Reagan presidency benefited not only from a spectacular main character and a useful team but also from talent and good fortune at enacting spectacle gestures. It is not difficult to find events during the Reagan years—the PATCO strike, the Geneva summit, the Libyan bombing, and others—whose significance primarily lay in their spectacle value. The most striking Reagan spectacle of all was the invasion of Grenada. Grenada deserves a close look, as it can serve as the archetypal presidential spectacle.

American forces invaded the island of Grenada in October 1983. Relations had become tense between the Reagan administration and the Marxist regime of Grenada's Maurice Bishop. When Bishop was overthrown and murdered by a clique of more militant Marxists, the Reagan administration began to consider military action. It was urged to invade by the Organization of Eastern Caribbean States, composed of Grenada's island neighbors. And it had a pretext for action in the safety of the Americans—most of them medical students—on the island. Once the decision to invade was made, U.S. troops landed in force, evacuated most of the students, and seized the island after encountering unexpectedly stiff resistance. Reagan administration officials announced that in the course of securing the island U.S. forces had discovered large caches of military supplies and documents, indicating that Cuba planned to turn Grenada into a base for the export of revolution and terror.

Examination of the details that eventually came to light cast doubt on the Reagan administration's claims of a threat to the American students and a buildup of "sophisticated" Cuban weaponry in Grenada. Beyond such details, there was sheer incongruity between the importance bestowed on Grenada by the Reagan administration and the insignificance that the facts seemed to suggest. Grenada is a tiny island, with a population of 100,000, a land area of 133 square miles, and an economy whose exports totaled $19 million in 1981.[18] That U.S. troops could secure it was never in question; as Richard Gabriel has noted, "In terms of actual combat forces, the U.S. outnumbered the island's defenders approximately ten to one."[19] Grenada's importance did not derive from the facts of the event or from the military, political, and economic implications of America's actions, but from its value as a spectacle.

What was this spectacle about? Its meaning was articulated by a triumphant President Reagan: "Our days of weakness are over. Our military forces are back on their feet and standing tall."[20] Reagan, even more than the American military, came across in the media as "standing tall" in Grenada.

The spectacle actually began with the president on a weekend golfing vacation in Augusta, Georgia. His vacation was interrupted first by planning for an invasion of Grenada and then by news that the U.S. Marine barracks in Beirut had been bombed. Once the news of the Grenada landings replaced the tragedy in Beirut on the front page and television screen, the golfing angle proved to be an apt beginning for a spectacle. It was used to dramatize the ability of a relaxed and laid-back president to rise to a grave challenge. And it supplied the White House with an unusual backdrop to present the president in charge, with members of his team by his side. As Francis X. Clines reported in the *New York Times,*

The White House offered the public some graphic tableaux, snapped by the White House photographer over the weekend, depicting the President at the center of various conferences. He is seen in bathrobe and slippers being briefed by Mr. Shultz and Mr. McFarlane, then out on the Augusta fairway, pausing at the wheel of his golf cart as he receives another dispatch. Mr. Shultz is getting the latest word in another, holding the special security phone with a golf glove on.[21]

Pictures of the president as decision-maker were particularly effective because pictures from Grenada itself were lacking; the Reagan administration had barred the American press from covering the invasion. This move outraged the press but was extremely useful to the spectacle, which would not have been furthered by pictures of dead bodies or civilian casualties or by independent sources of information with which congressional critics could raise unpleasant questions.

The initial meaning of the Grenada spectacle was established by Reagan in his announcement of the invasion. The enemy was suitably evil: "a brutal group of leftist thugs." American objectives were purely moral—to protect the lives of innocent people on the island, namely American medical students, and to restore democracy to the people of Grenada. And the actions taken were unmistakably forceful: "The United States had no choice but to act strongly and decisively."[22]

But the spectacle of Grenada soon expanded beyond this initial definition. The evacuation of the medical students provided one of those unanticipated occurrences that heighten the power of spectacle: When several of the students kissed the airport tarmac to express their relief and joy at returning to American soil, the resulting pictures on television and in the newspapers were better than anything the administration could have orchestrated. They provided the spectacle with historical as well as emotional resonance. Here was a second hostage crisis—but where Carter had been helpless to release captive Americans, Reagan had swiftly come to the rescue.

Rescue of the students quickly took second place, however, to a new theme: the claim that U.S. forces had uncovered and uprooted a hidden Soviet-Cuban base for adventurism and terrorism. In his nationally televised address, Reagan did not ignore the Iran analogy: "The nightmare of our hostages in Iran must never be repeated." But he stressed the greater drama of defeating a sinister communist plot. "Grenada, we were told, was a friendly island paradise for tourism. Well, it wasn't. It was a Soviet-Cuban colony being readied as a major military bastion to export terror and undermine democracy. We got there just in time."[23] Grenada was turning out to be an even better spectacle for Reagan: He had rescued not only the students but the people of all the Americas as well.

As the spectacle expanded and grew more heroic, public approval increased. The president's standing in the polls went up. *Time* reported that "a post-invasion poll taken by the *Washington Post* and ABC News showed that 63% of Americans approve the way Reagan is handling the presidency, the highest level in two years, and attributed his gain largely to the Grenada intervention."[24] Congressional critics, although skeptical of many of the claims made by the administration, began to stifle their doubts and chime in with endorsements in accordance with the polls. An unnamed White House aide, quoted in *Newsweek*, drew the obvious lesson: "You can scream and shout and gnash your teeth all you want, but the folks out there like it. It was done right and done with dispatch."[25]

In its final gestures, the Grenada spectacle commemorated itself. Reagan invited the medical students to the White House and, predictably, basked in their praise and cheering. The Pentagon contributed its symbolic share, awarding some eight thousand medals for the Grenada operation—more than the number of American troops that had set foot on the island. In actuality, Gabriel has shown, "the operation was marred by a number of military failures."[26] Yet these were obscured by the triumphant appearances of the spectacle.

That the spectacle of Grenada was more potent and would prove more lasting in its effects than any disconfirming facts was observed at the time by Anthony Lewis. Reagan "knew the facts would come out eventually," wrote Lewis. "But if that day could be postponed, it might make a great political difference. People would be left with their first impression that this was a decisive President fighting communism."[27] Grenada became for most Americans a highlight of Reagan's first term. Insignificant in military or diplomatic terms, as spectacle it was one of the most successful acts of the Reagan presidency.

A Schizoid Spectacle: George H. W. Bush

Time magazine accorded George Herbert Walker Bush a unique honor: it named him its "Men of the Year" for 1990. There were really two President Bushes, the magazine explained, a strong and visionary leader in international affairs and a fumbling and directionless executive at home.[28] The split in Bush's presidency that *Time* highlighted was as evident in the realm of spectacle as in the realm of policy. The foreign affairs spectacle of the first Bush presidency featured a masterful leader, a powerhouse team, and thrilling gestures. The domestic spectacle featured a confused leader, a colorless team, and gestures of remarkable ineptitude. Together, they created a schizoid spectacle.

Critics could find much to fault in the substance of Bush's foreign policy, but as spectacle, his foreign policy leadership was a great triumph.[29] The main character in the Bush administration's foreign policy spectacle was experienced, confident, decisively in charge. Bush seemed bred to foreign policy stewardship in a patrician tradition dating back to Theodore Roosevelt and Henry Stimson. He came across to the public as the master diplomat, successfully cajoling and persuading other world leaders through well-publicized telephone calls; in truth, he moved easily among international elites, obviously in his element. He was an even more triumphant spectacle character when featured in winning tableaux as commander in chief of Operation Desert Storm.

The foreign policy team made a superb contribution to the global side of the Bush spectacle. Not since the administration of Richard Nixon had a president's skill at diplomacy been so effectively magnified by his top civilian advisers; not since World War II had a commander in chief been blessed with such popular military subordinates. James Baker, Bush's one-time Houston neighbor and longtime political manager, was both courtly and canny as secretary of state. Richard Cheney was a cool, cerebral secretary of defense, with an air of mastery reminiscent of Robert McNamara. Colin Powell, chair of the Joint Chiefs of Staff, radiated dignity and authority as the highest ranking African American in the history of the military and was almost universally admired. Gen. Norman Schwarzkopf was a feisty commander for Desert Storm—an appealing emblem for a military finally restored to glorious health after two decades of licking its Vietnam wounds.

More than anything else, military gestures produced exciting drama in the Bush foreign affairs spectacle. Panama was the prelude to the Persian Gulf War. It featured, in Manuel Noriega, a doubly immoral adversary—a drug smuggler as well as a dictator. The U.S. military operation to depose Noriega was swift and efficient, and a victorious outcome was assured once the Panamanian strongman was seized and transported to the United States to face drug-trafficking charges.

The Gulf War victory dwarfed Panama, not only as significant policy accomplishment but also as spectacle. Bush depicted Iraqi dictator Saddam Hussein as a second Hitler, a figure whose immense record of evil made Noriega look like a small-time thug. To be sure, Operation Desert Storm lacked the satisfying climax of destroying the evil adversary, but as a military display, it provided Americans with numerous scenes to cheer. The indisputable favorites were Defense Department videos of laser-guided bombs homing in on Iraqi targets with pinpoint accuracy. In the cinematic terms that President Reagan had made popular, Desert Storm was not the cavalry rescue of Grenada or the capture of the pirate captain in Panama; it was high-tech epic, the return of the American Jedi.

Bush's foreign policy spectacle was successful—perhaps too successful. Once the Soviet Union crumbled and Iraq was militarily humiliated, foreign policy seemed much less relevant to most Americans. According to Walter Dean Burnham, "In 1992 foreign policy issues and public concerns about them played the smallest role in any American presidential election since 1936."[30] As Americans began to focus almost exclusively on the home front, they witnessed a domestic Bush spectacle utterly unlike the foreign affairs version.

The domestic Bush was an uncertain, awkward character, especially in the electorally decisive field of economic policy. Inheriting what he had once derided as Reagan's "voodoo economics," Bush presided over an economic crisis when the policy's magic failed. In the face of this crisis, which was evident by the second year of his administration, Bush drifted, seemingly without a clue as to how to restore the economy to health. The only economic prescription he ever put forward with any conviction was a cut in the capital gains tax rate that would have most directly benefited wealthy investors. Comfortable dealing with the problems that beset international elites, Bush seemed ill at ease with the economic problems plaguing ordinary Americans.

Bush's economic team only magnified his weaknesses. His secretary of the Treasury, Nicholas Brady, and chair of the Council of Economic Advisers, Michael Boskin, were pale, dim figures who barely registered in the public's consciousness. To the extent that anyone did notice them, they seemed to epitomize inaction. A more visible economic team member was the budget director, Richard Darman. But he was portrayed in the media as arrogant and abrasive, epitomizing the antagonism between the Bush White House and Capitol Hill that resulted in domestic policy gridlock.

It was through a series of small gestures, some intended and others inadvertent, that Bush's disengagement from the economic difficulties of ordinary people was most dramatically demonstrated. Touring a grocery store, the president expressed amazement at the electronic scanners that read prices. To those who stood by every week as these scanners recorded their food purchases, here was a president unfamiliar with how families struggled to pay their grocery bills. Visiting a suburban mall on the day after Thanksgiving (the busiest shopping day of the year) in 1991, Bush brought along reporters who publicized his purchases: athletic socks for himself, Christmas presents for his family. Bush's shopping expedition seemed designed to convey the message that Americans could lift themselves out of recession just by taking a few more trips to the local mall. The most telling gesture of disengagement came early in 1992 at a campaign stop in New Hampshire, when Bush blurted out a stage cue from one of his speechwriters: "Message: I care." The message that came through instead was that the president had to be prompted to commiserate with the economic woes of the American people.

Real economic fears and pains denied Bush reelection in 1992. But the fears and pains were made worse by the ineptitude of his domestic spectacle. A president who lacked not only a credible economic plan but also credible gestures that would communicate concern and effort to restore economic health went down to a landslide defeat, with 63 percent of the electorate voting against him. The schizoid spectacle of George Bush, triumphant in its foreign policy performance, disastrous in its domestic policy performance, was over.

A Postmodern Spectacle: Bill Clinton

George Bush had two disparate spectacles; Bill Clinton had many. Clinton's was a postmodern spectacle. A postmodern spectacle, heretofore more familiar in popular culture than in presidential politics, features fleeting images and fractured continuity, surfaces without depths, personae rather than personalities. Characters in a postmodern spectacle do not succeed by capturing the lasting admiration or trust of their audience but by personifying artfully the changing fashions that fascinate it.

Depictions of Clinton by close observers in the media tended to agree on his shape-shifting presidential performance but to differ as to whether it should evoke moral indignation or neutral evaluation. One constantly caustic Clinton watcher, *New York Times* columnist Maureen Dowd, called the president "the man of a thousand faces."[31] Other commentators preferred cool postmodern terms such as *makeover* and *reinvention,* the same words used to describe the diva of contemporary pop culture, Madonna.[32]

Clinton's presidency had important elements of constancy, including the successful economic course first charted in 1993 and the president's underlying attachment to government as a potentially positive force in society. And the frequent changes during Clinton's two terms owed as much to the formidable political constraints he faced as to the opportunities for spectacle he seized.[33] Moreover, historical precedents for Clinton's "mongrel politics" may be found in the administrations of presidents such as Woodrow Wilson and Richard Nixon, who also were accused of opportunistic borrowings from ideological adversaries in eras when the opposition party had established the reigning terms of political discourse.[34] Nonetheless, Clinton's repeated redefinitions of himself and his presidency made these predecessors seem almost static by comparison. Sometimes awkwardly, sometimes nimbly, Clinton pirouetted across the presidential stage like no one before him.

Clinton's first two years in power were largely a failure of spectacle. The promising populist intimacy of the 1992 campaign quickly gave way to a spectacle of Washington elitism, of social life among the rich and famous (the infamous $200 haircut by a Beverly Hills stylist) and politics among the entrenched and arrogant (the cozy alliance with the Democratic congressional leadership). The new president seemed simultaneously immature (the undisciplined decision delayer aided by a youthful and inexperienced White House staff) and old-fashioned (the big-government liberal with his bureaucratic scheme to reform the health care system). The crushing rebukes that Clinton suffered in 1994—the failure of his health care plan even to reach the floor of either house of Congress and the Republican takeover of both houses in the midterm elections—showed how little he had impressed his audience. Yet a postmodern irony was at work for Clinton, for his defeats freed him. Not having to implement a large-scale health care plan, Clinton was able to dance away from the liberal label. Not having to link himself with his party's congressional leadership in a bid for legislative achievement, he was able to shift his policy stances opportunely to capitalize on the weaknesses of the new Republican agenda.

In his first two years Clinton lacked an important ingredient for many presidential spectacles: a dramatic foil. Bush had used Manuel Noriega and Saddam Hussein, but the post–cold war world was too uninteresting to most Americans to supply foreign leaders ripe for demonization. The hidden blessing of the 1994 elections for Clinton was that they provided him with a domestic foil of suitably dramatic proportions: Newt Gingrich. Gingrich was often compared to Clinton—and the comparison worked mostly in Clinton's favor. Shedding the taint of liberalism, Clinton pronounced himself a nonideological centrist saving the country from Gingrich's conservative extremism. Before, Clinton had talked and shown off too much in public; now, in comparison to the grandiose garrulousness of Gingrich, he seemed almost reticent—and certainly more mature. Attacked as too soft in his first two years, Clinton could turn the image of compassion into a strength by attacking a foil who proposed to reduce spending for seniors on Medicare and Medicaid and to place the children of welfare mothers in orphanages. Lampooned as spineless in his first two years, Clinton could display his backbone in winning the budget showdown with the Republicans in the winter of 1995–1996.[35]

In a postmodern spectacle, a president can try on a variety of styles without being committed to any one of them. As the 1996 election season commenced (and as Gingrich fled the spotlight after his budget defeat), Clinton executed another nimble pirouette by emulating the patron saint of modern Republicans, Ronald Reagan. Clinton's advisers had him watch Reagan videotapes to study "the Gipper's bearing, his aura of command."[36] His campaign team found a model for 1996 in the 1984 Reagan theme of "Morning in America," in which a sunny president capitalized on peace and prosperity while floating serenely above divisive issues. Like Reagan in 1984, Clinton presented himself in 1996 as the benevolent manager of economic growth, the patriotic commander in chief comfortable with military power, and the good father devoted to family values. Unlike Reagan, he added the images of the good son protecting seniors and the good steward protecting the environment. Clinton's postmodern appropriation of Reagan imagery helped to block the Republicans from achieving their goal of a unified party government fulfilling Reagan's ideological dreams.

Clinton's postmodern spectacle shaped public impressions of his team. With a man of uncertain character in the White House, strong women in the cabinet drew special attention: Attorney General Janet Reno at the outset of his first term, Secretary of State Madeleine Albright at the outset of his second. But no members of Clinton's cabinet or staff played as important supporting roles in his spectacle as his wife, Hillary, and his vice president, Al Gore. Hillary Rodham Clinton appeared as an updated, postfeminist version of Eleanor Roosevelt, a principled liberal goad pressing against her husband's pragmatic instincts. Like Eleanor, she was a hero to the liberal Democratic faithful and a despised symbol of radicalism to conservative Republican foes. Al Gore's spectacle role was to be the stable and stolid sidekick to the quicksilver president. Even his much-satirized reputation as boring was reassuring when counterpoised to a president who appeared all too eager to charm and seduce his audience.

A postmodern spectacle is best crafted by postmodern spectacle specialists. When Clinton's presidential image began taking a beating, he turned for help to image makers who previously had worked for Republicans but who were as ideologically unanchored as he was. In 1993 Clinton responded to plunging polls by hiring David Gergen, the White House communications chief during Ronald Reagan's first term. But the amiable Gergen could not reposition Clinton as a centrist nearly so well as Dick Morris, Clinton's image consultant after the 1994 electoral debacle. Morris had worked before for Clinton but also for conservative Republicans such as Senate Majority Leader Trent Lott. As a *Newsweek* story described him, Morris "was a classic mercenary—demonic, brilliant, principle-free."[37] It was Morris's insight, as much as Clinton's, that rhetoric and gesture, supported by the power of the veto, could turn a seemingly moribund presidency after 1994 into a triumphant one in 1996.

The remarkable prosperity of Clinton's second term purchased an unusual stretch of calm (some called it lethargy) for his administration—until the Monica Lewinsky storm threatened to wreck it early in 1998. Numerous Americans of all political persuasions were appalled by Clinton's sexual escapades and dishonest explanations in the Lewinsky affair. But for Clinton-haters on the right, long infuriated by the successful spectacles of a character who symbolized (for them) the 1960s culture they despised, the Lewinsky scandal produced a thrill of self-confirmation: See, they proclaimed, his soul *is* the moral wasteland we always claimed it to be. The fact that the majority of Americans did not concur with conservative Republicans that Clinton's moral failures necessitated his ouster from the presidency only made his impeachment and conviction more urgent for the right. If strong support for Clinton in the polls indicated that the public was following him down the path toward moral hollowness, removing him became a crusade for the nation's soul, an exorcism of moral rot jeopardizing the meaning of the Republic.

But the moralistic fulminations of the right were no match for the power of spectacle. It was not spectacle alone that saved the Clinton presidency. Clinton was protected by prosperity and by Americans' preference for his centrist policies over the conservative alternatives. He was aided, too, by the inclination of most Americans to draw a line between public rectitude and private freedom. Nonetheless, Clinton's eventual acquittal by the Senate owed much to spectacle. To be sure, his own spectacle performance in the Year of Lewinsky was hardly his best. Perhaps no role so little suited Clinton as repentant sinner. But he was blessed by even worse performances from his adversaries. Just as Newt Gingrich was necessary to resuscitate Clinton from the political disaster of 1994, so was Kenneth Starr essential to his rescue from the personal disaster of 1998. Starr's self-righteous moralism disturbed most Americans more than Clinton's self-serving narcissism.

In the end, the shallowness of the postmodern spectacle that had characterized the Clinton presidency from the start supplied an ironic benefit in the Lewinsky scandal. Had Clinton possessed a stable, respected character, revelations of secret behavior that violated that character might have startled the public and shrunk its approval of his performance in office. His standing in the polls might have plummeted, as President Reagan's did after the disclosure that his administration was selling arms to terrorists. But a majority of Americans had long believed, according to the polls, that Clinton was not very honest or trustworthy, so his misbehavior in the Lewinsky affair came as less of a shock, and was quickly diluted by reminders of his administration's popular achievements and agenda. Postmodern spectacle is not about character, at least not in a traditional sense; it is about delivering what the audience desires at the moment. Personality, political talent, and a keen instinct for survival made Bill Clinton the master of postmodern spectacle.

From Recycled Spectacle to War on Terrorism: George W. Bush

After reaching the White House through one of the closest and most intensely disputed elections in the history of the presidency, George W. Bush began his administration with a recycled spectacle. Promising the novelty of a "compassionate conservatism" during the campaign, the Bush administration's original agenda mainly followed the familiar priorities of the Republican right. But its conservatism ran deeper than its policy prescriptions. In its characters, its styles, its gestures, the Bush administration was determined to reach back past the postmodern spectacle of Bill Clinton and restore the faded glories of contemporary conservatism by recycling them.

One fund of recycled images and themes upon which Bush drew was the Reagan spectacle. As a presidential character, Bush enjoyed many affinities with Reagan. Bush presented himself as a Reagan-style nonpolitician whose sunny optimism and embracing bonhomie would brighten a harsh and demoralizing political environment. His principal prescriptions for the nation also recycled Reaganesque themes and gestures. Like Reagan, Bush rapidly pushed through Congress a massive tax cut that favored the wealthy in the guise of an economic stimulus, using "fuzzy math" to promise Americans the pleasure of prosperity without the pain of federal deficits. Like Reagan, Bush promoted a national missile defense that would use cutting edge (and still nonexistent) technology to restore the ancient dream of an innocent America invulnerable to the violent quarrels of the world. Even the Bush administration's most politically costly stance in its early months—presidential decisions favoring private interests over environmental protection—was couched in the Reagan claim of protecting the pocketbooks of ordinary citizens. Revising a Clinton rule that would mandate higher efficiency for central air conditioners, Bush's secretary of energy, Spencer Abraham, indicated that his goal was to save low-income consumers from having to pay more to cool their homes or trailers.[38]

Recycled images and themes from his father's administration were equally evident in the early months of Bush's presidency. They were especially useful as emblems of the "compassionate" side of the new chief executive. Like his father, "W" trumpeted his conciliatory stance toward congressional opponents. Like his father, W set out to be an "education president." The recycling of paternal gestures also was apparent in his meetings with representatives of the groups that had opposed his election most strongly. Just as the father had met with Jesse Jackson after winning the White House, the son invited in the Congressional Black Caucus. Neither Bush expected to win over African American voters through these gestures. Instead, each hoped to signal to moderate white voters that they were "kinder, gentler" conservatives who exuded tolerance and good will.

The new Bush administration also reached even farther back in time in its bid to dramatize its repudiation of Clinton's postmodern character and style.

Two of the new administration's most important figures—Vice President Richard Cheney and Secretary of Defense Donald Rumsfeld—were prominent alumni of the Ford administration; Cheney and Rumsfeld represented Bush's "That '70s Show," although they no longer sported the sideburns and wide lapels of Ford's day. Leaping back before the hated 1960s, the Bush administration also evoked an even earlier time, as Cheney, echoing the 1950s theme of "our friend, the atom," praised nuclear energy as "the cleanest method of power generation we know."[39] Maureen Dowd, the most savage yet perceptive critic of Clinton's postmodern character, has been no less troubled by the "retro" nature of the Bush spectacle. After watching Bush speak at his alma mater, Yale, Dowd wrote that the president "seemed like a throwback" and described him as "Eisenhower with hair."[40]

Bush's presidential team draws upon Republican characters and themes of the past to provide a reassuringly mature, veteran cast in contrast to the youthful self-indulgence associated with the postmodern Clinton. It also drains some of the political danger out of the widespread doubts about Bush's lack of preparation and seriousness in the presidency. Initially, the most visible team member was the vice president, who played the role of the wise and experienced father to the reformed playboy son, even though Cheney is only five years older than Bush. But Cheney's time in the spotlight was cut short when jokes and cartoons proliferated about him being the real White House decision-maker. Once Cheney declined in visibility (although not in influence), various members of the Bush cabinet emerged to signal compassion or conservatism as the situation seemed to require. On the compassionate end of the spectrum, the most interesting figure was Secretary of State Colin Powell, conveying the warm image of moderation and multilateralism otherwise absent from the administration's approach to foreign affairs. On the conservative end, the most striking figure was Attorney General John Ashcroft, conveying the dour image of the Christian right's culture wars. The fundamental conservatism of the Bush spectacle was even evident in the first lady. As a demure traditional wife who eschews a political role, Laura Bush quietly renounces the feminist activism of Hillary Rodham Clinton.

Perhaps the most revealing spectacle gesture in the early months of the Bush presidency was the speech on stem-cell research on August 9, 2001. Speaking from his Texas ranch in his first televised address to the American public since his inauguration, Bush ended weeks of fevered media speculation by announcing that he would permit federal tax dollars to be used for research on existing stem-cell lines but not for research on lines established after August 9. Balancing the public's hope for miracle cures to an array of severe illnesses with the conservatives' insistence on preserving the life of embryos, Bush's decision was meant to epitomize compassionate conservatism. Yet the heart of the spectacle lay in the presentation of his decision more than in its substance. Reminiscent of Reagan at the launch of the Grenada spectacle, Bush's speech countered criticisms of a disengaged presidency by presenting a highly serious chief executive sacrificing his vacation time to make the gravest of decisions. A president under fire in the media as an intellectual lightweight who was the captive of his advisers was presented (by his advisers) as the real decision-maker, confronting a policy dilemma worthy of a moral philosopher. To make sure that the public grasped the gesture, the day after the speech, presidential communication director Karen Hughes provided the press with a detailed briefing on how Bush had wrestled with the decision. She portrayed the president, in the words of the *New York Times,* as "a soul-searching, intellectually curious leader."[41]

Although the stem-cell speech was politically effective, by late summer of Bush's first year in office the recycled spectacle was wearing a bit thin. Polls revealed a downward drift in public approval, and media commentary suggested a policy drift after the enactment of the Bush tax program. In early August, word came from the White House that the fall would witness a new Bush focus on "values."[42] Just as Bill Clinton, following the advice of Dick Morris, had turned to the rhetoric and gestures of values to overcome public unhappiness about his liberalism, so Bush was being urged to stress values to change the subject from his administration's increasingly unpopular conservatism. By early September, however, a sharp downturn in economic indicators had overshadowed the values campaign and redirected the Bush team's attention to the economy. On September 9 the *New York Times* reported that "as White House officials move to refocus President Bush's energies on the precarious economy, they are working to present him as a more commanding leader in what may be the most treacherous stretch of his first year in the White House."[43]

As the Bush White House scrambled to adjust to changing political issues and fashions, it contemplated the same kind of reinventions that it had denounced in its postmodern predecessor. But the reinvention it was actually to undergo was completely unscripted. The terrorist attacks of September 11 and their aftermath hurled the Bush presidency into a crisis for which none of its previous images and gestures seemed particularly appropriate.

The terrorists who piloted hijacked airliners into the World Trade Center and the Pentagon meant to kill thousands of Americans, but they also had a twisted spectacle of their own in mind by striking at symbols of American capitalism and military might. In the person of Osama bin Laden, the attack on America has featured a demonic villain far more menacing than the Manuel Noriega or Saddam Hussein who served as foils for the first Bush presidency. No one has accused the younger Bush of exaggerating when he labeled bin Laden "the evil one." But if the ingredients for a drama of extraordinary proportions were readily available, the horror of September 11 seemed too elemental for the contrivances characteristic of spectacle. The spectacle with which the Bush presidency commenced had recycled conservative themes from the past five decades to portray him as the opposite of a narcissistic Clinton presiding over a self-indulgent society. The war on terrorism that began on September 11 offered Bush the chance to be the opposite of Clinton in a more novel and profound sense.

In the first weeks after the terrorist attacks, Bush at times seemed to leave behind the gestures of recycled spectacle and rise to this extraordinary occasion. His impressive speech to Congress on September 20 struck a delicate balance between a forceful response to terrorism, a compassionate response to tragedy, and a teaching of tolerance toward followers of the Islamic faith. Many observers were impressed by Bush's demeanor during the speech. Less stiff and more articulate than in prior national addresses, Bush appeared animated by the gravity of the crisis. His associates began to describe a transformation of the heretofore laid-back president. As Frank Bruni wrote in the *New York Times*, one Bush friend reported that Bush "clearly feels he has encountered his reason for being, a conviction informed and shaped by the president's own strain of Christianity."[44] Of course, in an age of spectacle any characterization of the president from his aides and associates has been carefully "spun" for public consumption.

Although at times after September 11 Bush appeared a changed president, the habits of spectacle are too ingrained in the modern White House to allow the abandonment of its characteristic contrivances. Bush often turned the war on terror into a personal duel with bin Laden, playing the hero locked in mortal combat with the avatar of evil. Evoking Ronald Reagan doing his best Clint Eastwood imitation (and employing the title of a classic TV western starring Steve McQueen), Bush pledged that bin Laden would be hunted down: "There's an old poster out West, as I recall, that said 'Wanted: Dead or Alive.' "[45] White House spectacle specialists, such as Karen Hughes, Ari Fleischer, and Karl Rove, worked furiously to stifle criticisms of their boss, using media-management techniques, as Dowd observed, to "spoon-feed the press the image of an In-Charge, Focused, Resolute President."[46] At first, Bush's war on terrorism seemed to be fought most effectively on the terrain of television: the White

House prevailed on the networks to edit bin Laden's videotapes before showing them, while arranging for the popular "America's Most Wanted" show to feature the administration's hunt for his accomplices.[47]

With the unexpectedly swift success of the military campaign in Afghanistan, the delicate balance in Bush's initial response to September 11 gave way to a consistently martial tone. Paced by Secretary of Defense Rumsfeld, the Bush administration began to feature a spectacle of muscular globalism. In his State of the Union address in January 2002, the commander in chief previewed an expansion of the war on terror to combat "an axis of evil," composed of North Korea, Iran, and especially Iraq.[48] Bush's dramatic phrase, which made headlines around the world, rhetorically recalled U.S. enemies in World War II and the cold war to amplify the peril from adversaries in the Middle East and Asia. In its emphasis on Iraq, it gestured toward the spectacular completion by the son of the mission in which the father had sadly fallen short. But as Bush looked to exemplary global crusades of the past to build support for an escalation of his own war on terror, messy modern realities, especially in the Middle East, began to complicate his strategy. As of this writing in April 2002, they threaten to call into question the crusading imagery of good versus evil that has become the central spectacle of the Bush presidency.[49]

Conclusion

It is tempting to blame the growth of spectacle on individual presidents, their calculating advisers, and compliant journalists. It is more accurate, however, to attribute the growth of spectacle to larger structural forces: the extreme personalization of the modern presidency, the excessive expectations of the president that most Americans have, and the voluminous media coverage that fixes on presidents and treats American politics largely as a report of their adventures. Indeed, presidential spectacles can be linked to a culture of consumption in which spectacle is the predominant form that relates the few to the many.

Spectacle, then, is more a structural feature of the contemporary presidency than a strategy of deception adopted by particular presidents. In running for the presidency, then carrying out its tasks, any contemporary chief executive is likely to turn to spectacle. Spectacle has become institutionalized, as specialists in the White House routinely devise performances for a vast press corps that is eager to report every colorful detail. Spectacle is expected by the public as the most visible manifestation of presidential leadership. A president who deliberately eschewed its possibilities would probably encounter the same kind of difficulties as a president who tried to lead by spectacle and failed.

Still, the rise of spectacle in the presidency remains a disturbing development. It is harmful to presidents, promoting gesture over accomplishment and appearance over fact. It is even more harmful to the public, because it obfuscates presidential activity, undermines executive accountability, and encourages passivity on the part of citizens. The presentation of leadership as spectacle has little in common with the kind of leadership that American democratic values imply.

Notes

1. George C. Edwards III, *The Public Presidency: The Pursuit of Popular Support* (New York: St. Martin's Press, 1983), 1.

2. Samuel Kernell, *Going Public: New Strategies of Presidential Leadership*, 3d ed. (Washington, D.C.: CQ Press, 1997), 106. For historical perspective on the president's relationship with the public, see Jeffrey K. Tulis, *The Rhetorical Presidency* (Princeton: Princeton University Press, 1987); and Richard J. Ellis, ed., *Speaking to the People: The Rhetorical Presidency in Historical Perspective* (Amherst: University of Massachusetts Press, 1998).

3. Daniel Dayan and Elihu Katz, "Electronic Ceremonies: Television Performs a Royal Wedding," in *On Signs*, ed. Marshall Blonsky (Baltimore: Johns Hopkins University Press, 1985), 16.

4. Roland Barthes, *Mythologies* (New York: Hill and Wang, 1972), 15–25.

5. David L. Paletz and Robert M. Entman, *Media Power Politics* (New York: Free Press, 1981), 21.

6. Theodore J. Lowi, *The Personal President* (Ithaca: Cornell University Press, 1985), 96.

7. See Stephen J. Wayne, "Great Expectations: What People Want from Presidents," in *Rethinking the Presidency*, ed. Thomas E. Cronin (Boston: Little, Brown, 1982), 185–199; and Thomas E. Cronin, *The State of the Presidency*, 2d ed. (Boston: Little, Brown, 1980), 2–25.

8. Guy Debord, *Society of the Spectacle* (Detroit: Black and Red, 1983), para. 60.

9. On the confidence of the public personality and the anxiety of his audience, see Richard Sennett, *The Fall of Public Man* (New York: Knopf, 1977).

10. Erving Goffman, *The Presentation of Self in Everyday Life* (Garden City, N.Y.: Anchor Books, 1959), 104.

11. See Michael Rogin, *Ronald Reagan, the Movie, and Other Episodes in Political Demonology* (Berkeley: University of California Press, 1987), 1–43.

12. Paul D. Erickson, *Reagan Speaks: The Making of an American Myth* (New York: New York University Press, 1985), 49, 51, 52.

13. Quoted in ibid., 100.

14. Lou Cannon, *Reagan* (New York: Putnam, 1982), 371–401.

15. "Meet David Stockman," *Newsweek*, February 16, 1981.

16. Nicholas Lemann, "The Peacetime War," *Atlantic*, October 1984, 88.

17. "Coolly Taking Charge," *Time*, September 6, 1982.

18. "From Bad to Worse for U.S. in Grenada," *U.S. News and World Report,* October 31, 1983.

19. Richard A. Gabriel, *Military Incompetence: Why the American Military Doesn't Win* (New York: Hill and Wang, 1985), 154.

20. Quoted in "Fare Well, Grenada," *Time,* December 26, 1983.

21. *New York Times,* October 26, 1983.

22. Ibid.

23. Ibid., October 28, 1983.

24. "Getting Back to Normal," *Time,* November 21, 1983.

25. " 'We Will Not Be Intimidated,' " *Newsweek,* November 14, 1983.

26. Gabriel, *Military Incompetence,* 186.

27. Anthony Lewis, "What Was He Hiding?" *New York Times,* October 31, 1983.

28. "A Tale of Two Bushes: One Finds a Vision on the Global Stage; The Other Still Displays None at Home," *Time,* January 7, 1991.

29. See, for example, Larry Berman and Bruce W. Jentleson, "Bush and the Post–Cold War World: New Challenges for American Leadership," in *The Bush Presidency: First Appraisals,* ed. Colin Campbell and Bert A. Rockman (Chatham, N.J.: Chatham House, 1991), 93–128.

30. Walter Dean Burnham, "The Legacy of George Bush: Travails of an Understudy," in *The Election of 1992: Reports and Interpretations,* ed. Gerald M. Pomper et al. (Chatham, N.J.: Chatham House, 1993), 21.

31. Maureen Dowd, "Bubba Don't Preach," *New York Times,* February 9, 1997.

32. Howard Fineman and Bill Turque, "How He Got His Groove," *Newsweek,* September 2, 1996; Garry Wills, "The Clinton Principle," *New York Times Magazine,* January 19, 1997.

33. See Bert A. Rockman, "Leadership Style and the Clinton Presidency," in *The Clinton Presidency: First Appraisals,* ed. Colin Campbell and Bert A. Rockman (Chatham, N.J.: Chatham House, 1996), 325–362.

34. Stephen Skowronek, *The Politics Presidents Make: Leadership from John Adams to Bill Clinton* (Cambridge: Harvard University Press, 1997), 447–464.

35. Elizabeth Drew, *Showdown: The Struggle between the Gingrich Congress and the Clinton White House* (New York: Simon and Schuster, 1996).

36. Fineman and Turque, "How He Got His Groove."

37. Evan Thomas et al., "Victory March," *Newsweek,* November 18, 1996.

38. Matthew L. Wald, "Bush Relaxes Clinton Rule on Central Air-Conditioners," *New York Times,* April 14, 2001.

39. Joseph Kahn, "Cheney Promotes Increasing Supply as Energy Policy," *New York Times,* May 1, 2001.

40. Maureen Dowd, "From A to Y at Yale," *New York Times,* May 23, 2001.

41. Katherine Q. Seelye and Frank Bruni, "A Long Process That Led Bush to His Decision," *New York Times,* August 11, 2001.

42. Frank Bruni, "After Six Months, Bush Team Plans Change of Focus," *New York Times,* August 5, 2001.

43. Richard L. Berke and David E. Sanger, "Bush's Aides Seek to Focus Efforts on the Economy," *New York Times,* September 9, 2001.

44. Frank Bruni, "For Bush, a Mission and a Defining Moment," *New York Times,* September 22, 2001.

45. Quoted in *New York Times,* September 18, 2001.

46. Maureen Dowd, "We Love the Liberties They Hate," *New York Times*, September 30, 2001.

47. Alessandra Stanley, "President Is Using TV Show and the Public in Combination to Combat Terrorism," *New York Times*, October 11, 2001.

48. Quoted in *New York Times*, January 30, 2002.

49. James Gerstenzang, "A Newly Hamstrung Bush Faces 'Bumps in the Road,'" *Los Angeles Times*, April 21, 2002.

12 The Presidency and the Press: The Paradox of the White House Communications War

Lawrence R. Jacobs*

Most contemporary presidents face a conundrum: high expectations from the public about what they can and should do to remedy the nation's problems and a limited ability to meet these expectations without the cooperation of an often-recalcitrant Congress. The standard approach presidents take to overcome this conundrum is to "go public"—that is, to appeal directly to the American people in the hope of rousing them to pressure members of Congress to support the president. Chief executives and their advisers devote much of their time to trying to shape news coverage of their policy initiatives, often in hopes of crowding out congressional voices. But as Lawrence R. Jacobs's case studies of health care reform and Social Security reform during the Clinton presidency indicate, a strategy of "pounding the press" by launching a unilateral "communications war" is much less likely to succeed than less adversarial and more cooperative strategies of media relations.

The opening months of Bill Clinton's first term in 1993 foretold the lost opportunities and disappointments that would mark so much of his presidency. Indeed, the first six months of 1993 serve as a case study of how *not* to begin a presidency. The gays-in-the-military dust-up, the infamous designer haircut, and the near-defeat of his first significant legislative proposal (the budget and package of economic stimulus proposals) vaporized whatever "honeymoon" presidents are supposed to enjoy. The inaugural bunting was only just coming down, yet Clinton's political bank account was already overdrawn, even though this president had started with what most modern presidents only dream of—majorities for his party in both houses of Congress.

*I greatly appreciate the timely assistance of Eric Ostermeier. A thank you is also due to Greg Shaw and Melanie Burns.

Clinton's aides and friends traced his political problems to hostile media coverage and his team's failure—as Sen. Jay Rockefeller privately counseled Hillary Rodham Clinton—to bring journalists into a "crafted information flow" that incorporated friendly sources and supportive messages.[1] Health care reform—one of the top issues of Clinton's 1992 campaign—epitomized the president's political quagmire. Clinton's advisers blamed the rough going on the opposition's success in portraying reform as "more taxes and government control"; the critics out-maneuvered the White House in recruiting reporters who were "ripe for manipulation" to "serve as the vehicle for attacks." White House aides criticized the press for not only spewing forth the attack messages of the opposition but also for using a "horse race" "prism for all the coverage" about the president. Clinton's actions were either reduced to his "concern about getting elected" or ignored because "it's not confrontational [and] it's not conflict."[2] The debilitating outcome of this cycle of damaging media coverage was to "fuel" the public's "fears" that they would "pay more [and] get less."[3]

The solution, the White House decided, was to launch a "communications war" that would "use the power of the White House to control the message" through presidential speeches and actions to dominate press reporting and drown out critical commentary by journalists and political opponents.[4] The key to political success, Clinton explained after his first year in office, was the president's unparalleled "access to the people through the communications network." The ability to dominate press coverage, he believed, gave any chief executive the ability to "create new political capital all the time."[5] Clinton's aides were more blunt: the president and his advisers could "get away with anything provided you believe in something, you say it over and over again, and you never change."[6] Political redemption, then, lay in a "massive public communications campaign" that was aimed at the press and that "deliberately and relentlessly communicate[d]" the president's "program to the public."[7]

Clinton launched a communications war that would bombard the press with friendly messages as the antidote to political vulnerability and hostile news reporting, but his use of this strategy was not unique in domestic politics. Modern presidents believe, and many political observers agree, that one of the primary political tools available to the White House is the ability to issue "messages" and get the media to frame debate in ways that favor the president and disadvantage his opponents. Resort to communications warfare arises out of a fundamental conundrum that all modern presidents share: they are elected to satisfy the nation's expectations for peace and prosperity but operate in a constitutional system and political process that disperses power and invites political rivalry, division, and stalemate.

Needing to augment their scarce political power, modern presidents routinely "go public" to promote themselves and their policies. Presidents zero in on the press as the decisive tool to pry themselves loose from an institutional stranglehold and mobilize public support.[8] This media-based strategy translates into an everyday White House concern with tightly calibrating events and speeches to shape press reporting and "attract favorable news stories and direct press attention to particular issues and policies."[9] The routinization of "going public" by flooding the press with messages has motivated successive presidents to develop within the White House a "full-time rhetorical manufacturing plant." Analysis of presidential public statements shows that the "modern president now spends much of his time trying to out-think the media" by "grabbing at persuasive opportunities [and] constructing persuasive ground rules before their opponents or the media have a chance to do so."[10] Pounding the press defines the operational core of modern presidential political strategy.

Presidential media campaigns (especially on domestic policy initiatives) rest on three expectations. First, presidents plan their activities and speeches to increase the volume of media coverage devoted to specific policy areas. The Clinton White House had two purposes for the relentless communication of its health care reform proposal. One was to increase coverage of the administration's proposals, and the other was to shift media attention from more troublesome issues such as the president's abandoned campaign promise of a middle class tax cut and the Whitewater land deal in Arkansas.

Second, presidents expect their communications offensive to increase the media's use of administration allies as sources and to keep the opposition from making news. The calculus is that getting the media to select members of the president's team as sources will generate stories that put the president in the best possible light. "Friendly" sources are counted on to promote and publicize the president's ideas and interests, while opponents or disinterested sources attempt to raise hostile, unhelpful, or distracting questions. Think of Senator Rockefeller's dictum to create an "information flow" in which journalists would rely upon President Clinton's friends for their stories.

Third, presidents declare a "communications war" but, ironically, expect the press to steer away from coverage of political strategizing in favor of reports on the substance of their initiatives. Presidents calculate that press stories framed in terms of political strategy and conflict breed cynicism among Americans, but news stories that portray presidential actions in terms of substantive policy convey seriousness and constructiveness in promoting the nation's interests rather than their own.[11] Flash back to the Clinton administration's efforts to gear up a "massive public communications campaign" even as it schemed to shift news coverage from the "horse race" of political competition to "substantive questions."[12]

Modern presidents and many political observers agree, then, that presidents enjoy a unique vantage point from which to dominate news reporting. Presidents are confident that they can exploit this advantage to augment their scarce political resources in the face of defiant individuals and institutions. Pounding the press is the means by which presidents succeed politically. It enables them to determine the subjects of news reports, frame priority issues in substantive terms, and boost the media's selection of friendly sources while depressing their use of hostile voices.

Costs of Communications Warfare

The ubiquitous confidence in pounding the media as a strategy for presidential success is, however, greatly overstated. On contentious issues that divide the political parties, presidential efforts to win the media wars increase coverage of their policy initiatives but in ways that contradict presidential goals. Perversely, these efforts boost press attention to opposition sources and political strategy rather than to friendly sources and policy substance. The paradox is that the more the president publicly promotes divisive policies to create favorable news, the more likely the press is to increase its volume of damaging coverage. The flaw in the White House strategy is a radical underestimation of the costs—namely, expansion of the media's coverage of these strategies and of oppositional viewpoints—and an unrealistic confidence in its own ability to "get away with anything." One of the troubling consequences of this excessive confidence is that it can seduce presidents into embracing policy proposals that are outside the vital policy center in which legislation is enacted.

Appreciating the paradoxical effects of the presidential strategy of pounding the press requires understanding not only the White House communications strategy but also the norms, organizational dynamics, and procedures of the press. The overly optimistic estimates of the president's ability to generate positive news coverage stem from an insufficient understanding of the standards and practices that guide the news media.[13]

Three factors govern how reporters cover presidential initiatives. First, economic competition to expand audience size and increase profits motivates the media to cover what they expect to be the audience-grabbing "big" political story.[14] Second, journalists are expected by their colleagues to adhere to the professional norm that they are guardians of the public welfare and therefore are responsible for informing citizens about government deliberations in an objective and nonpartisan manner. Third, the media's assignment of reporters to "beats"—namely, sites of government activity where power routinely resides—creates standard organizational routines and operations that structure the subject, sources, and flow of news reports. For instance, more journalists are assigned to cover the White House than the Supreme Court, and as a result it is the subject of more press reports.[15]

The interaction of media routines and competing politicians in turn generates three patterns in press coverage of presidential efforts to pound the press and win good news for divisive policy initiatives.[16] First, an escalation in presidential communications on controversial policy initiatives increases the volume of press reports on them. By contrast, the president's de-escalation of his "communications war" decreases the volume of press coverage. This pattern fulfills, in part, the strategic intentions of presidents.

Second, the larger number of presidential statements on a contentious issue paradoxically results in a notable rise in press interviews and reports on the reactions of independent voices, such as policy experts and, especially, of authoritative critics, such as members of Congress who are in positions to influence legislation. Although the president generally dominates news reporting,[17] contentious presidential initiatives open the news gate to more appearances by independent or critical sources. The media's monitoring of other official newsbeats (especially Congress) and journalists' adherence to the norm of informing citizens with critical but not partisan coverage help to explain why the press opens its news reports to authoritative sources who conflict with the White House message. The president's political opponents eagerly welcome the media's intensified attention as an opportunity to advance their interests, promote their ideas, and put their faces in the news. When presidential campaigns and the conflict over a particular issue diminish or remain muted, the number of stories reporting opposition viewpoints also declines or remains low.

Third, the president's declaration of a communications war to promote a contentious policy prompts the press to diminish its reporting on substantive policy issues and expand its coverage of the motivations, intentions, and strategic behavior of policy advocates. When faced with partisan acrimony, journalists avoid taking sides by ducking judgments about goals in favor of describing and evaluating the success of the president's strategy.

When the White House launches a communications war on contested policies, it provokes just the kind of press coverage that it set out to avoid—an increase of media attention to opposition voices and political maneuverings. In the next section, I consider the media's coverage of two highly contentious social welfare issues on which Bill Clinton placed a high priority: reform of health care in 1993 and 1994 and the reform of Social Security in 1997 and 1998.

Belligerence and Détente in the Media Wars

President Clinton adopted quite different communications strategies on reforming health care and reforming Social Security. The divergence in the president's strategies and in the reactions of the Washington political community produced important differences in the sources and framing of press reports. On health care, the president's effort to hammer home his message provoked a strong political counteraction that was reflected in a sharp rise in press coverage of "unfriendly" sources and in reports on political strategy instead of policy substance. By contrast, Clinton's Social Security campaign did not focus on promoting a particular programmatic solution but instead pursued an accommodating strategy. Press reports were noticeably substantive and less focused on the views of opponents.

Clinton's campaigns to reform health care and Social Security offer striking illustrations of high-profile efforts by a president to use his unique "access," as Clinton put it, to the media. Press reporting was tracked from January 1993 to December 1994 in the case of health care reform and from July 1997 to June 1998 for Social Security reform. Examination of press coverage of these issues was based on a detailed content analysis of a diverse set of media outlets.[18] I used the Nexis database to track nineteen print and broadcast media outlets for the Social Security episode and twelve outlets for the health care debate; these analyses included national broadcast media as well as local and national print media.[19] Press reports were examined in terms of dozens of separate and quite diverse issues raised during the debates on both topics. This approach made it possible to examine individual statements or "messages" within each news story and to provide a detailed account of the number of lines of media coverage devoted to Social Security and health policy issues.[20]

In addition to tracking the volume of press reporting, I also tracked the sources that journalists cited and determined whether they presented or framed their reports in substantive terms (for example, the content of Clinton's proposed health care plan) or in terms of political conflict and strategy (the horse race prism that bothered Clinton's aides—and many critics of the press).[21] The frequency with which the press used a source or presented a substantive frame as opposed to a strategic frame was determined by tallying the number of lines devoted to each. I calculated the use of a particular source or frame as a proportion of the total number of lines the press devoted to reporting on health care issues or Social Security policy each month. This proportional measure controls for the overall upsurges in coverage that periodically catapulted health care or Social Security into the spotlight; it makes it possible to detect changes in coverage over time that were independent of the rising volume of reports on either issue. Finally, the media content analysis was checked independently for reliability and found accurate.[22]

The Health Care Wars

Bill Clinton came into office in January 1993 committed to a comprehensive reform of the American health care system as one of his top legislative priorities. Although candidate Clinton effectively articulated the strong opposition to the existing health care system (a "negative consensus"), as president he faced a dense thicket of organized opposition. The president's allies were not the kind to rely upon. To start, congressional Democrats split into warring factions. Organized labor and senior citizens, who were long-standing Democratic Party constituents, backed Clinton's goal of universal health insurance coverage but were unwilling to commit enthusiastic support until each wrung additional concessions for its members. Then came the die-hard opponents: organizations representing small health insurers and small businesses who saw their very survival at stake and partisan Republicans who presciently equated the demise of the president's reform with their electoral victory.

In Sync: The White House Media Campaign and the Volume of Press Reports. President Clinton got bogged down during much of his first half-year in office with passing his budget and designing his proposal for health care reform, but, by September the budget was approved and the outlines of his health reform proposal were set. The White House now switched gears and prepared an elaborate "launch" of the proposal that culminated with the quintessence of the media-based promotional presidency: an electrifying, prime-time presidential speech to the nation from the House of Representatives and a deluge of public presidential statements about health care reform.[23] Carefully staged visits to congressional committees by the first lady continued the administration's choreographed trumpeting of its health reform initiative.

The White House campaign ignited counterstrategies by other political actors. The president's closest congressional allies—members of his own party—quickly splintered into different camps and, in some cases, conspired against him. Democrats who were miffed at the president's direction on health care reform capitalized on the media's hunger for leaks by feeding a politically damaging early draft of the president's plan to reporters. Other Democrats battled over which committee would review the legislation and share the national spotlight with the president. Some Republican members of Congress rushed forward with their own bill to prevent the White House from monopolizing press coverage. More than half of the Republican senators and House members endorsed their party's proposal, but the Republicans (including some of those who endorsed the plan) had no intention of passing a health care reform bill that President Clinton would sign. In addition, interest groups—especially opponents of the president's proposal—launched their own national media campaign, including a series of television advertisements featuring "Harry and Louise," a fictional couple that offered folksy criticism.[24]

Press reporting of health issues paralleled the political and policy developments. Figure 12.1, which shows the total monthly volume of press coverage, indicates that the first of three main periods of extensive reporting occurred in September 1993, which was the peak of media coverage of the president's efforts. It corresponds with the high point in Clinton's public comments on health care along with the explosion of activity by government officials in both political parties and by interest group opponents.

The decline and bottoming out of press reports in November and then more fully in December reflect the rarely acknowledged but intrinsic weakness in presidential media campaigns: they are nearly impossible to sustain. What had been meticulously planned in the White House as a seamless campaign to "deliberately and relentlessly communicate" the president's plan was tripped up by unplanned delays in transmitting the administration's legislative proposal to Congress, foreign policy emergencies (such as the attack on American troops in Somalia), and domestic controversies, including the Whitewater charges that followed the Clintons from Arkansas. While the president was distracted from promoting his health care proposal, his critics remained "on message" and eager to take advantage of his absence to hammer his plan and outline their alternative plans. What had fit together seamlessly in the White House "launch plans" for its communications war quickly came apart in the real world of policy complexity, unexpected interruptions, and an opposition that was motivated and equipped to wage the kind of

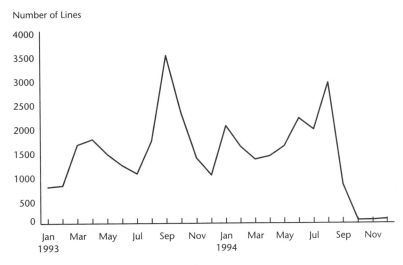

Figure 12.1 Total Number of Lines of Press Coverage of Health Care Issues, 1993–1994

Number of Lines

Source: Compiled by the author: see notes 18 and 19.

all-consuming and unrelenting assault that presidential planners had dreamed of but could not deliver.

The second peak in press reporting, shown in Figure 12.1, occurred in January 1994, when Clinton attempted to restart his stalled media campaign for health care reform and the opposition stiffened. Clinton used his televised, prime-time State of the Union address to reemphasize the importance of reform and to focus Congress on moving his legislation through hearings. His dramatic attempt to rouse Americans through the press included the theatrical flourish of a veto threat for any legislation that fell short of universal coverage.

Senate Minority Leader Robert Dole, head of the Republican Party, stepped into the spotlight that Clinton had shone on health care reform. In his most direct and open challenge to Clinton's crusade, Dole downplayed the urgency of reform, insisting that there "isn't a crisis" in health care and emphasizing the theme of the Harry and Louise ads that the president's plan was bureaucratic and overly complicated. January ended with the nation's governors meeting in Washington and agreeing that the federal government was not moving fast enough on health care reform. Press reports reflected Clinton's renewed media campaign and the counteroffensive by the opposition. National and local press outlets substantially increased the volume of their coverage. Figure 12.1 shows a doubling of news reports on health care from December to January.

The White House communications war was interrupted again in the spring. Clinton was eager to keep the media (and therefore the public) focused on health care reform, but his proposal disappeared into the Byzantine world of the legislative process as committees geared up for hearings. The health subcommittee of the House Ways and Means Committee met in March, and the Congressional Budget Office (CBO) released several studies, but members of Congress were not yet prepared to begin formal deliberations. Press coverage reflected this lull in policy-making activity, dipping to one of its lowest levels during the spring (see Figure 12.1). Yet again, the administration's carefully scripted plans for its media onslaught faltered as health care reform was held captive and out of sight.

The third and final surge in press coverage of Clinton's campaign to reform health care came in the May to August 1994 period in response to the quickening pace and seriousness of the congressional lawmaking process. All the major committees met and voted; several of them approved the major components of the Clinton proposal, but the most important committees voted down critical components of the plan. The Senate conducted a heated floor debate but did not approve any legislation. Throughout this period, Senate Majority Leader George Mitchell and other leaders conducted intense but ultimately futile meetings to stitch together a coalition supportive of health care reform. Clinton once again escalated his public statements as a means to pressure Congress, but the Republicans remained steadfast opponents, backing away from the proposal they had embraced earlier and from far more minor reforms such as revising insurance rules. Several Democrats also defected from the president's corner. In the end, a Congress that was controlled by the president's party never even voted on one of his top domestic priorities.

The greater intensity and seriousness of the actual debate among authoritative government officials was matched by a rise in press reports from May to August. The press positioned itself to carry the dénouement of Clinton's health reform campaign. After August and the failure of Senator Mitchell's efforts to find a supportive congressional coalition and the administration's later acknowledgment that its plan was dead, media reporting on health care plummeted and was nearly nonexistent during the 1994 midterm election campaigns.

In short, the volume of press coverage of health care reform in 1993 and 1994 paralleled the cycles of debate among authoritative government officials in ways that defied well-hatched White House plans. Clinton's fervent public campaign in 1993 and 1994 to promote his ideas through press coverage succeeded in drawing unusual press attention to the issue, as the White House hoped. But that success opened the door for critics of Clinton's plan to grab the spotlight and exploit legislative maneuvering and unexpected events.

Sharing the Mike. The tempo and character of the policy debates on health care reform changed not only in the volume of press reports but also in the media's sources and framing—variations that contradicted the administration's plans. A principal motivation for the Clinton White House communications war was to create an "information flow" that connected journalists with friendly sources—namely, the president, administration officials, and Democratic Party allies—who would deliver supportive messages. Close analysis of press reports shows that the White House strategy did capture significant attention for the president, but it also increased press attention to opponents and to journalists and policy experts who raised questions that took attention from the president's message.

From January 1993 to December 1994 the president and administration officials were the source of 14 percent of news reports on health reform, as measured by lines of coverage. Members of the Democratic Party (such as Senators Rockefeller and Mitchell) drew another 8 percent of the media's references. By margins of 3 to 1 and even 4 to 1, the press cited congressional Democrats as offering more supportive than critical comments. But the "friendly" sources that the White House hoped would infiltrate news reports were not entirely dependable: the president's partisans and subordinates were also sources of a substantial number of critical press reports, leaking damaging information to the press.

The success of the White House juggernaut in attracting press attention created an opportunity for the president's critics. The press turned to interest groups, who usually criticized the Clinton plan, in 22 percent of its coverage. Most of these interest groups represented hospitals and doctors or were advocacy groups such as AARP, the seniors lobby. An additional 6 percent of press reports used Republican Party officials as sources. In the battle over whom journalists turned to for interviews and information, the White House declaration of war created a slight edge for its opponents or, at best, fought critics to a draw.

In addition to the sources most prone to criticize Clinton's plan, the press also regularly used sources who were inclined to offer "nonpartisan" reactions that tended to raise questions and issues that distracted or contradicted the administration's carefully planned message. The media's search for independent arbiters of an acrimonious debate meant that 7 percent of journalists' sources were policy experts. On top of that, journalists, press commentators, and political pundits were the source in 22 percent of media coverage. The willingness of journalists to narrate or insert their own observations about the health reform debate into news coverage is part of a larger pattern of reporters' substituting their own commentary and interpretations for "standard sources" and the actual words of politicians.[25] In 1993 and 1994 journalists were not shy about offering their rendition of what they saw as the White House's staged contrivances and in doing so in a critical tone.

The media's selection of sources varied with the dynamics of the health reform debate. During the White House "roll-out" of its plan in September 1993, the proportional attention that the press devoted to Clinton, administration officials, and to Democratic Party officials soared, amounting to 40 percent of journalists' sources. In addition, the relative attention to critics or independent voices declined or remained muted: the relative attention to Republicans increased but remained around 10 percent, and the interest group share fell to under 5 percent; journalists pulled back significantly. After September 1993, however, the White House attempt to dominate whom journalists used as sources went downhill. Except for a slight uptick in January 1994, when the president delivered the State of the Union address, his and his administration officials' relative presence steadily declined during this period. Meanwhile, journalists' use of opponents (Republicans and interest groups) and of themselves dominated press reports. When the action shifted to Congress in the spring and summer of 1994, journalists tended to ignore Clinton and administration officials as sources (their share hovered between 5 percent and 10 percent from April to the November elections) in favor of Democratic Party officials, mostly members of Congress.

The reality of press sources is far from the White House's initial strategy of cajoling reporters to use friendly sources who would control the message, pass the White House's finely tuned rhetoric through the press, and ignite public support. The media's actual reaction flipped White House expectations—the president's communications offensive led the press to expand the range of partisan and sectional viewpoints as evident in the greater attention devoted to Republicans and interest groups. Once again, choreographed plans by the White House hit an unexpected roadblock: its "message" was shot down by hostile return fire or obscured in a haze of expert or journalist commentary.

The End of the Hidden-Hand Presidency. Part of the art of politics is to present policies that benefit particular groups as the actions of a beneficent and

Figure 12.2 Proportion of Press Coverage Dedicated to Strategic and Substantive Problem Framing of Health Care Issues, 1993–1994

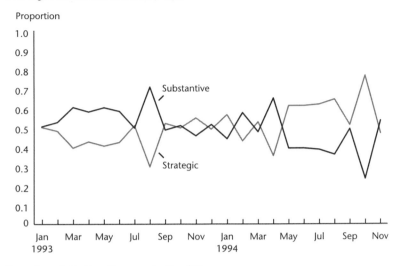

Source: Compiled by the author: see notes 18 and 19.

Note: The proportions are calculated with lines of frame mentions for each month as the numerator and the total number of lines per month as the denominator.

public-spirited leader who has put aside crass political calculations in the interests of the country's good. One of the core objectives of the Clinton White House was to focus reporters on the substance of its health care reform proposal rather than on the administration's self-serving political strategizing. Here again White House expectations were reversed and its plans to dominate press reporting frustrated.

The proportion of attention that the press devoted to framing the debate in terms of substantive issues as opposed to political strategy and conflict was evenly split over the 1993 to 1994 period. This overall pattern, however, masks critical variations over time. The failure of determined efforts by the White House to keep the press focused on policy substance rather than on the strategy of the horse race is evident in Figure 12.2. The figure shows that during the first nine months of Clinton's term, when his health care reform plan was under design, the media devoted greater attention to substantive issues than to the politics of the president's initiative, drawing 70 percent of press reports in August. The White House offensive fell apart, however, after September when press reports tended to be dominated by accounts of political strategy and bickering. Consider the *Washington Post*'s coverage on September 23, 1993, following Clinton's prime-time appeal. Ruth Marcus and Ann Devroy kicked off their report by highlighting the "fundamental differences" and "grueling fight" that had already developed; Spencer Rich literally catalogued the positions of competing interest groups.[26]

The November and January surges in the media's strategic framing of the health reform debate reflect its increasingly political character. Dole shifted his comments from receptiveness to Clinton's plan to direct opposition, and Clinton countered the Republican and interest group attacks with his carefully crafted State of the Union address. Far from deferring to the White House script of rich substantive content, the press conveyed the genuine acceleration of political disagreement and maneuvering. Journalists covered the artifice and behind-the-scenes stagecraft of the president-sponsored Kabuki Theatre.

The third and largest spike in strategic framing began in May 1994, paralleling the culmination of the policy debates among members of Congress. The press conveyed the genuine struggle between the Democratic leaders' frantic but vain efforts to build a supportive coalition and the reform opponents' maneuverings to suffocate these efforts. No amount of White House stage managing could prevent the press from focusing on the real clashes among authoritative government officials over a divisive and highly visible domestic policy initiative.

Little in the health care reform episode resembles the elaborate step-by-step White House plan for presidential dominance of press coverage. The White House consistently underestimated the media's tendency to cover controversial presidential initiatives by increasing their use of critics or distracting independent voices as sources and their focus on political conflict and strategy.

The Search for Common Ground on Social Security

Clinton's Social Security initiative shared important features with his health care reform campaign. In both cases, Clinton was strongly motivated to tackle these contentious social policies as a means to cement his domestic legacy.[27] But he conducted his campaign to reform Social Security during his second term in a manner significantly different from his health reform offensive. The shift in presidential strategy generated a different reaction from his political opponents and a different pattern of press reporting. In addition, the president's efforts on Social Security benefited from the relatively widespread concern about the program that already existed among authoritative government officials, including members of Congress in both parties and Alan Greenspan, the chairman of the Federal Reserve Board.

What distinguished Clinton's actions on Social Security is that he started by acknowledging and attempting to accommodate the viewpoints of a diverse set of political actors who had already expressed interest in reforming the program. In contrast to their health reform initiative, Clinton and his aides launched their efforts on Social Security by asking how they could enact "compromise" legislation; they had decided that "the main problem . . . is about nurturing a political environment in which Congress and the administration can make changes without being punished by voters."[28] The president concluded—as the *Washington Post* reported in January 1998—that it was "unwise for him to offer his own solution to the impending Social Security crisis on the grounds that this would politicize the issue and make it harder to reach a compromise." Abandoning his position as commander in chief in a communications war, Clinton now defined his role, according to the *Post,* as "coax[ing] along a bipartisan dialogue" that "search[ed] with him for common ground" and "buil[t] a bipartisan consensus." He also sought to "raise public awareness of the program's rising costs . . . [and find] ways for accommodating the huge influx of baby-boom retirees."[29]

Joint Efforts to Gain Press Attention. Social Security drew increased media attention in 1997 and 1998 because of actions by President Clinton and an array of other authoritative government officials. In contrast to the health care reform episode, however, the debate over Social Security did not grow out of White House efforts to dominate and control press reporting. Instead, the program drew attention in the summer and fall of 1997 because a number of influential government officials called for action to solidify its long-term financing. Figure 12.3, which indicates the number of lines the press devoted to covering Social Security from July 1997 to June 1998, shows that news coverage increased in August when journalists reported complaints by members of Congress and other political actors that the balanced budget legislation signed by Clinton on August 11 failed to address the program's future financial challenges. The uptick in press reporting during the second half of November was fuelled by Greenspan's congressional testimony and his recommendation that Congress consider privatizing Social Security in the course of addressing the future financing of the program.

Figure 12.3 shows that the first major peak in press reporting on Social Security occurred during the second half of January 1998. The rise in media coverage reflected the actions of an array of government officials during the previous six months, particularly since the second half of December when the

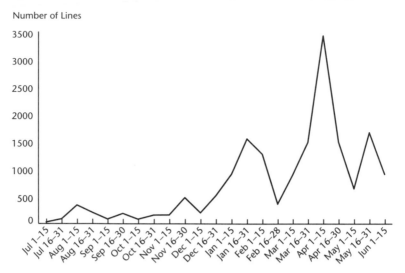

Figure 12.3 Total Number of Lines of Press Coverage of Social Security, 1997–1998

Source: Compiled by the author: see notes 18 and 19.

government indicated that the federal budget deficit was falling faster than previously projected. Media coverage of Social Security continued to rise in January when Clinton announced that he would propose a balanced budget in 1998 (three years earlier than required by the budget legislation he had signed into law in August) and the CBO projected that the federal deficit would end in 1998 and be replaced in three years by surpluses.

Clinton ratcheted up the political stakes in Social Security reform by featuring it in his January 27 State of the Union address and insisting that Congress join with him to "save Social Security first" before reducing federal taxes. The president forcefully argued that any budget surplus should be held in reserve until after a national dialogue and Social Security reforms had been enacted. The media reflected the heightened attention to Social Security by boosting coverage still higher. The combined effect of Clinton's speech and the actions of others was to raise press reports sevenfold between the first half of December and the second half of January.

The critical point is that the press was drawn to Social Security *before* Clinton's State of the Union address by real world events (namely, the brightening budgetary outlook for Social Security) and by the actions of a diverse group of influential government officials—members of Congress, Greenspan, CBO officials, and others. In contrast to health reform, Social Security did not arrive at the top of the government's policy agenda because of an orchestrated communications war by the president.

Social Security drew its strongest media attention in April 1998 (as shown in Figure 12.3) when the president served as a convener of major players in the debate rather than as a communicator-in-chief who was intent on smothering opposing voices. An early April forum in Kansas City, Missouri, which was hosted by a Washington odd-couple—a seniors advocacy group (AARP) and a fiscal watchdog organization (Concord Coalition), brought Clinton together with members of Congress to explain the substantive challenges facing Social Security and to debate specific reforms. In response, between the second half of March and the first half of April, journalists more than doubled their coverage of Social Security, boosting it nearly tenfold since the low in late February.

The third principal peak in press reporting came in the second half of May (see Figure 12.3) when news coverage more than doubled its level during the first half of the month (though still half the level of the April high). The May surge was fuelled by another confluence of actions by a diverse set of government officials. The White House reported higher budget surpluses, and Clinton insisted on saving them until reforms of Social Security were identified. The House Budget Committee passed a budget that used the surpluses to cut taxes. And a national commission established by the Center for Strategic and International Studies recommended committing 2 percent of Social Security's payroll tax to establishing individual investment accounts along with other reforms.

Sharing the Limelight. The media's sources for its reports on Social Security largely followed the contours of the Washington debate among authoritative decision-makers. Clinton's success in the Social Security case suggests that he did not gain much (if anything) from White House efforts to dominate media sources during the debate on reforming health care.

Indeed, Clinton's less adversarial and more cooperative approach to Social Security reform corresponds with some press practices that were friendlier to the White House. In comparison to news coverage of the health care debate, press reports on Social Security reform were significantly less likely to use interest groups as sources and were somewhat more prone to use the president and administration officials. Republicans and policy experts were cited a bit more frequently than during the health reform debate, and journalists cited themselves during the Social Security debate at about the same rate as during the health reform episode.

Reaffirming the general fidelity of news reports to the contours of the actual policy debate, the proportional share of attention that journalists gave to different sources generally paralleled the developments in the debate over Social Security. Not surprisingly, the president and administration officials drew the largest share of press sources during the second half of January not because of a crafty communications strategy but rather because the president devoted his most visible policy statement of the year—his 1998 State of the Union address—to Social Security reform.

Press Reports on Substance over Strategy. The administration's decision not to roll out the public relations guns and instead to engage in a constructive public discussion of Social Security reform generated press reports that overwhelmingly focused on substantive policy issues instead of political strategy and conflict. Figure 12.4, which is based on a proportional measure of news coverage, shows that journalists conveyed the substantive policy issues facing the country three times as often as the behind the scenes maneuvering. The media's focus on policy substance is the most noticeable feature of media framing in Figure 12.4. The attention to political strategy and conflict did rise modestly when authoritative officials devoted significant attention to Social Security, but this coverage of the horse race never seriously encroached on the media's predisposition toward policy content. Press reports on political jockeying picked up noticeably during the second half of the summer when Social Security became embroiled in late-round sparring over the budget legislation.

The next uptick in press attention to political maneuvering came in late January 1998 as Clinton challenged the Republicans. Clinton's call to "save Social Security first" was calculated to derail Republican efforts to use projected budget surpluses for tax cuts. The Republicans could hardly launch a full-scale partisan assault on Clinton for preaching fiscal conservatism, a long-standing Republican mantra. Press reports on political maneuvering also rose a bit during the Kansas City meeting in April. This uptick captures the fact that authoritative policymakers initiated the discussion of *how* to reform Social Security, but the muted nature of press attention to the politics of reform and the overwhelming focus on policy substance echoed the emphasis by Clinton as well as by Republican and Democratic legislators on their joint interest in avoiding partisan squabbling in favor of outlining reform options on which they had significant agreement.

The actual character of political dynamics accounts for the nature of press coverage of Social Security. The White House retreat from communications warfare on Social Security and its focus on accommodation generated more substantive (and less horse race) coverage. A comparison of press framing of

Figure 12.4 Proportion of Press Coverage Dedicated to Strategic and Substantive Problem Framing of Social Security Issues, 1997–1998

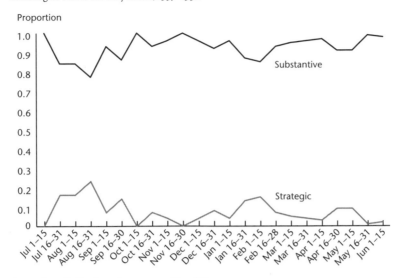

Source: Compiled by the author: see notes 18 and 19.

Note: The proportions are calculated with lines of each frame for each two-week period as the numerator and the total number of lines per two-week period as the denominator.

Clinton's crusade for health care reform (Figure 12.2) and his facilitation of Social Security reform (Figure 12.4) reveals the costs of communications war. The White House media blitz on health care reform produced a press focus on political strategy and conflict rather than policy substance; its more accommodating approach on Social Security produced nearly opposite results.

Collaborative Presidential Leadership

Presidents and their advisers enter the White House as political victors. They have overcome stiff competition, long odds, and often several well-founded predictions of imminent defeat. Once ensconced in the West Wing, they quickly come to appreciate that because of the institutional and political constraints on governing, the stratospheric expectations they fed during the campaign are very difficult to satisfy. The blend of supreme confidence and inadequate political resources both motivates the White House to expand the president's support among Washington's political elites and ordinary Americans and convinces it that administration officials possess the skills and temperament to win the communications war.

The reality, however, is that concerted efforts by presidents to dominate press coverage and portray themselves and their policies in a good light is unlikely to produce the results they anticipated. Such efforts are more likely to generate political opposition and press coverage that captures the strategic gamesmanship and conflict among the president, his allies, and his opponents. Analysis of press reporting of Clinton's campaigns to reform Social Security and health care, as well as previous research, suggests that the content and cycle of media coverage largely mirror the intensity, content, and relative degree of dissensus in the actual policy debates among authoritative government officials.[30] Clinton's crusade for health care reform generated press reports that were preoccupied with political conflict and strategy in a way that his more accommodating approach to Social Security reform did not.

The exaggerated confidence of presidents and their advisers in their communications capacity routinely produces two surprises for them. First, the White House's fixation on the potential benefits of media-based warfare distorts and overtakes its evaluation of the significant costs of this style of leadership—namely, significant press attention to critics and to the unattractive business of strategizing.[31] No amount of "spin control" or bulletins from White House "war rooms" will consistently override the standard journalistic approach to news coverage of conveying the strategy and conflict inherent in presidential crusades. Presidents who opt to become communications warriors invariably inflict political damage on themselves.

Second, presidential schemes to dominate press coverage of divisive domestic policies often result in wasted opportunities and political deadlock. White House hubris in its ability to control information encourages it to embrace policy initiatives that overreach what the public is willing to accept. Unquestioned faith in spin control was one of the reasons the Clinton White House produced a health plan in 1993 that lacked sufficient political support among the public and in Congress.

The net political gain of presidential campaigns to dominate press coverage is much more ambiguous than the White House and many political observers appreciate. Nevertheless, the president and the country can benefit from presidential public appeals. For the president, public leadership through the press is a tool for setting the policy agenda by directing attention to his priority policy areas. For the country, public presidential leadership expands the volume of information distributed to the public and broadens the range of voices and viewpoints that are heard. This in turn increases the probability that Americans will be able to identify various policy advocates and their interests, understand the costs and benefits of proposed policy changes (and how these are distributed), and, because of the increased scrutiny of public claims, evaluate the reliability of information. Presidential leadership pulls into the light of day policy that is normally cloistered in government offices and congressional committees.

The implication of the paradox of presidential media campaigns—namely, that increased public appeals generate press attention to critics and to political conflict and strategy—is not that presidents should abandon the bully pulpit. Instead, they should reconsider one particular leadership style (communications warfare) in favor of another—institutionally-based cooperative leadership. Cooperative leadership rests on a philosophy of shared governance, common institutional interests, and a focus upon issues already of interest to other government officials. Cooperative presidential leadership means sharing the national spotlight, rather than scheming to smother critics and their viewpoints, and using this common platform to accommodate competing perspectives in a spirit of compromise. Cooperative leadership by presidents increases the volume of press coverage, broadens the range of its sources, and encourages news reports about substantive issues. Presidents who fully appreciate the constraints and costs of communication warfare will place a greater premium on the modest (but realistic) benefits of cooperative leadership.

Notes

1. Memo to first lady from Sen. Jay Rockefeller, 5/26/93, regarding "Health Care Reform Communications," confidential.

2. Interview with administration official (No. 2) by Lawrence R. Jacobs (LRJ), 12/6/94; interview with No. 16 by LRJ, 12/6/94, in person, White House, Washington D.C.; interview with No. 10 by LRJ, Washington, D.C., 6/19/95; interview with No. 21 by LRJ, 8/2/94, in person, Washington, D.C.; interview with No. 23 by LRJ, 6/28/94, in person, White House, Washington, D.C.; interview with No. 9 by LRJ, Washington, D.C., 12/8/94; interview with administration official by LRJ, No. 7; interview with No. 20 by LRJ, 8/31/94, telephone; interview with No. 1 by LRJ.

3. "A Winning Strategy for Health Care Reform" for first lady by Ira Magaziner, Jeff Eller, and Bob Boorstin, 7/93; memo to first lady from Michael Lux, regarding "positioning ourselves on health care," 5/3/93.

4. Memo from Lux to the president, 12/15/93.

5. Sidney Blumenthal, "The Education of a President," *New Yorker,* January 24, 1994, 31–43; interview with No. 20 by LRJ, 8/1/4, in person, Washington D.C.; interview with No. 18 by LRJ, Washington, D.C., 7/17/95; interview with No. 7.

6. Interview with No. 1 by LRJ, 12/6/94; interview with No. 15 by LRJ, 6/28/94, in person in Washington, D.C.; interview with No. 16; interview with No. 21 by LRJ, 8/2/94, in person, Washington, D.C.

7. Interview with No. 9 by LRJ, Washington, D.C., 12/8/94; interview with No. 16 by LRJ, 12/6/94, in person, White House, Washington, D.C.; report by Magaziner, "Preliminary Work Plan for the Interagency Health Care Taskforce," 1/26/93; memo to first lady from Magaziner, 5/3/93, regarding, "what is ahead and how to organize for it;" memo to distribution from Jennings and Ricchetti, 4/14/93, regarding "congressional update and strategy for health care reform"; interview with No. 1 by LRJ; memo to first lady from Boorstin and Lois Quam, 2/6/93, regarding health care communications 100 day strategy.

8. William Bennett and Robert Entman, "Mediated Politics: An Introduction," in *Mediated Politics: Communication in the Future of Democracy*, ed. William Bennett and Robert Entman (New York: Cambridge University Press, 2001); Timothy Cook, "The Future of the Institutional Media," in *Mediated Politics*, ed. Bennett and Entman; Timothy Cook, *Governing with the News: The News Media as a Political Institution* (Chicago: University of Chicago Press, 1998); Samuel Kernell, *Going Public: New Strategies of Presidential Leadership*, 3d ed. (Washington, D.C.: CQ Press, 1997).

9. Kernell, *Going Public*, 96.

10. Roderick Hart, "Some Footnotes on the Role of Public Communication in Incumbent Politics" in *Communications Yearbook*, ed. Margaret McClaughlin (Beverly Hills: Sage, 1987), 143 and 120.

11. Cappella and Jamieson presents evidence that press reporting on political strategy and conflict does correspond with increased cynicism among Americans. Joseph N. Cappella and Kathleen H. Jamieson, *Spiral of Cynicism: The Press and the Public Good* (New York: Oxford University Press, 1997).

12. Interview with No. 2; interview with No. 10 by LRJ, Washington, D.C., 6/19/95.

13. Grossman and Kumar's appreciation of both the presidency and the media are among the notable exceptions. Michael Grossman and Martha Kumar, *Portraying the President* (Baltimore: Johns Hopkins University Press, 1980).

14. The press assumption that audience clamor for "big" political stories that can be conveyed like a "horse race" is not entirely supported by scholars of political communication. Kathleen H. Jamieson, *Dirty Politics* (New York: Oxford University Press, 1992).

15. Herbert Gans, *Deciding What's News* (New York: Vintage, 1980), 132–133; Mark Fishman, *Manufacturing the News* (Austin: University of Texas Press, 1980); Timothy Cook, "Domesticating a Crisis: Washington Newsbeats and Network News After the Iraqi Invasion of Kuwait," in *Taken by Storm: The Media, Public Opinion, and U.S. Foreign Policy in the Gulf War*, ed. W. Lance Bennett and David Paletz (Chicago: University Chicago Press, 1994).

16. These expectations build on Lawrence R. Jacobs and Robert Y. Shapiro, *Politicians Don't Pander: Political Manipulation and the Loss of Democratic Responsiveness* (Chicago: University of Chicago Press, 2000); William Bennett, "Toward a Theory of Press-State Relations in the United States" *Journal of Communication* 40 (1990): 103–125; M. Alexseev and William Bennett, "For Whom the Gates Open: Journalistic Norms and Political Source Patterns in the United States, Great Britain, and Russia" *Political Communication* 12 (1995): 395–412.

17. Gans, *Deciding What's News;* Bennett, "Toward a Theory of Press-State Relations in the United States"; Timothy Cook, *Making Laws and Making News: Media Strategies in the U.S. House of Representatives* (Washington, D.C.: Brookings Institution, 1989); Leon Sigal, *Reporters and Officials* (Lexington, Mass.: D. C. Heath, 1973); Gaye Tuchman, *Making News* (New York: Free Press, 1978).

18. The Social Security analysis was conducted as part of a project with Fay Cook, and the health care analysis draws on data collected for a book that Bob Shapiro and I wrote. Fay Lomax Cook and Lawrence Jacobs, "Evaluation of Americans Discuss Social Security: Deliberative Democracy in Action," Report to the Pew Charitable Trusts, 1999; Jacobs and Shapiro, *Politicians Don't Pander,* chaps 5 and 6.

19. In terms of Social Security coverage, we examined major national print media (*Wall Street Journal, New York Times,* and Associated Press) and television (CNN and ABC), as well as the following leading state newspapers: *Albuquerque Journal, Arizona Republic, Boston Globe, Denver Post, Detroit News, San Francisco Chronicle, Austin American Statesman, Buffalo News, Des Moines Register, Minneapolis Star Tribune, Seattle Times, Idaho Statesman, Lexington Herald-Leader,* and *Tallahassee Democrat.* Our health care analysis also focused on major national print media (*USA Today, New York Times, Washington Post, Newsweek,* and *Fortune*) and television (CNN, ABC News), as well as leading state newspapers *(Atlanta Journal-Constitution, Dallas Morning News, Sacramento Bee, Minneapolis Star Tribune).*

20. Our use of the NEXIS database means that lines from different print and broadcast media were of equivalent length and therefore were comparable.

21. For instance, a news account of Clinton's health care reform campaign that focused on the president's calculation that passing his plan would boost the Democratic Party's prospects in the 1994 election represents a strategic frame, while a news report on the content of the president's plan or on the national health care expenditures on hospital and physician services and their rate of increase over the past decade would be coded as substantive frames.

22. Intercoder reliability for the Social Security and health care analyses was assessed by having two coders who had not previously been involved in the research analyze a sample of news stories that had also been coded by the two primary coders. Comparisons of the codings across all variables for all the researchers produced correlation coefficients that fell in the .7 range or higher. Based on these checks, the content analysis was considered accurate.

23. Jacobs and Shapiro, *Politicians Don't Pander,* 112–114, 173.

24. Lawrence R. Jacobs, "Manipulators and Manipulation: Public Opinion in a Representative Democracy" *Journal of Health Politics, Policy and Law* 26 (December 2001): 1361–74.

25. Cappella and Jamieson, *Spiral of Cynicism;* Jamieson, *Dirty Politics;* Thomas E. Patterson, *Out of Order* (New York: Knopf, 1994); Catherine Steele and Kevin Barnhurst, "The Journalism of Opinion: Network News Coverage of U.S. Presidential Campaigns, 1968–1988," *Critical Studies in Mass Communications* 13 (September 1996): 187–209.

26. Ruth Marcus and Ann Devroy, "Clinton Stamps 'Urgent Priority' on Health Plan," *Washington Post,* September 23, 1993; Spencer Rich, "Who Stands Where on Health Care," *Washington Post,* September 23, 1993.

27. John Harris, "Clinton Looks to Political Center to Revive Domestic Agenda," *Washington Post,* December 7, 1998.

28. John Harris, "Clinton Plan: Push Social Security Fix; President Considers a Special Session To Prod Lawmakers," *Washington Post,* January 4, 1998.

29. Harris, "Clinton Plan"; Harris, "Clinton Looks to Political Center"; Amy Goldstein and George Hager, "Clinton Promises Push on Social Security; Search for Common Ground Urged; Plan May Be Sent to Hill," *Washington Post,* December 9, 1998.

30. For instance, Jacobs and Shapiro, *Politicians Don't Pander;* Bennett, "Toward a Theory of Press-State Relations in the United States"; Alexseev and Bennett, "For Whom the Gates Open."

31. Past research on presidential impact on press reporting repeatedly points to constraints due to outside events as well as alternative interpretations by other elites and the media's framing of these outside developments and alternative interpretations. Edwards, George and B. Dan Wood, "Who Influences Whom? The President, Congress, and the Media," *American Political Science Review* 93 (1999): 327–344. Nadeau, Richard, Richard Niemi, David Fan, and Timothy Amato, "Elite Economic Forecasts, Economic News, Mass Economic Judgments, and Presidential Approval," *Journal of Politics* 61 (1999): 597–611.

13 The Presidency and Interest Groups: Programmatic Ambitions and Contentious Elites

Daniel J. Tichenor

Presidents occupy a prominent place in American iconography—just think of memorials like the Washington Monument and Mount Rushmore or of the faces of presidents that dominate American coins and currency. Interest groups enjoy a less favorable status in American popular culture. Candidates campaign for office by branding their opponents, not themselves, as "tools" of the "special interests." Yet interest groups have political resources that presidents need in their pursuit of domestic policy accomplishment. As Daniel J. Tichenor uses historical evidence to show, two important variables affect the likelihood that interest groups will provide presidents with necessary political support. One is whether powerful organized interests are affiliated or unaffiliated with the president's political party. The other is whether historical circumstances afford the president a broad or narrow capacity to exercise policy leadership. The four situations produced by combining these two variables range from the productive "collaborative breakthrough politics" to the stagnant "adversarial politics-as-usual."

The national interest group system is as much a fixture in contemporary Washington politics as is the modern presidency. Both were born in the protean decades of the early twentieth century, and their relationship to one another has often been uneasy, if not contentious. At first blush, modern chief executives appear to have ample incentive to keep their distance from organized interests. Although millions of ordinary citizens either belong to or contribute to specific interest groups, most Americans view organized interests in national politics with a level of contempt and suspicion not unlike that of the Constitution's wary architects.[1] As the only U.S. official elected by the entire nation, modern presidents often have cast themselves as guardians of the common good against a welter of selfish vested interests. "Fifteen million people in the United States are represented by lobbyists," Harry S. Truman was fond of saying.

"The other 150 million have only one man who is elected at large to represent them—that is, the President of the United States."[2] Likewise, administrations that seem too closely aligned with particular interest groups risk being charged with serving special interests, as George W. Bush learned early in his presidency when his stands on issues such as Arctic drilling, arsenic levels in drinking water, and global warming provoked criticism that he was cozying up to well-heeled corporate powers.[3] Presidential wariness of organized interests is accentuated by the fact that entrenched Washington lobbies routinely frustrate the president's programmatic goals.

For their part, interest groups would appear to have good reasons to concentrate their energies on government institutions other than the presidency. Congressional members and federal bureaucrats typically enjoy long tenures in office, but an individual president's hold on power is comparatively brief. The tenure of postwar presidents averages less than six years. Furthermore, gaining access to the White House can be a tall order for a lobbyist because of the enormous constraints on the time and attention of presidents and their advisers. In contrast, the size and specialized work of Congress and federal agencies make them more accessible than the White House to interest groups. As one political insider put it, "There are 535 opportunities in Congress and only one in the White House. Where would you put your effort?"[4] In short, interest group relationships with congressional members and federal bureaucrats are likely to be longer lasting and more reliable than those with presidents and their top aides.

Despite these significant disincentives to close presidential-interest group relations, rarely can either disregard the other. Indeed, they do so at their political peril. Organized interests are crucial elements of executive electoral coalitions. In an era of candidate-centered campaigns, interest groups provide money, organizational support, and votes for presidential hopefuls during their primary and general election bids.[5] Once in office, modern presidents stake their claim as successful leaders largely on whether they can build supportive coalitions for their policies with any regularity. Along with political parties, organized interests can offer the White House a potent and efficient means of expanding support for the president's agenda in Congress and other venues. Presidents must also consider, however, that interest groups can just as surely serve as continuous sources of mobilized opposition.

In turn, interest groups cannot ignore the enormous power modern executives wield over public agenda-setting, policy formation, federal budgets, and crucial details of implementation. Presidents also have the capacity to alter the prevailing interest group system they encounter. They can encourage the creation of new organized interests, actively work to demobilize others, and even influence how interest groups frame their preferences in the first place.[6] In short, the modern presidency presents interest groups with significant structural opportunities and constraints to which they must attend. Whether as allies or rivals, policy-minded presidents and interest groups cannot discount each other in a political system constitutionally designed to "counteract ambition with ambition."[7]

A comprehensive treatment of presidential-interest group relations would explore election campaigns, party politics, executive appointments, judicial nominations and confirmations, executive orders, major legislation, and related issues. My purposes here are more modest. In the pages that follow, I focus on the interactions of presidents and interest groups in domestic policymaking. I begin by presenting a theoretical model of presidential-interest group interactions based on the relationship of organized interests to presidents' parties (affiliated versus unaffiliated) and on the relative capacities of different presidents to exercise policy leadership in varying historical circumstances (broad versus narrow). From this model, I identify four distinctive forms of presidential-interest group interaction: collaborative breakthrough politics, adversarial breakthrough politics, collaborative politics-as-usual, and adversarial politics-as-usual. The remainder of the chapter offers historical case studies that illuminate each type of interactive politics.

As we shall see, collaboration with the president is frequently less rewarding (and opposition more beneficial) for interest groups than is commonly presumed. Indeed, modern executives have good reason to frustrate the policy ambitions of even their strongest interest group allies, and group opponents sometimes can translate White House antagonism into new sources of organizational vitality. At the same time, modern presidents find that the national interest group system can pose major extraconstitutional impediments to their programmatic goals, compounding the challenges of policy leadership in a political system replete with barriers to change. It is little wonder that tensions and resentments abound in presidential-interest group interactions concerning domestic policymaking, with each prone to blame the other for lost opportunities.

Friends, Foes, and Policy Leadership: A Framework of Presidential-Interest Group Relations

The first decades of the twentieth century witnessed an evolution in the presidency, one that tied executive authority and power to previously scorned forms

Figure 13.1 Appearances of Private Corporations and Interest Groups at Congressional Hearings, 1833–1917

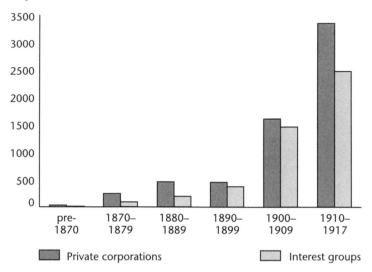

Source: Based on data created by the author from the CIS Index for Congressional Hearings, 23d–64th Congresses (Washington, D.C.: Government Printing Office, 1985).

of rhetorical leadership.[8] During the same period, an unprecedented number and variety of organized interests became actively engaged in Washington lobbying.[9] As Figure 13.1 illustrates, never before had so many organized interests attempted to influence federal policymaking. Conflict and ambivalence characterized modern presidential-interest group relations from the start. Early activists such as Theodore Roosevelt and Woodrow Wilson frequently warned the public of the sinister influence of organized interests in national politics and spoke eloquently of the president's duty to champion the public good. "The business of government is to organize the common interest against the special interest," Wilson told appreciative voters.[10]

Both Roosevelt and Wilson, however, found it difficult to ignore organized interests that could help them govern. During his second term, Roosevelt confided to a close friend that his principled refusal to nurture relationships with corporate interests made leadership challenging. "I am genuinely independent of the big monied men in all matters where I think the interests of the public are concerned . . .," he noted. "But . . . it is out of the question for me to expect them to grant favors to me in return. The sum of this is that I can make no private or special appeals to them, and I am at my wits' end how to proceed."[11] Wilson's administration, by contrast, nurtured close working relationships with business and labor groups during the First World War in order to coordinate industrial production. As the political scientist E. Pendleton Herring noted soon after the war, "In mobilizing the full strength of the country these special interest units gave the government cohesive and responsible organizations with which to deal."[12]

Likewise, more than a few organized interests in the Progressive Era perceived the rise of the modern presidency as a potentially important opportunity to advance their agendas. Consider, for example, the considerable energy and resources that women's suffrage groups such as the National American Woman Suffrage Association and the Congressional Union focused on winning White House support in the 1910s. Inspired by Roosevelt's transformation of the presidency into a "popular steward" of the people, suffragists saw the executive office as a new source of policy dynamism in an often staid American polity. "We knew that [the presidency], and perhaps it alone, would ensure our success," suffragist leader Alice Paul later explained.[13] Wilson was hounded by suffragist groups from his first inauguration in 1913 until the waning stages of his second term. Significantly, the tactics suffragist organizations employed in their pursuit of presidential support included not only conciliatory lobbying but also highly disruptive anti-administration protests.[14] As modern presidents and interest groups emerged as fixtures in national political life, their ability to recast each other's political calculations and policy fortunes was unmistakable.

To capture presidential-interest group relations in their full richness and complexity would require separate accounts of how each individual executive has dealt with interest groups. But one way to generalize about the interactions between modern presidents and interest groups—that is, to identify patterns and draw analytical insights about their reciprocal relations—is to focus on two factors that help structure presidential-interest group politics: (1) the relationship of interest groups to the president's party and (2) the relative opportunities for presidential policy leadership.

It is an old saw of political science that vigorous political parties and interest groups are fundamentally at odds with one other.[15] In truth, both major American parties are linked to interest groups, and both nurture interest group coalitions that will help its candidates win office and its officeholders govern. "Whether observed in the electoral or lobbying arenas," Mark Peterson notes, "a significant portion of the interest group community reflects ideological positions, takes stands on the issues of the day, or represents constituencies whose orientations are at least compatible with one of the two major parties."[16] While reassuring the general public of their eagerness to stand up to "special interests," modern presidents and their political advisers readily understand the importance of party-affiliated interest groups in constructing successful electoral coalitions and governing majorities. Franklin D. Roosevelt, for example, established mechanisms by which White House staff members could attend to the groups comprising his loose New Deal coalition, including organized labor, nationality groups, and small farmers.[17] Subsequent presidents have followed suit.[18] Naturally, not every interest group pursues access to or alliances with the White House. For ideological and strategic reasons, groups unaffiliated with the president's party may advance outsider strategies, such as campaigns to garner media attention and public support. For the purposes of our analytical model, the relationship of interest groups to the president's party (ranging from closely affiliated to staunchly unaffiliated) is crucial because it takes stock of both *collaborative* and *adversarial* forms of interaction.

What are the implications of collaborative and adversarial relations when the opportunities for modern executives to advance their domestic policy agendas are broad or narrow? By most accounts, few presidents have enjoyed broad opportunities to dominate the policy-making process and to advance their agendas (*breakthrough politics*). Presidential scholars tend to agree that the political context was exceptionally favorable for Woodrow Wilson, Franklin Roosevelt, Lyndon Johnson, and Ronald Reagan to exercise policy leadership.[19] Most modern presidents have had to struggle with more challenging leadership circumstances in which their opportunities to reshape public policy have been relatively narrow (*politics-as-usual*).

As Table 13.1 illustrates, four types of interactive politics emerge when we consider together the relationship of interest groups to the president's party (affiliated or unaffiliated) and the relative capacity of a president to exercise policy leadership (broad or narrow).[20] One may predict that *collaborative breakthrough politics* will involve White House sponsorship and co-optation of interest group allies. When the agendas or behavior of supportive groups are at odds with politically dominant presidents, these groups are likely to be marginalized.

Adversarial breakthrough politics places interest group opponents in the difficult position of challenging presidents who have enormous political capital. If these groups are politically effective, they likely will face intense White House assaults. Even when confronted by powerful White House antagonism, oppositional groups may find alternative sources of support in Congress or the bureaucracy because of the fragmented structure of our political system. Indeed, White House antagonism may inspire sympathy for a threatened cause that groups can use to attract new supporters and draw fresh resources.

Table 13.1 Presidents and Interest Groups: A Model of Interactive Politics

President's Capacity to Exercise Policy Leadership	Relationship of Interest Groups to the President's Party	
	Affiliated *(Collaborative Strategies)*	Unaffiliated *(Adversarial Strategies)*
Broad *(Breakthrough politics)*	Collaborative breakthrough politics *Roosevelt's New Deal for labor* *Reagan and the Christian Right*	Adversarial breakthrough politics *Roosevelt and the Liberty League* *Reagan's assault on liberal citizens groups*
Narrow *(Politics-as-usual)*	Collaborative politics-as-usual *G.H.W. Bush, clean air, and the Competitiveness Council* *Clinton and NAFTA*	Adversarial politics-as-usual *Carter and energy reform* *Clinton and health care reform*

The dynamics of *collaborative politics-as-usual* can produce either weak or strong ties between presidents and party-affiliated interest groups. Weak alliances are likely when the president offends affiliated groups by moving toward the political center to secure policy achievements and an independent public image. Presidents who pursue this strategy may presume that, as captives of the president's party, affiliated groups have few alternatives but to maintain at least tacit support for the administration. Nevertheless, strong alliances are possible if the constrained presidents are eager to shore up support from their ideological base by pursuing the policy initiatives endorsed by affiliated interest groups. Collaborative politics-as-usual seems likely to be inhospitable to affiliated groups seeking major policy innovations and more opportune for groups satisfied with incremental policy change.

Finally, *adversarial politics-as-usual* predictably affords oppositional interest groups numerous chances to frustrate the policy designs of politically constrained presidents by mobilizing grassroots resistance, exploiting alliances with supporters in other branches and levels of government, and pursuing other forms of veto-politics. When presidents do not dominate the policymaking process, we may also anticipate that oppositional groups will play a significant role in helping to set the public agenda and shape new policy initiatives. Under these circumstances, the White House may decide to follow the lead of interest groups championing popular causes. To illuminate these distinctive patterns of interactive politics, the chapter next examines several cases of presidential-interest group relations.

Roosevelt and Industrial Unionism:
Collaborative Breakthrough Politics

Interest groups are often attentive to new political openings for their policy goals. During the 1930s organized labor could not resist linking its fortunes to the activist presidency of Franklin Roosevelt and his ambitious New Deal agenda. Labor leaders such as John L. Lewis of the United Mine Workers (UMW) particularly welcomed opportunities to translate New Deal legislative and administrative initiatives into growth for unions. In particular, labor leaders hoped to organize unskilled industrial workers who had been largely neglected by the American Federation of Labor (AFL). In 1933 the Roosevelt administration invited a large number of organized interests—including business and labor groups—to participate in drafting the National Industrial Recovery Act (NIRA). Labor activists such as W. Jett Lauck, a Lewis lieutenant, persuaded the White House to include a vague provision in NIRA, Section 7(a), that recognized the right of workers to bargain collectively. Although corporate leaders were reassured by their lawyers that the provision included no administrative mechanism for enforcement, Lauck reported to Lewis that Section 7(a) "will suit our purposes." After NIRA sailed through Congress, Lewis and other union organizers aggressively exploited the popularity of Roosevelt and NIRA to attract more miners to the UMW. "The president wants you to join the union," UMW literature and speakers told workers.[21] Tens of thousands of miners signed union cards and formed lodges with names such as "New Deal" and "Blue Eagle." After only one year of invoking the celebrated names of Roosevelt and the New Deal, the UMW's membership rolls had swollen from 150,000 to more than 500,000.[22]

Lewis and other labor organizers orchestrated a dramatic break with the AFL in 1934, forming the Congress of Industrial Organizations (CIO) to represent millions of unskilled industrial workers.[23] Publicly, CIO leaders professed unwavering support for Roosevelt and the New Deal. In private, they noted the aloof posture assumed by the White House when Sen. Robert Wagner, D-N.Y., championed legislation that would fundamentally protect unionizing efforts. Roosevelt tepidly endorsed the Wagner Act of 1935, organized labor's "Magna Carta," only at the eleventh hour.[24] Although he understood that organized labor was a crucial element of his electoral and governing coalitions, the president took pains to publicly assert his independence of both labor and business interests. During major strikes, for example, Roosevelt was known to tell reporters that labor activists "did silly things," and he often sounded centrist tones in urging employers and disgruntled laborers to embrace "common sense and good order."[25]

Lewis and the CIO recognized Roosevelt's lack of enthusiasm for union radicalism but also appreciated that labor reforms such as the Wagner Act and the National Labor Relations Board (NLRB) were powerful catalysts for union organizing and collective bargaining. In 1936 Lewis, David Dubinsky, George Berry, Sidney Hillman, and other labor activists entered into an electoral marriage of convenience between the CIO and the Democratic Party to reelect Roosevelt. CIO unions contributed significant financial and logistical support to the president's reelection campaign; in fact, Lewis's UMW was the Democratic Party's largest financial benefactor in 1936. In forming the Labor Nonpartisan League, however, Lewis hoped that union votes could be marshaled in future elections to support whichever party or candidate best served the CIO's interests.[26]

After his landslide victory, it became clear that Roosevelt expected organized labor to follow his lead and not the reverse. Like other presidents who have dominated the policy process, Roosevelt intended to dictate the terms of any alliances between the White House and interest groups. Amid labor confrontations with "little steel" in 1937 and 1938, Roosevelt stunned many labor supporters with his comment on the killing of ten steelworkers who were demonstrating in Chicago against Republic Steel Corporation. Denouncing management and unions alike as sponsors of senseless violence, Roosevelt declared "a curse on both your houses." In a Labor Day radio address to millions of listeners, Lewis rebuked the president: "It ill behooves one who has supped at labor's table and who has been sheltered in labor's house to curse with equal fervor and fine impartiality both labor and its adversaries when they become locked in deadly embrace."[27] By the end of the 1930s, Lewis and a few other CIO leaders were convinced that the NLRB, the courts, and the White House were limiting the labor movement's larger aims. During the 1940 election, Lewis worked in vain to derail FDR's reelection, fearing that it would bring about American entry into war and the concomitant demise of labor's agenda for progressive change. After vain efforts to launch a third party challenge and to back the Republican candidate Wendell Willkie in the 1940 election, Lewis stepped down as CIO president.[28]

Eager to marginalize and defuse Lewis-style CIO militancy, the Roosevelt White House embraced moderate "labor statesmen" like Sidney Hillman, president of the Amalgamated Clothing Workers of America and a founder of the CIO. Hillman, in contrast to Lewis, was an unflinching Roosevelt loyalist. He would oversee the creation of the CIO's political action committee, which further cemented ties between organized labor and the Democratic Party.

After Pearl Harbor, war imperatives called for extraordinary industrial production and coordination. Labor leaders such as Philip Murray, the new CIO president, and Walter Reuther of the United Auto Workers proposed "industrial councils" that would facilitate efficient wartime production while giving organized labor real influence—along with business and government—in supervising industries and the workforce. The Roosevelt administration eschewed such ideas. In the end, the AFL, the CIO, and other unions agreed to a "no-strike pledge" during the war and merely hoped that the war agencies would exercise their robust power over industrial workers benevolently.[29] "Instead of an active participant in the councils of industry," historian Alan Brinkley notes, "the labor movement had become, in effect, a ward of the state."[30] As the war drew to a close, Lewis's vision of an independent labor movement engaged in militant activities was overshadowed by broad CIO and AFL support for a more conciliatory posture. Heartened by the gains and protections secured during Roosevelt's administration, leaders of organized labor pinned their hopes on a permanent alliance with the Democratic Party.

Presidents with broad opportunities to shape domestic policy are unlikely to leave the interest group system the way they found it. If they have the ability to remake American politics and governance, it is hardly surprising that these chief executives would not be equally capable of reconstructing the interests that are closest to them. Although Roosevelt did not explicitly favor union expansion or the meteoric rise of the CIO, his influence in these developments was unmistakable. Organized labor had benefited a great deal from its ties to a president blessed with the exceptional opportunity to advance major policy changes, but Roosevelt exercised enormous control over the terms of their alliance and the nature of reform. Co-optation was the price of labor's programmatic collaboration, as union militancy and independence gave way to a moderate, bureaucratic style of labor organization.

Reagan and the Christian Right: Collaborative Breakthrough Politics II

During the late 1970s the Christian Right emerged from a long political slumber to assert itself as a new force in conservative politics. For decades following the Scopes trial of 1925 and the repeal of Prohibition in 1933, religious conservatives had retreated from the political sphere into a separate subculture of churches and sectarian educational and social institutions.[31] In the 1960s and 1970s many social and political changes deeply offended Christian fundamentalists, evangelicals, Pentecostals, and charismatics, who strongly believed that they must resist culturally liberal government policies that favored "secular humanism" over faith-based morality. Organizations formed to advocate what leaders of the new Christian Right described as a pro-family agenda, including tax credits for private school tuition, promotion of school prayer, and restrictions on abortion and pornography. The most prominent new group was the Moral Majority, led by televangelist Jerry Falwell. Other new organizations included the Religious Roundtable, which brought together reform-minded fundamentalist and evangelical clergy, the National Christian Action Council, Christian Voice, and Pat Robertson's Freedom Council.[32]

During the presidential campaign of 1980, Ronald Reagan openly courted conservative Christian leaders by sharing their enthusiasm for restoring traditional values and pledging his support for their social agenda. He won an early endorsement from Christian Voice, which organized an effective political action committee—Christians for Reagan—on his behalf. The Religious Roundtable invited Reagan to address more than fifteen thousand ministers at one of its public affairs briefings in the summer of 1980, another event that helped coalesce conservative Christian support behind his candidacy. The Moral Majority and other groups encouraged voter mobilization at the fundamentalist and evangelical grassroots, urging followers to express their religious convictions at the polls.[33] Reagan openly appealed to conservative religious leaders and constituents by supporting the removal of a pro–Equal Rights Amendment plank from the Republican platform and the insertion of an anti-abortion plank.[34] His 1980 presidential bid served as an important catalyst for unifying and mobilizing the Christian Right, making it a feared electoral force in American politics.

As president, Reagan appointed a number of Christian Right activists to visible administration positions. Morton Blackwell, who served as a liaison between evangelicals and the Reagan campaign organization, was named a special assistant on the White House staff. Robert Billings, former executive director of the Moral Majority, received a prominent post in the Department of Education. Gary Bauer, a future director of the Family Research Council, became the head of the domestic policy team in Reagan's second term. Reagan also used his "bully pulpit" to speak out on behalf of Christian Right causes, including frequent endorsements of constitutional amendments to prohibit abortion and restore school prayer.[35] Reagan exercised his executive powers to bar the disbursement of public funds to any family planning organization that discussed abortion as an option with patients (the so-called "gag rule"). The White House also threw its support behind fundamentalist Bob Jones University in its lawsuit against the IRS, which had revoked the institution's tax-exempt status because of its racially discriminatory practices.[36]

If Christian Right activists expected the Reagan administration to expend significant political capital on behalf of their social reform agenda, however, they soon discovered that the White House had other priorities. Reagan strategists aggressively streamlined the president's reform agenda to focus on economic issues and a defense buildup. Political liabilities and distractions were minimized or eliminated. James Baker, the politically moderate White House chief of staff, and Robert Michel, the House Republican leader, set the tone early by serving notice that social issues would not be the Reagan administration's top priority. Reagan even reneged on a campaign promise to appear at the 1981 March for Life in Washington, offering instead to meet privately with anti-abortion leaders in the Oval Office. Several of them boycotted the meeting in protest. Paul Weyrich, a central figure in the Christian Right movement, organized a conference call among conservative religious leaders in hopes of rallying them to press their social policy goals with the president. Yet few of these leaders were prepared to battle the Reagan White House. Falwell and his Moral Majority loyalists, for instance, argued that to antagonize the administration would be self-defeating.[37] Significantly, at the same time the White House was placing Christian Right issues on the back burner, the Moral Majority and other conservative religious organizations dutifully joined a broad coalition of conservative interest groups in rallying behind the 1981 Omnibus Budget Reconciliation Act and the Economic Recovery Tax Act.[38] Although they had few tangible policy gains to show for their alliance with Reagan, prominent Christian Right groups threw their full support behind the president's reelection campaign in 1984.

The Reagan presidency gave the Christian Right and its conservative social agenda enormous symbolic recognition. It also forged an enduring alliance between conservative religious groups and the Republican Party: in every presidential election since 1980, the Christian Right has focused its energies on electing the Republican candidate. Ralph Reed, a prominent movement figure, credits Reagan with leading religious conservatives "out of the wilderness" and "giving their concerns a viability in the political system that they had never had before."[39] To be sure, he and many other Christian Right activists also lament that they received little more from the Reagan administration than "consolation prizes like speeches by the Gipper to their annual conventions or schmooze sessions in the Roosevelt Room."[40] Yet the Christian Right had few alternatives but to remain loyal. Presidents who dominate the political system for a time, such as FDR and Reagan, largely control the terms of their sponsorship of interest group allies. Co-optation is often the price interest groups pay for their engagement in collaborative breakthrough politics. Sometimes the price is high. Unlike organized labor in the 1930s, which benefited from the reform program framed by Roosevelt, the Christian Right accepted a form of co-optation from Reagan that ensured the frustration of its policy goals.

Roosevelt and the American Liberty League: Adversarial Breakthrough Politics

When a president dominates the national policy-making process as thoroughly as Roosevelt did during his first term as president, oppositional groups often have little choice but to shift their political efforts from working with the administration to challenging it with aggressive publicity campaigns and electoral battles. In short, disgruntled interest groups must shift from "insider" to "outsider" tactics. The American Liberty League's crusade against Roosevelt and the New Deal provides an apt illustration of adversarial breakthrough politics.

Early in his presidency, Roosevelt hoped that his administration and its economic recovery experiments would earn the approval of a broad coalition of interests. He was particularly eager to win the support of the business community. But business leaders began to mobilize against Roosevelt when New Deal reformers unveiled a 1934 stock exchange measure that made clear the administration's determination to regulate high finance.[41] In the summer of 1934, defiant business leaders launched the Liberty League to serve as an anti–New Deal interest group. The new organization was dominated by prominent executives and corporate lawyers from banking, oil, steel, transportation, auto, and other industries.[42] The league boasted especially close ties to General Motors and the Du Pont family's financial empire. Claiming to be nonpartisan, the league took pains to include among its officers a handful of conservative Democrats who loathed the New Deal, most notably Al Smith, the 1928 Democratic presidential nominee.[43] Each of these officers, including Smith, soon bolted from the Democratic Party, however, which led Arthur Krock of the *New York Times* to conclude that the league's nonpartisanship was a fiction. Instead, he informed readers that the Liberty League was the aegis of Republican patricians determined to guard business civilization.[44]

League officers initially crowed that their organization would enlist 2 million to 4 million in its crusade to defend nineteenth-century economic liberalism against the New Deal. Their efforts went nowhere: at its peak, the league could claim roughly 75,000 members. Its principal activities focused on reshaping what one leader called "the collective expression of public opinion."[45] The league established offices in the National Press Club building; issued a profusion of pamphlets, bulletins, and newspaper editorials; and made extensive use of the radio to challenge New Deal principles. League spokespersons warned radio listeners that the New Deal threatened "the individual freedom of the worker . . . to sell his own labor on his own terms" and unfairly seized "the accumulation of the thrifty" in order to distribute it to "the thriftless and unlucky."[46]

Roosevelt handled the league adeptly. He told reporters that he was delighted to learn that league officers were evaluating the New Deal in light of the Ten Commandments. Unfortunately, he noted, they had forgotten the commandment from Jesus to "love thy neighbor as thyself."[47] In his January 1936 message to Congress, Roosevelt declared his pride in having "earned the hatred of entrenched greed," "the unscrupulous money-changers," and the "discredited special interests." In a much-publicized speech to well-heeled members of the Liberty League at Washington's Mayflower Hotel a few weeks later, Al Smith excoriated New Dealers for betraying traditional American ideals in favor of socialist notions of government control and radical collectivism.[48] The choice was clear, he declared. Was it to be "Washington or Moscow, the Stars and Stripes or the red flag and the hammer and sickle, the Star Spangled Banner or the Internationale?"

While the Republican National Committee and its presidential candidate, Alfred M. Landon, attempted to strike moderate to liberal postures during the 1936 election, the Liberty League provided Roosevelt a perfect foil. Landon hoped to distance his party from the Liberty League by running on progressive issues, and he pointedly asked the organization not to publicly endorse his candidacy. Nevertheless, league members contributed lavish sums to defeat Roosevelt in 1936 and stepped up their anti–New Deal publicity efforts during the campaign. To the chagrin of the Landon team, these high-profile election activities only helped New Dealers brand the Republican Party the tool of wealthy antigovernment elites. Throughout the 1936 campaign, Roosevelt railed against "economic royalists" who cared little about the plight of most Americans. For his last campaign address outside New York in 1936, FDR chose Wilmington (the Delaware home of the Du Pont empire) to speak about liberty. He took the opportunity to recount a parable of Lincoln's about a wolf who, having been pulled from the neck of a lamb by the shepherd, denounced the shepherd for destroying liberty. "Plainly, the sheep and the wolf are not agreed upon a definition of the word liberty," he quipped.[49]

Not long after Roosevelt won his landslide reelection, the Liberty League chose to shut down rather than retreat into the political wilderness. Its failed effort to derail the New Deal illustrates the difficulties oppositional groups can face when squaring off against breakthrough presidents. The lack of a large membership base also limited the effectiveness of the league's outsider tactics. However, as we shall see in President Reagan's struggle with liberal citizen organizations, oppositional groups sometimes can prove resilient and even mount effective challenges to breakthrough presidents.

Reagan's Assault on Liberal Citizen Groups: Adversarial Breakthrough Politics II

Ronald Reagan, the first modern conservative president with abundant political tools, declared war on liberal advocacy groups. Reaganites made no effort to conceal their disdain for liberal interest groups, viewing them as "a bunch of ideological ambulance chasers" who profited from bloated government and stood in the way of "regulatory relief."[50] Government retrenchment, the Reagan White House resolved, would require a concerted effort to decrease the resources, size, and influence of liberal advocacy groups concerned with the environment, consumer protection, civil rights, poverty, and other policy issues. According to Mark Peterson and others, the Reagan administration set out to demobilize its interest group opponents in 1981 by cutting government programs favored by liberal groups, limiting their access to important federal agencies, and eliminating federal grants and contracts supporting their activities.[51]

The Reagan offensive was devastating for some advocacy groups, especially antipoverty organizations. The administration's social welfare budget cuts of 1981 spared programs aimed at the elderly, thereby neutralizing senior citizens lobbies that might have served as powerful allies of advocacy organizations for the poor.[52] Instead, Reagan's effort to "defund the left" by eliminating government grant programs that supported liberal groups took its heaviest toll on a small cluster of poor people's lobbies.[53] Nevertheless, even as many antipoverty organizations shifted their energies from political advocacy to providing services, a number of groups concerned with the homeless made the Reagan administration's assault on the welfare state the focal point of contentious politics. Organizations associated with the emerging homeless movement of the 1980s engaged in confrontational anti-Reagan protests, building shantytown "Reaganvilles," reminiscent of the Hoovervilles of the Great Depression, and staging demonstrations that drew extensive media attention casting the White House as insensitive to the poor.[54] Ironically, the Reagan administration's constriction of established antipoverty organizations dating back to the Great Society opened the door for new groups to challenge the president's agenda. Presidential antagonism inadvertently served as an impetus for liberal interest group formation.

Beyond its effective assault on a handful of antipoverty organizations, the White House plan to enervate liberal groups failed. Reagan strategists largely ignored the possibility that resourceful oppositional groups might transform the open hostility of a powerful conservative president into a catalyst for liberal organizational growth. National environmental groups, for example, prospered during the 1980s. Although denied access to once friendly federal agencies,[55] environmental organizations launched an effective drive that included aggressive fund-raising, publicity, and coordinated action with congressional allies. As private donations to these groups increased, environmental leaders quipped that James Watt, Reagan's unpopular anti-conservation secretary of the interior, was the "Fort Knox of the environmental movement."[56] Organizations such as the Wilderness Society and the Sierra Club watched their membership rolls double in size between 1980 and 1985.[57] Finally, environmental groups drove from office two prominent Reagan appointees (Watt and Environmental Protection Agency Director Anne Gorsuch) and mounted a successful challenge to the administration's plans for environmental deregulation. Clearly, adversarial breakthrough politics can give oppositional groups the chance to expand and exert influence if they enjoy strong mass-based constituencies and alternative sources of support within government.

Bush, Centrist Reform, and the Competitiveness Council: Collaborative Politics-as-Usual

Presidents with narrow opportunities to exercise domestic policy leadership often have strong political incentives to embrace centrist reforms. By moving toward the political center, these presidents can gain credit among voters for advancing popular bipartisan initiatives. In the process, however, they may alienate their party's core interest group allies. George H. W. Bush's endorsements of popular bipartisan measures on the environment and civil rights illustrate this tradeoff.

Bush's opportunities for policy leadership were severely limited when he became president in 1989. His party held only 175 seats in the House of

Representatives, the fewest of any modern president at the start of a term. Operating within this constrained political environment, the Bush administration hoped to prove its capacity to govern by introducing major environmental reform legislation that would draw considerable congressional, media, and popular support. During his 1988 election campaign, Bush pledged a "kinder and gentler" America and promised to be an "environmental president." As he proclaimed on the campaign trail, "Those who think we are powerless to do anything about the 'greenhouse effect' are forgetting about the 'White House effect.' "[58]

Once in office, Bush stayed on the environmental bandwagon; like Richard Nixon before him, Bush hoped to outmaneuver—or at least keep pace with—congressional Democrats on an issue of enormous popular concern. In July 1989 he sent to Congress an ambitious clean air bill, which was enacted in early 1990 after successful negotiations between the White House and with Senate Majority Leader George Mitchell, D-Maine. The Clean Air Act amendments proved to be Bush's most significant policy achievement.[59] Along the way, however, his administration was required to marginalize traditional Republican interest group allies in business and industry.

At about the same time, the Bush White House endorsed another major centrist reform—the Americans with Disabilities Act (ADA), which had the solid support of the public and liberal political actors but was viewed with dread by many in the business community. The ADA sought to add the disabled to the groups protected against discrimination by the 1964 Civil Rights Act. At the urging of a broad coalition of advocates for disability rights, civil rights, and labor, the ADA also required that new or remodeled facilities be made accessible to disabled persons seeking jobs or hoping to make use of public accommodations; existing facilities were to be made accessible whenever "readily achievable." The potential financial costs arising from ADA requirements were enormous, and Bush administration officials attempted to soften the blow on business interests by pressuring legislators to eliminate language from the bill permitting aggrieved parties to sue for damages. Congressional Democrats refused to make any concessions to the administration and passed the ADA unaltered. With polls indicating overwhelming public support for civil rights reform on behalf of the disabled, Bush signed the ADA into law.[60]

Conservative critics assailed the Bush administration for approving the Clean Air Act amendments and the ADA.[61] Business groups and other conservative organizations warned administration officials that, at the start of a recession, new regulatory burdens placed "significant drags on the country's economic recovery."[62] Troubled by those attacks, Bush hoped to appease business groups outside the gaze of the media by limiting the regulatory reach of the Clean Air Act, the ADA, and other initiatives in the implementation process. To this end, Bush created the Council on Competitiveness within the Executive Office of the President. The council, chaired by Vice President Dan Quayle, was to review regulations issued by government agencies and make them less burdensome for the relevant industry. "The president would say that if we keep our hand on the tiller in the implementation phase," recounted a member of the council, "we won't add to the burdens of the economy."[63]

In closed-door meetings, the Competitiveness Council focused on agency regulations that industry representatives complained were excessive. When the Department of Housing and Urban Development issued ADA-related regulations on how to make apartments more accessible to the disabled, for instance, the council pressured the department to ease the regulations at the behest of construction and real estate interests. As Jeffrey Berry and Kent Portney found, "The new rules were more sympathetic to the industry, and lobbyists for the home builders claimed that hundreds of millions of dollars would be saved each year in aggregate building costs."[64]

The success of some business groups in winning regulatory relief from the Bush administration illustrates perhaps the most promising strategy for interest group allies of politically constrained presidents to achieve incremental policy gains. Avoiding the glare of television lights, interest groups are most likely to benefit from collaborative politics-as-usual by mobilizing White House pressure on federal agencies for friendly implementation of existing laws. The Competitiveness Council, however, was ultimately unable to operate in secrecy. Liberal public interest groups, media scrutiny, and congressional opponents eventually hamstrung its activities.[65] As the Bush years suggest, the relationship between presidents with limited political power and the interest group coalitions of their party is often unproductive. And it does not matter which party controls the White House. Liberal interest groups closely aligned to the Democratic Party also were frustrated during the Clinton administration when popular centrist reforms were on the table. Clinton's support for the North American Free Trade Agreement (alienating organized labor), the Personal Responsibility and Work Opportunity Reconciliation Act (alienating antipoverty and civil rights groups), and the Defense of Marriage Act (alienating gay and lesbian groups) underscores the significant incentives for constrained executives to associate themselves with centrist initiatives even if they estrange interest group allies.

Clinton and Health Care Reform:
Adversarial Politics-as-Usual

Shortly after his unexpected 1948 election, President Truman launched an aggressive campaign to secure national health insurance. Hoping to make the most of his modest political opportunity for programmatic leadership, Truman vigorously nurtured popular support for his ambitious health proposal. The American Medical Association (AMA) and other groups that viewed national health insurance as anathema to their interests launched an intense public relations campaign designed to depict Truman's plan as socialistic and corrosive of quality medical care. Spending what was then an unprecedented $1.5 million for its publicity counteroffensive, the AMA ran ads that portrayed how national health insurance would place government bureaucrats between patients and their physicians. Already constrained by the slim Democratic majorities in Congress and by strong resistance from the conservative southern wing of his party, Truman was helpless to save his health plan when public support dwindled.[66]

More than four decades later, Bill Clinton, another Democrat constrained by limited political capacities to remake domestic policy, chose universal health care coverage as the centerpiece of his administration's reform agenda. He ran effectively on the issue during the 1992 election, receiving a warm reception from large numbers of voters who agreed that the health care system was in crisis. After a lengthy policy-planning process, Clinton unveiled his much-anticipated Health Security Act in late 1993, using language intended to associate his proposal with one of the federal government's most popular programs, Social Security. In substance, the act called for a new public-private partnership involving "managed competition" and employer mandates.[67] Politically, it made important concessions to large companies and health care insurance providers to win their support, while promising universal coverage and checks on soaring medical costs to attract the elderly, consumer groups, unions, religious organizations, and groups representing women, children, and minorities. When the AMA, the U.S. Chamber of Commerce, and several large employers voiced support for principal features of the Health Security Act, the Clinton administration seemed to have assembled a powerful left-right coalition of unions, big business, health-care providers, and the elderly.

By mid-1994 Clinton's crusade for sweeping health care reform was dead. Critics point to the plan's eye-glazing complexity, resistance from Democrats on the relevant congressional committees, Clinton's failure to streamline his policy agenda, his unwillingness to work with reform-minded Republicans, high levels of public distrust in government, among other explanations.[68] For our purposes, however, it is useful to concentrate on the significant role that Clinton's interest group adversaries played in derailing health care reform.

Initially, the strongest group opposition to the administration's health care package came from two national organizations with large grassroots constituencies: the Health Insurance Association of America (HIAA) and the National Federation of Independent Businesses (NFIB). The HIAA represented midsize and small health insurance companies, many of which would go out of business if the Health Security Act became law. Large employers stood to benefit from the Clinton plan, but small businesses represented by the NFIB found intolerable the proposal's mandate that employers pay 80 percent of employee health premiums.[69] The Pharmaceutical Research and Manufacturers of America (PRMA), representing drug companies that stood to lose profits under the Clinton scheme, also joined the cause. Then, late in 1993 Republican strategists led by William Kristol of the Project for the Republican Future began to persuade a broad set of conservative interest groups to mobilize in opposition to the Health Security Act. Anything but an all-out effort to defeat health care reform, Kristol argued, would seriously compromise the political future of the Republican Party and its interest group coalition. Passage of the Clinton plan, he insisted, would "relegitimize middle-class dependence for 'security' on government spending and regulation" and thereby revive the Democratic Party's appeal "as the generous protector of middle-class interests."[70] Before long, the Christian Coalition, antitax groups, and variety of other conservative interest groups devoted new resources to kill health care reform, coordinating their activities with HIAA, NFIB, and PRMA.

Clinton's interest group adversaries devoted considerable resources to advertising. The HIAA spent approximately $14 million on its public relations blitz, which included the well-known "Harry and Louise" television ads expressing middle class angst about the Clinton proposal. The PRMA devoted roughly $20 million to its political advertising campaign. The antireform advertising crusade was designed to minimize public concerns about a health crisis while arousing fears that the president's plan would compromise the quality of medical care, eliminate individual choice of health care providers, encourage bloated government, and dramatically increase taxes to cover the cost of universal coverage. For its part, the 600,000-member NFIB focused on grassroots mobilization, including direct mail and phone bank assaults on the Clinton plan.[71] Against this backdrop, the White House received only modest support for its health care initiative from traditionally Democratic interest group allies.

The AFL-CIO and other labor groups, for example, had already expended considerable resources fighting one of Clinton's treasured centrist achievements, NAFTA.[72]

Adversarial politics took its toll on public support for the health care reform, which drifted downward from 67 percent in a September 1993 *Washington Post*/ABC News poll to 44 percent in February 1994.[73] Destined for defeat, the Health Security Act was never put to a vote in either the House or the Senate. The failure of Clinton's major domestic policy initiative presaged the Republican takeover of Congress in November. Many analysts trace the demise of health care reform in 1993 and 1994 to the Clinton administration's strategic missteps, of which there were many. Placed within the context of our theoretical model, however, Clinton's failure to achieve major health care reform reflects the formidable challenges faced by politically constrained presidents who pursue large-scale policy change. It also illustrates the enormous opportunities for interest group adversaries to block the programmatic ambitions of modern presidents in periods of politics-as-usual.

Conclusion

The political interactions between presidents and national interest groups are facts of contemporary American political life. By studying presidential-interest group relations in light of executive leadership opportunities and the partisan and ideological affiliations of interest groups, we can draw comparisons and recognize patterns across time, much as Stephen Skowronek's emphasis on regime cycles enables us to analytically link together presidents from different historical periods facing similar political circumstances (see Chapter 5).[74] The existing scholarly literature tends to underscore the recent development of the institutional resources and political strategies the White House can use to deal with the interest group system.[75] These valuable empirical insights sometimes have led students of the presidency to perceive all modern presidents as being equally well situated to orchestrate successful relations with organized interests. For example, according to Peterson, "Modern presidents have the institutional means, and have demonstrated the willingness, to influence the interest group system to their own advantage"—including considerable resources to punish opponents and reward allies in the interest group community.[76] Our model of interactive politics offers a decidedly different portrait of presidential-interest group relations, one in which modern executives are frequently confounded in their efforts both to coax allies into supportive coalitions and to thwart opposition groups.

Except for rare moments of presidential dominance, interest groups engage in their own orchestration of effective strategic politics.

Presidents with transformational policy aspirations but ordinary leadership opportunities have routinely found interest group relations to be trying. Oppositional groups are usually in a good position to frustrate the president's most ambitious programmatic goals, as Clinton's ill-fated crusade for health care reform illustrates. Nurturing and aiding interest group allies can also prove difficult for politically constrained presidents. These executives have strong incentives to endorse popular centrist measures because enactment allows them to point to tangible policy achievements. In the process, however, they routinely alienate affiliated interest groups, as Bush learned from his support of the Clean Air Act amendments and the ADA. Indeed, the political allure of such popular centrist initiatives frequently saps the ability of politically constrained presidents to build strong coalitions behind their more partisan measures. During periods of politics-as-usual, executives instead may quietly provide succor to their interest group allies through administrative means, but the intense scrutiny devoted to White House activities by the media and organized opposition means that such efforts rarely remain secret. When publicized, they may subject the president to charges of catering to special interests and may be contested by interest group adversaries in federal courts and Congress.

Although most interest groups allied to presidents with constrained leadership opportunities receive fewer tangible benefits than many assume, oppositional groups often find the adversarial politics that prevail during such presidencies to be hospitable to vibrant and effective activism. As interest groups opposed to Clinton's Health Security program discovered in the 1994 midterm election, countermobilization can have surprising transformational possibilities.

Obviously, interest groups are most rewarded for collaborative relations with the White House during those rare historic moments when breakthrough presidents dominate American governance. But as the Christian Right found during the Reagan revolution, such alliances are no guarantee of programmatic achievement. Breakthrough presidents set the terms of collaboration, and allied interest groups whose goals may jeopardize more important White House objectives may find themselves marginalized in the policy process. Even when the transformational goals of breakthrough presidents and allied interest groups are nearly the same, as was the case with Roosevelt New Dealers and labor activists in the 1930s, co-optation is typically the price these groups pay to secure dramatic gains for their constituencies.

The sorry history of the American Liberty League illustrates the desperate straits faced by organized interests that oppose the programmatic ambitions of politically dominant presidents. It is telling, however, that Ronald Reagan, the most recent breakthrough president, dominated domestic policymaking for only a year and that his interest group adversaries prospered during most of his tenure. The scale and variety of the interest group system since the 1970s has been greater than ever before. This important development, as Graham K. Wilson argues, forces presidents today to contend with "a thicker structure of constraining institutions (in this case, interest groups)."[77] Thus, the promise of strained relations between modern presidents and interest groups is more certain than ever. As our investigation of presidential-interest group relations suggests, the most significant and enduring bias of the American political system is its hostility toward nonincremental reform.

Notes

1. See Jeffrey Berry, *The Interest Group Society* (Glenview, Ill.: Scott, Foresman, 1989), 2–3; and Mark Petracca, "The Rediscovery of Interest Group Politics," in *The Politics of Interests: Interest Groups Transformed,* ed. Mark Petracca (Boulder: Westview, 1992), 7–11.

2. Quoted in James Deakin, *The Lobbyists* (Washington, D.C.: Public Affairs Press, 1966), 7.

3. "Is Bush Poisoning His Well," *National Journal,* April 14, 2001, 1120–1.

4. Lyndon Johnson adviser, quoted in Paul Light, *The President's Agenda* (Baltimore: Johns Hopkins University Press, 1999).

5. Stephen Wayne, "Interest Groups on the Road to the White House: Traveling Hard and Soft Routes," in *The Interest Group Connection,* ed. Paul Herrnson, Ronald Shaiko, and Clyde Wilcox (Chatham, N.J.: Chatham House Publishers, 1998), 65–79.

6. See Benjamin Ginsburg and Martin Shefter, "The Presidency and the Organization of Interests," in *The Presidency and the Political System,* 5th ed., ed. Michael Nelson (Washington, D.C.: CQ Press, 1988).

7. See Alexander Hamilton, James Madison, and John Jay, *The Federalist Papers,* ed. Clinton Rossiter (New York: New American Library, 1961).

8. Jeffrey Tulis, *The Rhetorical Presidency* (Princeton: Princeton University Press, 1987).

9. See Elisabeth Clemens, *The People's Lobby: Organizational Innovation and the Rise of Interest Group Politics in the United States, 1890–1925* (Chicago: University of Chicago Press, 1997); and Richard Harris and Daniel Tichenor, "Organized Interests and American Political Development," *Political Science Quarterly* (spring 2003).

10. Quoted in Lewis Eigen and Jonathan Siegel, *The Macmillan Dictionary of Political Quotations* (New York: Macmillan, 1993), 382.

11. Ibid., 381.

12. E. Pendleton Herring, *Group Representation Before Congress* (Baltimore: Johns Hopkins University Press, 1929), 51.

13. Quoted in Christine Lunardini and Thomas Knock, "Woodrow Wilson and Woman Suffrage: A New Look," *Political Science Quarterly* 95 (winter 1981): 671.

14. Daniel Tichenor, "The Presidency, Social Movement, and Contentious Change: Lessons from the Woman's Suffrage and Labor Movements," *Presidential Studies Quarterly* 29 (March 1999): 14–25.

15. Robert Dahl, *Dilemmas of Pluralist Democracy* (New Haven: Yale University Press, ed., Petracca, 1982), 190.

16. Mark Peterson, "Interest Mobilization and the Presidency," in *Politics of Interests*, 239–240.

17. Joseph Pika, "Interest Groups and the White House under Roosevelt and Truman," *Political Science Quarterly* 102 (fall 1987): 4, 647–668.

18. Bradley Patterson Jr., *The Ring of Power* (New York: Basic Books, 1988), 200–212.

19. William Lammers and Michael Genovese, *The Presidency and Domestic Policy* (Washington, D.C.: CQ Press, 2000); David Mayhew, *Divided We Govern* (New Haven: Yale University Press, 1991); and Erwin Hargrove and Michael Nelson, *Presidents, Politics and Policy* (New York: Knopf, 1984).

20. For an excellent typology of interest group liaison (governing party, consensus building, outreach, and legitimation), see Mark Peterson, "The Presidency and Organized Interests: White House Patterns of Interest Group Liaison," *American Political Science Review* 86 (September 1992): 3.

21. Robert Zeiger, *John L. Lewis: Labor Leader* (Boston: Twayne, 1988), 64.

22. William Leuchtenburg, *Franklin Roosevelt and the New Deal* (New York: Harper and Row, 1963), 106–107.

23. Ibid., 86.

24. Bruce Miroff, *Icons of Democracy* (New York: Basic Books, 1993), 262.

25. Ibid., 260–262.

26. Leuchtenburg, *Franklin Roosevelt*, 189.

27. Zeiger, *John L. Lewis*, 105–106.

28. Marc Landy, "FDR and John L. Lewis: The Lessons of Rivalry," in *Modern Presidents and the Presidency*, ed. Marc Landy (Lexington, Mass.: D. C. Heath, 1985), 106–112; and Zeiger, *John L. Lewis*, 109.

29. Alan Brinkley, *The End of Reform: New Deal Liberalism in Recession and War* (New York: Knopf, 1995), 201–226.

30. Ibid., 212.

31. Eric Larson, *Summer for the Gods* (Cambridge: Harvard University Press, 1997), 232–235.

32. John C. Green, "The Spirit Willing: Collective Identity and the Development of the Christian Right," in *Waves of Protest*, ed. Jo Freeman and Victoria Johnson (New York: Rowman and Littlefield, 1999), 156–159.

33. Kenneth Wald, *Religion and Politics in the United States* (Washington, D.C.: CQ Press, 1992), 234–235.

34. See Ralph Reed, *Active Faith: How Christians Are Changing the Soul of American Politics* (New York: Free Press, 1996), 113–114.

35. A. James Reichley, *Religion in American Public Life* (Washington, D.C.: Brookings Institution, 1985), 324–325.

36. Duane Oldfield, *The Right and the Righteous: The Christian Right Confronts the Republican Party* (New York: Rowman and Littlefield, 1996), 118–121.

37. See Reed, *Active Faith*, 114–115.

38. Reichley, *Religion in American Public Life,* 325.

39. Reed, *Active Faith,* 116.

40. Ibid., 115.

41. Leuchtenburg, *Franklin Roosevelt,* 90.

42. See Frederick Rudolph, "The American Liberty League, 1933–1940," *American Historical Review* 56 (October 1950): 19–33.

43. Albert Fried, *FDR and His Enemies* (New York: St. Martin's Press, 1999), 90–91, and 120–125.

44. Krock is quoted in Rudolph, "American Liberty League," 22–23.

45. Ibid., 25.

46. Ibid., 24, 28.

47. Fried, *FDR and His Enemies,* 90.

48. Leuchtenburg, *Franklin Roosevelt,* 178–179.

49. Rudolph, "American Liberty League," 25.

50. The quote is Reagan's; see Michael S. Greve, "Why 'Defunding the Left' Failed," *Public Interest* 89 (fall 1987): 91.

51. Peterson, "Interest Mobilization and the Presidency," 226–230.

52. Douglas R. Imig, "American Social Movements and Presidential Administrations," in *Social Movements and American Political Institutions,* ed. Ann Costain and Andrew McFarland (New York: Rowman and Littlefield, 1998), 151–162.

53. Douglas R. Imig, *Poverty and Power* (Lincoln: University of Nebraska Press, 1996), 49–54.

54. Imig, "American Social Movements," 167–169.

55. Mark Peterson and Jack Walker have shown that Reagan ushered in "a virtual revolution" in the access of interest groups to bureaucratic agencies of the federal government. See Peterson and Walker, "Interest Group Responses to Partisan Change," in *Interest Group Politics,* 2d ed., ed. Allan J. Cigler and Burdett A. Loomis (Washington, D.C.: CQ Press, 1986), 172.

56. Greve, "Why 'Defunding the Left' Failed," 99.

57. See Christopher Bosso, "The Color of Money: Environmental Groups and the Pathologies of Fund Raising," in *Interest Group Politics,* 4th ed., ed. Allan J. Cigler and Burdett A. Loomis (Washington, D.C.: CQ Press, 1995), 104; and Richard Waterman, *Presidential Influence and the Administrative State* (Knoxville: University of Tennessee Press, 1989), 134.

58. John Holusha, "Bush Pledges Aid for Environment," *New York Times,* September 1, 1988.

59. Richard Cohen, *Washington at Work: Back Rooms and Clean Air* (New York: Macmillan, 1992); Norman Vig, "Presidential Leadership and the Environment From Reagan to Clinton," in *Environmental Policy: New Directions for the Twenty-First Century,* 4th ed., ed. Norman Vig and Michael Kraft (Washington, D.C.: CQ Press, 2000), 104–107.

60. See David Mervin, *George Bush and the Guardianship Presidency* (New York: St. Martin's Press, 1996), 98–101.

61. See Richard Harris and Sidney Milkis, *The Politics of Regulatory Change: A Tale of Two Agencies* (New York: Oxford University Press, 1996), 292–293.

62. Mervin, *George Bush,* 100.

63. Quoted in Harris and Milkis, *Politics of Regulatory Change,* 289.

64. Jeffrey Berry and Kent Portney, "Centralizing Regulatory Control and Interest Group Access: The Quayle Council on Competitiveness," in *Interest Group Politics* 4th ed., ed., Cigler and Loomis, 320.

65. Ibid., 336–340.

66. One of the best accounts of this struggle is provided by Paul Starr, *The Social Transformation of American Medicine* (New York: Basic Books, 1982), 350.

67. Jacob Hacker, *Road to Nowhere: The Genesis of President Clinton's Plan for Health Security* (Princeton: Princeton University Press, 1997).

68. Theda Skocpol, *Boomerang: Health Care Reform and the Turn Against Government* (New York: W. W. Norton, 1997), 133–188; Allen Schick, "How a Bill Didn't Become a Law," in *Intensive Care: How Congress Shapes Health Policy,* ed. Thomas Mann and Norman Ornstein (Washington, D.C.: Brookings Institution, 1995), 240–251; Darrell West and Burdett Loomis, *The Sound of Money* (New York: W. W. Norton, 1999), 75–108.

69. West and Loomis, *Sound of Money,* 78–82.

70. Skocpol, *Boomerang,* 143–146.

71. West and Loomis, *Sound of Money,* 83–85.

72. Ibid., 79–80.

73. Ibid., 92–93.

74. Stephen Skowronek, *The Politics Presidents Make* (Cambridge: Harvard University Press, 1993).

75. For an excellent review of this literature, see Joseph Pika, "Interest Groups: A Doubly Dynamic Relationship," in *Presidential Policymaking: An End-of-Century Assessment,* ed. Steven Shull (New York: M. E. Sharp, 1999), 59–78.

76. It is telling that Peterson focuses on the political activities of Lyndon Johnson and Ronald Reagan, presidents with exceptional opportunities to advance policy breakthroughs. See Peterson, "Interest Mobilization and the Presidency," 237.

77. Graham K. Wilson, "The Clinton Administration and Interest Groups," in *The Clinton Presidency: First Appraisals,* ed. Colin Campbell and Bert Rockman (Chatham, N.J.: Chatham House, 1996), 231.

14 The Presidency and Political Parties

Sidney M. Milkis

The modern presidency has been anything but supportive of today's Republican and Democratic Parties. According to Sidney M. Milkis, most presidents, starting with Franklin D. Roosevelt, have found the traditional party system to be too grounded in state and local organizations to be of much help in the effort to forge presidential policies and programs. Indeed, to the extent that the parties have exercised influence through Congress, presidents have sometimes perceived them to be an impediment to national leadership. FDR, Lyndon B. Johnson, and Richard M. Nixon each took steps to replace party influence with centralized administration in the bureaucracy and the White House. Ronald Reagan and George H. W. Bush tried to restore some (but not all) of the traditional importance of the political parties, Milkis argues, by "refashioning them into highly untraditional but politically potent national organizations." Their efforts were uneven and met with limited success, and their successors, Bill Clinton and George W. Bush, have done little to sustain them.

The relationship between the presidency and the American party system has always been difficult. The architects of the Constitution established a non-partisan president who, with the support of the judiciary, was intended to play the leading institutional role in checking and controlling the "violence of faction" that the Framers feared would rend the fabric of representative democracy. Even after the presidency became a more partisan office in the early nineteenth century, its authority continued to depend on an ability to transcend party politics. The president is nominated by a party but, unlike the British prime minister, is not elected by it.

The inherent tension between the presidency and the party system reached a critical point during the 1930s. The institutionalization of the modern presidency, arguably the most significant constitutional legacy of Franklin D. Roosevelt's New Deal, ruptured the limited, albeit significant, bond that linked presidents to their parties. In fact, the modern presidency was crafted with the intention of reducing the influence of the party system on American politics. In this sense Roosevelt's extraordinary party leadership contributed to the decline of the American party system. This decline continued—even accelerated—under the administrations of subsequent presidents, notably Lyndon B. Johnson and Richard M. Nixon. Under Ronald Reagan, however, the party system showed signs of transformation and renewal. Reagan and his successor, George H. W. Bush, supported efforts by Republicans in the national committee and congressional campaign organizations to restore some of the importance of political parties by refashioning them into highly untraditional but politically potent national organizations. Yet recent developments—virulent institutional clashes between the executive and legislature, the decline of public authority, the impeachment of a popular president presiding over the most prosperous economy in three decades, and the controversial conclusion to the 2000 presidential contest—have raised serious doubts about the capacity of these emergent national parties to build popular support for political principles and programs.[1]

These developments were suspended for a time after the September 11, 2001, attacks on the World Trade Center and the Pentagon and the launch of the war on terrorism. George W. Bush's command of a more unified and patriotic nation in the aftermath of the attacks appeared to revitalize the modern presidency, only to discredit further the raw and disruptive factionalism that has characterized the nationalized party politics of the past two decades.

New Deal Party Politics, Presidential Reform, and the Decline of the American Party System

The New Deal seriously questioned the adequacy of the traditional natural-rights liberalism of John Locke and the Framers, which emphasized the need to limit constitutionally the scope of government's responsibilities. The modern liberalism that became the public philosophy of the New Deal entailed a fundamental reappraisal of the concept of rights. As Roosevelt first indicated in a 1932 campaign speech at the Commonwealth Club in San Francisco, effective political reform would require, at a minimum, the development of "an economic declaration of rights, an economic constitutional order," grounded in a commitment to guarantee a decent level of economic well-being for the American people. Although equality of opportunity had traditionally been promoted by limited government interference in society, recent economic and social changes, such as the closing of the frontiers and the growth of industrial combinations, demanded that America now recognize "the new terms of the old social contract."[2]

Establishing a new constitutional order would require a reordering of the political process. The traditional patterns of American politics, characterized by constitutional mechanisms that impeded collective action, would have to give way to a more centralized and administrative government. As Roosevelt put it, "The day of enlightened administration has come."[3]

The concerns Roosevelt expressed at the Commonwealth Club are an important guide to understanding the New Deal and its effects on the party system. The pursuit of an economic constitutional order presupposed a fundamental change in the relationship between the presidency and the party system. In Roosevelt's view, the party system, which was essentially based on state and local organizations and interests and therefore suited to congressional primacy, would have to be transformed into a national, executive-oriented system organized on the basis of public issues.

In this understanding, Roosevelt was no doubt influenced by the thought of Woodrow Wilson. The reform of parties, Wilson believed, depended on extending the influence of the presidency. The limits on partisanship inherent in American constitutional government notwithstanding, the president represented the party's "vital link of connection" with the nation: "He can dominate his party by being spokesman for the real sentiment and purpose of the country, by giving the country at once the information and statements of policy which will enable it to form its judgments alike of parties and men."[4]

Wilson's words spoke louder than his actions; like all presidents after 1800, he reconciled himself to the strong fissures within his party.[5] Roosevelt, however, was less willing to work through existing partisan channels, and more important, the New Deal represented a more fundamental departure than did Wilsonian progressivism from traditional Democratic policies of individual autonomy, limited government, and states' rights.

As president-elect, Roosevelt began preparations to modify the partisan practices of previous administrations. For example, convinced that Wilson's adherence to traditional partisan politics in staffing the federal government was unfortunate, Roosevelt expressed to Attorney General Homer S. Cummings his desire to proceed along somewhat different lines, with a view, according to the latter's diary, "to building up a national organization rather than allowing patronage to be used merely to build Senatorial and Congressional machines."[6] Roosevelt followed traditional patronage practices during his first term, allowing the chair of the Democratic National Committee (DNC), James Farley, to coordinate appointments in response to local party organizations and Democratic senators. After Roosevelt's reelection in 1936, however, the recommendations of these organization people were not followed as closely. Beginning in 1938, especially, as Edward Flynn, who became the DNC chair in 1940, indicated in his memoirs, "the President turned more and more frequently to the so-called New Dealers," so that "many of the appointments in Washington went to men who were supporters of the President and believed in what he was trying to do, but who were not Democrats in many instances, and in all instances were not organization Democrats."[7]

Wilson had taken care to consult with legislative party leaders in the development of his policy program, but Roosevelt relegated his party in Congress to a decidedly subordinate status. He offended legislators by his use of press conferences to announce important decisions and, unlike Wilson, eschewed the use of the party caucus in Congress. Roosevelt rejected as impractical, for example, the Wilsonian suggestion of Rep. Alfred Phillips Jr. "that those sharing the burden of responsibility of party government should regularly and often be called into caucus and that such caucuses should evolve party policies and choice of party leaders."[8]

The most dramatic aspect of Roosevelt's attempt to remake the Democratic Party was his twelve-state effort, involving one gubernatorial and several congressional primary campaigns, to unseat conservative Democrats in 1938. Such intervention was not unprecedented; William H. Taft and Wilson had made limited efforts to remove recalcitrants from their parties. But Roosevelt's campaign took place on a scale that was unprecedented and, unlike previous efforts, made no attempt to work through the regular party organization. His action was viewed as such a shocking departure from the norm that the press labeled it "the purge," a term associated with Adolf Hitler's attempt to weed out dissension from Germany's National Socialist Party and Joseph Stalin's elimination of "disloyal" party members from the Soviet Communist Party.

In 1936 the Roosevelt administration successfully pushed to abolish the Democratic National Convention rule that required support from two-thirds of the delegates for the nomination of the president and vice president. This rule had been defended in the past because it guarded the most loyal Democratic region—the South—against the imposition of an unwanted ticket by the less habitually Democratic North, East, and West.[9] To eliminate the rule, therefore, would weaken the influence of southern Democrats (whom Thomas Stokes, a liberal journalist, described as "the ball and chain which hobbled the Party's forward march") and facilitate the adoption of a national reform program.[10]

After the 1938 purge campaign, columnist Raymond Clapper noted that "no President ever has gone as far as Mr. Roosevelt in striving to stamp his policies upon his party."[11] This massive partisan effort began the process of transforming the party system from local to national and programmatic party organizations. At the same time, the New Deal made partisanship less important. Roosevelt's partisan leadership ultimately was based on a personal link with the public that would better enable him to make use of his position as leader of the nation, not just of the party that governed the nation.[12] For example, in all but one of the 1938 primary campaigns in which he participated personally, Roosevelt chose to make a direct appeal to public opinion rather than attempt to work through or to reform the regular party apparatus. This strategy was encouraged by earlier reforms, especially the direct primary, which had begun to weaken the grip of party organizations on the voters. Radio broadcasting also had made direct presidential appeals an enticing strategy, especially for as popular a president with as fine a radio presence as Roosevelt. After his close associate Felix Frankfurter urged him to go to the country in August 1937 to explain the issues that gave rise to the bitter Court-packing controversy, Roosevelt, perhaps in anticipation of the purge campaign, responded, "You are absolutely right about the radio. I feel like saying to the country— 'You will hear from me soon and often. This is not a threat but a promise.' "[13]

In the final analysis, the "benign dictatorship" that Roosevelt sought to impose on the Democratic Party was more conducive to corroding the American party system than to reforming it. His prescription for party reform—extraordinary presidential leadership—posed a serious, if not intractable, dilemma: on the one hand, the decentralized character of politics in the United States can be modified only by strong presidential leadership; on the other, a president determined to alter fundamentally the connection between the executive and the party eventually will shatter party unity.[14]

Roosevelt, in fact, was always aware that the extent to which his goals could be achieved by party leadership was limited. He felt that a full revamping of partisan politics was impractical, given the obstacles to party government that are so deeply ingrained in the American political experience. The immense failure of the purge campaign reinforced this view: in the dozen states in which the president acted against entrenched incumbents, he was successful in only two—Oregon and New York.[15] Moreover, Roosevelt and his fellow New Dealers did not view the welfare state as a partisan issue. The reform program of the

1930s was conceived as a "second bill of rights" that should be established as much as possible in permanent programs beyond the vagaries of public opinion and elections. The new rights that Roosevelt pledged the federal government to protect included "the right to a useful and remunerative job" and "the right to adequate protection from the fears of old age, sickness, accident and unemployment."[16] These new rights were never formally ratified as part of the Constitution, but they became the foundation of political dialogue, redefining the role of the national government and requiring major changes in American political institutions.

Thus, the most significant institutional reforms of the New Deal did not promote party government but fostered instead a program that would help the president to govern in the absence of party government. This program, as embodied in the 1937 executive reorganization bill, would have greatly extended presidential authority over the executive branch, including the independent regulatory commissions. The president and the executive agencies would also be delegated extensive authority to govern, making unnecessary the constant cooperation of party members in Congress. As a presidential committee report put it, with administrative reform the "brief exultant commitment" to progressive government that was expressed in the elections of 1932 and, especially 1936, would now be more firmly established in "persistent, determined, competent, day by day administration of what the Nation has decided to do."[17]

It is interesting to note that the administrative reform bill, which was intended to make politics less necessary, became, at Roosevelt's urging, a party government-style "vote of confidence" for the administration in Congress. Roosevelt initially lost this vote in 1938, when the reorganization bill was defeated in the House of Representatives, but he did manage, through the purge campaign and other partisan actions, to keep administrative reform sufficiently prominent in party councils that a compromise version passed in 1939. Although considerably weaker than Roosevelt's original proposal, the 1939 Executive Reorganization Act was a significant measure. It not only provided authority for the creation of the Executive Office of the President, which included the newly formed White House Office and a strengthened and refurbished Bureau of the Budget, but also enhanced the president's control of the expanding activities of the executive branch. As such, the reorganization act represents the genesis of the institutional presidency, which was equipped to govern independently of the constraints imposed by the regular political process.

The civil service reform carried out by the Roosevelt administration was another important part of the effort to replace partisan politics with executive administration. The original reorganization proposals of 1937 contained provisions to make the administration of the civil service more effective and to expand the merit system. The reorganization bill passed in 1939 was shorn of this controversial feature; but Roosevelt found it possible to accomplish extensive civil service reform through executive action. He extended merit protection to personnel appointed by the administration during its first term, four-fifths of whom had been brought into government outside of merit channels.[18] Patronage appointments had traditionally been used to nourish the party system; the New Deal celebrated an administrative politics that fed instead an executive department oriented to expanding liberal programs. As the administrative historian Paul Van Riper has noted, the new practices created a new kind of patronage, "a sort of intellectual and ideological patronage rather than the more traditional partisan type."[19]

Roosevelt's leadership transformed the Democratic Party into a way station on the road to administrative government. As the presidency developed into an elaborate and ubiquitous institution, it preempted party leaders in many of their limited, but significant, duties: providing a link from government to interest groups, staffing the executive department, contributing to policy development, organizing election campaigns, and communicating with the public.[20] Moreover, New Deal administrative reform was directed not just to creating presidential government but to embedding progressive principles (considered tantamount to political rights) in a bureaucratic structure that would insulate reform and reformers from electoral change.

Lyndon Johnson's Great Society and the Transcendence of Partisan Politics

Presidential leadership during the New Deal prepared the executive branch to be a government unto itself and established the presidency rather than the party as the locus of political responsibility. This shift was greatly augmented by World War II and the cold war. With the Great Depression giving way to war, another expansion of presidential authority took place, as part of the national security state, further weakening the executive's ties with the party system. As the New Deal prepared for war, Roosevelt spoke not only of the government's obligation to guarantee "freedom from want" but also its responsibility to provide "freedom from fear"—to protect the American people, and the world, against foreign aggression. The obligation to uphold "human rights" became a new guarantee of security, which presupposed a further expansion of national administrative power.[21]

But the modern presidency was created to chart the course for, and direct the voyage to, a more liberal America. Roosevelt's pronouncement of a "second bill of rights" had begun this task, but it fell to Johnson, as one journalist noted, to "codify the New Deal vision of a good society."[22] This program entailed expanding the economic constitutional order with policy innovations such as Medicare and, even more significant, extending these benefits to African Americans.

Johnson's attempt to create the Great Society marked a significant extension of programmatic liberalism and accelerated the effort to transcend partisan politics. Roosevelt's ill-fated efforts to guide the affairs of his party were well remembered by Johnson, who came to Congress in 1937 in a special House election as an enthusiastic supporter of the New Deal. He took Roosevelt's experience to be the best example of the generally ephemeral nature of party government in the United States, and he fully expected the cohesive Democratic support he received from Congress after the 1964 election to be temporary.[23] Johnson, like Roosevelt, looked beyond the party system toward the politics of "enlightened administration."

Although Johnson avoided any sort of purge campaign and worked closely with Democratic congressional leaders, he took strong action to deemphasize the role of the traditional party organization. For example, the Johnson administration undertook a ruthless attack on the DNC beginning in late 1965, slashing its budget to the bone and eliminating several of its important programs, such as the highly successful voter registration division. The president also ignored the pleas of several advisers to replace the amiable but ineffective John Bailey as DNC chair. Instead, he humiliated Bailey, keeping him on but turning over control of the scaled-back committee's activities to Marvin Watson, the White House political liaison.[24]

Journalists and scholars explain Johnson's lack of support for the regular party organization by referring to his political background and personality. Some have suggested that Johnson was afraid the DNC might be built into a power center capable of challenging his authority in behalf of the Kennedy wing of the party.[25] Others have pointed to Johnson's roots in the one-party system in Texas, an experience that inclined him to emphasize a consensus style of politics, based on support from diverse elements of the electorate that spanned traditional party lines.[26]

These explanations are not without merit. Yet to view Johnson's failures as a party leader in purely personal terms is to ignore the imperative of policy reform that influenced his administration. Like Roosevelt, Johnson "had always regarded political parties, strongly rooted in states and localities, capable of holding him accountable, as intruders on the business of government."[27] Moreover, from the beginning of his presidency Johnson had envisioned the creation of an ambitious program that would leave its (and his) mark on history in the areas of government organization, conservation, education, and urban affairs. Such efforts to advance not only the New Deal goal of economic security but also the "quality of American life" necessarily brought Johnson into sharp conflict with unreconstructed elements of the Democratic Party, such as the national committee and local machines.[28] As one Johnson aide put it, "Because of the ambitious reforms [LBJ] pushed, it was necessary to move well beyond, to suspend attention to, the party."[29]

Considerable evidence exists that the Johnson administration lacked confidence in the Democratic Party's ability to act as an intermediary between the White House and the American people. For example, an aide to Vice President Hubert Humphrey wrote to Marvin Watson that "out in the country most Democrats at the State and local level are not intellectually equipped to help on such critical issues as Vietnam and the riots." After a meeting with district party leaders of Queens, New York, the White House domestic adviser Joseph Califano reported that "they were . . . totally unfamiliar with the dramatic increases in the poverty, health, education and manpower training areas."[30] The uneasy relationship between the Johnson presidency and the Democratic Party was particularly aggravated by the administration's aggressive commitment to civil rights, which created considerable friction with local party organizations, especially, but not exclusively, in the South. It is little wonder, then, that when riots began to erupt in the cities in the mid-1960s, the president had his special assistants spend time in ghettos around the country instead of relying on the reports of local party leaders.[31]

Lack of trust in the Democratic Party encouraged the Johnson administration to renew the New Deal pattern of institutional reform. In the area of policy development, one of the most significant innovations of the Johnson administration was to create several task forces under the supervision of the White House Office and the Bureau of the Budget. These working groups were made up of leading academics throughout the country who prepared reports in virtually all areas of public policy. The specific proposals that came out of these groups, such as the Education Task Force's elementary education proposal, formed the heart of the Great Society program. The administration took great care to protect the task forces from political pressures, even keeping their existence secret. Moreover, members were told to pay no attention to political considerations; they were not to worry about whether their recommendations would be acceptable to Congress and party leaders.[32]

The deemphasis of partisan politics that marked the creation of the Great Society was also apparent in the personnel policy of the Johnson presidency. As his main talent scout, Johnson chose not a political adviser but John Macy, who was also chair of the Civil Service Commission. Macy worked closely with the White House staff, but, especially during the earlier days of the administration, he was responsible for making recommendations directly to the president. As the White House staff rather grudgingly admitted, Macy's "wheel ground exceedingly slow but exceedingly fine."[33] Candidates with impressive credentials and experience were uncovered after careful national searches.

The strong commitment to merit in the Johnson administration greatly disturbed certain advisers who were responsible for maintaining the president's political support. James Rowe, who was Johnson's campaign director in 1964 and 1968, constantly hounded Macy, without success, to consider political loyalists more carefully. Rowe believed that Johnson's personnel policy was gratuitously inattentive to political exigencies. At one point he ended a memo to Macy by saying, "Perhaps you can train some of those career men to run the political campaign in 1968. (It ain't as easy as you government people appear to think it is.)" Macy never responded, but the president called the next day to defend the policies of his personnel director and to chastise Rowe for seeking to interfere in the appointment process.[34]

The rupture between the presidency and the party made it difficult to sustain political enthusiasm and organizational support for the Great Society. The Democrats' poor showing in the 1966 congressional elections precipitated a firestorm of criticism about the president's inattention to party politics, criticism that continued until Johnson withdrew from the presidential campaign in 1968. Yet Johnson and most of his advisers felt that they had to deemphasize partisanship if the administration was to achieve programmatic reform and coordinate the increasingly unwieldy activities of government. During the early days of the Johnson presidency, one of his more thoughtful aides, Horace Busby, wrote the president a long memo in which he stressed the importance of establishing an institutional basis for the Great Society. About a year later, Busby expressed great satisfaction that the Johnson presidency had confounded its critics by achieving notable institutional changes. In fact, these changes seemed to mark the full triumph of the Democrats as the party to end party politics:

Most startling is that while all recognize Johnson as a great politician his appointments have been the most consistently free of politics of any President—in the Cabinet or at lower levels.

On record, history will remember this as the most important era of nonpartisanship since the "Era of Good Feeling" more than a century ago at the start of the nineteenth century. Absence of politics and partisanship is one reason the GOP is having a hard time mounting any respectable offense against either Johnson or his program.[35]

As in the case of the New Deal, however, the institutional innovations of the Great Society did not eliminate "politics" from the activities of the executive branch. Rather, the Great Society extended the merging of politics and administration that had characterized executive reform during the 1930s. For example, to improve his use of the appointment process as a tool of political administration, Johnson issued an executive order to create a new category of positions in the executive branch, called noncareer executive assignments (NEAs). In recognition of their direct involvement in policymaking, the NEAs were exempted from the usual civil service requirements.

To be sure, the NEAs gave Johnson a stronger foothold in the agencies.[36] But the criteria his administration used to fill these positions emphasized loyalty to Johnson's program rather than a more narrow, personal commitment to the president. As a consequence, Johnson's active role as manager of the federal service, which John Macy considered unprecedented for a "modern-day Chief Executive," helped to revive the high morale and programmatic commitment that had characterized the bureaucracy during the 1930s.[37] As White House aide Bill Moyers urged in a memo to the president with respect to the newly created Department of Housing and Urban Development, the goal of the Great Society was to renew "some of the zeal—coupled with sound, tough executive management of the New Deal days."[38]

The legacy of Johnson's assault on party politics was apparent in the 1968 election. By 1966 Democratic leaders no longer felt that they were part of a national coalition. As 1968 approached, the Johnson administration was preparing a campaign task force that would work independently of the regular party apparatus.[39] These actions greatly accelerated the breakdown of the state and local Democratic machinery, placing party organizations in acute distress in nearly every large state.[40] By the time Johnson withdrew from the election in March 1968, the Democratic Party was already in the midst of a lengthy period of decay that was accentuated, but not really caused, by the conflict over the Vietnam War.

Thus, the tumultuous 1968 Democratic convention and the party reforms, spawned by the McGovern-Fraser Commission, that followed in its wake should be viewed as the culmination of long-standing efforts to free the presidency from traditional partisan influences. In many respects, the expansion of presidential primaries and other changes in nomination politics initiated by the commission were a logical extension of the modern presidency. The very quietness of the revolution in party rules that took place during the 1970s is evidence in itself that the party system was forlorn by the end of the Johnson era. These changes could not have been accomplished over the opposition of alert and vigorous party leaders.[41]

Johnson was well aware that elements were in place for the collapse of the regular party apparatus by 1968. From 1966 on, his aides bombarded him with memos warning of the disarray in the Democratic Party organization. Johnson also was informed that reform forces in the states were creating "a new ball game with new rules." These memos indicated that the exploitation of a weakened party apparatus by insurgents would allow someone with as little national prominence as antiwar senator Eugene McCarthy to mount a head-on challenge to Johnson.[42] The president expressed his own recognition of the decline of party politics in a private meeting with Humphrey on April 3, 1968, a few days after he announced his decision not to run for reelection. Although indicating his intention to remain publicly neutral, Johnson wished the vice president well. But he expressed concern about Humphrey's ability to win the support of the party organization: "This the president cannot assure the vice president because he could not assure it for himself."[43] Like Roosevelt, Johnson had greatly diminished his political capital in pursuit of programmatic innovation.

Richard Nixon, Nonpartisanship, and the Demise of the Modern Presidency

Considering that the New Deal and Great Society were established by replacing traditional party politics with administration, it is not surprising that when a conservative challenge to liberal reform emerged, it entailed the creation of a conservative "administrative presidency."[44] This development further contributed to the decline of partisan politics.

Until the late 1960s, opponents of the welfare state were generally opposed to the modern presidency, which had served as the fulcrum of liberal reform. Nevertheless, by the end of the Johnson administration it was clear that a strong conservative movement would require an activist program of retrenchment to counteract the enduring effects of the New Deal and Great Society. Opponents of liberal public policy, primarily housed in the Republican Party, decided that, ideologically, the modern presidency could be a two-edged sword.

The administrative actions of the Nixon presidency were a logical extension of the practices of Roosevelt and Johnson. The centralization of authority in the White House and the reduction of the regular Republican organization to perfunctory status during the Nixon years were hardly unprecedented.[45] The complete autonomy of the Committee for the Re-Election of the President (CREEP) from the Republican National Committee (RNC) in the 1972 campaign was but the final stage of a long process of White House preemption of the national committee's political responsibilities. And the administrative reform program that was pursued after Nixon's reelection, in which executive authority was concentrated in the hands of White House operatives and four cabinet "supersecretaries," was the culmination of a long-standing tendency in the modern presidency to reconstitute the executive branch as a formidable and independent instrument of government.[46]

Thus, just as Roosevelt's presidency anticipated the Great Society, Johnson's presidency anticipated the administrative presidency of Richard Nixon. Indeed, the strategy of pursuing policy goals through administrative capacities that had been created for the most part by Democratic presidents was considered especially suitable by a minority Republican president who faced a hostile Congress and bureaucracy intent on preserving those presidents' programs. Nixon actually surpassed previous modern presidents in viewing the party system as an obstacle to effective governance.

Yet, mainly because of the Watergate scandal, Nixon's presidency had the effect of strengthening opposition to the unilateral use of presidential power, even as it further attenuated the bonds that linked presidents to the party system. The evolution of the modern presidency now left the office in complete institutional isolation. This isolation continued during the Ford and Carter years, so much so that by the end of the 1970s scholars were lamenting the demise of the presidency as well as of the party system.

The Reagan Presidency and the Revitalization of Party Politics

The development of the modern presidency fostered a serious decline in the traditional local and patronage-based parties. Yet some developments during the Reagan presidency suggested that a phoenix had emerged from the ashes. The erosion of old-style partisan politics had allowed a more national and issue-oriented party system to develop, forging new links between presidents and their parties.

The Republican Party in particular developed a formidable organizational apparatus, which displayed unprecedented strength at the national level. The refurbishing of the Republican organization was largely due to the efforts of William Brock, who, during his tenure as chair of the RNC from 1976 to 1980, set out to rejuvenate and ultimately to revolutionize the national party. After 1976 the RNC and the two other national Republican campaign bodies, the National Republican Senatorial Committee and the National Republican Congressional (House) Committee, greatly expanded their efforts to raise funds and provide services at the national level for the party's state and local candidates. Moreover, these efforts carried the national party into activities, such as the publication of public policy journals and the distribution of comprehensive briefing books for candidates, that demonstrated its interest in generating programmatic proposals that might be politically useful. The Democrats lagged behind in party-building efforts, but the losses they suffered in the 1980 elections encouraged them to modernize the national political machinery, openly imitating some of the devices used by the Republicans. As a result, the traditional party apparatus, based on patronage and state and local organizations, gave way to a more programmatic party politics, based on the national organization. Arguably, a party system had finally evolved that was compatible with the national polity forged on the anvil of the New Deal.[47]

The revival of the Republican Party as a force to counter government by administration seemed to complete the development of a new American party system. The nomination and election of Ronald Reagan, a far more ideological conservative than Nixon, galvanized the Republican commitment to programs, such as "regulatory relief" and "new federalism," that challenged the institutional legacy of the New Deal. Had such a trend continued into the 1990s, the circumvention of the regular political process by administrative action may well have been displaced by the sort of full-scale debate about political questions usually associated with critical realignments.

Reagan broke with the tradition of the modern presidency and identified closely with his party. The president worked hard to strengthen the Republicans' organizational and popular base, surprising his own political director with his "total readiness" to shoulder partisan responsibilities such as making numerous fund-raising appearances for the party and its candidates.[48] Apparently, after having spent the first fifty years of his life as a Democrat, Reagan brought the enthusiasm of a convert to Republican activities.

The experience of the Reagan administration suggests how the relationship between the president and the party can be mutually beneficial. Republican

Party strength provided Reagan with the support of a formidable institution, solidifying his personal popularity and facilitating the support of his program in Congress. As a result, the Reagan presidency was able to suspend the paralysis that seemed to afflict the executive office in the 1970s, even though the Republicans still lacked control of the House of Representatives. In turn, Reagan's popularity served the party by strengthening its fund-raising efforts and promoting a shift in voters' party loyalties, placing the Republicans by 1985 in a position of virtual parity with the Democrats for the first time since the 1940s.[49] It may be, then, that the 1980s marked the watershed both for a new political era and for a renewed link between presidents and the party system.

In the final analysis, however, the emergence of strong national party organizations in the 1980s could not fundamentally alter the limited possibilities for party government under the U.S. Constitution, a fact that would continue to encourage modern presidents, particularly those intent on ambitious policy reform, to emphasize popular appeals and administrative action rather than "collective responsibility." It is not surprising, therefore, that the Reagan presidency frequently pursued its program with acts of administrative discretion that short-circuited the legislative process and weakened efforts to carry out broadly based party policies. The Iran-contra scandal, for example, was not simply a matter of the president's being asleep on his watch; rather, it also revealed the Reagan administration's determination to assume a more forceful anticommunist posture in Central America in the face of a recalcitrant Congress and bureaucracy.[50]

Sen. Richard Lugar, R-Ind., who as chair of the Foreign Relations Committee from 1985 to 1987 acted as Reagan's Senate floor leader in matters of foreign policy, has said that he considers the Iran-contra affair to have been a "glaring exception" to Reagan's general willingness to consult with Congress and to work closely with the Republican leadership. The irony, according to Lugar, is that this uncharacteristic inattention to partisan responsibility made possible the president's "most signal policy failure."[51]

Yet a close examination of policymaking during the Reagan years provides other examples of the administration's resorting to unilateral executive action. From the start, in fact, the Reagan White House often pursued programmatic change by using the administrative tactics that characterized the Nixon years. Not only was policy centered in the White House Office and other support agencies in the Executive Office of the President, but much care was taken to plant White House loyalists in the departments and agencies—people who could be relied on to ride herd on civil servants and carry forth the president's program. Most significant, a wide range of policies to deregulate business were pursued, not through legislative change but by administrative inaction, delay, and repeal. President Reagan's Executive Orders 12291 and 12498 mandated a comprehensive review of proposed agency regulations and centralized the review process in the Office of Management and Budget (OMB).[52] Reagan also appointed the Task Force on Regulatory Relief, headed by Vice President George Bush, to apply cost-benefit analyses to existing rules. In this light, the Iran-contra scandal may be seen not as an aberration but as an extreme example of how the Reagan administration reacted when it anticipated or was confronted with congressional resistance to its proposals.

Indeed, the importance of presidential politics and executive administration in the Reagan presidency may actually have weakened the prospects for a Republican realignment. Journalist Sidney Blumenthal argued that Reagan "did not reinvent the Republican party so much as transcend it. His primary political instrument was the conservative movement, which inhabited the party out of convenience."[53] Blumenthal's observation is only partly correct—Reagan's commitment to strengthening his party was sincere and, in many respects, effective. Nevertheless, his administration's devotion to certain tenets of conservative ideology led it to rely on unilateral executive action and on the mobilization of conservative citizens groups in a way that ultimately compromised the president's support for the party. "Too many of those around [the president] seem to have a sense of party that begins and ends in the Oval Office," William Brock, then secretary of labor, lamented in 1987. "Too many really don't understand what it means to link the White House to a party in a way that creates an alliance between the presidency, the House, and the Senate, or between the national party and officials at the state and local level."[54] This criticism was echoed by many Republican officials during the final two years of the Reagan presidency.

In sum, Reagan did not transform Washington completely. Rather, he strengthened the Republican beachhead in the nation's capital, solidifying his party's recent dominance of the presidency and providing better opportunities for conservatives in the Washington community. Reagan's landslide reelection in 1984 did not prevent the Democrats from maintaining control of the House of Representatives; nor did his plea to the voters during the 1986 congressional campaign to elect Republican majorities prevent the Democrats from recapturing control of the Senate.

Reagan's two terms witnessed a revitalization of the struggle between the executive and legislative branches; indeed, his conservative program became the foundation for more fundamental philosophical and policy differences between them than in the past. The Iran-contra affair and the battles to control regulatory policy were marked not just by differences between the president and Congress about policy but also by each branch's efforts to weaken the other. The efforts of Republicans to compensate for their inability to control Congress by seeking to circumvent legislative restrictions on presidential conduct were matched by Democratic initiatives to burden the executive with smothering legislative oversight.[55] The opposition to liberal reform, then, did not end in a challenge to national administrative power but in a raw and disruptive battle to control its services.

A major, if not the main, forum for partisan conflict during the Reagan years was a sequence of investigations in which Democrats and Republicans sought to discredit one another. To be sure, the legal scrutiny of public officials was in part a logical response to the Watergate scandal. To prevent another Nixon-style "Saturday Night Massacre," Congress passed the Ethics in Government Act of 1978, which provided for the appointment of independent counsels to investigate allegations of criminal activity by executive officials. Not surprisingly, divided government encouraged the exploitation of the act for partisan purposes. In the 1980s congressional Democrats found themselves in a position to demand criminal investigations and possible jail sentences for their political opponents. When Bill Clinton became president in 1993, congressional Republicans turned the tide with a vengeance. As a consequence, political disagreements were readily transformed into criminal charges. Moreover, investigations under the special prosecutor statute tended to deflect attention from legitimate constitutional policy differences and to focus the attention of Congress, the press, and citizens alike on scandals. Disgrace and imprisonment thus joined electoral defeat as a risk of political combat in the United States.[56]

Reagan's Legacy and the Accession of George H. W. Bush

The 1988 election revealed the limits of the Reagan revolution, reflecting in its outcome the underlying pattern that had characterized American politics since 1968: Republican dominance in the White House, Democratic ascendancy almost everywhere else. In fact, the 1988 election represented an extreme manifestation of this pattern. Never before had a president been elected while the other party gained ground in the House, Senate, the state legislatures, and the state governorships. Never before had voters given a newly elected president fewer fellow partisans in Congress than they gave George H. W. Bush.[57]

Bush's first year as president revealed both his skill as a political conciliator and the continuing obstacles to the restoration of partisanship to the presidency. Facing a Democratic Congress and lacking his predecessor's rhetorical ability, Bush had little choice but to reach across party lines to accomplish his goals. His "kinder, gentler" approach to Congress was often reciprocated during his first year. After intensive negotiations, Bush managed to reach agreements with Congress on two of the most troublesome issues he faced on taking office—aid to the contra rebels in Nicaragua and the crisis of the savings and loan industry. The president won high marks from many legislators for his give-and-take approach to domestic and foreign policy, as well as for the personal attention he paid to the political needs of Democrats and Republicans alike.

In many ways, however, Bush's conciliatory approach camouflaged an aggressive partisanship aimed at extending the political effects of the Reagan revolution beyond the presidency. Having served as a Republican county chair in Texas during the 1960s and as RNC chair during the Watergate scandal (the first president ever to have served as national party chair), Bush came to the White House with a zest for his partisan duties. He not only continued Reagan's practice of campaigning for fellow Republicans and of raising funds for the regular party apparatus, but also he gave his party's national organization a higher profile than any modern president. Bush placed his principal political adviser, Lee Atwater, not in the White House—the usual practice of modern presidents—but in the national party chair.[58]

With the president's approval Atwater did not confine himself to the customary role of presiding over the party's institutions. Instead, he sought to transform the RNC into an aggressive political organization that would highlight the differences between Republicans and Democrats on economic, social, and foreign policy issues at every level of government. Atwater's combative partisanship provided balance to a presidency that otherwise preferred consultation and compromise to confrontation.

Yet the Bush administration's efforts to consolidate and extend the Republican gains of the Reagan years were not successful. In the final analysis, the failure of this objective can be explained by fundamental disagreements between liberals and conservatives that defied Bush's efforts to forge a more inclusive Republican Party. In fall 1990 a serious intraparty struggle developed over the 1991 budget. Seeking to work out a compromise with the Democratic congressional leadership, Bush accepted a fiscal package that included excise tax hikes on gasoline and home heating oil. In turn, the Democratic leadership agreed to cut Medicare spending. The deal left liberal Democrats and conservative

Republicans furious. Especially strong resistance arose in the House, where the Democratic opposition abhorred the Medicare cuts and the regressive nature of the new taxes, and many Republicans, led by Minority Whip Newt Gingrich, felt betrayed by Bush's willingness to abandon his celebrated campaign pledge to oppose new taxes.[59]

At the urging of Democratic and Republican supporters of the tax agreement, Bush went on television to try to sell the package to the American people. This speech was the president's first attempt to mobilize public opinion to pressure Congress; it was a dismal failure. Despite Bush's rhetorical appeal and feverish administration lobbying efforts on Capitol Hill, a majority of House Republicans followed Gingrich in opposing the compromise, dooming it to defeat. The subsequent budget agreement that passed the House and the Senate included a hike in the tax rate on high-income taxpayers, a proposal that Bush had bitterly opposed. The agreement passed with the support of Democratic majorities, but most Republicans in Congress voted against it.[60]

The bitter feud over the 1991 budget left the Republican Party in a state of disarray during the 1990 midterm election campaign. Bush's offers to help his fellow partisans were spurned by some candidates who could not forgive the president for reneging on his "no new taxes" pledge. Conservatives believed that Bush had abandoned not only a sacred pledge but also the party's best hope of winning a majority in the House and Senate. The budget debacle obscured the differences between the parties, undercutting Republican congressional candidates' chances to campaign in 1990 on what they considered the party's most effective issue. Finally, in late October, Bush became embroiled in a feud with the cochair of the Republican Congressional Campaign Committee, Ed Rollins, who circulated a memo urging Republican House candidates not to hesitate to distance their campaigns from the president. This spectacle embarrassed the White House, which pressured Rollins to resign in early 1991. But the damage had been done—Republicans had lost their philosophical compass along with further ground in the House and Senate.[61]

In sum, the closer ties that Reagan and Bush tried to forge between the modern presidency and the Republican Party did not alter the unprecedented partisan and electoral divisions that characterized the era of divided government. Indeed, the persistence of divided government itself retarded the restoration of partisanship to the presidency. During the early days of his presidency, Bush attempted to reach out to Democrats in Congress to restore the badly frayed consensus in American politics. But he gave no reasonable defense of his pragmatism. Once he abandoned his antitax pledge, Bush's presidency floated adrift. His search for agreement with Congress in the absence of any clear principles threatened the modern presidency with the same sort of isolation and weakness that had characterized the Ford and Carter years.[62]

Bill Clinton and the Politics of Divided Democracy

The 1992 election contained both optimistic and pessimistic portents for the modern presidency. The Democrats ran an effective campaign; the party not only captured the presidency but also preserved its majorities in the House and Senate, ending twelve years of divided rule in American politics. Indeed, Bill Clinton's victory over Bush seemed to represent more than a rejection of the incumbent president; in part, it expressed the voters' hope that the institutional conflict they had witnessed during the era of divided government would now come to an end.[63] This hope was encouraged by Clinton's promise to govern as a "new Democrat," as an "agent of change" who would restore consensus to American politics.

Nevertheless, the strong support for independent candidate H. Ross Perot reflected the continuing erosion of partisan loyalties in the electorate. Indeed, Perot's campaign, which garnered 19 percent of the popular vote (the most serious electoral challenge to the two-party system since Theodore Roosevelt's 1912 Progressive Party campaign), suggested just how much presidential politics had been emancipated from the constraints of party. Perot, a successful businessman, had never held political office of any kind, and his campaign, dominated by thirty-minute "infommercials" and hour-long appearances on talk shows, set a new standard for direct, plebiscitary appeals that threatened to sound the death knell of the party campaign. "Perot hints broadly at an even bolder new order," historian Alan Brinkley wrote in July 1992, "in which the president, checked only by direct expressions of popular desire, will roll up his sleeves and solve the nation's problems."[64]

In the end, however, the American people invested their hope for constructive change more cautiously, in the possibility that Clinton embodied a new form of Democratic politics that could correct and renew the progressive tradition as shaped by the New Deal. During the mid-1980s, Clinton had headed the Democratic Leadership Council (DLC), a group of party moderates who developed many of the ideas that became the central themes of his run for the presidency. As Clinton declared frequently during the campaign, these ideas represented a new philosophy of government, a "new covenant" that in the name of responsibility and community would seek to constrain the demands for economic rights that had been unleashed by the New Deal. The essence of Clinton's message was that the long-standing liberal commitment to guaranteeing economic welfare through entitlement programs such as Social Security, Medicare, Medicaid, and Aid to Families with Dependent Children had gone too far. The main objective of the new covenant was to correct the tendency of Americans to celebrate individual rights and government entitlements without acknowledging the mutual obligations they had to each other and to their country.[65]

Clinton pledged to dedicate his party to the new concept of justice he espoused. But his commitment to control government spending and recast the welfare state was obscured during the early days of his presidency by many traditional liberal actions. No sooner had he been inaugurated than Clinton announced his intention to lift the long-standing ban on homosexuals in the military. The president soon learned, however, the difficulty of resolving such a divisive social issue through "the stroke of a pen." To be sure, the development of the administrative presidency gave chief executives more power to exercise domestic policy autonomously. Yet with the expansion of national administration to issues that shaped the direction and character of American public life, this power proved to be illusory.[66]

Most damaging for Clinton was that the issue became a symbol of his inability to revitalize progressive politics as an instrument to redress the economic insecurity and political alienation of the middle class. The bitter partisan fight in the summer of 1993 over the administration's budget served only to reinforce doubts about Clinton's ability to lead the nation in a new, more harmonious direction. Even though his budget plan promised to reduce the deficit, it involved new taxes and an array of social programs that Republicans and conservative Democrats perceived as standard "tax and spend" liberalism. In August 1993 Congress enacted a modified version of the plan, albeit by a razor-thin margin and without any support from Republicans, who voted unanimously against it in the House and Senate. Clinton won this narrow, bruising victory only after promising moderate Democrats that he would put together another package of spending cuts in the fall. But this uneasy compromise failed to dispel the charge of his political opponents that Clinton was a wolf in sheep's clothing—a conventional liberal whose commitment to reform had expired at the end of the presidential campaign.[67]

The apologetic stance that Clinton displayed in the face of traditional liberal causes was, to a point, understandable; it was a logical response to the modern institutional separation between the presidency and the party. The moderate wing of the party that he represented—including the DLC—was a minority wing. The majority of liberal interest group activists and Democratic members of Congress still preferred "entitlements" to "obligations" and "regulations" to "responsibilities." The media-driven caucuses and primaries, a legacy of the McGovern-Fraser reforms, had given him the opportunity to seize the Democratic label as an outsider candidate, but they offered no means to effect a transformation of his party when he took office. To bring about the new mission of progressivism that he advocated during the election, Clinton would have had to risk a brutal confrontation with the major powers in the Democratic Party.[68]

No president had risked such a confrontation with his party since Roosevelt's failed purge campaign in 1938. It is not surprising, therefore, that Clinton's allies in the DLC urged him to renew his "credentials as an outsider" by going over the heads of the party leadership in Congress and taking his message directly to the people. The new president could "break gridlock," they argued, only by appealing to the large number of independents in the electorate who had voted for Perot—that is, by "forging new and sometimes bipartisan coalitions around an agenda that moves beyond the polarized left-right debate."[69]

In fall 1993 Clinton took a page from his former DLC associates in his successful campaign to secure congressional approval of the North American Free Trade Agreement (NAFTA) with Canada and Mexico. The fight for NAFTA caused Clinton to defend free enterprise ardently and to oppose the protectionism favored by labor unions, one of the most important constituencies in the national Democratic Party. Clinton's victory owed partly to the support of Republican congressional leadership. No less important was Vice President Al Gore's inspired performance in a debate with Perot, the leading opponent of NAFTA. Gore's optimistic defense of free markets was well received by a large television audience, rousing enough public support for the treaty to persuade a majority of legislators in both houses of Congress to approve it.[70]

But health care, not trade policy, became the defining issue of Clinton's early presidency. The administration's health care proposal promised to "guarantee all Americans a comprehensive package of benefits over the course of an entire lifetime." The formulation of this program appeared to mark the apotheosis of New Deal administrative politics; it was designed by first lady Hillary Rodham Clinton and the president's longtime friend Ira Magaziner behind closed doors. Moreover, it would have created a new government entitlement program and administrative apparatus that signaled the revitalization rather than the reform of the traditional welfare state.[71] Although the administration made conciliatory overtures to the plan's opponents, hoping to forge bipartisan cooperation on Capitol Hill and a broad consensus among the general public, the possibilities for comprehensive reform hinged on settling differences about the appropriate role of government that had divided the parties and the country for the past two decades. In the end, this proved impossible.[72]

By proposing such an ambitious health care reform bill, Clinton angered conservatives. By failing to deliver on his proposal, he dismayed the ardent liberals of his party. Most significant, the defeat of the president's health care program created the overwhelming impression that he had not lived up to his campaign promise to transcend the bitter philosophical and partisan battles of the Reagan and Bush years.

Clinton and his party paid dearly for this failure in the 1994 midterm elections. The Republicans gained fifty-two seats in the House and eight in the Senate, taking control of Congress. Moreover, they won dramatic victories at the state and local levels: Republicans increased their share of governorships to thirty, their first majority since 1970; they also approached parity in state legislatures, a status they had not enjoyed since 1968. The Republicans achieved this victory in an off-year campaign that was unusually partisan and ideological, thanks largely to the remarkable ascent of Newt Gingrich. Having fought against Bush's efforts to soften the hard edges of the Reagan revolution, Gingrich now positioned himself to fulfill its failed promise—to get government off the backs of the American people. Gingrich, his party's choice to be the new Speaker of the 104th Congress, persuaded more than three hundred House candidates to sign a Republican Contract with America, a "covenant" with the nation that promised to rein in government by eliminating programs, ameliorating regulatory burdens, and cutting taxes. Clinton's attack on the Republican program during the campaign seemed to backfire, serving only to abet Republicans in their effort to highlight the president's failure to reinvent government.[73]

The dramatic Republican triumph in the 1994 midterm election brought back divided government and with it the institutional confrontation that Clinton had promised to resolve. Indeed, the first session of the 104th Congress quickly degenerated into the same sort of administrative politics that had corroded the legitimacy of political institutions in the United States since Nixon's presidency. This time, however, the struggle between the branches assumed a novel form: institutional confrontation between a Democratic White House and a Republican Congress.

The battle between Clinton and Congress became especially fierce over legislation to balance the budget. More than any idea celebrated in the Contract with America, Republicans believed that a balanced budget bill would give them their best opportunity to control Congress for years to come. The most controversial part of the GOP's program was a proposal to scale back the growth of Medicare, a federal health insurance program for the elderly and disabled, by encouraging beneficiaries to enroll in health maintenance organizations and other private, managed health care systems. Rallied by their militant partisan members in the House, Republicans sought to pressure Clinton to accept their budget priorities by twice shutting down government offices and even threatening to force the U.S. Treasury into default. These confrontation tactics backfired. Clinton's veto of a sweeping budget bill in December 1995, which not only would have overhauled Medicare but also remade decades of federal social policy, roused popular support for the administration. In attacking Medicare and Democratic social policy, such as environmental programs, the Republicans' militant assault on programmatic liberalism went beyond what was promised by the Contract with America and gave Clinton the opportunity to take a political stand that most of the country supported.

When Congress returned for the second session of the 104th Congress in January 1996, it was not to Speaker Gingrich's agenda of reducing the role of Washington in the society and economy but to the measured tones of Clinton's third State of the Union message. The president, having outmaneuvered the Republican Congress, now co-opted its most popular theme, declaring "the era of big government is over."[74] This was not merely a rhetorical flourish. Withstanding furious criticism from liberal members of Congress and interest group activists, Clinton signed welfare reform legislation in August that replaced the existing entitlement to cash payments for low-income mothers and their dependent children with temporary assistance and a strict work requirement.[75] Clinton conceded that the act was flawed, cutting too deeply into nutritional support for low-income working people and denying support unfairly to legal immigrants. Nevertheless, by requiring welfare recipients to take jobs, it served the fundamental principle Clinton championed in the 1992 campaign of "recreating the Nation's social bargain with the poor."[76]

Warning that "we cannot go back to the time when our citizens were left to fend for themselves," however, Clinton called for a halt to Republican assaults on popular liberal programs dedicated to providing economic security, educational opportunity, and environmental protection.[77] Using DNC funds, the White House had orchestrated a national media blitz toward the end of 1995 that excoriated the Republicans' program to reform Medicare and presented the president as a figure of national reconciliation who favored welfare reform and a balanced budget but who also would protect middle-class entitlements, education, and the environment.[78] Clinton's carefully modulated State of the Union message underscored this media campaign, revealing the president as a would-be healer eager to bring all sides together.

Throughout the 1996 election campaign, Clinton held firmly to the centrist ground he had staked out after the 1994 elections, campaigning on the same "new" Democratic themes of "opportunity, responsibility, and community" that had served him well during his first run for the White House. He won 49 percent of the popular vote to the Republican nominee Robert Dole's 41 percent and Perot's 8 percent, and 379 electoral votes to Dole's 159.

Clinton was the first Democratic president since FDR to be elected to a second term, but his candidate-centered campaign, abetted by a strong economy, did little to help his party. The Democrats lost two seats in the Senate and gained only a modest nine seats in the House and thus failed to regain control of either chamber. In truth, Clinton's campaign testified to the fragility of the nationalized party system that arose during the 1980s. The president's remarkable political comeback in 1995 was supported by so-called soft money that was designated for party-building activities and not covered by campaign finance laws.[79] These funds were used mostly to mount television advertising campaigns that championed the president's independence from partisan squabbles. Indeed, Clinton scarcely endorsed the election of a Democratic Congress in 1996; moreover, he raised funds for the party's congressional candidates only late in the campaign. Adding insult to injury, the administration's controversial fund-raising methods led to revelations during the final days of the election that reduced Clinton's margin of victory and undermined the Democrats' effort to retake the House.[80]

Clinton's wayward effort to forge a "third way" is suggestive of the modern presidency's dominant but uneasy place in contemporary American politics. The disjuncture between the bitter partisanship within the Capitol and the weakening of partisan affiliation outside of it won Clinton—along with his skill in combining doctrines—a certain following in the country.[81] His gift for forging compromise was displayed in May 1997, when the White House and the Republican leadership agreed on a tentative plan to balance the budget by 2002. In part, this uneasy deal was made possible by a revenue windfall caused by the robust economy, which enabled the negotiators to avoid the sort of hard choices over program cuts and taxes that had animated the bitter struggles of the 104th Congress.[82] Even so, this rapprochement, which brought about the first balanced budget in three decades, testified to the potential of modern presidents to advance principles and pursue policies that defy the sharp cleavages characteristic of the nationalized party system.

Yet as the House impeachment and Senate trial of Clinton dramatically revealed, the "extraordinary isolation" of the modern presidency has its limits.[83] Hoping to become a great president in the tradition of Franklin Roosevelt, Clinton became the first elected president to be impeached by the House of Representatives. (Andrew Johnson, the only other president to suffer such an indignity, inherited the executive office after Lincoln was assassinated.)

Just as Reagan and Bush were plagued by independent counsels who investigated abuses in their administrations under the authority of the Ethics in Government Act, so did Clinton have troubles of his own with independent counsels.[84] In early January 1998 Kenneth Starr was authorized to expand the scope of the Whitewater inquiry to pursue allegations that the president had an affair with a White House intern, Monica Lewinsky, and that at Clinton's urging his close associate Vernon Jordan had encouraged Lewinsky to lie under oath about the matter. Remarkably, as the Lewinsky scandal unfolded throughout 1998, the public continued to express overwhelming approval of Clinton's performance in office, especially his management of the economy. In addition, the public generally disapproved of Starr's tenacious investigation into Clinton's peccadilloes and the eagerness with which the Republican-controlled Congress exploited the results. Nevertheless, Clinton paid dearly; many, although sympathetic, appeared to lose all confidence in his ability to provide moral leadership. Voters distinguished sharply between Clinton, the chief executive, of whom they approved, and Clinton, the man, whom they regarded as immoral and untrustworthy.[85]

With the decline of Clinton's personal stature, nearly every political expert predicted that the Republicans would emerge from the 1998 elections with a tighter grip on Congress and, by implication, on the president's political fate.[86] But having been preoccupied by the Lewinsky scandal for the entire year, the Republicans were left without an appealing campaign message. They were unable to increase their 55–45 majority in the Senate and lost five seats in the House, leaving them with a slim 223–211 majority. Just as Clinton was the first Democrat since FDR to be reelected, so did he now become the first president since Roosevelt in 1934 to see his party gain seats in a midterm election. Bitterly disappointed by the results, the Republicans fell into soul-searching and recriminations. Ironically, it was Gingrich, the hero of their 1994 ascent to power, and not Clinton, who was forced from office. After the elections, Gingrich announced that he was giving up not only his leadership position but also his seat in Congress.

Clinton's job was safe. But whatever authority the president had at the beginning of his administration to establish a new covenant of rights and responsibilities between citizens and their government was shattered by the public disrespect for his morality. Indeed, the virulent partisanship that characterized the impeachment process forced Clinton to seek fellowship among his fellow Democrats in Congress and to abandon plans to pursue entitlement reform as the capstone of his presidency.[87] In the wake of the impeachment debacle, Clinton positioned himself as the champion of Social Security and Medicare, urging Congress to invest a significant share of the mounting budget surplus in these traditional liberal programs.[88] Clinton's extraordinary resilience, it seemed, was achieved at the cost of failure to fulfill his promise to correct and renew the progressive tradition.

The 2000 Election, September 11, and Beyond: George W. Bush and the Modern Presidency

The political realignment of the 1930s established the president, rather than party organizations or Congress, as the principal agent of popular rule. But recent history shows that it may be unreasonable, even dangerous, to rely so heavily on presidents to determine the contours of national political action. As the sensational media treatment of the Lewinsky scandal revealed, the modern presidency operates in a political arena that is seldom congenial to meaningful political debate and that all too often is guilty of deflecting attention from painful but necessary struggles about the relative merits of contemporary liberalism and contemporary conservatism. With the rise of the mass media and the liberation of the executive from many of the constraints of party leadership, presidents have resorted to rhetoric and administration, tools with which they have sought to forge new, more personal ties with the public. But as the nation has witnessed all too clearly since the 1960s, this form of populist presidential politics can too easily degenerate into rank opportunism. Moreover, it risks exposing the people to the sort of public figures who will exploit popular impatience with the difficult tasks involved in sustaining a healthy constitutional democracy.

The 2000 election testified to the growing weaknesses of American democracy. Neither the Democratic nominee, Vice President Gore, nor the Republican,

Governor Bush of Texas, took positions that suggested a way out of the fractious state of American politics. Instead, both candidates took centrist pragmatic positions during the general election campaign that were designed to shore up the principal programs of the welfare state. The activists of the Democratic and Republican Parties differed starkly on issues such as abortion and the environment, reflecting their fundamental disagreements about the role of government and the relationship between church and state. But the two candidates sought to distance themselves from their parties, seeking a strategic center between Democratic liberalism and Republican conservatism. The election ended in a virtual tie, a deadlock ultimately resolved by the Supreme Court. Even the conclusion to the election failed to arouse popular passions. The controversy bitterly divided policy activists, but not the American people, many of whom, following the recent pattern of low turnout elections and public indifference toward politics, had stayed away from the polls.

Bush's presidency began inauspiciously. Bush started out with Republicans in control of Congress, albeit by the narrowest of margins. Indeed, the Senate was evenly split between Democrats and Republicans, with Vice President Richard Cheney breaking the tie. But, like Clinton at the beginning of his administration, Bush chose to cooperate with his party's strongly ideological leaders in the legislature. Like Clinton, too, Bush may have preferred to solidify the base support of his party before reaching out to independent voters. The president's emphasis on traditional conservative issues such as tax cuts, regulatory relief, energy production, and missile defense risked alienating moderate Republicans, a dwindling, but pivotal group in the closely divided House and Senate. The president and his party paid dearly for this risk in May 2001, when Sen. James Jeffords of Vermont announced that he was transferring his allegiance from the Republican to the Democratic caucus, giving control of the Senate to the Democrats.[89]

Facing the prospect of partisan obstruction in the Senate, the Bush administration intensified its efforts to consolidate political and policy responsibility within the White House. In serving the first President Bush, Lee Atwater had gone to the RNC rather than the White House, helping to sustain for a time the status and independence of the national party organization. In contrast, George W. Bush's top political consultant, Karl Rove, became a top White House adviser, assuming political responsibility that undercut the power of RNC head James S. Gilmore III, then the governor of Virginia. Politics was joined to policy as Rove sought to position the president for late 2001 as a nontraditional Republican. By the end of his first summer in the White House, Bush was prepared to stress education and values, not taxes and defense.[90]

At its best, Clinton's "third way" sought consensus for a limited but energetic national government. All too often, however, this approach degenerated into a politics of expediency that substituted polls and focus groups for leadership. Bush's "compassionate conservatism" seemed to have the same strengths and weaknesses as Clinton's "new covenant." Indeed, Bush's campaign speeches, proclaiming the values of "responsibility," "community," and "education," bore a striking resemblance to Clinton's rhetoric during the 1992 and 1996 elections. And the Bush administration programs that embodied these values—especially his reform proposals for education, social services, and welfare—invoked many of the ideas incubated in the DLC that gave rise to Clinton's policy initiatives.[91]

To be sure, important differences between Clinton and Bush can be identified. Clinton never made clear how his third-way politics would serve the core principles of the Democratic Party; in fact, Clinton and the DLC were highly ambivalent, if not avowedly hostile, to partisanship. But Bush embraced "compassionate conservatism." His rhetoric and policy proposals, Rove argued, were a deliberate attempt to play to conservative values, but not in a way that was reflexively antigovernment.[92] Bush's call for substantial tax cuts appealed to the right's hostility toward government, but the president acknowledged, columnist E. J. Dionne observed, "that most people do not draw meaning from the marketplace alone, and that the marketplace is not the sole test or most important source of virtue."[93] "The invisible hand works many miracles," Bush said in July 1999. "But it cannot touch the human heart. . . . We are a nation of rugged individuals. But we are also the country of the second chance—tied together by bonds of friendship and community and solidarity."[94]

In part, this moral commitment would be served by empowering nonmarket institutions that worked outside of government. For example, Bush proposed changes in federal and state regulations that would allow private "faith-based" organizations to play a larger role in providing government social services to the poor. The national government would have an important role to play in sustaining moral values as well. Although conservatives once talked of eliminating the Department of Education, Bush proposed that the nation's public schools be made more accountable to the department by linking federal aid to secondary and elementary schools to national standards of student learning. Social conservatives had long sought to advance morality by opposing abortion. Bush professed to be staunchly "pro-life," but he called for a more "incremental" attack on abortion. More important, he proposed to associate conservative religious values with an affirmative government responsibility to help the poor, promote marriage, and ensure that "every child will be educated."[95]

Bush-style "compassionate conservatism" promised to soften the harsh antigovernment edge of the Republican Party. It also appeared to give the president a platform to act independently of his party. Programs such as faith-based initiatives and educational reform were not pursued within Republican councils. Rather, as has been the custom since the development of the modern presidency, the White House pursued these objectives through executive orders and bipartisan cooperation.[96] The education bill particularly seemed less a use of government to serve conservative principles than it did an uneasy compromise between liberal demands for more spending and conservative insistence on standards. Bush trumpeted his alliance with the liberal Democratic icon, Sen. Edward M. Kennedy, in passing education reform legislation.

No less than the third way, then, compassionate conservatism promised to transcend the long-standing contest in American politics between the righteous claims of entitlement and the virtues of individual responsibility. As Bush noted in February 2001, in his first major address to Congress and the nation, "Our new governing vision says government should be active, but limited, engaged but not overbearing." Bush's rhetorical but vague pragmatism showed the same tendency as Clinton's to deflect the country's attention from hard choices. Bush denied, for instance, that the American people needed to choose between a $1.5 trillion tax cut and a laundry list of programs, including the same middle-class entitlements that Democrats championed.[97]

Similarly, Bush's first prime-time televised address to the nation on a specific issue—stem cell research—represented a serious but awkward effort to satisfy all sides. Many religious conservatives viewed stem cell research as a form of abortion that violated the rights of the unborn. Even Pope John Paul II had offered his counsel when President Bush visited the Vatican a few weeks before his August 2001 address. "A free and virtuous society, which America aspires to be, must reject practices that devalue and violate human life at any stage from conception, until natural death," the pontiff lectured the president during their meeting.[98] But most Americans, including a majority of Roman Catholics, supported stem cell research, viewing it as a matter of scientific progress toward better health care that was beyond the church's jurisdiction.

Bush's remarks tried to bridge the two sides of the debate. In a solution that the president characterized as careful and prayerful—but detractors dismissed as clumsy and calculating—he announced that federal grants could be used to conduct studies on stem cells that already had been extracted from embryos left over at fertility clinics. But he prohibited federal support of research that involved the creation or destruction of additional embryos. By splitting the difference on this moral issue, the president's critics complained, Bush had obscured rather than illuminated the proper role of the national government in protecting life and health.[99]

More to the point, Bush's attempt to resolve the stem cell controversy highlighted the tension between the modern executive and popular sovereignty. The rules governing stem cell research will continue to be debated within the Washington community, but it is doubtful that the stem cell controversy will arouse much attention from those outside the nation's capital. After all, if public debate is truly required, why should the issue be resolved by a lone executive and administered by unelected bureaucrats? Arguably, democracy requires public debate and resolution that is better done by numerous and representative assemblies, namely Congress and the state legislatures.

The Bush administration's policy came in the form of an executive order, which delegated ultimate authority for overseeing stem cell research to the new President's Council on Bioethics. The delegation of policy responsibility to "monitor stem cell research, to recommend appropriate guidelines and regulations, and to consider all the medical and ethical ramifications of biomedical innovation" to an administrative board confirmed in important respects the legacy of the New Deal and the modern presidency—namely, a more active and better-equipped national state but one without adequate means for common deliberation and public judgment.[100]

The president's attention shifted dramatically away from issues such as abortion and stem cell research when the United States was attacked on September 11, 2001. In the aftermath of the first attack on the American continent since the War of 1812, and the most deadly in the nation's history, the country appeared to unite overnight. Citizens gave generously to relief funds to aid the families of those who lost their lives. The American flag was unfurled everywhere, and patriotic hymns, especially, "God Bless America," were sung repeatedly. Polls showed a remarkable jump in support for Bush, and a strong consensus formed behind his military response to the terrorist assault.

Some skeptics predicted that this national unity would dissolve once partisan bickering began in Congress over how the government should stimulate the economy, which was showing signs of decline before September 11 and seemed likely to be weakened by the catastrophic events of that day. In the short term, however, the war on terrorism strengthened the modern presidency and greatly tempered the polarized partisanship that had held it hostage during the previous three decades. Hardly a discouraging word was heard when the Bush administration created an Office of Homeland Security, imposed tighter restrictions on airports, and embraced deficit spending to ease the economic disruptions caused by the terrorist attacks. Accustomed to seeking the middle ground between liberal compassion and conservative disdain for government, Bush found himself justifying the war against terrorism in words that echoed Franklin Roosevelt. "Freedom and fear are at war," Bush told a joint session of Congress on September 20. "The advance of human freedom—the great achievement of our time, and great hope of every time—now depends on us. Our nation—this generation—will lift a dark threat of violence from our people and our future. We will rally the world to this cause by our efforts, by our courage."[101]

Nearly a century ago, the philosopher William James wrote that progressives were obliged to search for "the moral equivalent of war." One possible solution, he suggested, was to conscript youth into a national service corps, in which "they might get the childishness knocked out of them" and "come back into society with healthier sympathies and soberer ideas."[102] Since John F. Kennedy, presidents have been attracted to the idea of national service; indeed, Bill Clinton viewed it as one of the defining elements of his "new covenant." But Clinton's community service program, which led to the creation of Americorps, fell far short of James's ambitious proposal.[103]

The remarkable and horrific events of September 11 renewed hope among public intellectuals and government officials that a moral substitute for war could be found. In February 2002, in his first State of the Union address, Bush called on Americans not to let pass the patriotism aroused by the war against terrorism. He urged them to embrace "a new ethic and a new creed," and "to commit at least two years—4,000 hours over a lifetime—to the service of your nation."[104] Yet this plea for national service was preceded, indeed, overshadowed by the president's warning that "our war against terror is only beginning."[105] Such a sober call to arms, preparing the country for a protracted struggle against an elusive and seemingly implacable enemy, inevitably raised the intriguing and troubling possibility that there may not be a moral equivalent of war in the modern administrative state.

Notes

1. For a more detailed treatment of the issues discussed in this chapter, see Sidney M. Milkis, *The President and the Parties: The Transformation of the American Party System Since the New Deal* (New York: Oxford University Press, 1993); and Sidney

M. Milkis, *Political Parties and Constitutional Government: Remaking American Democracy* (Baltimore: Johns Hopkins University Press, 1999).

2. Franklin D. Roosevelt, *Public Papers and Addresses*, 13 vols. (New York: Random House, 1938–1950), 1:751–756.

3. Ibid., 752.

4. Woodrow Wilson, *Constitutional Government in the United States* (New York: Columbia University Press, 1908), 68–69.

5. Arthur S. Link, "Woodrow Wilson and the Democratic Party," *Review of Politics* 18 (April 1956): 146–156. Wilson effectively established himself as the principal spokesperson for the Democratic Party. But he accepted traditional partisan practices concerning legislative deliberations and appointments to gain support for his program in Congress, thus failing to strengthen either the Democratic Party's national organization or its fundamental commitment to progressive principles. After 1914, Wilson embraced many elements of progressive democracy, such as the direct leadership of public opinion, national administration of commercial activity, and civil service reform. But this conversion to advanced progressivism only exposed the yawning gap between, on the one hand, Wilson's pretense to serving as a national progressive leader, and, on the other hand, his allegiance to a decentralized and patronage-based party. See Daniel Stid, *The President as Statesman: Woodrow Wilson and the Constitution* (Lawrence: University Press of Kansas, 1998), esp. chaps. 6, 8.

6. *Personal and Political Diary of Homer Cummings*, January 5, 1933, box 234, no. 2, 90, Homer Cummings Papers (no. 9973), Manuscripts Department, University of Virginia Library, Charlottesville.

7. Edward J. Flynn, *You're the Boss* (New York: Viking, 1947), 153.

8. Alfred Phillips Jr. to Franklin D. Roosevelt, June 9, 1937; and Roosevelt to Phillips, June 16, 1937, President's Personal File, 2666, Franklin D. Roosevelt Library, Hyde Park, New York.

9. Franklin Clarkin, "Two-Thirds Rule Facing Abolition," *New York Times*, January 5, 1936, IV 10.

10. Thomas Stokes, *Chip Off My Shoulder* (Princeton: Princeton University Press, 1940), 503. For an assessment of Roosevelt's role in the abolition of the two-thirds rule that also addresses the significance of this party reform, see Harold F. Bass Jr., "Presidential Party Leadership and Party Reform: Franklin D. Roosevelt and the Abrogation of the Two-Thirds Rule" (paper presented at the annual meeting of the Southern Political Science Association, Nashville, Tennessee, November 7–9, 1985).

11. Raymond Clapper, "Roosevelt Tries the Primaries," *Current History*, October 1938, 16.

12. Morton Frisch, *Franklin D. Roosevelt: The Contribution of the New Deal to American Political Thought and Practice* (Boston: S. T. Wayne, 1975), 79.

13. Frankfurter to Roosevelt, August 9, 1937, box 210, Papers of Thomas G. Corcoran; Roosevelt to Frankfurter, August 12, 1937, reel 60, Felix Frankfurter Papers; both in Manuscript Division, Library of Congress, Washington, D.C.

14. Herbert Croly, a fellow Progressive, criticized Wilson's concept of presidential party leadership along these lines. Although he shared Wilson's view that executive power needed to be strengthened, Croly argued that the "necessity of such leadership [was] itself evidence of the decrepitude of the two-party system." A strong executive would not reform parties but instead would establish the conditions in which partisan responsibility would decline and a more direct and palpable link between the president and public opinion would be created. The emergence of a modern executive and the

destruction of the two-party system, Croly wrote, "was an indispensable condition of the success of progressive democracy." *Progressive Democracy* (New York: Macmillan, 1914), 345, 348.

15. The purge campaign galvanized opposition throughout the nation, apparently contributing to the heavy losses the Democrats sustained in the 1938 general elections.

16. The term "second bill of rights" comes from Roosevelt's 1944 State of the Union message, which reaffirmed the New Deal's commitment to an economic constitutional order. Roosevelt, *Public Papers and Addresses*, 13:40.

17. *Report of the President's Committee on Administrative Management* (Washington, D.C.: U.S. Government Printing Office, 1937), 53. This committee, headed by Louis Brownlow, played a central role in the planning and politics of executive reorganization from 1936 to 1940. For a full analysis of the commission, see Barry Karl, *Executive Reorganization and Reform in the New Deal* (Cambridge: Harvard University Press, 1963).

18. Memorandum, "Extending the Competitive Classified Civil Service," Herbert Emmerich to Louis Brownlow, June 29, 1938; and Civil Service Commission, statement regarding executive order of June 24, 1938, extending the merit system; both in *Papers of the President's Committee on Administrative Management,* Roosevelt Library; see also Richard Polenberg, *Reorganizing Roosevelt's Government* (Cambridge: Harvard University Press, 1966), 22–23, 184. With the passage of the Ramspeck Act in 1940, this convulsive movement to reshape the civil service was virtually completed. The Ramspeck Act authorized the president to extend the merit system to nearly 200,000 positions previously exempted by law, many of them occupied by supporters of the New Deal. Roosevelt took early advantage of this authorization in 1941. By executive order he extended the coverage of the civil service protection to include about 95 percent of the permanent service. Leonard White, "Franklin Roosevelt and the Public Service," *Public Personnel Review* 6 (July 1945): 142.

19. Paul Van Riper, *History of the United States Civil Service* (Evanston, Ill.: Row, Peterson, 1958), 327. The merging of politics and administration took an interesting course as a result of the 1939 Hatch Act. Until passage of this bill, which barred most federal employees from participating in campaigns, the Roosevelt administration made use of the growing army of federal workers in state and local political activity, including some of the purge campaigns. Even though the Hatch Act curtailed Roosevelt's ability to continue these activities, the president signed the legislation. He was more interested in orienting the executive branch as an instrument of programmatic reform than he was in developing a national political machine, and the insulation of federal officials from party politics was not incompatible with such a task.

20. The task of communicating with the public encouraged FDR and those who staffed the newly created Executive Office of the President to make use of surveys. With the help of the respected pollster, Hadley Cantril, the Roosevelt administration learned that the American people viewed the idea of "second bill of rights" favorably. Oscar Cox to Hadley Cantril, May 3, 1943; Hadley Cantril to Oscar Cox, April 30, 1943; Memorandum, Hadley Cantril to David Niles, James Barnes, and Oscar Ewing, April 30, 1943; "Public Opinion: The NRPB Report and Social Security, Office of Public Opinion Research, April 28, 1943. Roosevelt Library, Oscar Cox Papers, Box 100, Lend-Lease Files. On the Roosevelt administration's use of polls, see Robert Eisenger and Jeremy Brown, "Polling as a Means Toward Presidential Autonomy: Emil Hurja, Hadley Cantril and the Roosevelt Administration," *International Journal of Public Opinion Research* 10 (1998):

239–256; and Theodore Lowi, *The Personal President: Power Invested, Promise Unfulfilled* (Ithaca: Cornell University Press, 1985), 62–66.

21. Roosevelt, *Public Papers and Addresses*, vol. 9, 671–672.

22. Richard A. Rovere, "A Man for This Age Too," *New York Times Magazine*, April 11, 1965, 118. For an account of the influence of Roosevelt and the New Deal on Johnson's presidency, see William E. Leuchtenburg, *In the Shadow of FDR: From Harry Truman to Ronald Reagan*, rev. ed. (Ithaca: Cornell University Press, 1985), chap. 4; and Milkis, *President and the Parties*, chaps. 7 and 8.

23. Lyndon Baines Johnson, *The Vantage Point: Perspectives of the Presidency, 1963–1969* (New York: Holt, Rinehart and Winston, 1971), 323.

24. Theodore White, *The Making of the President, 1968* (New York: Atheneum, 1969), 107.

25. Rowland Evans and Robert Novak, "Too Late for LBJ," *Boston Globe*, December 21, 1966, 27.

26. David Broder, "Consensus Politics: End of an Experiment," *Atlantic Monthly*, October 1966, 62.

27. Doris Kearns, *Lyndon Johnson and the American Dream* (New York: New American Library, 1976), 256.

28. In a memorandum on one of the early strategy sessions that led to the Great Society, Larry O'Brien, Johnson's chief legislative aide, expressed concern about the acute political problems he anticipated would result from such an ambitious program. Memorandum, Larry O'Brien to Henry Wilson, November 24, 1964, Henry Wilson Papers, box 4, Lyndon Baines Johnson Library, Austin, Texas.

29. Interview with Horace Busby, June 25, 1987.

30. Memorandum, William Connel to Marvin Watson, August 27, 1967, Marvin Watson Files, box 31; Memorandum, Joseph Califano to the president, March 27, 1968, Office Files of the President (Dorothy Territo), box 10; both in Johnson Library.

31. Memorandum, Harry C. McPherson Jr. and Clifford L. Alexander to the president, February 11, 1967, Office Files of Harry McPherson; Memorandum, Sherwin Markman to the president, February 17,1968, White House Central Files, Subject File, "WE9 (welfare), Exec. February, 1968," Box 38; Sherwin J. Markman, Oral History, by Dorothy Pierce McSweeny, tape 1, May 21, 1969, 24–36; both in Johnson Library. Many local Democrats felt threatened by the community action program with its provision for "maximum feasible participation." See Daniel P. Moynihan, *Maximum Feasible Misunderstanding* (New York: Free Press, 1970), 144–145.

32. William E. Leuchtenburg, "The Genesis of the Great Society," *Reporter*, April 21, 1966, 38.

33. Memorandum, Hayes Redmon to Bill Moyers, May 5, 1966, box 12, Office Files of Bill Moyers, Johnson Library. For an excellent book-length treatment of Johnson's personnel policy, see Richard L. Schott and Dagmar S. Hamilton, *People, Positions, and Power: The Political Appointments of Lyndon Johnson* (Chicago: University of Chicago Press, 1983).

34. Memorandum, James Rowe to John W. Macy Jr., April 28, 1965, John Macy Papers, box 504; James H. Rowe, Oral History, by Joe B. Frantz, interview 2, September 16, 1969, 46–47; both in Johnson Library. Rowe's battles with Macy are noteworthy and ironic: as a charter member of the White House Office, he performed Macy's role for the Roosevelt administration, upholding the principle of merit against the patronage requests of the DNC chair James Farley and his successor, Ed Flynn.

35. On the importance of institutional reform, see Draft Memorandum, Horace Busby to Mr. Johnson, n.d., box 52, folder of memos to Mr. Johnson, June 1964; Busby quote is from Memorandum, Horace Busby for the president, September 21, 1965, box 51, Office Files of Horace Busby, Johnson Library.

36. Terry Moe, "The Politicized Presidency," in *The New Direction in American Politics*, ed. John E. Chubb and Paul E. Peterson (Washington, D.C.: Brookings Institution, 1985), 254.

37. Memorandum, Horace Busby to the president, April 21, 1965, and attached letter from John Macy (April 17, 1965), box 51, Office Files of Horace Busby, Johnson Library; Joseph Young, "Johnson Boost to Career People Called Strongest by a President," *Washington Post,* May 16, 1965; Eugene Patterson, "The Johnson Brand," *Atlanta Constitution,* April 30, 1965; and Raymond P. Brandt, "Johnson Inspires the Civil Service by Appointing His Top Aides from Among Career Officials," *St. Louis Dispatch,* May 2, 1965. For a comprehensive treatment of Johnson's management of the bureaucracy, see James A. Anderson, "Presidential Management of the Bureaucracy and the Johnson Presidency: A Preliminary Exploration," *Congress and the President* 1 (autumn 1984): 137–163.

38. Memorandum, Bill Moyers to the president, December 11, 1965, box 11, Office Files of Bill Moyers, Johnson Library.

39. James Rowe became quite concerned on hearing of the task force proposal. He warned the White House staff that this might further weaken the regular party apparatus, which was "already suffering from shellshock both in Washington and around the country because of its impotent status." James Rowe, "A White Paper for the President on the 1968 Presidential Campaign," n.d., Marvin Watson Files, box 20, folder of Rowe, O'Brien, Cooke, Criswell Operation, Johnson Library.

40. Allan Otten, "The Incumbent's Edge," *Wall Street Journal,* December 28, 1967.

41. Byron E. Shafer, *Quiet Revolution: The Struggle for the Democratic Party and the Shaping of Post-Reform Politics* (New York: Russell Sage Foundation, 1983). In 1969 the DNC, acting under the mandate from the 1968 Chicago Convention, established the Commission on Party Structure and Delegate Selection. Under the chairmanship first of Sen. George McGovern and, after 1971, of Rep. Donald Fraser, the commission developed guidelines for the state parties' selection of delegates to the national conventions. Their purpose was to weaken the prevailing party structure and to establish a more direct link between presidential candidates and the voters. The DNC accepted all the commission's guidelines and declared in the call for the 1972 convention that they constituted the standards that state Democratic Parties, in qualifying and certifying delegates to the 1972 Democratic National Convention, must make "all efforts to comply with." The new rules eventually caused a majority of states to change from selecting delegates in closed councils of party regulars to electing them in direct primaries. Although the Democrats initiated these changes, many were codified in state laws that affected the Republican Party almost as much. For a discussion of the long-term forces underlying the McGovern-Fraser reforms, see David B. Truman, "Party Reform, Party Atrophy, and Constitutional Change," *Political Science Quarterly* 99 (winter 1984–1985): 637–655.

42. Memorandum, John P. Roche for the president, December 4, 1967, White House Central Files, PL (Political Affairs) folder; Memorandum, Ben Wattenberg to the president, December 13, 1967, Marvin Watson Files, box 10; Memorandum, Ben Wattenberg to the president, March 13, 1968, Marvin Watson Files, box 11; all in Johnson Library.

43. Memorandum of conversation, April 5, 1968, White House Famous Names, box 6, Robert F. Kennedy folder, 1968 Campaign, Johnson Library.

44. Richard Nathan, *The Administrative Presidency* (New York: Wiley, 1983).

45. On Nixon's party leadership as president, see the Ripon Society and Clifford Brown, *Jaws of Victory* (Boston: Little, Brown, 1973), 226–242.

46. Nathan, *Administrative Presidency*, 43–56. Toward the end of the Johnson presidency, the administration made an effort to consolidate further the president's control of the activities of the executive branch. Johnson's second task force on government organization—the Heineman task force—made many recommendations in 1967 that formed the basis of the Nixon administrative reform program. For example, it called for the regrouping of executive departments and agencies into a smaller number of "superdepartments" that would be "far more useful and much more responsive to, and representative of, Presidential perspectives and objectives than the scores of parochial department and agency heads who now share the line responsibilities of the executive branch." Johnson favored the Heineman task force's central recommendations and planned to implement some of them after his reelection in 1968, but Johnson's retirement came sooner than expected. Task Force on Government Organization, "The Organization and Management of the Great Society Programs," June 15, 1967, and "A Recommendation for the Future Organization of the Executive Branch," September 15, 1967, both reports located in Outside Task Forces, box 4, Task Force on Government Organization folder, Johnson Library. See also Peri Arnold, *Making the Managerial Presidency: Comprehensive Reorganization Planning, 1905–1980* (Princeton: Princeton University Press, 1986), 268.

47. A. James Reichley, "The Rise of National Parties," in *New Direction in American Politics,* ed. Chubb and Peterson, 191–195. By the end of the 1980s, Reichley was less hopeful that the emergent national parties were well-suited to perform the parties' historic function of mobilizing public support for political values and government policies. See his richly detailed study, *The Life of the Parties: A History of American Political Parties* (New York: Free Press, 1992), esp. chaps. 18–21.

48. Rhodes Cook, "Reagan Nurtures His Adopted Party to Strength," *Congressional Quarterly Weekly Report,* September 28, 1985, 1927–30; David S. Broder, "A Party Leader Who Works at It," *Boston Globe,* October 21, 1985, 14; and personal interview with Mitchell Daniels, assistant to the president for political and governmental affairs, June 5, 1986.

49. Thomas E. Cavanaugh and James L. Sundquist, "The New Two-Party System," in *New Direction in American Politics,* ed. Chubb and Peterson.

50. As the minority report of the congressional committees investigating the Iran-contra affair acknowledged, "President Reagan gave his subordinates strong, clear, and consistent guidance about the basic thrust of the policies he wanted them to pursue toward Nicaragua. There is some question and dispute about *precisely* the level at which he chose to follow the operational details. There is no doubt, however, . . . [that] the President set the U.S. policy toward Nicaragua, with few if any ambiguities, and then left subordinates more or less free to implement it." *Report of the Congressional Committees Investigating the Iran-Contra Affair,* 100th Cong., 1st sess., House Report 100–433, Senate Report 100–216 (Washington, D.C.: U.S. Government Printing Office, 1987), 501 (emphasis in original).

51. Interview with Sen. Richard Lugar, August 7, 1987.

52. Nixon transformed the Bureau of the Budget into the Office of Management and Budget by executive order in 1970, adding a cadre of presidentially appointed assistant directors for policy to stand between the OMB director and the bureau's civil servants. As a consequence, the budget office attained additional policy responsibility and

became more responsive to the president. In the Reagan administration, the OMB was given a central role in remaking regulatory policy. See Richard A. Harris and Sidney M. Milkis, *The Politics of Regulatory Change: A Tale of Two Agencies,* 2d ed. (New York: Oxford University Press, 1996).

53. Sidney Blumenthal, *The Rise of the Counter-Establishment: From Conservative Ideology to Political Power* (New York: Times Books, 1986), 9.

54. Interview with William E. Brock, August 12, 1987.

55. Benjamin Ginsberg and Martin Shefter, *Politics by Other Means: The Declining Importance of Elections in America* (New York: Basic Books, 1990).

56. Linda Greenhouse, "Ethics in Government: The Price of Good Intentions," *New York Times,* February 1, 1988; and Cass R. Sunstein, "Unchecked and Unbalanced: Why the Independent Counsel Act Must Go," *The American Prospect* (May–June, 1998): 20–27.

57. Michael Nelson, "Constitutional Aspects of the Elections," in *The Elections of 1988,* ed. Michael Nelson (Washington, D.C.: CQ Press, 1989), 195.

58. Burt Solomon, "Bush's Zeal for Partisan Duties Tempered by His Bipartisan Style," *National Journal,* October 28, 1989, 2651.

59. On the budget battles of 1990, see Barbara Sinclair, "Bush and the 101st Congress," in *The Bush Presidency: First Appraisals,* ed. Colin Campbell and Bert Rockman (Chatham, N.J.: Chatham House, 1991), 174–183.

60. Bush's problems were compounded by the loss of Atwater, who had collapsed in early March while delivering a speech. He was diagnosed with a brain tumor, and, although he continued to occupy the party chair, had to abandon his political responsibilities. Atwater's absence left the Republican headquarters without effective leadership for almost a year, before Bush, after receiving several rejections, finally tapped Secretary of Agriculture Clayton Yeutter to replace him. Harold F. Bass, "George Bush: Party Leader" (paper presented at the annual meeting of the American Political Science Association, Washington, D.C., August 29–September 1, 1991), 10–11.

61. The Democrats added one seat in the Senate, strengthening their majority to 56 to 44, and eight seats to their already lopsided advantage in the House, yielding an advantage of 268 to 167. The losses were mild by historical standards; indeed, some Republicans argued that by losing only eight seats in the House and one in the Senate, their party fared rather well in the midterm campaign. But this argument ignored the fact that the GOP was starting from a very low base in the legislature and that it suffered disappointing defeats in the Florida and Texas gubernatorial races. James A. Barnes, "Back to Square One," *National Journal,* November 10, 1990, 2704–9.

62. On the institutional conflicts and partisan estrangement that characterized the final two years of the Bush presidency, see Milkis, *President and the Parties,* chap. 11.

63. An exit poll revealed that a plurality of voters now preferred to have the presidency and Congress controlled by the Democratic Party. See William Schneider, "A Loud Vote for Change," *National Journal,* November 7, 1992, 2544.

64. Alan Brinkley, "Roots," *New Republic,* July 27, 1992.

65. William Clinton, "The New Covenant: Responsibility and Rebuilding the American Community" (speech delivered at Georgetown University, Washington, D.C., October 23, 1991).

66. On President Clinton's use of executive orders, his attempt to carry out policy "with the stroke of a pen," see Thomas Friedman, "Ready or Not, Clinton Is Rattling the Country," *Washington Post,* January 31, 1993, IV 1. The proposal to lift the ban on gays and lesbians in the military plagued Clinton throughout the critical early months of his

presidency. Intense opposition from the respected head of the Joint Chiefs of Staff, Colin Powell, and the influential chair of the Senate Armed Services Committee, Sam Nunn, R-Ga., forced Clinton to defer his executive order for six months while he sought a compromise solution. But the delay and the compromise aroused the ire of gay and lesbian activists, who had given strong financial and organizational support to Clinton during the election. The controversy also forced the president to betray his campaign promise to focus "like a laser" on the economy. Ann Devroy and Ruth Marcus, "President Clinton's First Hundred Days: Ambitious Agenda and Interruptions Frustrate Efforts to Maintain Focus," *Washington Post,* April 29, 1993, A1.

67. Douglas Jehl, "Rejoicing Is Muted for the President in Budget Victory," *New York Times,* August 8, 1993, 1, 23; David Shribman, "Budget Battle a Hollow One for President," *Boston Globe,* August 8, 1993, 1, 24.

68. Indeed, during the early days of his presidency, Clinton sought to identify with his party's leadership in Congress and the national committee—partly, one suspects, to avoid the political isolation from which Carter had suffered. Whereas Carter kept party leaders in Congress and the national committee at arm's length, Clinton sought both to embrace and to empower the national organization. The White House lobbying efforts on Capitol Hill focused almost exclusively on the Democratic caucus; and the administration relied heavily on the DNC to marshal public support for its domestic programs. Interviews with David Wilhelm, chair, Democratic National Committee, October 18, 1993, and Craig Smith, political director, Democratic National Committee, October 19, 1993; Rhodes Cook, "DNC Under Wilhelm Seeking a New Role," *Congressional Quarterly Weekly Report,* March 13, 1993, 634. For a critical analysis of the DNC's lobbying efforts on behalf of Clinton, see Kathryn Dunn Tenpas, "Promoting President Clinton's Policy Agenda: DNC as Presidential Lobbyist," *The American Review of Politics* 17 (fall 1996): 283–298.

69. Al From and Will Marshall, "The Road to Realignment: Democrats and the Perot Voters," in *The Road to Realignment: Democrats and the Perot Voters* (Washington, D.C.: Democratic Leadership Council, 1993), 1-3–1-5.

70. A majority of Republicans in the House and Senate supported the free trade agreement, whereas a majority of Democrats, including the House majority leader and majority whip, opposed it. David Shribman, "A New Brand of D.C. Politics," *Boston Globe,* November 18, 1993, 15; Gwen Ifill, "56 Long Days of Coordinated Persuasion," *New York Times,* November 19, 1993, A27.

71. Address to Congress on health care plan, printed in *Congressional Quarterly Weekly Report,* September 25, 1993, 2582–6; Robin Toner, "Alliance to Buy Health Care: Bureaucrat or Public Servant?" *New York Times,* December 5, 1993, 1, 38.

72. Adam Clymer, "National Health Program, President's Greatest Goal, Declared Dead in Congress," *New York Times,* September 27, 1994, A1. For a comprehensive treatment of the Clinton health care program, see Cathie Jo Martin, "Mandating Social Change within Corporate America" (paper presented at the annual meeting of the American Political Science Association, New York, 1994). Martin's study shows that health care reform became the victim of "radically different world views about the state and corporation in modern society," 1.

73. Examining exit polls that suggested that a "massive anti-Clinton coalition came together" to produce the "revolution" of 1994, the political analyst William Schneider wrote of the voters' desire for change, "If the Democrats can't make government work, maybe the Republicans can solve problems with less government." Schneider, "Clinton, the Reason Why," *National Journal,* November 12, 1994, 2630–2.

74. William Clinton, State of the Union address, January 23, 1996, printed in *Congressional Quarterly Weekly Report*, January 27, 1996, 258–262.

75. Many public officials and journalists claimed that the new law put an end to "a sixty-one year old entitlement to welfare." In truth, the Aid to Families with Dependent Children program (AFDC) never existed as an entitlement in the sense that Social Security and Medicare did. The program only guaranteed federal matching funds to states that established AFDC programs. See R. Shep Melnick, "The Unexplained Resilience of Means-Tested Programs" (paper delivered at the annual meeting of the American Political Science Association, Boston, September 3–6, 1998).

76. William Jefferson Clinton, "Remarks on Signing the Personal Responsibility and Work Opportunity Reconciliation Act," August 22, 1996, *Weekly Compilation of Presidential Documents*, no. 1484.

77. Clinton, State of the Union address, January 23, 1996.

78. Bob Woodward, *The Choice* (New York: Simon and Schuster, 1996), 344.

79. Anthony Corrado, "Financing the 1996 Elections," in *The Election of 1996*, ed. Gerald Pomper (Chatham, N.J.: Chatham House, 1997).

80. Michael Nelson, "The Election: Turbulence and Tranquility in Contemporary American Politics," in *The Elections of 1996*, ed. Michael Nelson (Washington, D.C.: CQ Press, 1997), 52; Gary Jacobson, "The 105th Congress: Unprecedented and Unsurprising," in *Elections of 1996*, ed. Pomper, 161; and Kathryn Dunn Tempas, "The Clinton Reelection Machine: Placing the Party Organization in Peril," *Presidential Studies Quarterly*, vol. 28, no. 4 (fall 1998): 761–768.

81. Indeed, Clinton's third way was emulated abroad as well, with leaders in Britain, Germany, Italy, and Holland attempting to fashion programs that combined market efficiency and social justice. See Jim Hoagland, "Third Way Politics," *Washington Post*, May 20, 1999. In the face of these developments, DLC president Al From, who had often been critical of Clinton's inconsistent commitment to "the third way," credited the president with "modernizing progressive politics for the world." Interview with Al From, June 7, 1999. For a more critical and historical analysis of Clinton's third-way politics, see Stephen Skowronek, *The Politics Presidents Make: Leadership from John Adams to Bill Clinton* (Cambridge: Harvard University Press, 1997), 447–464.

82. Richard W. Stevenson, "After Years of Wrangling, Accord Is Reached on Plan to Balance the Budget by 2002," *New York Times*, May 3, 1997, 1.

83. The term *extraordinary isolation* is Woodrow Wilson's. See *Constitutional Government in the United States*, 69.

84. Republicans had long opposed reauthorization of the independent prosecutor statute, considering it an unconstitutional infringement on the executive's prosecutorial authority, but their resistance to Democratic efforts to reauthorize the statute came to an end in 1993, when the Whitewater scandal emerged. Katy J. Harriger, "Independent Justice: The Office of the Independent Counsel," in *Government Lawyers: The Federal Bureaucracy and Presidential Politics* (Lawrence: University Press of Kansas, 1995), 86.

85. Just 20 percent of those interviewed in a January 1999 Gallup poll thought Clinton provided good moral leadership, and only 24 percent characterized him as honest and trustworthy, new lows for his presidency. "Good Times for Clinton the President, but Personal Reputation Hits New Low," Gallup News Service, January 23, 1999, htpp://www.Gallup.com.

86. Janny Scott, "Talking Heads Post-Mortem: All Wrong, All the Time," *New York Times*, November 8, 1998, A22.

87. Interview with Will Marshall, president, Progressive Policy Institute, June 14, 1999.

88. David E. Rosenbaum, "Surplus a Salve for Clinton and Congress, *New York Times,* June 29, 1999.

89. Tish Durkin, "The Scene: The Jeffords Defection and the Risk of Snap Judgments," *National Journal,* May 26, 2001.

90. Fred Barnes, "The Impresario: Karl Rove, Orchestrator of the Bush White House," *Weekly Standard,* August 20, 2001. Rove indicated that he believed Atwater, a friend of his for twenty years, had made a mistake in going to the RNC. Political power fell into the hands of White House Chief of Staff John Sununu. "Parties are of great importance in the tactical and mechanical aspects of electing a president . . .," Rove said. "But they are less important in developing a political and policy strategy for the White House. Parties are an important means to the president's end. But the White House has to determine the administration's objectives." Interview with Karl Rove, November 15, 2001. A leading conservative in Washington indicated that he strongly urged Rove to work at the White House, not the RNC, "where organizational frustrations were rampant." Interview with conservative journalist, not for attribution, November 13, 2001.

91. New Democrats accused Bush of trying to steal their politics. As DLC president Al From wrote in spring 1999, Bush's effort to call himself a "compassionate conservative" appeared to be an effort by Republicans "to do for their party what New Democrats did for ours in 1992—to redefine and capture the political center." Al From, "Political Memo," *The New Democrat,* 11 (May/June 1999): 35. Many Republicans agreed. One skeptical conservative revealed that if he wanted to know the Bush campaign's position on a particular issue, he would consult the DLC magazine, *The New Democratic Blueprint.* Interview with Bush campaign adviser, not for attribution, November 13, 2001.

92. Rove interview; Michael Gerson, Bush's principal speechwriter, argued that the president's rhetoric did not try to "split the difference" between liberalism and conservatism. Rather, Bush's speeches sought to convey how "activist government could be used for conservative ends." Interview with Michael Gerson, November 15, 2001.

93. E. J. Dionne Jr., "Conservatism Recast," *Washington Post,* January 27, 2002.

94. George W. Bush, "Duty of Hope," speech, Indianapolis, Indiana, July 22, 1999, www.georgewbush.com.

95. Rove interview; remarks by Gov. George W. Bush, June 12, 1999, Cedar Rapids, Iowa, www.georgewbush.com.

96. On January 29, 2001, Bush created a White House office to, among other things, "eliminate unnecessary legislative, regulatory, and other bureaucratic barriers that impede faith-based and other community efforts to solve social problems." Executive Order 13199, "Establishment of Faith-Based and Community Initiatives." He also ordered the Departments of Labor, Education, Health and Human Services, and Housing and Urban Development, as well as the attorney general's office, to establish Centers for Faith-Based and Community Initiatives within their departments. These centers would perform internal audits, identifying barriers to the participation of faith-based organizations in providing social services and forming plans to remove these barriers. Executive Order 13198, "Agency Responsibilities with Respect to Faith-Based and Community Initiatives," January 29, 2001. As for education, from the start Bush and his advisers viewed it as the central issue distinguishing Bush as a different kind of Republican. George W. Bush, State of the Union address, January 29, 2002, www.whitehouse.gov; and Rove interview.

97. George W. Bush, "Address to Joint Session of Congress," February 27, 2001, *Washington Post,* February 28, 2001, A10.

98. "Pope Warns Bush on Stem Cells," BBC News, July 23, 2001, www.news.bbc.com.

99. Alan Wolfe, "Bush's Gift to America's Extremists," *New York Times,* August 19, 2001.

100. "President Names Members of Bioethics Council," statement by the press secretary, January 16, 2002, www.whitehouse.gov.

101. George W. Bush, address to a joint session of Congress and the nation, January 20, 2002, www.whitehouse.gov.

102. William James, *The Moral Equivalent of War and Other Essays,"* ed. John K. Roth (New York: Harper and Row, 1971), 13–14.

103. Steven Waldman, "Nationalize National Service," *Blueprint* (spring 1999).

104. Bush, State of the Union address.

105. Ibid.

Part V Presidents and Government

15 The Institutional Presidency

John P. Burke

Not until 1857 did Congress appropriate funds for a White House staff—one clerk. More than a half-century later President Woodrow Wilson had only seven full-time aides. Growth in the size of the White House staff began in earnest during the presidency of Franklin D. Roosevelt, and, with occasional lapses, the growth has yet to abate. The major challenge for presidents—not just for Roosevelt and his Democratic successors, such as Bill Clinton, but also for conservative Republicans like Ronald Reagan and both Bushes—has been to keep pace with an ever-expanding bureaucracy. Ironically, John P. Burke argues, the size and complexity of the modern presidential staff have caused the White House itself to take on "the character of a bureaucratic organization." Presidents, with varying success, have adopted a number of strategies to make good use of their staffs, which Burke chronicles.

Analysis of the workings of the White House staff, both by those who have served on it and by scholars, has a peculiar if not schizophrenic quality. For some, the staff system is simply a reflection of the personality, style, and managerial skills of the incumbent president. Others emphasize characteristics of the presidency that seem to endure from administration to administration. Both of these perspectives have some merit. Presidents do seem to leave their imprint—for better or for worse—on the office. The formal and hierarchical arrangements of the Dwight D. Eisenhower, Richard M. Nixon, and Ronald Reagan presidencies and the more collegial, informal, ad hoc patterns in the John F. Kennedy, Lyndon B. Johnson, and Bill Clinton White Houses can be linked to the organizational preferences and "work ways" of each of these chief executives. Today's White House staff, made up of some two thousand employees in significant policymaking positions, serves as an organizational context that can—just as in any bureaucracy—set limits on what a president can do and sometimes thwart even the best of presidential intentions. For the skillful president, the White House staff is like very hard clay that can be molded with great effort, patience, and understanding; for the less skilled it can become a hard rock, if not a brick wall, that resists presidential management and control.

A full analysis of how presidents have succeeded or failed at this "organizational artistry" would require a detailed account of the presidential staff system that has evolved since the late 1930s and a close examination of the efforts of each of the presidents from Franklin D. Roosevelt through George W. Bush to organize and manage the institutional presidency. What follows, therefore, is only part of this larger project: an outline of some of the institutional characteristics of the modern presidency and the managerial challenges they present to incumbent presidents.[1]

One point that deserves mention is how odd the need for organizational leadership would have seemed to presidents in the nineteenth and early twentieth centuries. Thomas Jefferson managed his office with one secretary and a messenger. Sixty years later, in the administration of Ulysses S. Grant, the size of the staff had grown to three. By 1900 the staff consisted of a private secretary (now formally titled "secretary to the president"), two assistant secretaries, two executive clerks, a stenographer, three lower level clerks, and four other office personnel. Under Warren G. Harding the size of the staff grew to thirty-one, but most staff members were clerical. Herbert Hoover managed to persuade Congress to approve two more secretaries to the president, one of whom he assigned the job of press aide.

It was common practice for early presidents to hire immediate family and other relatives as their secretaries, an indication that their few staff members functioned as personal aides rather than as substantive policy advisers. John Quincy Adams, Andrew Jackson, John Tyler, Abraham Lincoln, and Ulysses Grant all engaged their sons as private secretaries. George Washington, James K. Polk, and James Buchanan employed their nephews. James Monroe employed his younger brother and two sons-in-law. Zachary Taylor hired his brother-in-law.

Early presidents also paid the salaries of their small staffs out of their own pockets. Not until 1857 did Congress appropriate money ($2,500) for a presidential clerk—one. As recently as the Coolidge presidency, the entire budget for the White House staff, including office expenses, was less than $80,000.[2] By 1963 it had climbed to $12 million. In 1998 the corresponding figure for the Executive Office of the President was estimated at $233 million.

As demands on the presidency mounted, more help was needed. Grappling with the Great Depression of the 1930s, President Roosevelt's solution was to "muddle through." Early in his administration he experimented with a form of cabinet government but quickly became dissatisfied with its members' parochial perspectives, in-fighting, and tendency to leak information to the press—problems that would be encountered by many of Roosevelt's successors who also took office thinking that the cabinet would play a central role in their policymaking. Roosevelt then moved to a series of coordinating bodies that included relevant cabinet officers and the heads of the new agencies that were created as part of the New Deal. Another of FDR's managerial strategies was to borrow staff from existing departments and agencies; these employees remained on their home agencies' personnel budgets while they were "detailed" to the White House. In fact, the legislative whirlwind of Roosevelt's first hundred days was the product of a loosely organized group of assistants, many of whom did not have formal positions on the White House staff.

Roosevelt's patchwork arrangement worked, but just barely. In an interview with a group of reporters shortly after his reelection in 1936, Roosevelt publicly attributed his victory to the failure of his Republican opponent, Gov. Alfred P. Landon of Kansas, to seize on the president's chief weakness. "What is your weakness?" one of the reporters asked. "Administration," replied the president.[3] Clearly something needed to be done.

Roosevelt had already taken steps to rectify his administrative problems by forming the Committee on Administrative Management, headed by Louis Brownlow. Roosevelt's creation of the Brownlow Committee was not the first presidential effort to seek administrative advice on how to make the presidency work more effectively.[4] But it was the Brownlow Committee that most clearly and directly focused on the need for a larger, reorganized White House staff.[5]

Concluding that "the President needs help," Brownlow and his associates proposed that "to deal with the greatly increased duties of executive management falling upon the president, the White House staff should be expanded."[6] After initial rejection of the then-controversial proposal, Congress passed the revised recommendations of the Brownlow Committee in the Reorganization Act of 1939.[7] Significant increases in the staff resources available to the president also followed passage of the Employment Act of 1946, which created the Council of Economic Advisers, and the National Security Act of 1947, which led to the development of the National Security Council, and recommendations of the 1947 Hoover Commission on the Reorganization of the Executive Branch.[8] During Eisenhower's presidency, existing units within the White House Office (the core unit of the White House staff) were more clearly defined and new offices were created. Eisenhower also designated Sherman Adams as the first

White House chief of staff and assigned him significant authority to oversee and coordinate the domestic policy component of the staff system.[9]

From the handful of aides that Roosevelt and his predecessors could appoint, the numbers have steadily increased in each succeeding administration. By 1953 the size of the White House Office was about 250. Twenty years later, it had grown to almost five hundred. In 1977, criticizing the size of the staff as a symptom of the "imperial presidency," Jimmy Carter reduced it by a hundred employees, mostly by moving them to other parts of the executive bureaucracy. By 1980, Carter's last year in office, the size of the staff had inched back up to five hundred, and it has remained at about that size ever since. When other administrative units under direct presidential control (the larger Executive Office of the President) are included—such as the Office of Management and Budget, the National Security Council, and the Council of Economic Advisers—the number swells to about two thousand appointees. Physically, the Executive Office of the President has spilled out from the East and West wings of the White House, first to occupy the Old Executive Office Building next door, which was once large enough to house the Departments of State, War, and Navy, and then to encompass the New Executive Office Building on the north side of Pennsylvania Avenue as well as other, smaller buildings in the vicinity.

A marked change in the character of the presidency has thus occurred. By recognizing that the American executive is an institution—a presidency, not merely a president—we can better understand the office, how it operates, what kinds of challenges it faces, and how it affects our politics.

The Institutional Presidency

If the presidency is best understood as an institution, then clearly it should embody some of the characteristics of an institution. But what do we mean by terms such as *institution, institutional,* and *institutionalization?* Our concern is the organizational character of the presidency—its growth in size, the complexity of its work ways, and the general way in which it resembles a large, well-organized bureaucracy. More specifically, an institution is complex in what it does (its functions) and how it operates (its structure); and it is well-bounded—that is, differentiated from its environment.[10]

Complex Organization

Institutions are complex: they are relatively large in size; each part performs a specialized function; and some form of central authority coordinates the

Table 15.1 The White House Office, 1939

Secretary to the president	Stephen Early
Secretary to the president	Brig. Gen. Edwin M. Watson
Secretary to the president	Marvin H. McIntyre
Administrative assistant	William H. McReynolds
Administrative assistant	James H. Rowe, Jr.
Administrative assistant	Lauchlin Currie
Personal secretary	Marguerite A. LeHand
Executive clerk	Rudolph Forster

Source: United States Government Manual, 1939 (Washington, D.C.: U.S. Government Printing Office, 1939).

parts' various contributions to the work of the whole. The first aspect of complexity—the increase in size of the institutional presidency—can easily be seen by comparing the White House staff available to President Roosevelt in 1939, before the adoption of the Brownlow Committee's recommendations, with the staff at work in the Clinton or Bush White House. The eight individuals that the *United States Government Manual* for 1939 lists as members of the White House staff (see Table 15.1) are clearly dwarfed by the long list of staff members currently serving under President George W. Bush. A comparison of the Roosevelt and Bush staffs also illustrates the second aspect of organizational complexity: increasing specialization of function. Roosevelt's aides were, by and large, generalists; they were simply called "secretary to the president" or "administrative assistant." If one were to look at the staff list for the Bush White House, one would find titles such as deputy assistant to the president for communications, deputy assistant to the president for legislative affairs, deputy assistant to the president and director of media affairs, special assistant to the president for public liaison, and associate counsel to the president.

Many other units of the White House staff operate within functionally defined, specialized areas, such as national security or environmental quality. In fact, one of the primary causes of the growth of the White House staff has been the addition of these units: the Bureau of the Budget (created in 1921, transferred from the Treasury Department in 1939, and reorganized as the Office of Management and Budget in 1970), the Council of Economic Advisers (1946), the National Security Council (1947), the Office of the United States Trade Representative (1963), the Office of Policy Development (1970), the Council on Environmental Quality (1970), the Office of Science and Technology Policy (1976), the Office of Administration (1977), the National Critical Materials Council (1984), and the Office of National Drug Control Policy (1989).[11] All told, the once relatively simple tasks of presidents' staff—writing speeches, handling correspondence, and orchestrating the daily schedule—have evolved into substantive duties that affect the policies presidents propose and how they deal with the steadily increasing demands placed on the office.

The final characteristic of institutional complexity is the presence of a central authority that coordinates the contributions of the institution's functional parts. For the presidency, such authority nominally resides in the president. Since the 1950s, however, coordinating authority has gradually been taken over by the White House chief of staff—Sherman Adams under Eisenhower; H. R. Haldeman under Nixon; Hamilton Jordan under Carter; James Baker, Donald Regan, Howard Baker, and Kenneth Duberstein under Reagan; John Sununu and Samuel Skinner under George H. W. Bush; Thomas F. "Mack" McLarty III, Leon Panetta, Erskine Bowles, and John Podesta under Clinton; and Andrew Card Jr. under George W. Bush—with substantive roles in policymaking and, in most cases, day-to-day authority over the workings of the White House staff.

Differentiation from Environment

The complexity of the presidency and its reliance on expert advice have given the institution a unique place in the policy process, differentiating it from its political environment. One way this has occurred is through increased White House control of new policy initiatives. Presidents now routinely try to shape the nation's political agenda, and the staff resources they have at their disposal make it possible for them to do so. John Kennedy, Lyndon Johnson, and especially Richard Nixon, with his creation of the Domestic Council, all emphasized White House control of policy proposals, deemphasizing the involvement of the cabinet and the bureaucracy. Carter and Reagan both began their terms of office with calls for more presidential reliance on the cabinet. They quickly found that goal to be unworkable in practice and turned inward to the White House staff for policy advice. Clinton also followed this pattern. Although one of the major initiatives of his administration—health care reform—was largely crafted by an ad hoc commission led by his wife, Hillary Rodham Clinton, most of his other efforts were mainly the work of his immediate staff.

Those outside the White House—Congress, the bureaucracy, the news media, and the public—have responded to presidential direction of the national agenda by expecting more of it. Political lobbying and influence seeking, especially by those directly involved in Washington politics, focus on the president. American politics remains highly decentralized, incremental, and open to multiple points of access, but those seeking to influence national politics try to cultivate the people who have most to do with policy proposals: the White House staff.

A second aspect of the presidency that differentiates it from the surrounding political environment is the way parts of the staff are organized explicitly to manage external relations with the media, Congress, and different constituencies. The press secretary and staff coordinate and in many cases control the presidential news passed on to the media.[12] Since 1953 specific staff assistants also have been assigned solely to lobby Congress on the president's behalf. Today, White House lobbying efforts are formally organized within the large, well-staffed Office of Legislative Affairs. The establishment of special channels of influence for important constituent groups is another way presidents manage relations with the political environment. This practice began in the administration of Harry S. Truman, when David Niles became the first staff aide explicitly assigned to serve as a liaison to Jewish groups. Eisenhower hired the first black presidential assistant, E. Frederic Morrow, and added a special representative from the scientific community as well. In 1970 Nixon created the Office of Public Liaison as the organizational home within the White House staff for the aides serving as conduits to particular groups. By the time Jimmy Carter left office in 1981, special staff members were assigned to groups such as consumers, women, the elderly, Jews, Hispanics, white ethnic Catholics, Vietnam veterans, and gay men and lesbians, as well as such traditional constituencies as African Americans, labor, and business.[13] In George W. Bush's White House, liaison to constituency groups took on particular importance with the appointment of Karl Rove as "senior adviser" to the president. Rove was not only placed in charge of the public liaison and political affairs offices in the White House, but also he has been the contact for conservative, business, and religious groups.

The increasing differentiation of the presidency as a discrete entity thus complements its increasing complexity and reliance on expertise as evidence of its status as an institution.

Effects of an Institutional Presidency

Even if the presidency bears the marks of an institution, do its distinctly institutional characteristics—as opposed to the individual styles, practices, and idiosyncrasies of each president—matter? Despite the tremendous growth in the size of the president's staff, perhaps it remains mainly a cluster of aides and supporting personnel, with their tasks, organization, and tenure varying greatly from administration to administration, even changing within the term of a particular president. After all, observers of the presidency, both scholarly and journalistic, have noted enormous differences between the Kennedy and

Eisenhower White Houses, between Johnson and Nixon, Carter and Reagan, Reagan and Bush, and even Bush father and Bush son. It is the personality, character, and individual behavior of each of these presidents that have generally attracted the attention of press and public.

Some of these observations are accurate, but to the extent that the institutionalized daily workings of the presidency transcend the personal ideologies, character, and idiosyncrasies of those who work within it (especially the president), it makes sense to analyze the presidency from an institutional perspective. Not only do many of the presidency's institutional characteristics affect the office, but also the effects are negative as well as positive: the institutional presidency can help determine the success or failure of a particular presidency.

External Centralization: Presidential Control of Policymaking

The creation of a large presidential staff has centralized much policymaking power within the confines of the presidency. This development has both positive and negative aspects. On the positive side, an institutional presidency that centralizes the control of policy can protect the programs that presidents wish to foster. The Washington political climate is not receptive to new political initiatives, which must compete for programmatic authority and budget allocations against older programs that are generally well established in agencies and departments, have strong allies on Capitol Hill, and enjoy a supportive clientele of special interest groups.

In creating the Office of Economic Opportunity (OEO), Lyndon Johnson, a president whose legislative skills were unsurpassed, recognized precisely this problem. The OEO was designed to be a central component of Johnson's War on Poverty. As Congress was considering the legislation to create the OEO, three departments—Commerce, Labor, and Health, Education, and Welfare— all lobbied to have it administratively housed within their respective bailiwicks. Johnson, recognizing that this would subordinate the OEO to whatever other goals a department might pursue, lobbied Congress to set up the OEO so that it would report directly to the president. Johnson was especially swayed by the views of Harvard economist John Kenneth Galbraith, who warned, "Do not bury the program in the departments. Put it in the Executive offices, where people will know what you are doing, where it can have a new staff and a fresh man as director."[14]

The centralization of power in presidents' staffs has not always redounded to their advantage. One of the worst effects of increasing White House control of the policy process, especially in foreign policy, has been to diminish or even exclude other sources of advice. Since the creation of the National Security Council (NSC) in 1947, presidents have tended to rely for policy recommendations on the council's staff, especially the president's special assistant for national security. Ironically, Congress's intent in creating the NSC was to check the foreign policy power of the president by creating a deliberative body whose members would provide an alternative source of timely advice to the president.

Except during Eisenhower's presidency, the NSC has not generally functioned as an effective deliberative body. What has developed is a large, White House–centered NSC staff, headed by a highly visible national security assistant, that often dominates the foreign policy making process. The reasons why the NSC staff and the national security assistant have come to dominate are plain: proximity to the Oval Office, readily available staff resources, and a number of presidents whose views about decision-making processes differed from Eisenhower's. Beginning with McGeorge Bundy under Kennedy and continuing with Walt W. Rostow under Johnson, Henry Kissinger under Nixon, and Zbigniew Brzezinski under Carter, most national security assistants have not only advocated their own policy views but also have eclipsed other sources of foreign policy advice, especially the secretary of state and his or her department.

Perhaps the best testimony to the problems created by centralized control of foreign policy by the NSC staff can be found in the memoirs of three recent secretaries of state. Cyrus Vance, who served under Carter, repeatedly battled Brzezinski. Vance's resignation as secretary of state, in fact, was precipitated in 1980 by the administration's ill-fated decision—from which Vance and the State Department were effectively excluded—to try to rescue the American hostages in Iran.[15]

Alexander Haig, Reagan's first secretary of state, encountered similar problems with the NSC. In his memoirs, Haig claims he had only secondhand knowledge of many of the president's decisions. In a chapter tellingly titled, "Mr. President, I Want You to Know What's Going on Around You," Haig reported,

William Clark, in his capacity as National Security Adviser to the President, seemed to be conducting a second foreign policy, using separate channels of communications . . . bypassing the State Department altogether. Such a system was bound to produce confusion, and it soon did. There were conflicts over votes in the United Nations, differences over communications to heads of state, mixed signals to the combatants in Lebanon. Some of these, in my judgment, represented a danger to the nation.[16]

George P. Shultz, Haig's successor as secretary of state, also found himself cut out of a number of important policy decisions by the NSC staff. The most notable was the Reagan administration's secret negotiations with Iran to exchange arms for the release of American hostages in Lebanon and its covert use of the profits generated by the arms sales to fund the contra rebels in Nicaragua. The arms deal violated standing administration policy against negotiating for hostages, and the disclosure of the secret contra funds undermined congressional support for Reagan's policies in Central America. The affair not only indicated Shultz's conflicts with the NSC but was also politically damaging to the president.

Some exceptions have been noted to the general pattern of NSC dominance in foreign policy making—one occurred during the Ford administration, another in the first Bush presidency. In both cases a reasonable balance was struck in the advisory roles of the State Department and the NSC. But the two cases are revealing about the conditions under which excessive centralization can be avoided. In both presidencies the same individual, Brent Scowcroft, served as the NSC adviser, and he deliberately crafted his job to be a "neutral broker" of the foreign policy making process rather than a policy advocate. Furthermore, in both administrations the secretaries of state had extensive White House staff experience. Kissinger had served under Nixon as NSC special assistant, and for part of his tenure in the Nixon and Ford administrations he was simultaneously NSC special assistant and secretary of state. Bush's secretary of state, James Baker, had served as White House chief of staff and as secretary of the Treasury under Reagan.

Clinton's national security apparatus during his first term offered yet another twist. NSC special assistant Anthony Lake served, like Scowcroft, in the role of neutral broker but with a secretary of state, Warren Christopher, who largely failed to articulate a broader vision of America's foreign policy in the post–cold war world. Both served under a president who had more interest and experience in domestic than foreign affairs. This arrangement generated criticisms of "policy drift" and a "foreign policy vacuum."

Clinton's second term began auspiciously with the appointment of Madeleine Albright as secretary of state, Sandy Berger as NSC adviser, and former senator William Cohen, a Republican from Maine, as defense secretary. Yet criticisms were voiced about intelligence-gathering failures, the lack of contingency planning, and a decision-making process that was at times secretive and restricted to a small group. These charges were raised especially in the aftermath of the August 1998 bombing of a pharmaceutical factory in Sudan that appeared to be linked—although the evidence would later seem less conclusive—to attacks on two U.S. embassies in East Africa.[17] In early 1999 Clinton undertook a more serious venture when he decided to have NATO respond with military force against the Serbian government's atrocities in Kosovo. Although the Serbs eventually backed down, the administration was taken to task for its problems with its contingency planning, military options, and exit strategy.[18]

Foreign and national security policy making in George W. Bush's presidency may offer still another variant. NSC adviser Condoleezza Rice is a longtime Bush confidant who, like her mentor Brent Scowcroft, is considered both a neutral broker and a policy adviser. Bush, however, clearly has other powerful voices in his inner circle: Secretary of State Colin Powell, Defense Secretary Donald Rumsfeld, and Vice President Richard Cheney, all of whom served in previous administrations. Rumsfeld and Cheney were chief of staff under Ford, and Powell the NSC adviser under Reagan. Rumsfeld and Cheney also served as defense secretary, and Powell was chairman of the Joint Chiefs of Staff. Rice, it has been reported, can hold her own within such experienced company, even chairing meetings of the administration's foreign policy principals.[19]

In domestic and economic policy, Bush centralized policymaking in some areas but not in others. For example, early in the new administration Vice President Cheney was asked to develop a comprehensive energy program. Bush also chose a special task force to flesh out his campaign proposals for Social Security reform. In other areas, such as tax reform, education, patients' bill of rights, and the faith-based initiatives proposal, the White House staff was the dominant force. In fact, in at least one of the issue areas, education policy, reports surfaced indicating that the secretary of education was not pleased with the dominant role taken by the White House.[20]

The events of September 11, 2001, radically transformed many of the internal dynamics of the Bush presidency. The more deliberate and orderly decision-making channels of the preceding months were replaced by more fluid, time-constrained, and ad hoc procedures. A "war cabinet" consisting of White House and cabinet officials took center stage. According to one account, "The war effort has White House advisers enmeshed in a new coalition with the State, Defense, Treasury and Justice departments, speaking hourly with officials they hardly knew before."[21] The domestic agenda was largely put on hold, replaced by efforts to revive the economy and adequately defend the home front.

Although a policy process with more balanced participation by the cabinet and the White House staff developed after September 11, the White House remained a powerful force. The "outline of the war plan often emerge[d] from the private conversations" of President Bush and Rice.[22] The NSC added two new offices to deal with counterterrorism and computer security. Bush signed an executive order creating the Office of Homeland Security, with a mandate to prevent and respond to domestic terrorism, and appointed former Pennsylvania governor Tom Ridge to lead it. On June 6, 2002, President Bush proposed that the office be reorganized as a cabinet-level department. Josh Bolten, a longtime Bush policy adviser and deputy chief of staff, took the chair of the new Domestic Consequences Committee, reflecting the shift in the national agenda.

Internal Centralization: Hierarchy, "Gate-Keeping," and Presidential Isolation

The general centralization of policymaking power by the White House staff has been accompanied by a centralization of power within the staff by one or two chief aides. This internal centralization is further evidence of the institutional character of the presidency, and it too can affect the way the institutional presidency operates, providing both opportunities and risks for a president.

On the positive side, centralization of authority within a well-organized staff system can ensure clear lines of responsibility, well-demarcated duties, and orderly work ways. When presidents lack a centralized, organized staff system, the policymaking process suffers.

The travails of Franklin Roosevelt's staff illustrate the problems that can arise from lack of effective organization. Roosevelt favored a relatively unorganized, competitive staff system, one in which the president acted as his own chief of staff. But rather than establishing regular patterns of duties and assignments and an orderly system of reporting and control, Roosevelt often gave several of his staff assistants the same assignment, in effect pitting them against each other.

Some analysts have argued that redundancy—two or more staff members doing the same thing—can benefit an organization.[23] But in Roosevelt's case, staff resources were minimal. Worse, his staff arrangements generated competitiveness, jealousy, and insecurity among his aides, none of which is conducive to sound policy advice or effective administration. Patrick Anderson wrote, "Roosevelt used men, squeezed them dry, and ruthlessly discarded them. . . . The requirement [for success] was that they accept criticism without complaint, toil without credit, and accept unquestioningly Roosevelt's moods and machinations."[24]

In addition to making the staff more effective, a system in which one staff member serves as chief of staff or is at least *primus inter pares* (first among equals) is advantageous to a president for other reasons. It can protect the president's political standing, for example. A highly visible staff member with a significant amount of authority within the White House can act as a kind of lightning rod, handling politically tough assignments and deflecting political controversy from the president to himself or herself.

Perhaps the best example of this useful division of labor comes from the Eisenhower presidency. Part of Eisenhower's success as president derived from a leadership style in which he projected himself as a chief of state who was above the political fray, while allowing his assistants, especially Sherman Adams, the flinty former governor of New Hampshire and Eisenhower's chief of staff, to seem like prime ministers concerned with day-to-day politics. A 1956 *Time* magazine feature on Eisenhower's staff, reported that Adams's scrawled "O.K., S.A." was tantamount to presidential approval. Although in reality it was Eisenhower who made the decisions, Adams's reputation as the "abominable 'No!' man" helped to "preserve Eisenhower's image as a benevolent national and international leader" and protect his standing in the polls.[25]

A well-organized, centralized staff can also work against a president. Corruption and the abuse of power are among the dangers in elevating one assistant to prominence and investing that person with a large amount of power. Sherman Adams proved politically embarrassing to Eisenhower when he was accused of accepting gifts from a New England textile manufacturer. Eisenhower found it personally difficult to ask his trusted aide to resign and delegated the job to Vice President Nixon. In fact, the political and personal problems Eisenhower experienced by relying on, then having to fire, Adams seem to be part of a pattern: Truman and Harry Vaughan, Johnson and Walter Jenkins, Nixon and Haldeman, Reagan and Donald Regan, and Bush and John Sununu.

Another two-edged consequence of a centralized staff system is that a highly visible assistant with a large amount of authority can act as a "gatekeeper," controlling and filtering the flow of information to and from the president. Both Jordan under Carter and Regan under Reagan were criticized for limiting access to the president and selectively screening the information and advice their presidents received. Joseph Califano Jr., Carter's secretary of Health, Education, and Welfare, had repeated run-ins with Jordan. While lobbying Dan Rostenkowski, the Democratic representative from Illinois and influential chair of the Health Subcommittee of the House Ways and Means Committee, on a hospital cost containment bill, Califano found that Rostenkowski also resented the treatment he was receiving from Jordan. "He never returns a phone call, Joe," Rostenkowski complained. "Don't feel slighted," Califano replied. "He treats you exactly as he treats most of the Cabinet."[26] In July 1979 Carter fired Califano and promoted Jordan.

Donald Regan, who succeeded James Baker as Reagan's chief of staff in 1985, acquired tremendous power in domestic policy, played a major role making important presidential appointments, and was even touted in the media as Reagan's prime minister. Immediately on taking office, Regan flexed his political muscles by revamping the cumbersome cabinet council system, substituting instead two streamlined bodies: the Economic Policy Council and the Domestic Policy Council. Regan retained control of the two councils' agendas. According to Becky Dunlap, an aide to Attorney General Edwin Meese III, "Don Regan more than anyone else has the authority to say this issue has to be dealt with by the Cabinet council. And he does that on a regular basis." Subsequent council reports to President Reagan also flowed through Regan: "The simplified system strengthened Regan's direct control over policy, establishing him as a choke point for issues going to the President."[27]

Regan certainly was effective in centralizing power in his hands, but his attempts to exercise strong control over the policymaking process did not always serve the president's ends. In the realm of domestic policy, the tactics of Regan and his staff frequently upset House Republicans: Regan "ignored them while shaping a tax bill with [Democratic] House Ways and Means Chairman Dan Rostenkowski." President Reagan salvaged tax reform with a personal appeal to his party in Congress, "but the specter of the president traveling to Capitol Hill like a supplicant to plead for Republican House votes plainly raised doubts about the quality of White House staff work."[28]

In the realm of foreign affairs, Regan was the first chief of staff to play a major role in both making and implementing policy. His attempts to influence foreign policy precipitated the resignation of Robert McFarlane, the national security adviser, and led to the selection of Adm. John Poindexter, a Regan ally, as his replacement. The Regan-dominated, Poindexter-led NSC soon embroiled the Reagan administration in the politically embarrassing Iran-contra affair.

Although George H. W. Bush was more personally involved in the policy process than Reagan, his management style fared little better. In foreign affairs, he tended to operate with a close-knit group of advisers, especially his trusted and longtime associate, Secretary of State James Baker. Although simultaneously at the center of the decision process and avoiding "micro-management" of his decisions in the U.S. effort to depose Panamanian dictator Manuel Noriega and in the Persian Gulf War, Bush appears to have been vulnerable to some of the problems Irving Janis has identified in his theory of "groupthink": a tendency for the leader to announce his preferences before the group has fully explored alternatives, exclusion of dissenting views (for example, Colin Powell, chairman of the Joint Chiefs of Staff, was absent from several meetings soon after Iraq invaded Kuwait), and a certain degree of like-mindedness in the views of the participants.[29] Bush may have avoided decision fiascoes, however, because of his own foreign policy expertise and experience and his ability to reach out to other world leaders in forging effective coalitions, especially during the Gulf War.

Bush clearly preferred foreign affairs to domestic, largely turning the latter over to Chief of Staff John Sununu. Early in his presidency, published reports likened Bush's domestic policy style to Alexander George's theory of multiple advocacy—an approach that Roger Porter, one of Bush's top domestic aides, embraced.[30] Sununu and the OMB director, Richard Darman, however, quickly asserted control over Bush's domestic and economic policy operations, leading to, according to Walter Williams, a "domestic policy regency."[31]

Centralized authority of the kind Regan and Sununu practiced is clearly preferable to organizational anarchy. But as hierarchy and centralization develop within the White House staff, presidents can find themselves isolated, relying on a small, core group of advisers. If that occurs, the information the president gets will already have been selectively filtered and interpreted. Discussions and deliberations will be confined to an inner circle of like-minded advisers. Neither development is beneficial to the quality of presidential decision making or to the formulation of effective policy proposals.

It will be interesting to see how much centralized authority develops in George W. Bush's White House. Drawing on their shared experience of the elder Bush's management style, the president and his chief of staff, Andrew Card, are aware of the dangers of investing too much power in the chief of staff position. Moreover, in planning for the new administration, Bush and Card sought to build stronger political and communications operations into the White House policy process than had existed in the first Bush White House. These operations were initially headed by Karl Rove (politics) and Karen Hughes (communications), both of whom are longtime aides and advisers to Bush. The division of labor proved reasonably effective, although Rove's political contacts and advice have been subject to media scrutiny. Hughes's resignation in April 2002 also changed the equation, and it is unclear whether her successor, Daniel Bartlett, will be able to match her considerable skills. Like the "troika" of the early Reagan years, success will depend on the ability of Bush's top aides to manage conflict, work together harmoniously, and avoid shutting out other channels of information and advice.

President Bush's response to the events of September 11 also may work against the tendency to vest too much power in one or two principal aides. Most accounts of his decision making stress his deeper involvement in the details of policy, close monitoring of developing events, and frequent meetings with his war cabinet. Bush continues to delegate some areas "to more experienced advisers but keep[s] others to himself."[32]

Bureaucratization

As the top levels of the White House staff have gained authority and political visibility, the rest of the staff has taken on the character of a bureaucratic organization. Among its bureaucratic characteristics are complex work routines, which often stifle originality and reduce differences on policy to their lowest common denominator. Drawing on his experience in the Carter White House, Greg Schneiders complained that if one feeds "advice through the system . . . what may have begun as a bold initiative comes out the other end as unrecognizable mush. The system frustrates and alienates the staff and cheats the President and the country."[33] Schneiders also noted that the frustrations of staffers do not end with the paper flow:

There are also the meetings. The incredible, interminable, boring, ever-multiplying meetings. There are staff meetings and task force meetings, trip meetings and general schedule meetings, meetings to make decisions and unmake them and to plan future meetings, where even more decisions will be made.[34]

"All of this might be more tolerable," Schneiders suggested, "if the staff could derive satisfaction vicariously from personal association with the President." But few aides have any direct contact with the president: "Even many of those at the highest levels—assistants, deputy assistants, special assistants—don't see the President once a week or speak to him in any substantive way once a month."[35]

What develops as a substitute for work satisfaction or personal proximity to the president are typical patterns of organizational behavior: "bureaucratic" and "court" politics. With regard to court politics, for example, White House staff members often compete for assignments and authority that serve as a measure of their standing and prestige on the staff and ultimately with the president. Sometimes these turf battles are physical in character, with staff members competing for larger office space and closer proximity to central figures in the administration, especially to the president and the Oval Office in the West Wing. At the beginning of each presidential term, journalists take an intense interest in the size of staff offices and their location in relation to the president; these are taken as signs of relative power and influence by the Washington political community.

Not only are staff members concerned about their standing within the White House, but also they are attentive to how they are perceived by outsiders. Patterns of behavior—bureaucratic politics—can develop that relate to a staff member's place in the organization: "Where one stands depends on where one sits." Staff members often develop allies on the outside—members of the press, members of Congress, lobbyists, and other political influentials—who can aid the programs and political causes of particular parts of the institutional presidency or the personal careers of staffers. Conversely, they can also create hostility and enmity among those outside the staff who compete with them for presidential attention. One classic example of this is the "us versus them" attitude that develops between the Office of Policy Development (inside) and regular departments (outside) in domestic policy and between the NSC staff (inside) and the State Department (outside) in foreign policy. In part, such attitudes may stem from different orientations and perspectives: "Political appointees seem to want to accomplish goals quickly while careerists opt to accomplish things carefully."[36] But these attitudes may also inhere in simple bureaucratic competition and politics, generated by a complex, bureaucratic institution.

Politicization

As a response to the bureaucratization of the White House staff, presidents are increasingly politicizing the institutional presidency. That is, they are attempting to make sure that staff members heed their policy directives and serve their political needs, rather than their own.

In most cases, the presidents' reasons for politicizing their staffs are understandable. The Constitution's system of shared powers deals presidents a weak hand. Furthermore, presidents should expect broad agreement among their aides and assistants with their political programs and policy goals. President Nixon, for example, created the Domestic Council as a discrete unit within the White House staff to serve as his principal source of policy advice on domestic affairs because he feared that the agencies and departments were staffed with unsympathetic liberal Democrats.

The difficulty for presidents comes in determining to what extent they should politicize their staff. Excessive politicization can limit the range of opinions among (and thus the advice from) the staff; taken to extremes, politicization may result in a phalanx of like-minded sycophants.

Excessive politicization can also weaken the objectivity of the policy analysis at the president's disposal, especially if the newly politicized staff unit has a tradition of neutral competence and professionalism. As Terry Moe summarized the argument, "Politicization is deplored for its destructive effects on institutional memory, expertise, professionalism, objectivity, communications, continuity, and other bases of organizational competence."[37]

One part of the president's staff in which politicization has been most noticeable—and the debate over politicization most charged—is the Office of Management and Budget. The same Nixon effort that created the Domestic Council also led to the reorganization of the old Bureau of the Budget into the present OMB. Although an arm of the executive branch and certainly not wholly above politics, the BOB was regarded as a place where neutral competence was paramount, "a place where the generalist ethic prevailed . . . a place where you were both a representative for the President's particular view and the top objective resource for the continuous institution of the Presidency."[38]

Nixon increased the number of political appointees in the OMB. Moreover, some functions once assigned to professionals were given to political appointees; for example, presidentially appointed program associate directors were placed in the OMB's examining divisions.[39] The effects of these changes have been noticeable: greater staff loyalty to political appointees, less cooperation with other parts of the White House staff and with Congress, and reduced impartiality and competence in favor of ideology and partisanship. The role of the OMB in the policy process has also changed: it now gives substantive policy advice—not just objective budget estimates—and has taken an active and visible role in lobbying Congress.

The experience of the Reagan administration is particularly revealing on the risks of excessive politicization in budget making, an area where expertise and objective analysis must complement the policy goals expressed in the president's budget proposal. Reagan relied heavily on the OMB, especially during the directorship of David Stockman, both in formulating Reaganomics and trying to get its legislative provisions passed by Congress. Stockman himself concluded—and announced that conclusion in the title of his memoirs—that the so-called Reagan revolution failed.[40] Part of Stockman's thesis was that Reagan was done in by normal Washington politics, which is particularly averse to a budget-conscious president. But Stockman's own words reveal a politicized, deprofessionalized OMB, which may not have been able to give the president the kind of objective advice that he needed, at times, to win over his critics and political opponents:

The thing was put together so fast that it probably should have been put together differently. . . . We were doing the whole budget-cutting exercise so frenetically . . . juggling details, pushing people, and going from one session to another. . . . The defense program was just a bunch of numbers written on a piece of paper. And it didn't mesh.[41]

The politicization of the OMB cannot explain all of Stockman's difficulties. But as Stockman's account attests, Reagan and his advisers needed hard questioning, objective analysis, and criticism of the sort that the old bureau, but not the new OMB, could provide a president.

The numerous scandals that plagued the Clinton presidency offer another twist: efforts not just to control policy but to protect the president's legal position and engage in damage control. According to George Stephanopoulos, "We had a team of lawyers nicknamed the Masters of Disaster, whose sole job was to handle Whitewater and related inquiries—responding to grand jury subpoenas, preparing congressional testimony, answering questions from the press." There were negative consequences. In Stephanopoulos' view,

I'd learned that simply gathering facts to answer allegations could spawn new inquiries and additional avenues of attack, creating a cycle that was the political equivalent of a perpetual-motion machine. Anyone anywhere near the activity risked getting sucked into the swirl and spit out with a tarnished reputation and a ton of debt.[42]

In part as a response to these legal difficulties, a wall of separation developed within the White House between those attending to the president's legal troubles and those attempting to serve the president's policy and political needs. Many of the latter floundered in the dark, most notably press secretary Mike McCurry. In the opinion of Michael Isikoff, the *Newsweek* reporter who first uncovered the Lewinsky matter, the White House staff nonetheless became enmeshed in the scandal:

The lies were told at first by Clinton and then spread and magnified by everybody around him—his top aides, his lawyers, his spin doctors. The lies were easily rationalized on the grounds that it was Clinton's private life that was at issue. . . . But lying, engaged in often enough, can have a corrosive effect. . . . A culture of concealment had sprung up around Bill Clinton and, I came to believe that summer, it had infected his entire presidency.[43]

Putting the President Back In

During the past fifty years the institutional presidency has undoubtedly offered presidents some of the important resources they need to meet the complex policy tasks and expectations of the office. But as we have seen, the effects of an institutional presidency—centralization of policymaking in the president's staff, hierarchy, bureaucratization, and politicization—have detracted from as well as served presidents' policy goals.

Presidents are not, however, simply at the mercy of the institution. Having emphasized the institutional character of the presidency, we should not neglect the presidential character of the institution. Although the presidency is an institution, it is an intensely personal one, which can take on a different character from administration to administration, from one set of staff advisers to another. Presidents and their staffs are by no means hostage to the institution; they have often been able to benefit from the positive resources it provides while deflecting or overcoming institutional forces that detract from their goals.

The most obvious management task a president faces is the basic recognition on first being elected that the organization and staffing of the White House are matters of highest priority. All of Washington and the media wait in eager anticipation for the president-elect to announce the names of the new cabinet. However, it is early and careful study about how presidents-elect organize the White House staff—whether they favor the more formal system of Eisenhower, Nixon, or Reagan or the more collegial arrangement of Kennedy, Johnson, or Carter—and select the people who work for them that will make or break their presidencies.

Clinton's difficulties during his first years as president can be attributed in great measure to a failure, during the transition period before he took office, to understand what it takes to create an effective staff system. According to one report, "Though it had studied the operations of every other major government agency, [the transition team] assigned no one to study the workings of the White House."[44] This failure was "an insane decision," according to one senior Clinton aide. "We knew more about FEMA [Federal Emergency Management Agency] and the Tuna Commission than we did about the White House. We arrived not knowing what was there, had never worked together, had never worked in these positions."[45]

Clinton's early appointments of top aides exhibits another pattern of which presidents need to be wary: the tendency to offer staff positions to longtime political loyalists and campaign workers. As one Clinton aide noted, "Unable to shift from a campaign mode, it [the Clinton transition team] made staffing decisions with an eye to rewarding loyal campaign workers instead of considering the broader task of governing."[46] Presidents surely need assistants who are personally loyal to them and share their deeply held political views, but presidents also need aides who are adept in Washington politics or have substantive expertise in a particular policy area. Too many friends from Little Rock, Sacramento, or rural Georgia can doom a presidency very quickly.

In contrast, George W. Bush enjoyed a more successful transition to office, even with the unusual circumstances of determining who won the election. Much preliminary planning had been undertaken before the election, including the selection of a chief of staff. Furthermore, even as the uncertainty over Florida rolled on (not to be settled until December 12), transition planning was well under way in the Bush camp. Bush placed Cheney in charge of the transition. Cheney was not only a veteran of past administrations but also a participant in the outgoing Ford and senior Bush transitions. Bush's early selection of Card as chief of staff enabled White House planning and organization to proceed on course. By the end of the first week of January, Bush was only a week behind where Clinton had been in picking his cabinet, and he was well ahead in announcing White House appointments.

Unlike some of his predecessors, Bush also did a good job of melding loyalty and political experience. Several members of his Texas inner circle were appointed to prominent positions, particularly on the White House staff. But, throughout the administration, there were an unusually high number of appointees with prior Washington experience.

Beyond striking a good balance between loyalty, on the one hand, and Washington experience and policy expertise, on the other, presidents must also be aware of the strengths and, especially, the weaknesses of the various ways of organizing the staff members they have selected. For example, to reduce some of the negative effects of relying on a large-scale White House staff, Eisenhower complemented his use of the formal machinery of the NSC and Adams's office with informal channels of advice. In foreign affairs, he turned not just to his trusted secretary of state, John Foster Dulles, but also to a network of friends with political knowledge and experience, such as Gen. Alfred M. Gruenther, the supreme allied commander in Europe. Eisenhower also held regular meetings with his cabinet and with congressional leaders to inform them of his actions, to garner their support, and to hear their views and opinions.[47]

When dealing with his staff, Eisenhower encouraged his aides to air their disagreements and doubts and to be candid and straightforward in their comments. He especially emphasized the need to avoid expressing views that simply reflected departmental or other bureaucratic interests. Herbert Brownell, his attorney general from 1953 until 1957, recalls that Eisenhower "time after time" would tell his cabinet members, "You are not supposed to represent your department, your home state, or anything else. You are my advisers. I want you to speak freely and, more than that, I would like to have you reflect and comment on what other members of the cabinet say."[48] Minutes of Eisenhower's NSC meetings reveal a president who was exposed to the policy divisions within his staff and who engaged in lively discussions with Dulles, Nixon, Harold Stassen, Henry Cabot Lodge, and others. But Eisenhower was also careful to reserve the ultimate power of decision for himself; although they had a voice in the process, neither the NSC nor Adams decided for the president.

Kennedy dismantled most of the national security staff that had existed under Eisenhower, preferring instead to use smaller, more informal and collegial decision-making forums. Kennedy's abandonment of more formal procedures may have been unwise, but his experience with the Ex-Com (his executive committee of top foreign policy advisers) offers lessons about how presidents can work effectively with informal patterns of advice seeking and giving. In April 1961 Kennedy's advisers performed poorly, leading him into an ill-conceived, poorly planned, hastily decided, and badly executed invasion of Cuba—the Bay of Pigs disaster. In the aftermath of that fiasco, Kennedy commissioned a study to find out what had gone wrong; on the basis of its findings, he reorganized his decision-making procedures—including major changes in the Central Intelligence Agency—and explored the faults in his own leadership style. By the time of the Cuban missile crisis in October 1962, Kennedy and his advisers had become an effective decision-making group. Information was readily at hand, the assumptions and implications of policy options were probed, pressures that could lead to a false group consensus were avoided, and Kennedy deliberately did not disclose his own policy preferences—sometimes absenting himself from meetings—to facilitate candid discussions and to head off a premature decision.

In addition to developing a suitable leadership style, presidents can also take steps to deal with the bureaucratic tendencies that can crop up in their staffs. Kennedy's New Frontier agenda, for example, included a number of unbureaucratic programs, such as the Peace Corps; and his personal style generated loyalty and trust. Eisenhower lacked the youthful vigor of his successor, but his broad organizational experience made him a good judge of character with a sure instinct for what and how much he could delegate to subordinates and how best to organize and use their respective talents. As with members of his cabinet, Eisenhower emphasized to his staff aides that they worked for him, not for the NSC, Adams, or others.

Finally, although the tendencies toward centralization of policymaking power within the White House and politicization of the advisory process have been powerful, all presidents have the capacity to choose how they will act and react within a complex political context populated by other powerful political institutions, processes, and participants. Too much politicization weakens any special claims of expertise, experience, and general institutional primacy that the president might make in a particular policy area. Too much centralization eclipses the role of other political actors in a system that is geared to share, rather than exclude, domains of power; it may also set in motion a powerful antipresidential reaction.

In fact, President Bush faced a painful lesson in this regard following the defection of Vermont senator James Jeffords from the Republican Party in May 2001. It was a move that caused the GOP to lose control of the Senate. Jeffords's disenchantment with his party was, at least in part, the result of his treatment by the White House. For Bush, it created an even more difficult barrier to legislative success.

Presidents would be well advised not to neglect the observation about presidential success that Richard Neustadt made more than forty years ago: "Presidential power is the power to persuade."[49] But what presidents also need to know is that the character and intended audience of that persuasion must be tailored, not just to the requirements of legislative bargaining and enhancing popular support but to the institutional character of the presidency itself.

Notes

1. For a fuller account, see John P. Burke, *The Institutional Presidency: Organizing and Managing the White House from FDR to Clinton* (Baltimore: Johns Hopkins University Press, 2000).

2. Stephen J. Wayne, *The Legislative Presidency* (New York: Harper and Row, 1978), 30.

3. Quoted in Louis Brownlow, *A Passion for Anonymity: The Autobiography of Louis Brownlow*, vol. 2 (Chicago: University of Chicago Press, 1958), 392.

4. For fuller discussion of earlier efforts, see Peri Arnold, *Making the Managerial Presidency: Comprehensive Reorganization Planning, 1905–1980* (Princeton: Princeton University Press, 1986).

5. I use the term "larger" to refer to the Brownlow Committee's recognition that the president needed greater staff resources and its recommendations that the Bureau of the Budget be brought over from the Treasury Department and that the Executive Office of

the President be created. In its advice on increasing the size of the president's immediate staff, the committee's recommendations were rather modest: the addition of six administrative aides who would avoid the political spotlight and have a "passion for anonymity." These new positions added a more formal structure to the Roosevelt White House and set out new responsibilities for the once–ad hoc staffing arrangement. It is also interesting to note that Roosevelt rejected Brownlow's recommendations that the position of a chief of staff be created and that a more hierarchical, formally organized White House be established; their implementation would await FDR's successors. For further analysis of FDR and the institutional presidency, see Matthew J. Dickinson, *Bitter Harvest: FDR, Presidential Power, and the Growth of the Presidential Branch* (Cambridge: Cambridge University Press, 1997).

6. President's Committee on Administrative Management, *Administrative Management in the Government of the United States* (Washington, D.C.: U.S. Government Printing Office, 1937), 4.

7. The initial Brownlow Committee recommendation for reorganizing the executive branch also included proposals to redefine the jurisdiction of cabinet departments, regroup autonomous and independent agencies and bureaus, and give the president virtually unchecked authority to determine and carry out the reorganization and any needed in the future. The more controversial proposals were either dropped or made more palatable in the reorganization act passed by Congress in 1939.

8. For further discussion of the Brownlow and Hoover Commissions, as well as other efforts at reorganizing the presidency, see Arnold, *Making the Managerial Presidency.*

9. On the growth of the White House staff during the Eisenhower presidency, see John Hart, "Eisenhower and the Swelling of the Presidency," *Polity* 24 (1992): 673–691.

10. The characteristics of institutionalization are adapted, in part, from Nelson Polsby, "The Institutionalization of the U.S. House of Representatives," *American Political Science Review* 52 (1968): 144–168. On the notion of the presidency as an institution, also see Lester Seligman, "Presidential Leadership: The Inner Circle and Institutionalization," *Journal of Politics* 18 (1956): 410–426; *The Institutionalized Presidency,* ed. Norman Thomas and Hans Baade (Dobbs Ferry, N.Y.: Oceana Press, 1972); Robert S. Gilmour, "The Institutionalized Presidency: A Conceptual Clarification," in *The Presidency in Contemporary Context,* ed. Norman Thomas (New York: Dodd, Mead, 1975), 147–159; John Kessel, *The Domestic Presidency: Decision-Making in the White House* (North Scituate, Mass.: Duxbury Press, 1975); Lester Seligman, "The Presidency and Political Change," *Annals* 466 (1983): 179–192; John Kessel, "The Structures of the Carter White House," *American Journal of Political Science* 27 (1983): 431–463; John Kessel, "The Structures of the Reagan White House," *American Journal of Political Science* 28 (1984): 231–258; Colin Campbell, *Managing the Presidency* (Pittsburgh: University of Pittsburgh Press, 1986); and Peri Arnold, "The Institutionalized Presidency and the American Regime," in *The Presidency Reconsidered,* ed. Richard Waterman (Itasca, Ill.: F. E. Peacock, 1993), 215–245.

11. Until 1977 the Office of Policy Development was named the Domestic Council.

12. On White House relations with the media, see Michael Grossman and Martha J. Kumar, *Portraying the Presidency* (Baltimore: Johns Hopkins University Press, 1981).

13. For further discussion, see Joseph Pika, "Interest Groups and the Executive: Federal Intervention," in *Interest Group Politics,* ed. Allan J. Cigler and Burdett A. Loomis (Washington, D.C.: CQ Press, 1983), 298–323.

14. Galbraith, quoted in Lyndon Johnson, *Vantage Point: Perspectives of the Presidency, 1963–69* (New York: Holt, Rinehart and Winston, 1971), 76.

15. Cyrus Vance, *Hard Choices: Critical Years in America's Foreign Policy* (New York: Simon and Schuster, 1983), 409–410.

16. Alexander Haig, *Caveat: Realism, Reagan, and Foreign Policy* (New York: Macmillan, 1984), 306–307.

17. Tim Weiner and James Risen, "Decision to Strike Factory in Sudan Based on Surmise," *New York Times,* September 21, 1998.

18. Elaine Sciolino and Ethan Bronner, "How a President, Distracted by Scandal, Entered Balkan War," *New York Times,* April 18, 1999.

19. See, for example, Martha Brant and Evan Thomas, "A Steely Southerner, *Time,* August 6, 2001; and Jane Perlez, "Rice on Front Line in Foreign Policy Role," *New York Times,* August 19, 2001.

20. See, for example, Noam Scheiber, "Rod Paige Learns the Hard Way," *New Republic,* July 2, 2001; and Diana Schemo, "Education Chief Seeks More Visible Role," *New York Times,* August 5, 2001.

21. Dana Milbank and Bradley Graham, "With Crisis, White House Style Is Now More Fluid," *Washington Post,* October 10, 2001.

22. Jane Perlez, David Sanger, and Thom Shanker, "From Many Voices, One Battle Strategy," *New York Times,* September 23, 2001.

23. Martin Landau, "Redundancy, Rationality, and the Problem of Duplication and Overlap," *Public Administration Review* 29 (1969): 346–358.

24. Patrick Anderson, *The President's Men* (Garden City: Anchor Books, 1969), 10.

25. Fred I. Greenstein, *The Hidden-Hand Presidency* (New York: Basic Books, 1982), 147. Adams's counterpart in foreign affairs was Secretary of State John Foster Dulles.

26. Joseph A. Califano Jr., *Governing America: An Insider's Report from the White House and the Cabinet* (New York: Simon and Schuster, 1981), 148.

27. Ronald Brownstein and Dick Kirschsten, "Cabinet Power," *National Journal,* June 28, 1986, 1589.

28. Bernard Weinraub, "How Donald Regan Runs the White House," *New York Times Magazine,* January 5, 1986, 14.

29. Irving Janis, *Groupthink: Psychological Studies of Policy Decisions and Fiascoes,* 2d ed. (Boston: Houghton Mifflin, 1982). On possible problems with Bush's small group decision making in the Gulf War, see Bob Woodward, *The Commanders* (New York: Simon and Schuster, 1991); Daniel P. Franklin and Robert Shepard, "Analyzing the Bush Foreign Policy" (paper presented at the annual meeting of the American Political Science Association, Washington, D.C., August 29–September 1, 1991); and Cecil V. Crabb Jr. and Kevin V. Mulcahy, "The Elitist Presidency: George Bush and the Management of Operation Desert Storm," in *The Presidency Reconsidered,* ed. Richard Waterman (Itasca, Ill.: F. E. Peacock, 1993), 275–300. On problems in the Panama invasion of 1989, see John Broder and Melissa Healy, "Panama Operation Hurt by Critical Intelligence Gaps," *Los Angeles Times,* December 24, 1989, 1.

30. Michael Duffy, "Mr. Consensus," *Time,* August 21, 1989, 19. George's theory also found its way into Porter's book analyzing Gerald Ford's Economic Policy Board; see Roger Porter, *Presidential Decision Making* (Cambridge: Cambridge University Press, 1980).

31. Walter Williams, "George Bush and White House Policy Competence" (paper presented at the annual meeting of the American Political Science Association, Chicago, September 3–6, 1992), 12–13.

32. Doyle McManus and James Gerstenzang, "Bush Takes CEO Role in Waging War," *Los Angeles Times,* September 23, 2001.

33. Greg Schneiders, "My Turn: Goodbye to All That," *Newsweek*, September 24, 1979, 23.

34. Ibid.

35. Ibid.

36. Thomas P. Murphy, Donald E. Neuchterlein, and Ronald J. Stupak, *Inside the Bureaucracy: The View from the Assistant Secretary's Desk* (Boulder: Westview Press, 1978), 181.

37. Terry M. Moe, "The Politicized Presidency," in *The New Direction in American Politics*, ed. John Chubb and Paul Peterson (Washington, D.C.: Brookings Institution, 1985), 235.

38. Hugh Heclo, "OMB and the Presidency: The Problem of 'Neutral Competence,'" *Public Interest* 38 (1975): 81.

39. Ibid., 85.

40. David A. Stockman, *The Triumph of Politics: Why the Reagan Revolution Failed* (New York: Harper and Row, 1986).

41. Quoted in William Greider, *The Education of David Stockman and Other Americans* (New York: Dutton, 1982), 33, 37.

42. George Stephanopoulos, *All Too Human* (Boston: Little, Brown, 1999), 416.

43. Michael Isikoff, *Uncovering Clinton* (New York: Crown, 1999), 168.

44. Jack Nelson and Robert Donovan, "The Education of a President," *Los Angeles Times Sunday Magazine*, August 1, 1993, 14.

45. Quoted in ibid.

46. Ibid.

47. On Eisenhower's "binocular" use of informal and formal patterns of advice, see Greenstein, *Hidden-Hand Presidency*, 100–151. On his decision-making processes, see John P. Burke and Fred I. Greenstein, with Larry Berman and Richard Immerman, *How Presidents Test Reality: Decisions on Vietnam, 1954 and 1965* (New York: Russell Sage Foundation, 1989).

48. Herbert Brownell with John P. Burke, *Advising Ike: The Memoirs of Attorney General Herbert Brownell* (Lawrence: University Press of Kansas, 1993), 294.

49. Richard E. Neustadt, *Presidential Power: The Politics of Leadership* (New York: Wiley, 1960).

16 The Presidency and the Bureaucracy: The Presidential Advantage

Terry M. Moe

Separation of powers guarantees that presidents will face a fragmented bureaucracy whose centrifugalism and autonomy are protected by Congress, Terry M. Moe explains. This situation seriously limits presidential leadership and control. Yet, Moe argues, the system also endows presidents with important advantages— some arising from their unilateral powers of discretionary action, others from Congress's vulnerability to collective action problems—that allow them to shape the structure of government, gain greater control over bureaucracy, and shift the balance of power in their favor. Although they cannot hope to remove all obstacles to their leadership, presidents can make "a bad situation better." Moe illustrates his thesis with case studies on civil service reform, congressional oversight of the institutional presidency, and regulatory review.

In the U.S. system of separation of powers, it is inevitable that the president and Congress will struggle over the bureaucracy. Both have legitimate roles to play in creating and designing public agencies, staffing them, funding them, and overseeing their behavior. But what they want from them is often very different. Presidents have their own agendas, addressing the needs and aspirations of a national constituency. Legislators are driven by localism and the narrow demands of special interest groups. Both need bureaucracy to get what they want. And so they struggle.

During the nineteenth century, there was little bureaucracy; the departments and agencies of the executive branch were few in number and small in size and scope. Presidents tended to be weak and Congress strong. But as government began actively addressing the burgeoning problems of industrial society during the early decades of the twentieth century, particularly during the New Deal, American bureaucracy grew enormously. And as the bureaucracy grew, so did the presidency, which has evolved into a complex institution whose specialized components—from the Office of Management and Budget to the National Security Council to the White House domestic policy staff to the White House appointments unit and many others—are largely devoted to providing presidents with a capacity for coherent, centralized control of the bureaucracy.[1] These developments are the defining structural features of modern American government. It is bureaucratic and presidentially led.

This is not to say that presidents somehow reign supreme over the bureaucracy. Far from it. For reasons discussed later in the chapter, separation of powers virtually guarantees that they will face a fragmented bureaucracy whose centrifugalism and autonomy are protected by Congress. Under the circumstances, the best presidents can do is make a bad situation better—and it is by reference to this grim baseline that they have been successful. Rather than take an unfavorable system as a given and accept the way it stacks the political game against them, presidents have moved to restructure the system itself and, in so doing, to transform the game into one more hospitable to their leadership and control. Separation of powers is naturally brutal to presidents. But they have made it less so.

The question posed in this chapter is this: how have presidents been able to do this? If Congress and the president share authority, if they are both broadly powerful, and if both want to control the bureaucracy, then why has their struggle allowed presidents to restructure the system in their own favor?

A detailed historical account would suggest that various factors have been at work. A common claim, for example, is that Congress has simply deferred to presidents, recognizing that they are better suited to provide the expertise, coordination, and dispatch necessary for effective government in an era of complex policy. There is surely some truth to this, especially for cases in which their interests have not been in conflict. But a more interesting and consequential claim is the following: even when the interests of presidents and Congress are in conflict, which is much of the time, presidents have inherent advantages in the realm of institution building that allow them, slowly but surely, to strengthen their hand in the ongoing battle with Congress for control of the bureaucracy.

This is the claim I want to argue in this chapter. The discussion is divided into two parts. In the first, I offer a perspective on how decisions about bureaucratic control are made in the U.S. system, the relative roles that presidents and Congress play, and the forces that give rise to the presidential advantage in restructuring the system. Notable among these forces are the president's unilateral powers of discretionary action and Congress's debilitating collective action problems.

In the second part, I illustrate this argument with three cases that bear directly on the institutional balance of power: the Civil Service Reform Act of 1978, congressional oversight and funding of the institutional presidency, and presidential review of regulatory rule making.

Why Bureaucratic Control Is So Difficult

In a world defined by separation of powers, the bureaucracy is destined to be difficult for presidents to control.[2] Indeed, the bureaucracy is not designed for coherent, central control by the president or anyone else. In one way or another, most of it arises out of fragmented, decentralized processes of congressional politics and is slowly put together piece by piece over time. Each piece is a separately conceived and orchestrated political product, fashioned by a unique coalition of legislators and interest groups, and designed to promote a particular set of interests.

The designers of public agencies take a steadfastly myopic and parochial approach to bureaucracy. As individual actors in a fragmented system, interest groups and members of Congress are not held responsible for the performance of the system as a whole, as the president is. And they have no serious concern for broad issues of management, efficiency, and coordination, as the president does. Interest groups have their eyes on their own interests, and little else. Legislators have their eyes on their own electoral fortunes, and thus on the special (often local) interests that can bring them security and popularity. Groups and legislators need each other, and they work well together. For both, politics is not about the system. It is about the pieces and about special interests.

What kind of pieces do they build? Specifically, how do they go about designing public agencies? In any given case a legislative coalition wants an agency that can do its bidding most effectively. But this is not simply a matter of creating structures that promote effective organization in the usual sense. For whether the agency actually pursues coalition objectives through time, effectively or not, depends on who controls it and what they want it to do. If control falls into the wrong hands, all the effectiveness in the world will not help. The central political challenge a coalition faces, then, is not to build an effective organization per se, but rather to ensure its own control and insulate against the control of others.

To some extent, the solution is to identify the obvious opponents—an unfriendly president, say, or a powerful business group—and adopt structures that protect the agency from their influence. But the control problem actually runs much deeper than this. In fact, it is rooted in democracy and in the political uncertainty that goes along with it. Under democratic rules, a new agency is subject to control by whoever happens to hold public authority. Today's friendly authorities may be replaced by enemies tomorrow, as electoral and other shifts in political fortunes bring new players into positions of power—and give them the legal right to control the agency and to ruin everything. In a democracy, then, the only sure way to insulate an agency against unwanted control by others is to insulate it against future authority in general, and thus against democratic accountability.

This strategy may sound pernicious, but the forms it takes are exceedingly common and widely accepted in U.S. politics. The most direct approach is for a coalition to impose detailed formal restrictions on its agency—via decision procedures, standards, timetables, personnel rules, and the like—that tell it by law precisely what to do and how to do it, thus removing much of its behavior from ongoing democratic control. In so doing, the coalition is able to exercise its own control *ex ante,* embedding its interests in strategically chosen structures that essentially put the agency on autopilot, resistant to future control by others. The benefits of insulation do not come cheap: these same structures tend to bury the agency under an avalanche of formalism and undermine its effectiveness. But in a world of political uncertainty, this is a price worth paying if the agency is to be protected.

Presidents are prime targets of this strategy, even when coalitions regard the current incumbent as friendly. The reason is that all presidents, for institutional reasons, use their power in ways that are threatening to legislators and groups. Their interests are different. As national leaders with broad, heterogeneous constituencies, they think in grander terms about social problems and the public interest, and they tend to resist specialized appeals. Moreover, because they are held uniquely responsible by the public for virtually every aspect of national performance, and because their leadership and their legacies turn on effective governance, they have strong incentives to seek coherent, central control of the federal bureaucracy for themselves and their national agenda.

Legislative coalitions have ample reason to fear presidents, then, and to insulate agencies against presidential influence. All the formal restrictions mentioned previously help to do that: by insulating agencies from external control in general, they help to shut out presidents. But other restrictions are aimed directly at presidents. The independent regulatory commission, for example, is a popular structural form that restricts presidential removal and managerial powers. Similarly, legislation often limits the number of presidential appointees in an agency and uses civil service and professionalism to insulate personnel from presidential direction.

Presidents have every incentive, whatever their party or agenda, to oppose these restrictions and to press for a bureaucracy they can control—and institutions that allow them to do it better. One strategy is to participate actively in the legislative process, using their political clout to push, bargain, and logroll their way toward somewhat better structures when agencies are created or reorganized. Another is to avoid the legislative process as much as possible and instead to use their executive powers to cobble together the structures they want. Both strategies, but especially the second, have been major forces animating the growth and elaboration of the institutional presidency—which represents, in structural form, a continuing effort by modern presidents to strike back and gain the upper hand.

This is how the institutional battle lines are drawn. Legislators and groups, motivated by parochial concerns, routinely go about the piecemeal construction of a bureaucracy that is buried in formalism, poorly designed for its tasks, and insulated from coherent control. Presidents, motivated to lead, find this unacceptable. They take aggressive action to modify the "congressional bureaucracy," to develop their own institutional capacity for control, and to presidentialize the system. Legislators and groups resist, presidents counter, and so it goes. The central dynamic of the American bureaucratic system derives from this tension between presidents who seek control and the legislative and group players who want to carve out and defend their own small pieces of turf.

Presidential Advantage: Discretion and Unilateral Power

This is a dynamic in which presidents hold certain advantages. In time, these advantages allow them to move the structure of the system, however haltingly and episodically, along a presidential trajectory.

Presidents are greatly advantaged by their position as chief executive, which gives them the right to make unilateral decisions about structure and policy. If they want to develop their own institution, review or revise agency decisions, coordinate agency actions, make changes in agency leadership, or otherwise impose their views on government, they can simply proceed—and it is up to Congress (and the courts) to react. For reasons discussed later, Congress often finds this difficult or impossible to do, and the president wins by default. The ability to win by default is a cornerstone of the presidential advantage.

Why do presidents have powers of unilateral action?[3] Part of the answer is constitutional. The Constitution, rather than spelling out their authority as chief executive in great detail—a strategy favored by those among the Framers who were most concerned with limiting the executive—remains largely silent on the nature and extent of presidential authority, especially in domestic affairs. It broadly endows presidents with the "executive power" and gives them responsibility to "faithfully execute the laws," but says little else. This very ambiguity, as Richard Pious notes, "provided the opportunity for the exercise of a residuum of unenumerated power."[4] The proponents of a strong executive at the Constitutional Convention, who won out on this language, were well aware of that.

The question of what the president's formal powers really are, or ought to be, will always be controversial among legal scholars. But two things seem reasonably clear. One is that if presidents are to perform their duties effectively under the Constitution, they must be (and in practice are) regarded as having certain legal prerogatives that allow them to do what executives do: manage, coordinate, staff, collect information, plan, reconcile conflicting values, and so on. This is what it means, in practice, to have the executive power.[5] The other is that, although the content of these prerogative powers is often unclear, presidents have been aggressive in pushing an expansive interpretation: rushing into gray areas of the law, asserting their rights, and exercising them—whether other actors, particularly in Congress, happened to agree or not.[6]

The courts, which have the authority to resolve ambiguities about the president's proper constitutional role, have not chosen to do so. Certain contours of presidential power have been clarified by major court decisions—on the removal power, for instance, and executive privilege—and justices have sometimes offered their views on the president's implied or inherent powers as chief executive. But the political and historical reality is that presidents have largely defined their own constitutional role by pushing out the boundaries of their prerogatives.[7]

Congress can do nothing to eliminate the executive power of presidents. They are not Congress's agents. They have their own constitutional role to play and their own constitutional powers to exercise, powers that are not delegated to them by Congress and cannot be taken away. Any notion that Congress makes the laws and that the presidents' job is simply to execute them—to follow orders, in effect—overlooks what separation of powers is all about: presidents have authority in their own right, coequal to Congress and not subordinate to it.

Precisely because presidents are chief executives, however, what they can and cannot do is also shaped by the goals and requirements of the laws they are charged with executing. And Congress has the right to be as specific as it wants in designing these laws, as well as the agencies that administer them. If it likes, it can specify policy and structure in enough detail to narrow agency discretion considerably, and with it the scope of presidential control. It can also impose requirements that explicitly qualify and limit how presidents may use their prerogative powers, as it has done, for example, in protecting members of independent commissions from removal and in mandating civil service protections.[8]

Yet these sorts of restrictions ultimately cannot contain presidential power. To begin with, presidents are powerful players in the legislative process, and they will fight for statutes that give them as much discretion as possible. In addition, the legislative authors of statutes cannot eliminate all discretion from their delegations of authority to bureaucracies and presidents, and they would not want to even if they could. Their concern, politics aside, is still the effective provision of benefits to their constituents. For problems of even moderate complexity, especially in an ever-changing world, this requires putting most aspects of policy and organization in the hands of agency professionals and allowing them to use their expert judgment to flesh out the details. Once the authority is delegated, however, it is the president and the agencies who govern, not Congress. Short of new legislation, Congress can only oversee from the outside. The presidents are chief executives, and they call the shots.

Thus although legislators and groups may try to protect their agencies by burying them in rules and regulations, a good deal of agency discretion will remain, and presidents cannot readily be prevented from turning it to their own advantage. They are centrally and supremely positioned in the executive, they have great flexibility to act, they have a vast array of powers and mechanisms at their disposal—not to mention informal means of persuasion and influence— and they, not Congress, are ultimately responsible for day-to-day governance. Even when Congress directly limits a presidential prerogative (the removal power, say), presidents have the flexibility simply to shift to other means of control.

In part, Congress's problem is analogous to the classic problem a board of directors faces in trying to control management in a private firm.[9] The board, representing owners, tries to impose rules and procedures to ensure that management will behave in the owners' best interests. But managers have their own interests at heart, and their expertise and day-to-day control of operations allow them to strike out on their own. Much the same is true for Congress and presidents. However much Congress tries to structure things, presidents can use their own institution's—and through it, the agencies'—informational and operational advantages to promote the presidential agenda.

But the corporate analogy is not quite on target. Owners have control problems even though their authority is supreme: their agents are managers whom they hire and over whom they have authority. Congress's problem is far more severe. Presidents possess all of the resources for noncompliance that corporate managers do, but their position is far stronger because they are not Congress's agents in the scheme of government. They have authority in their own right. Congress does not hire them, it cannot fire them, and it cannot structure their powers and incentives in any way it might like. Yet it is forced to entrust them with the execution of the laws. From a control standpoint, this is a nightmare come true for Congress.

It is also important to recognize that, although Congress can try to limit presidential prerogatives through statute, presidents are greatly empowered through statutory law whether Congress intends it or not. Some grants of power to the presidency are explicit, such as the negotiation of tariffs and the oversight of mergers in the foreign trade field. But the most far-reaching additions to presidential power are implicit. When new statutes are passed, almost regardless of what they are, they increase presidents' total responsibilities and give them a formal basis for extending their authoritative reach into new realms. At the same time, they add to the total discretion available for presidential control, as well as to the resources contained within the executive.

It may seem that the proliferation of statutes would tie presidents up in knots as they pursue the execution of each one. But the aggregate effect is liberating. Presidents, as chief executives, are responsible for *all* the laws—and, inevitably, those laws turn out to be interdependent and conflicting in ways that the individual statutes themselves do not recognize. As would be true of any executive, the president's proper role is to rise above a myopic focus on each statute in isolation, to coordinate policies by taking account of their interdependence, and to resolve statutory conflicts by balancing their competing requirements. All of this affords presidents substantial discretion, which they can use to impose their own priorities on government.[10]

Regulatory review is but one example. Since the presidency of Richard M. Nixon, all presidents have insisted on reviewing the proposed rules of regulatory agencies (particularly those of the Environmental Protection Agency), causing a number of important rules to be delayed, modified, or shelved.[11] Critics in Congress have complained loudly that regulatory review prevents the agencies from single-mindedly pursuing their mandates. And they are right. Yet presidents are responsible not just for each particular statute, but for all statutes—including those that direct them to reduce inflation and unemployment, promote economic growth, conserve energy, and otherwise enhance the nation's economic well-being. Thus presidents have a statutory (as well as a constitutional) basis for asserting their coordinating-and-balancing prerogatives in bringing these other values to bear on the regulatory agencies. What this means in political practice is that they have a legal argument for imposing presidential priorities and expanding the scope of their own discretionary action. The greater the proliferation of congressional legislation over the years, the greater the president's opportunities to find just this sort of conflict and interdependence—and to assert control.

Presidential Advantage: Congress's Collective Action Problems

Another major source of presidential advantage deserves equal emphasis. Presidents are unitary actors who sit alone atop their own institution. What they say goes. In contrast, Congress is a collective institution that can make decisions only through the laborious aggregation of members' preferences. As such, it suffers from serious collective action problems that presidents not only avoid but can exploit.

This crucial fact of political life is too often overlooked. Scholars and journalists tend to reify Congress, to treat it as if it were an institutional actor like the president, and to analyze their interbranch conflicts accordingly. The president and Congress are portrayed as fighting it out, head to head, over matters of institutional power and prerogative. Each is seen as defending and promoting its institutional interests. The president wants power, Congress wants power, and they struggle for advantage.

This misconstrues things. Congress is made up of hundreds of members, each a political entrepreneur in his or her own right, each dedicated to his or her reelection and therefore to serving his or her district or state. Although all have a common stake in the institutional power of Congress, this is a collective good that, for well-known reasons, can only weakly motivate their behavior.[12] They are trapped in a prisoner's dilemma: all might benefit if they could cooperate in defending or advancing Congress's power, but each has a strong incentive to free ride if support for the collective good is politically costly to them as individuals. Just as most citizens, absent taxation, would not voluntarily pay their shares of national defense costs, so most legislators will not flout the interests of their constituencies (and their own electoral interests) if that is the price of protecting congressional power. If a legislator were offered a dam or a veterans' hospital or a new highway to vote for a bill that, among other things, happened to reduce Congress's power somewhat relative to the president's, there would be little mystery as to where the stronger incentives lie.

The internal organization of Congress, especially its party leadership, imposes a modicum of order and authority on member behavior and gives the institution a certain ability to guard its power.[13] But disabling problems still run rampant, and they are built in. Party leaders are notoriously weak—and they are weak because their "followers" want them to be. Good leadership means promoting the reelection prospects of members by decentralizing authority, expanding their opportunities to serve special interests, and giving them the freedom to vote their constituencies' preferences.[14]

Presidents are not hobbled by these collective action problems and, supreme within their institution, can simply make authoritative decisions about what is best. Although their interests as individuals may sometimes conflict with those of the presidency as an institution—for example, if their desire for responsiveness and loyalty in an agency like the Office of Management and Budget (OMB) undercuts the presidency's long-term capacity for expertise and competence[15]—their drive for leadership almost always motivates them to promote the power of their institution. Thus not only is the presidency a unitary institution, but there is also substantial congruence between the president's individual interests and the interests of the institution.

This sets up a basic imbalance. Presidents have both the will and the capacity to promote the power of their own institution, but individual legislators have neither and cannot be expected to promote the power of Congress as a whole in any coherent, forceful way. This means that presidents will behave imperialistically and opportunistically, but that Congress will not do the same in formulating an offensive of its own, and indeed will not even be able to mount a consistently effective defense against presidential encroachment.

Congress's situation is all the worse because its collective action problems do more than disable its own will and capacity for action. They also allow presidents to manipulate legislative behavior to their own advantage—getting members to support or at least acquiesce in the growth of presidential power. One basis for this has already been established by political scientists: in any majority-rule institution with diverse members, so many different majority coalitions are possible that, with the right manipulation of the agenda, outcomes can be engineered to allow virtually any alternative to win against any other.[16] Put more simply, agenda setters can take advantage of the collective action problems inherent in majority-rule institutions to get their own way.

Presidents have at least two important kinds of agenda power. First, precisely because Congress is so fragmented, presidentially initiated legislation is the most coherent force in setting Congress's legislative agenda. The issues Congress deals with are fundamentally shaped each year by the issues presidents decide will be salient.[17] Second, presidents set Congress's agenda when they or their appointees in the bureaucracy take unilateral action to alter the status quo—by changing the direction of an agency's policy, for example. This happens all the time, and Congress is simply forced to react or acquiesce. In either case, presidents can choose their positions strategically, with an eye to the various majorities in Congress, and engineer outcomes more beneficial to the presidency than they could if dealing with a unified opponent.[18]

Presidential leverage is enhanced by the many obstacles that stand in the way of each congressional decision. A bill must pass through subcommittees, committees, and floor votes in both houses; it must be endorsed in identical form by each house; and it is threatened along the way by rules committees, filibusters, holds, and executive vetoes. Every veto point must be overcome if Congress is to act. But presidents need to succeed with only one to ensure the status quo—and their own veto will usually suffice if the others don't.

More generally, the transaction costs of congressional action are enormous. Not only must coalitions somehow be formed among hundreds of legislators across two houses and a variety of committees—which calls for intricate coordination, persuasion, trades, promises, and all the rest—but, owing to scarce time and resources, members must also be convinced that the issue at hand is more deserving than the hundreds of other issues competing for their attention. Party leaders and committee chairs can help, but the veto-filled process of generating legislation remains incredibly difficult and costly. And because it is, the best prediction for most issues most of the time is that Congress will take no positive action at all. Whatever members' positions on an issue, the great likelihood is that *nothing will happen.*

When presidents are able to use unilateral powers and discretion to shift the status quo, what they want most from Congress is no formal response at all—which is exactly what they are likely to get. This would be so in any event, given the multiple veto points and high transaction costs that plague congressional choice. But it is especially likely when presidents and their agents weigh into the legislative process on their own behalf—dangling rewards, threatening sanctions, directing the troops, unsticking legislative deals with side payments.[19]

Presidents are especially well-situated and endowed with political resources to do this. And again, blocking is fairly easy.

Whether presidents are trying to block or to push for positive legislation, the motivational asymmetry between them and Congress adds mightily to their cause. I referred to this earlier, but it is important enough to need underlining. Presidents are strongly motivated to develop an institutional capacity for controlling the bureaucracy as a whole, and, when structural issues are in question, they take the larger view. How do these structures contribute to or detract from the creation of a presidential system of control? Legislators are driven by localism and special interests, and they are little motivated by these sorts of system concerns. This basic motivational asymmetry has a great deal to do with what presidents are able to accomplish in their attempts to block or steer congressional outcomes.

On issues affecting the institutional balance of power, presidents care intensely about securing changes that promote their institutional power, whereas legislators typically do not. They are unlikely to oppose incremental increases in the relative power of presidents unless the issue in question directly harms the special interests of their constituents—which, if presidents play their cards right, can often be avoided. On the other hand, legislators are generally unwilling to do what is necessary to develop Congress's own capacity for strong institutional action. Not only does it often require that they put constituency concerns aside for the common good, which they have strong incentives not to do, but it also tends to call for more centralized control by party leaders and less member autonomy, which they find distinctly unattractive.

When institutional issues are at stake in legislative voting, then, presidents have a motivational advantage: they care more. This asymmetry means that they will invest more of their political clout in getting what they want. It also means that the situation is ripe for trade. Legislators may fill the airwaves with rhetoric about the dangers of presidential power, but their weak individual stakes allow them to be bought off with the kinds of particularistic benefits (and sanctions) that they really do care about. This does not mean that presidents can perform magic. If what they want requires affirmative congressional action, the obstacles are many and the probability of success is low. But their chances are still much better than they otherwise would be, absent the motivational asymmetry. And if all they want to do is block, which often is all they need, then the asymmetry can work wonders in cementing presidential *faits accomplis*.

Presidential Advantage: Three Cases

The weight of all these factors, taken together, points to a decided presidential advantage in the battle for institutional power. Presidents are unitary decision-makers: they can take unilateral action in imposing their own structures; their individual interests are largely congruent with the institutional interests of the presidency; and they are dedicated to gaining control of the bureaucracy. Congress is hobbled by collective action problems, vulnerable to agenda manipulation by presidents, and populated by individuals whose interests diverge substantially from those of the institution. The result is an imbalance in the dynamic of institutional change, yielding an uneven but relentless shift toward a more presidential system.

To illustrate this argument, let us now take a brief look at three important cases in recent institutional politics, all of them involving attempts by presidents to expand their own powers at the expense of Congress. The first explores the politics of the Civil Service Reform Act of 1978, in which President Jimmy Carter sought a significant increase in presidential control over federal employees, and asks how Congress responded. The second looks at congressional oversight and funding of the institutional presidency and asks how effectively Congress has used its own powers to prevent presidents from increasing theirs. The third spotlights regulatory review, in which presidents have imposed their own rules and priorities on agency decision making, and asks what Congress has done to stop them.

Civil Service Reform

The career civil service, whose members are neither hired nor fired by presidents, is obviously a major impediment to presidential leadership. But until Jimmy Carter, no modern president had invested much effort in trying to alter the system. Civil service reform had been contemplated in broad reorganization packages, notably under Franklin D. Roosevelt (via the Brownlow Committee) and Dwight D. Eisenhower (via the second Hoover Commission), but it had never been a high priority on its own.[20] This is hardly surprising. Genuine reform calls for new legislation of the first magnitude, which is extraordinarily difficult and politically costly to achieve. With so many other ways to enhance their power through unilateral action, presidents had little incentive to pursue it.

Carter's situation was different from that of his predecessors, however. He oversaw a government much bigger, more bureaucratic, and more expensive than theirs. Moreover, by the mid-1970s, in a worsening atmosphere of stagflation and energy shortages, Americans were fed up. Strong antigovernment, antitax sentiments swelled within the electorate, and politicians—including Jimmy Carter—responded with pledges of reform.[21]

It was easy to portray civil service reform as part of this broad movement for better, more effective government. But for Carter it was much more than that: it was a way to make the civil service system an arm of the presidency and thus to enhance the president's capacity for controlling the bureaucracy. The kind of reform he had in mind amounted to nothing less than a clear shift in the balance of institutional power.

In the early spring of 1978, barely a year after assuming office, Carter placed a comprehensive proposal for civil service reform before Congress. Together with Alan Campbell, the chair of the Civil Service Commission, he turned loose a small army of White House staffers, cabinet members, and OMB officials to mobilize support within Congress.[22] The proposal involved five major changes in the federal personnel system.[23] These would

1. Divide the Civil Service Commission, long a nonpartisan independent agency, into two parts. One, the Office of Personnel Management (OPM), would be headed by a single presidential appointee and would determine personnel policies for federal employees. The other, the Merit Systems Protection Board (MSPB), would be an adjudicatory agency for handling appeals and grievances.

2. Create a Senior Executive Service (SES), a flexible corps of high-level administrators (about 9,200 in number) who could be moved from job to job and would qualify for substantial merit pay.

3. Move from automatic pay raises for supervisors and managers toward performance evaluations and merit pay.

4. Substantially curtail veterans' preferences, which, since World War I, had given them the inside track for federal jobs.

5. Codify the arrangements for unionization and collective bargaining by federal employees and place responsibility for these matters in a new agency, the Federal Labor Relations Authority (FLRA).

There was nothing here to fool legislators into seeing civil service reform as an impartial attempt to achieve "good government." The OPM would be an arm of the presidency and would be granted a great deal more discretion than the old Civil Service Commission—discretion that could be turned to this president's, and any future president's, advantage. There would be a large corps of senior executives (whose personal views, loyalties, and partisanship are easily identified) that the OPM could allocate at its discretion across pivotal jobs in agencies throughout government. And these executives, as well as others not in the SES, would be subject to performance evaluations and merit pay—which would be determined, inevitably, by the discretionary judgments of the president's appointees within the OPM and the agencies.

How did Congress respond? It responded just as we would expect. Legislators simply did not care much about the balance-of-power issue, and, with a few exceptions, did not oppose this clear shift in authority and discretion to the president. Virtually all the political controversy was stimulated by the intense opposition of special interest groups—labor unions and veterans' organizations—to the provisions of the act that specifically affected them.[24]

The committees with primary jurisdiction for civil service reform were the Governmental Affairs Committee in the Senate and the Post Office and Civil Service Committee in the House. The Senate committee was not tied to any particular interest groups, because its mandate was to oversee government organization generally and because it attracted senators from various constituencies. These senators, like all politicians during the late 1970s, knew that supporting almost anything labeled "reform" would have its electoral advantages. And there were few direct effects on their constituencies to worry about. Meanwhile, Carter was pushing hard, using the resources at his disposal to win the committee over. The result was almost total support, among both Democrats and Republicans, for the core provisions of the president's bill.

Even this committee, however, was not immune to group influence. Aware of the broadly based power of veterans' groups in Congress, committee members feared a bloody floor fight that could derail the whole bill. They also may have responded to direct pressure—veterans in every state are numerous, organized, and active. In any event, the committee reported a bill that substantially weakened the offensive provision about veterans, but otherwise preserved what the president wanted.[25]

On the Senate floor, two Republicans who had opposed the bill in committee, Charles Mathias Jr. of Maryland and Ted Stevens of Alaska, argued the dangers of politicization of the civil service by the president. This was the only serious opposition that was couched in institutional rather than interest group terms.[26] They were appeased, however, with minor amendments that left the essence of the bill unchanged. The amended bill was then approved by the Senate by a vote of 87 to 1, hardly an indication that senators were staying up nights worrying about the balance of institutional power.[27]

In the House, there was more of a political struggle—but not over institutional issues. The House Post Office and Civil Service Committee was a friendly place for interest groups. Because of the nature of its jurisdiction, it was a high-priority setting for federal employees' unions and the politicians who sought to serve them. And they were not happy with this act.[28]

Initially, the president had attempted to buy off the opposition with provisions codifying important aspects of federal labor relations and creating the FLRA. But the unions found these concessions too weak and not enough to compensate for the act's threatened expansions of executive discretion and merit pay, which directly eroded the kinds of rule-based protections that unions consistently demand for their members.

The federal employees' unions did not have enough support to defeat the bill in the House, but they were strong enough to cause trouble. Their fallback was to have Rep. William Clay, a Democrat from Missouri, attach an amendment that relaxed existing Hatch Act limitations on political activities by federal employees. Although this left the remaining provisions unaffected, it was something the unions desperately wanted, and it had actually passed the House the year before. Altering the Hatch Act was vehemently opposed by Republicans, however, who were generally quite supportive of Carter's original bill. Clay's amendment gave Republicans the incentive to launch strategic maneuvers of their own, leading to a complicated battle whose intricacies can be appreciated only by seasoned parliamentarians.[29]

In the end, the Clay amendment was dropped. Labor did persuade the House to attach an amendment limiting the SES to a small pilot program, and Republicans went along, knowing it would be dropped from the bill at the conference committee stage. More concretely, labor also succeeded in strengthening the provision on collective bargaining a bit. Veterans left their mark, too: the House accepted the Senate's wording, which retained most veterans' preferences. The resulting bill passed the House by a vote of 385 to 10.[30] As in the Senate, the House decision had nothing to do with general concerns about the balance of power. Once the interest groups were satisfied, the legislators were willing to go along.

The conference committee, with Republican support, restored the full SES program. To mollify labor Democrats, it tacked on a two-house legislative veto to this provision alone. After five years, Congress could overturn the SES provision if both houses voted (within a prescribed sixty-day period) to do so. Aside from this change—and the victory by veterans—the bill that came out of conference was almost exactly what President Carter had requested: an act radically transforming the civil service system by granting the president substantial new discretion and power. It passed both houses without controversy.[31]

While all this was happening, a revealing decision was being made along a separate track. The president had sought most of his changes in the civil service through new legislation, but he had asked for authority to divide the Civil Service Commission into two parts, the OPM and the MSPB, through a reorganization plan that, by law, would take effect unless vetoed by either the House or the Senate.

The reaction of legislators to this aspect of the proposal is especially telling evidence of how they approach matters of institutional power, because this Carter reorganization plan was an issue shorn of all special-interest provisions. It simply called for an up-or-down vote on whether presidents should bring personnel more fully under their control throughout the government. Did members of Congress rise up to stop this presidential power grab? Hardly. The House at least voted on the matter: a resolution to kill the president's plan was defeated, 19 to 381. The Senate did not even vote.[32]

In sum, the president cared a great deal about the issues of institutional power embedded in civil service reform, but members of Congress did not. The few political fireworks were supplied by the only special interest groups directly affected by this legislation: unions and veterans.

Congressional Oversight of the Presidency

Under our constitutional system, Congress's powers are vague at the margins, just as the president's powers are. Although Congress has the right to make the laws, it is unclear how far it can go in making laws that undermine presidents' abilities to carry out their duties as chief executives. Similarly, Congress has the power of the purse, but it cannot be too draconian in denying presidents funds without encroaching on their proper responsibilities.

Still, an aggressive Congress bent on defending and increasing its own power would do what presidents have done: it would push its prerogatives to the limit and use every ambiguity in the Constitution to its own advantage. If threatened, as it clearly has been, by the growing scope and reach of the institutional presidency, Congress has the formal power to reduce funding, withhold authorization, stifle appointments, and engage in aggressive oversight. Indeed, it could just as well try to nip all its problems in the bud by preventing the emergence of a powerful institutional presidency in the first place. Presidents cannot build a powerful institution with no money.

Yet Congress has done nothing of the sort. Not only has it failed to act aggressively in asserting its own powers, but it has also largely stood on the sidelines and allowed presidents to do what they want in building their own institution in their own way. John Hart sums it up this way:

Ever since the Executive Office of the President was established in 1939, Congress has shown a marked reluctance to enforce, let alone strengthen, its oversight of the presidential branch. Even the events of Watergate, which helped to crystallize a great deal of criticism of the White House staff, did little to increase enthusiasm for improving congressional oversight in this area. Those efforts that were made came from a handful of legislators who were never able to convince the majority of their colleagues on Capitol Hill to share their concerns with the same intensity, and, today, the presidential branch remains relatively immune from congressional scrutiny of any kind.[33]

Hart explained Congress's reticence by pointing to the norm of comity, an understanding among legislators that, in the interests of harmony between the branches, presidents should be given latitude to develop their institution as they see fit. Even if there is such a norm, however, deeper questions remain. Why would legislators find it compatible with their interests? Why would they leave presidents alone when they have the power to go after them?

The answer is rooted in Congress's collective action problems. Legislators do not care much about incremental changes in the institutional presidency unless their constituents are directly affected. There are no interest group "fire alarms" to prod them into action, no clear electoral benefits to be gained from opposing the president. Meantime, presidents care intensely, and they dedicate their resources to getting what they want.

The creation of the Office of Management and Budget, the workhorse of the institutional presidency, illustrates what Congress is up against when presidents take the offensive on purely institutional issues. The vehicle was President Nixon's Reorganization Plan no. 2, which sought to transform the Bureau of the Budget (BOB) into a more powerful presidential agency. Political appointees would replace careerists as heads of operating divisions; the bureau's functions in program management, coordination, and information would be expanded; and all functions vested by law in the BOB would be transferred to the president. The whole point of this plan was to give the OMB greater managerial control of the bureaucracy, and to make the OMB more responsive to the president.[34] Legislators saw this proposal for what it was, but the institutional issues were not sufficient to galvanize opposition. The Senate never even voted on a resolution of disapproval. The House did, but the Nixon forces put together a coalition of Republicans and southern Democrats to win.[35]

In time, Congress would put up more resistance. But until the early 1970s, Congress had little success in braking the institutional presidency and showed little interest in doing so. It did try to influence the kind of advice presidents received—creating the Council of Economic Advisors (CEA) and the National Security Council (NSC), for example, within the Executive Office of the President (EOP)—but this was futile as a control mechanism, because presidents can refuse to take any advice they do not want. The CEA and NSC, like all other units in the EOP, quickly became creatures of the sitting president anyway, because each president was given a free hand to organize, employ staff, assign jobs, and allocate resources.[36] Congress was largely in the dark, moreover, about exactly what presidents were doing. It did not even know how many people were employed within the White House Office, where they came from, which units of government paid their salaries, or what their jobs were. Congress was funding all this, routinely and without question. But it literally did not know what it was funding.[37]

Things changed in the early 1970s. By then Nixon had transformed the BOB, dramatically increased (or so it appeared) the size and power of his White House staff, and in a variety of ways antagonized the Democrats and their interest group supporters. In response, a small number of legislators began to press for closer congressional oversight. These sorts of isolated challenges normally would not pose much of a threat. But then Watergate hit with full force, generating a public backlash against the "imperial presidency" and turning up the political heat. More and more legislators found that attacking the presidency was a popular thing to do, at least for a short while.

The most notable struggles to come out of all this had their roots in a 1972 study by the House Post Office and Civil Service Committee, which, for the first time, collected simple data documenting the growth of the presidency and the centralization of power in the White House. It decried these developments and called for more intensive efforts by Congress to amass information about the presidency and to restrict its institutional development.[38]

The next year, Rep. John Dingell, a Democrat from Michigan, tried to unhinge the presidential budget by revealing an amazing discovery: although Congress was regularly funding some five hundred White House employees, a 1948 statute still in effect authorized only six presidential assistants and eight secretaries! President Nixon mobilized enough support in Congress to gain authority and funding for his staff in the short term, but a permanent legislative solution obviously had to be found. His opponents, meanwhile, had been accidentally empowered beyond their wildest dreams.[39]

During the next several years, various legislators tried to engineer a bill that would both authorize a reasonably sized White House staff and provide Congress with better information and control. After a series of failed attempts, the House Post Office and Civil Service Committee came up with a bill that, with much modification, was passed into law as the White House Personnel Authorization Employment Act of 1978. The committee's original proposal was highly threatening to the president. It imposed strict ceilings on the total number of White House staff, as well as the number of senior presidential aides and executives; it also required presidents to submit an annual report to Congress with detailed information about who works in the White House, what they do, and who pays their salaries. As we would expect, however, resisting this bill proved to be a top-priority for President Carter. He maneuvered House members into supporting a friendly, largely symbolic final bill—one that authorized a large White House staff and gutted the ceiling and reporting requirements.

Specifically, Carter got the House committee to remove its limit on total staff and to accept an unconstraining ceiling on senior officials. (Indeed, the "ceiling" would have allowed a fully staffed Carter White House to double its senior staff if it wanted.) He then persuaded the Senate, whose members cared even less about the issue, to reduce the reporting requirements further: instead of detailed records on individual employees, the White House would need to report only the total amounts spent on different types of staff. Information that was genuinely revealing would remain hidden, as before. In the conference committee, the Senate version prevailed, and the fully gutted bill became law. The president got his authorization. Congress got next to nothing.[40]

Since then, relations between the two branches have been anything but harmonious, and Congress has had ample reason—were it truly concerned with protecting its institutional power—to take further legislative action to rein in the presidency. During the Reagan years, Congress faced a president intent on pursuing his conservative agenda through an aggressive expansion of executive power. And during the post-1994 Clinton years, Republicans gained control of Congress for the first time in forty years and faced a Democratic president whose opposition threatened their plans to reshape the fundamentals of American public policy. These periods of intense institutional conflict, however, generated no congressional action of any consequence to strengthen its oversight of the executive. To date, the 1978 law has been Congress's most coherent attempt to get a grip on the institutional presidency. And it is little more than a symbolic gesture.

Legislation is not Congress's only avenue of attack, however. There is also its annually exercised power of the purse, which is clearly capable of eviscerating the institutional presidency if used strategically. How has Congress wielded this formidable power? It has barely put it to use. Until the 1970s, presidential budgets were lightly scrutinized and typically passed through Congress unchanged. Presidents provided almost no information about the White House and its operations, or even about the details of EOP agencies, and Congress simply appropriated whatever presidents said was necessary. During the 1970s, matters became more contentious, peaking during the Watergate era but never entirely subsiding thereafter.[41]

Presidents have to work a little harder for their money now. Appropriations committees demand more information, scrutinize it more carefully, and are more critical than they used to be. But there is much less here than meets the eye. Presidents continue to get virtually everything they request, legislative rhetoric aside.[42] This was even the norm during the Reagan era, and it continued during the tumultuous years of struggle between Democrat Clinton and the conservative Republican Congress. The information presidents provide to Congress, moreover, is next to useless for genuine control purposes. For the most part, their requests take the form of lump-sum amounts pertaining to entire EOP units or to broad categories of employees or activities, with no information about the details of presidential organization, programs, or staffing. Even during the conflictual years of divided government, then, the presidency is treated with kid gloves when it comes to oversight, and Congress remains largely in the dark about what happens inside the executive.

Regulatory Review

Regulatory review is often spotlighted as an issue that captures what the institutional battle between the president and Congress is all about. Presidents have imposed new procedures on regulatory agencies in a sustained attempt to gain control of agency rule making and assert presidential priorities. Meanwhile, the agencies and their legislative supporters have vigorously protested, claiming that the bureaucracy is being denied the autonomy and discretion it needs to fulfill its legislative mandates. What could better reflect the struggle for institutional power and advantage than this?

Yet regulatory review is quite different from most institutional issues in one crucial respect: it has entailed direct presidential attacks on interest groups, notably environmental groups. Unlike civil service reform or congressional oversight of the presidency, where the effects are broad and general, the effects of regulatory review have been concentrated on a few powerful targets. Not surprisingly, these targets have fought back. As a result, legislators' normally weak incentives to protect Congress's institutional interests against presidential onslaughts have been bolstered, enormously so, by powerful groups demanding legislative action. Regulatory review, then, is an unusual—and, for Congress, quite fortunate—case in which interest groups are actually pressuring Congress to protect its own institutional interests.[43]

The controversy began in the early 1970s, when President Nixon instituted the Quality of Life review program under the OMB. His real target was the Environmental Protection Agency (EPA), newly created in 1970, which was devising antipollution rules that stood to cost industry billions of dollars a year at a time when the national economy—Nixon's main concern—was headed for trouble. The administration adopted procedures requiring the EPA to submit its rules for prepublication review so that other agencies (notably the Department of Commerce) could comment, economic costs could be analyzed, conflicting views could be reconciled, justifications could be required—and pressure could be applied to bring EPA rules more in line with the president's program.

During this period, however, new legislation deepened the presidency's regulatory problems. As Robert Percival notes,

Seven new regulatory agencies had been created, including EPA, OSHA [Occupational Safety and Health Administration], and the Consumer Product Safety Commission. Between 1970 and 1974, twenty-nine major regulatory statutes had been enacted and the number of pages in the Federal Register had more than doubled from 20,036 to 42,422 per year.[44]

When Gerald Ford became president in 1974, he faced a rising tide of costly regulations, along with serious inflation and energy problems that demanded action. He responded by creating a more extensive system of regulatory review. The Quality of Life program was continued. In addition, with the consent of an inflation-concerned Congress, he established the Council on Wage-Price Stability (COWPS) in the EOP and ordered regulatory agencies to submit their proposed rules, along with "inflation-impact statements," to COWPS for review. The aim, once again, was to use procedure, analysis, and pressure to get regulatory agencies to recognize economic costs and modify their rules accordingly.

When Jimmy Carter, a Democrat, took office, environmental and labor groups looked forward to a relaxation that would give their agencies a freer hand. But Carter faced virtually the same problems that the Republicans Nixon and Ford had, and his response was distinctly presidential: he took even more aggressive action along the same general path. In Executive Order 12044, agencies were told to prepare "regulatory analyses" for all rules having major economic effects by rigorously evaluating their cost-effectiveness. Proposed rules would then be reviewed by the new Regulatory Analysis Review Group (RARG), made up of representatives from seventeen executive agencies, led by the OMB, COWPS, and the CEA, and staffed by economists who were committed to cost-benefit analysis.

It is clear from insider accounts that the regulatory agencies—led by presidential appointees—responded by moderating some of their rules, at times against their own best judgment.[45] The most affected interest groups and agencies, particularly the environmentalists and the EPA, complained loudly, and members of Congress, led by Sen. Edmund Muskie, a Democrat from Maine, obliged with sympathetic hearings but little else. Near the end of the Carter administration, however, the insistent pressure finally bore fruit: Carter pledged to go easier on the EPA, and RARG backed off.[46]

This was the calm before the storm. In little more than a year, Ronald Reagan took office and pushed regulatory review well beyond the bounds of his predecessors. He began quickly, appointing a Task Force on Regulatory Relief (chaired by Vice President George H. W. Bush), which promptly suspended some two hundred pending regulations and prepared a hit list of current regulations to be targeted for review. He followed up with his ground-breaking Executive Order 12291, which brought regulatory agencies under presidential control as never before.

The executive order required agencies to submit all proposed rules to the OMB's Office of Information and Regulatory Affairs (OIRA) for prepublication review, accompanied by rigorous cost-benefit analyses and evaluations of alternatives. In a departure from past practice, the OMB now allowed agencies to issue rules only when the benefits could be shown to exceed the costs; it also required them to choose among alternatives in such a way as to maximize the net benefits to society as a whole. Moreover, the OMB now asserted the right to delay proposed rules indefinitely while review was pending.[47]

The Reagan scheme imposed severe constraints on the EPA, OSHA, and other regulatory agencies.[48] Environmental groups, especially, were furious, and launched all-out attempts to persuade Congress to break the hold of regulatory review. This pressure had been building for more than ten years, as frustration with past presidents had prompted demands for a congressional counterattack. But now, with the Reagan agenda so aggressive, the groups were pulling out the stops.

How did Congress respond? It did not take on the president directly in an all-out assault—say, through major legislation that declared Executive Order 12291 null and void. Instead, its approach was piecemeal and fragmented, and it generated just what we would expect from a group-dominated institution: special interest legislation—such as the 1982 amendments to the Endangered Species Act, the 1984 amendments to the Hazardous and Solid Waste Act, and the 1986 Superfund amendments—that, through countless new restrictions, further narrowed the EPA's discretion, hobbled it with even more cumbersome administrative burdens, and, on very specific items, directed the president and the OMB not to interfere. For the most part, then, legislators and groups attacked the president by burying the EPA in more bureaucracy. As Percival describes it, "Congress has expressed its dissatisfaction with the consequences of regulatory review by adding more specific statutory controls on agencies' discretion every time it has reauthorized the environmental laws. The result has been a distinct trend toward reduced flexibility."[49]

At the same time all this was going on, another drama was unfolding. OIRA, as it happens, was not really a Reagan invention. It had been created at the tail end of the Carter period as part of the Paperwork Reduction Act of 1980, and only later did Reagan, through an executive order, put regulatory review into its hands.[50] The problem was that as a statutory agency OIRA had to weather the budgetary process every year to get funding—and to make matters worse, its authorization was set to run out in 1983. In principle, then, OIRA was vulnerable to attack.

What happened? OIRA's opponents had a perfect chance to shoot it down in 1983 because reauthorization called for an affirmative act of Congress and they needed only to block. And, in fact, the act was not reauthorized. The House went along, but the Senate did not.[51] Reagan countered by instructing OIRA to do what it had always done. But it was now acting without legislative authorization, which meant that, merely on a parliamentary point of order, legislators could move to deny the agency funding. No authorization, no funding.

Yet opponents were not able to make this tactic work. In 1984 and 1985 OIRA was funded. In 1986 Representative Dingell credibly threatened to use the point-of-order strategy, and a bargain was struck with the White House: the act would be reauthorized and OIRA would receive funding, but future agency heads would require Senate confirmation and OIRA would have to increase public disclosures about its review process.[52] These were concessions by Reagan, but not serious ones considering that, if legislative opponents really had been able to exercise power, they could have put OIRA out of business. The president clearly had the upper hand. The regulatory review system churned on, shaping and delaying regulations—and infuriating interest groups and agencies.

The Bush years witnessed more of the same. Although Bush was not as committed to regulatory review as his predecessor, the basic structure of Executive Order 12291 remained in place, a less zealous OIRA continued to do its presidential job, and the interest groups continued to nibble away at their nemesis through piecemeal congressional action. Environmentalists scored an indirect success (with Bush's assistance) through the new Clean Air Act of 1990, which buried the EPA in more bureaucratic constraints, directives, and timetables. This bill, as Jonathan Rauch put it, "is one of the most expensive and complicated regulatory measures of the postwar years. It runs to almost 800 pages."[53]

They also took direct shots at OIRA. Its authority, which had been renewed in 1986, ran out again in three years, which gave opponents yet another opportunity to kill it. In 1990 legislators agreed to reauthorize the Paperwork Reduction Act if Bush would accept certain restrictions on OIRA's powers, among them a sixty-day deadline for reviewing rules and a requirement that it provide detailed explanations for any substantive changes in rules. These, again, were not major concessions, because they would leave the entire regulatory review apparatus in place. Although Bush was willing to go along, some Republican senators opposed the bill (for reasons of their own), and it was defeated.[54] The result left OIRA without authorization and thus vulnerable to extinction. Yet the Bush (and later the Clinton) administration in subsequent years succeeded in getting funding for the agency.

In short, OIRA's legislative opponents had everything going for them, and still they failed to stop regulatory review. They did, however, make trouble: they defeated Bush's nominee to head OIRA. The president then relied on his executive flexibility, choosing not to submit another candidate and instead to ask an OIRA careerist to serve as acting head. He also took a look at all the problems surrounding OIRA as a statutory agency and decided to change strategy, shifting major responsibility for regulatory review from OIRA to the Competitiveness Council, a purely presidential unit headed by Vice President Dan Quayle.[55]

The Competitiveness Council, which originally had been given a broad presidential mandate to look into issues ranging from legal reform to job training, dove quickly into regulatory review and, with staff assistance from OIRA, became an influential and controversial force. For the remainder of the Bush presidency, legislative opponents shifted their ire to the council, and went after it in the usual ways.[56] But they were never able to deny it funding; they had no basis for affecting its personnel or appointments; and they never passed legislation challenging the council's right to do what it did.[57]

When the Democrats regained the White House in 1993, one of the first things President Bill Clinton did was to get rid of the Competitiveness Council. This evoked a joyous response from many legislators and interest groups, but it was largely symbolic—for he most assuredly did not get rid of regulatory review. Indeed, he made it clear that regulatory review was essential to presidential leadership and that he intended to keep it—precisely what we should expect of all presidents, whatever their partisanship.

Before his first year was out, Clinton issued Executive Order 12866, which, although repealing Reagan's Executive Order 12291, reimposed a structure of presidential review very similar to Reagan's—even retaining, for instance, cost-benefit requirements—but better adapted to the new president's own agenda and constituency, which were more proregulation and probureaucracy than Reagan's. Accordingly, under the Clinton regime, regulatory review functions were returned to OIRA; procedures were revamped to grant greater access to environmentalists, labor, and other Clinton supporters; and only the most costly regulatory matters were targeted for review, leaving greater scope for agency discretion.[58]

If there is anything unusual about the Clinton years, it is that Congress did a turnabout. When the Republicans gained control in 1995, the constellation of legislative forces shifted against government regulation, and the president was actually under pressure from congressional conservatives to use his powers of regulatory review more forcefully than he wanted to. With Clinton resisting, Republicans pushed ahead with legislative proposals to impose heavy new restrictions on the regulatory agencies.[59] These failed to become law because Congress, as usual, was unable to take bold action, and the president ultimately prevailed—another reflection of the presidential advantage.

The controversial election of 2000 that sent Republican George W. Bush to the White House gave the Democrats greater clout in Congress and put regulatory review and its politics back on more familiar footing. On the day of his inauguration, Bush issued an order delaying a spate of last-minute Clinton regulations and calling for further review, with the clear intent of derailing those that conflicted with his conservative agenda. In response, liberal legislators and their interest group allies put the spotlight on certain rules with public appeal—regarding, for instance, the level of arsenic in drinking water—and met with some success in portraying Bush as probusiness and insensitive to the environment. Bush then sought moderate ground on some issues to soften his image, but he did not change his goals. Agency heads were still under pressure to keep regulation to a minimum. And by midsummer of his first year in office, despite much conflict, he had succeeded in getting the Democrat-controlled Senate to confirm John Graham—known for being skeptical of regulation and an advocate of aggressive cost-benefit analysis—as the head of OIRA.[60]

With the tragedy of September 11, 2001, the Bush administration was quickly overwhelmed by national security issues, and domestic policy took a back seat. How long this state of affairs will last, and what it will mean for the administration's program of regulatory reform, is difficult to say. But it is clear that President Bush is intent on keeping the costs and burdens of regulation to a minimum and that the tools of presidential control are in place—however much Congress may complain—to allow him to move forcefully when he chooses to do so.

Overall, the story of regulatory review is more riddled with outright conflict than the others we have told. In this case, attempts by presidents to expand their institutional powers have taken the form of attacks on specific groups, and these groups have launched counterattacks. It is Congress's good fortune to have been caught in the middle, for the groups have been pressuring legislators to take actions that, coincidentally, defend the interests of Congress as an institution. This is why Congress has been more active and successful in regulatory review than in the other areas we have looked at.

Nevertheless, Congress's limited success is nothing to brag about. Regulatory review is now a routine part of the executive process. Presidents began it, built it up, and regularly exercised its powers in the face of interest group and legislative hostility. Congress did not rise up and pass major legislation to stop them, although it had the power to do so. It did not refuse to fund the review agencies, although it also had the power to do that. Instead, it succeeded only in imposing minor restrictions on regulatory review—and burying the EPA still further in bureaucracy.

Conclusion

This is not an account of presidential triumph. Separation of powers creates a governmental system that is distinctly unfriendly to presidents. It fragments authority, multiplies opposition and conflict, promotes inertia, generates a bureaucracy resistant to central control, and, in a host of other ways, produces an environment hostile to any kind of forceful, coherent leadership.

But presidents are strongly motivated to try to overcome as much of this as they can. And their best bet is not to accept a system that is stacked against them, but rather to do what they can to modify the architecture of the system itself—making it more presidential, more conducive to the leadership they strive to exercise. It is here that the story looks brighter for them. For whatever separation of powers does to frustrate their leadership, it also ensures that they will benefit from certain critical advantages over Congress in the politics of institution building and bureaucratic control. In time, they can create a friendlier system.

Some of these advantages arise from their unilateral powers of discretionary action as chief executive. These are powers that Congress does not possess and, except at the margins, cannot readily stop presidents from exercising. They give presidents tremendous flexibility in designing and developing their institutional capacity for control. They also enable presidents to take aggressive action in shifting the status quo, allowing them to win by default if Congress cannot react effectively.

Equally important advantages accrue to presidents because, as unitary decision makers, they have the good fortune to face a Congress that is inherently vulnerable to serious collective action problems. One manifestation is the motivational asymmetry: presidents care much more about institutional issues than legislators do, and they are far better able to take action. Another is that multiple veto points and high transaction costs make it extremely difficult for Congress to take decisive action at all, especially in the face of presidential opposition. When presidents use their powers of unilateral action to change the status quo, Congress often cannot do anything about it, and presidents win by default.

The case studies serve to illustrate how these presidential advantages play out in American politics. Whether we look at civil service reform, congressional oversight, or regulatory review, presidents have clearly been aggressive in building their own institutions for controlling the vast government bureaucracy. And Congress has typically been disorganized, ineffective, and even passive in response. Presidents did not always get their way in these cases, and Congress did not always fail to act, but changes in the institutional balance of power came about because presidents were pushing and shoving to occupy new institutional terrain, and Congress did not have what it takes to stop them.

Inevitably, I have not been able to discuss everything that may seem relevant to these cases or to the general theme of this chapter. Politics is complicated, and complete histories would show that many influences have been at work.

Each president is different, for example, and their personalities, ideologies, and agendas surely help to explain why some of them (Reagan, say) place more emphasis on strategies of institution building and control than others (such as the elder Bush). Similarly, divided government contributes to the pattern of conflict we have observed: Republican presidents are less likely than Democrats to find support for their agendas in a Democratic Congress, and they are thus more likely to pursue an "administrative presidency" that places a premium on control of the bureaucracy.[61] Finally, there is the familiar argument that Congress defers to presidents, which may sometimes be valid, especially for foreign policy issues that have little effect on constituency interests. Most of the time, however, deference is just another way of saying that legislators do not have strong incentives to act on institutional issues.

I have also had to neglect Congress's own attempts at institution building. A more extensive analysis would examine, for example, the political origins of the Congressional Budget Office, the War Powers Act, the tremendous growth in legislative staff, and other developments that may seem to counterbalance the institutional presidency. Still, such an analysis would be unlikely to challenge the thesis of presidential advantage. The new congressional budgetary process is a disaster of fragmentation and irresponsibility. Presidents largely ignore the War Powers Act. And legislative staff members spend most of their time pursuing the parochial interests that so animate their bosses. Were the picture more fully drawn, Congress still would not be nearly as well equipped to defend or promote its interests as the president is.

What does the future hold? Most obviously, it promises continued gains by presidents and continued movement toward a more presidential system. Although this trend may raise legitimate concerns among those who fear excessive presidential power (or certain presidents' agendas), on the whole it can be regarded as a healthy development. The American system has always been fragmented and decentralized, and the institutions favored by today's legislators and interest groups are cut from this same mold. Whether they intend to be or not, they are protectors of the institutional status quo. Were they to prevail consistently, they would entrench an outdated brand of centrifugal government that cannot address the burgeoning problems of a modern, complex society.

What is new and different in the modern period is the presidency. Presidents are the ones who are out of step with tradition, pushing for leadership, control, responsibility, and effectiveness—and for new institutional arrangements that fly in the face of old-style practice and parochialism. They are the ones, conservatives and liberals alike, who represent the driving force for change in the structure of American government, change that is needed if government is to work at all well.

This does not mean that, over time, presidents are somehow destined to take over. It does not even mean that they will have enough authority or control to govern effectively. Separation of powers sets up too many impediments, from the legal requirements of the Constitution to the competitive dynamics of modern politics, to allow for such a one-sided shift in the institutional balance. The most reasonable expectation is for some sort of equilibrium to be reached in future years, an equilibrium more presidential than we have now—but still a far cry from what presidents would like and what effective leadership of government would require.

Notes

1. Terry M. Moe, "The Politicized Presidency," in *The New Direction in American Politics,* ed. John E. Chubb and Paul E. Peterson (Washington, D.C.: Brookings Institution, 1985); John P. Burke, *The Institutional Presidency* (Baltimore: Johns Hopkins University Press, 1992).

2. For a more fully developed discussion of these issues, see Terry M. Moe, "The Politics of Structural Choice: Toward a Theory of Public Bureaucracy," in *Organization Theory: From Chester Barnard to the Present and Beyond,* ed. Oliver E. Williamson (New York: Oxford University Press, 1990). For empirical evidence on the political design of bureaucracy, see Terry M. Moe, "The Politics of Bureaucratic Structure," in *Can the Government Govern?* ed. John E. Chubb and Paul E. Peterson (Washington, D.C.: Brookings Institution, 1989).

3. For a detailed attempt to develop a theory of the presidential power of unilateral action, along with an overview of the relevant historical evidence, see Terry M. Moe and William G. Howell, "The Presidential Power of Unilateral Action," *Journal of Law, Economics, and Organization* 15 (1999): 132–179. See also Kenneth Mayer, *With the Stroke of a Pen* (Princeton University Press, 2001); Joel Fleishman and Arthur Aufses, "Law and Orders: The Problem of Presidential Legislation," *Law and Contemporary Problems* 40 (1976): 1–45; Phillip Cooper, "By Order of the President: Administration by Executive Order and Proclamation, *Administration and Society* 18 (1986): 233–262.

4. Richard Pious, *The American Presidency* (New York: Basic Books, 1979), 38.

5. Harold H. Bruff, "Presidential Power and Administrative Rulemaking," *Yale Law Journal* 88 (1979): 451–508; Harold H. Bruff, "Presidential Management of Agency Rulemaking," *George Washington Law Review* 57 (1989): 533–595; Lloyd N. Cutler, "The Case for Presidential Intervention in Regulatory Rulemaking by the Executive Branch," *Tulane Law Review* 56 (1982): 830–848; Peter Strauss, "The Place of Agencies in Government: Separation of Powers and the Fourth Branch," *Columbia Law Review* 84 (1984): 573–669.

6. Pious, *American Presidency.*

7. On how the courts have approached presidential power, and particularly presidential powers of unilateral action, see, for example, Fleishman and Aufses, "Law and

Orders"; Thomas Cronin and Michael Genovese, *The Paradoxes of the American Presidency* (New York: Oxford University Press, 1998); and Gordon Silverstein, *Imbalance of Powers: Constitutional Interpretation and the Making of American Foreign Policy* (New York: Oxford University Press, 1997).

8. Louis Fisher, *The Politics of Shared Power* (Washington, D.C.: CQ Press, 1993); Strauss, "Place of Agencies in Government."

9. Eugene Fama and Michael Jensen, "Separation of Ownership and Control," *Journal of Law and Economics* 26 (1983): 301–325.

10. Pious, *American Presidency;* Bruff, "Presidential Power and Administrative Rulemaking"; Bruff, "Presidential Management of Agency Rulemaking"; Strauss, "Place of Agencies in Government"; Cutler, "Case for Presidential Intervention."

11. Robert V. Percival, "Checks Without Balance: Executive Office Oversight of the Environmental Protection Agency," *Law and Contemporary Problems* 54 (1991): 127–204.

12. Mancur Olson, *The Logic of Collective Action,* 2d ed. (Cambridge: Harvard University Press, 1971).

13. Gary Cox and Mathew McCubbins, *Legislative Leviathan* (Berkeley: University of California Press, 1993).

14. David Mayhew, *Congress: The Electoral Connection* (New Haven: Yale University Press, 1974).

15. Hugh Heclo, "The OMB and the Presidency: The Problem of Neutral Competence," *Public Interest* 38 (winter 1975): 80–98.

16. Richard D. McKelvey, "Intransitivities in Multidimensional Voting: Models and Some Implications for Agenda Control," *Journal of Economic Theory* 12 (June 1976): 472–482.

17. See John Kingdon, *Agendas, Alternatives, and Public Policies* (Boston: Little, Brown, 1984); Paul Light, *The President's Agenda* (Baltimore: Johns Hopkins University Press, 1982).

18. Thomas H. Hammond, Jeffrey S. Hill, and Gary J. Miller, "Presidents, Congress, and the 'Congressional Control of Administration' Hypothesis" (paper presented at the annual meeting of the American Political Science Association, Washington, D.C., 1986).

19. George C. Edwards III, *Presidential Influence in Congress* (San Francisco: W. H. Freeman, 1980); Stephen J. Wayne, *The Legislative Presidency* (New York: Harper and Row, 1978).

20. Richard Polenberg, *Reorganizing Roosevelt's Government 1936–1939* (Cambridge: Harvard University Press, 1966); Peri E. Arnold, *Making the Managerial Presidency* (Princeton: Princeton University Press, 1986).

21. Felix A. Nigro, "The Politics of Civil Service Reform," *Southern Review of Public Administration* 20 (1979): 196–239.

22. Patricia W. Ingraham, "The Civil Service Reform Act of 1978: The Design and Legislative History," in *Legislating Bureaucratic Change: The Civil Service Reform Act of 1978,* ed. Patricia W. Ingraham and Carolyn Ban (Albany: State University of New York Press, 1984); Harlan Lebo, "The Administration's All-Out Effort on Civil Service Reform," *National Journal,* May 27, 1978, 837–838.

23. Nigro, "Politics of Civil Service Reform."

24. Arnold, *Making the Managerial Presidency;* Ann Cooper, "Carter Plan to Streamline Civil Service Moves Slowly Toward Senate, House Votes," *Congressional Quarterly Weekly Report,* July 15, 1978, 1777–84.

25. Cooper, "Carter Plan to Streamline Civil Service."

26. It may well be that their rhetoric was really just a vehicle for defending group interests. Mathias, in particular, had every reason to be keenly sensitive to what the federal employees' unions wanted, because many of their members live in his state.

27. Ann Cooper, "Carter Military Bill Veto Could Slow Senate Action on Civil Service Measure," *Congressional Quarterly Weekly Report,* August 19, 1978, 2174; Ann Cooper, "Senate Approves Carter Civil Service Reforms," *Congressional Quarterly Weekly Report,* August 26, 1978, 2239, 2299.

28. Nigro, "Politics of Civil Service Reform."

29. Ann Cooper, "Carter Civil Service Plan: Battered but Alive," *Congressional Quarterly Weekly Report,* July 22, 1978, 1839–41, 1890–94.

30. Ann Cooper, "House Civil Service Debate Slowed by Bill Opponents," *Congressional Quarterly Weekly Report,* September 9, 1978, 2441; Ann Cooper, "Civil Service Reforms Likely This Year," *Congressional Quarterly Weekly Report,* September 16, 1978, 2458–62.

31. Ann Cooper, "Enactment of Civil Service Reforms Nears," *Congressional Quarterly Weekly Report,* October 7, 1978, 2735–36.

32. Ann Cooper, "Civil Service Reorganization Plan Approved," *Congressional Quarterly Weekly Report,* August 12, 1978, 2125–27.

33. John Hart, *The Presidential Branch* (New York: Pergamon, 1987), 169.

34. Hugh Heclo, "The OMB and the Presidency"; Moe, "Politicized Presidency"; Arnold, *Making the Managerial Presidency.*

35. "Congress Accepts Four Executive Reorganization Plans," *Congressional Quarterly Almanac, 1970* (Washington, D.C.: Congressional Quarterly, 1971), 462–467.

36. Edward S. Flash Jr., *Economic Advice and Presidential Leadership: The Council of Economic Advisers* (New York: Columbia University Press, 1965); I. M. Destler, *Presidents, Bureaucrats, and Foreign Policy* (Princeton: Princeton University Press, 1972); Bert Rockman, "America's Department of State: Irregular and Regular Syndromes of Policymaking," *American Political Science Review* 75 (1981): 911–927.

37. Dean L. Yarwood, "Oversight of Presidential Funds by the Appropriations Committees: Learning from the Watergate Crisis," *Administration and Society* 13 (1981): 299–346.

38. House Committee on Post Office and Civil Service, *A Report on the Growth of the Executive Office of the President 1955–1973,* Committee Print 19, 92d Cong., 2d sess., 1972.

39. "Executive Office, Treasury Funds," *Congressional Quarterly Weekly Report,* August 4, 1973, 2155–57.

40. "White House Staff," *Congressional Quarterly Almanac, 1978* (Washington, D.C.: Congressional Quarterly, 1979), 796–798; Hart, *Presidential Branch.*

41. Yarwood, "Oversight of Presidential Funds."

42. If there is an exception, it is in the controversial (and special interest) area of regulatory review, discussed in the next section. For data on presidential budgets, see the accounts of Treasury, Post Office, and Civil Service appropriations in *Congressional Quarterly Almanac* (Washington, D.C.: Congressional Quarterly, 1970–present).

43. The basic history of regulatory review is well known. The following account relies largely on William F. West and Joseph Cooper, "The Rise of Administrative Clearance," in *The Presidency and Public Policy Making,* ed. George C. Edwards III, Steven A. Shull, and Norman C. Thomas (Pittsburgh: University of Pittsburgh Press, 1985); Elizabeth Sanders, "The Presidency and the Bureaucratic State," in *The Presidency and the Political System,* 3d ed., ed. Michael Nelson (Washington, D.C.: CQ Press, 1990), 409–442;

Thomas O. McGarity, *Reinventing Rationality: The Role of Regulatory Analysis in the Federal Bureaucracy* (Cambridge: Cambridge University Press, 1991); and Percival, "Checks without Balance."

44. Percival, "Checks Without Balance," 139.

45. See, for example, John Quarles, *Cleaning Up America* (New York: Houghton Mifflin, 1976).

46. Christopher C. De Muth, "Constraining Regulatory Costs—Part I: The White House Review Program," *Regulation 4* (January/February 1980): 13–26.

47. To this already stringent set of procedures, Reagan later added Executive Order 12498, which required agencies to submit annually a program outlining all significant regulatory actions planned for the coming year so that the OMB would have plenty of time to review them without the pressure of statutory deadlines.

48. Peter M. Benda and Charles H. Levine, "Reagan and the Bureaucracy: The Bequest, the Promise, and the Legacy," in *The Reagan Legacy: Promise and Performance,* ed. Charles O. Jones (Chatham, N.J.: Chatham House, 1988).

49. Percival, "Checks Without Balance," 175.

50. Benda and Levine, "Reagan and the Bureaucracy."

51. Ann Cooper, "Paperwork Reduction," *Congressional Quarterly Almanac, 1983* (Washington, D.C.: Congressional Quarterly, 1984), 590–591.

52. Ann Cooper, "OMB Regulatory Review," *Congressional Quarterly Almanac, 1986* (Washington, D.C.: Congressional Quarterly, 1987), 325.

53. Jonathan Rauch, "The Regulatory President," *National Journal,* November 30, 1991, 2902–6.

54. Kitty Dumas, "Administration Deal Pushes Paperwork Reduction Act," *Congressional Quarterly Weekly Report,* October 27, 1990, 3602; Janet Hook, "101st Congress Leaves Behind Plenty of Laws, Criticism," *Congressional Quarterly Weekly Report,* November 3, 1990, 3699.

55. Rauch, "Regulatory President."

56. Kirk Victor, "Quayle's Quiet Coup," *National Journal,* July 6, 1991, 1676–80.

57. On the failed attempt to deny the council funding, see Susan Kellam, "Social Security Riders Thrown from Senate Treasury Bill," *Congressional Quarterly Weekly Report,* September 12, 1992, 2712–13; Kellam, "Conferees Cut $200 Million, Pave Way to Approval," *Congressional Quarterly Weekly Report,* September 26, 1992, 2936.

58. Executive Order 12866, 58 Fed. Reg. 51735 (1993). This order also repeated Reagan's Executive Order 12498.

59. See, for example, John H. Cushman Jr., "Republicans Plan Sweeping Barriers to New U.S. Rules," *New York Times,* December 25, 1994, A1.

60. See, for example, Stephen Labaton, "Bush Is Putting Team in Place for a Full-Bore Assault on Regulation," *New York Times,* May 23, 2001; Douglas Jehl, "Regulations Czar Prefers New Path," *New York Times,* March 25, 2001; Susan E. Dudley, "Bush's Regulatory Record," *Intellectual Ammunition,* July/August 2001, on the Web at www.heartland.org/ia/julaug01/regulation.htm.

61. Richard Nathan, *The Administrative Presidency* (New York: Wiley, 1983).

17 The President and Congress

Matthew Dickinson

Renowned presidential scholar Richard Neustadt describes the American system of constitutional government as one of "separated institutions sharing powers." One implication of this description is that it is difficult for the president to accomplish much without the support or at least the acquiescence of Congress. Political parties developed as a bridge between the constitutionally separated branches early in American history. A president usually could count on the support of his fellow partisans in Congress, and they usually constituted a majority in both the House of Representatives and the Senate. Recent decades, however, have been marked by "divided government," in which the opposition party controls one or both houses of Congress. In addition, argues Matthew J. Dickinson, the two parties have become more ideologically polarized, which makes it even harder for the president to find allies across the political divide. Dickinson suggests that the president's best strategy in the current political environment may be to "speak softly and carry a big veto."

The September 11, 2001, terrorist attacks on New York City's World Trade Center and the Pentagon near Washington, D.C., dramatically altered the political climate in the nation's capital.[1] In the hours and days after the strikes, bipartisan consensus replaced the partisan bickering that had dominated presidential-congressional relations during the first months of George W. Bush's presidency. Political leaders of both parties promised to work together to pursue the war against terrorism. Some observers speculated that this new-found spirit of cooperation might herald the dawning of a "kindler, gentler" political era.

In this chapter I argue that such a shift is unlikely to be the case. Presidential influence in Congress—always problematic in the American system of government—has become even less effective than before. This development is largely due to the growing ideological polarization of the political parties,

458

especially since 1992. Against a backdrop of persistent divided government during the post–World War II era, polarized parties continue to exacerbate the constitutional divide that separates the presidency from Congress. Unless the war on terrorism reverses this process of polarization, Bush's influence in Congress will benefit only marginally from his elevated political stature.

To explain why, I first sketch the dynamics of Bush's relationship with Congress prior to the terrorist strikes. I then examine the fundamental forces shaping that relationship, beginning with the constitutional design of the government and the creation and evolution of political parties. Although parties helped to ameliorate some of the centrifugal political tendencies inherent in the U.S. political system during the nation's first century, they peaked in influence in the last third of the nineteenth century and slowly declined in importance thereafter. More recently, a series of developments, some dating to the early 1960s, transformed the role of parties within Congress and among the electorate. By the 1990s congressional politics was dominated by two ideologically cohesive political parties that supported increasingly divergent policies. Under these conditions, I argue, Bush faces a legislative "catch-22." Partisan strategies designed to appeal to the Republican core will divide Congress and alienate the more moderate electorate. But any attempt to govern from the ideological center will be opposed by party purists from both ends of the political spectrum. What, then, is Bush's optimal legislative strategy? I conclude the chapter by exploring the limited options for the exercise of presidential influence in Congress during the contemporary era.

The Bush Presidency: A Tepid and
Short-Lived Honeymoon

In May 2001 Congress passed, largely on the strength of Republican votes, a ten-year, $1.35-trillion tax reduction plan supported by President Bush.[2] After that, Bush's political momentum, never very robust, began to dissipate. Moderate Republican legislators proved reluctant to support many of his other legislative initiatives, including an energy plan that called for drilling in environmentally sensitive areas, grants of federal aid to religious charities, a scaled-back patients' "bill of rights," and an expanded missile defense system. This resistance was exemplified most dramatically when a leading Republican moderate, Sen. James M. Jeffords of Vermont, left his party in May because he felt it had become too conservative. By agreeing to vote with the Democrats, Jeffords cost the Republican Party control of the Senate.[3] Meanwhile, in the

House the Republicans held a tenuous nine-vote majority, but threats of defection among party moderates threatened Bush's legislative agenda there as well.[4]

Congressional Democrats, emboldened by their sudden majority status in the Senate and upset over what they perceived to be Bush's failure to pursue a more bipartisan governing strategy, became more confrontational. When economic projections forecast a smaller than expected budget surplus, Democrats went on the attack, targeting the newly enacted Bush tax cut as too large, too favorable to the wealthy, and irresponsible, given his promise to increase spending for defense and education. They also accused the Bush administration of raiding the Social Security and Medicare trust funds to pay for other government programs and of trying to privatize a portion of the Social Security program. As an alternative to Bush's policy agenda, Democrats began pursuing their own legislative program, including an expanded patients' rights bill, an alternative energy plan that focused on conservation, and more stringent campaign finance laws.

Bush sought to regain the initiative by mobilizing public support for his legislative initiatives. His efforts were hampered, however, by the perception that he lacked an electoral mandate: he had lost the popular presidential vote in 2000 and won the presidency only because of a controversial Supreme Court ruling that awarded him Florida's disputed electoral votes. After the brief surge in public support typically experienced by newly elected presidents (the "honeymoon effect"), Bush's job performance approval rating, as measured by Gallup Polls, dropped from a high of 63 percent in May to a low of 51 percent in early September.[5] Moreover, that support did not translate into public backing on many of the issues that formed the core of Bush's legislative agenda in Congress.[6]

Just eight months into his presidency, Bush's already tepid political honeymoon with the 107th Congress and the public appeared to be even cooler. The chances for legislative compromise on his agenda seemed remote, as Democratic and Republican legislators forsook bipartisanship and instead advocated the positions designed to mobilize their core electoral constituencies in preparation for the 2002 midterm elections. Because the midterm election usually costs the president's party seats in Congress, it appeared likely that Bush would face at least two more years of an opposition-controlled Senate and perhaps the loss of his party's majority in the House.[7]

Then came the tragic events of September 11. A suddenly somber Congress temporarily put aside partisan politics, immediately passing an almost unanimous resolution supporting the president's declaration of a war on terrorism.

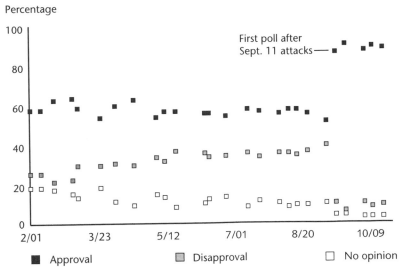

Figure 17.1 Bush's Gallup Poll Approval Ratings, February 2–October 10, 2001

Percentage

First poll after
Sept. 11 attacks

■ Approval   □ Disapproval   □ No opinion

Source: Gallup Poll opinion surveys.

Three days after the attacks, Congress approved a $40 billion emergency spending bill supporting Bush's prosecution of the war. In a matter of weeks the House and the Senate passed additional legislation, including a $7 billion airline bailout bill recommended by Bush to combat the economic fallout from the attacks and an antiterrorism bill that gave law enforcement agencies more power to prevent future attacks. On October 7, when Bush authorized the bombing of targets in Afghanistan, aimed at eliminating Osama Bin Laden's al Qaeda terrorist network and the forces of the ruling Taliban government, congressional leaders quickly reaffirmed their support for the president's actions.

So did the public. After September 11 Bush's approval ratings soared to unprecedented heights, fueled in large part by Americans' support for his war on terrorism.[8] His approval ratings, as shown in Figure 17.1, rose from 51 percent September 7–10, to 90 percent September 21–22, and remained high through the beginning of October, with no indication that they would wane anytime soon.

Faced with this dramatic turnabout in presidential-congressional relations, some pundits wondered whether a new bipartisan political era might be under way. Events soon suggested otherwise. Partisan sniping between the president and Congress was evident within a month of the terrorist strike, when Bush chided congressional leaders for leaking intelligence reports to the news media.

The sniping soon developed into full-scale legislative warfare with Bush and his Republicans supporters in Congress squaring off against congressional Democrats on bills involving airport security and an economic stimulus package. Partisan conflict between the president and Congress, at least on domestic issues, was back.

Journalists and other observers often characterize these struggles as unseemly pursuits that do not address the national interest. It is worth remembering, however, that the Framers saw virtues in the institutional clash between the president and Congress. Indeed, they designed a government that invited such conflicts, a government of "separated institutions sharing powers," to use Richard Neustadt's well-known phrase.[9] Ironically, as I describe in the next section, political parties were initially established to help soften some of the sharper edges of this institutional rivalry. Today, however, in conjunction with divided government, parties are more likely to exacerbate that rivalry.

Congress, the President, and Political Parties, 1789–1960

The Constitution sets out the basic parameters that govern the president's relationship with Congress. For these two branches to fulfill their constitutional obligations, from legislating to conducting foreign policy to managing the bureaucracy, they must actively collaborate. Consider their most significant function: making laws. Article I, Section 1, specifies that "all legislative Powers herein granted shall be vested in a Congress of the United States" consisting of "a Senate and House of Representatives." Article I, Section 7, establishes the president's legislative role: before bills passed by the House and Senate can become law they must be signed by the president or vetoed and passed again by at least two-thirds of the members in each congressional chamber. Article II, Section 3, states that the president shall recommend to Congress "such Measures as he shall judge necessary and expedient." Modern presidents have routinely interpreted this phrase as an invitation to submit a legislative program, and legislators have come to expect this service. To be sure, proposing legislation is no guarantee it will be enacted, but doing so provides the president with very significant power to set the congressional agenda.[10]

So it goes across the range of the national government's functions. In foreign affairs, Congress declares war, but the president is commander in chief of the armed forces. Presidents appoint ambassadors and negotiate treaties, but only with the Senate's advice and consent. Congress establishes a bureaucracy and a system of courts below the Supreme Court, but presidents appoint their members, including the Supreme Court's—again with Senate approval. More-over, Congress establishes and funds all lower level government bureaucracies, as well as determining who controls appointments to these agencies.

Clearly, the Constitution requires the Congress and the president to work together if the "shared powers" of the national government are to be exercised. The Constitution also ensures that these branches will do so from decidedly different perspectives because the president, the House, and the Senate represent distinct constituencies and serve different terms of office.

To become president, one must win a majority of electoral college votes, which are apportioned according to each state's representation in Congress. Because of the evolution of a winner-take-all presidential selection system, in which the candidate with a plurality receives all of a state's electoral votes, presidential candidates typically hew to the ideological center of the political spectrum.[11] For would-be presidents, there is no electoral payoff for attracting a significant minority of a state's popular vote.[12]

Representatives are selected through a single-member, simple-plurality voting system, from electoral districts where constituencies are much smaller and typically more homogenous than the nation as a whole.[13] Depending on a district's constituency, a candidate for the House might be successful by staking out a relatively extreme ideological position. Moreover, because the entire House is up for election every two years, it tends to be more responsive than the president to prevailing political passions.[14]

Senators act on yet a third set of political imperatives. Although they also are chosen by a simple plurality of a state's popular vote, Senate constituencies vary considerably depending on the size and diversity of each state's population.[15] Generally speaking, the constituencies senators represent are more heterogeneous than in House districts, which reduces the likelihood that senators will be beholden to ideologically extreme viewpoints.[16] In addition, because senators serve for six years, with only one-third of the chamber up for election at any time, the whole Senate is unlikely to be as responsive to the political forces that influence presidential or House elections.

The upshot is that presidents, senators, and representatives come to their shared constitutional tasks with different political needs and goals. This was the Framers' original intent: as Madison explained in *Federalist Paper* no. 51, with power apportioned among the branches in this way, it will be more difficult for any branch to abuse its authority.[17] But the Framers also hoped to establish an effective government, and in this respect the original constitutional scheme had several defects.

First, the presidential selection system did not provide the presidency with a strong enough electoral base to resist congressional encroachment. By 1800 presidential nominations were determined by congressional caucuses controlled by a single political faction. Moreover, as James Sterling Young documents, the Framers' emphasis on limited government, together with the tendency for each branch to jealously protect its institutional prerogatives, prevented the president and Congress from addressing national problems during the nation's early years. Citizens, in turn, failed to develop a strong attachment to a government that seemed largely ineffectual.[18]

To address these problems in the decade after the Constitution's ratification, the nation's leading politicians gravitated toward a single solution: political parties. The Constitution makes no mention of parties, but their precursors were already evident during George Washington's administration, when debates broke out among his advisers on issues such as the constitutionality of the Neutrality Proclamation and the creation of a central bank. These disputes highlighted the growing ideological divide between those, led by Secretary of the Treasury Alexander Hamilton, who favored a strong presidency and a more powerful national government and those, led by Secretary of State Thomas Jefferson and Rep. James Madison, who sought to limit national authority, particularly presidential authority.

By the Third Congress (1793–1795), voting within the chambers was along clearly discernable party lines, as the two major political factions sought to mobilize support among legislators on important issues. These attempts spilled over into the electoral arena as well. Following Washington's retirement, the presidential election of 1796 showed early evidence of party cleavages among the political elite, and by 1800 the presidential race had become clearly partisan.

Parties developed despite the Framers' deep antipathy toward them, because they performed a number of useful functions. First, by providing the presidency with a popular base of support, parties rescued the office from its dependence on Congress. The process by which the presidency gained an independent electoral base involved several steps. First, the electoral college was transformed from an independent body that both nominated and elected the president to an instrument of parties. By 1800 potential presidential electors in each state were pledging before the election to vote as a bloc on behalf of a particular candidate.[19] This change provided the means for parties to aggregate electoral support across state lines behind a single candidate, with the greater possibility that their candidate would win a majority in the electoral college.

The use of the party ballot increased the likelihood of electing a national figure as president; without it, electoral votes would have been scattered among a host of local favorites. But to provide the president with a truly independent electoral base, an additional link to the voting public was required. The connection was established by the development of mass-based political parties that chose presidential candidates and mobilized the electorate to support them. The advent of the national convention-based nominating system, first used by a major party in 1832, took the presidential nominating process out of the hands of the congressional caucus and put it into the hands of local and state politicians.

Meanwhile, the growth of mass-based campaigns organized by parties had helped create an attachment within the citizenry to the national government. By the 1820s, spurred by the sharper competition for the presidency, popular participation in elections began to rise.[20] In the 1824 presidential election, less than 30 percent of the eligible electorate voted. Sixteen years and four elections later, turnout had jumped to almost 80 percent. The presidency and the national government were now a visible and durable part of the political landscape.

Parties served an additional function: they provided a means to bridge the constitutional gap between president and Congress. If voters' choices in presidential and congressional elections were driven by party allegiances, a single party would likely control both branches after each election. And if candidates elected on the same party label shared a similar ideological outlook, presidents might capitalize on these shared preferences to convince Congress to pass their legislative program. Voters could then reasonably hold the government accountable for the policies it produced. In this way political parties might partially compensate for the centrifugal tendencies inherent in the Constitution.[21]

In fact, throughout the nineteenth century, the promise of "responsible party" government proved greater than the reality. For one thing, parties were loosely knit federations of partisan factions led by state and local chieftains— not unified bodies organized around a coherent party program. Second, presidents possessed few tools for enforcing party discipline in Congress. They had to share their most potent weapon, political patronage, with the legislative branch. And with the rise of the nonpartisan civil service and the decline of patronage-based parties beginning in the twentieth century, even this tool became less effective as a source of presidential leadership. Third, unified government could not be taken for granted: even when political parties reached their apex of influence during the sixty-eight years from 1832 to 1900, divided government existed in some form for thirty-two of those years. Nor did unified party control always translate into congressional support for a president's policies. As we noted above, presidents, senators, and representatives from the same party respond to different political incentives because of their different constituencies and terms of office. In short, what the Constitution set apart, the parties did not necessarily put together.

Except for dramatic periods of electoral realignments, when presidential and congressional races were subject to the same intense political pressures, legislators did not feel a shared sense of political fate with presidents. Moreover, the ties that bound the two branches began to fray during the first half of the twentieth century, as the traditional services provided by the mass-based parties were gradually undermined by progressive reforms. The advent of the direct primary weakened party leaders' control over the nomination of political candidates.[22] The party ballot gave way to the Australian, or secret ballot, making it harder for party officials to enforce discipline in elections. Civil service reforms, beginning in 1883 with the Pendleton Act, reduced the utility of patronage as a source of presidential influence in Congress. Collectively, these developments sent the parties into a slow but inexorable decline that extended through the twentieth century. The result was a further unraveling of the weak bonds linking the presidency and Congress.

The Era of Incumbency and Insulation, 1960–1990

In the 1960s political parties reached their nadir of influence. Congress entered what Morris Fiorina describes as the "era of incumbency and insulation," in which the outcomes of presidential and congressional races became less unified.[23] As Figure 17.2 indicates, voting studies revealed a growing tendency for voters to split their ticket between a presidential candidate of one party and a congressional candidate of the other. At the same time, Figure 17.3 shows that the number of self-identified independent voters was on the rise. Although scholars dispute how to interpret this development, it suggests at the very least that partisanship was becoming less important to voters.

Electoral reforms and other developments after the 1968 elections further diminished the importance of parties in the presidential nominating process. In the 1972 election a majority of party delegates to the presidential nominating conventions were selected through primaries, in which voters cast secret ballots. The primaries weakened the party leaders' traditional role of gatekeeper to nominations. Meanwhile, campaign finance reforms designed to minimize the influence of private money in elections helped to elevate the

Figure 17.2 Split-Ticket Votes, Presidential Election Years

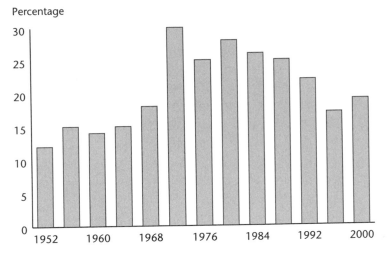

Source: National Election Studies, 1952–2000.

importance of single-issue interest groups as sources of candidate funding. The rise of the electronic media allowed congressional candidates to take their campaigns directly to the people, with minimal reliance on party organizations. The result was that the candidate-centered campaign replaced the party-mediated campaign.

Figure 17.3 Self-Identified Independent Voters (in percent)

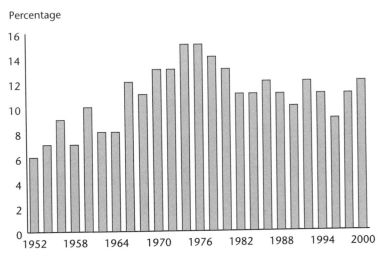

Source: National Election Studies, 1952–2000.

No longer needing to cater to the party's interests, members of Congress proved particularly adept at putting together their own coalitions to win re-election. The benefits of incumbency for senators and representatives began rising. The percentage of the popular vote that incumbents gained between their first and second election to Congress—the "sophomore surge" attributable to incumbency—went up from about two percentage points in the 1950s to seven percentage points in the 1970s. In the same period, the number of marginal congressional races in which the winning candidate won with 55 percent or less of the popular vote declined, signifying a decrease in party competition.[24] The congressional swing ratio, formally defined as the number of seats a party gains in Congress for every 1 percent increase in its national popular vote, also declined—another indication that congressional races were less responsive to shifts in national political forces than in the past.

According to Fiorina, at least part of this heightened incumbency effect was a reflection of legislators' effective use of casework to bolster their name recognition and support among their constituents. Because helping people solve their problems with government is nonpartisan and nonideological, it also contributed to the voters' sense that parties mattered less than ever.[25] Finally, incumbents proved more adept than challengers at using the new campaign regulations to raise money, even though studies showed that money was more crucial to the challenger's chances of electoral success. This further padded the incumbent advantage.

Whatever the explanation for the rise in incumbency reelection rates, Democrats, as the majority party in Congress at the time these changes were under way, benefited disproportionately, especially in the House. In the forty years from 1954 to 1994 the Democrats never lost control of the House, even though Republicans won the presidency six times in ten elections and increased their share of the popular vote in congressional races.[26] The Republicans had better luck in the Senate, winning control of that chamber from 1980 to 1986, but the outcomes of senatorial elections also diverged from the national trends influencing presidential races.

By the mid-1980s, then, Congress and the presidency appeared more separated from each other than ever. Presidential coattails, never very strong in American history, were diminishing. The number of congressional districts carried by a congressional candidate of one party and the presidential candidate of the other jumped from less than 5 percent in 1900 to more than 40 percent in 1984. As a result, sweeping presidential victories no longer guaranteed large gains for the president's party in Congress. In 1972 Richard Nixon was reelected overwhelmingly, winning 520 electoral votes and 62 percent of the popular vote, but the Republicans gained only twelve House seats and lost two Senate seats; the Democrats retained control of both chambers. Similarly, in 1984 Reagan won a landslide reelection with 525 electoral votes and 59 percent of the popular vote, but his party gained only fifteen House seats—not nearly enough to capture control—and the Republican majority in the Senate fell by two seats. Two years later Reagan's party lost the Senate as well. The result was an increased occurrence of divided government.

From 1947 to 1991 the parties divided control of Congress and the presidency in some form for twenty-four of the forty-four years.[27] Without a sense of collective responsibility or shared political fate, members of Congress saw little virtue in working closely with the president to address national issues. For example, both branches failed throughout the 1980s to address the burgeoning budget deficit. As Fiorina observed, "[U]ntil members of Congress believe that their personal fates coincide with that of the president, and that both depend on doing well by the country, the political failure that has become familiar in recent decades will continue."[28]

For many scholars, the solution to divided government and legislative gridlock was a return to strong political parties. But not everyone agreed that divided government meant gridlock. David Mayhew's study showed that from 1946 to 1990 the legislative process was no more prone to deadlock under divided government than it was under unified control.[29] One reason was that neither the Democrats nor the Republicans were a homogenous party in the post–World War II era. Conservative Democrats rarely faced opposition in elections in the one-party South, and they had accrued enough seniority in Congress to become a potent conservative force within their otherwise liberal party. The Republicans, too, although a mostly conservative party, included a moderate wing of legislators centered predominantly in the Northeast.

Party labels, therefore, did not clearly distinguish legislators' ideological preferences. Democratic conservatives and Republican centrists frequently crossed party lines to vote with the opposition, and presidents could cultivate bipartisan coalitions of support. In particular, the heterogeneous nature of the Democratic Party allowed Republican presidents to mobilize bipartisan coalitions on certain issues, which explains Mayhew's finding that Richard Nixon, Gerald Ford, and Ronald Reagan were able to persuade a Congress controlled by Democrats to pass significant legislation. They did so by mobilizing coalitions of a majority of Republicans and the conservative wing of the Democratic Party.

Even as the scholarly community debated Mayhew's findings, however, changes were under way that threatened to undercut the implications of his research.[30] First, the two parties had started shedding their more moderate members beginning as early as 1964. As they each became more ideologically cohesive over the next three decades, they also grew more distinct from one another. In the 1970s congressional races started becoming attuned to national political trends. Although district-level factors were still critical in determining outcomes of House races, by the 1990s it was no longer true that, in the words of Thomas P. "Tip" O'Neill Jr., "all politics is local." Congress had entered a new, more partisan era.

Congress and the President in the Post–Reform Era: Toward More Responsible Party Government?

Scholars were slow to recognize the changing nature of congressional elections and political parties. With hindsight, it is clear that by the mid-1970s the decline of parties had been arrested. Split-ticket voting peaked in 1972, when 30 percent of voters supported a congressional candidate of one party and the presidential candidate of the other. From then on it declined, falling to 19 percent of voters in the 2000 election.

Similarly, the percentage of voters labeling themselves "pure" independents—that is, those who did not even lean toward one party—peaked at 15 percent in 1976, then dropped to between 9 percent and 12 percent throughout the next two decades. Self-identified strong Democrats, meanwhile, edged up from a low of 15 percent in 1972 to 19 percent in 2000. Those identifying themselves as strong Republicans increased from a low of 8 percent in 1978 to 12 percent in 2000.

At the same time, congressional races became increasingly responsive to national forces, although local factors still dominated. By regressing the current House district vote on the previous House district and presidential vote, and using the presidential vote as a proxy for national political trends, Fiorina constructed a rough measure of the relative importance of national and local forces in House elections. As Figure 17.4 indicates, by 1976 the influence of national forces in House elections in the presidential election year had begun rebounding after declining through the 1960s. This finding holds for House midterm elections. Indeed, as Figure 17.5 shows, in the House midterm elections of 1982 and 1994, the influence of the national component actually equaled the local component.

Figure 17.4 Decomposition of Presidential-Year House Elections (Contested and Uncontested Seats)

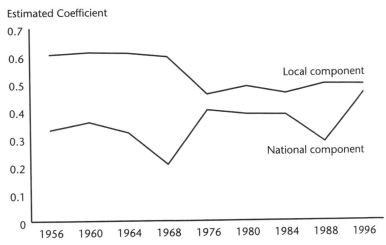

Estimated Coefficient

Source: David Brady, John Cogan, and Morris Fiorina, "Epilogue: The Era of Incumbency and Insulation," in *Continuity and Change in House Elections,* ed. David Brady et al. (Stanford: Stanford University Press, 2000), 141.

What explains this turnabout in party influence? Scholars cite several factors that collectively transformed and revitalized the parties and made members of Congress more responsive to national forces. First, the Republicans began making inroads among voters in the once solidly Democratic South, which in turn

Figure 17.5 Decomposition of Midterm House Elections (Contested and Uncontested Seats)

Estimated Coefficient

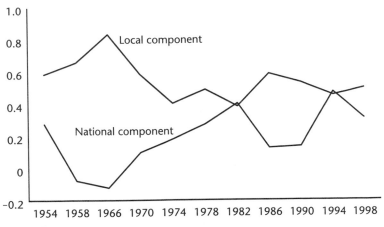

Source: David Brady, John Cogan, and Morris Fiorina, "Epilogue: The Era of Incumbency and Insulation," in *Continuity and Change in House Elections,* ed. David Brady et al. (Stanford: Stanford University Press, 2000), 139.

altered the geographical location of the parties' core constituencies. A precipi-
tating event was the Democratic Party's embrace of civil rights under President
Lyndon Johnson, fueled by the surge of liberal Democrats into Congress in the
1958 and 1964 elections. Some conservative southern voters reacted to the 1964
Civil Rights Act and 1965 Voting Rights Act by switching parties, and young voters just entering the electorate were more likely to become Republicans. In 1964
only 17 percent of southern voters called themselves Republicans. Twenty years
later the number had increased to 31 percent, and in 2000 it was 37 percent—the
same proportion of self-professed Republicans as outside the South. This trend
was encouraged by the Republicans' "southern strategy," which was designed to
split the Democratic Party by emphasizing party differences on social issues
like school busing, affirmative action, and crime and punishment. At the same
time, thanks in large part to the Voting Rights Act, African American electoral
participation in the South was on the rise, and they voted overwhelmingly
Democratic.

Population shifts from the East and Midwest to the West and South (from
the "Rustbelt" to the "Sunbelt") accentuated these trends. Moderate Republicans in the East found themselves marginalized in a party moving its center to
the more conservative South and the Rocky Mountain states. The decennial re-
districting process, in which congressional seats are reapportioned to take account of population shifts, contributed to the partisan restructuring. In
particular, the creation of majority-minority congressional districts, in which a
majority of eligible voters belong to racial or ethnic minorities, helped accen-
tuate the party divisions. First established by the Justice Department after
Congress amended the Voting Rights Act in 1982, these districts were successful
at increasing minority representation in Congress.[31] But they also helped to
consolidate the Republican vote in neighboring districts. The result was further
ideological polarization between the two parties: representatives elected in
majority-minority districts, particularly African Americans, were typically to
the extreme left of the Democratic Party. At the same time, by "bleaching" the
surrounding area of minority voters, these outside districts were more likely to
elect conservative Republicans.

The changing nature of campaign finance also contributed to the parties'
transformation. In the early 1970s Congress passed the first of a series of reforms
designed to mitigate the influence of big money by providing public funding for
presidential races, capping individual contributions to political campaigns, and
requiring public disclosure of campaign expenses. Decisions by the Supreme
Court equating some types of campaign spending with free speech, however,

allowed single-issue interest groups whose views were frequently outside the ideological center of the electorate to become an important source of campaign funding.[32] The influx of special interest money and the increased participation of issue activists, particularly in congressional nominating contests, tended to reward more ideologically extreme candidates. Much of this money flowed from groups outside a candidate's state or district. No longer were congressional races purely local affairs; rather, they were buffeted by national trends.

At the same time, the parties took advantage of campaign regulations allowing them to raise unlimited amounts of money for "party-building" exercises. These "soft" money contributions became an important source of campaign funds and helped transform the role of political parties. Instead of the loose federations of locally controlled, vote-mobilizing organizations of a century ago, parties became synonymous with their national party committees, which focused on fund-raising and candidate recruitment and training. These committees became adept at targeting resources in ways that maximized their party's seats in Congress, a transformation that further contributed to the nationalization of congressional elections.

The transformation of the major parties affected the electorate. Faced with candidates espousing widely divergent political views, voters were left to choose between extremes or not participate at all. For a growing number of voters the second option seemed more palatable. Political scientists began attributing some of the lower turnout numbers in presidential and congressional elections since 1960 to public dissatisfaction with the partisan and ideological tone of public debate.

The purging of both parties' moderate wings created the conditions in Congress for what David Rohde and John Aldrich call "conditional party government." When political parties in a legislative body are evenly matched and internally unified, Rohde and Aldrich argue, rank and file legislators may find it in their electoral interest to strengthen their party's leadership. In the House, institutional reforms pushed primarily by liberal Democrats from 1970 to 1977 helped facilitate strong party leadership. These included a "subcommittee bill of rights" that weakened the power of committee chairs, rule changes that enhanced the Speaker's powers, and a revitalization of the majority party caucus as a decision-making forum.[33] The Democrats were the first to capitalize on these reforms in the 1970s and 1980s by granting more power to Speakers Tip O'Neill, Jim Wright, and Tom Foley.[34]

The House Republicans, under the leadership of Minority Leader Newt Gingrich, fought back. They began an aggressive campaign to retake both chambers of Congress. By 1994, as a result of population shifts, effective candidate recruitment, a focused agenda, and extensive fund-raising, the Republicans were well positioned in the midterm elections to capitalize on voter dissatisfaction with the Clinton administration. In dramatic fashion, they picked up fifty-three House seats and eight Senate seats to take control of both chambers for the first time in forty years. The Republican takeover provided compelling evidence that congressional races were more susceptible to national forces than in the 1960s. Subsequent events revealed just how partisan Congress had become. Legislators in the Republican-controlled House could not persuade their Senate counterparts to sign on fully to their conservative "Contract with America," and in the winter of 1995/1996 partisan wrangling over the federal budget led to several government shutdowns. This fight was followed by the bitterly partisan impeachment and trial of President Bill Clinton in 1998/1999.

Other data support these highly visible indicators of partisan conflict. The difference between Republican and Democratic mean party ideology scores in Congress reached a low from 1968 to 1972, and climbed steadily thereafter.[35] Party unity scores, a measure of votes in Congress in which a majority of legislators from one party vote against a majority from the other, also increased in this period. So did the number of individual party votes, defined as the percentage of times the average Democrat or Republican voted with his or her party during votes that split the two parties.[36] Moreover, since 1968 the importance of party affiliation in explaining roll call voting by legislators has grown stronger.[37] Clearly, partisan politics now dominates congressional proceedings. This development has had a profound and troubling effect on presidential leadership of Congress.

Politics, Partisanship, and Presidential Influence in Congress: Speak Softly and Carry a Big Veto

Under unified government, the development of ideologically distinct, internally cohesive parties and the nationalization of congressional elections would conceivably strengthen the president's hand on Capitol Hill. This is particularly true because the correlation between House members' roll call votes and the level of support for the president among voters in their House districts has been increasing steadily since 1978.[38] Under divided government, however, strong parties have the opposite effect. They exacerbate the constitutional divide between the president and Congress.

Facing a divided government in which the Senate is controlled by a party with strongly opposing policy views, what legislative strategy could President Bush pursue to maximize his influence in Congress? One strategy is make public appearances to promote his agenda. Beginning in the 1980s, several scholars noted a tendency for presidents to "go public," to use mass appeals to mobilize public support for their policy proposals.[39] Woodrow Wilson first articulated the logic of this approach in 1908:

Let [the president] once win the admiration and confidence of the country, and no other single force can withstand him, no combination of forces will easily overpower him. His position takes the imagination of country. He is the representative of no constituency, but of the whole people.... [I]f he rightly interprets the national thought and boldly insist upon it, he is irresistible.[40]

Conceivably, Bush could capitalize on his status as a wartime president to mobilize public support for his domestic policies. Although he began his term by making a conspicuous effort to limit his public appearances, since the terrorist strikes he has been a ubiquitous and, by most accounts, effective presence on television.[41] But Bush's strategy of going public has unfolded against unique circumstances that are unlikely to persist and may reveal the limits of this presidential strategy. Such efforts can succeed only when four conditions are met. First, the president must be in good standing with the public. Second, the public must be attentive to and understand the arguments the president is making. Third, presidential popularity must be fungible, that is, it must translate into public support for the president's stance on specific issues. Finally, members of Congress must not be equally adept at or willing to mobilize countervailing support among their own publics. All of these conditions were in place after September 11, but how long will they last? Moreover, will public appeals by the president succeed with Congress on issues other than the war on terrorism? As noted above, within two months of the terrorist strikes, cracks in the facade of bipartisanship were already evident in Washington.

In this regard, it is telling that political scientists trying to demonstrate the effectiveness of going public usually cite the same example: Ronald Reagan's first-term success in getting Congress to pass his tax and spending bills.[42] Even in this case, the evidence that Reagan's rhetorical appeals carried the day is questionable.[43] More general studies of the influence of presidential popularity on legislative success suggest that it has only a marginal effect.[44] In short, although President Bush became more popular after September 11, it was never certain that his public support would translate into more influence in Congress, particularly on domestic issues.

For further evidence of the limited fungibility of war-induced popularity, President Bush need only consult his father's experience. George H. W. Bush also enjoyed stratospheric popularity when he led a successful international coalition against Iraq, which had invaded neighboring Kuwait, in the Persian Gulf War. But that support quickly dissipated in the economic downturn that followed, and Bush was voted out of office in 1992.

The senior Bush's experience shows that the bipartisan aura of wartime success can quickly evaporate as normal politics reasserts itself and ideological divisions among voters and politicians resume center stage. Indeed, in November 2001, less than two months after the terrorist strikes, normal politics was already reasserting itself in the partisan divisions on Capitol Hill over the airport security and economic stimulus bills.

Facing a divided government and finding popularity a poor substitute for bipartisan support in Congress, Bush is likely to spend the rest of his term caught between the proverbial rock and hard place. Any legislative strategy designed to appease the Republican core in Congress will likely polarize the national political debate and cost Bush support among the more centrist portion of the electorate. President Clinton suffered this fate. He passed a budget and pursued health care reform in 1993 and 1994 by relying on his Democratic majority in Congress, but his overtly partisan strategy boomeranged when the Republicans gained control of Congress in 1994. At this point, moreover, Bush lacks the majority in the Senate necessary even to make a purely partisan strategy feasible.

By moving to the ideological center to appeal to moderates in both parties, however, Bush could lose the support of his conservative base, much as his father's decision to compromise his "no new taxes" pledge cost him considerable Republican support when he sought renomination in 1992. In an era of divided government and polarized politics, governing from the center is risky. President Clinton pursued this strategy after the Republicans' historic takeover of Congress in 1994. Although it paid dividends for Clinton at the polls in 1996, critics argued that Clinton sacrificed his party in the process. Clinton largely adopted Republican policies on trade, welfare reform, and law enforcement, and the Democrats failed to regain their traditional majorities in either legislative chamber.

On many issues it may be impossible for Bush to "triangulate" between the ideological extremes of the two parties, even if he tries. As ideologically extreme voters and activists have come to dominate the nomination process for members of Congress, legislators who support a centrist policy agenda risk defeat by opponents whose views are closer to their party's ideological median. Considering the cohesiveness of the Republican right wing, "triangulation" may be a more difficult strategy for Bush to pursue than it was for Clinton. Most measures of legislators' ideology indicate that the number of Republican moderates in Congress is much smaller than the number of Democratic conservatives.[45] On most issues, therefore, Bush lacks enough Republican votes in Congress to pursue a centrist strategy.

Faced with divided government, Bush's most potent weapon may be the veto. It was a tool his father exercised effectively: The elder Bush vetoed forty-five bills in four years and was overridden only once. Clinton also used the veto as an important tool in his struggle with the Republican-controlled Congress after 1994. Although the veto is a powerful instrument for shaping legislative outcomes, it is also a very blunt weapon; presidents can use it to block unwanted bills, but it is less helpful in getting the president's policies through Congress. Moreover, Congress has become adept at passing omnibus legislation that contains enough politically untouchable items to make it difficult for presidents to exercise a veto.

Ultimately, Bush's legislative strategy will be dictated in large part by the outcome of the 2002 midterm elections. It may be that Republicans will gain enough seats in Congress to allow him to govern by relying primarily on a party majority. Toward this end, Bush may be tempted to use public support for his prosecution of the war to persuade voters to return a Republican Congress. But this is a dangerous game because the Democrats surely would accuse Bush of playing politics with national security.

Moreover, an overtly partisan electoral strategy risks alienating the mostly moderate electorate, which could retaliate by voting to divide control of the government once again. Ultimately, Bush's most feasible tactic may be to try to convince legislators that it is in their electoral interest to pursue a politics of accommodation and compromise. His ability to do so, however, will depend on the willingness of voters to reward legislators of their own party who support conciliation over conflict. In this regard, the events of September 11 may prove to be a turning point in American politics. Hereafter, the president and leaders of both parties may feel stronger pressure from their constituents to settle their differences and work together. The early signs, however, are not hopeful. Lacking significant and enduring changes in the political incentives members of Congress face, Bush may discover that in an era of polarized politics and divided government, fighting terrorism abroad is easier than confronting Congress at home. If so, Bush's best legislative strategy may be to quietly seek out policies that have the potential for bipartisan consensus and carry a big veto stick.

Notes

1. Passengers on a fourth hijacked jet evidently overpowered their attackers before the plane reached its intended target. The jet crashed in a field in Pennsylvania, killing all aboard.

2. Bush had initially sought a $1.65-trillion tax reduction bill, but Democratic resistance in the Senate pared that back. The final bill passed the House by 240 to 125, and the Senate by 62 to 38, with the unanimous support of Republicans in both chambers.

3. The Senate was split evenly, with fifty seats in each party caucus, at the beginning of Bush's term. The Republicans controlled the chamber thanks to Vice President Richard Cheney, who, as presiding officer, casts the deciding ballot in case of tie votes. Jeffords's decision to vote with the Democrats thus cost the Republicans Senate control.

4. The Republicans held 221 seats, Democrats 212, and there were two independents.

5. Bush's peak approval rating prior to September 11 came during polls taken March 5–7. Thereafter, it ranged between 52 percent and 57 percent through September 2001. By September 7–10, it had dropped to its lowest point in his presidency, 51 percent. The president's approval rating consists of all positive responses to the question, "Do you approve or disapprove of the way George W. Bush is handling his job as president?"

6. A random survey conducted September 6–9 indicated that "the public favors Democrats over the president on the economy, the environment, energy, patients' rights, Social Security and prescription drugs." Dan Balz and Richard Morin, "It's the Economy, Mr. President," *Washington Post National Weekly Edition*, September 17–23, 2001, 34.

7. With one exception, the party of every president since Franklin Roosevelt in 1934 has lost seats in the midterm congressional elections. The exception was 1998, when the Democrats gained five seats in the House, and broke even in the Senate.

8. A *Washington Post*/ABC News Poll conducted the week of October 8–14 found that 92 percent of those interviewed approved of the way Bush was handling his job as president, the highest job approval rating ever recorded in *Post*/ABC surveys. *Washington Post National Weekly Edition*, October 15–21, 2001, 35.

9. Richard Neustadt, *Presidential Power and the Modern Presidents* (New York: Free Press, 1990), 29.

10. See George C. Edwards III and Andrew Barrett, "Presidential Agenda Setting in Congress," in *Polarized Politics*, ed. Jon R. Bond and Richard Fleisher (Washington, D.C.: CQ Press, 2000), 109–133.

11. The exceptions are Maine and Nebraska; in both states it is possible to split electoral votes between candidates, though in practice this rarely happens.

12. The classic case is Ross Perot, who received more than 18 percent of the popular vote in 1992, but did not win a single electoral college vote.

13. This is not mandated in the Constitution, but gradually became the norm in the United States and is now based in statute.

14. Since the Twenty-second Amendment was ratified, presidents can be reelected only once.

15. Senators were not popularly elected until 1914, after ratification of the Seventeenth Amendment.

16. See Gerald C. Wright and Michael Berkman, "Candidates and Policy in U.S. Senatorial Elections," *American Political Science Review* 80 (June 1986): 576–590.

17. James Madison, *Federalist Papers*, no. 51 (Norwalk, Conn.: Easton Press, 1979), 347.

18. James Sterling Young, *The Washington Community, 1800–1828* (New York: Columbia University Press, 1966).

19. See Richard McCormick, *The Presidential Game: The Origin of American Presidential Politics* (New York: Oxford University Press, 1984).

20. Ibid.

21. E. E. Schattschneider, *Party Government* (New York: Farrar and Rinehart, 1940).

22. In 1901 Florida became the first state to use a presidential primary.

23. Morris Fiorina, "Epilogue: The Era of Incumbency and Insulation," in *Continuity and Change in House Elections*, ed. David Brady, John Cogan, and Morris Fiorina (Stanford: Stanford University Press, 2000).

24. On the incumbency advantage, see Andrew Gelman and Gary King, "Measuring the Incumbency Advantage Without Bias," *American Journal of Political Science* 34 (1990): 1142–64. On the declining marginals, see David Mayhew, "Congressional Elections: The Case of the Vanishing Marginals," *Polity* 6 (spring 1973): 295–318.

25. The classic statement of this thesis is Morris Fiorina's *Congress: Keystone of the Washington Establishment*, 2d ed. (New Haven: Yale University Press, 1989).

26. Republican popular support in congressional elections peaked at 48 percent in 1968 and reached 46 percent in 1980.

27. For a readable overview of the issues, see Morris Fiorina, *Divided Government* (New York: Macmillan, 1992).

28. Morris Fiorina, "The Presidency and Congress: An Electoral Connection?" in *The Presidency and the Political System*, 5th ed., ed. Michael Nelson (Washington, D.C.: CQ Press, 1988), 431.

29. David Mayhew, *Divided We Govern: Party Control, Lawmaking, and Investigations, 1946–1990* (New Haven: Yale University Press, 1991).

30. Looking at new data through 1997, for instance, Sarah Binder finds that policy gridlock is higher under conditions of divided government. Sarah H. Binder, "Congress, the Executive, and the Production of Public Policy," in *Congress Reconsidered*, 7th ed., ed. Lawrence C. Dodd and Bruce I. Oppenheimer (Washington, D.C.: CQ Press, 2001), 293–314.

31. Fifteen new black majority districts and nine new Latino majority districts were established in 1992.

32. In 1976 the Supreme Court ruled in *Buckley v. Valeo* that campaign finance regulations prohibiting individuals from making campaign expenditures independent from a candidate's campaign violated constitutionally protected free speech.

33. See David W. Rohde, *Parties and Leaders in the Post-Reform House* (Chicago: University of Chicago Press, 1991); and John H. Aldrich and David W. Rohde, "The Logic of Conditional Party Government: Revisiting the Electoral Connection," in *Congress Reconsidered*, ed. Dodd and Oppenheimer, 269–292.

34. Steven S. Smith and Gerald Gamm, "The Dynamics of Party Government in Congress," in *Congress Reconsidered*, ed. Dodd and Oppenheimer, 259–260.

35. Gary Jacobson, "Party Polarization in National Politics: The Electoral Connection," in *Polarized Politics*, ed. Bond and Fleisher, 13.

36. Roger H. Davidson and Walter J. Oleszek, *Congress and Its Members*, 8th ed. (Washington, D.C.: CQ Press, 2001), 274–275.

37. Jacobson, "Party Polarization in National Politics," 27.

38. Ibid.

39. The most cogent summary is by Samuel Kernell, *Going Public: New Strategies of Presidential Leadership*, 3d ed. (Washington, D.C.: CQ Press, 1997).

40. Woodrow Wilson, *Constitutional Government in the United States* (New York: Columbia University Press, 1908), 68.

41. Howard Kurtz, "Return of the Television Presidency," *Washington Post*, November 9, 2001.

42. For example, Kernell, *Going Public*, 140–167; Theodore Lowi, *The Personal Presidency: Power Invested, Promise Unfulfilled* (Ithaca, N.Y.: Cornell University Press, 1985).

43. Marc Bodnick, "Going Public Reconsidered: Reagan's 1981 Tax and Budget Cuts," *Congress and the Presidency* 17 (spring 1990): 13–28.

44. See, for instance, Jon R. Bond and Richard Fleisher, *The President in the Legislative Arena* (Chicago: University of Chicago Press, 1990).

45. See, for example, Richard Fleisher and Jon Bond, "Partisanship and the President's Quest for Votes," in *Polarized Politics*, ed. Bond and Fleisher, 166.

18 The Presidency and the Judiciary

David A. Yalof

Richard Nixon's election as president in 1968 marks a great political divide in presidential history. Until then, Americans almost always elected a "united party government"—that is, they gave the president (at least initially) a Congress con- trolled by his political party. Nixon's election was the first in more than a century in which a new president faced a Congress controlled entirely by the opposition party. It also marked the beginning of the current era of "divided government," in which split-party control of the presidency and Congress is the rule rather than the exception. As David Yalof shows, divided government, along with several other factors, has affected the politics of Supreme Court nominations. Prior to 1968, most nominees to the Court were chosen from the political arena; since then, they have come almost exclusively from the ranks of sitting jurists. Yalof finds that a court dominated by justices without extensive political experience has been less willing than high courts of the past to defer to Congress and the presi- dency on matters of constitutional and political importance.

A century from now, legal scholars will probably treat the Supreme Court case of *Bush v. Gore* (2000) as a historic anomaly of sorts—a railroad ticket good for that day and place only.[1] The Court's December 13, 2000, decision, which assured George W. Bush's victory in the electoral college by ending the hand recounts of election ballots in Florida, hardly signified a new direction in jurisprudence. Indeed, nothing that happened before or since that controver- sial decision gives any indication that the five justices in the majority plan to in- sert into other substantive areas of the law the novel vision of equal protection they applied that day. Moreover, *Bush v. Gore* provides a hopelessly limited fac- tual precedent: it is hard to imagine how such an unusual set of circumstances

Some of the discussion in this chapter is borrowed from my work on Supreme Court appointments. David Yalof, *Pursuit of Justices: Presidential Politics and the Selection of Supreme Court Nominees* (Chicago: University of Chicago Press, 1999, pbk 2001).

(state supreme court involvement, conflicting statutory provisions governing manual recounts, and so on) might ever again coalesce to such a degree that the Court's *Bush v. Gore* decision would somehow be "controlling." In all likelihood, *Bush v. Gore* will take its place in the annals of Supreme Court history alongside a case such as *Korematsu v. United States*, which, although precipitated by dramatic events, has been all but ignored as precedent by subsequent Courts.[2]

From the perspective of social scientists, however, more can be gleaned from *Bush v. Gore* than what is found in the controversial doctrines and reasoning of its written opinions. Certainly, the Court dramatically divided on clear ideological (and some would argue partisan) lines: the five justices most often associated with adopting "conservative" approaches to the law—Chief Justice William Rehnquist and Associate Justices Sandra Day O'Connor, Antonin Scalia, Anthony Kennedy, and Clarence Thomas—accepted Bush's arguments that the hand recounts must be stopped immediately, and the four justices more commonly linked to "moderate" or "liberal" positions in legal disputes—Associate Justices John Paul Stevens, David Souter, Ruth Bader Ginsburg, and Stephen Breyer—voted to resume the hand counts, albeit with some disagreement about the proper standard that should thereafter be applied.[3] The fact that two justices nominated by Republican presidents, Stevens and Souter, sided with the Democratic presidential candidate hardly undermines the starkness of these divisions. Stevens and Souter had long before been dismissed from the fold by conservative Republicans frustrated by their tendency to vote with liberals on hot button issues such as abortion, school prayer, affirmative action, and racial districting. Still, *Bush v. Gore* blazes no new ground on this front either. For decades leading political scientists have gathered statistical support for the notion that justices' votes are consistent with their political leanings, notwithstanding the words of the statutes, constitutional text, or judicial precedents that they purport to be interpreting.[4]

Rather, what makes *Bush v. Gore* so politically significant (apart from its decisive effect on the presidential contest) was that the decision boldly proclaimed the ascendancy of a new relationship between two of the three branches of the federal government. The Court's willingness to enter the national "political thicket" jettisoned all popular notions that as an institution the Supreme Court transcended politics: the partisan cliques that emerged among the justices were simply too neat to be dismissed as a matter of coincidence. In fact, the justices' willingness to hear the case in the first place shocked most Court watchers accustomed to seeing that institution stay as detached as possible from such heated political battles.

To be sure, the Supreme Court has routinely intervened in sensitive state political matters since the Warren Court era of the 1950s and 1960s, asserting its authority to shape state education systems, state prison systems, and even the political makeup of state legislatures. But the workings of the federal government—and in particular matters surrounding the presidency—have been treated mostly as off-limits by the Court. This restriction was self-imposed, and the Court has been willing to abandon it only when one of the core liberties found in the Constitution comes under attack from the executive branch.[5] Thus, when innovative lawsuits arrived at the Court to challenge the president's power to terminate foreign treaties, or to challenge the president's immunity from civil liability for acts committed as president, these suits received little sympathy from the justices.[6] And even when a president committed such outrageous acts that the Court did hand him a rare defeat, it always came saddled with mounds of qualifications. For example, in *Youngstown Sheet & Tube Co. v. Sawyer* (1952), President Truman's seizure of the steel mills was declared invalid, but future presidents were given "implied powers" to act outside the express responsibilities articulated in the Constitution.[7] Similarly, President Richard Nixon was ordered to hand over tapes of White House conversations in *United States v. Nixon* (1974), but the Court still confirmed the existence of a limited "executive privilege" under the Constitution, the first time it had ever formally recognized such a privilege.[8] Thus, even when the Court handed a president a loss, the justices proceeded cautiously, and with an eye to the ramifications their decision would have in the greater political context.

The Supreme Court did not arrive at this level of deference to the president by accident. As recently as the 1960s, the justices, as well as many lower federal court judges, came from the same political environment that surrounded the Court. Governors, senators, cabinet members, and other White House advisers were commonly tapped for Supreme Court nominations, which meant that the Court would have a substantial contingent of justices with a well-honed sensitivity to this environment. Between 1937 and 1967, twelve of the twenty-two Supreme Court appointments went to individuals who came directly from the executive or legislative branches of the federal government. Three other nominees during this period—Felix Frankfurter, Abe Fortas, and Earl Warren—also qualify as "political insiders" by most definitions: Frankfurter and Fortas were close personal advisers to Presidents Franklin Roosevelt and Lyndon Johnson, respectively, and Warren had been a Republican vice-presidential candidate in 1948. Not surprisingly, political scientist Robert Dahl's well-known discovery that the Court ultimately goes along with the dominant national political coalition proved true even during the aggressive Warren Court era, when the Court limited its interventions to cases in which individual rights were under direct assault, and then mostly by state authorities.[9]

Nixon's succession to the presidency in January 1969 marked the beginning of a new era in presidential-judicial relations. Outspoken in his criticism of Warren Court precedents during the 1968 campaign, Nixon determinedly ignored loyal Republican friends and stalwarts when making Supreme Court appointments, choosing instead federal circuit court judges he barely knew.[10] In doing so, Nixon helped to establish a trend: seventeen of the last nineteen nominees to the Court have been sitting jurists, compared to just one who came from either the executive or legislative branches (Rehnquist, who was an assistant attorney general) and one who was in private practice (Lewis Powell). Certainly all nineteen were better known for their legal or judicial acumen than for their recent political triumphs. In the meantime, senators, governors, cabinet members, and Washington insiders have been routinely ignored. Few presidential campaigns have turned on the issue of future nominations to the Court; as a consequence, presidents have been relieved of any responsibility to name particular justices to fulfill campaign promises. At the same time, the more intense political atmosphere that surrounds the confirmation of prospective justices has encouraged presidents to choose nominees with well established legal reputations, rather than those who sport political records that lend themselves to easy partisan and ideological attack.

This newly professionalized Court of career jurists has sowed its oats through confrontations with, rather than deference to, the president and Congress. Both Democrats and Republicans in Congress have been taken aback by the conservative Rehnquist Court's willingness to overturn longtime precedents supporting federal initiatives to fight criminal activity and regulate the environment.[11] The powers of the presidency also have been shaped by the current Court. In 1988 the justices upheld the controversial Independent Counsel Act, giving its stamp of approval to an institutional check on executives that is only barely accountable to normal political forces.[12] Ten years later, the Supreme Court unanimously required the sitting president of the United States, who was sued over a sexual harassment incident that occurred *prior* to his presidency, to defend himself against that suit while he was still in office.[13] It seemed the only thing this bold Court had not yet done was to insert itself into the election of a president. With *Bush v. Gore,* the circle is now complete.

In truth, Robert Dahl's hypothesis that the Court represents an "affirming" (and therefore democratic) branch of government deserves some reconsideration in light of the past thirty years of judicial activity concerning the conduct of the president. *Bush v. Gore* takes up space in the law books as a legal aberration, but it also provides social scientists and legal commentators with symbolic confirmation of the change in the relationship between these two branches of the federal government.

Presidential Campaigns and the Judiciary

Even before a president takes office, he must address critical questions concerning his views on controversial legal precedents and the way he hopes to shape the judiciary. Occasionally during the nineteenth and twentieth centuries, the Supreme Court and related issues figured prominently in campaigns for the presidency.[14] In the 1800 race between President John Adams and Vice President Thomas Jefferson, the latter owed his victory largely to his party's steadfast denunciation of the controversial Alien and Sedition Acts of 1798, which criminalized the act of criticizing government officials. The Federalist Party had supported the legislation, and Adams signed it. The law provided a forum for Federalist judges to rail against Republican editors and publishers at sedition trials. The voters put the judiciary on trial in the election of 1800, and the judiciary lost.

A half-century later, the Supreme Court's decision in *Dred Scott v. Sandford* served as the whipping boy for a new Republican Party during the election campaign of 1860.[15] The *Dred Scott* decision invalidated the Missouri Compromise of 1820, which had divided U.S. territories among free and slave states; in the process the Court aggressively articulated a theory of the slave as personal property. In the 1860 campaign Republican Abraham Lincoln alleged that the timing and substance of *Dred Scott* pointed to a conspiracy by the Democrats to nationalize slavery. According to political scientist Donald Grier Stevenson, the 1860s are widely viewed today as the nadir of Supreme Court influence, largely because Lincoln's 1860 victory placed the Court on the losing side of the presidential election.[16]

During the twentieth century, the Court was only infrequently a factor in presidential elections. In many ways the Court's low profile in election campaigns stands in marked contrast to the high profile it assumed during that century as a national policymaker. The Court was certainly on Franklin Delano Roosevelt's mind during the 1936 election campaign because the justices had stymied the president's New Deal initiatives by invalidating the National Industrial Recovery Act and the Agricultural Adjustment Act, among other pieces of federal legislation.[17] Surprisingly, Roosevelt maintained a "studied silence" about the Court during the campaign. As historian William Leuchtenberg points out, Roosevelt enjoyed only a five-point lead in the Gallup poll that summer, and, with some other surveys predicting his defeat, "deliberately raising the Court question seemed foolhardy."[18] Later, it would appear as if Roosevelt had fumbled away the opportunity to create a mandate for the Court-packing plan he unveiled after the election, a bold initiative to expand the Court that went down to a narrow but embarrassing defeat in 1937. Thus, at one of those rare moments in history when ordinary Americans were as focused on Court issues as were political elites, voters were denied a rich debate among the presidential candidates about how they would address the constitutional crisis that was brewing.

The same pattern prevailed in subsequent decades, as the Court and judiciary-related matters provided mostly side stories in presidential election contests. Harry Truman, John Kennedy, and Lyndon Johnson barely discussed the Court during their campaigns. Dwight Eisenhower occasionally sought to distinguish his preferred method of judicial selection from that of the Democrats, who he believed awarded judgeships on the basis of patronage and partisanship. Yet he rarely highlighted this point in his most important campaign speeches. And when President Eisenhower nominated California governor Earl Warren (chosen to pay back a campaign debt) and circuit court judge John Marshall Harlan (pushed by close friend and former legal partner Attorney General Herbert Brownell) to the Court, critics barely stirred.

Richard Nixon's campaign for the presidency in 1968 marked the first concerted attempt by a major party candidate in the twentieth century to place the Supreme Court and its recent rulings squarely before the voters. Blaming the Warren Court and its "pro-felon" rulings such as *Miranda v. Arizona* for the civil unrest that was sweeping the country, Nixon promised that he would appoint only conservative "law and order" judges who would "strictly interpret" the Constitution and not "make law."[19] Nixon's campaign strategy made sense, especially in the South, where resentment against civil rights initiatives had spilled over into resentment against the Warren Court as well. In securing a Republican plurality in the South for the first time in the century-long history of the Republican Party, Nixon demonstrated that when legal issues were couched in the right electoral rhetoric, they could make a difference.

Although Nixon's 1968 campaign changed the rhetoric of future campaigns, subsequent election outcomes were not affected by Court-related issues to nearly the same degree. Running for reelection in 1972, President Nixon could point to his selection of four moderate-to-conservative justices as proof of his sincerity. But it was the relative prosperity of the country that propelled Nixon into office for a second term. Eight years later, Ronald Reagan went a step further in his campaign by targeting Supreme Court decisions that were politically divisive, even among Republican voters. Reagan directed his fiercest criticism at *Roe v. Wade,* which created a constitutional right to abortion, observing that the decision was "an abuse of power worse than Watergate."[20] Reagan also decried other controversial rulings banning Bible readings and prayer in the public schools, protecting nonobscene pornography as a free expression right, approving busing as a means of facilitating racial integration in the schools, and upholding certain affirmative action programs. Reagan even borrowed from Nixon's playbook of a decade earlier, denouncing Supreme Court decisions that protected the rights of the accused. In truth, Reagan's anti-Court rhetoric may have shored up the support of the most socially conservative Republicans, but those voters were certain to vote Republican in any case. Reagan's 1980 and 1984 election victories were due to the state of the country's economy more than anything else. Still, it was telling that Reagan was not punished for such rhetoric by more moderate Republican voters. Democratic presidential nominee Walter Mondale's repeated harping on the conservative leanings of the Supreme Court proved little match for the peace and prosperity the country enjoyed in 1984. And when Massachusetts governor Michael Dukakis hammered Vice President George H. W. Bush on social issues and the future composition of the Court in 1988, his attacks barely registered with the crucial swing voters who had elected Reagan twice and then elected Bush despite his controversial social agenda.

Arkansas governor Bill Clinton's successful effort to bring many of these same swing voters back to the Democratic Party in 1992 was notable for its lack of emphasis on Court-related issues. During President Bush's term the Supreme Court had curtailed abortion rights, first in *Webster v. Reproductive Health Services* (1989) and then in *Planned Parenthood v. Casey* (1992).[21] In these decisions the Court narrowly saved *Roe v. Wade* from its seemingly inevitable demise, while opening the door to more government restrictions. Clinton and the Democrats had been handed a golden opportunity to make the Court an issue in the 1992 election campaign, but chose instead to focus on the economy.

Perhaps Clinton's advisers had learned something from the Dukakis and Mondale failures: although Court-related rhetoric is now considered an essential aspect of every presidential campaign, it sways few voters. Since 1968 each presidential candidate has been asked to provide his views on the right to abortion (Republicans candidates have all opposed the right; Democrats have supported it), affirmative action (Republicans oppose; Democrats support with qualifications), and the "philosophy of judging" the candidate favors (Republicans support "strict interpretation"; Democrats support the notion of a "living Constitution"). How these campaign positions convert into the actual practice of selecting judges is less certain.

This type of Court-related campaigning has significant implications, however, because, in general, all of the winning presidential candidates have kept their promises. The socially conservative Republican presidents Nixon, Reagan, and Bush appointed conservative jurists to the Court. President Clinton, the only Democrat to appoint justices since the 1960s, appointed two moderate-to-liberal jurists to the Court. The one aberration during this period—President Bush's appointment of moderate-to-liberal David Souter to the Court in 1990—is notable because it proved to be such a clear exception to the rule. Thus, although presidents may not be elected because of their positions on the judiciary, they still attempt to fulfill their campaign promises.

Like "A Bolt of Lightning?" Presidential Appointments to the Federal Judiciary

Selection to any federal court—but especially the Supreme Court—has been likened to the spin of a roulette wheel or a bolt of lightning that can strike anywhere without warning. Esteemed Harvard law professor Thomas Reed Powell summed it up this way: "The selection of Supreme Court Justices is pretty much a matter of chance."[22] Certainly, the composition of the federal judiciary—at least until recently—could have been fairly characterized as a collection of friends and allies of senators from the president's party (lower court judges) and a collection of friends and allies of presidents (Supreme Court justices). Because no one can know very far in advance who will one day become a senator or a president, being in the right place at the right time demands political acumen, expert networking, and even luck. In the case of the Supreme Court, those nominees whom the president did not personally know were often friends of someone well connected in the administration. Eisenhower's selection of Harlan, a long-time friend of the attorney general, provides a case in point.

Today, lower federal court appointments are still often the product of well-honed connections with U.S. senators. Jimmy Carter's short-lived attempt to displace this patronage system with merit-based "nominating commissions" ran into political obstacles and was quickly disbanded by his successor, Ronald Reagan. Subsequent presidents have tried to shape the appointment of some lower court judges, especially at the circuit court level. Merit and ideology played a significant role in the elevation of numerous law professors to the courts of appeals during the 1980s and 1990s. Yet patronage, especially with regard to district court judgeships, still plays a central role when filling positions in the lower federal courts.[23]

In contrast, the process for identifying and selecting candidates for the Supreme Court has undergone a dramatic transformation. The identification of Supreme Court nominees by presidents originated as a private affair, handled entirely by the president and perhaps a small coterie of his closest advisers. George Washington worked alone after his first inauguration in 1789 to sort through the multitude of written suggestions he received concerning whom he should place on the still-empty United States Supreme Court.[24] Thomas Jefferson consulted with legislators from his party, while Ulysses S. Grant and Woodrow Wilson sought the advice of cabinet members. Sitting Supreme Court justices have managed to break into this inner circle of advisers on occasion; most notably, Chief Justice William Howard Taft exerted considerable influence over the Court appointments made by Presidents Warren Harding and Calvin Coolidge during the 1920s. To the extent that the attorney general played a role, it was simply as an adviser, with no special resources to draw on other than his own expertise on Court-related issues. Presidents huddled with the attorney general and any other trusted advisers to toss around the names of potential nominees. Once a shortlist was identified, little research was conducted, other than perhaps to provide a "heads up" to congressional leaders or officials in the organized bar.

Beginning in the mid-twentieth century, however, a confluence of factors served to transform the political landscape that shapes the recruitment of candidates to the Supreme Court. These factors include:[25]

1. *Growth and bureaucratization of the Justice Department.* From a modest-sized agency in the late nineteenth century, the Justice Department has grown into a mammoth enterprise, assuming many litigation functions on behalf of the federal government that previously had been performed by the individual agencies. Especially significant was the creation of the Office of Legal Counsel (OLC) in the 1930s. The OLC was conceived of as a bureaucratic resource for the attorney general, serving him in his role as legal adviser to the president.

In recent years, the heavily politicized OLC has been headed by an assistant attorney general with a staff of about twenty lawyers. During the 1980s and early 1990s Presidents Reagan and Bush relied heavily on the OLC and other Justice Department lawyers to generate lists of candidates for the federal judiciary, including the Supreme Court.

2. *Growth and bureaucratization of the White House staff.* Not to be outdone by agencies such as the Justice Department, the White House staff underwent a growth spurt of its own, expanding from just thirty-seven employees in the early 1930s to more than nine hundred staffers by the late 1980s.[26] Beginning with President Kennedy, who consulted regularly with White House counsel Theodore Sorenson, presidents have increasingly relied on staff lawyers to assist in the vetting of prospective judicial candidates and, more recently, as a source of independent legal research.

3. *Growth in the size and influence of the federal judiciary.* Congress's creation of new federal judgeships during the twentieth century has affected the process of judicial recruitment in significant ways. With 862 federal judgeships in existence today, modern presidents enjoy far more opportunities than their predecessors to place their imprint on judicial policymaking. The president may have to fill on average as many as thirty to forty vacancies on the federal bench during each year of his term—upon taking office in January 2001 President Bush was greeted with approximately one hundred vacancies, including thirty-one on the U.S. courts of appeals. Moreover, a large number of those judgeships, including all of those on the Court of Appeals for the D.C. Circuit, are unencumbered by normal considerations of senatorial courtesy, the legislative norm that allows senators of the president's party to dictate local appointments. These judgeships are readily available as a testing ground for future Supreme Court justices. Federal appellate judges who prove to be ideologically compatible with the president's agenda may find themselves on shortlists for elevation to the Supreme Court, either by the president who appointed them or by a later administration of the same party. President Reagan followed this practice, nominating to the Court two judges, Robert Bork and Antonin Scalia, whom he had earlier appointed to the D.C. Circuit. President Clinton nominated two jurists to the Court, Ruth Bader Ginsburg and Stephen Breyer, who had been appointed to circuit court judgeships by President Carter more than a decade earlier. Because these prospective justices have already issued multiple rulings from the federal bench, they have fashioned a judicial portfolio that usually makes their behavior on the Supreme Court more predictable.

4. *Divided party government.* Between 1896 and 1946, opposing parties controlled the White House and the Senate during just two sessions of Congress, but since then divided party control has become a routine feature of government. The president has faced a hostile U.S. Senate in fifteen of twenty-eight Congresses since World War II, and in seven of the eight Congresses since 1986. Control of the Senate confirmation process confers significant benefits on those who might want to defeat a judicial nomination. By creating witness lists stacked against the nominee, establishing ground rules for the hearings that encourage open-ended debates, and delaying the scheduling of hearings until interest group opposition can mobilize, the chair of the Senate Judiciary Committee can greatly increase the odds that a nominee will not be confirmed. Had Robert Bork been tapped for the Supreme Court in 1986, he would have been steered through a committee led by ardent Reagan supporters Strom Thurmond of South Carolina and Orrin Hatch of Utah; instead, a year later, he faced Delaware senator Joseph Biden's Democrat-controlled committee and was rejected. An administration's approach to Supreme Court recruitment is necessarily altered by the likelihood that an opposition-controlled Senate Judiciary Committee lies in wait.

5. *Increased participation by interest groups, including the organized bar, in the selection process.* Although organized interests occasionally mobilized to defeat Supreme Court nominees in the nineteenth and early twentieth centuries, the level and intensity of interest group participation in the process today is unprecedented. Since World War II, interest groups have extended their influence into the early stages of judicial selection. The American Bar Association has been rating nominees to all federal courts since the early 1950s; negative or even unenthusiastically positive recommendations can damage a nominee substantially, if not derail the nomination altogether. Other groups, such as the Alliance for Justice, People for the American Way, and the Leadership Conference on Civil Rights, have made Supreme Court appointments a high priority for their organizations.

6. *Increased media attention before and during Supreme Court confirmation hearings.* In the not-so-distant past, the media's spotlight would fall on a prospective Supreme Court justice only after he or she was officially nominated, and even then the process of confirming the nominee—including the conduct of Senate committee hearings—was mostly an inside-the-beltway diversion. Today, the process extends from rumors of a pending vacancy to the final confirmation vote and is a thoroughly public matter. National reporters assigned to cover the Supreme Court provide their readers with updated

shortlists of the candidates the president is considering. In a nod to this reality, Bill Clinton strategically floated the names of candidates to a hungry media contingent even before he had decided on his final selections. This practice of "politics by trial balloon" provided Clinton with advance warning of the opposition he was inviting, but it may have also given the administration's enemies too much influence over the selection process. For example, in 1994 Senator Hatch and Senate Minority Leader Robert Dole of Kansas torpedoed the prospective Supreme Court nomination of Interior Secretary Bruce Babbitt with their not-so-subtle public hints about Babbitt's lack of judicial experience.[27] President Clinton's failure to commit to Babbitt before he underwent that rhetorical assault may have rescued the administration from considerable embarrassment, but it also invited public attacks from critics who might otherwise have feared the wrath of a White House already significantly invested in that one candidate.

7. *Advances in legal research technology.* In 1956 Herbert Brownell sought to investigate the record of a prospective candidate for the Court, William Brennan, a New Jersey Supreme Court justice. To perform the task Brownell did what any first-year law student would have done at that time: he manually went through the New Jersey court reports, skimming Brennan's written opinions. By the 1980s this traditional method of legal research had been replaced by legal research programs such as LEXIS/NEXIS and WESTLAW, which allow officials to gather all of a prospective candidate's past judicial opinions, scholarship, and public commentary in the blink of an eye. Justice Department officials can even construct elaborate word searches to hone in on the candidate's most controversial statements about the issues that most interest opposition senators. Naturally, these advances in research technology are a double-edged sword: media outlets and opposition interest groups are as likely to discover negative information about prospective candidates as is the administration itself. Shocking eleventh-hour revelations, such as the news that Supreme Court nominee G. Harrold Carswell had given a speech at a Ku Klux Klan rally (which helped to undermine his nomination in 1970), seem much less likely in the computer age. The ease of information gathering may also contribute to a streamlining of the selection process to favor lackluster, plain vanilla candidates who are capable of surviving intense scrutiny of their backgrounds. For all the conservative critics' frustrations at some of Justice Souter's rulings, many have forgotten that it was Souter's complete lack of a controversial, substantive record on important legal issues—and thus the difficulty of attacking him—that made his candidacy so appealing to Bush administration officials.

These changes in the political landscape have profoundly influenced the process by which prospective Supreme Court nominees are first identified and eventually selected. In recent administrations, high-level political operatives, who did not want to expend all of the president's political capital on a confirmation fight, have battled ardent ideologues hell-bent on transforming the constitutional landscape through the selection of right-thinking Supreme Court justices. Such arguments bring out the worst in both groups: by underselling the others' preferences and overselling their own, administration officials corrupt the advice they offer to the president and undermine his unique interests in the process.

The factors that have shaped the political environment for Supreme Court recruitment have pulled the Court toward professional judges whose long records on the bench satisfy the administration's ideologues, but whose lack of political experience and relatively noncontroversial public profile satisfy only the most cautious members of the president's inner circle. As we shall see, many of these variables came into play during President Reagan's second term, highlighting the modern tendency to produce a Court of political "outsiders."

The Reagan Administration and the Modern Era of Judicial Recruitment

During Reagan's first term in office, conservative lawyers in the Justice Department—determined to alter the constitutional landscape in a conservative direction—were forced to cool their heels and wait. The only Supreme Court vacancy arose when Potter Stewart informed officials that he intended to retire at the conclusion of the Court's 1980–1981 term, just six months into the Reagan presidency. As a candidate in 1980, Reagan had on more than one occasion professed his desire to name the first woman justice to the Supreme Court, and that promise was still fresh in the public's mind at the time of Stewart's decision. Attorney General William French Smith immediately went to work on a list of prospective candidates that was topped by female jurists, most of whom were more moderate than conservative insiders desired. Smith was the driving force behind the selection of Judge O'Connor of the Arizona Court of Appeals, even though her views on critical issues such as school prayer, affirmative action, and abortion were very much in question. Nevertheless, on the basis of extensive research gathered by Smith's associates and the recommendations of O'Connor's Stanford Law School network, which included classmate William Rehnquist and Assistant Attorney General William F. Baxter, among others,

O'Connor's name was approved for nomination by the president in July 1981. If the Reagan administration was preparing to fight for a more hard-core conservative Court, it did not plan any bold moves so early in the president's term.

Soon after Reagan secured his landslide reelection victory in 1984, administration lawyers began preparing in earnest for the next Supreme Court vacancy. Beginning in February 1985, an informal group of Justice Department officials was formed, led by OLC head Charles J. Cooper and William Bradford Reynolds, head of the Civil Rights Division. Together, these officials reviewed potential nominees on a near weekly basis. In defining the attributes of the so-called "ideal candidate," the group worked from a list of twelve criteria:[28]

1. "awareness of the importance of strict justiciability and procedural requirements"
2. "refusal to create new constitutional rights for the individual"
3. "deference to states in their spheres"
4. "appropriate deference to agencies"
5. "commitment to strict principles of 'nondiscrimination' "
6. "disposition towards 'less government rather than more' "
7. "recognition that the federal government is one of enumerated powers"
8. "appreciation for the role of free market in our society"
9. "respect for traditional values"
10. "recognition of the importance of separations of power principles of presidential authority"
11. "legal competence" and
12. "strong leadership on the court/young and vigorous"

In searching for individuals who met these criteria, administration lawyers followed a familiar path. Their attention quickly focused on four appellate court judges whom President Reagan had appointed during his first term in office: Robert Bork and Antonin Scalia of the D.C. Circuit, Patrick Higginbotham of the Fifth Circuit, and Judge Ralph K. Winter Jr. of the Second Circuit. Joining these four on the Justice Department's shortlist were two earlier Republican appointees to the U.S. Court of Appeals for the Ninth Circuit: J. Clifford Wallace, appointed by Nixon in 1972, and Anthony M. Kennedy, appointed by Ford in 1975. All six jurists were relatively young (Bork at fifty-eight was by far the oldest), and all were strong proponents of conservative principles. None was a politician of the traditional sort: Scalia and Bork had served brief stints in the Justice Department, but the group consisted mainly of academics and jurists. In fact, the administration's intense review of their judicial records revealed few surprises. Kennedy was a stalwart conservative, but had strayed occasionally on privacy issues, where his "easy acceptance of privacy rights as something guaranteed by the Constitution" was viewed as "really distressing."[29] Perhaps this was a harbinger of Kennedy's eventual reluctance to overturn *Roe v. Wade*.

Scalia and Bork stood out as the most consistently conservative of the lot. Scalia, a fifty-year-old Italian American, was described by Justice Department attorneys as "especially creative and successful in transforming the common intuition that 'courts are running the country' into a set of coherent principles about what courts should not do."[30] His opinions on separation of powers and jurisdictional questions in particular were deemed brilliant. In addition, a thorough computer search of Scalia's record on the D.C. Circuit uncovered not a single opinion in which either the result or the ground of decision seemed problematic from a conservative legal perspective. Bork was the more controversial figure, both because he had obeyed President Nixon's order to fire the Watergate special prosecutor, Archibald Cox, during a stint as solicitor general in 1973, and for his colorful and controversial academic writings decrying landmark Supreme Court rulings that protected the right to abortion and an expanded right of free speech. But as a judicial conservative, Bork had few equals. According to one Justice Department report, Bork's guiding philosophy was that "if the judiciary overrules democratically sanctioned choices by creating rights not found in the constitutional text, it has engaged in an illegitimate—indeed, tyrannical—suppression of self-government."[31]

More important, Bork and Scalia were considered ideal candidates to survive the partisan sniping that was expected during the Senate confirmation process. They were circuit court judges who had survived Senate confirmation a few years earlier. And like many other circuit judges, their written opinions tended to disprove outsiders' perceptions of them as sharp ideological extremists. Even Bork's fiercest opponents would later admit that his circuit court opinions were on the whole both "balanced in judgment" and "fair in treatment of the arguments of losing parties and dissenters."[32] In short, these two court of appeals judges represented the administration's greatest hope of "sneaking" a true conservative onto the Supreme Court.

Several critical differences between the candidates ultimately vaulted Scalia ahead of Bork on the Reagan administration's Supreme Court promotion list. First, Scalia was eight years younger than Bork, giving him more staying power on the Court. Second, Scalia carried less pre-judicial baggage than Bork, who was still (perhaps unjustifiably) saddled with the legacy of having fired the Watergate prosecutor. Finally, Scalia would be the first Italian American justice, a fact that officials hoped would provide him with political cover among Senate Democrats.

In late spring 1986, more than a year after the administration's pre-screening process began, Chief Justice Warren Burger informed White House officials of his intention to retire. Once Attorney General Edwin Meese began to press for Justice Rehnquist's elevation to chief justice, all eyes turned to Scalia as Rehnquist's replacement. In truth, Rehnquist's appointment carried some baggage of its own: Democrats were eager to revive accusations that he had harassed African American voters in Arizona during the 1960s, a charge that was never proven, and that he had written memos critical of school desegregation when he was serving as a clerk to Justice Robert Jackson in the early 1950s. In discussions with the president, White House Chief of Staff Donald Regan pointed out that nominating Rehnquist together with Bork might create too difficult a battle to win, even with the help of a Republican-controlled Senate Judiciary Committee. Convinced that Regan was correct, the president on June 17, 1986, announced his selections of Rehnquist to be chief justice and Scalia to be associate justice. Scalia glided to confirmation in the Senate by a 98–0 vote. Rehnquist's confirmation, however, bogged down in debates about his conservative opinions and drew the highest number of negative votes ever cast against a successful nominee for chief justice; Rehnquist was confirmed, 65–33.

Lewis Powell's decision to retire a year later, on June 26, 1987, precipitated another battle, but not within the administration. Bork was the highest ranking candidate remaining from the previous year, and nothing had happened since then to alter the administration's preference. At least one outside factor had changed, however. In January 1987 the Democrats had taken control of the Senate for the first time since 1981, and the Senate Judiciary Committee was now led by Senator Biden, who planned to run for president in 1988. Lawyers in the White House Counsel's Office foresaw some problems for Bork, but they did not forcefully argue against his selection. After all, Biden had stated that he would vote to confirm Bork if he were ever nominated to the Supreme Court. But immediately after the nomination was announced on July 1, liberal interest groups began to mobilize against Bork. His nomination would eventually become a watershed in confirmation politics. Senator Biden exercised the majority party's prerogative to delay confirmation hearings until September, and the long paper trail Bork had left—more as a law professor than as a judge—was dissected by critics in a way that few had anticipated. During his testimony before the Judiciary Committee, Bork's lecture-like academic discourses about a range of constitutional issues began to convince moderate Republican senators, including Arlen Specter of Pennsylvania and John Warner of Virginia, that the bearded jurist lacked compassion for the problems of ordinary people. Few were surprised when, on October 23, the Senate defeated Bork's nomination by a 58–42 vote.

President Reagan turned to two more court of appeals judges in the wake of Bork's rejection: first, Douglas Ginsburg of the D.C. Circuit, who withdrew amid allegations that he had used marijuana as a law professor, and then Anthony Kennedy, who was easily confirmed. Thus, all five of the candidates Reagan nominated to the Court were sitting judges on federal or state courts, and in his second term all four were judges on the U.S. Courts of Appeals. Although Bork, Scalia, and Ginsburg had logged time working in the Justice Department for Republican administrations, they were, by the time of their nominations, political outsiders in every real sense. None represented the type of political insider (senator, attorney general, governor) that had been more commonly tapped for Supreme Court appointments during the early and middle twentieth century (see Table 18.1).

Political scientist Mark Silverstein has correctly identified 1968 and the Nixon campaign as a pivotal moment in Supreme Court politics.[33] It was not until the early to mid-1980s, however, that the Court underwent a more complete transformation into a bench of outsiders, more isolated from the rough and tumble of national politics than most Courts of the past. The post–World War II Court was heralded as a collection of intellectual giants—Felix Frankfurter, Hugo Black, Robert Jackson, and William O. Douglas—but their intellects had served presidents and their administrations, whether informally—Frankfurter was Roosevelt's private confidante, Black his loyal foot soldier in the Senate—or formally—Jackson was Roosevelt's attorney general, and Douglas was head of the Securities and Exchange Commission. In contrast, the justices appointed since 1969 have enjoyed little if any direct interaction with the presidents who appointed them. The first President Bush continued this trend by tapping two federal circuit court judges, Clarence Thomas and David Souter, for the Court during his single term in office.[34] President Clinton tried to buck the pattern by seriously considering New York governor Mario Cuomo, Senate Majority Leader George Mitchell, and Secretary of Education Richard Riley, in addition to Babbitt, for the Supreme Court during his first two years in office. But when political push came to shove (threats of stalled confirmation, the loss of political capital, and so forth), Clinton also turned to two federal circuit judges, Ginsburg and Breyer. Although these judges were well known in legal circles, they had remained outside the trenches of political warfare for well over a decade.

Table 18.1 Positions Held by Supreme Court Nominees at the Time of Their Nominations, 1937–1994

Nominee	Year	Appointing President	Position Previously Held
Hugo Black	*1937*	*Roosevelt*	*U.S. senator*
Stanley Reed	*1938*	*Roosevelt*	*U.S. solicitor general*
Felix Frankfurter	1939	Roosevelt	Law professor
William O. Douglas	*1939*	*Roosevelt*	*SEC chairman*
Frank Murphy	*1940*	*Roosevelt*	*U.S. attorney general*
James Byrnes	*1941*	*Roosevelt*	*U.S. senator*
Harlan Stone (C.J.)	1941	Roosevelt	U.S. Supreme Court associate justice
Robert Jackson	*1941*	*Roosevelt*	*U.S. attorney general*
Wiley Rutledge	1943	Roosevelt	Federal appellate judge
Harold Burton	*1945*	*Truman*	*U.S. senator*
Fred Vinson (C.J.)	*1946*	*Truman*	*U.S. secretary of the Treasury*
Tom C. Clark	*1949*	*Truman*	*U.S. attorney general*
Sherman Minton	1949	Truman	Federal appellate judge
Earl Warren (C.J.)	*1953*	*Eisenhower*	*Governor of California*
John M. Harlan	1954	Eisenhower	Federal appellate judge
William Brennan	1956	Eisenhower	N.J. Supreme Court judge
Charles Whittaker	1957	Eisenhower	Federal appellate judge
Potter Stewart	1958	Eisenhower	Federal appellate judge
Byron White	*1962*	*Kennedy*	*Deputy attorney general*
Arthur Goldberg	*1962*	*Kennedy*	*U.S. secretary of labor*
Abe Fortas	1965	Johnson	Private practice, presidential adviser
Thurgood Marshall	*1967*	*Johnson*	*U.S. solicitor general*
Abe Fortas (C.J., withdrew)	1968	Johnson	U.S. Supreme Court associate justice
Homer Thornberry (withdrew)	1968	Johnson	Federal appellate judge
Warren Burger (C.J.)	1969	Nixon	Federal appellate judge
Clement Haynsworth (rejected)	1969	Nixon	Federal appellate judge
G. Harrold Carswell (rejected)	1970	Nixon	Federal appellate judge
Harry Blackmun	1970	Nixon	Federal appellate judge
Lewis Powell	1971	Nixon	Private practice
William Rehnquist	*1971*	*Nixon*	*Asst. attorney general*
John Paul Stevens	1975	Ford	Federal appellate judge
Sandra Day O'Connor	1981	Reagan	Arizona appellate judge
William Rehnquist (C.J.)	1986	Reagan	U.S. Supreme Court associate justice
Antonin Scalia	1986	Reagan	Federal appellate judge
Robert Bork (rejected)	1987	Reagan	Federal appellate judge
Douglas Ginsburg (withdrew)	1987	Reagan	Federal appellate judge
Anthony Kennedy	1987	Reagan	Federal appellate judge
David Souter	1990	Bush I	Federal appellate judge
Clarence Thomas	1991	Bush I	Federal appellate judge
Ruth Bader Ginsburg	1993	Clinton	Federal appellate judge
Stephen Breyer	1994	Clinton	Federal appellate judge

Source: Compiled by the author.

Note: Nominees who came directly from executive or legislative branches are highlighted in bold italics.

The factors that shape the modern process of selecting Supreme Court nominees have thus come home to roost on the Rehnquist Court, which stands as independent of the other two branches of the federal government as any other Supreme Court in history. Justices who never attended cabinet meetings may be understandably naïve about how the executive branch really works. It is little wonder that the modern Supreme Court is willing to wade so boldly into deep political waters and render judgments that represent highly controversial exercises of judicial power.

"May It Please the Court": Presidential Influence on the Judicial Process

The growth and bureaucratization of the Justice Department has facilitated more than just a thorough vetting of prospective Supreme Court candidates. It has also made possible greater White House involvement in the litigation that flows to the Supreme Court, the lower federal courts, and the various state courts. The federal government has long been the most frequent litigant in the federal courts and the Supreme Court; each day countless new lawsuits are filed against federal agencies such as the Department of Health and Human Services. Executive Branch lawyers settle many such lawsuits; others go to trial either before an administrative law judge or before a federal court.

Drawing on social scientist Marc Galanter's landmark framework for understanding the systematic features of a legal system, the executive branch is a "repeat player": it is a litigating actor engaged in many similar cases over time.[35] Accordingly, the federal government enjoys a number of advantages in the litigation process, including expertise, informal relationships with other actors, a prior "bargaining reputation," and the ability to "play the odds" for advantages that may accrue only in later cases. All of these factors weigh heavily in the government's favor in most forms of litigation.

In recent years the White House has sought to parlay these advantages to gain through the courts what it could not attain elsewhere, whether because of congressional inertia, concerted interest group opposition, or the president's fears that legislative solutions would redound to the detriment of fellow party members in Congress. Unable to enact conservative modifications to the Voting Rights Act, in the early 1990s the Bush administration supported private legal efforts to overturn congressional districts that were drawn to protect certain racial groups. The Clinton administration switched sides and, beginning in 1993, supported upholding many of those same districts. The Justice

Department under Clinton also aggressively prosecuted Microsoft Corporation for antitrust violations in the late 1990s and managed to attain a stunning judicial order in 2000 to break up the company, which was subsequently overturned on appeal. George W. Bush, Clinton's successor in office, encouraged his Justice Department to adopt a less aggressive approach to the Microsoft litigation. Executive branch agencies with litigation expertise may also lend behind-the-scenes assistance in "private litigation" matters. The Clinton administration lent support to private plaintiffs suing tobacco companies and gun manufacturers during the mid- to late-1990s.

The federal government's "repeat-player" advantage in court also pays dividends for the White House when it takes an interest in cases before the Supreme Court. The solicitor general, who represents the United States in most cases in court, enjoys an especially close relationship with the justices, no matter which party controls the White House. Not surprisingly, the solicitor general's office has an extraordinary level of success before the Court, as reflected in the Court's rulings on cases and even more dramatically in the Court's selection of which cases to hear.[36]

Although frequently a petitioner or respondent before the Supreme Court, the solicitor general influences matters more subtly by submitting amicus curiae (friend of the court) briefs filed in cases in which the U.S. government is not directly involved, but nonetheless takes an interest in the outcome. In the 1960s Archibald Cox became the first solicitor general to aggressively involve his office in the filing of amicus briefs. From 1961 through 1965 Cox's office filed an average of seventeen amicus briefs per year, including twenty-eight amicus briefs in 1963 alone.[37] During the 1970s and 1980s, the federal government routinely filed amicus briefs in 20 percent to 30 percent of all cases decided by the Court, and sometimes in as many as half.

This high level of amicus filings by the U.S. government, which has held steady in recent years, is driven largely by perceptions that the Supreme Court serves as an important venue for deciding a range of politically significant legal issues. The Reagan administration in particular sought to use the amicus brief as a tool of constitutional change, and it achieved considerable success in this regard under its first solicitor general, Charles Fried. The solicitor general and the president at times may differ on legal strategy. During the Nixon administration, Solicitor General Erwin Griswold declined to argue for the government before the Supreme Court in two cases involving national security and the draft. The Carter administration's attorney general, Griffin Bell, engaged in a well-reported feud on the president's behalf with Solicitor General Wade

McCree concerning how to handle the controversial affirmative action case, *Regents of California v. Bakke* (1978).[38] Still, most solicitors general are chosen in the first place for their compatibility with the president's agenda, and they act accordingly to defend the president's interests. The president thus enjoys considerable influence in the Supreme Court.

Presidential Powers and the Supreme Court: Limited Checks and Tenuous Balances

On rare occasions, the president finds himself in the Supreme Court battling over the metes and bounds of his own constitutional and statutory powers. Traditionally, the president has enjoyed considerable success in these circumstances. For reasons both practical and political, the Court is poorly situated to control the president through its rulings. Even the members of the Court not appointed by the sitting president understand that the president's status as a nationally elected official and his position at the reins of every executive branch agency make him a formidable foe under any circumstance. President Andrew Jackson famously declined to enforce the Supreme Court's 1832 ruling in *Worcester v. Georgia*, declaring—perhaps apocryphally—of the chief justice: "John Marshall has made his decision—*now let him enforce it!*"[39] Even unpopular presidents considered throwing down similar gauntlets. During the Watergate crisis, immediately after the Supreme Court had voted 8–0 against the president's claim that he retained an absolute executive privilege to protect White House communications, a politically weak President Nixon still weighed alternatives to compliance. According to one report, Nixon openly wondered if to preserve the power of the office he did not have a "constitutional duty" to reject the Court's order.[40]

Faced with this reality, the Supreme Court has traditionally proceeded with caution when considering attempts to curtail presidential authority. In *Marbury v. Madison*, Chief Justice Marshall cleverly established a power of judicial review for the Supreme Court by invalidating a 1789 law that the plaintiff was invoking to secure an overdue judicial commission from the Jefferson administration.[41] Marshall's fear of noncompliance by Jefferson persuaded him not to order the new administration to deliver the commission. Sixty years later, during the Civil War, the Supreme Court upheld President Lincoln's seizure of ships in *The Prize Cases* (1863), even though he issued those orders nearly three months before Congress had authorized him to declare that a state of insurrection existed.[42] Although the Supreme Court appeared to show more backbone in *Ex parte Milligan* (1866) when it invalidated Lincoln's suspension of habeas corpus, the Court's ruling was handed down only after the war was ended and the commander in chief in question was dead.[43]

Like Congress, the Supreme Court of the early to mid-twentieth century stood little chance of prevailing against a presidency that was increasingly involved in domestic and international politics. In 1936 the Court declared that a president has "plenary and exclusive power . . . as the sole organ of the federal government in the field of international relations."[44] With the conduct of foreign relations and war lying squarely within the domain of the chief executive, few were surprised either by the Supreme Court's deference to President Roosevelt's internment of Japanese Americans during World War II or by its acquiescence when President Carter terminated a defense treaty (without Senate approval) nearly a half century later.

In domestic affairs, Supreme Court deference to the president's conduct of the executive branch has prevailed as well, albeit with a few exceptions. In *Myers v. United States* (1926), the Court granted the president unbridled discretion to fire executive officials, a generous reading of presidential power that was only partially undone by its decision a decade later to restrict presidential terminations of independent agency commissioners.[45] President Truman was deeply angered by the Court's 1952 ruling invalidating his administration's seizure of the steel mills to avert a labor strike, but complied with the Court's order to return the mills to their owners. Yet the Court gave far more to the presidency in *Youngstown Sheet & Tube Co. v. Sawyer* (1952) than it took away.[46] A majority of justices formally accepted the theory that the president enjoys "inherent powers" not expressly found in the Constitution. The same could be said of *United States v. Nixon* (1974), in which the Court recognized for the first time that presidents have an executive privilege to protect documents in many circumstances, albeit not in Nixon's specific case.

In each of these instances, the Supreme Court expanded presidential powers far more than it constricted them: those contemporaneous presidential excesses did not become an excuse to limit future executives who exercised a bit more caution. In contrast, no such two-edged sword emerged from *Nixon v. Fitzgerald* (1982), in which the Court narrowly decided that a president is immune from lawsuits concerning any of his official acts. Notably, it was the new arrivals on the Court (Burger, Powell, Rehnquist, Stevens, and O'Connor) who sided with former president Nixon in *Fitzgerald*. Yet in the two decades that followed, those same justices crafted a majority far more willing to interfere with, rather than defer to, the chief executive.

Two cases in particular exemplify the current Court's willingness to cast away traditional notions of deference to the president in favor of other concerns such as "efficiency" and "fairness." Little of value was provided to the president in *Morrison v. Olson* (1988), in which the Court upheld a statute providing for an independent counsel to investigate possible federal criminal violation by high-level executive officials, including the president. Because the specially chosen counsel, although an "executive officer," was deemed an "inferior" officer by the Supreme Court, Congress could constitutionally preclude the president from firing him or her without due cause.[47] As Justice Scalia noted in his passionate dissent, the statute essentially deprived the president of the exclusive control over the exercise of executive power that the Constitution vests in him alone.[48] (In 1999 Congress discontinued the controversial statute, a political nod to the harsh consequences it had wrought on both political parties since its inception.) Scalia, however, joined with a unanimous court in *Clinton v. Jones* to deny President Clinton's request to delay a civil suit brought against him until after he left office. Writing for the Court, Justice Stevens confidently asserted that "if the past is any indicator, it seems unlikely that a deluge of litigation will ever engulf the presidency."[49] The fact that this lawsuit did engulf the presidency, spawning the Lewinsky investigation, among other matters, simply highlights how the current Court has grown unsympathetic to the plight of modern presidents.

Morrison v. Olson and *Clinton v. Jones* also underscore the degree to which changes in personnel have desensitized the Supreme Court to the political realities surrounding the modern presidency. A Court that traditionally has been careful not to straitjacket future presidents now shows little hesitancy to do so, and with little explanation of how others are to deal with the consequences of its decisions. What constituted "good cause" enabling a president to fire an independent counsel under the (now defunct) independent counsel statute? Is the test the same as it is for termination of independent agency heads? Additionally, what criteria should a district court use in weighing presidential requests for delays in litigation against the desire of a plaintiff to move expeditiously to trial? Does a regularly scheduled cabinet meeting justify delaying a presidential response to a subpoena for documents, for example?

The world the justices have left for others to sort out is complex indeed. It has been wrought by a Court manned by nine justices, six of whom have never served in any capacity in the executive branch (Rehnquist, Scalia and Thomas are the exceptions) and seven of whom have never even worked for Congress (all but Breyer and Thomas). The Court's willingness to involve itself in the *Bush v. Gore* litigation seems almost inevitable under such circumstances. And until the political environment cools down enough to encourage presidents to again mix politicians with jurists on the Court, the confident—perhaps even arrogant—streak of independence exhibited by the modern Court may grow even more striking, with consequences that will continue to reverberate throughout the political system.

Notes

1. *Bush v. Gore*, 531 U.S. 98 (2000).

2. *Korematsu v. United States*, 323 U.S. 214 (1944). In *Korematsu*, the Court upheld the removal of Japanese Americans living on the West Coast and their internment during World War II. Although the decision has been derided by commentators, legal scholars, and even many justices during recent decades—see, for example, *Adarand Constructors, Inc. v. Pena*, 515 U.S. 200 (1995), in which a majority of the Court referred to the case as an "error" produced by a retreat from "the most searching judicial inquiry"—the technical precedent in *Korematsu* has never been formally overruled.

3. Justices Breyer and Souter technically agreed with the conservatives that the recount ordered by the Florida Supreme Court violated the Fourteenth Amendment's Equal Protection Clause because it failed to establish a consistent standard for counting the disputed ballots. But those two justices thought there was still time for recounts with a more explicit standard, and they ruled accordingly. Justices Stevens and Ginsburg found no constitutional problems at all with the Florida Supreme Court's ruling that recounts should continue under the vague "intent of the voter" criterion established by each individual county canvassing board.

4. This model of judicial decision making has been labeled by many scholars as "the attitudinal model." Two of its leading proponents, Jeffrey Segal and Harold Spaeth, argue that "the Supreme Court decides disputes in light of the facts of the case vis-à-vis the ideological attitudes and values of the justices. Simply put, Rehnquist votes the way he does because he is extremely conservative; [Thurgood] Marshall voted the way he did because he [was] extremely liberal." Jeffrey A. Segal and Harold J. Spaeth, *The Supreme Court and the Attitudinal Model* (New York: Cambridge University Press, 1993), 65. The attitudinal model has been challenged in recent years by scholars concerned that it pays insufficient attention to bargaining among the justices and strategic opinion writing, among other factors. See Lee Epstein and Jack Knight, *The Choices Justices Make* (Washington, D.C.: CQ Press, 1998); Forrest Maltzman, James F. Spriggs, and Paul Wahlbeck, *Crafting Law on the Supreme Court: The Collegial Game* (Cambridge: Cambridge University Press, 2000).

5. This philosophy of judicial intervention even in a democratic republic was most eloquently articulated in footnote four of *United States v. Carolene Products Co.*, 304 U.S. 144, n. 4 (1938). Justice Stone, writing for four of the seven justices deciding the case, announced that "there may be a narrower scope for operation of the presumption of constitutionality when legislation appears on its face to be within a specific prohibition of the Constitution, such as those of the first ten Amendments."

6. See *Goldwater v. Carter*, 44 U.S. 996 (1979), and *Nixon v. Fitzgerald*, 457 U.S. 731 (1982).

7. *Youngstown Sheet & Tube Co. v. Sawyer*, 343 U.S. 579 (1952).

8. *United States v. Nixon*, 418 U.S. 683 (1974).

9. See Robert Dahl, "Decision-making in a Democracy: The Supreme Court as a National Policy-maker," *Journal of Public Law* 6 (1957): 279–295. The Warren Court overturned twenty-five acts of Congress in its sixteen-year tenure, but it more aggressively directed its attention to state authorities. In total, more state laws (150) were overturned during the Warren Court era than under any other chief justice before or since. See David M. O'Brien, *Storm Center: The Supreme Court in American Politics,* 4th ed. (New York: W. W. Norton, 1996), 54.

10. Nixon barely even knew his own assistant attorney general, William Rehnquist; among his close advisers, the president had occasionally referred to him as "Renchberg."

11. Most dramatically, in *United States v. Lopez,* 514 U.S. 549 (1995), the Court held for the first time in nearly sixty years that Congress had exceeded its power under the Commerce Clause in Article I, Section 8, Clause 3, of the Constitution. Specifically, the Court invalidated the Gun Free School Zones Act of 1990, which made it a federal crime for any individual to possess a firearm within a school zone. In recent years the Court has also drawn a line against certain federal regulations governing state government activities. See, for example, *New York v. United States,* 505 U.S. 144 (1992); *Printz v. United States,* 521 U.S. 898 (1997).

12. *Morrison v. Olson,* 487 U.S. 654 (1988).

13. *Clinton v. Jones,* 520 U.S. 681 (1997).

14. For a full discussion of the preconditions for such Court-related campaigns, see Donald Grier Stevenson Jr.'s excellent book, *Campaigns and the Court: The U.S. Supreme Court in Presidential Elections* (New York: Columbia University Press, 1999).

15. *Dred Scott v. Sanford,* 60 U.S. 393 (1857).

16. Stevenson, *Campaigns and the Court,* 103.

17. See *United States v. Butler,* 297 U.S. 1 (1936); and *Schechter Poultry Corp. v. United States,* 295 U.S. 495 (1935).

18. William Leuchtenberg, *The Supreme Court Reborn: The Constitutional Revolution in the Age of Roosevelt* (New York: Oxford University Press, 1995), 107.

19. *Miranda v. Arizona,* 384 U.S. 436 (1966).

20. *Roe v. Wade,* 410 U.S. 113 (1973); Reagan is quoted in Stevenson, *Campaigns and the Court,* 204.

21. *Webster v. Reproductive Health Services,* 492 U.S. 490 (1989), and *Planned Parenthood v. Casey* 505 U.S. 833 (1992).

22. Quoted in O'Brien, *Storm Center,* 59.

23. For a fuller discussion of Carter's nominating commissions, as well as the politics of lower court appointments in general, one should consult Sheldon Goldman's excellent book, *Picking Federal Judges: Lower Court Selection from Roosevelt Through Reagan* (New Haven: Yale University Press, 1997).

24. John Anthony Maltese, *The Selling of Supreme Court Nominees* (Baltimore: Johns Hopkins University Press, 1995), 24.

25. The discussion that follows of these factors and of the Reagan administration's practice of selecting Supreme Court nominees is borrowed largely from David Yalof, *Pursuit of Justices: Presidential Politics and the Selection of Supreme Court Nominees* (Chicago: University of Chicago Press, 1999).

26. Stephen Hess, *Organizing the Presidency* (Washington, D.C.: Brookings Institution, 1988), 5.

27. Richard Berke, "Hatch Assails Idea of Justice Babbitt," *New York Times,* June 9, 1993, A17.

28. These criteria are listed in a memo written by Roger Clegg, a special assistant to the attorney general, defining the attributes of a so-called ideal Supreme Court candidate. Although Clegg's paper has not yet been made available to the public (see Withdrawal Sheet, 6 August 1996, Supreme Court/Rehnquist/Scalia General Selection Scenario [1 of 3] file, Box 14287, Peter Wallison Files, Ronald Reagan Presidential Library), its contents may be reconstructed by examining judicial profiles tailored to adhere to the terms of the criteria he discusses. See, for example, Report on Patrick Higginbotham paper, Supreme Court-Rehnquist/Scalia Notebook (2 of 4) file, Peter Wallison files, Ronald Reagan Presidential Library.

29. Memo, Steven Matthews to Special Projects Committee, May 23, 1986, Supreme Court Rehnquist/Scalia Notebook I (3 of 4) file, OA 14287, Peter Wallison Files, Ronald Reagan Presidential Library.

30. Report on Antonin Scalia, Supreme Court-Scalia (3 of 5) file, Peter Wallison Files, Ronald Reagan Presidential Library.

31. Report on Robert Bork, Supreme Court-Rehnquist/Scalia Notebook (1 of 2) file, Peter Wallison files, Ronald Reagan Presidential Library.

32. For example, the American Bar Association's Committee on the Judiciary opposed Bork's candidacy but praised the tone of his circuit court opinions. See Letter, Harold R. Tyler to Joseph Biden, September 21, 1987, reprinted in U.S. Congress, Senate, Committee on the Judiciary, *The Nomination of Robert H. Bork to be Associate Justice of the Supreme Court of the United States,* 100th Cong., 1st sess., September 21, 1987, 1232.

33. Mark Silverstein, *Judicious Choices: The New Politics of Supreme Court Confirmations* (New York: W. W. Norton, 1994), 10–12.

34. Thomas had served in the executive branch as an assistant secretary of education and head of the Equal Employment Opportunity Commission during the Reagan administration, but he had limited direct contact with the president.

35. See Marc Galanter, "Why the 'Haves' Come Out Ahead: Speculations on the Limits of Legal Change," *Law and Society Review* 9 (fall 1974): 95–151.

36. Rebecca Mae Salokar, *The Solicitor General: The Politics of Law* (Philadelphia: Temple University Press, 1992), 106–150.

37. Lincoln Caplan, *Tenth Justice* (New York: Vintage Books, 1987), 197.

38. *Regents of California v. Bakke,* 438 U.S. 265 (1978).

39. *Worcester v. Georgia,* 6 Pet. (31 U.S.) 515 (1832); Jackson quoted in Horace Greeley, *The American Conflict,* vol. 1 (Hartford, Conn.: O. D. Case, 1864), 106 (emphasis in original).

40. Bob Woodward and Carl Bernstein, *The Final Days* (New York: Avon Books, 1976), 300.

41. *Marbury v. Madison,* 1 Cr. (5 U.S.) 137 (1803).

42. The Prize Cases, 22 Black (67 U.S.) 635 (1863).

43. *Ex parte Milligan,* 24 Wall. (71 U.S.) 2 (1866).

44. *United States v. Curtiss-Wright Export Corp.,* 299 U.S. 304, 320 (1936).

45. *Myers v. United States,* 272 U.S. 52 (1926). The later case is *Humphrey's Executor v. United States,* 295 U.S. 602 (1935).

46. *Youngstown Sheet & Tube Co. v. Sawyer,* 343 U.S. 579 (1952).

47. According to Article II, Section 2, Clause 2, of the Constitution, "the Congress may by Law vest the Appointment of such inferior Officers, as they think proper, in the President alone, in the Courts of Law, or in the Heads of Departments."

48. *Morrison v. Olson,* 487 U.S. 654, 728 (1988) (Scalia, J., dissenting).

49. *Clinton v. Jones,* 520 U.S. 681, 702 (1997).

19 Divided Government and Policymaking: Negotiating the Laws

Paul J. Quirk and Bruce Nesmith

In recent years divided government has become the norm in Washington, sometimes (as since May 2001) with a Republican in the White House and the Democrats in control of one or both houses of Congress, and sometimes the reverse. A large and confusing literature has developed in political science in answer to the following question: Does it make any difference to public policymaking whether the same political party controls both elected branches or control is divided between the parties? James Sundquist is among those who say yes, it does matter; David Mayhew and others say no. By looking at the relationship between the president and Congress through the lens of negotiation theory, Paul J. Quirk and Bruce Nesmith demonstrate that each group of scholars is correct regarding some circumstances and incorrect regarding others. In this chapter Quirk and Nesmith specify what those circumstances are.

The voters in national elections often deliver a split verdict, handing the presidency to one political party and one or both houses of Congress to the other party. In recent decades, in fact, such split verdicts have been the most frequent result. The Democrats controlled both institutions for two years after the 1992 election. The Republicans did so (by one vote) for four months after the 2000 election, until Vermont senator James Jeffords quit the Republican Party, handing control of the Senate to the Democrats. The voters have divided control of the legislative and executive branches after every other presidential and midterm election from 1980 to 2000. As of 2002 divided government had prevailed for thirty-four of the fifty years since 1953. As long as the two parties continue to have roughly equal electoral support, divided party control is likely to remain a recurring feature of American government.

No consensus has emerged about what difference it makes whether control of government is unified or divided. Many commentators view divided government with alarm. In an influential essay, James Sundquist pointed out that divided government flies in the face of long-standing conventional wisdom about how American government is able to work—namely, that potentially excessive conflict between Congress and an independently elected president is overcome by the ties of a common party affiliation. Lacking these ties, he argued, divided government is prone to stalemate, incoherence, and irresponsibility.[1] By the end of George H. W. Bush's presidency, this view was widely accepted. In the 1992 campaign, both he and his opponent, Bill Clinton, blamed divided government for causing "gridlock." Most of the voters who were questioned in an election day exit poll said they preferred unified party control.[2]

Other commentators, however, come to the defense of divided government. They point out that divided control offers protection against the potential abuses of an "imperial presidency." They also deny that partisan differences necessarily prevent cooperation between the president and Congress.[3] Indeed, political scientist David Mayhew claimed that divided control makes little difference to government performance.[4] Many citizens actually prefer divided government. According to a 1996 poll, a majority of independent voters and even 19 percent of the Democrats preferred a Republican Congress if President Clinton were reelected.[5]

In this chapter we attempt to cast some new light on the consequences of divided government, mostly by taking a closer look at the theoretical issues. We interpret the legislative process as a negotiation between the president and Congress. We take into account both the policy and the electoral dimensions of party competition. And we consider how the nature of that competition varies with the issues at stake.

The State of the Debate

Critics and defenders of divided government both have been prone to make sweeping claims.[6] Critics argue that divided control creates three fundamental obstacles to effective government.[7] First, the president and an opposition party Congress have clashing views on national policy. Second, because the president and an opposition party congressional majority each want to prevent the other from gaining credit with the voters, they have strong incentives to block each other's legislative initiatives. In a sense, opposing the president is the other party's job in a two-party system. Third, because each party controls only part of the policymaking machinery, the voters cannot hold either party accountable for results. For all these reasons, the critics conclude, divided government is indecisive, incompetent, and irresponsible.

To support their view, the critics point out that sweeping changes in national policy have been accomplished mainly under unified government—especially when strong presidents, such as Woodrow Wilson, Franklin Roosevelt, and Lyndon Johnson, have had large same-party majorities in Congress. They also associate divided control with failures of policymaking, such as the massive budget deficits during the Reagan and Bush administrations and the government shutdowns during the divided government period of the first Clinton administration.

Defenders of divided government, most prominently David Mayhew, have challenged this critique. In a major empirical study, Mayhew identified 267 important laws that Congress enacted between 1946 and 1990. He found that these laws were passed with almost identical frequency under the two forms of party control.[8] In addition, Mayhew identified numerous examples of incoherent or irresponsible policymaking that occurred under unified control, and he showed that, apart from the singular experience of the 1980s, divided government has not produced larger budget deficits. In short, Mayhew concluded, divided party control makes no important difference to the performance of government.

In turn, other scholars have answered Mayhew. Studies by John Coleman and Sarah Binder find that since World War II, unified government has been both more productive and more responsive to the public mood.[9] Others claim that the adverse effect of divided control has been exacerbated in recent years by increased partisanship in Congress. Studies of enactments in the post–World War II era find that the parties are less likely to reach agreement when they are more ideologically polarized.[10]

The debate is far from over.[11] It is clear that the worst fears of critics of divided government are not supported by the evidence. Yet the view that divided government makes no difference is hardly plausible. Whether the president and the majority in Congress have compatible ideological and electoral goals or conflicting goals almost certainly matters. The question is how. Does divided government lead to deadlock or just cause some friction and delay? Does it change policy outcomes in other ways? Does divided party control have any advantages? And do the answers to these questions depend on anything else—such as the issues at stake or the state of the parties?

Presidential-Congressional Negotiation

The legislative process, we suggest, is fundamentally a negotiation between the president and Congress. Most centrally, it is a negotiation between the president and those members of Congress who are at the center of congressional opinion on the subject of the legislation and who will therefore cast the pivotal votes.[12] On a civil rights bill, for example, the pivotal members are the civil rights moderates. The partisan identity of these members depends on the political cleavages on the legislative issue. If the issue divides the two parties, then the pivotal members are in the majority party; in effect, the president must negotiate with the majority party. If an issue cuts across party lines, however, the pivotal members may come from both parties.

The relation between the president and Congress has the three features of any negotiation.[13] First, the president and Congress are interdependent: they need each other to achieve their interests. Apart from the rare overriding of a president's veto, neither branch can achieve legislative policy change unless Congress passes a bill and the president signs it. Second, the president and Congress are generally in "mixed-interest conflict." That is, they have both conflicting interests (something to fight about) and complementary interests (a basis for reaching agreement). These interests may concern policy goals, electoral goals, or both. For example, President Richard M. Nixon and the congressional Democrats wanted to pass a strong clean air bill; but each side wanted to claim the credit for introducing the stronger measure. President George W. Bush and the Democratic Senate favored an economic stimulus package in late 2001, but Bush favored tax cuts, and the Democrats wanted more spending. Third, the president and Congress communicate with each other to seek agreement. They make offers and counteroffers. To win concessions, either side may threaten to block action. But this communication is not all demands and threats: just as important, the president and Congress use communication to promote joint learning. They evaluate alternatives, clarify their respective interests, and often invent new solutions.[14] If successful, they reach an agreement and carry it out by enacting a bill.

To understand how the president and Congress interact in the legislative process, one must take into account two properties of negotiation: bargaining power and bounded efficiency.[15] Then one must consider how these properties play out—the prospects for cooperation—under different circumstances of policy conflict.

Bargaining Power

The relative success of actors in a negotiation reflects their bargaining power. For the most part, each side's bargaining power depends on how well its interests will be served in the absence of an agreement.[16] Whichever side can walk away from the bargaining table more easily can be more demanding and will take away more of the gains from an agreement.

The relative power of the president and Congress depends, therefore, on how badly each wants to enact a bill. Suppose that a Democratic Congress wants a large spending increase for a domestic entitlement program but a Republican president wants only a small one. Because the president is more satisfied than Congress with current spending, he can insist on a smaller increase. If Congress holds out for more spending and no bill is passed, spending continues at current levels. The president, in effect, wins—getting almost the amount he or she wanted, while Congress gets much less than it wanted. On the other hand, suppose they have the same disagreement concerning a discretionary program whose funding requires annual appropriations. In that case, the president and Congress will negotiate on equal terms. Unless the president is willing to close down the program, he or she needs to pass the appropriation just as much as Congress does.

The relative success of competing negotiators also depends on bargaining skill. For example, if presidents are skilled at figuring out how far they can push Congress, they can win more favorable terms than if their judgments are off the mark.

Bounded Efficiency

Within certain bounds, negotiation can overcome conflicts and produce efficient agreements—agreements that take advantage of opportunities for mutual gain. This important property comes from negotiators' ability to exchange information about their interests, undertake joint deliberations, and make binding commitments to a course of action.

The president and Congress can use a variety of methods to resolve their conflicts and achieve action. They can work out a compromise on issues where they have conflicting goals to forge an agreement that serves their common goals. For example, they may compromise on the shape of a tax cut to pass an economic stimulus measure they both want. They can look for improved solutions to policy problems, providing a more satisfactory outcome to both branches.

To some degree, a divided-control president and Congress can even negotiate the electoral benefits of legislative action. In the simplest case, the president may promise to share credit with the opposition party, for example, by inviting some members to participate in a public signing ceremony. In some cases, the president and Congress may adjust the division of a bill's benefits between their respective party constituencies to even out electoral effects that would other-wise hinder agreement. If passing a tax cut will tend to help a Republican president, a Democratic congressional majority may demand that its constituency groups get the larger share of the cuts. In sum, negotiation can overcome even serious conflict to permit action on common interests. That is what negotiation is for.

The efficiency of negotiation is bounded and variable, however, because conflicting interests cause friction. Negotiators compete for larger shares. They become angry, fear to appear weak, or are deterred from cooperating by constituencies that do not recognize the advantages of doing so. Even with important common interests at stake, therefore, negotiators may fail to agree. Or they may settle for a "lowest-common-denominator" agreement—one that requires only the easiest concessions but fails to exploit the available opportunities for mutual gain. All these barriers to cooperation may be important in legislative negotiations between the president and Congress.

Circumstances and Cooperation

Whether negotiation succeeds or fails depends on various circumstances. Above all, it depends on what is at stake. The more important the negotiators' complementary interests, in relation to their conflicting interests, the less friction they will have to deal with and the better the prospects for cooperation.[17] By the same token, the more they have to disagree about, and the less they have to gain by agreeing, the more likely they will fight. For example, a Republican president and a Democratic Congress may negotiate constructively to avert an impending calamity, such as the threatened insolvency of the Social Security system in the early 1980s, but they may have far more difficulty resolving a less urgent long-term problem such as excessive spending on entitlement programs.

Negotiations may go through alternating periods of conflict and cooperation. Tough negotiating tactics sometimes elicit even tougher responses, leading to a spiral of increasing hostility. (This is why negotiations are sometimes suspended for a "cooling-off period.") Alternatively, a cooperative gesture may induce a cooperative reply, causing a deescalation of conflict. A divided-control president and Congress may go through some periods of partisan rancor and other periods of cooperation.

Negotiators may have a fragile commitment to certain goals that arise from a sense of responsibility as opposed to tangible self-interest. If they can work out a mutually acceptable sharing of the burdens, negotiators may make large sacrifices for the sake of such goals. If they cannot come to acceptable terms, they may abandon those goals entirely. So the president and Congress sometimes act in a high-minded, principled manner—for example, passing an unpopular treaty to cede control of the Panama Canal to Panama—and other times cave in to political pressure.[18]

In any case, the success of negotiators in resolving conflict, like their bargaining power, also depends on their skills and strategies. An effective negotiator who is interested in achieving cooperation can defuse tensions and discover opportunities for mutual gain.[19] Political leaders have varying skills and dispositions for such efforts. That President Clinton was personally disliked by many Republicans made negotiations with them more difficult. President Bush appears more capable of negotiating constructively with congressional Democrats.

In the end, negotiations have a large element of unpredictability.[20] Skilled negotiators disguise their strategies to avoid being at a disadvantage. As a result, some negotiations fail because the participants misperceive each others' intentions. Other negotiations surprise everyone when, seemingly against the odds, they succeed.

Legislative Performance Under Unified and Divided Government: Interests and Issues

How, then, does divided government affect negotiations between the president and Congress? In general, it increases the prominence of conflicting interests between the two branches and decreases that of complementary interests. Inevitably, it will sometimes make cooperation more difficult, but this increased conflict is not always an important obstacle to reaching agreement.

Policy Interests

To begin with, divided party control leads to policy disagreement between the president and Congress, but only on *ideological* issues, and mainly in the absence of major changes in policy conditions or constituency demands. Democrats and Republicans consistently differ on ideological issues—those on which liberals and conservatives and their respective constituency groups also differ. Democrats push for bigger government, providing more services, and Republicans for smaller government and fewer services, among other differences. A divided president and Congress will therefore often be at odds on many issues.[21]

Nevertheless, a divided president and Congress will often agree on policy. Even on ideological issues, the two parties will respond the same way to a major change in the balance of political pressures or policy demands.[22] Despite partisan differences over environmental regulation, for example, both will respond to a widespread alarm about toxic pollution. In such cases, a Republican president and a Democratic Congress will have common goals for legislative action—even though they may disagree on how far to go.

Moreover, many policy issues cut across the liberal-conservative divide, either eliciting a broad consensus among politicians or causing divisions within both ideological groupings. Conflicts may arise between different industries, regions, or ethnic groups, or a broad range of groups may largely agree. Such issues include immigration, agricultural commodity subsidies, the deregulation of certain industries, and support for Israel. In some cases, officeholders of both parties have a common conception of national needs, which they may pursue even at the risk of offending important constituencies. These issues may include foreign aid, trade policy, and the reduction of budget deficits.

Because cross-cutting issues are relatively free of partisan differences over policy, they do not cause great difficulties for divided government. A complication arises, however, when cross-cutting issues are linked with ideological issues in the same piece of legislation. For example, a decision on reducing a budget deficit (a cross-cutting issue) cannot be separated from ideological conflicts about spending and taxes. In such a case, a divided-control president and Congress may agree on the cross-cutting issue, but, to take action, they will have to negotiate their conflicting interests on the ideological issues.

Electoral Interests

Much as with policy conflict, divided control also leads to interbranch electoral conflict—but only in certain respects. At the collective level, party electoral competition is zero-sum: if the Republicans gain support, the Democrats lose it. For this reason Sundquist argues that a congressional opposition party almost inevitably will try to defeat the president's initiatives.[23]

But two aspects of the situation help get around this difficulty. One is that, as noted previously, partisan effects are negotiable. If Democrats and Republicans both must act, they can work out a deal that avoids harm to either party. If the president needs opposition-party support to pass a popular public works bill, for example, he can either agree to share the credit with opposition leaders or adjust the bill's provisions to do more for the opposition's constituencies. In short, the president can make cooperating worth their while.[24]

The second and more important consideration is that this zero-sum conflict is between the parties as collectivities, not between the president and opposition-party members of Congress as individuals. They do not run for reelection against each other; rather, they all run against their own challengers. If the president and opposition members have compatible constituency interests on a given issue, they can all strengthen their reelection prospects by supporting the same measure.[25] Congressional Democrats were happy to share credit with President Reagan for the 1986 Tax Reform Act.[26] Indeed, because American politicians notoriously look out for themselves more than their parties, they can often cooperate across party lines.

The intense partisanship of the most recent Congresses may suggest that such cooperation is becoming either more difficult or less rewarding. In fact, as a result of realignment in the electorate, liberal Republicans and conservative Democrats have become almost nonexistent in Congress, depleting the natural base for moderate policies.[27] In their 1994 "Contract with America," the Republicans outlined and then vigorously pursued a vision of the country that was radically different from the Democrats' vision. The bitter partisanship of the Clinton impeachment debate of 1998 and early 1999 was a further sign of deepening conflict. If the ideological differences between the two parties continue to grow, divided government is likely to work less well in the future than it did in the past.

Ideological Issues

Because of the ideological differences between the parties—the Democrats' liberalism and the Republicans' conservatism—the effects of divided government are most pronounced on ideological issues, but the amount of conflict depends on the circumstances. In fact, the bogeyman of gridlock brought about by divided government appears only under certain conditions—namely, when the political pressures and policy demands on an ideological issue do not change very much.[28] In such a period, a divided-control president and Congress typically want to move in opposite directions. Even if both then become slightly more liberal or slightly more conservative in response to a change in demands, they may still disagree about the direction of change, resulting in deadlock. For example, a modest uptick in public support for a liberal social program will not generate support for expansion from a Republican president who thinks the program is already too large. In contrast, a unified-control president and Congress will make policy as they want it. If a small change then occurs in the political demands, they will respond together, producing action. The president and Congress agreed to strengthen gun control during a two-year period of unified Democratic control of government. The "Brady Bill" of 1993 required a waiting period for the purchase of handguns, and this law was followed by ban on assault weapons in 1994.[29] No gun control measures ensued during periods of divided government or unified Republican control, despite repeated Democratic attempts to raise the issue.

This difference in responses to modest changes in political demands was apparent in the politics of welfare in the 1970s and 1980s. Polls showed an increase in support for welfare in the early 1970s, a downward turn from the mid-1970s to the early 1980s, and a rebound toward more liberal views in the late 1980s. The fluctuations were not dramatic, however, with the proportion saying that "too much" was being spent on welfare ranging between 40 percent and 60 percent.[30] As expected, divided government has dampened the response to these modest shifts in political demand. Despite the rise in popular support, the divided-government administrations of Richard Nixon and Gerald Ford did not significantly increase welfare spending.[31] Instead, ignoring the modest liberal trend in opinion, both presidents took a hard line on welfare. By the beginning of the unified Democratic administration of Jimmy Carter, the public was becoming less patient with welfare recipients, and neither branch wanted much change. The House in 1979 passed a bill setting an income floor for welfare families, but the Senate killed it.

The rightward shift on welfare after 1975 produced action in 1981, Ronald Reagan's first year in office, in a brief period of "quasi-unified" party control. The Republicans controlled the presidency and the Senate, and, despite a nominal Democratic majority in the House, the Republicans and conservative Democrats formed a working majority that largely controlled that body, too. Reagan's initiatives, embodied in the Omnibus Budget and Reconciliation Act of 1981, dropped 400,000 families from the welfare rolls and reduced benefits to 300,000 others, mainly by eliminating Aid to Families with Dependent Children (AFDC) allowances for the working poor.

The Democrats recaptured genuine control of the House in the 1982 midterm election, beginning ten years of clear-cut divided control. About the same time, the public mood on welfare shifted again, becoming somewhat more liberal during the rest of the 1980s. But the Republican presidents were not swept away by the moderately generous public mood, and divided government did not respond to it.

When the demands on an ideological issue change dramatically, however, the presence of divided government may not make much of a difference. In the face of sufficiently powerful demands, a divided-control president and Congress will see which way the wind is blowing and set their sails accordingly. For example, public fears about rising energy costs in 2001 forced President Bush to agree to Democratic calls for expanded price controls on electricity.[32] The parties may fight over political credit or disagree about exactly how far to go, but, because such demands create an important shared interest in action, the parties are usually able to reach agreement.

Clearly, divided party control made little difference in the legislative response to the consumer and environmental movements of the 1960s and 1970s. The unified-control Johnson presidency yielded major legislation on fair packaging and labeling, meat and poultry inspection, wilderness protection, highway beautification, automobile emissions, and water quality. But the divided-control Nixon presidency went even further, producing several landmark laws on consumer and environmental matters: the Consumer Product Safety Act of 1974, the Magnuson-Moss Act of 1974, the National Environmental Policy Act of 1969, the Clean Air Act of 1970, and the Water Pollution Control Act of 1972, among others. As Mayhew pointed out, the strong public sentiment on these issues made the difference between unified and divided control virtually irrelevant.[33]

By the same token, divided control has not kept the president and Congress from reacting to sea changes in the political demand for defense spending. As the United States withdrew from Vietnam and experienced improved relations with the Soviet Union and China from 1969 to the mid-1970s, Americans who favored reductions in military spending outnumbered by at least three to one those favoring increases. The divided-control Nixon and Ford administrations as well as the unified-control Carter administration cut defense spending, in relation to domestic spending, every year from 1969 to 1977. Disillusionment with *détente* in the mid-1970s began to reverse the trend, and, after the Soviet Union invaded Afghanistan, respondents in a 1980 poll favored defense increases over cuts by five to one.[34] The result was eight straight real increases in defense spending—under unified Democratic control (Carter, 1978–1980), quasi-unified Republican control (Reagan, 1981), and divided control (Reagan, 1982–1985). The late 1980s brought yet another broad shift. With the Soviet Union in eclipse, public sentiment went back to the parsimonious mood of the early 1970s. The divided governments under Reagan, Bush, and Clinton allowed real defense spending to drop substantially. In 2001 the war on terrorism produced a dramatic increase in support for the military, and the Democrats in Congress backed the Bush administration's plan to spend more on defense.

In its most recent phase, welfare policy is a similar case. After the relatively liberal late 1980s, public opinion on welfare turned to the right again—and quite sharply after 1991—a turn underlined by the Republican victory in the

1994 congressional elections.[35] Despite a Democratic president and divided government, the change in opinion produced a corresponding rightward shift in policy. The Welfare Reform Act of 1996 ended sixty years of legally guaranteed assistance to the poor, set a time limit of five years on payments to any family, and gave state governments broad discretion on welfare policy.

The expectation that unified and divided government will respond similarly to major changes in political demand largely accounts for the central finding of Mayhew's study—that the two situations produced about the same number of important laws. For the most part, then, important laws are the result of major changes in political demand, no matter whether the government is divided or unified.

One effect of divided control on ideological issues concerns not whether government can act but rather what kind of action it takes. Because the president and Congress both have bargaining power, divided control requires compromise between the parties and leads to ideologically moderate outcomes. This effect has been apparent, for example, in how tax bills have treated different income groups. Not surprisingly, unified governments of either party have imposed new taxes primarily on the constituency groups of the other party: Democrats "soak the rich," whereas Republicans collect more from lower- and middle-income groups. In contrast, divided governments have kept the distribution of the tax burden roughly constant. The quasi-unified Republican government of Reagan's first year passed a huge tax cut, with the benefits heavily slanted toward wealthier citizens.[36]

Recession and the 1982 congressional elections ended conservative control of the House, and the divided government of the rest of the Reagan-Bush era was more evenhanded on tax issues. The Tax Equity and Fiscal Responsibility Act of 1982, the first of a series of tax increases aimed at reducing budget deficits, was a balanced package. New rules for the alternative minimum tax and the sale of corporate tax benefits extracted revenues from the wealthy. Increased excise taxes for cigarettes and telephones mostly affected lower-income persons.[37] In the same manner, the 1990 budget agreement raised taxes in several ways but took very nearly the same percentages of total revenues from most income groups as before the bill.[38]

In 1993 the unified Democratic Clinton presidency brought back partisan tax policy, imposing a hefty tax increase primarily on upper-income groups. The Clinton tax program raised the top personal rate by 5 percent, with an additional 10 percent surtax on incomes over $250,000. It also raised the alternative minimum tax and took more from well-to-do retirees. The only major provision that hit all income groups was a modest boost in the gasoline tax, accounting for just one-eighth of the new revenue.[39]

After the Republicans gained control of Congress in 1994, tax policy again became more balanced. A 1997 tax cut included cuts in capital gains and estate taxes for wealthier Americans, as well as education incentives and a partially refundable child tax credit for lower- and middle-income constituents.[40]

During the brief period of unified control of government after the 2000 election, Republicans were able to enact a ten-year tax cut in early 2001 that primarily benefited upper-income groups. Its major provisions included cuts in the top income tax rates, repeal of estate and gift taxes, "marriage penalty" relief that primarily affected higher-income individuals, and lower taxes on pensions and individual retirement accounts. President Clinton had vetoed a very similar tax package passed by congressional Republicans under divided government in 1999.[41]

Cross-Cutting Issues

Divided control should matter less on issues that cut across the liberal-conservative cleavage. Democrats and Republicans are not at odds on these issues, although each party may be internally divided. Partisan rivalry for political credit may obstruct action in some cases, but a divided-control president and Congress can usually negotiate around that rivalry. A divided government therefore should be almost as likely to act on such issues as a unified one.

Divided government has not caused much trouble, for example, on efforts to cut back wasteful agricultural subsidies or anticompetitive regulatory programs—reforms supported by consumer-oriented liberals, free-market conservatives, and academic policy analysts and opposed by the affected industries and their employees.[42] Dramatic reforms of anticompetitive regulation in transportation, financial services, and other industries were initiated in the abbreviated divided-control Ford administration and adopted soon afterward in the unified-control Carter administration.

Progress on reforming agricultural subsidies has actually been more rapid under divided government than under unified government. The Republican Nixon administration worked with the Democratic Congress to pass a 1970 law that trimmed subsidized acreage, lowered price supports, and limited payments to individual farmers.[43] They collaborated again on a 1973 law that abolished "parity," the practice of basing farm support on 1910–1913 prices.[44] Neither Carter's unified Democratic administration nor Reagan's 1981 quasi-unified Republican administration made more than a few changes. The Reagan and Bush divided governments, however, resumed the attack with a 1985 law that scaled down farm loan programs and reduced target prices and a 1990 law that took 15 percent of farmland out of the commodity support system. Most dramatically, President Clinton signed the Republican-initiated Freedom to Farm Act of 1996, which was intended to abolish the system of target prices and production limits altogether and to phase out payments on most commodities, although subsequent legislation in 2002 reversed course and reestablished heavy subsidies.

The main difficulty for divided government occurs when cross-cutting issues are directly linked to ideological issues and both must be decided in the same measure. Such cases are quite common: liberals and conservatives both want to increase access to health care, but liberals favor a national health care plan, and conservatives would rely on tax credits and private insurance. Liberals and conservatives both want to avoid budget deficits, but liberals favor higher taxes, and conservatives want reduced spending.

The dynamics of linked cross-cutting demand and ideological conflicts have been apparent in how the president and Congress have dealt with economic recessions. If an economic slump is severe and other economic conditions favor a fiscal stimulus package, the parties have a strong cross-cutting interest in taking such action. If a downturn is mild or other conditions stand in the way of fiscal action, that interest is weaker. A strong shared interest in fiscal action will overcome ideological conflicts about taxes and spending, but a weak one may not.

Presidents Nixon and Ford faced lagging economies in periods of manageable budget deficits and moderate inflation; the cross-cutting interest in fiscal action during their administrations was quite strong.[45] As we would expect, divided government posed no major obstacle to such action. In each case, the president and Congress fought a partisan battle over how to respond but eventually passed a substantial stimulus bill. With the president having a disproportionate political stake in a healthy economy, the Democrats got much of what they wanted in these measures. In the 1971 agreement with Nixon, they successfully demanded increases in domestic spending and public works projects, along with their long-sought wage and price controls (which Nixon ordered unilaterally). In the deal with Ford four years later, Democrats won a larger stimulus than Republicans wanted and blocked Republican demands to link tax cuts with spending limits. For both Nixon and Ford, who enjoyed strengthened economies in time to help with their reelection bids, the price was worth it.

In contrast, during the two recessions of the 1980s, troublesome inflation or massive deficits made fiscal stimulus hard to justify economically; the cross-cutting interest in stimulation was, therefore, virtually nonexistent. Both Carter's unified government and Reagan's divided government were stymied.[46]

Divided government appeared to make a real difference only in the in-between case of the mild but prolonged economic slump during the last two years of the Bush administration. Congress and the president showed only an ambivalent, slowly emerging cross-cutting interest in fiscal action. In this circumstance, the parties could not easily resolve their ideological differences, and divided control led to stalemate. In the early stages of the recession in 1991 especially, most economists cautioned against a deficit-increasing fiscal stimulus, and both parties were internally divided on the issue. Through most of the year, President Bush and significant Republican and Democratic factions in Congress opposed any such action. As the slump dragged on, the president and the Democrats gradually came around to favoring a stimulus measure, at least in principle. But they had serious ideological conflicts about specific tax cuts and spending increases, and neither party was sufficiently committed to a bill to make major concessions on those issues. In March 1992 the Democrats pushed a highly partisan stimulus measure through Congress. Bush vetoed it. No serious negotiations were undertaken before Congress recessed for that year's election campaign.[47] Bush paid heavily for the lack of action on the economy in his losing campaign for reelection. In the next recession, which began in 2001, divided government prevented the enactment of an economic stimulus bill.

Autonomy Issues

The consequences of unified or divided control are hardest to sort out when policymakers try to overcome popular or interest group pressure on cross-cutting issues and act responsibly according to their own view of the public interest—that is, to exercise autonomy. In such cases, divided government actually has both advantages and disadvantages, and the overall effect is far from obvious.

Suppose, for example, that both parties see a need to cut entitlement spending or to increase foreign aid—actions that have weak political constituencies and are strongly disapproved by many voters. As critics have often pointed out, divided control creates two obstacles to such action. First, the president and Congress will each want the other to take the lion's share of the responsibility. Each has an incentive to hang back and wait for the other to act. Second, they will fight about any linked ideological issues that may be at stake, such as how much to cut middle-class as opposed to low-income entitlements. Preoccupied with such tensions, the president and Congress may neglect their shared goal of acting responsibly.

On the positive side, however, divided government also defuses the electoral risks of autonomous action. Because both parties must get on board for any bill to pass, they share the blame for taking action opposed by powerful constituencies. A divided-control president and Congress can act autonomously, therefore, without requiring either party to pay dearly in loss of support.[48] Moreover, with votes coming from both parties, their leaders can tolerate numerous defections by individual members of Congress and still assemble a winning coalition. In particular, they can allow many of the politically vulnerable members of each party to play it safe and vote against the leadership position.

Without any clear-cut advantage for either unified or divided control, the president and Congress seem likely to have roughly the same ability to act autonomously in each situation. As we have mentioned, for example, divided government does not lead to larger budget deficits. To be sure, from 1946 to 1988 the average annual deficit was much larger under divided government ($65 billion) than under unified control ($16 billion). But the difference results almost entirely from the massive deficits of the Reagan years. Take away the peculiar experience of those years—presumably the result of other causes—and the average deficits under unified and divided control are just about the same.[49]

Moreover, the president and Congress have succeeded in cutting deficits under both forms of party control. Significant cuts were made during two recent periods of unified Democratic control. President Carter pushed tight, deficit-reducing budgets through Congress in 1979 and 1980, although his budget-balancing aspirations were defeated by a sinking economy.[50] President Clinton carried out a 1992 campaign promise by enacting a deficit-reduction plan with substantial spending cuts and upper-income tax increases. With Republicans solidly opposed, the Clinton plan passed by narrow margins in the House and the Senate, and only after numerous concessions to Democratic members. Nevertheless, it reduced the deficit by $490 billion over five years. For their trouble, Carter and Clinton lost popular support.

Similar deficit reductions have also occurred under divided government— even before Clinton and the Republican-controlled Congress achieved a fiscal 1999 budget with a projected $70 billion surplus. In 1969 President Nixon and the Democratic Congress agreed on expenditure ceilings that allowed Nixon to make specific spending cuts.[51] During the Reagan presidency, Senate Republicans mediated between the president and congressional Democrats to achieve significant deficit reductions. A 1982 bipartisan package strengthened tax enforcement, repealed business deductions, and cut spending by $17 billion; a 1984 measure pared away a smaller chunk of the deficit. The Senate Republicans tried again in 1985, but Reagan and the Democrats struck a deal to pass a looser budget. In 1990, after Bush had recanted a 1988 campaign pledge not to raise taxes, a deficit-cutting bipartisan budget was soundly defeated on the House floor. Despite the inauspicious beginning, however, a revised bipartisan bill was enacted that raised taxes, cut spending, and reduced the deficit by about one-quarter.[52]

Even if divided party control has little or no overall effect on the ability of the president and Congress to act autonomously, it may change the dynamics of autonomy issues in another way: the performance of divided government may be more volatile. On the one hand, a divided-control president and Congress can in effect conspire with each other to override popular or interest group demands and largely avoid the risk of either party's losing electoral support. On the other hand, they can become so embroiled in partisan and ideological warfare that they essentially abandon efforts to act responsibly. Which response occurs depends on the complex and somewhat unpredictable dynamics of negotiation, with its potential for upward and downward spirals of conflict.

A dramatic episode of escalating conflict occurred during the divided-control Nixon presidency. As we have mentioned, the Democratic Congress in 1972 reacted against Nixon's cuts in domestic programs by refusing to pass a new spending ceiling. Responding aggressively, Nixon tried to enforce a ceiling of his own by vetoing popular legislation, pocket vetoing appropriations bills, and impounding funds that Congress had appropriated.[53] Congress turned up the heat even further, taking the president to court to undo his impoundments and passing new statutory restrictions on the president's discretion in carrying out the budget. The acrimonious dispute may even have strengthened Congress's disposition to impeach and remove Nixon during the Watergate affair.

Another escalation of partisan conflict contributed to the deficits during the Reagan and Bush years. Casting off the electoral burden of the Republicans' traditionally austere economics, Reagan in 1981 pushed a massive tax reduction, setting aside any genuine concern for the fiscal consequences.[54] The Democrats, angered by Reagan's strategy and unwilling to bear the burden of fiscal responsibility alone, mounted a vehement defense of domestic spending. The result, accepted by both sides, was a soaring national debt.

Naturally, a president and Congress of the same party will also vary in their willingness to act autonomously. But their ability to do so will not depend on volatile interparty negotiations.

Because the president is the main focus of accountability, enacting a bill that runs against public opinion or rejects interest group demands will usually be somewhat more costly to the president's party than to an opposite-party congressional majority. As compensation, the president will do relatively well on any linked ideological issues in the dispute. In 1999, for example, President Clinton and the Republican Congress reached agreement, after several years of failed effort, on a bill overhauling regulation of the financial services industry.[55] The bill, strongly favored by economists, was politically risky because some sectors of the industry disliked it and it ran up against public antipathy toward large banks. At the last stage, there remained a linked ideological issue: Texas Republican senator Phil Gramm's attempt to repeal a 1977 law requiring banks to make loans in low-income areas. Clinton threatened to veto the overhaul bill if it contained Gramm's amendment. The Republicans agreed to drop most of Gramm's proposal in the conference committee.

The Question of Reform

Reformers have suggested various means to ensure, or at least make it more likely, that the same political party ends up in control of both the presidency and Congress. Their proposals range from eliminating midterm congressional elections, to giving the president's party bonus seats in Congress, to mandating a straight party vote for the offices of president, vice president, senator, and representative.[56]

None of these reforms has ever had widespread support. But dissatisfaction with "gridlock" and criticism of divided government reached new heights during the 1992 campaign. With divided government a certainty until 2003, such criticism may resume. We must therefore ask: Is the propensity toward divided control of the presidency and Congress a serious malady of American government, one for which reformers should indeed seek a cure?

Judging by our theoretical analysis and various examples, probably not. Contrary to the clean-bill-of-health view issued by Mayhew, divided government does have costs in reduced efficiency and responsiveness. But contrary to Sundquist's grim assessment, those costs are inherently limited and balanced by compensating advantages.

Recent developments have made it more likely that a divided-control president and Congress will have completely incompatible policy objectives, resulting in deadlock. But this should generally occur only on ideologically salient issues—and even then, only in the absence of broad public agreement on the desired direction of change. If a Democratic president wants to expand social programs and a Republican Congress wants to contract them, nothing will happen. This result usually reflects a corresponding division in national opinion.[57] When such a division exists, deadlock is arguably appropriate; it does not count as a cost.

Allegations to the contrary notwithstanding, divided control probably has no significant, overall effect on the ability of the president and Congress to act autonomously in the face of misguided or narrowly based political demands. Divided government may be stymied by partisan and ideological squabbling between the branches, but unified government may be paralyzed by the majority party's fear of giving the opposition an issue to exploit in the next election. In addition, too much government autonomy would be dangerous. But there is evidently little difference, in this respect, between the two forms of control.

The real costs of divided party control lie elsewhere. In many cases, a president and Congress of different parties will have a hard time reaching agreement and taking action, even though they share a common interest, substantively and politically, in policy change. Either their competing electoral interests or their conflicting ideological preferences get in the way. In 2001 and 2002 such blocking or delaying of action was apparent on several bills related to the war on terrorism and the economic recession, which affected policy on airport security, the investigation and prosecution of suspected terrorists, and economic stimulation measures. The possibility that bipartisan, perhaps widely shared, policy objectives will not be served because of partisan conflict on other matters is the principal cost of divided government.

That divided government imposes this cost is not a damning indictment, however, for two reasons. First, negotiation limits the damage. In general, the more important the bipartisan policy interests at stake, the more readily the president and Congress can overcome their conflicts and reach agreement. Just as labor negotiations usually avoid prolonged strikes, legislative negotiations usually avoid costly policy stalemate. Divided government will block action in certain cases when the perceived need to act is neither clear-cut nor urgent. The prototype of this situation is the 1991–1992 economic slump: because the parties were not fully convinced of the need for a fiscal stimulus package, they would not compromise to achieve one.

Second, the losses from destructive partisan conflict are balanced by what is arguably an important advantage. Divided party control of the presidency and Congress ensures that both liberal and conservative views are influential and that the policies adopted are ideologically moderate. In an important sense, these middle-of-the-road policies are more in tune with the public's wishes than the one-sided outcomes that either party would impose if left to its own devices. In short, under divided government American citizens put up with a great deal of partisan bickering and with a certain amount of genuine failure to act on common interests in order to avoid the excesses that may lie at either end of the political spectrum.

Notes

1. James L. Sundquist, "Needed: A Political Theory for a New Era of Coalition Government in the United States," *Political Science Quarterly* 103 (winter 1988–1989): 613–635.

2. Voter Research and Surveys, General Election Poll, November 3, 1992.

3. Roger H. Davidson, "Invitation to Struggle: An Overview of Legislative-Executive Relations," *Annals of the American Academy of Political and Social Science* 499 (September 1988): 9–21.

4. David R. Mayhew, *Divided We Govern: Party Control, Lawmaking, and Investigations, 1946–1990* (New Haven: Yale University Press, 1991).

5. Scott Keeter, "Public Opinion and the Election," in *The Election of 1996: Reports and Interpretations,* ed. Gerald M. Pomper et al. (Chatham, N.J.: Chatham House, 1997), 125–126.

6. For a useful set of essays on the debate, see James A. Thurber, ed., *Divided Democracy* (Washington, D.C.: CQ Press, 1991). For a critical commentary, see Morris P. Fiorina, *Divided Government* (New York: Macmillan, 1992), chap. 6.

7. See especially, Sundquist, "Needed: A Political Theory." For additional critical views, see Michael L. Mezey, "The Legislature, the Executive, and Public Policy: The Futile Quest for Congressional Power," in *Divided Democracy,* ed. Thurber, chap. 6; and the essays in *The Politics of Divided Government,* ed. Gary W. Cox and Samuel Kernell (Boulder: Westview Press, 1991).

8. Mayhew found a slightly greater frequency of important laws under unified government. But he argued that his measure understated the policy change under divided government because Reagan's 1981 tax and budget measures, representing a sweeping reorientation of federal policy, were embodied in just two laws; see *Divided We Govern,* chap. 4.

9. John J. Coleman, "Unified Government, Divided Government, and Party Responsiveness," *American Political Science Review* 93 (December 1999): 821–835; and Sarah A. Binder, "The Dynamics of Legislative Gridlock, 1947–96," *American Political Science Review* 93 (September 1999): 519–533.

10. John H. Aldrich and David W. Rohde, "The Consequences of Party Organization in the House: The Role of the Majority and Minority Parties in Conditional Party Government," in *Polarized Politics: Congress and the President in a Partisan Era,* ed. Jon R. Bond and Richard Fleisher (Washington, D.C.: CQ Press, 2000), 31–72; George C. Edwards III and Andrew Barrett, "Presidential Agenda Setting in Congress," in *Polarized Politics,* 109–133; and Barbara Sinclair, "Hostile Partners: The President, Congress, and Lawmaking in the Partisan 1990s," in *Polarized Politics,* 134–153.

11. The existing empirical evidence is by no means definitive. See Fiorina, *Divided Government,* chap. 6. Among the difficulties, the number of important laws is a limited

indicator of government performance. Nor has anyone measured the demand for policy change in different periods. In any case, Mayhew's historical record is too short for reliable inferences. Although his decision to study the post–World War II era was reasonable, one or two highly productive or unproductive presidencies could change the average performance of unified or divided government significantly for such a period. Some authors have taken a long-term perspective or used evidence from the American states. See James E. Alt and Charles Stewart, "Parties and the Deficit: Some Historical Evidence" (paper presented at the National Bureau of Economic Research Conference on Political Economics, Cambridge, Mass., February 2–3, 1990); and James E. Alt and Robert C. Lowry, "Divided Government and Budget Deficits: Evidence from the States," manuscript, Harvard University, Cambridge, 1993. Mayhew offers a cogent theoretical discussion to support his empirical findings. In our view, however, he is more successful in explaining why the difference in performance between unified and divided government may be obscured by other forces (what he calls "constancy" and "alternative variation") than in arguing that the difference does not exist at all (owing to "compensation"). See Mayhew, *Divided We Govern*, chaps. 5 and 6.

12. We rely here on a loose form of median-voter theory. For an accessible introduction to this theory and the larger body of spatial theory, see Gerald Strom, *The Logic of Lawmaking: A Spatial Theory Approach* (Baltimore: Johns Hopkins University Press, 1991). We refer to moderate members (in the plural), instead of the single median member, for several reasons: to reflect the uncertainties of the legislative process; to avoid the implication that the president can negotiate with a single pivotal member (and perhaps win his or her support with a side payment); and to allow for the possibility that the group of moderate members is bipartisan. Our analysis ignores the structures and procedures of Congress (committees, leadership positions, the filibuster, and so on) and the complexities of coalition building. We do not argue that it is a full account of congressional behavior, but only that it provides the best simple understanding of Congress's positions in negotiations with the president. For a defense of the median-voter perspective in interpreting Congress, see Keith Krehbiel, *Information and Legislative Organization* (Ann Arbor: University of Michigan Press, 1992). Because median-voter theory does not apply in a straightforward way to legislative decisions with more than one major dimension, our assumption is somewhat more shaky in those cases. Very roughly, we assume that members whose preferences are near the median on any of the major dimensions are especially influential.

13. Paul J. Quirk, "The Cooperative Resolution of Policy Conflict," *American Political Science Review* 83 (September 1989): 905–921; compare Thomas C. Schelling, *The Strategy of Conflict* (Cambridge: Harvard University Press, 1980). Two collections of essays provide a good overview of the contemporary literature on negotiation: H. Peyton Young, ed., *Negotiation Analysis* (Ann Arbor: University of Michigan Press, 1991); and J. William Breslin and Jeffrey Z. Rubin, *Negotiation Theory and Practice* (Cambridge: Program on Negotiation at Harvard Law School, 1991).

14. Howard Raiffa, *The Art and Science of Negotiation* (Cambridge: Harvard University Press, 1982).

15. Our perspective on negotiation is influenced partly by rational-choice analyses but also by social-psychological theories and by the large practical literature on conflict resolution. See Steven J. Brams, *Negotiation Games: Applying Game Theory to Bargaining and Arbitration* (New York: Routledge, 1990); Dean G. Pruitt, *Negotiation Behavior* (New York: Academic Press, 1981); J. Z. Rubin and B. R. Brown, *The Social Psychology of*

Bargaining and Negotiation (New York: Academic Press, 1975); R. Fisher and W. Ury, *Getting to YES: Negotiating Agreement Without Giving In* (Boston: Houghton-Mifflin, 1981); and Susan L. Carpenter and W. J. D. Kennedy, *Managing Public Disputes* (San Francisco: Jossey-Bass, 1988). For an attempt to apply a conflict-resolution perspective in a general analysis of public policymaking, see Quirk, "Cooperative Resolution of Policy Conflict." Our treatment of the negotiation perspective is a new synthesis of the broad themes of the negotiation literature.

16. More precisely, what matters is the strength of each side's "best alternative to a negotiated agreement." See Fisher and Ury, *Getting to YES*.

17. This is Robert Axelrod's notion of "conflict of interest." We avoid his term, however, because of its misleading connotations of financial impropriety. Robert Axelrod, *Conflict of Interest: A Theory of Divergent Goals, With Applications to Politics* (Chicago: Markham, 1970).

18. This variability is also stressed, but explained differently, by R. Douglas Arnold in *The Logic of Congressional Action* (New Haven: Yale University Press, 1990).

19. This is a major theme of practical literature about negotiation. See Fisher and Ury, *Getting to YES*; Raiffa, *The Art and Science of Negotiation;* and I. William Zartman and Maureen R. Berman, *The Practical Negotiator* (New Haven: Yale University Press, 1982).

20. See Otomar J. Bartos, "How Predictable Are Negotiations?" in *The 50% Solution,* ed. I. William Zartman (New Haven: Yale University Press, 1983), 485–509. Also see Oran Young, ed., *Formal Theories of Negotiation* (Urbana: University of Illinois Press, 1975), especially the editor's introductory essays.

21. Some of our reasoning appeals to a casual and implicit spatial analysis of negotiation games. Other aspects of our argument would not lend themselves to a spatial representation.

22. We assume that the two parties maintain a fairly constant distance from each other on any given ideological issue, but that they move in the same direction in response to unidirectional changes in public opinion, interest group demands, or objective policy conditions, such as poverty rates or evidence of environmental hazards.

23. Sundquist, "Needed: A Political Theory."

24. Roughly speaking, the president will have to reduce the opposition party's political costs of passing his bill enough that opposition members would prefer to accept that collective cost rather than take the risk, individually, of being blamed for obstructing it.

25. Mayhew makes a similar point about individual electoral incentives in *Divided We Govern,* 102–103.

26. Timothy J. Conlon, Margaret T. Wrightson, and David R. Beam, *Taxing Choices: The Politics of Tax Reform* (Washington, D.C.: CQ Press, 1990).

27. David W. Rohde, *Parties and Leaders in the Postreform House* (Chicago: University of Chicago Press, 1991); and Roger H. Davidson, ed., *The Postreform Congress* (New York: St. Martin's, 1992).

28. Roughly, the condition required for divided government to produce deadlock is that fluctuations in the parties' positions, due to changing conditions, must be smaller than the difference between the president's position and those of the pivotal members of the House and Senate (relatively moderate members of the opposition party).

29. Robert J. Spitzer, *The Politics of Gun Control* (Chatham, N.J.: Chatham House, 1995), chap. 5.

30. Richard G. Niemi, John Mueller, and Tom W. Smith, *Trends in Public Opinion: A Compendium of Survey Data* (New York: Greenwood, 1989), 89.

31. Our account of changes in welfare policy is based largely on James T. Patterson, *America's Struggle Against Poverty* (Cambridge: Harvard University Press, 1986), 192–207, 212–214.

32. Chuck McCutcheon, "FERC Move to Expand Price Controls Means Energy Policy Debate Can Now Focus on Long Term," *CQ Weekly*, June 23, 2001, 1514; Jeff Gerth, "U.S. Agency Widens Its Curbs on Price of Power in West," *New York Times*, June 19, 2001, A1, 19.

33. Mayhew, *Divided We Govern*, 58–60, 85–86.

34. Niemi, Mueller, and Smith, *Trends in Public Opinion*, 87.

35. R. Kent Weaver, Robert Y. Shapiro, and Lawrence R. Jacobs, "The Polls—Trends: Welfare," *Public Opinion Quarterly* 59 (1995): 606–627.

36. Howard E. Shuman, *Politics and the Budget: The Struggle Between the President and Congress*, 3d ed. (Englewood Cliffs, N.J.: Prentice-Hall, 1992), 129–131.

37. Karen W. Arenson, "Ramifications of Tax Law Affect Many," *New York Times*, August 23, 1982, D7. Lower-income people spend a larger share of their incomes on cigarettes and telephones.

38. Shuman, *Politics and the Budget*, 328–329.

39. David S. Cloud, "New Levies on Gas and the Rich Would Yield $240 Billion," *Congressional Quarterly Weekly Report*, August 7, 1993, 2132–3.

40. "Reconciliation Package: Tax Cuts," *Congressional Quarterly Almanac, 1997* (Washington, D.C.: Congressional Quarterly, 1998), 30–46.

41. Daniel J. Parks, with Bill Swindell, "Tax Debate Assured a Long Life as Bush, GOP Press for New Cuts," *CQ Weekly*, June 2, 2001, 1304–9; Robert Greenstein and Isaac Shapiro, "Who Would Benefit From the Tax Proposal Before the Senate?" Center on Budget and Policy Priorities, May 21, 2001, http://www.centeronbudget.org/5-15-01tax.htm (June 26, 2001); Randy Wynn, "A Year of Grudging Compromises and Unfinished Business," *CQ Weekly*, November 27, 1999, 2846–7.

42. Martha Derthick and Paul J. Quirk, *The Politics of Deregulation* (Washington, D.C.: Brookings Institution, 1985).

43. "1970 Agricultural Act Cleared After 16-Month Debate," *Congressional Quarterly Almanac, 1970* (Washington, D.C.: Congressional Quarterly, 1971), 634–636.

44. Willard W. Cochrane and Mary E. Ryan, *American Farm Policy, 1948–1973* (Minneapolis: University of Minnesota Press, 1976), 69, 83.

45. "Bold Moves on Economy by Nixon Administration," *Congressional Quarterly Almanac, 1971* (Washington, D.C.: Congressional Quarterly, 1972), 58; Herbert Stein, *Presidential Economics: The Making of Economic Policy from Roosevelt to Reagan and Beyond* (New York: Simon and Schuster, 1984), 215.

46. With inflation running as high as 18 percent in 1980, Carter urged Congress to focus on cutting the budget to fight inflation rather than stimulating the economy. See "Carter Seeks 'Prudent' 1981 Spending Plan," *Congressional Quarterly Almanac, 1980* (Washington, D.C.: Congressional Quarterly, 1981), 131–132. In the severe recession of 1982–1983, in the Reagan era, it was the combination of an unprecedented peacetime federal budget deficit and Republican opposition to spending increases and "make-work jobs" that precluded action. Reagan pleaded with the public to "stay the course" while the government waited out the recession. See Stein, *Presidential Economics*, 276.

47. Paul J. Quirk and Bruce Nesmith, "Explaining Deadlock: Domestic Policymaking in the Bush Presidency," in *New Perspectives on American Politics,* ed. Lawrence C. Dodd and Calvin Jillson (Washington, D.C.: CQ Press, 1994), 200–201.

48. See Kent Weaver and Burt Rockman, *Do Institutions Matter?* (Washington, D.C.: Brookings Institution, 1993), 451–452.

49. Fiorina points out in *Divided Government,* 94–95, that congressional Democrats restrained Reagan's tax cuts and defense buildup and that even many Republicans opposed his cuts in domestic spending. Thus, he suggests, a unified Republican government during the early 1980s might have enacted even larger tax cuts and defense increases, accomplished no greater spending cuts, and therefore produced even larger budget deficits.

50. "Budget and Appropriations," *Congressional Quarterly Almanac, 1979* (Washington, D.C.: Congressional Quarterly, 1980), 172.

51. John B. Gilmour, *Reconcilable Differences: Congress, the Budget Process, and the Deficit* (Berkeley: University of California Press, 1990), 46–47.

52. Paul J. Quirk, "Domestic Policy: Divided Government and Cooperative Presidential Leadership," in *The Bush Presidency: First Appraisals,* ed. Colin Campbell and Bert A. Rockman (Chatham, N.J.: Chatham House, 1991), 69–92.

53. Gilmour, *Reconcilable Differences,* 46–49.

54. Stein, *Presidential Economics,* chap. 7.

55. "Major Overhaul Enacted of Rules Governing the Financial Services Industry," *Congressional Quarterly Almanac, 1999* (Washington, D.C.: Congressional Quarterly, 2000), 3–36. See also the discussion in Quirk and Nesmith, "Explaining Deadlock," 203–205.

56. For a thorough discussion of these and other proposals to strengthen the linkage between the president and Congress, see James L. Sundquist, *Constitutional Reform and Effective Government* (Washington, D.C.: Brookings Institution, 1986), chap. 4.

57. Gary C. Jacobson, "Party Polarization in National Politics: The Electoral Connection," in *Polarized Politics,* ed. Bond and Fleisher, 930, finds that recent partisanship in Congress is traceable to divergence in the parties' electoral coalitions, partly (but not entirely) the result of realignment among southern whites.

Index

Krock, Arthur, 341
Kumar, Martha J., 10, 326*n*13, 422*n*12

Labor Nonpartisan League, 337
Lake, Anthony, 408
Lance, Bert, 9, 147, 283
Landon, Alfred M., 342, 401
Lau, Richard R., 255*n*26
Lauck, W. Jett, 336
Lawson, Nigel, 40
Lee, Jong R., 14
Lemann, Nicholas, 286
Leuchtenberg, William, 389*n*22, 486
Lewinsky, Monica, 10, 68, 104, 179, 181, 210,
    295–296, 380
Lewis, Anthony, 290
Lewis, John L., 336–337
Lewis-Beck, Michael, 60
Libya, 15, 283
Life magazine, 1
Likud coalition (Israel), 63
Lincoln, Abraham, 225, 400
    as monocratic president, 33
    assassination, 116
    campaign, 220, 485
    judiciary and, 501
    leadership style, 202
    personality and psychology, 202
    ranking, 1
Line-item veto, 18
Lipset, Seymour Martin, 192
Lisagor, Peter, 11
Locke, John, 356
Long, Huey, 221
Lott, Trent, 295
Lowi, Theodore J., 281, 387*n*20
Lugar, Richard, 369

Mackenzie, G. Calvin, 185*n*18
Mackuen, Michael B., 254*n*11
Macmillan, Harold, 36, 46
Macy, John, 364, 389*n*34
Madison, James, 80, 218. *See also*
    Federalist, The
    as president, 113
    cabinet and, 219
    executive independence, 88
    on need for Senate, 108*n*25
    opposition to demagoguery, 82, 106*n*7
    personality and psychology, 198
    political philosophy, 464
    presidential psychology, 192
    separation of powers, 109*n*39, 463
    views on representation, 85–86
Madonna, 293
Magaziner, Ira, 180, 376
Major, John, 35, 64
Marbury v. Madison, 501
Marcus, Ruth, 318, 392*n*66

Marshall, John, 88, 501
Martin, Cathie Jo, 393*n*72
Matheson, Sean C., 188*n*62
Mathias, Charles, Jr., 439, 456*n*26
Mayhew, David, 16, 469–470, 479*n*24,
    508–509, 518, 524, 526*n*8, 527*n*11
McCain, John, 227, 243
McCarthy, Eugene, 222, 366
McCarthy, Joseph, 82
McCree, Wade, 501
McCurry, Mike, 417
McFarlane, Robert, 412
McGarity, Thomas O., 456*n*43
McGovern, George, 190, 226, 231, 234, 390*n*41
McGovern-Fraser Commission, 222, 366,
    390*n*41
McKinley, William, 227
McLarty, Mack, 179, 404
McQueen, Steve, 300
Media
    "body watch," 8–9
    Clinton health care plan and, 310–318,
        327*n*21
    Clinton Social Security plan and, 318–323
    communications warfare, 306–310, 323–324
    factors governing coverage, 308–309
    "horse race" phenomenon, 317–318,
        322–323, 326*n*14
    journalistic commentary, 316
    nominating process and, 229
    presidential influence on reporting, 328*n*31
    presidential spectacle, 280–281
    selection of judicial nominees and, 491–492
Medicare, 362, 378
Meese, Edwin, 286, 412, 496
Melnick, R. Shep, 394*n*75
Meredith, James, 135
Merit Systems Protection Board, 438, 441
Merolla, Jennifer, 255*n*35
Mexican War, 129–131
Mezey, Michael L., 526*n*7
Michel, Robert, 340
Military
    defense spending, 164–165, 286, 517
    homosexuals in the military, 375, 392*n*66
    missile defense, 103, 173, 297
    officers as presidential prospects, 227
Milkis, Sidney, 386*n*1, 389*n*22, 391*n*52,
    392*n*62
Ministry of Agriculture, Fisheries, and Food
    (Britain), 44
Miranda v. Arizona, 486
Mississippi, University of, 135
Missouri Compromise of 1820, 143, 485
Mitchell, George, 314, 345, 497
Mitterrand, François, 31–32, 43, 44
Moe, Terry M., 21, 74*n*18, 416, 454*n*n*2, 3
Mondale, Walter, 226, 229, 231, 487
Monroe, James, 113, 218–219, 400